D0931232

Popular Anti-Catholicism

in Mid-Victorian England

Popular Anti-Catholicism in Mid-Victorian England

D. G. Paz

Stanford University Press
Stanford, Califonia
1992

RANDALL LIBRARY UNC-W

Stanford University Press
Stanford, California

© 1992 by the Board of Trustees of the
Leland Stanford Junior University

Printed in the United States of America

CIP data are at the end of the book

The Press gratefully acknowledges
the work of the author in preparing
camera-ready copy for this book.

BR
759
.P388
1992

For my teachers

Lucy M. Brown
London School of Economics

Irby C. Nichols, Jr.
University of North Texas

Jacob M. Price
University of Michigan

ACKNOWLEDGMENTS

FOR PERMISSION TO quote Crown-copyright papers, I thank the Controller of H. M. Stationery Office; for permission to use papers in their charge, I thank his Grace the Lord Archbishop of Canterbury, the Duke of Norfolk, the Most. Rev. the Roman Catholic Archbishop of Birmingham, the Rt. Rev. the Bishop of Mississippi, the Rt. Rev. the Roman Catholic Bishop of Northampton, the Dean and Chapter of Exeter Cathedral, Mrs. F. E. Copleston, and Dr. David Ransome.

I am indebted to the librarians, archivists, and other staff of the British Library's Bloomsbury Reading Room and Newspaper Library at Colindale, the Public Record Office at Kew and Portugal Street, the Southampton Record Office, Manchester Central Library, Birmingham Reference Library, Northampton City Library and County Record Office, the Yale Center for British Art, and the University Libraries of Clemson, Duke, Emory, Georgia, London, Michigan, Nebraska at Omaha, and Yale. I thank the following people, who helped me in many ways: Dr. and Ms. J. L. Alexander, Prof. Josef L. Altholz, Prof. Walter L. Arnstein, Dr. Marc Baer, Ms. Linda Berri, Dr. John Bohstedt, Dr. Lucy M. Brown, Dr. Gerard Connolly, Mr. Jay Crawford, Prof. Richard M. Golden, Dr. and Ms. John Hurt, the Rev. Dr. John P. Marmion, Dr. and Ms. Hugh Mcleod, Prof. David Nicholas, Ms. Lisa Ridenour, Prof. R. K. Webb, Ms. Marian Withington, and Dr. John R. Wolffe (I hope that I have been as helpful to him as he has been to me).

Portions of this book were given as papers at meetings of the American Historical Association, Carolinas Symposium on British Studies, Catholic Record Society, Midwest Conference on British Studies, Missouri Valley History Conference, and the Southern Conference on British Studies, and to Prof. F.M.L. Thompson's seminar at the Institute of Historical Research, Mrs. Dorothy Thompson's seminar at the University of Birmingham, Dr. Lynn Hunt's and Dr. Thomas Walter Laqueur's summer seminar (funded by the National Endowment for the Humanities) at the University of California at Berkeley, and the History Department's seminar at Clemson University. The criticism of the participants at these meetings and seminars was very helpful. Portions of this book have appeared as articles in *Albion*, the *Historian*, and *Historical Research*. I thank the editors of these journals for permission to republish.

Research for this book was supported by a Fellowship for College Teachers from the National Endowment for the Humanities, and a Provost's Research Award and a Faculty Research Grant from Clemson University; a sabbatical leave and a lightened teaching load allowed its writing. The University of Nebraska at Omaha and Clemson University provided computer time.

CONTENTS

ABBREVIATIONS

Boase	Frederick Boase, *Modern English Biography*
CH	*Church History*
DNB	*Dictionary of National Biography*
EHR	*English Historical Review*
Hansard	*Hansard's Parliamentary Debates*, 3rd Ser.
HJ	*Historical Journal*
JEH	*Journal of Ecclesiastical History*
MCL	Manchester Central Library
PP	*Parliamentary Papers*
PRO	Public Record Office
TRHS	*Transactions of the Royal Historical Society*

Popular Anti-Catholicism

in Mid-Victorian England

INTRODUCTION

IN STAVE THREE of *A Christmas Carol*, Dickens makes the Ghost of Christmas Present take Scrooge to a market, just about to be shut down before Church on Christmas morning. The people are bustling about, doing their last shopping, "jovial and full of glee; calling out to one another." The half-closed shops groan with provender—chestnuts, pears, apples, grapes, filberts, oranges, lemons, and Norfolk Biffins. Dickens describes the physical appearance of these foods with his usual orotund adjectives; the one foodstuff that he *personifies*, however, is the onion. "There were ruddy, brown-faced, broad-girthed Spanish Onions, shining in the fatness of their growth like Spanish Friars; and winking from their shelves in wanton slyness at the girls as they went by, and glanced demurely at the hung-up mistletoe."[1] When Dickens saw an onion, he did not just see an onion; he saw a swarthy Franciscan friar from the Mediterranean world, overweight from gluttony, lusting for sex with passing women. The difference between ordinary people and creative artists is that when we see an onion, we see an onion, but when they see an onion, they also see something far different and perhaps even new and wonderful. Yet although the power of their imaginations determines that they will transform the things of their world, it is the cultural context of the day that determines which images they use. The fear and loathing of Roman Catholicism was a major part of the nineteenth-century cultural context.[2]

The question of the extent to which Roman Catholics should be granted civil rights matching those of Anglicans was one of the hottest political questions of the nineteenth century. Not until Roman Catholic Emancipation in 1829 could Roman Catholics vote or stand for election to town government and to Parliament, hold commissions in the army and navy, or qualify for ministerial office. And many laws that discriminated against Roman Catholics remained on the books. Their churches could not have steeples; their priests could not wear clerical garb in public; their schools were denied state funding; they could not leave charitable bequests for purposes judged "superstitious" by Protestant standards. Roman Catholics also faced social discrimination. They were physically shunned; and the mass media of the day produced a torrent of tracts, books, magazines, and newspaper stories that reviled their beliefs, challenged their political loy-

---

[1] Charles Dickens, *The Annotated Christmas Carol*, ed. Michael Patrick Hearn (New York, 1989; orig. pub. 1843), p. 114.
[2] Victor Sage makes this point in *Horror Fiction in the Protestant Tradition*, arguing that the contemporary audience could read the "hidden, allegorical structure" in Gothic fantasy because both authors and audience shared "a deeply sown, deeply contested set of theological expectations in nineteenth-century culture" (London, 1988, p. 18). As he develops the argument, however, he gives it neither evidentiary rigor nor rootedness in Victorian culture.

alty, and depicted them as the deluded dupes of men who lusted for sex, money, and power.

For instance, Charles Chiniquy, an apostate priest from Lower Canada, travelled around the English-speaking world, publicizing the evils of Roman Catholicism. His autobiography, *Fifty Years in the Church of Rome*, narrates, among other things, how the U. S. President Abraham Lincoln was assassinated as the result of a Jesuit plot. The Roman Catholic Church had started the Civil War by promoting Southern secession. Jefferson Davis, President of the Confederate States, was married to a Roman Catholic; General P.G.T. Beauregard was a Roman Catholic. (Never mind that another Confederate general, Leonidas Polk, was an Anglican bishop.) The Jesuits determined to kill Lincoln as punishment for his having defeated the South.[3]

Chiniquy's earlier book, *The Priest, the Woman, and the Confessional*, describes how priests use the confessional to seduce women.

> The husband respectfully requested the friends to leave the room with him, and shut the door, that the holy confessor might be alone with his penitent during her general confession.
>
> One of the most diabolical schemes, under the cover of auricular confession, had perfectly succeeded. The mother of harlots, the great enchantress of souls, whose seat is on the city of the "seven hills," had, there, her priest to bring shame, disgrace, and damnation, under the mask of Christianity.
>
> The destroyer of souls, whose masterpiece is auricular confession, had, there, for the millionth time, a fresh opportunity of insulting the God of purity through one of the most criminal actions which the dark shades of night can conceal.
>
> But let us draw the veil over the abominations of that hour of iniquity, and let us leave to hell its dark secrets.[4]

Anti-Catholicism, in one form or another, has been an English characteristic since the Reformation and was especially marked in the nineteenth century. It rests upon three fundamental ideas: that of the Protestant Constitution, that of the Norman Yoke, and that of Providentialism.

England's experiences from the Reformation to the Glorious Revolution embedded in the people's historical consciousness a distinct view of Roman Catholicism that was the bedrock on which the Victorians built. This view advanced theological, moral, and political objections to Roman Catholicism. Theologically, Roman Catholicism stood for a sacrificial priesthood that interposed itself between God and humankind, and an overweening spiritual domination condemned in the apocalyptic Scriptures. Morally, Roman Catholicism claimed the power to dispense from the moral law, and indeed blurred the supposedly clear distinction between right and wrong. Victorian anti-Catholics often misrepresented the casuist moral theology of St. Alphonsus Liguori and Peter Dens as being the justification

---

[3] Charles Chiniquy, *Fifty Years in the Church of Rome* (Chino, Cal., 1985; orig. pub. 1886), pp. 291-317. Joseph George, Jr., analyzes this claim in "The Lincoln Writings of Charles P.T. Chiniquy," *Journal of the Illinois State Historical Society*, LXIX (1976), 17-25. Chiniquy's story reappeared in a pamphlet that was handed out in the streets of Cambridge when the Pope visited Britain in 1983 (Sage, *Horror Fiction*, pp. 68-69), and in a comic book sold in Christian bookshops in the United States (*The Big Betrayal*, Chick Publications, 1981).

[4] Charles Chiniquy, *The Priest, the Woman, and the Confessional* (Chino, Cal., 1979; orig. pub. 1874), p. 57.

for sexual and other sorts of immorality. Politically, Roman Catholicism stood for the arbitrary rule of absolute monarchs, and held that allegiance to the Pope was superior to allegiance to the state. England's "Protestant Constitution," it was believed, had attained its excellence at the Glorious Revolution of 1688, after a long struggle with popery. It was the Protestant nature of the Constitution that gave Britons both their religious and their civil freedoms. Therefore, the participation of Roman Catholics in political life threatened the integrity of the Constitution and opened the country to the dangers of subversion reminiscent of the fires of Smithfield, the Armada, and Guy Fawkes.[5]

The idea of the "Norman Yoke" complemented the idea of the Protestant Constitution. The Norman Yoke is the notion that the Saxons had governed themselves in primeval democratic folkmoots, but that the Normans had taken away that self-government by imposing a tyranny of foreign kings and landlords. The notion reinforced anti-Catholic constitutionalism when its adherents stressed the papal blessing on Duke William's invasion and various Plantagenet kings' acts of homage to the Pope, and imagined a Saxon Church less bound to papal authority than its Norman successor. The Norman Yoke theory reappeared in political discourse during the 1770s, and blended into the debates over Roman Catholic Emancipation during the thirty years before 1828.[6]

Finally, the idea of Providentialism linked together theology and politics. This is the idea that things happen, and happen the way they do, because God wants them to happen that way. God intervenes in the affairs of individuals to reward them for their faith or to punish them for their sins. A popular tract gives an example. When some holiday-makers spent a Sunday afternoon visiting Tintern Abbey and sailing on a pleasure-boat along the River Wye, God punished them for sabbath-breaking by summoning a storm, swamping the boat, drowning the people, and having the fishes eat the eyes and lips of the corpses.[7] God interferes similarly in the affairs of nations. Thus, the cholera epidemic of 1832, the potato famine of the 1840s, the Crimean War, and the Indian Mutiny all happened because God wanted them to happen, usually to punish the British people for their sins, but sometimes to use Britain as an instrument of divine purpose.[8] Providentialists argued that God had given Britain its world political and economic power in order to do God's will, which was the spread of British Christianity and institutions. Since Britain was Protestant, it therefore followed that God willed Protestantism.

[5] G.F.A. Best, "Popular Protestantism in Victorian Britain," *Ideas and Institutions of Victorian Britain: Essays in Honour of George Kitson Clark*, ed. Robert Robson (London, 1967), pp. 118-23; G.F.A. Best, "The Protestant Constitution and its Supporters, 1800-1829," *TRHS*, VIII (1958), 109-11; John Sharp, "The Influence of St. Alphonsus Liguori in Nineteenth-Century Britain," *Downside Review*, CI (1983), 60-76; Josef L. Altholz, "Truth and Equivocation: Liguori's Moral Theology and Newman's *Apologia*," *Church History*, XLIV (1975), 73-84.

[6] Gerald Newman, *The Rise of English Nationalism: A Cultural History, 1740-1830* (New York, 1987), pp. 184-91; Robert Hole, *Pulpits, Politics, and Public Order in England, 1760-1832* (Cambridge, 1989), pp. 232-47; G.I.T. Machin, *The Catholic Question in English Politics, 1820 to 1830* (Oxford, 1964).

[7] *The Broken Sabbath* (ca. 1840), in Louis James, *English Popular Literature, 1819-1851* (New York, 1976), pp. 158-61.

[8] Richard J. Janet, "The Decline of General Fasts in Victorian England, 1832-1857" (Ph.D. thesis, University of Notre Dame, 1984), pp. 81-84.

Did supporters of the Protestant Constitution "as a group disappear almost without a trace" after 1829 because the Irish Question made repeal of Roman Catholic Emancipation impossible as a matter of practical politics?[9] Or did the Protestant Constitution remain "a meaningful concept in public life" despite the fact that Roman Catholic Emancipation had eliminated the Constitution's Protestant nature?[10] Was Victorian anti-Catholicism merely "the last expression" of this tradition? Were Victorian anti-Catholics simply "men who clung to dying theories of the Constitution and to social *mores* which were changing faster than they imagined"?[11]

Was anti-Catholicism a stalking horse for anti-Irish prejudice? This argument holds that the English did not like Roman Catholics (most of whom were Irish) because they did not like the Irish. Was it primarily the Irish Question that pushed anti-Catholicism to the center of political life during the nineteenth century? Did the debates over Roman Catholic Emancipation in the 1820s, the growth of the Irish Roman Catholic population in England, and the ways that that growth irritated Anglo-Irish relations provide "the strongest stimulus" for the revival of "a more whole-hearted anti-Catholicism," in contrast to the indifference and latitudinarianism of the eighteenth century?[12]

Can anti-Catholic sentiments best be analyzed as a psychological phantasmagoria of paranoid sexuality, reflecting the "fears, prejudices, hopes, and perhaps even unconscious desires" of the people? Is it an attempt to resolve the "increasing anxiety and uncertainty over sexual values and the proper role of woman" that supposedly characterized the nineteenth century?[13]

Are cultural and geographical variables at work? Can one distinguish between European and American anti-Catholicism by arguing that in Europe, popish subversion was taken to threaten the established order of monarchs and aristocrats, while in the United States it was taken to threaten the "ideals or a way of life" of "free Americans"?[14] Or can one distinguish between Continental anti-Catholicism and the British variety by arguing that the Continental type reflected "varying class and regional discontents," while the British variety, transcending class and region, "was chauvinistic and almost general"?[15]

Nonconformists had been relatively quiet during the first third of the nineteenth century, partly to avoid charges of political disloyalty during wartime, partly because their energies were engaged by the Evangelical revival, and partly because of their own internal divisions. After 1828, however, they grew more militant in protesting the Established Church's privileged position and, by implication, their own inferiority. Repeal of the

[9] Best, "Protestant Constitution," pp. 122-24.
[10] E. R. Norman, *Anti-Catholicism in Victorian England* (London, 1968), p. 19.
[11] *Ibid.*, p. 21.
[12] *Ibid.*, p. 18; D. W. Bebbington, *Evangelicalism in Modern Britain: A History from the 1730s to the 1980s* (London, 1989), pp. 101-2 (quoted); Alan D. Gilbert, *Religion and Society in Industrial England: Church, Chapel and Social Change, 1740-1914* (London, 1976), pp. 172-73.
[13] David Brion Davis, "Some Themes of Counter-Subversion: An Analysis of Anti-Masonic, Anti-Catholic, and Anti-Mormon Literature," *Mississippi Valley Historical Review*, XLVII (1960), 217-20; Robert J. Klaus, *The Pope, the Protestants, and the Irish: Papal Aggression and Anti-Catholicism in Mid-Nineteenth Century England* (New York, 1987), pp. 290-94.
[14] Davis, "Counter-Subversion," p. 205.
[15] Norman, *Anti-Catholicism*, p. 20.

Test and Corporation Acts, as is well known, was but "a nominal and formal concession" of "purely legal equality"; only the remedying of Dissenters' grievances would turn the concession into "practical reality."[16] The Grey, Peel, and Melbourne ministries attempted to pacify both Dissent and Roman Catholicism during the 1830s by exempting chapels from the poor-rate, granting civil registration of births, deaths, and marriages, repealing Lord Hardwicke's Marriage Act of 1753, and chartering the nondenominational University of London. Nonconformists, however, remained dissatisfied because these concessions whetted their appetite for further concessions, especially with respect to religious tests at Oxford and Cambridge universities, burial in churchyards according to the Anglican rite, and the collection of church rates. The Church Rate Abolition Society's campaign in 1837 produced petitions bearing 674,719 signatures (as against pro-Anglican petitions with 330,123 signatures). The Melbourne Ministry did propose the abolition of church rates, but abandoned it when it could muster a majority of only five on its second reading. Dissenters became increasingly frustrated with Whig inaction, for not until 1866 did a government again support church-rate abolition.[17]

Religious tensions increased markedly during the period 1837-50, as conflicts among Anglicans, Nonconformists, and Roman Catholics converged on several issues. The focus of church-rate disputes shifted from Parliament to vestries with refusals to levy rates, or to pay them when levied. In the celebrated Braintree (Essex) Case, the churchwardens tried to levy a rate after the vestry refused to do so; the litigation that followed lasted until 1853. Simultaneously, John Thorogood, a Chelmsford shoemaker, was imprisoned for nonpayment of church rates in 1839-40; other cases of nonpayment followed, especially at Leicester and Rochdale. Edward Miall, the Leicester Congregationalist, began publishing the *Nonconformist* in 1841, and organized the Anti-State Church Association in 1844. Although Dissent was thus becoming more militant, it was also becoming more divided, between those who wanted the relief of grievances and those who came to believe that only disestablishment and disendowment of the Church of England would elevate the Nonconformists to first-class citizenship.[18]

The High-Church wing of the Established Church fought back, not only by defending church rates, but also by expanding its claims on public revenues for the support of parochial schools. The Church had managed to defeat the Melbourne Ministry's attempt to create a system of nondenominational teacher-training and Erastian school-inspection in 1839 (with the help of the Wesleyans, who feared that the plan would place Roman Catholic schools on an equal footing with Protestant schools). Then the Peel Ministry, more favorably disposed to Anglican claims, introduced the Factory Bill, 1843. This measure contemplated a network of church-controlled schools funded by a local rate, but the government was compelled to withdraw it after an outpouring of mainly Nonconformist protest. Finally, the Russell Ministry bowed to the inevitable and issued the Educa-

---

16 G.I.T. Machin, *Politics and the Churches in Great Britain, 1832 to 1868* (Oxford, 1977), p. 55; Paul Adelman, *Victorian Radicalism: The Middle-Class Experience, 1830-1914* (London, 1984), pp. 67, 69.
17 Machin, *Politics and the Churches*, pp. 42-43, 51, 56-61.
18 *Ibid.*, pp. 46, 103-8; Adelman, *Victorian Radicalism*, p. 70.

tion Minutes of 1846, which authorized extensive funding for teacher-training on a denominational basis, of which the Church would get the largest share. Nonconformists again mounted a massive protest when the Minutes were presented to Parliament in 1847, but this time failed to change state policy. The results of this decade-long dispute were that militant Nonconformists added another major grievance to their list, while Anglicans mistrusted the motives of both Whigs and Dissent.[19]

At the same time, relations between the state and the Roman Catholic Church were unstable, because the Roman Catholic Relief Acts of 1778, 1791, and 1829 only suspended penal legislation, and many Roman Catholic activities remained illegal. Some laws worked a real hardship. Philanthropists after 1832 could endow Roman Catholic charities, but any bequests that allocated funds for "superstitious" purposes such as Masses or candles for the dead were void. Roman Catholics were excluded from the government's education grants until 1847; thereafter they could qualify for aid only under conditions that they deemed insulting. Other laws, although unenforced, symbolized their legal and social inferiority. Roman Catholic chapels could not have steeples, Jesuits could not live in England, public religious processions were illegal, nuns had to register with the government, and those who stayed away from the parish church on Sunday were subject to fines. Roman Catholic M.P.s complained about these matters throughout the 1840s, and charges of forced conversions to Anglicanism enlivened debates on the poor law and the factory law. The Peel Ministry, however, resolutely opposed any modification of the Roman Catholic Emancipation Act.[20]

Ireland, however, required special treatment. There, religious grievances combined with nationalism to create a militance that could be ignored only at the peril of revolution. The Whigs had sought to ease tensions by awarding state aid to parochial schools in the 1830s. The Peel Ministry went further in principle by relaxing somewhat the restrictions on Roman Catholic charities with the Charitable Bequests Act, 1844, and by creating a permanent endowment for the Maynooth seminary, the main trainer of Irish priests, in 1845. The Parliament at Westminster had given annual grants to Maynooth since 1801, as had the Irish Parliament before, but the conversion of the annual grant into a permanent endowment provoked savage parliamentary debates, a furor of public meetings, and the desertion of Peel by his backbenchers. He remained in power thereafter only through Whig support, and the Maynooth endowment, not repeal of the Corn Laws, marks the fatal split of the Conservative Party.[21]

The Russell Ministry, which came to power in 1846, believed that the Roman Catholic clergy were the key to pacifying the island and hoped to play on the differences between the lower clergy and the prelates. The

[19] D. G. Paz, *The Politics of Working-Class Education in Britain, 1830-50* (Manchester, 1980), pp. 79-87, 114-22, 132-33.

[20] D. G. Paz, "Another Look at Lord John Russell and the Papal Aggression, 1850," *Historian*, XLV (1982-83), 48-49.

[21] Gilbert A. Cahill, "The Protestant Association and the Anti-Maynooth Agitation of 1845," *Catholic Historical Review*, XLIII (1957), 273-308; G.I.T. Machin, "The Maynooth Grant, the Dissenters and Disestablishment, 1845-1847," *EHR*, LXXXII (1967), 61-85; E. R. Norman, "The Maynooth Question of 1845," *Irish Historical Studies*, XV (1967), 407-37; Frank Howard Wallis, "The Anti-Maynooth Campaign: A Study in Anti-Catholicism and Politics in the United Kingdom, 1851-69" (Ph.D. thesis, University of Illinois, 1987), pp. 12-17.

former, although nationalistic and allegedly an influence for sedition at the polls, were also concerned with the mundane issues of salary, tenure, and freedom from episcopal domination; the latter, becoming increasingly ultramontane throughout the period, might be willing to sacrifice nationalism for increased social status and a free hand over the lower clergy. Thus, Russell developed four policies designed to gain the support of the Irish Roman Catholic Church.

The first was to appoint Irish Roman Catholics to office. R. L. Sheil, considered for a cabinet post, became Master of the Mint; the wealthy landowner R. More O'Ferrall became governor of Malta in 1847. But those Irishmen likely to be acceptable to the government were not likely to carry much weight among Irish nationalists. Thus Russell's second measure was as bold as his first had been picayune; he firmly grasped the nettle of concurrent endowment. A tour of Ireland in the autumn of 1833 had convinced him that the tithe should be supplanted by a land tax, to be used for the concurrent endowment of Roman Catholic, Presbyterian, and Church of Ireland clergymen. Russell brought it up from time to time thereafter, and proposed a concrete scheme to the Cabinet in October 1848 for an annual grant of £340,000 to a body of Irish Roman Catholic commissioners, to be used as they pleased for glebes, stipends, and the repair of chapel fabric. Although the Pope approved such a plan, the Irish Roman Catholic bishops, fearful of losing their independence, vetoed it. Russell still talked endowment a year later, but the proposal was a dead issue.[22]

The third policy was as cheap as the second was dear. The Irish Roman Catholic Church during this period asserted its claim to be the "legitimate" church of Ireland as against the Anglican Establishment; one sign of this claim was the Roman prelates' practice of using the same titles as those of the Anglican prelates. Russell, acting on the advice of Lord Clarendon, Lord Lieutenant of Ireland, required Dublin Castle to adopt this usage. "The importance of enlisting the RC Clergy thru their Bishops on the side of Govt. & the legitimate objects of Govt. cannot be exaggerated, & it is fortunate that the Bishops can be rendered less hostile by such puerilities as empty titles. The fact is however that they set great store by them . . . & their pleasure at being My Lorded . . . is quite curious."[23] Such a practice was illegal, for the Roman Catholic Emancipation Act forbade the use of Anglican titles. This was one of those galling implications of inferiority that Roman Catholics had attempted to remove in 1845 and 1846, but which the Peel Ministry had defended as part of the inviolable pact of Roman Catholic Emancipation. Lord John Russell, on the other hand, struck a good latitudinarian note, maintaining that it was desirable to "repeal those disallowing clauses which prevented a Roman Catholic bishop assuming a title held by a bishop of the Established Church. He could not conceive any good ground for the continuance of this restriction. . . . As to preventing persons assuming particular titles, nothing could be more absurd and puerile than to keep up such a distinction."[24] The value of this policy in easing Anglo-Irish relations is problematical.

[22] Paz, "Another Look," p. 50; Machin, *Politics and the Churches*, p. 36.
[23] Clarendon to Russell, 30 Oct. 1847, Russell Papers, PRO, quoted in Paz, "Another Look," p. 50.
[24] Conflated from 3 *Hansard*, LXXXII (1845), 290, and LXXXIII (1846), 501.

Russell's last policy was to circumvent the Irish hierarchy entirely by establishing diplomatic relations with Rome. Britain had maintained sporadic contacts through representatives of other courts and had seconded an attaché of the Florentine legation to live in Rome since 1832. But such expedients were not enough to further Russell's goals—the encouragement of Italian liberalism and papal cooperation in restraining Irish ultramontanes—so the ministry introduced a bill in 1848 to establish formal diplomatic relations. Although Russell claimed that the measure touched the Papacy only in its temporal role, both ultramontanes and Ultra-Tories, for their own reasons, charged that the Pope as prince was inseparable from the Pope as pontiff. Thus, the enacted measure referred to the Pope as "the Sovereign of the Roman States," not the usual "Supreme Pontiff," and required his representative at London to be a layman. Russell accepted these amendments, which came from the Ultra-Tory side, rather than lose the bill, but they made the measure unacceptable to the Papacy. The Pope refused to exchange envoys on such terms, and Russell's last attempt at good church-state relations had come to naught.[25]

At this juncture there occurred the Papal Aggression, an ebullition of anti-Catholic sentiment during the winter of 1850-51. On 29 September 1850, Pope Pius IX[26] created a territorial hierarchy of twelve bishoprics and declared that the new divisions would hold "notwithstanding the rights and privileges of the ancient English sees."[27] English Roman Catholic bishops now ruled dioceses styled after English place-names rather than after points of the compass, and bore titles derived from their sees rather than from extinct Levantine cities. Although England remained a mission in the Vatican's eyes,[28] this change marked "a critical discontinuity in the history of the [Roman Catholic] community."[29] A day later, Pius elevated Nicholas Wiseman,[30] vicar apostolic of the Central District,[31] and the most prominent leader of the English Roman Church, to head the new hierarchy as the first Cardinal Archbishop of Westminster. Having received his red hat, Wiseman issued his first pastoral letter, and took the high road to London on 12 October to assume his duties.

Neither Wiseman nor Pius appeared to have anticipated more than token British protests, but their expectations turned out to be illusory and, perhaps, naive. When news of Pio Nono's and Wiseman's proclamations reached London, about a week after the new Cardinal had departed from

---

[25] Paz, "Another Look," p. 51; Julian Reynolds, "Politics vs. Persuasion: The Attempt to Establish Anglo-Roman Diplomatic Relations in 1848," *Catholic Historical Review*, LXXI (1985), 372-93; Donal A. Kerr, "England, Ireland, and Rome, 1847-1848," *Studies in Church History*, XXV (1989), 259-77.

[26] Giovanni Maria Mastai Ferretti (1792-1878); Pope, 1846-78. Vaguely reformist, vaguely nationalist, vaguely Romantic, vaguely humanitarian; the reality of the 1848 Revolution turned him into a political and theological reactionary. *New Catholic Encyclopedia*, VI, 405-8; Giacomo Martina, *Pio IX (1846-1850)* (Rome, 1974).

[27] *Annual Register*, XCII (1851), 405-11.

[28] The Propaganda continued to handle English affairs until 1908—a sure sign that the Vatican still regarded England as a mission.

[29] John Bossy, *The English Catholic Community, 1570-1850* (London, 1975), pp. 4-5, 360-63.

[30] Nicholas Patrick Stephen Wiseman (1802-1865), first Cardinal Archbishop of Westminster; born at Seville of Irish parents; lived in Ireland (1805-10) and England (1810-18); at Rome as student, scholar, and Rector of the English College, 1818-40; leading Roman Catholic prelate in England, 1840 to his death (*DNB*, XXI, 714-17).

[31] The vicar apostolic governs missionary areas where the Roman community is too small to support regular diocesan organization, and has a courtesy title taken from North African or Near Eastern sees that the Muslims had extinguished.

Rome, the *Times*'s leader-writers reflected for five days, then launched a series of attacks against the new hierarchy. Since Westminster, the seat of Parliament, symbolized British liberties, Wiseman's use of that title was an insult. The hierarchy, moreover, would encourage "the wanton interference of a band of foreign priests" in domestic affairs. Although a few "weak minds" had converted, the Pope was mistaken in believing that England would ever return to "Romish bondage." Thus Pius's illegal exercise of spiritual power would be to no avail.[32]

Roman Catholics themselves added fuel to the Protestant fire. The London press took the text of the papal decree, published between 22 and 26 October, to be both an assumption of supreme spiritual authority over the nation and a denial of the validity of Anglican orders.[33] (The provincial press published the text a day or so later,[34] and it is wrong to think that the subsequent furor was the creation of the metropolitan press, or of the *Times* alone.[35]) On the 27th, John Henry Newman preached what can only be described as an inflammatory sermon at the enthronement of the new Roman Catholic Bishop of Birmingham, proclaiming that God was leading England back to the true church, which possessed both "divine prerogatives and . . . high destiny."[36] But Wiseman's first pastoral letter to his flock caused the most serious damage. The document was read in London chapels on Sunday, 28 October, and appeared in the newspapers the next day.[37] "[W]e govern, and shall continue to govern," Wiseman declared, "the counties of Middlesex, Hertford, and Essex as ordinary thereof, and those of Surrey, Sussex, Kent, Berkshire, and Hampshire . . . as administrator with ordinary jurisdiction." Turning to the hierarchy's significance, he declared movingly to his flock:

> The great work, then is complete. . . . Your beloved country has received a place among the fair Churches, which . . . form the splendid aggregate of Catholic Communion; Catholic England has been restored to its orbit in the ecclesiastical firmament, from which its light had long vanished, and begins now anew its course of regularly adjusted action round the centre of unity, the source of jurisdiction, of light and vigour. . . .
>   Then truly is this day to us a day of joy and exhaltation of spirit, the crowning day of long hopes, the opening day of bright prospects. How must the Saints of our country, whether Roman or British, Saxon or Norman, look down from their seats of bliss, with beaming glance, upon this new evidence of the faith and Church which led them to glory, sympathising with those who have faithfully adhered to them through centuries of ill repute for the truth's sake, and now reap the fruit of their patience and longsuffering. And all those blessed martyrs of these latter ages, . . . who mourned . . . over the departure of England's religious glory; oh! how must they bless God, who hath again visited his people.—how take part in our

32 *Times*, 9, 14, 19 Oct. 1850.

33 *Ibid.*, 22 Oct. 1850; *Standard*, 14 Oct. 1850; *Illustrated London News*, 26 Oct. 1850.

34 *Manchester Courier*, 26 Oct. 1850; *Aris's Birmingham Gazette*, 28 Oct. 1850.

35 As do Klaus, *Pope, Protestants, and Irish*, p. 221; and Edward Norman, *The English Catholic Church in the Nineteenth Century* (Oxford, 1984), pp. 103-4. A survey of newspaper comment on the assumption of titles is in Thomas P. Joyce, *The Restoration of the Catholic Hierarchy in England and Wales, 1850: A Study of Certain Public Reactions* (Rome, 1966).

36 J. H. Newman, *Sermons Preached on Various Occasions*, new ed. (London, 1898), pp. 121-59; *Times*, 29 Oct. 1850.

37 *Times*, 29 Oct. 1850; *Standard*, 29 Oct. 1850. The *Times* commented sarcastically: "It will be seen that His Eminence the newly-appointed Cardinal has not been slow to exercise the authority of his recently acquired dignity."

joy . . . , as they behold the silver links of that chain which has connected their country with the see of Peter in its vicarial government changed into burnished gold; not stronger nor more closely knit, but more beautifully wrought and more brightly arrayed.[38]

It was unfortunate that this document transpired only a week before Guy Fawkes Day. The press vigorously attacked Wiseman's pastoral letter and Newman's sermon, damning their language as arrogant and their appraisal of English religious conditions as unrealistic. On the day itself the new hierarchy replaced "gunpowder, treason, and plot." Londoners awoke to see slogans such as "No Popery" and "No Wafer Gods" painted on walls. At noon, a monster procession, centered about a huge effigy of Wiseman and escorted by men dressed as monks and nuns, marched through the metropolis. Many parishes throughout England held services commemorating the day, and effigies of Pius and Wiseman often replaced the usual straw guys.[39]

Two days later, the press published the text of Lord John Russell's notorious open letter to the Bishop of Durham. The prime minister attacked the "insolent and insidious" Papal Aggression[40] because it challenged the Royal Supremacy and the Established Church by implying that Rome held authority over England. Russell did not fear this "outward attack," for a nation that had enjoyed freedom of speech and religion for so long had nothing to fear from the Pope. The greater threat were the Tractarians, who were leading their flocks to Roman "mummeries of superstition."[41]

> Clergymen of our own Church . . . have been most forward in leading their flocks "step by step to the very verge of the precipice." The honours paid to saints, the claim of infallibility for the Church, the superstitious use of the sign of the cross, the muttering of the liturgy so as to disguise the language in which it is written, the recommendation of auricular confession, and the administration of penance and absolution, all these things are pointed out by clergymen of the Church of England as worthy of adoption.
>   What then is the danger to be apprehended from a foreign ruler of no great power compared to the danger within the gates from the unworthy sons of the Church of England herself?

These pronouncements and counter-pronouncements resulted in nationwide protest meetings during the last two months of 1850.[42] The clergy of Westminster and the parishioners of St. George's, Hanover Square, petitioned their bishop only a few days after Pius's decree had appeared in the press. The Anglican hierarchy denounced the assumption of titles, urged their clergy to circulate protest petitions, and themselves petitioned the Queen, contending that the creation of a rival hierarchy "unchurched" the Church of England and usurped the Royal Supremacy. Clergy, following their episcopal leaders, sponsored parish meetings; by the

---

[38] English Historical Documents, 1833-1874, ed. G. M. Young and W. D. Handcock, English Historical Documents, David C. Douglas (gen. ed.), 12 vols. (New York, 1956), Vol. XII, Pt. 1, pp. 365-66.

[39] Times, 30 Oct., 6, 9 Nov. 1850; Illustrated London News, 2, 9 Nov. 1850.

[40] This phrase, which came to be the label for the brouhaha, first appeared in the national press in a letter from "A London Clergyman" (Times, 24 Oct. 1850).

[41] Russell to Edward Maltby, 4 Nov. 1850, Eng. Hist. Docs., pp. 367-69.

[42] For announcements and reports of meetings, see the Times for November and December, 1850, under the heading "The Papal Aggression."

middle of November, the movement had grown to include town and county assemblies. Societies and corporations, municipal, educational, and professional, also protested the Papal Aggression. The Scottish Episcopal Church, Church of Scotland, Protestant Dissenting Deputies, and Wesleyan Methodist Committee on Privileges joined in the protests, as did Nonconformist chapels throughout England. Some protests resulted in violence. Crowds disturbed Sunday services at the ritualist parish, St. Barnabas's, Pimlico, with hisses and cries of "No Popery!," and actual riots occurred in Cheltenham, Birkenhead, and Liverpool. The indignation prompted a massive petition drive that garnered 2,616 memorials to the Queen protesting the new hierarchy, bearing 887,525 signatures (roughly five percent of the English population).

Clearly the Papal Aggression had summoned up energies and feelings in an unexpected way. A vicar near East Retford, Notts, reported thusly on the mood in his parish to his archdeacon:

> [O]n Sunday afternoon I preached on the subject [of the Papal Aggression,] giving such an explanation as I was able to from what I had read of the Manchester meeting and others. I had a large Congregation, fully one third of my population, and a good muster of singers. The effect was like electricity. No sooner had I ended my sermon than the quire struck up with that beautiful hymn of Dr. Is. Watts'
> Soldiers of Christ arise
> And put your armour on
> now I think [that] shows us that even here our protestant people are alive to *Popish Insult*.[43]

Russell's denunciation of Romanism and Tractarianism in the Durham Letter could not end the government's involvement in Papal Aggression. The newspaper press and the Protestant public demanded that something be done to repel the Papal Aggression, and Russell, by the Durham Letter, appeared to have promised that something, indeed, would be done. Russell, however, had no idea of how to translate the Durham Letter into policy. Conflicting advice assailed him from all sides. Should mediæval or Tudor penal laws be resurrected? Should the Deanery of Westminster be turned into a diocese, thereby bringing Wiseman into violation of the Roman Catholic Emancipation Act? Would an order in council be appropriate? Moderate Cisalpine groups also proffered their advice. T. Chisholm Anstey, Francis Riddell, and Mark Tierney (domestic chaplain to the Duke of Norfolk) offered to help the government draft legislation that would keep charitable bequests out of the hands of the ultramontanes. At Rome, the Old Catholic Lord Edward Howard served as intermediary for discussions among Msgrs. Garibaldi and Fornari, Count Montalembert, and John Abel Smith, M.P., about a possible compromise bull.[44]

Russell, however, was moving in the direction of a concordat with the Papacy. He proposed to the cabinet on 2 November that the government "ask the Pope for an explanation." In concrete terms this meant appointing R. L. Sheil to the Florentine legation, from which he might ask the Pope to retract *Universalis Ecclesiæ*. The Queen objected to such a course

[43] Rev. John Goodacre to the Ven. George Wilkins, 12 Nov. 1850, Archdeaconry of Nottingham Manuscripts, University of Nottingham Library, Misc. 281a.
[44] Paz, "Another Look," p. 60.

and it was dropped. But Russell continued to dream of a concordat, asked Palmerston how other states organized their relations with the Papacy, and circulated another proposal to the cabinet in mid-December that the government "make known" its views of the matter in Rome. Palmerston opposed such a scheme, observing that the government neither possessed inducements attractive enough to bring the Pope to restore the vicars apostolic nor was strong enough to prevent penal legislation from being passed, that the negotiations must be kept secret—an impossible task—in order to prevent the inevitable objections, and that in any case it was too late to initiate talks in time to resolve the problem before Parliament met. As late as March 1851, Russell still hoped for a concordat, the trade-off being the withdrawal of *Universalis Ecclesiæ* and a royal veto over the appointment of Roman Catholic prelates in return for the free entry of papal bulls if they were registered with a board. Palmerston's comment on another of Russell's foreign policy schemes seems appropriate here: "This is all nonsense."[45]

Russell had been thinking simultaneously of legislation, and indeed had been urged on by the senior Whig politicians Ellice, Minto, Sir George Grey, and Lord Truro. The more easygoing Whig ministers—Lansdowne, Palmerston, Clarendon, and Earl Grey—thought that public agitation was folly and Russell's reaction witless. But they believed that the government had to propose some measure, or else public opinion would never forgive them and an anti-Catholic measure would be enacted anyway. By 11 December the cabinet, without consulting the Irish lord lieutenant, had agreed to introduce legislation making the assumption of territorial titles illegal and the conveyance of property under such titles void. Russell's legislation—the Ecclesiastical Titles Bill—was introduced in the House of Commons in February 1851. The Peelites, Irish, and Radicals, upon whom the ministry depended for important support, found the measure repugnant, while Conservatives and some right-wing Whigs considered it too weak to meet the problem, for its penalties were relatively mild and its ban did not extend to Ireland. Thus there was a second round of meetings, from March to July of 1851, that produced 1,914 petitions to the House of Commons, bearing 348,590 signatures, praying that the Ecclesiastical Titles Bill be made more stringent. The result was parliamentary chaos and the collapse of the government. Although Russell did return to office after a short time, because there was no alternative government, and although the Ecclesiastical Titles Bill was eventually enacted (with stronger language than Russell had wanted), his days were numbered.[46] Russell's Papal Aggression policy thus satisfied no one.

Concurrently with the public furor over Papal Aggression, several scandalous court cases further tarnished the Roman Catholic Church and provided evidence for anti-Catholic claims. A priest at Sheffield was compelled to pay child support in July 1850, after his servant testified that he had seduced her, heard her confession, and granted her absolution to quiet her scruples. A girl at Exeter claimed to have been coerced by Jesuits into converting to Rome in December.[47] The most notorious cases, which gained

    [45] *Ibid.*, pp. 60-61.
    [46] *Ibid.*, p. 61; D. G. Paz, "Lord John Russell's Anti-Catholic Dilemma: The Ministerial Crisis of 1851," *Proceedings of the South Carolina Historical Association, 1987*, pp. 33-43.
    [47] *Leeds Mercury*, 27 July, 28 Dec. 1850.

the widest publicity, however, were those of *Metairie v. Wiseman and Others*, the Talbot Case, *Connelly v. Connelly*, and *Achilli v. Newman*; they had to do with sex, money, and priestly domination.

Metairie, heard in March 1851, seemed to prove that popish priests used their inordinate spiritual powers to extract money from the dying. Mathurin Carré (1770-1847), a teacher of French who had lived in England since 1797, had accumulated a fortune of £10,000 by means of industry and "a miserly parsimony." Carré fell ill in February 1847 and was treated by a Roman Catholic physician, who learned of the old man's fortune. The physician told James Holdstock, pastor of St. Aloysius's chapel, Somers Town, who convinced Carré to give £7,000 to the girls' school connected with the chapel. Carré's next-of-kin, François Metairie, challenged the deed of gift on the grounds of improper influence. Although the parties settled out of court, the case allowed newspapers to denounce mercenary and exploitative practices over the dying, and to pin the charges to Wiseman's cassock even though he was a defendant only by virtue of his official capacity as Holdstock's superior.[48]

Hard on its heels came the Talbot Case, heard in Chancery in March and April, which was publicized as an example of unscrupulous priests trying to get their hands on an heiress's fortune by inveigling her into a nunnery. Augusta Talbot was the daughter of a Roman Catholic father (George Henry Talbot, half-brother of the Earl of Shrewsbury, a prominent Old Catholic peer) and an Anglican mother. When the parents, who had separated, died (the father in 1839 and the mother in 1841), the girl was made a ward of chancery and given to Lord Shrewsbury's care. The case arose when Craven Fitzhardinge Berkeley, who had married Augusta's mother, claimed that the Shrewsburys had attempted to force Augusta to marry the duc de Rochefoucault, and that when she refused, the Countess of Shrewsbury had put her in a nunnery at Taunton as a postulant. At issue was who would control Augusta's inheritance of £80,000. Lord Chancellor Truro dismissed Berkeley's petition as unfounded (he had made no effort to see Augusta since 1843), but the Protestant prints used the case to make further allegations about greedy priests, and the brilliant *Punch* cartoonists John Leech and John Tenniel drew sinister monks luring virginal girls into convents.[49] This case allowed anti-Catholics to dismiss vows of poverty in sisterhoods as "a grand scheme for relieving English ladies of their money."[50]

Connelly v. Connelly was used to demonstrate that Roman Catholicism had the power to destroy the bonds of matrimony itself. This case related to Pierce and Cornelia Connelly, American Episcopalians who had converted to Roman Catholicism in 1835. The two received a papal separation so that Pierce could become a priest and Cornelia a nun. They ended up

[48] *Times*, 6, 7, 8, 10, 11, 12, 13, 14, 18 Mar., 18 June 1851; *Huddersfield Chronicle*, 1 Feb., 22 Mar. 1851; *Leeds Mercury*, 8, 15, 22 Mar. 1851.

[49] *Times*, 17, 21, 22, 24, 28, 31 Mar., 1, 2 Apr. 1851; *Huddersfield Chronicle*, 22 Mar., 5 Apr. 1851; *Sunderland Herald*, 4 Apr. 1851; *Leeds Mercury*, 29 Mar., 5 Apr. 1851; Susan P. Casteras, "Virgin Vows: The Early Victorian Artists' Portrayal of Nuns and Novices," *Religion in the Lives of English Women, 1760-1930*, ed. Gail Malmgreen (Bloomington, 1986), p. 133; Lindsay Errington, *Social and Religious Themes in English Art, 1840-1860* (New York, 1984), pp. 341-44. Sage (*Horror Fiction*, p. 38) uses these cartoons to make a one-sentence point about the Antichrist, but the cartoons are solidly rooted in a real-life event related to an altogether different allegory, that of monkish greed.

[50] Walter Walsh, *The Secret History of the Oxford Movement*, 5th ed. (London, 1899), p. 170.

in England where Pierce was a chaplain in Lord Shrewsbury's household and Cornelia the foundress of a teaching order. When Pierce, overshadowed by more prominent converts, quarreled with Nicholas Wiseman, he left the Church and sued Cornelia for restitution of conjugal rights. The case was argued in the Arches Court, which ruled for Pierce in May 1849 and March 1850, and the appeal to the Judicial Committee of the Privy Council was heard in June 1851. The case hinged on the technical questions of how the marriage laws of Pennsylvania, Rome, and England affected the marriage, and of where the Connellys were domiciled when they separated, but the newspaper reports focused on the enormity of the Pope's claim to dispense from the vows of matrimony.[51]

Without a doubt, however, the most notorious of the cases was the libel trial *Achilli v. Newman* of June 1852. Giacinto Achilli, a former Dominican who had been arrested after the Pope's restoration to power at Rome in 1849, was freed after representations from leading Evangelicals and travelled around the British Isles in 1850 and 1851, lecturing on the doctrinal corruption of the Roman Catholic Church and the sexual wickedness of its clergy. But Nicholas Wiseman learned that the Inquisition had arrested him for being a notorious fornicator, and John Henry Newman repeated Wiseman's charges in a series of public lectures at Birmingham. Achilli charged Newman with criminal libel, and the trial was held in June 1852. For four days, the British reading public was treated to accounts of sordid sex with their breakfast kippers, as witnesses testified that Achilli had raped Italian penitents, rubbed his body against English servant girls, and played with his housekeeper's breasts. Despite the evidence, the jury found Newman guilty, but Protestants could take little pleasure from the verdict, for all but the most credulous anti-Catholics had come to realize that Achilli was a rogue.[52]

The revelations of the *Achilli* case appear to have brought some anti-Catholics—or the *Times*'s leader-writers, at least—to their senses. The *Times* had rejoiced in the *Metairie* settlement as having vindicated the anti-Catholic claims and had put the best Protestant face possible on the Talbot Case disappointment, but the *Achilli* verdict was too much for it. It declared that justice had not been done, and it moderated its treatment of subsequent litigation. The Norwood Nunnery Case, *Griffiths v. de l'Espinasse*, heard at the Guildford Assizes in August 1852, focused on nuns' alleged cruelty to a schoolgirl. The jury found for the nuns, and the *Times* deplored intolerance, complained that the courtroom had been filled with sensation-seekers, and professed to be pleased that justice had prevailed. Two years later, the *Times* treated the action *Boyle v. Wiseman*, in which a dissident priest sued Cardinal Wiseman for libel, very gingerly, passing up the chance to milk it for anti-Catholic purposes, even though Wiseman probably had uttered the libel complained of.[53] The provincial press, however, was more lurid in its coverage of these cases and continued to publish local cases for their smut value.[54]

[51] D. G. Paz, *The Priesthoods and Apostasies of Pierce Connelly: A Study of Victorian Conversion and Anticatholicism* (Lewiston, N.Y., and Queenston, Ont., 1986), p. 139-49; *Leeds Mercury*, 30 Mar. 1850, 5 July 1851; *Times*, 13 May, 7 June 1852.

[52] Paz, *Connelly*, pp. 18-25; *Leeds Mercury*, 26 June 1852, 26 Jan., 6, 23 July 1853.

[53] *Times*, 25, 26 June, 7 Aug. 1852, 14 Aug. 1854.

[54] *Leeds Mercury*, 14 Aug. 1852, 9 July 1853, 19 Aug., 18 Nov. 1854.

Two international causes célèbres of the 1850s added to the popular image of Romanism's persecutory tendencies: the Madiai Affair of 1852 and the Mortara Affair of 1858.

The Grand Duchy of Tuscany had maintained a relatively liberal religious policy during the second quarter of the century, permitting Protestant chapels to exist in connection with the Prussian and British legations, and tolerating Tuscans who converted to Protestantism, but the reaction to the 1848 Revolution reversed this policy. The Grand Duke banned Protestant proselytism, forbade Tuscan subjects to attend Protestant worship, and warned the two chapels not to allow Tuscans to attend their services. Among those Tuscan subjects who were arrested for violating these laws were Francesco and Rosa Madiai. The Madiai let lodgings to British travellers, and over the years had developed close connections with them. Thus they had champions; after their trial and imprisonment, their friends approached the Foreign Office, accounts of their fate appeared in the press, and Protestants organized mass meetings and petition drives. The agitation lasted from November 1851 to March 1853, when the Madiai were freed and expelled from the Grand Duchy.[55]

The Mortara Affair of 1858 reinforced the image of priestly obscurantism. Edgar Mortara, a Jewish child from Bologna in the Papal States, had been secretly baptized by one of the family servants. When this came to light, the child was removed from his family, taken to Rome, and there placed in a convent to be raised as a Christian. English reaction focused on the aspects of the case related to the breaking up of families, forcible conversion, and fears that Roman Catholic servants engaged in the surreptitious baptism of non-Catholic infants. The *Times* argued that the matter was none of Britain's business, and should be left to France and Austria.

> The Jews know how to take care of themselves; they are rich, united, and love their tribe; they are high in the Councils of Emperors, and they know that not even Popes and Cardinals are independent of their aid. They will, no doubt, carry the day, and restore the infant Mortara to his parents, and to the faith, the habits, and the antipathies of his race. So we may, with an easy conscience, consider the affair not to concern ourselves, and look at it merely with an eye of curiosity, as if we were studying the usages of some strange and newly discovered people.[56]

Anti-Catholics were less easy in their consciences, however much they may have agreed with the leader-writer's anti-Semitism, and protested the enormity of the affair. The Mortara Affair occasioned the same sorts of parliamentary and public debates, petition drives, and controversial literature that the Madiai Affair did.[57] Both affairs reinforced the belief that Roman Catholic obscurantism fitted well with authoritarian government.

Over the long term, there were three main domestic foci to anti-Catholic agitation during the 1850s and '60s: the abolition of church rates, the repeal of the Maynooth endowment, and the inspection of convents.

[55] Anne Lohrli, "The Madiai: A Forgotten Chapter of Church History," *Victorian Studies*, XXXII (1989-90), 30-43.
[56] *Times*, 26 Oct. 1858.
[57] Dr. Bruce S. Kupelnick, of Boston, Mass., is writing a book-length study of the Mortara Affair.

Church-rate abolition was connected with anti-Catholicism because the Church of England could be depicted as semi-papist, especially with the rise of Anglo-Catholicism. Miall's Anti-State Church Association, which changed its name to the Liberation Society in 1853, hoped that the call to disestablish the Church and confiscate its property would serve as the center of pan-Protestant unity, but that rally-cry did not work. It offended the more conservative or cautious Nonconformists, who were more interested in the remedying of practical grievances, and who resented the Liberation Society's sneers at mere amelioration. So, for tactical reasons the Liberation Society in 1853 gave its efforts over to the abolition of church rates, hoping that abolition would lead to disestablishment.

Abolition seemed close to fulfillment during the 1850s. Abolitionists got a majority in the House of Commons for an abolition bill in 1855, but the Palmerston government compromised by proposing to exempt non-Anglicans from the rate. Revelling in its newly-found influence as the leader of a broad Nonconformist coalition, the Liberation Society accepted the compromise. Exemption, however, was not good enough for the more hard-line disestablishmentarians, and abolition bills got majorities in the House in 1858 and 1859. Stung to defend the Establishment, Anglicans argued that abolition was a stalking horse for disestablishment, and a House of Lords select committee in 1859 heard Liberation Society spokesmen admit that it was so. The result was a setback for the abolition campaign and confusion on the part of the Liberation Society during the 1860s.[58]

Voluntaryism, church-rate abolition, and indeed separation of church and state all were issues that linked agitation about the Church of England with agitation for the repeal of the Maynooth endowment. Proposals to abolish the endowment were introduced in every session of the House of Commons between 1851 and 1863; they evoked fierce debate, charges of political disloyalty and sexual degradation, and petition campaigns. Opponents of the endowment seemed to come close to success in the mid-1850s, when the Aberdeen Ministry agreed to a royal commission of investigation in 1853, and when Richard Spooner, Tory M.P. for Birmingham, received leave to introduce an abolition bill, but the commission showed that the Maynooth faculty were if anything too moderate to suit the Irish Roman Catholic bishops,[59] and the abolition bill of 1856 never got a second reading.[60] Although there was much anti-Catholic placarding and oratory in provincial towns, the would-be molders of public opinion were decidedly negative. The *Illustrated London News* denounced "the theological rancour of those who care nothing for justice, nothing for peace, nothing for charity, nothing for the consciences of those who differ from them." The *Times,* which had dismissed Spooner's motion as a "vernal infliction," labelled his success "a sham for the benefit of the constituen-

[58] Jacob P. Ellens, "Lord John Russell and the Church Rate Conflict: The Struggle for a Broad Church, 1834-1868," *JBS,* XXVI (1987), 232-57; Jacob P. Ellens, "The Church Rate Conflict in England and Wales, 1832-1868" (Ph.D. thesis, University of Toronto, 1983); David M. Thompson, "The Liberation Society, 1844-1868," *Pressure from Without in Early Victorian England,* ed. Patricia Hollis (New York, 1974), pp. 210-38.

[59] Cardinal Cullen delated the faculty to the Propaganda for being too Gallican, and several lecturers were disciplined (Wallis, "Anti-Maynooth Campaign," pp. 128-30).

[60] *Ibid.,* pp. 69-116, 142-49; Frank Wallis, "The Revival of the Anti-Maynooth Campaign in Britain, 1850-52," *Albion,* XIX (1987), 527-48.

cies," and rightly predicted that, having put their Protestantism on record by voting for the motion, the majority would see to it that the bill would never get a second reading. The Palmerston government certainly did not take matters seriously: the only minister present during the debate was the Chancellor of the Exchequer—and he was asleep.[61]

By the mid-1860s, the anti-Maynooth campaign was in disarray. Spooner's health had failed, and its new parliamentary leaders, G. H. Whalley, M.P. for Peterborough, and the Warwickshire squire and Tory M.P. Charles Newdigate Newdegate, quarreled among themselves as to who was the better parliamentarian and Protestant. Their constant repetition of the most extreme anti-Catholic charges, charges that appeared to have little basis in fact, were wearing thin the patience of the House. Moreover, a good deal of their support came from Voluntaryists who wanted to see the abolition of all religious endowments (Edward Miall had hailed Spooner as an ally in 1856), and this somewhat backhanded support drifted away after 1865 as Maynooth became subsumed in the question of Irish Church disestablishment. Finally, abolition of the grant was widely seen as an unnecessary insult to Irish sensibilities. Petitioning drives out-of-doors declined as the hopelessness of parliamentary abolition became apparent.[62] Luckily for the anti-Catholics, however, another issue, convents, surfaced in the mid-1860s.

The question of inspecting convents, to make sure that no nuns were being entombed alive, exploited for the sake of their money, or otherwise abused, first arose as a response to the Papal Aggression episode and the convent cases of the early 1850s. Bills proposing inspection along the lines of the inspection of lunatic asylums were introduced in 1851 and 1852. Having failed to pass those measures, anti-Catholics attempted to create select committees to investigate convents in 1853 and 1854. These proposals occasioned acrimonious debate within the House of Commons, petition campaigns outdoors, and an extensive tract literature. Roman Catholics resented the implication that convents were dens of iniquity ("either prisons or brothels," said Henry Drummond in one of the most notorious anti-Catholic slurs ever uttered in the House of Commons[63]), and of course saw these measures as nothing more than attempts to restrict their freedom of religion.[64]

Thereafter, the parliamentary focus of anti-Catholics shifted to the Maynooth question, and the matter of nunneries was not raised again until 1863-64, when a dispute over the will of an Oxford Convert, who had left his estate of £5,000 to the Brompton Oratory rather than to his Protestant sister, led Newdegate to move for a select committee. He renewed the motion in 1865, 1869, and 1870. Once again, the proposals provoked acrimonious debates, petition drives, and exchanges in print; once again they provided a forum for accusations verging on the pornographic.[65] Newdegate eventually saw his motion pass, but, ironically, the committee did not do what he wanted—produce evidence that convents were wicked places

---

[61] *Illustrated London News*, 19 Apr. 1856; *Times*, 16, 17 Apr., 31 May 1856.
[62] Wallis, "Anti-Maynooth Campaign," pp. 170-94; *Times*, 31 May 1856.
[63] 3 *Hansard*, CXV (1851), 266.
[64] Walter L. Arnstein, *Protestant Versus Catholic in Mid-Victorian England: Mr. Newdegate and the Nuns* (Columbia, Mo., 1982), pp. 62-63.
[65] *Ibid.*, pp. 32-33, 63-64, 108-32.

that required registration and inspection—and after 1871 the convent question was increasingly seen as a joke.[66]

During the 1870s and later, anti-Catholicism gradually receded as a major public issue. On the one hand, it became increasingly limited to educated opinion rather than a topic of popular agitation. The reaction to the First Vatican Council's promulgation of doctrines related to papal infallibility and church-state relations took the form of a debate between W. E. Gladstone and Roman Catholic apologists, with little call for government involvement and little public agitation. Gladstone's pamphlet on the Vatican decrees made him more money than any other of his works, and sold more copies than any other save that on the Bulgarian Horrors, but the general public was unmoved.[67] And insofar as anti-Catholicism remained a topic of popular agitation, that agitation became increasingly limited to the port city of Liverpool, where its special mix of politics, religion, and ethnicity kept alive the traditional responses that were dying out elsewhere.[68]

That this narrative could have been written at all is evidence that considerable valuable and thoughtful research has been done on anti-Catholicism as a problem in the "high politics" of the nineteenth century, while some scholars, recognizing the importance of popular anti-Catholicism, have touched on how that sentiment influenced the development of Wesleyan Methodism and working-class Toryism. With few exceptions, the approaches are episodic, focusing on a specific event or person, and thus find it difficult to account in a systematic and comprehensive way for the persistence of anti-Catholicism over time, to distinguish it from anti-Irish sentiment, or to explain thoroughly its social, economic, political, and religious bases.[69]

I am interested in what led ordinary people to become anti-Catholic. I seek to define the political, social, economic, and religious backgrounds and concerns of those people who behaved in anti-Catholic ways (which I measure as committing violent acts against Roman Catholic targets, signing anti-Catholic petitions, joining anti-Catholic organizations, and reading anti-Catholic literature). My book takes the Papal Aggression Crisis of 1850-51 as its methodological starting-point, by using computer-aided statistical techniques to link the number of signatures generated by the petition drives of those years with the social, economic, and religious evidence in the 1851 Census. The results of this analysis produce hypotheses about the nature of anti-Catholicism that I then test in four ways: by connecting the quantitative evidence of petitioning with the literary evi-

[66] *Ibid.*, pp. 136-47, 154-62.

[67] Norman, *Anti-Catholicism*, pp. 80-81, 95, 98; Josef L. Altholz, "The Vatican Decrees Controversy, 1874-1875," *Catholic Historical Review*, LVII (1971-72), 593-605; Josef L. Altholz and John Powell, "Gladstone, Lord Ripon, and the Vatican Decrees, 1874," *Albion*, XXII (1990), 449-59.

[68] See John Bohstedt, "Authoritarian Populism: Protestant-Catholic Riots in Edwardian Liverpool," *Riot, Police and Popular Politics in Liverpool, 1800-1914*, ed. John C. Belchem (forthcoming, 1992); and G.I.T. Machin, "The Last Victorian Anti-Ritualist Campaign, 1895-1906," *Victorian Studies*, XXV (1981-82), 277-302.

[69] John Wolffe's study, *The Protestant Crusade in Great Britain, 1828-1860* (Oxford, 1991), is likely to be the definitive account of institutional anti-Catholicism from the perspective of national politics. I have read the thesis on which this work is based, and Dr. Wolffe graciously showed me page proofs of part of his book. His work is complementary to mine, but our interests and approaches differ.

dence of newspapers, religious periodicals, and manuscript sources; by identifying and looking closely at localities and at groups whose behavior diverges from the norm; by fixing in their social contexts the signatories of those petitions that have survived; and by analyzing the circumstances of collective behavior.

The book is limited to England, rather than using Britain for its geographical field of analysis. Scotland and Wales are distinct cultural entities, having their own institutions, histories, and concerns, all of which differ from England's. (And Wales has its own language, which I do not read.) Some historical problems demand a British perspective, but England, itself after all a distinct cultural entity with its own institutions, history, and concerns, sometimes is equally appropriate. All too often, however, English history, and even British history, turn out to be the history of what was happening in the West End, ignoring what was happening north of the Thames or north of the Trent. My book certainly addresses English-wide issues, but turns to certain localities to see how those issues worked themselves out at the local level. These localities are Manchester and other places in southwest Lancashire; Leeds and the West Riding; Birmingham and Derby in the West Midlands; Northamptonshire; and Cambridgeshire. I occasionally treat other places in the Northeast, the East Midlands, the West Country, and Greater London. I did not choose these places on a whim, but because they differed markedly from the statistical norm, or because they were spot on the norm, or because of some other reason relating to their history or their potential for comparison. In this book, England really is England.

This book covers the period from the early 1830s, when Roman Catholic Emancipation, governmental reform, the Oxford Movement, and Dissenters' claims seemed to challenge accepted institutions, to the early 1870s, when both Roman and Anglo-Catholicism had become prominent parts of the English religious scene, when the lack of significant public reaction to the First Vatican Council signalled a sea change in responses to Catholic claims, and when the anti-Catholic lecturer William Murphy was beaten to a pulp. Its thesis is that anti-Catholicism is a complicated issue that cannot be reduced simply to the residue of historical memory, or to not liking the Irish, or to the subconscious thirst for pornography, or to the imposition of hegemonic bourgeois social control. Rather, there were varieties of anti-Catholicisms that served several purposes, social, political, and theological, according to the needs and histories of specific groups and locales. Each of these needs analysis. Furthermore, Roman Catholics themselves provoked a Protestant reaction to their theological and political militance, and were not simply the passive victims of outside aggression.[70]

The middle classes, and to some extent the working classes, gave effect to their views about Roman Catholicism by means of anti-Catholic voluntary societies. These groups attempted to mold public opinion through public meetings, petition drives, cheap tracts, the newspaper press, and public lecturing. All these elements are interrelated, and are connected with modes of Victorian entertainment. I deal with them in Chapter I.

[70] I advanced this last point in 1979 and 1982 ("Popular Anti-Catholicism in England, 1850-1851," *Albion*, XI, 1979, 331, 355; "Another Look," p. 49); and Walter L. Arnstein came independently to the same conclusion in 1982 (*Protestant Versus Catholic*, pp. 3-4).

Anti-Catholicism is not simply about anti-Irish sentiment, and anti-Irish sentiment is not reducible to simple racism. Indeed, the Victorian middle and working classes were ambivalent about both Irish and Roman Catholics. Their attitudes towards Roman Catholicism were affected by the vigorous apologetical and controversial activities of English Roman Catholics, both individual and institutional. The growth of Roman Catholic self-confidence and triumphalism began early on in the nineteenth century; Cardinal Wiseman was not the sole, or even the primary, stimulus to that growth; and both laymen and ordinary priests were as active as bishops in defending their faith. English Roman Catholics were neither passive victims in the face of anti-Catholic abuse nor the obedient puppets of a few leaders in London. I analyze these issues in Chapters II and III.

The Church of England was one of the most anti-Catholic of institutions, in both theory and practice, for political, social, and theological reasons. The evolution of Evangelical theology during the first half of the century combined with challenges to the Church's legal status to prepare a ground in which anti-Catholicism flourished. Moreover, the development of Anglo-Catholicism, which had spread from the universities into the parishes by mid-century, rather earlier than is commonly thought, also stimulated anti-Catholicism. That movement cut the ground from under the Evangelicals by denying that Anglicanism was Protestant, challenged Evangelical acceptance of the economic status quo, and seemed to many to be the importation of alien, un-English religious ideas into the body politic. The anti-Catholicism of the several Nonconformist denominations had their own distinct natures and sources. During the first half of the nineteenth century, Nonconformity was evolving from a sectarian to a denominational structure, at a time when it was challenging the status of Anglicanism. These changes caused political, economic, social, and theological tensions that anti-Catholicism could resolve. I examine these issues in Chapters IV, V, and VI.

Anti-Catholicism also played a role in local political and recreational culture. Some anti-Catholics attempted to advance their goals by means of electoral politics, but found that local conditions often denied them success. Electoral politics, public lecturing, and campaigns to mold public opinion often blended into popular collective violence. Violence related to religion and ethnicity—bonfire riots, Irish rows, street riots, pub brawls—was common during the nineteenth century. The causes of riotous or violent behavior are complex and are rooted in local conditions, and cannot be reduced to simple dislike of the Irish, or even to class conflict. I deal with these issues in Chapters VII and VIII.

Anti-Catholic leadership in urban areas reflected the composition of their economic environments. The leadership came primarily from the middle classes. There was a hard core of committed activists, which called upon that great body of earnest Victorian joiners and do-gooders ready to support worthy voluntary societies for moral reform. From their perspective, anti-Catholicism was an engine of philanthropic moral reform no different from antislavery, anticruelty, or anti-Corn Law campaigns. Anti-Catholic leadership in rural areas, on the other hand, reflected traditional deferential community life. The roles of workers and of women are much less clear. Organized anti-Catholicism was more attractive to artisans, shopkeepers, and the upwardly mobile than it was to factory operatives and laborers. As for women, anti-Catholicism appears to have been a marked exception to the feminization of Victorian religious institutions. Chapter IX treats of these issues.

The book's broader significance is to be found in two areas. First, it firmly fixes an important religious issue in its political and social milieux, adds to our understanding of the role of extraparliamentary expressions of public opinion, and offers a new explanation of the nature of working-class violence. Beyond that, this study offers itself as a model of how historians should analyze the interplay between national issues and their local manifestations as molded by local conditions, and of how historians should meld together documentary, literary, and nonverbal evidence.

I

ORGANIZED ANTI-CATHOLIC PROTEST

> At the time when the Pope had "frightened the
> isle from its propriety," a friend of ours, who, in
> getting on to the top of an omnibus, said, "it is a
> wet day," was received by the coachman with
> "Thankye, Sir, for that very sensible information.
> You're the first gen'leman for a whole fortnight
> that has spoken about anything but the Papal
> Aggression!"[1]

ANTI-CATHOLICS SOUGHT TO spread their views by the "indirect
and traditional forms of pressure" so beloved of the Victorians: organizing
public opinion by means of mass meetings and demonstrations, petition
campaigns, and the distribution of printed propaganda; lobbying M.P.s
and ministers; and starting pressure groups. These tactics could become
electoral pressure when they acquired an electoral dimension, as when petitions were more pledges to vote in a certain way than requests that Parliament enact or abolish a certain law, or as when a pressure group attempted to influence the constituencies with an eye to creating a bloc
within Parliament.[2] The best known of these pressure groups are Liberal
and Radical ones such as the Anti-Corn Law League and the United
Kingdom Alliance, but Conservatives also made use of the tactic. Anti-
Catholics early on used the formal and informal methods of persuasion
available to the Victorian era: the meeting, the lecture, the newspaper, the
pressure group. Some tactics, especially those connected with petitioning,
were bound by formal rules, while other tactics, such as the public meeting, shaded off into the informal realm of public entertainment.

The Public Meeting and the Public Petition

The Victorian public meeting was a ceremony, planned in advance by
a committee, in which participants elected a chairman, moved and seconded resolutions, fought among themselves, turned out dissenters, and
adopted the petition to Parliament by acclamation. Almost any group assembled to express opinion on issues of the day—inhabitants of local areas,
professional and trade societies, religious congregations and synods, voluntary organizations, chambers of commerce, *ad hoc* political pressure
groups—even the friends of the Metropolitan Improved Hot Muffin Company. Public meetings of towns and counties, meetings of the "people"

---

[1] *Leeds Mercury*, 28 June 1851, quoting *The Builder*.
[2] D. A. Hamer, *The Politics of Electoral Pressure: A Study in the History of Victorian Reform
Agitations* (Hassocks, 1977), p. 9; Adelman, *Victorian Radicalism*, p. 6.

(usually defined as ratepayers or freeholders, but sometimes as inhabitants) enjoyed a quasi-official status; they offered the only constitutional way for the unenfranchised to express their opinions. (The riot, a tolerated part of the eighteenth-century Constitution, had gone out of favor since the Gordon Riots and the French Revolution, and politicians had not yet accepted the mass pressure group as an acceptable way of approaching Parliament.) Custom obliged lords-lieutenant and mayors to summon meetings at the request of freeholders or ratepayers, although the authorities sometimes declined to call meetings if they judged the requisition to be insufficiently signed. (In practice, this meant that the authorities might turn down requisitioners who lacked enough support from local notables or whose purposes were too radical.) These meetings were convened for the formal purpose of adopting addresses to the Queen or Parliament.[3]

Most public meetings, of course, were carefully orchestrated events that had as much to do with the balance of local political power as with the purpose for which they were ostensibly called, and mortal battles sometimes raged behind the scenes. (Thus the notables of Devonshire decided not to call a public meeting at all, lest the Evangelicals raise the question of Tractarianism and Dissenters attack the Establishment.[4]) The local notables first met in private to discuss how best to express their opinions. Some notables believed that it was better to have a lot of parish meetings, rather than one large town meeting, because of the effect of numbers.[5] Others believed that town or county meetings carried more prestige. And here civic pride played its part; a Southampton promoter wanted to hold a town meeting to protest the Papal Aggression because "so many *Inferior* places have set us the example."[6]

The Victorian public meeting could be lively, even dangerous, for ill-affected outsiders sometimes tried to amend the resolutions, raise extraneous issues, or even disrupt the proceedings. Secularist meetings often turned into entertainments. The secularists would say outrageous things; Protestant Evangelical missionaries, who almost always attended in search of souls, would debate; and occasionally Roman Catholic controversialists would contribute to make a jolly three-way dispute. Unwanted speakers bedeviled other meetings. When the Huddersfield branch of the National Public Schools Association held a meeting to promote state-supported secular education, a temperance lecturer gained the floor and argued that an education rate would not be necessary if workers stopped squandering their income on drink. The result was much uproar, before the meeting's organizers regained control.[7] Meetings in the Midlands and North during

---

[3] No adequate study of the Victorian public meeting exists. Besides studies of specific movements, see H. D. Jephson, *The Platform, Its Rise and Progress*, 2 vols. (London, 1892); B. Keith-Lucas, "County Meetings," *Law Quarterly Review*, LXX (1954), 109-14; Peter Fraser, "Public Petitioning and Parliament Before 1832," *History*, XLVI (1961), 195-211; Colin Leys, "Petitioning in the Nineteenth and Twentieth Centuries," *Political Studies*, III (1955), 45-64; and Robert L. Nicholls, "Surrogate for Democracy: Nineteenth Century British Petitioning," *Maryland Historian*, V (1974), 43-52. The public meeting in Charles Dickens, *Nicholas Nickleby* (London, 1978; orig. pub. 1839), pp. 71-76, was drawn from life.

[4] *Times*, 5 Nov. 1850.

[5] Charles Parsons to T. H. Croft Moody, 8 Nov. 1850, Messrs. Page & Moody, Solicitors (Protestant Defence Papers), Southampton City Record Office, D/PM/10/2/23.

[6] Joseph Toomer to T. H. Croft Moody, 2 Nov. 1850, *ibid.*, D/PM/10/2/26.

[7] Edward Royle, *Victorian Infidels: The Origins of the British Secularist Movement, 1791-1866* (Manchester, 1974), pp. 235-36; *Huddersfield Chronicle*, 1 Mar. 1851.

the 1830s and '40s often became battlegrounds between the working and middling classes.

Public meetings could be controlled, however. Careful preparation of the agenda and the assigning of tasks to movers and seconders of resolutions, in advance of the meeting, would prevent confusion and allow the meeting's organizers to maintain control of the proceedings.[8] Ensuring a friendly audience was another important method of control. Admission to the Manchester public meeting of 20 November 1850 was by ticket only; tickets were sold at 1s. for the platform, 6d. for reserved seats, and 3d. for the gallery. Free tickets for the floor were distributed to known Protestants. Acceptance of a ticket, moreover, was taken to mean agreement that only those called upon by the chairman should attempt to address the meeting. And when a heckler began to disrupt the proceedings, the police chucked him out.[9]

In this connection, two points need to be made. First, the line of demarkation between the public meeting (to express in a constitutional way the opinion of "the people") and the public lecture (to inform and entertain) was blurred. Second, the public meeting was a form of entertainment, at which attenders could see famous men, hear rousing oratory, and enjoy the excitement of being in a crowd.

The public lecture was a popular form of entertainment, on both sides of the Atlantic, during the middle of the nineteenth century. How could the middling classes and the upper reaches of the working classes fill up their leisure hours in a respectable way, now that the common lands had been enclosed and people were living in towns? Almost each night of the week, one could find, in big towns, public lectures in lyceums, mechanics' institutions, Dissenting chapels, and hired halls, on literary, historical, geographical, scientific, and religious topics; and men who for one reason or another chose not to enter one of the traditional professions made their livings by delivering public lectures in their fields of expertise.[10] Alessandro Gavazzi, the Italian nationalist and apostate priest, made much money by giving public lectures on the evils of the Papacy. His receipts were sufficient to make him a living, with enough left over to support penurious Italian exiles in Soho. Charles Bradlaugh was able to make a living in the late 1850s and early '60s by lecturing in London and the provinces on such topics as "The Existence of God," "The Divine Revelation of the Bible," and "Has Man a Soul?" He charged from 2d. to 1s. for admission to his lectures, keeping whatever was left over after the hall rental, advertising, and other expenses had been paid.[11]

---

[8] Page & Moody Papers, Southampton City Record Office, D/PM/10/1/16-24, shows the care with which the more experienced organizers of meetings proceeded.

[9] *Manchester Courier*, 23 Nov. 1850.

[10] Donald M. Scott, "The Profession that Vanished: Public Lecturing in Mid-Nineteenth-Century America," *Professions and Professional Ideologies in America*, ed. Gerald L. Geison (Chapel Hill and London, 1983), pp. 12-28; J. M. Golby and A. W. Purdue, *The Civilisation of the Crowd: Popular Culture in England, 1750-1900* (New York, 1985), pp. 88-98, 107-10; Norman McCord, *The Anti-Corn Law League, 1838-1846*, 2nd ed. (London, 1968), p. 60; Lilian Lewis Shiman, "Temperance and Class in Bradford, 1830-1860," *Yorkshire Archæological Journal*, LVIII (1986), 176; David Russell, "The Leeds Rational Recreational Society, 1852-59: 'Music for the People' in a Mid-Victorian City," *Thoresby Miscellany*, XVII (1981), 137-58; Howard M. Wach, "Culture and the Middle Classes: Popular Knowledge in Industrial Manchester," *JBS*, XXVII (1988), 375-404.

[11] *Leeds Mercury*, 1 Apr. 1854; Basil Hall, "Alessandro Gavazzi: A Barnabite Friar and the Risorgimento," *Studies in Church History*, XII (1975), 303-56; Walter L. Arnstein, *The Bradlaugh Case: Atheism, Sex, and Politics Among the Late Victorians* (Columbia, Mo., 1983), p. 10.

Itinerant anti-Catholic lecturers were fixtures of mid-Victorian public life. They combined entertainment (sometimes of a most prurient nature) with edification (sometimes of a most sanctifying nature); if they were foreigners, they offered the additional attractions of an exotic accent or dress, an evening's education in a foreign culture, and the opportunity to support a liberal cause such as Italian unification or Polish freedom. Because the Roman Catholic Church was a force for reaction in Italy and in much of the Austrian Empire, to be liberal was also to oppose that church and therefore to be at least potentially receptive to the messages of English domestic anti-Catholics. It was difficult, in the nineteenth century, to oppose the Roman Catholic Church without becoming anti-Catholic, just as it was difficult, in the twentieth century, to oppose the state of Israel without becoming anti-Semitic.

Some of the lecturers were honest men; some were desperate, penniless exiles; some were confidence men; it is wrong to dismiss them all as mountebanks, rogues, or "religious entertainers who did it for money."[12] Father Gavazzi, Antonio Gallenga,[13] and Piero Guicciardini[14] were honorable men led to anti-Catholicism by the logic of Italian nationalism. Johannes Ronge and Johan Czerski were rationalists and nationalists whom English Evangelicals, observing at a distance, turned into Evangelical Protestants.[15] John Victor Teodor, a former priest, and his colleagues Chylinski and Dobrogost claimed to be Polish nationalists hounded into England by Russian, Prussian, and Austrian forces; they found that they could make a living by pandering to the Evangelicals, lecturing, and performing, "in all its pomp, the Romish Mass" to paying customers ("Wafer Gods"[16] sold at the door for 1d. each).[17] Giacinto Achilli, William Murphy, and the mysterious André Massena (soi-disant Baron de Camin)[18] were corrupt demagogues, as were Patrick McMenemy, an Irish no-popery lecturer caught brawling in a Liverpool brothel, and James Mathison, who posed as a Roman Catholic while in the pay of an anti-Catholic society.[19] Their lurid handbills (see Fig. 1) were common sights on the hoardings.

---

[12] Best, "Popular Protestantism," p. 140 (quoted); Norman, Anti-Catholicism, pp. 17-18.

[13] Antonio Carlo Napoleone Gallenga (1810-1895) was an Italian nationalist, exile, and naturalized British subject who taught modern languages at University College, London, 1849-58, before becoming a Times correspondent, 1859-81 (Boase, V, 379-80).

[14] A Florentine count who became a Protestant in 1836 under the influence of the Plymouth Brethren; his arrest in 1849 stimulated public pressure in England. He was in England from 1851 to 1854. (Robert Sylvain, Alessandro Gavazzi: Garabaldien, Clerc, Prédicant des Deux Mondes, 2 vols., Quebec, 1962, I, 266-67, II, 443.)

[15] Huddersfield Chronicle, 22 Feb. 1851; Wayne Detzler, "Protest and Schism in Nineteenth-Century German Catholicism: The Ronge-Czerski Movement, 1844-5," Studies in Church History, IX (1972), 341-49; British Protestant, I (Sept. 1845), 216, (Oct. 1845), 221; Baptist Magazine, XXXVIII (June 1846), 334-37.

[16] I.e., the consecrated Host.

[17] Docketing on, and handbill encl. in, Doyle to Spencer Walpole, 30 July 1852, Home Office: Registered Papers, PRO, H.O. 45/4195; Teodor to Mrs. A. B. Hutchins, 2 Nov. 1850, Page & Moody Papers, Southampton City Record Office, D/PM/10/1/4. Prof. Roman Szporluk of Harvard University tells me that he thinks this lot were confidence men.

[18] Massena represented himself as both a Benedictine monk and a nobleman, and as a Roman Catholic but not a papist. An Anglo-Catholic vicar who met him concluded that he was "an unprincipled adventurer, gulling John Bull on his weak point, viz., his aptitude to believe any evil of the Church of Rome." (A Norfolk Diary: Passages from the Diary of the Rev. Benjamin John Armstrong, Vicar of East Dereham, 1850-85, ed. Herbert B. J. Armstrong, London, 1949, pp. 42-44.)

[19] Machin, Politics and the Churches, p. 253; Wolffe, Protestant Crusade, p. 186.

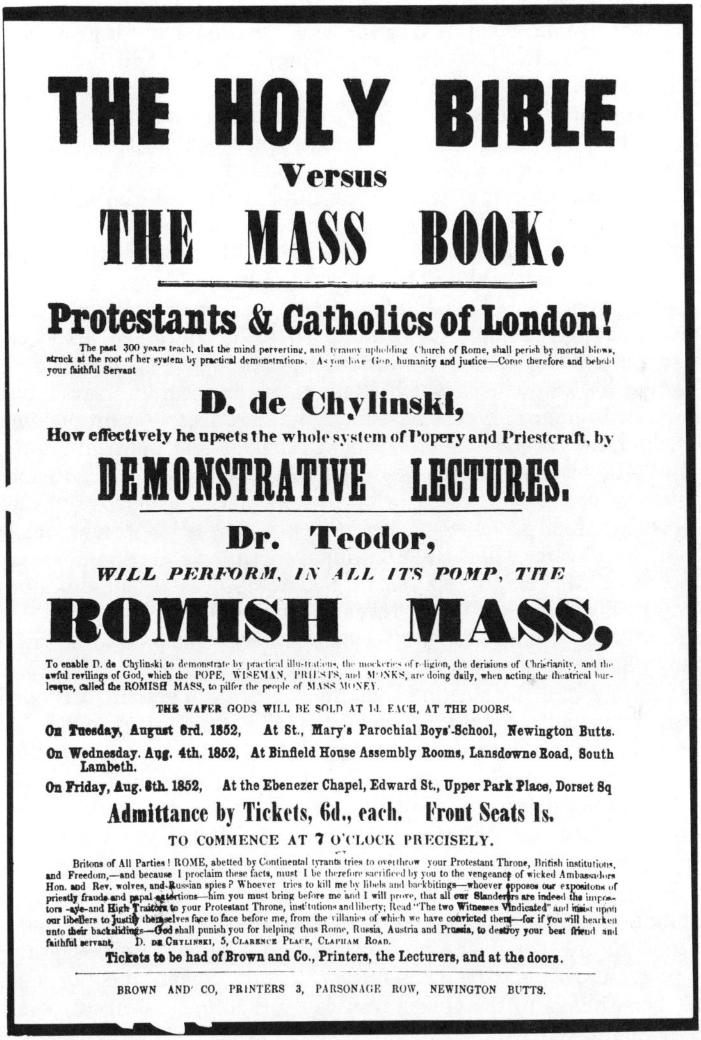

THE HOLY BIBLE

Versus

THE MASS BOOK.

Protestants & Catholics of London!

The past 300 years teach, that the mind perverting, and tyranny upholding Church of Rome, shall perish by mortal blows, struck at the root of her system by practical demonstrations. As you love God, humanity and justice—Come therefore and behold your faithful Servant

D. de Chylinski,

How effectively he upsets the whole system of Popery and Priestcraft, by

DEMONSTRATIVE LECTURES.

Dr. Teodor,

WILL PERFORM, IN ALL ITS POMP, THE

ROMISH MASS,

To enable D. de Chylinski to demonstrate by practical illustrations, the mockeries of religion, the derisions of Christianity, and the awful revilings of God, which the POPE, WISEMAN, PRIESTS, and MONKS, are doing daily, when acting the theatrical burlesque, called the ROMISH MASS, to pilfer the people of MASS MONEY.

THE WAFER GODS WILL BE SOLD AT 1d. EACH, AT THE DOORS.

On **Tuesday, August 3rd. 1852,** At St., Mary's Parochial Boys'-School, Newington Butts.

On **Wednesday. Aug. 4th. 1852,** At Binfield House Assembly Rooms, Lansdowne Road, South Lambeth.

On **Friday, Aug. 6th. 1852,** At the Ebenezer Chapel, Edward St., Upper Park Place, Dorset Sq

Admittance by Tickets, 6d., each.   Front Seats 1s.

TO COMMENCE AT 7 O'CLOCK PRECISELY.

Britons of All Parties! ROME, abetted by Continental tyrants tries to overthrow your Protestant Throne, British institutions, and Freedom,—and because I proclaim these facts, must I be therefore sacrificed by you to the vengance of wicked Ambassadors, Hon. and Rev. wolves, and Russian spies? Whoever tries to kill me by libels and backbitings—whoever opposes our expositions of priestly frauds and papal extortions—him you must bring before me and I will prove, that all our Slanderers are indeed the impostors -aye-and High Traitors to your Protestant Throne, institutions and liberty; Read "The two Witnesses Vindicated" and must upon our libellers to justify themselves face to face before me, from the villanies of which we have convicted them—for if you will hearken unto their backbitings—God shall punish you for helping thus Rome, Russia, Austria and Prussia, to destroy your best friend and faithful servant, D. de Chylinski, 5, Clarence Place, Clapham Road.

Tickets to be had of Brown and Co., Printers, the Lecturers, and at the doors.

BROWN AND CO, PRINTERS 3, PARSONAGE ROW, NEWINGTON BUTTS.

FIG. 1

Anti-Catholic Handbill, 1852

The most powerful of the mid-century lecturers were the apostate priests Giacinto Achilli and Alessandro Gavazzi. Achilli, a former Dominican from Viterbo, was dramatically snatched "from the jaws of the Inquisition" through the efforts of a group of ultra-Evangelical Churchmen (Lewis Tonna, Charles Cowan, M.P.) and Nonconformists (Sir Culling Eardley Eardley, Edward Steane, Baptist Noel), and brought to England in March 1850 as living proof of popish despotism. Until his past caught up with him (he had a history of seducing women), he gave devastating lectures that legitimized commonly held stereotypes of the Inquisition, Marian devotion, and the sexual habits of priests.[20] Gavazzi, in contrast, was a decent man whose Italian nationalism led him to reject, first, the Pope's temporal authority, and then his spiritual authority. Gavazzi electrified London audiences from January to May 1851 with his dramatic attacks on the Papacy, and then toured the Midlands and North from July 1851 to November 1852.[21] After a year's tour of the United States and Canada, Gavazzi returned to Britain, where he continued his attacks on Roman Catholicism, but also paid attention to Anglo-Catholicism.[22]

Despite his eloquence, which hypnotized his hearers even though he spoke only Italian, Gavazzi was not quite as effective a propagandist as was Achilli, for he was suspect on both religious and political grounds. In religion, Achilli professed to be regenerate, while Gavazzi was more an opponent of papal claims than a proponent of Evangelical Protestantism. Politically, Achilli professed to have been a simple colporteur during the Roman Revolution, while Gavazzi, highly visible as Garibaldi's chaplain, was suspected of being a republican. So, Achilli was accepted unquestioningly until his true nature was revealed, while Gavazzi was not fully accepted until he returned from his North American trip an adherent of the House of Savoy.

The lecture and the meeting sometimes blurred together. Although mechanics institutions usually steered clear of controversial topics, Roman Catholicism was an exception. The Rev. John Lord gave a series of lectures on monastic institutions at the Leeds Mechanics Institution in 1846. Although Lord attempted to balance the positive and negative aspects of monastic history, local observers fastened on the more lurid and bloodthirsty elements—the Spanish Inquisition. The Papal Aggression crisis saw more blurring. The Rev. R. P. Blakeney delivered a lecture on the errors in Roman Catholic doctrine, at the Assembly Rooms, Nottingham. But after the lecture was over, those present adopted an address asking the Pope to grant civil and religious liberty in Italy, Spain, and Portugal, and voted their thanks to the Queen and to Lord John Russell for being Protestant. Similarly, two clergymen at Huddersfield placarded the walls to advertise their "lectures" on the errors of Romanism. But in both cases,

---

[20] C. E. Eardley, *The Imprisonment and Deliverance of Dr. Giacinto Achilli, with some account of his previous history and labours* (London, 1850); *Leeds Mercury*, 22 Dec. 1849, 2 Feb., 9 Mar. 1850; *Times*, 8 Mar. 1850; *Evangelical Christendom*, III (Nov. 1849), 342, (Mar. 1850), 89-90; Paz, Connelly, pp. 18-26.

[21] Speaking at Northampton, Nottingham, Sheffield, Leeds, Newcastle, Carlisle, Manchester, Liverpool, Birmingham, in several Scottish towns, and in Dublin.

[22] Sylvain, *Gavazzi*, I, 262-63, 269-80, II, 287-441, 444-65; *Leeds Mercury*, 8 Feb. 1851; Hall, "Gavazzi," *passim*; Armstrong, *Norfolk Diary*, p. 30.

after they were done speaking, they circulated petitions to Parliament for signature.[23]

A corollary of this point is that people attended public meetings, as well as lectures, for their entertainment value. Some, of course, attended because they believed in the cause on behalf of which the meeting had been called, as was the case with James Bembridge, a lay evangelist employed by Evangelical Anglicans in Manchester. "Attended the great meeting in the evening of the Protestant Association, and was greatly interested with the telling & effective speeches delivered. It is high time for all classes to awake from slumber & to oppose the doings of the Man of Sin with all the means within their power."[24] Others, however, attended meetings as we today attend the cinema.

Charles Royce,[25] tutor to the children of Thomas Turner, surgeon, of Moseley Street and Pendleton, Manchester, during the mid-1840s, took full advantage of Manchester's intellectual ferment. Royce was a connoisseur of sermons. He attended Nonconformist chapels to hear prominent visiting preachers such as the Congregationalist John Angell James;[26] he admired the Anglican Hugh Stowell's preaching (one sermon, on "Balaam the son of Bosor who loved the wages of unrighteousness," he called "excellent").[27] Royce also attended as many public lectures as he could—Samuel Smiles on work, Elihu Burritt (the American linguist and peace activist), and Dr. William Benjamin Carpenter on the microscope, for instance.[28]

Royce also attended public meetings, but for the same reason as he went to lectures—to hear good speakers. He was at the Free Trade Hall to attend a monster meeting in favor of the early closing of shops; Dr. Robert Vaughan, Dr. William Ballantyne Hodgson, Baptist Noel, and the prominent politicians Lord John Manners, Joseph Brotherton, and William Ewart spoke. "I went not so much to be convinced of the desirableness of the object as to hear the men who were to advocate it. Nor was I disappointed. They all spoke well."[29] Royce loved oratory for its own sake, and easily tolerated markedly differing viewpoints. Royce attended, and enjoyed, a lecture by George Dawson, the theologically ultraliberal Dissenting minister from Birmingham. He also attended, and enjoyed, Hugh Stowell's swingeing attack on "Dawsonian tendencies."[30]

Another example is William Edwin Adams, editor of the *Newcastle Weekly Chronicle*. As a youth in Cheltenham Spa in the 1840s, he eagerly attended all sorts of lectures: on geology, astronomy, and poetry, on light subjects, and George Dawson on "the weaknesses and foibles of mankind."[31] People like Royce and Adams must have been in the audience at almost every public meeting, and many would have shared Royce's sentiments: "Tuesday evening we had Cowden Clarke at the Athenæum

---

23 *Leeds Mercury*, 17 Jan. 1846; *Times*, 23 Nov. 1850; *Huddersfield Chronicle*, 1 Feb., 5 Apr. 1851.

24 James Bembridge Journals, 4 Nov. 1850, MCL, BR MS 259.B1.

25 His brother, Henry, was the grandfather of the engineer Sir Frederick Henry Royce.

26 Charles Royce to George Royce, 31 Oct. 1845, Royce Family Papers, MCL, M70/3/6.

27 C. Royce to G. Royce, 23 July 1846, *ibid.*, M70/3/14.

28 C. Royce to G. Royce, 10 Dec. 1845, *ibid.*, M/70/3/7.

29 C. Royce to G. Royce, 6 Nov. 1846, *ibid.*, M70/3/18.

30 C. Royce to G. Royce, 23 Oct. 1845, *ibid.*, M70/3/17.

31 W. E. Adams, *Memoirs of a Social Atom*, ed. John Saville (New York, 1968), pp. 114-17.

on the Comic Writers & a comic genius he is. The next night I went to church & heard Mr. Stowell, a strange medley you will say, but I don't think so. We may cultivate wisely all our faculties & feel the more able to value each in particular."[32]

Organizers well understood the dual function of the public lecture. Aware that the desire for a sensation and the novelty of a "fresh new voice" attracted attention in real life, Margaret Oliphant made her fictional hero, Arthur Vincent, begin his ministry at Salem Chapel, Carlingford, by giving a course of public lectures intended both to inform the public of the virtues of Dissent and to publicize the existence of the chapel and its pastor.[33] The public lecture, then, was a fixture of urban life.

The ostensible object of the public meeting was to adopt a petition to some great constitutional authority—the Queen, the House of Lords, the House of Commons. Lithographed forms of petition were often available from some pressure group's London headquarters. After the petition was adopted and signed by those present at the meeting, it was circulated in order to obtain more signatures. The most common method of circulation was to lay it for signature at grocers' and other shops, booksellers and stationers, newspaper offices, and sometimes at the Town Hall. Other good places to lay it were in churches or chapels. When enough signatures had been gathered in that way, volunteers took it from house to house.[34]

The collection of signatures required organization. The especially well-organized Southampton branch of the Protestant Alliance identified strategic roads, and then assigned members to approach shopkeepers and clergymen and to be responsible for collecting the petitions.[35] (It cost the organization £2..10s. to collect signatures in 1850.[36]) Clergymen and ministers were especially important, for there was a direct relationship between the number of signatures to anti-Catholic petitions and the extent to which preachers worked on the fears of their congregations, as the Wesleyan John McLean put it to T. P. Bunting in 1839.[37]

To what extent were these signatures gathered by fraud or extracted by intimidation? Obviously, those who opposed the object of the petitions were ready to question the means by which signatures were collected. During the petition drive against the Factory Bill, 1843, reports appeared describing the taking of signatures from schoolboys and the indiscriminate taking of signatures outside a Roman Catholic chapel.[38] Overenthusiastic canvassers probably were willing to collect whatever signatures they could. But the Southampton branch, Protestant Alliance, at least, attempted to be honest, instructing its canvassers not to collect signatures from the very

[32] C. Royce to G. Royce, 6 Nov. 1846, Royce Family Papers, MCL, M70/3/18.

[33] Margaret Oliphant, *Salem Chapel* (London, 1986; orig. pub. 1863), p. 78.

[34] See instructions on how to collect signatures to petitions in the *Bulwark, or Reformation Journal*, II (July 1852); Printed paper, 26 Apr. 1845, Wordsworth Family Papers, Lambeth Palace Library, MS. 2143, ff. 145-46, is an example of a form. Local campaigns using these tactics can be seen in *The Protestant Watchman of the Midland District*, No. 10 (Dec. 1849), p. 117 (Birmingham); *Manchester Guardian*, 27 Nov. 1850 (Warrington); *Preston Guardian*, 23 Nov. 1850 (Over Darwen); *Preston Pilot*, 14, 28 Dec. 1850 (Ormskirk, Preston); *Reading Mercury*, 16 Nov., 28 Dec. 1850.

[35] Henry Taylor to T. H. Croft Moody, [6 Nov. 1850], Page & Moody Papers, Southampton City Record Office, D/PM/10/2/22; George Grey Cashman to Moody, [Nov. 1850], *ibid.*, D/PM/10/2/27; George Grey Cashman to Moody, [Feb. 1851], *ibid.*, D/PM/10/2/55.

[36] Memorandum of Moody, 30 Nov. 1850, *ibid.*, D/PM/10/1/7.

[37] R. Laishley to Moody, 5 June 1855, *ibid.*, D/PM/10/6/61; W. R. Ward, *Religion and Society in England, 1790-1850* (London, 1972), p. 213.

[38] *Times*, 28 Apr., 2 May 1843.

young, or to allow a person to sign for another without written authority from the one for whom he would sign.[39] Intimidation is equally likely; some canvassers probably did use their positions to extract signatures from the unwilling. William Griffiths, a worker from Birmingham, related an incident in 1851, when his employer asked him to sign an anti-Catholic petition held by a third man. When Griffiths refused, the third man accused him of being disloyal and of taking lessons from the ultraliberals George Dawson and Brewin Grant. Luckily for Griffiths, his employer respected his right to decline, and he kept his job. But Griffiths claimed that many factories and workshops in Birmingham had been visited in this manner, and that workers had signed, even though they opposed the petitions, for fear of losing their jobs.[40] If wholesale fraud or intimidation had characterized the massive petition drives of the 1840s and '50s, there would have been many more complaints from people like Griffiths. (After all, the radical working-class movement of the day did not hesitate to complain about much more serious repression.) Thus, it seems safe to conclude that fraud and intimidation were not the norm in the gathering of signatures.

Finally, one must ask what the purpose of the public petition was.[41] There was little reason, from a strictly parliamentary point of view, for pressure groups to invest time and energy in petitioning the House of Commons. The "gag" rule prevented any debate arising over the presentation of a petition, and most petitions were simply submitted to the Select Committee on Public Petitions, which classified them, decided which should be printed, and reported back to the House.[42] Memorials to the Queen probably brought even less advantage. The memorials in 1850 were submitted to the Home Secretary, who acknowledged receipt with a lithographed form letter.[43]

Some politicians thought that petitions were time-consuming nuisances. "I loathe the very smell and sight of *petitions*," Lord Strangford informed Lord Londonderry, "and I return yours, for that reason, *unread*. The fact is, I have enough to do to wade through those which are sent to myself, and have no time for those of others. *Devil take 'em*, is my constant prayer—however 'numerously and respectably signed' they may be."[44]

[39] Undated memorandum, [ca. Jan. 1851], Page & Moody Papers, Southampton City Record Office, D/PM/10/1/25.

[40] *Birmingham Mercury*, 22 Mar. 1851. For the intimidation of middle-class dissenters from social orthodoxy, see Walter E. Houghton, *The Victorian Frame of Mind, 1830-1870* (New Haven, 1957), pp. 398-99.

[41] Three sorts of topics attracted over ten thousand signatures. Radical political issues (franchise extension, the secret ballot, the reform of Parliament and of local government, the New Poor Law, and repeal of the Corn Laws and newspaper taxes) dominated petitioning in the 1830s and '40s, but virtually disappeared after about 1850. Religious issues emerged early on as a serious rival to Radical issues, and replaced the latter as the dominant type by the late 1850s. And finally there was a mélange of miscellaneous issues that came and went during the century—in the 1830s and '40s: postage, chimney sweeps, industrial safety, public health, and capital punishment; in the 1850s and '60s: master and servant laws, marriage with a deceased wife's sister; from the 1870s on: the Contagious Diseases Acts and animal rights. (Leys, "Petitioning in the Nineteenth and Twentieth Centuries," pp. 58-61.)

[42] Leys summarizes changes in the Standing Orders related to petitions in *ibid.*, pp. 48-54.

[43] The form letter appears in newspapers of the day, and a few are preserved in MS. collections. It reads: "I have had the honour to lay before the Queen, the address of the [_____], on the subject of the measures taken by the Pope, to establish a Roman Catholic hierarchy in this country. And I am to inform you that her Majesty was pleased to receive the same very graciously."

[44] Strangford to Londonderry, [Apr. 1843?], Londonderry Papers, Durham County Record Office, D/LO/C 100(378).

Anti-Catholic activists themselves were not quite sure about the value of petitioning. Some believed that petitioning influenced "unattached" or backbench M.P.s, who communicated their concern about public sentiment to their party leaders.[45] Others, who recognized that petitions to the House of Commons were ignored, thought that perhaps memorials to the Queen might be noticed more.[46] But Hugh Stowell, a leading Manchester anti-Catholic activist and reasonably shrewd political observer (when his religion did not cloud his judgement), doubted that petitioning of any sort did much good. He believed that ministers and party leaders paid much more attention to public meetings than to public petitions.[47]

A successful petition drive was at most a way of applying psychological pressure on the government of the day. Probably the most successful of the Victorian petition drives was that against the education clauses of the Factory Bill, 1843. The scenes in the House of Commons, where bundles of petitions swamped the clerks' table and clogged the aisles, clearly added to the tense atmosphere that the Peel Ministry tried to master, and made their task that much more difficult. But the large number of public petitions was neither the only nor the main reason for the ministry's decision to drop the bill.[48] Those who expected the House of Commons or the government to heed their petitions were doomed to disappointment.

In fact, both the public meeting and the public petition were ends in themselves. Colin Leys, who has studied the public petition closely, observes that the collection of signatures to petitions performed several important functions. It was a good way of mobilizing, involving, and keeping up the spirits of supporters. It was a good way of organizing public opinion around a concrete issue, of attracting publicity for the cause, and of seeming to be taking effective action. And a successful campaign provided evidence of public support for use in lobbying politicians.[49] The public meeting with its speeches and resolutions performed the same functions.[50] In the days before mass advertising by radio and television, the public meeting and public petition provided the only ways of gaining public attention, and even in the late twentieth century, pressure groups such as the nuclear disarmament movement resorted to meetings and petitions to boost their supporters' morale.

The public meeting and public petitioning enjoyed a symbiotic relationship with the newspaper (which, in Michael Brock's clever analogy, was to early Victorian politics what the transistor radio was to African politics in the 1950s[51]). Provincial newspapers needed news, partly because of the small size of their staffs, partly because of the nature of Victorian reporting. Small newspapers might be run by one or two men and a boy; newspapers in industrial towns and other largeish places might have an editor, leader-writer, subeditor, and two reporters. The great provincial papers had larger staffs; the *Manchester Guardian* grew from five reporters in 1838 to seven in 1868. (All figures exclude production staff.) None of

[45] *Watchman and Wesleyan Advertiser*, 26 Mar. 1851.
[46] *Protestant Magazine*, XI (Feb. 1849), 28.
[47] *Manchester Courier*, 18 Jan. 1851.
[48] Paz, *Politics of Working-Class Education*, pp. 119-21, 125.
[49] Leys, "Petitioning," pp. 58-59, 62-63.
[50] Hamer, *Politics of Electoral Pressure*, p. 17.
[51] Michael Brock, *The Great Reform Act* (London, 1973), p. 17.

the papers had the reportorial staff to cover their circulation area; they depended heavily on cutting and pasting and on stories submitted by interested parties. Nor was reporting investigative. The strength of Victorian reporting lay in the creation of "a body of solid and coherent information," in the same way as legal and parliamentary reporters did. But they were not good at dealing with unforeseen events; nor did they investigate events to establish what really happened.[52] (Thus it is that one gets more information about public disturbances, usually, from the law reporters' stenographic transcripts of trial testimony than from the news stories on the disturbances themselves.)

The public meeting, with its set speeches and resolutions, was perfectly suited for reporting. Such an event was much more likely to be reported than was a door-to-door petition campaign, and those who wanted to get publicity for their ideas were better off to hold a meeting than to placard a wall. This was especially true for religious news. Editors rarely reported on Sunday sermons, fearing that if they reported some sermons, then every denomination in their circulation area would demand space.[53] How the meetings were reported depended sometimes upon the newspaper's political views. Sometimes the organizers of meetings were reluctant to admit reporters from unsympathetic papers; and unsympathetic papers hoped that their reporters would be denied admission, in order to create a minor brouhaha.[54] So, in a sense, the public meeting happened in order to be reported as having happened, as much as to mobilize support for a cause.

Anti-Catholic Organizations

Meetings, petition drives, lecture tours, and the publication of books, pamphlets, and magazines all required money and organization; and several organizations existed (and still exist) to raise funds and provide services. They arose at different times for different purposes, and had different constituencies; and numerous smaller societies, with anti-Catholicism as a part of their agendas, had more ephemeral lives.[55]

The first and most problematical of the anti-Catholic organizations was the Orange Order, brought to Lancashire by militia and soldiers who had helped suppress the United Irish revolt of 1798. (Although Orange lodges were to be found all over England, the largest concentration of members was in Lancashire.) In 1835, however, the Order dissolved itself as the result of a Parliamentary investigation that revealed talk about a military coup, and that uncovered the existence of secret lodges in military barracks. But if the Order lost its Tory aristocratic support and its central organization after 1835, it did not cease to exist; it returned to its working-class roots in the northern industrial towns, loosely linked by the Loyal Orange Institution or the Grand Protestant Association of Loyal Orange-

---

[52] Lucy Brown, *Victorian News and Newspapers* (Oxford, 1985), pp. 82-83, 103.

[53] *Ibid.*, p. 99.

[54] *Leeds Mercury*, 21 Sept. 1839.

[55] It is thus wrong to say that most anti-Catholic societies were *ad hoc* responses to specific concessions to Roman Catholics, that they faded away after the momentary excitement passed, and that the Orange Order was the "only . . . recognizably significant permanent organization against Catholic claims." (Norman, *Anti-Catholicism*, p. 20.)

men.[56] It is tempting to dismiss the Orangemen as "little more than a joke, made up entirely of flunkeys,"[57] especially if one is uncomfortable with a working-class consciousness that does not quite fit into one's Marxist model. Throughout the period 1835-70, middle-class and aristocratic Tories avoided patronizing Orange lodges; the lodges remained pub-based societies under working-class control, clubs for drinking and for funeral benefits.[58] They also offered the opportunity for organized violence, as we shall see.[59] But throughout the period, Orangeism was marginal, geographically, politically, and socially.

More central were two Anglican societies, the British Society for Promoting the Religious Principles of the Reformation, founded in 1827, and the Protestant Association, founded in 1835. (The former group, commonly called the British Reformation Society or the Protestant and Reformation Society, changed its name to the Protestant Reformation Society in 1853.)

The British Reformation Society was the inspiration of the Scot James Edward Gordon, a retired Royal Navy captain, who had occupied his retirement with charitable work, and who turned to Ireland in the 1820s. Gordon came to believe that Ireland could be helped only by religious education of a specifically Protestant nature. These views were shared by the Anglican Evangelicals Hugh McNeile and Henry Drummond (who served on the British Reformation Society's committee) and by the religiously inclined Robert Jocelyn, third Earl of Roden. These men cooperated with Gordon to form the society, intending it to circulate tracts, to hold meetings for religious discussion, to collect information about the spread of Protestantism, and to educate Roman Catholics. Although the society tried to be nondenominational (by appointing token non-Anglicans to its committee), it in effect was Anglican.[60]

The British Reformation Society intended at first to proselytize in Ireland. Their aggressive program made it impossible for them to cooperate with the more moderate Dublin Readers' Society and London Hibernian Society. Moderate Irish Protestants were put off by the Reformation Society's loud, aggressive style, which offended the sensibilities of those they wanted to convert. But the society's Irish activities ended in 1832 because of increasing disturbances in Ireland, because the society's Irish auxiliaries were troubled by organizational and personality problems, and because of the growing need to promote Protestantism in Britain itself. So, the society focused increasingly on London, and attempted to found branches in the provinces.[61]

As the question of political rights for Roman Catholics was increasingly debated after 1828, anti-Catholics felt the need for a more purely political organization. Gordon put together two mass meetings at Exeter Hall in

[56] Frank Neal, *Sectarian Violence: The Liverpool Experience, 1819-1914: An Aspect of Anglo-Irish History* (Manchester, 1988), pp. 31-32, 68-72.

[57] John Foster, *Class Struggle and the Industrial Revolution: Early Industrial Capitalism in Three English Towns* (New York, 1974), p. 219.

[58] Neal, *Sectarian Violence*, pp. 167-72.

[59] *Inf.*, p. 253.

[60] Wolffe, *Protestant Crusade*, Ch. 2, pp. 34-41; John R. Wolffe, "Protestant Societies and Anti-Catholic Agitation in Great Britain, 1829-1860" (D.Phil. thesis, University of Oxford, 1985), pp. 26-30.

[61] Wolffe, *Protestant Crusade*, pp. 41-44, 49-61; Wolffe, "Protestant Societies and Anti-Catholic Agitation," pp. 30-36.

June and July of 1835 that resulted in the formation of the Protestant Association. This group taught that the British state was unlike any other in human history, save for ancient Israel, for it embodied divine law and expressed human duty to God rather than simply being a way of organizing society. In its view, Roman Catholic Emancipation had been a retrograde step, and its aim was to rectify this error by exposing Roman Catholicism as persecutory and as subversive of the British Constitution. The Protestant Association focused on the publication of tracts (over three-quarters of a million by 1842) and handbills, and put out a magazine, the *Protestant Magazine*, for middle-class readers. It also published cheap editions of works such as J.-H. Merle d'Aubigné's *History of the Reformation*.[62] Although claiming to be for all Protestants, its politics were closest to the Conservative Party's Ultra wing, thus prompting Daniel O'Connell to gibe that its opinions were "reproba-tory, or approba-tory, lauda-tory, or explana-tory, or any other tory you please."[63]

A decade later, in 1845, the decision of the Peel Ministry to make a permanent endowment for the Roman Catholic seminary at Maynooth, Ireland, precipitated the formation of two anti-Catholic organizations, the Evangelical Alliance and the National Club.

The Maynooth endowment offended a broad spectrum of interests, and thus offered the chance to create an anti-Catholic "united front." Anglican anti-Catholics hated the grant because it marked the Peel Ministry's betrayal of the Established Church. Moderate Nonconformists hated the grant because they were anti-Catholic, but also because they objected to the expenditure of public funds on non-Protestant activities. The more radical Nonconformists objected to the expenditure of public funds on any sectarian activity soever; they were called "Voluntaryists" in the political parlance of the day.

The Protestant Association organized the Central Anti-Maynooth Committee, chaired by Sir Culling Eardley Smith,[64] but dominated by Anglicans, in March 1845, to lead the united front. (The Committee had 39 Anglicans, 19 Congregationalists, nine Wesleyans, and four Presbyterians.) The Committee put on a mass meeting of Protestants to demonstrate unanimity on the issue. This met at Exeter Hall on 30 April and was supposed to last until 3 May, but split over the question of state aid for Protestant activities. The Voluntaryists, who were against any state aid, left and organized their own protest at Crosby Hall, because the moderates condemned aid for Roman Catholics while tolerating the Anglican Establishment. The Crosby Hall conference was absorbed into the Anti-State Church Association, while the Central Anti-Maynooth Committee led indirectly to the creation of the Evangelical Alliance.[65]

The Central Anti-Maynooth Committee, viewing itself as primarily political, focused on the campaign to repeal the Maynooth endowment,

---

[62] Wolffe, "Protestant Societies and Anti-Catholic Agitation," pp. 106-25, 128, 136-37; Wolffe, *Protestant Crusade*, Ch. 3, pp. 88-91.

[63] Wolffe, *Protestant Crusade*, pp. 95-96.

[64] Smith (1805-1863), 2nd bart., assumed the name of Eardley upon becoming head of the family in 1847. Treasurer of the London Missionary Society and closely connected with Congregational interests, he also promoted extremely Low Anglican interests. He was a Liberal in politics. (*DNB*, VI, 316-17.)

[65] Norman, *Anti-Catholicism*, pp. 29-30, 42-49; Wolffe, "Protestant Societies and Anti-Catholic Agitation," p. 187.

and disappeared after its failure to do so; but several of its leaders also hoped to see a more spiritual "Protestant confederation" to unite "Scriptural" Christians worldwide to combat popery. These people were mainly Scots—Thomas Chalmers and Robert Smith Candlish (Free Church) and David King (Secession)—who wanted to get support for the Free Church of Scotland, and who had contacts in England—especially the Birmingham Congregationalist John Angell James (who thought that the call for world union had to come from a non-English source). This fitted into the desires of several prominent foreign Protestants—especially the Swiss Jean-Henri Merle d'Aubigné, the Frenchman Adolphe Monod, and the Americans William Patton and Robert Baird. (The latter man had helped found the American and Foreign Christian Union, the leading anti-Catholic society in the United States.) These men, and other delegates, met in Liverpool in October 1845, and called for an organization that would promote the union of "Scriptural" Christians and combat popery.[66]

(That Evangelicalism and anti-Catholicism should have combined to produce the only nineteenth-century group to strive for Christian unity, and hence that laid the basis for the ecumenical movement of the twentieth century, is a circumstance that both conservative Evangelicals and liberal ecumenists in the late twentieth century wanted very much to forget.[67])

The Evangelical Alliance at once fell to quarreling over the criteria for membership. Some thought that the possession of membership in one's own denomination should be sufficient. Others wanted a way of excluding non-Evangelicals. Eventually, a nine-point statement of belief was drawn up, but the points produced more quarreling. They were too antinomian for the Wesleyans, but not Calvinist enough for the Free Church. They were too soft on slavery for the British, but too hard on it for the Americans.[68] Beyond this, the problem of defining a clear role vitiated the Evangelical Alliance; it never quite figured out what it was to *do*. It was not political, so it could not effectively lead interdenominational campaigns. It committed itself only to the collection of information, but serious anti-Catholics did not need or want facts. So, it followed the tried-and-true path of organizing local auxiliaries and holding meetings in which Roman Catholicism was excoriated in trenchant rhetoric.[69] But this was not enough.

The Maynooth grant had marked the final proof of the Peel Ministry's betrayal of its backbenchers, of the Church, and of the Protestant

[66] John Wolffe, "The Evangelical Alliance in the 1840s: An Attempt to Institutionalise Christian Unity," *Studies in Church History*, XXIII (1986), 338-40; Philip D. Jordan, *The Evangelical Alliance for the United States of America, 1847-1900: Ecumenism, Identity, and the Religion of the Republic* (New York and Toronto, 1982), pp. 33-45; Elihu Burritt, *Walks in the Black Country and its Green Borderland*, fwd. by Vivian Bird (Kineton, Warwick, 1976), p. 34; Ray Allen Billington, *The Protestant Crusade, 1800-1860: A Study of the Origins of American Nativism* (New York, 1938), pp. 264-69.

[67] Ruth Rouse and Stephen Charles Neill (eds.), *A History of the Ecumenical Movement, 1517-1948* (London, 1954), pp. 318-24, viewed the Evangelical Alliance's goals of Christian unity and anti-Catholicism as contradictory because they did not recognize that most nineteenth-century Evangelical Protestants denied that Roman Catholics were Christians. Jordan, *Evangelical Alliance*, pp. 187-89, shows that there was continuity of leadership between the American Branch, Evangelical Alliance, and the Federal Council of Churches.

[68] Jordan, *Evangelical Alliance*, pp. 48-52; Wolffe, "Evangelical Alliance," pp. 342-43; *Evangelical Christendom*, I (Oct. 1847), 318-19.

[69] *Evangelical Christendom*, I (Jan. 1847), 1, (Dec. 1847), 391-92, II (1848), iii, V (Jan. 1851), 6-7; Wolffe, "Evangelical Alliance," pp. 340-41, 344-46.

Constitution—at least, so thought the Ultra-Tories. In May 1845, a group of Ultras, led by J. C. Colquhoun and Sir Digby Mackworth, organized the National Club. Colquhoun was a Scottish Tory M.P. who had long been involved in anti-Catholic activities, who had pressed the Church of Scotland's claims to educational hegemony against Whiggish liberalism, and whom the Ultras had canvassed as a possible replacement for Sir Robert Peel as party leader during the late 1830s. Mackworth was a retired soldier and parliamentary hopeful. The National Club's purpose was to restructure the Conservative party along Ultra-Tory lines by stressing the Establishment even more strongly than did the Protestant Association. Non-Anglicans were excluded from membership (save for a few members of the Scots Kirk such as Colquhoun himself and John Cumming); by 1848, over half (254) of the club's 451 members were clergymen.[70] Although the National Club failed to play the leading role in restructuring Toryism that it aspired to, largely because the Tories restructured themselves over Protection, it exercised a modest influence behind the scenes. It issued pamphlets on topics of the day such as state aid to Roman Catholic schools and lobbied the Protectionist leadership; it organized its own members who were M.P.s and maintained contacts with the Tory press (especially with the *Morning Herald*, the *Standard*, and *John Bull*).[71]

Five years after Maynooth, the Papal Aggression crisis provoked the creation of three more societies, the Scottish Reformation Society, the Protestant Alliance, and the British Protestant League and Bible and Anti-Popery Mission.

Organized in 1850, the Scottish Reformation Society confined its meetings and proselytism north of the Border, but its monthly periodical, the *Bulwark*, was circulated widely throughout the island. Although it was intended to be a pan-Evangelical force, its leader was the Free Churchman James Begg[72] and the Free Church dominated its councils. Hence, both the Kirk and the Anglicans of the British Reformation Society suspected it of antiestablishmentarian tendencies.[73] Begg and the Scottish Reformation Society worked closely with the Protestant Alliance, organized in 1851 in an attempt to unite Anglicans and Nonconformists against popery. The two societies pushed the revived anti-Maynooth campaign in the 1850s and Charles Newdegate's convent inspection campaign in the 1860s. But as with the earlier anti-Maynooth agitations, the attempt to paper over the differences between Anglican establishmentarians and Nonconformist Voluntaryists produced groups that were long on rhetoric and short on action.[74]

The British Protestant League was organized in 1851 by the Rev. Tenison Cuffe, an apostate Anglican priest who had left the Church for the Countess of Huntingdon's Connexion the year before. Cuffe, who had in-

[70] Paz, *Working-Class Education*, pp. 37, 39, 95, 128, 158 n. 43; Wolffe, "Protestant Societies and Anti-Catholic Agitation," pp. 191-96.

[71] Wolffe, "Protestant Societies and Anti-Catholic Agitation," pp. 198-202.

[72] Begg (1808-1883), the son of a minister, was excluded from preferment in the Kirk because his anti-Catholicism was deemed too coarse and fanatical.

[73] Steve Bruce, *No Pope of Rome: Anti-Catholicism in Modern Scotland* (Edinburgh, 1985), pp. 31-36; *Bulwark*, III (Feb. 1854), 199, IV (Mar. 1855), 256-57; Wolffe, "Protestant Societies and Anti-Catholic Agitation," pp. 281-83.

[74] Wolffe, "Protestant Societies and Anti-Catholic Agitation," pp. 303-7; Wallis, "Anti-Maynooth Campaign," pp. 30-35; Wolffe, *Protestant Crusade*, Ch. 5; Arnstein, *Protestant Versus Catholic*, p. 73.

habited the fringes of London Anglican Evangelicalism as minister of the Carlisle proprietary chapel, was active in Protestant Association affairs as early as 1840. But his Protestant League was looked upon with suspicion; the Protestant Alliance feared that it was a rival, and the *Bulwark* charged that it was a fraud, existing solely for the purpose of collecting money. Cuffe failed to find prominent patrons, and his society died within a few years.[75]

Finally, two other societies appeared in 1865: the Protestant Evangelical Mission and Electoral Union, and the Church Association. The Protestant Evangelical Mission had its start as the sponsor of public lectures by William Murphy, an itinerant lecturer whose violent anti-Catholic rhetoric kept England north of the Trent in an uproar from 1866 until his ultimately fatal beating in 1871. After the loss of its champion, the group continued a shadowy existence into the early 1900s, reprinting salacious tracts by Pierce Connelly, Blanco White, and Maria Monk.[76] The Church Association was an Evangelical society that focused exclusively on Anglican matters, and that funded many of the anti-Ritualist legal prosecutions of the 1870s, '80s, and '90s.[77]

All these societies arose in successive waves as attempts to resolve two tensions inherent in organized anti-Catholicism. One tension was that between a more purely religious approach and a more purely political approach. The other tension was that between Anglicans and Nonconformists. Both tensions in the end proved to be unresolvable.

Problems in Measuring Anti-Catholicism

The anti-Catholic societies attempted to mobilize public opinion during the 1850s and '60s by means of petition drives over two related questions: repeal of the Maynooth endowment and the government inspection of convents. The Protestant Alliance, Scottish Reformation Society, and Protestant Association cooperated in organizing petition drives, and the National Club lobbied in the background. In addition, the societies used Italian affairs to keep interest alive. Petition drives and protest meetings were sparked by the Madiai Affair of 1852-53 (when a Protestant couple who kept a guest house in Florence were arrested for proselytism), the visit to England of King Victor Emmanuel I of Sardinia in 1855, the Mortara Affair of the late 1850s (in which a Jewish child in the Papal States, who had been secretly baptized, was removed from his family to be raised a Roman Catholic) and the visit to England of Giuseppi Garibaldi in 1863. The most successful of these petition drives, that against Maynooth in 1852, produced 322,921 signatures to 942 petitions.[78] In contrast, the public meetings during the winter of 1850-51 produced 2,616 memorials to the

[75] Wolffe, "Protestant Societies and Anti-Catholic Agitations," p. 310; *Penny Protestant Operative*, I (1840-41), *passim*; Moody to Cuffe, 1 Mar. 1852, Page & Moody Papers, Southampton City Record Office, D/PM/10/5/44; Cuffe to Moody, 3 Mar. 1852, *ibid.*, D/PM/10/5/45; Henry M. May to Moody, 3 Mar. 1852, *ibid.*, D/PM/10/2/59; handbills in *ibid.*, D/PM/10/5/50-56; *Bulwark*, I (May 1852), 291.

[76] *Circular of the Protestant Electoral Union*, I (1866)-V (1870); its tracts are in the British Library. For the Murphy Riots, see *inf.*, pp. 256-59.

[77] *Inf.*, pp. 150-51.

[78] Lohrli, "Madiai," pp. 28-50; Wolffe, "Protestant Societies and Anti-Catholic Agitations," pp. 317-36, 340-44; Wallis, "Revival of the Anti-Maynooth Campaign," pp. 527-48; Wallis, "Anti-Maynooth Campaign," pp. 45-58, 69-88; *Times*, 12 Nov. 1858.

Queen, bearing 887,525 signatures, and 1,914 petitions to the House of Commons, bearing 348,590 signatures.[79] Thus, the memorializing of 1850 and petitioning of 1851 produced more signatures than the anti-Maynooth petitioning of the 1850s and '60s; and, as we have seen, they were a more spontaneous expression of public opinion, in the sense that they were not produced from a central office.

How good a source are these memorials and petitions, and to what conclusions can they lead the historian? (And note here that in this book the word "memorial" refers invariably to the addresses to the Queen produced in 1850, and the word "petition" invariably to addresses to the House of Commons produced in 1851.) Can they be classified in any meaningful way? Can Can accurate count of signatures be made? Are they a meaningful measure of public opinion?

The memorials and petitions emanated from four basic sorts of meetings. Some came from explicitly Nonconformist bodies like Dissenting chapels and Sunday schools, Wesleyan class meetings, regional Congregational and Baptist unions. Others came from professional or occupational groups such as legal and medical societies. These are easy to catalogue.

It is more difficult to distinguish between public meetings and those dominated by the Church of England, especially in the smaller, rural areas. I classified the memorials and petitions described as from the "inhabitants of X parish" or from the "churchwardens and inhabitants of X" as public. (In the case of the latter designation, Nonconformists sometimes controlled vestries, especially in large towns and in the North.) Those described as from the "incumbent, churchwardens, and inhabitants of X parish," or otherwise mentioning clergymen, I classified as Anglican. But this method undercounts somewhat Anglican participation, for the purely Anglican meeting merged by degrees into the public meeting.

Some meetings were clearly Anglican, as when the clergy of Liverpool, or Manchester, or the Rural Deanery of Blackburn met to address the Queen.[80] Other meetings that involved laity were also clearly Anglican in nature. A public meeting at Bolton adopted a memorial from "the clergy, magistrates, gentry, and other inhabitants of the borough"; of the twelve speakers, seven were Anglican clergymen.[81] At Rochdale, the public meeting adopted a memorial to the Queen from "the Vicar of Rochdale, and undersigned clergy, and Inhabitants of Rochdale and its vicinity" and an address to the Bishop of Manchester from "clergymen and laymen of your lordship's diocese."[82] Other examples of public meetings clearly Anglican in nature are those of the Church Institute at Warrington, the parishioners of St. John's Hey, the Anglicans of Preston, and the "ministers, churchwardens, seat-holders, and inhabitants" of St. Katharine's, Northampton.[83]

[79] The memorials are found in "Return of the Number of Addresses which have been presented to Her Majesty on the subject of the Recent Measures taken by the Pope for the Establishment of a Roman Catholic Hierarchy in this Country," *PP*, 1851, LIX (84), 649-739; the petitions are found in *Report of the Select Committee of the House of Commons on Public Petitions* (Session 1851).

[80] *Manchester Guardian*, 6, 20, 27 Nov., 14 Dec. 1850.

[81] *Manchester Courier*, 23 Nov. 1850.

[82] *Ibid.*, 9 Nov. 1850.

[83] *Manchester Guardian*, 30 Nov. 1850; *Preston Pilot*, 14 Dec. 1850; *Northampton Herald*, 23 Nov. 1850.

Other meetings were clearly public in nature, open to all inhabitants regardless of religious adherence. The Nottingham town meeting, for instance, which met to petition the House of Commons, was chaired by the Mayor; of the eleven speakers, seven were borough officials or local notables, two were clergymen, and two were Baptist ministers.[84] Other examples are the public meetings at Leeds and Lancaster.[85] In some places, clearly, the effort was made to maintain a balance of speakers and to represent a variety of confessional views.

On the other hand, some Anglican meetings in a sense masqueraded as public. The public meeting at Ashton-under-Lyne was held at the town hall and chaired by former alderman Booth Mason (a death in Mayor R. Kershaw's family prevented his taking the chair). Each of the three resolutions was moved by an Anglican priest and seconded by a layman.[86] The public meeting at Altrincham, also held at the town hall and chaired by Mayor Richard Broadbent, heard one token Wesleyan minister, five Anglican clergymen, and four laymen.[87] At Liverpool, where Anglicans long had been active as a confessional group in politics, a proposed "protestant meeting," organized by the Rev. Hugh McNeile, the leading Anglican anti-Catholic in the borough, was merged into a public meeting called by the mayor in pursuance of a requisition.[88] The big Manchester meeting on 20 November is also instructive. The chairman, senior warden Richard Birley, began the proceedings by reading a letter from the Rev. Hugh Stowell, incumbent of Christ Church, Salford, Evangelical, and prominent anti-Catholic. Stowell "thought that the proceedings should be conducted entirely by laymen; in order to refute the calumny that this was merely a clerical movement."[89] It is, however, difficult to distinguish between this meeting, which ostensibly was for all Protestants in Manchester, and those of the Manchester and Salford Protestant Operative Association on 4 November and the Manchester and Salford Protestant Reformation Society on 8 March 1851, which were showcases for Stowell's rhetoric. Five clergymen and fifteen laymen prominent enough to be mentioned in the newspaper accounts of the public meeting, and five of the twelve speakers, also attended one of the Stowell rallies or were officers of the Manchester branch of the Evangelical, anti-Tractarian Church Pastoral Aid Society.[90]

A few other examples make the point that the line between an Anglican and a public meeting is not clear. The public meeting at Poulton-le-Fylde addressed both the Queen and the Bishop of Manchester; that at Stockport, chaired by Mayor George Turner, met at the Wellington Road National (i.e., Anglican) School and had ten clergymen in attendance.[91] The public meeting at Fleetwood heard a token Methodist, and that at Runcorn heard a Congregationalist, but both were dominated by Anglicans.[92] A "protestant meeting" at Astley was convened in the National School

84 *Times*, 22 Mar. 1851.
85 *Ibid.*, 28 Mar. 1851; *Preston Pilot*, 30 Nov. 1850.
86 *Manchester Guardian*, 7 Dec. 1850.
87 *Ibid.*, 23 Nov. 1850.
88 *Ibid.*, 16, 20, 23 Nov. 1850.
89 *Ibid.*, 23 Nov. 1850.
90 *Ibid.*, 6 Nov. 1850; *Manchester Courier*, 9, 16, 23 Nov. 1850, 1, 8, Mar. 1851.
91 *Preston Pilot*, 23 Nov. 1850; *Manchester Guardian*, 30 Nov. 1850.
92 *Preston Pilot*, 30 Nov. 1850; *Manchester Courier*, 7 Dec. 1850.

and included the presentation of a purse (£280 in gold) to the vicar.[93] At Glossop, the vicar directed the preparation and circulation of a memorial to the Queen.[94]

The *Manchester Courier* echoed Hugh Stowell's claim that the protests against the Papal Aggression enjoyed broad-based lay support: "The character of the memorials most distinctly proves that the movement is not one of the clergy only, as was recently alleged; for the signatures that are appended are nearly all those of the laity, clergy only, as in duty bound, heading the movement by their example and their names."[95] But in fact, many of the ostensibly public meetings were dominated by clergymen and represent in reality an Anglican voice.

A second problem is that of the counting of signatures. On balance, the figures for memorialists and petitioners are somewhat understated. There is no guaranty that the number of signatures given is accurate; the parliamentary clerks may have guessed at the numbers. How likely is it that Bristol produced precisely 15,000 memorialists?) The printed sources omit the number of signatures in only seven instances, none from large towns. The memorials from over half of the county meetings, and addresses from not a few parochial and town meetings, were signed only by the presiding officer on behalf of the meeting.[96] In the case of Lancashire, eight memorials, from the inhabitants of Walton-on-the-Hill, St. Simon's parish of Liverpool, Padiham, Liverpool, Leigh, Childwall, Manchester, and Burnley, were signed only by the chairmen of the meetings, as was the memorial of the Liverpool British Reformation Society. (Each of these memorials thus adds only one signature to the total, as do the memorials from the Wigan, Lancaster, and Liverpool corporations.) The number of signatures from the inhabitants of Bolton-by-the-Sands and Prince's Park parish of Liverpool was omitted from the parliamentary paper by clerical or typographical error. Presumably these omissions tend to underrate Lancashire's anti-Catholic sentiment.

Newspaper reports do not supply the missing figures, for estimates of crowd size were vague. We learn that the town hall at Leigh "was densely crowded in every part, and the avenues and staircases were also filled with people. Several hundreds went away unable to get into the hall."[97] The inhabitants of Mossley, Ashton-under-Lyne, met in the schoolroom attached to the church, "the room being well filled"; their memorial bore 775 signatures.[98] At Altrincham, "the hall was densely crowded with persons of all ranks, and the ante room of the large room of the Unicorn Inn, which was joined to it, by a partition dividing them being taken away, was filled; and many persons who were unable to get into these rooms, stood in an ante-room of the hall."[99] When the "Protestant Working Men of Man-

---

[93] *Manchester Guardian*, 9 Apr. 1851.
[94] *Ibid.*, 23 Nov. 1850.
[95] *Manchester Courier*, 30 Nov. 1850.
[96] The county meetings for which only the presiding officer signed are randomly distributed and therefore probably do not distort the geographical distribution of signatories to any significant degree, except for the West Country, East Anglia, and the West Midlands. (These counties are Cornwall, Devon, Somerset, Wilts, Berks, Oxford, Surrey, Essex, Norfolk, Suffolk, Hunts, Gloucester, Worcester, Warwick, Staffs, Leicester, Derby, Notts, York, Cumberland, Westmoreland, and Cheshire.)
[97] *Manchester Guardian*, 20 Nov. 1850.
[98] *Ibid.*, 14 Dec. 1850.
[99] *Ibid.*, 23 Nov. 1850.

chester" met at the Corn Exchange, the reporter mentioned that "the hall was not more than two-thirds full."[100] Now one could visit those buildings that still exist, to see how many they would hold, but even that will not supply the missing figures, for as we have seen, more people signed petitions and memorials than attended the meetings that adopted them.

The three memorials from the mayors and councils of Wigan, Lancaster, and Liverpool also contribute but one signature each to the total. Rarely, reports are full, as when the Nottingham borough council adopted a memorial by a vote of 21 to 16.[101] But all that we know for Wigan is that three councillors spoke in favor of the memorial, three spoke against, and nineteen were present.[102] As for Lancaster, we only know that fourteen councillors were present; the newspaper report does not indicate if there was any opposition to the memorial.[103]

The third major problem is that of whether the memorials and petitions are good indicators of what we really want to measure—anti-Catholicism. The memorials are the only countable evidence to emerge from the mass meetings of 1850, but the petitions allow of more choice. Parliament in 1851 received 1,686 petitions with 264,864 signatures protesting Roman Catholic encroachments, 28 petitions with 5,225 signatures praying for the passage of the Ecclesiastical Titles Bill, and 2,541 petitions with 756,578 signatures praying that the penalties for violation of the Ecclesiastical Titles Bill be made more stringent. The last set of petitions is the most appropriate indicator for two reasons. First, to ask for more stringent penalties was to reject Lord John Russell's attempt to soften penal legislation by eliminating Ireland from the measure; that was a common reaction in 1851, according to the literary evidence. Second, as the set largest in number of signatories, it has the best chance of reflecting accurately the distribution of the population. Thus, the indicator is *valid* (it measures what it claims to measure).

Despite the problems of enumeration and validity, these signatures are a broadly accurate measure—indeed, the only countable measure—of public sentiment in 1850-51. In order to speak accurately about public opinion, one needs a *good sample* (which reflects precisely the social, political, sexual, religious, age, educational, etc., distribution of the population) and a measuring instrument that is *reliable* (which produces the same response for the same subject each time that it is administered). Present-day polling organizations with difficulty meet these criteria; historians must make do with the evidence that has survived. But petitioning was a common way for the Victorians to express their opinion. (The House of Commons in 1851 received a total of 12,536 petitions on all subjects, bearing 2,686,491 signatures; over ten thousand petitions a year went to the House for the rest of the century.[104]) Thus the protest signatures are at least as good a measure of public opinion as are newspapers, which historians customarily use; when combined with literary evidence, they illuminate the subject of mass-based anti-Catholicism.

[100] *Ibid.*, 24 Dec. 1850.
[101] *Times*, 19 Nov. 1850.
[102] *Manchester Guardian*, 18 Dec. 1850.
[103] *Preston Pilot*, 7 Dec. 1850.
[104] Leys, "Petitioning," p. 54.

TABLE 1

Memorialists and Petitioners per Thousand People,
with Rank by County, 1850 and 1851

County	Memorialists		Petitioners	
	‰	Rank	‰	Rank
Bedford	14.10	38	9.26	30
Berkshire	20.16	35	11.65	22
Buckingham	28.21	29	9.06	31
Cambridge	34.26	26	8.00	33
Cheshire	33.78	27	14.99	17
Cornwall	18.33	36	11.39	23
Cumberland	35.90	25	15.19	16
Derby	54.94	15	46.23	2
Devon	61.12	11	10.50	27
Dorset	22.54	33	14.92	18
Durham	21.29	34	11.00	25
Essex	39.25	21	3.22	41
Gloucester	64.42	9	41.52	5
Hampshire	82.02	2	7.23	34
Hereford	17.21	37	11.03	24
Hertford	26.55	31	4.91	40
Huntingdon	30.02	28	12.32	21
Kent	58.00	14	34.28	6
Lancashire	74.10	4	42.14	4
Leicester	69.18	7	19.75	12
Lincoln	39.15	23	20.79	10
London	75.00	3	14.85	19
Middlesex	48.98	20	5.81	37
Norfolk	13.08	40	5.37	38
Northampton	120.35	1	6.96	35
Northumberland	27.28	30	6.88	36
Nottingham	39.16	22	52.61	1
Oxford	25.79	32	10.30	28
Rutland	6.26	42	0.00	42
Shropshire	49.18	19	10.99	26
Somerset	58.56	12	19.64	13
Stafford	49.73	17	30.00	7
Suffolk	13.49	39	5.06	39
Surrey	58.29	13	45.23	3
Sussex	69.90	6	15.77	15
Warwick	62.81	10	8.21	32
Westmoreland	64.71	8	29.02	8
Wiltshire	52.76	16	13.02	20
Worcestershire	37.31	24	10.14	29
East Riding	70.94	5	21.13	9
North Riding	49.70	18	18.55	14
West Riding	13.07	41	19.85	11

Source: "Return of the Number of Addresses . . . presented to Her Majesty on the subject of the Recent Measures taken by the Pope for the Establishment of a Roman Catholic Hierarchy in this Country," *PP*, 1851, LIX (84), 649-739; *Report of the Select Committee of the House of Commons on Public Petitions* (Session 1851); "Census of Great Britain, 1851: Population Tables, I," *PP*, 1852-3, LXXXV [1631], 106.

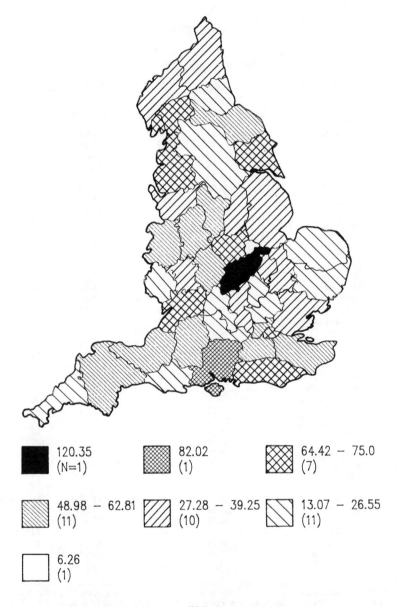

■	120.35 (N=1)	▨	82.02 (1)	▧	64.42 – 75.0 (7)
▨	48.98 – 62.81 (11)	▨	27.28 – 39.25 (10)	▨	13.07 – 26.55 (11)
□	6.26 (1)				

FIG. 2

Map of Memorialists by County in England, 1850

TABLE 2

Sources of Memorialists and Petitioners, England, 1850 and 1851

	Memorialists		Petitioners	
Source	N	%	N	%
Public meetings	541,544	61.02	221,254	63.47
Anglican meetings	318,675	35.91	12,325	3.53
Wesleyan Methodist	1,825	0.20	107,566	30.86
Other Dissent	17,846	2.01	6,782	1.94
Other	7,635	0.86	663	0.19
Total	887,525	100.00	348,590	100.00

Source: See Table 1

Patterns of Prejudice in 1850-1851

When tabulated, the figures show that memorializing in 1850 sprang from different sources and motives than did petitioning in 1850. Certainly far fewer people protested in 1851 than in 1850, and they came from different parts of the country. Only four counties occupied the same rank in both years, three were one or two ranks higher or lower, five were four ranks higher or lower, and 71 percent were five or more ranks higher or lower. (See Table 1 for the rank order of the counties.) Northampton and Hampshire ranked first and second in terms of memorializers per thousand of population, but thirty-fifth and thirty-fourth for petitioners per thousand. Nottingham, first among petitioners, was just below the median of the memorialists. Those counties that memorialized in 1850 were only reasonably likely also to petition in 1851.

The difference between the two instances of protest may be ascribed to the different sources that produced them. (See Table 2 above.) Wesleyan Methodists, quiet about protesting the hierarchy itself, contributed 73 percent of the petitions and 30 percent of the signatures in favor of making the Ecclesiastical Titles Bill more stringent. Anglicans, on the other hand, played a much more important role in 1850 than they did in 1851. In neither instance did non-Wesleyan Dissenters figure, except insofar as they may have participated in public meetings. Thus we must treat the two protest episodes separately and focus on Anglicans and Methodists in our analysis.

A map (Fig. 2) showing how the memorialists were distributed by county suggests that there seem to have been three, or possibly four, centers of memorializing. From Hampshire east along the south coast, we find the counties ranking second, third, sixth, thirteenth, and fourteenth in terms of signatures per thousand of population. From Northampton a second center of anti-Catholicism extended northwest to include the first, seventh, ninth, tenth, fifteenth, seventeenth, and nineteenth ranking counties. Lancashire (ranking fourth) and Westmoreland (eighth) formed a third locus; and from Devon east we see the counties ranking eleventh, twelfth, and sixteenth in memorialists. The centers of memorializing from Hampshire east and from Devonshire east were strong centers of Anglican church-attendance in the 1851 Religious Census, and had been so since Anglo-Saxon times. The direction of memorializing emanating from Northamptonshire followed counties that were less strongly Anglican. Lanca-

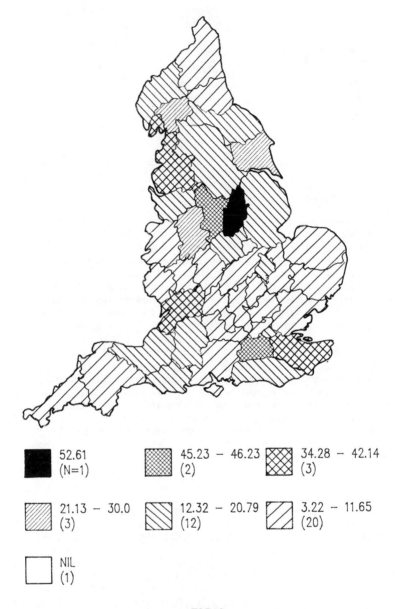

■	52.61 (N=1)	▨	45.23 – 46.23 (2)

FIG. 3

Map of Petitioners by County in England, 1851

TABLE 3

Sources of Memorialists and Petitioners, Lancashire, 1850 and 1851

	Memorialists		Petitioners	
Source	N	%	N	%
Public meetings	100,886	72.97	74,773	85.74
Anglican meetings	37,283	26.97	48	0.06
Wesleyan Methodists	0	0	12,392	14.21
Other Dissent	87	0.06	1	0.00
Other	1	0.00	0	0
Total	138,257	100.00	87,214	100.01

Source: See Table 1

shire, the religious needs of which had been ill provided for since Anglo-Saxon times, was the largest center of native Recusancy, had a weak Anglican presence, and was one of the strongest centers of Methodist life. Westmoreland, on the other hand, was a strong Anglican outpost in the Northwest.[105] All this suggests that several elements will turn out to govern the variation in memorializing.

A map of petitioners (Fig. 3) presents a different picture. Lancashire and Westmoreland retained their ranks of fourth and eighth; Gloucester moved from ninth to fifth; from Nottingham west we see three counties ranking first, second, and seventh. In the south, Surrey (third) and Kent (sixth) were the only major centers of petitioning. The counties that took the most prominent roles in petitioning were those in which Anglicanism was not very strong (save Westmoreland, Surrey, and Kent).[106] As for those counties that did not participate significantly in the protests, we note Cornwall, a band running southwest from East Anglia to Berkshire, and in the North Northumberland and Durham. The Midlands and the agricultural West Country appear to be the most inconsistent.

The Lancashire evidence parallels that for the nation. (See Table 3 below.) The bulk of the meetings in Lancashire were public—that is, from the inhabitants of an area. Self-proclaimed Anglican meetings generated only a quarter of the memorialists and less than 1 percent of the petitioners. (However, the number of Anglican meetings is somewhat understated, as we have seen.) Nonconformists were, for all practical purposes, inactive as distinct groups in 1850, but Wesleyans participated in the 1851 agitation, producing about 15 percent of the petitioners (as compared with 30 percent nationwide.)

So, we must pay close attention to differences and to localities—to differences among issues and denominations, and to the local concerns and issues that governed anti-Catholic attitudes. Moreover, we must begin our examination of popular anti-Catholicism by looking closely at the relationship that the popular mind drew between Roman Catholicism and Irish immigration to England.

[105] B. I. Coleman, *The Church of England in the Mid-Nineteenth Century: A Social Geography* (London, 1980), pp. 9-10, 20-21.
[106] *Ibid.*

II

CULTURAL IMAGES

> All the Milesians shipped over here are grad-
> ually displacing Englishmen. . . . The Milesians
> will supplant the Scandinavians, just as sheep eat
> out the noble red deer. . . . Their numbers are
> increasing. They now amount to one-third our
> population; and it is this third, of whom not one
> in ten thousand has anything to lose, that Mr.
> Mastai Ferretti is now marshalling for the sub-
> version of our Protestant institutions, the over-
> turn of our present distribution of property, and
> substitution of the old Roman worship of that
> Venus Astarte, blasphemously designated as the
> Virgin Mother of our Lord, of whom he claims
> to be the High Priest and Supreme Pontiff, by
> grant of the last Emperors, for the pure and
> Christian worship of our Apostolic Church.[1]

IRELAND, THE IRISH, and Irish immigration, it is often argued,
were at the heart of mid-Victorian anti-Catholicism. "[T]o the English
Protestant," Robert Klaus asserts, "the faith of the Irish was simply an
extension of their nationality. . . ."[2] David Hempton argues that the traditional English anti-Catholic mythology of the sixteenth and seventeenth
centuries was revived, reinforced, and raised to higher virulence by the
combination of Irish immigration, Irish political nationalism, and the
Evangelical revival.[3] Patrick Joyce and Neville Kirk both believe that ethnic tension and violence in southeast Lancashire and northeast Cheshire
increased during and after the late 1840s, that that increase "followed the
pattern of the arrival and dispersal" of Irish immigrants, and that the Papal Aggression controversy intensified the conflict.[4] L. P. Curtis, Jr., agrees
that the mid-nineteenth century is important, for it was then, he argues,
that the stereotype, based on scientific racism, of the Irish as an inferior
race, was "finally assembled and reproduced for a mass reading public

[1] *Kentish Observer*, 31 Oct. 1850.
[2] Klaus, *Pope, Protestants, and Irish*, p. 28.
[3] David Hempton, *Methodism and Politics in British Society, 1750-1850* (Stanford, 1984), pp.
116-17. See also Arnstein, *Protestant Versus Catholic*, pp. 49-50; and Norman, *Anti-Catholicism*,
p. 18.
[4] Patrick Joyce, *Work, Society, and Politics: The Culture of the Factory in Later Victorian England* (New Brunswick, N.J., 1980), p. 251; Neville Kirk, "Ethnicity, Class and Popular Toryism,
1850-1870," *Hosts, Immigrants and Minorities: Historical Responses to Newcomers in British Society, 1870-1914*, ed. Kenneth Lunn (Folkestone, 1980), p. 66.

which was by then ready to believe almost anything of a derogatory nature about the Irish people."[5] The English image of the Irish

> was bound up with the idea of race or with that amalgam of ostensibly scientific doctrines, subjective data, and ethnocentric prejudices which was steadily gaining respectability among educated men in Western Europe during the first half of the century. In England the idea of race as *the* determinant of human history and human behavior held an unassailable position in the minds of most Anglo-Saxonists. . . .[6]

Curtis admits that the Victorians used the word "race" loosely,[7] that anti-Irish "prejudice" had class and religious, as well as racist, bases, and that working-class "prejudice" "was a compound of economic insecurity, xenophobia, and . . . authoritaranism." But he fails to explore these non-racist elements; his argument rests on the evidence of Victorian anthropological writings; he clearly believes that anti-Irish racism bears explanatory primacy. He confines his discussion of what he calls "anti-Irish prejudice," "for reasons of space," to the writings of anthropologists, historians, "publicists," and "members of the British 'political nation.'" But he asserts without proof that these examples of anti-Irish sentiment "represent only a fraction" of the prejudices held by Victorians.[8]

Sheridan Gilley has shown that Curtis oversimplified what Victorian anthropologists actually wrote and ignored those anthropologists who do not fit his racist model. Gilley finds especially troubling Curtis's comparison of antiblack racism in the modern United States with English dislike of the Irish in Victorian times. "Curtis's argument has its attractions for liberal Americans obsessed with their own national tragedy, and not unpleased to learn that in the Irish, England had a long-standing 'colour problem' of her own." This comparison does not work. Celts are not black; that is, the "objective criterion" of skin color cannot be used to identify Celts. Anglo-Saxon judges of physical beauty never denied that Celts could be beautiful, while white racists deny all possibility of beauty to blacks. Nor did Victorians object to Protestant-Catholic or English-Irish marriages on grounds of "miscegenation." Rather, the terms "Celt" and "Anglo-Saxon" were as much cultural as racial labels; that is, for many anthropologists, "Anglo-Saxon" meant "English-speaking." The English disliked the Irish because the latter rejected English national religious, cultural, political, and economic values, not because they took the latter to be an alien and inferior race. The Irish themselves, moreover, formulated their grievances in nonracial terms, demanding political and religious rights, not racial equality. "They suffered as [Roman] Catholic republicans, not Celts; and they could pass the so-called barrier of 'race' by a change of idea, apostasy to imperialism and Protestantism."[9]

It is worthwhile to look closely at these issues, for the notion that pseudo-scientific racist ideology, based on "the axiom of unchanging racial at-

[5] L. P. Curtis, Jr., *Anglo-Saxons and Celts: A Study of Anti-Irish Prejudice in Victorian England* (Bridgeport, Conn., 1968), pp. 5-6.
[6] *Ibid.*, p. 19.
[7] See Christine Bolt, *Victorian Attitudes to Race* (London and Toronto, 1971), pp. ix-x, on this point.
[8] Curtis, *Anglo-Saxons and Celts*, pp. 19-20, 23-24, 125.
[9] Sheridan Gilley, "English Attitudes to the Irish in England, 1780-1900," *Immigrants and Minorities in British Society*, ed. Colin Holmes (London, 1978), pp. 85-94.

tributes," came to dominate English thinking during the period between the 1770s and 1850s continues to appear in the historical literature. A recent history of blacks in Britain advances that hypothesis, and an Open University set reader accepts Curtis's argument: "virulent racial categorization clearly set the Irish aside from, and inferior to, the English."[10] (A kind of fantasy of Celtic racism even appears in attempts to explain the distinctive nature of the U. S. South.[11]) Moreover, both Curtis and Gilley argue only about the ideas of the Victorian well-educated and scientific classes; neither says much about what racist ideas the vast majority of the English may have held. Finally, it is the case that both the Irish and the Roman Catholic populations of England were growing during the first half of the century, and that most of the latter were Irish. The Irish-born population grew from 290,891 in 1841 to 519,959 in 1851; the Roman Catholic population in 1851 amounted to something between 750,000 and 768,000. Of that Roman Catholic population, about half a percent (3,500) were converts, about a quarter (181,300) were native English Old Catholics, and the other 75 percent were Irish immigrants and their children.[12] Thus it is true that the Roman Catholics whom English Protestants met in daily life were most likely to be Irish, even in the 1860s and '70s, when Irish immigration slowed down.

The statistics do not bear out the hypothesis that the larger the presence of Irish in an area, the greater the manifestations of anti-Catholic and anti-Irish sentiment. We can measure this relationship precisely by using Pearson's product-moment correlation. Pearson's r measures the strength and direction of the relationship between two variables by determining how both vary together and how well the variation in one predicts ("explains") the variation in the other. (One might determine, for example, whether the proportion of the Irish population per county "explains" petitioning per county.) These calculations produce coefficients that range from $+1.0$ to -1.0, indicating a perfect relationship, with .0 indicating no relationship. Statisticians generally interpret coefficients above $\pm.6$ as showing strong relationships; anything below $\pm.2$ they consider weak; anything in between is moderate. In this instance, I shall correlate the number of signatures on memorials to the Queen protesting the creation of the Roman Catholic hierarchy in 1850 with the number of Irish-born in the total population, as revealed in the 1851 census.[13]

[10] Peter Fryer, *Staying Power: The History of Black People in Britain* (London, 1984), reviewed by Michael Banton, "Following the Colour Line," *TLS*, 20 July 1984, p. 813; *"Race" in Britain: Continuity and Change* ed. Charles M. Husband (London, 1982), p. 12. See A. J. Barker, *The African Link: British Attitudes to the Negro in the Era of the Atlantic Slave Trade, 1550-1807* (Totowa, N.J., 1978), for a corrective.

[11] Grady McWhiney, *Cracker Culture: Celtic Ways in the Old South* (University, Alabama, 1988); Grady McWhiney and Perry D. Jamieson, *Attack and Die: Civil War Military Tactics and the Southern Heritage* (University, Alabama, 1982), pp. 170-91; Forrest McDonald and Grady McWhiney, "The South from Self-Sufficiency to Peonage: An Interpretation," *American Historical Review*, LXXXV (1980), 1107-11.

[12] Jean-Alain Lesourd, "Les Catholiques dans la Société Anglaise, 1765-1865," 2 vols. (Ph.D. thesis, University of Lille, 1978), I, 6-7, 480-83, 495-96, II, 722-26. John D. Gay's estimate of 800,000 to one million Roman Catholics in 1851 errs on the high side (*The Geography of Religion in England*, London, 1971, p. 97). Klaus grossly overestimates the number of converts, at a thousand p.a. between 1840 and 1849 (*Pope, Protestants, and Irish*, pp. 17-18).

[13] Figures are from "Census of Great Britain, 1851: Population Tables, II," *PP*, 1852-3, LXXXVIII, Pt. 1 [1691], 304-10.

Correlating Irish-born per thousand of population by county with signatures per thousand produces a coefficient of .19—which indicates a very weak statistical relationship. The elimination of outliers from the equation—Northampton, the West Riding, Northumberland, Durham, Cumberland, and Cheshire—produces a bigger coefficient of .52—which indicates a fairly strong relationship between the presence of Irish-born in a county and that county's likelihood of generating anti-Catholic signatures. Northampton, however, had the highest rate of memorializing for all counties, but only eight Irish per thousand; the other five counties fall among the top seven counties in terms of Irish-born per thousand. Moreover, Northampton, Cheshire, and Cumberland were among the four counties that showed the most rapid rate of growth in numbers of Roman Catholics between the Papist Returns of 1767 and the Religious Census of 1851 (the other was Devon).[14] It does not make sense to have to ignore counties with large Irish populations, or with a rapid growth of Roman Catholic populations, in order to show that large Irish populations explain variation.

Lancashire follows the nationwide pattern. Correlating Irish-born per thousand of population by registration district with signatures per thousand non-Irish males produces a coefficient of .11. Removing an outlier—Liverpool, which has the largest number of Irish-born per thousand, but which falls considerably below the mean number of signatures per thousand—produces a coefficient of .32. There is another way to look at the relationship between the presence of Irish and anti-Catholic memorializing. (See Fig. 4.) The *top* ten registration districts of Lancashire, in terms of memorializing per thousand males not Irish, include only four of the top ten in terms of Irish per thousand (Manchester, Ashton-under-Lyne, Preston, and Wigan). The *bottom* ten in terms of memorializing include the other six of the top ten in terms of Irish (Liverpool, Prescot, West Derby, Warrington, Salford, and Chorlton). Now Liverpool is underrepresented because the memorial from the mass meeting of the local Protestant Reformation Society was signed only by its chairman; West Derby may also be underrepresented, for the memorials from Walton-on-the-Hill and Childwall parishes were signed only by the chairman. But that argument cannot be made for the other districts, and therefore one cannot say that a linear relationship between the presence of Irish and anti-Catholic sentiment would be clearer if only our sources were better. In short, the hypothesis, the more Irish, the more anti-Catholics, does not explain the evidence.

What, then, is the positive explanation? In order to understand the relationship between anti-Catholic and anti-Irish sentiment, one must attempt to enter the minds of the people by turning to the images of Roman Catholicism, Anglo-Catholicism, and Irish in the best-selling fiction, non-fiction, poetry, and art of the day. When one sees what the mass audience was told about those groups, one finds that working-class and middle-class readers were getting different images.

[14] Lesourd, "Catholiques dans la Société Anglaise," I, 10.

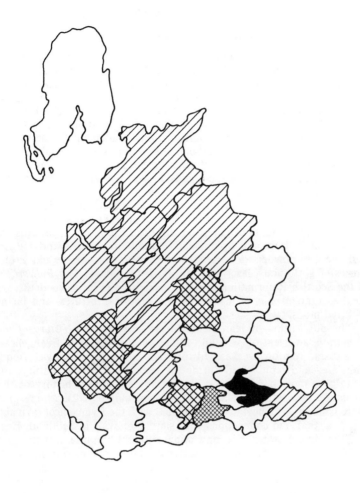

■	474.23 (N=1)	▨	358.15 (N=1)	▧	190 – 230 (N=3)
▨	97 – 179 (N=8)	☐	2 – 86 (N=13)		

FIG. 4

Map of Memorialists by Registration District in Lancashire, 1850

The Anti-Catholic and Religious Press

Anti-Catholicism was one of many issues addressed in the Nonconformist denominational periodicals of the day; it was central to the periodicals
of the anti-Catholic societies, both national and local. The people who organized and attended anti-Catholic rallies and who circulated anti-Catholic petitions in the 1840s and '50s read, or at least received, these periodicals. Charles Carill Worsley, of Platt Hall, Rusholme, Manchester, is
not too untypical of the local anti-Catholic leadership—he served on the
committee of his local anti-Catholic association, spoke at public meetings,
and belonged to the British Reformation Society and the Evangelical Alliance. Judging by his bookseller's bills, he was reading Evangelical theology
and anti-Catholic periodicals.[15]

Readers of these publications received frequent reminders of Roman
Catholicism's persecutory past in the form of historical articles that retold,
with varying amounts of gore, the stories of the Albigensian crusade, the
Inquisition in Italy and Spain, persecutions of Lollards and Huguenots,
and the Gunpowder Plot. Readers were reminded of the old Protestant
stories of gluttonous, lascivious, and sadistic monks. The *Bulwark*, organ
of the Scottish Reformation Society, specialized in lurid woodcuts, verging
on the pornographic, of massacres, martyrdoms, tortures, and fat monks
with red noses.[16]

The publication of Jean-Henri Merle D'Aubigné's *History of the Reformation*, an event of profound influence on worldwide Evangelical Protestantism, reinforced these history lessons. His work was frequently
translated and republished during the second half of the century, and became "the most popular supernatural and Protestant history of the Reformation ever written."[17] Merle D'Aubigné (1794-1872), a minister of the
State Church at Geneva, was associated with the Evangelical revival there,
a revival that had connections with similar revivals in Scotland, England,
and the United States. His connections brought him international speaking
engagements and his writings international attention during the 1840s,
'50s, and '60s, and made his book "more widely influential than any other
single Evangelical contribution."[18] His account combines the traditional
Protestant view of the late mediæval Catholic Church with the new eschatology of the Victorian Evangelical revival.[19]

These publications depicted nineteenth-century Roman Catholicism as
not all that much changed from the more distant past. Readers could see
for themselves the parallels between the historical lessons and the contemporary church's doctrine and practice with respect to purgatory, saints,
images, the Bible, and worship, and with respect to the travails of Protes-

---

[15] Bills to Thomas Anderson & Son, April 1858-April 1859, Carill Worsley Papers, MCL, M
35/9/52/7-9.
[16] Besides the *Bulwark*, see *Wesley Banner*, II (Oct. 1850), 372-73, (Dec. 1850), 449-50, III (Jan.
1851), 10-13; *Primitive Methodist Magazine*, XXXI (June 1850), 362-64, (Aug. 1850), 479-83.
[17] Harry Elmer Barnes, *A History of Historical Writing*, 2nd ed. (New York, 1963), p. 133.
[18] A. G. Dickens and John Tonkin, with Kenneth Powell, *The Reformation in Historical Thought*
(Cambridge, Mass., 1985), p. 189.
[19] Timothy Stunt, "Geneva and British Evangelicals in the Early Nineteenth Century," *JEH*,
XXXII (1981), 36; J.-H. Merle D'Aubigné, *History of the Great Reformation of the Sixteenth
Century in Germany, Switzerland, &c.* (Philadelphia, 1847). For an example of the reception of
Merle D'Aubigné's work, see *Leeds Mercury*, 21 Feb. 1846.

tants in Tahiti, Latin America, and Spain.[20] The lesson to be drawn was that the moral character of the Roman clergy had not changed. "There are two classes of Romish priest," said the *Bulwark*. "There is your sleek, oily, rolicking, leering, capon-lined emissary of Babylon, whose priestcraft is a mere trade; and there is your lean, intellectual, intense, credulous devotee."[21]

Turning to Ireland, the publications drew a terrible picture of rural unrest, poverty, indolence, ignorance, violence, murder, and seditious conspiracies.[22] They universally attributed the political and economic problems of Ireland to that island's dominant religious faith. The contrast between Protestant Ulster and the rest of the island proved it,[23] but the problem was more than that of the priests inciting the peasantry to commit crimes.[24] Roman Catholicism dulled the intellect, degraded the conscience, promoted idle and licentious holy days, and exalted poverty as a virtue.[25]

> The Gospel alone can remedy what coercion bills, and poor-laws, and railroads, and tenant right, and repeal, and all outward institutions and measures, never can reach, the moral degradation and moral prostration of Ireland, through the curse of Popery, with its degrading idolatry and corrupting priesthood. Popery, body-debasing and soul-destroying Popery, is the root of Ireland's misery.[26]

The organ of the Baptist Union, taking a more liberal view, did recognize that English exploiters must bear a share of the responsibility for Ireland's problems, that Protestantism there was a persecuting religion of tithes and distraints, and that Dissenters silently assented in these persecutions. But for it, too, popery was the root of Ireland's ills.[27]

That portion of these publications' Christian and uplifting fiction that dealt with the Irish offers a positive view of their national character. Here we see three themes. First, in story after story, told in a stage-Irish brogue,[28] Paddy, the simple but shrewd peasant, sees through the priest's tricks. (The priest wants a shilling to hear Paddy's confession. Paddy learns that the priest pays the bishop to be confessed, who pays the archbishop, who pays the cardinal, who pays the Pope, who confesses to God for free. Paddy decides to keep his shilling and deal directly with God.[29]) Second, we learn that the Irish, both in Ireland and in England, are gen-

---

[20] *Christian's Penny Magazine*, VI (Apr. 1851), 95-104; *Wesley Banner*, I (1849), 71-72, 205-6, II (1850), 480, III (1851), 18-19, 123, 142; *Bulwark*, IV (Feb. 1855), 211-13, V (Jan. 1856), 190, (Feb. 1856), 218-20.

[21] *Bulwark*, I (Jan. 1852), 175.

[22] *Church*, n.s., I (Sept. 1846), 64-65; *Evangelical Christendom*, III (Jan. 1849), 4; *Protestant Witness*, I (24 Mar. 1849), 118; *Protestant Magazine*, XI (May 1849), 73, (Aug. 1849), 122, (Dec. 1849), 183; *Primitive Methodist Magazine*, XXXI (Apr. 1850), 232-34; *Bulwark*, V (Dec. 1855), 167.

[23] *Penny Protestant Operative*, IX (Dec. 1848), 141; *English Presbyterian Messenger*, n.s., I (Jan. 1848), 29.

[24] *Protestant Witness*, I (18 Nov. 1848), 44.

[25] *Ibid.*, p. 45; *Christian Witness*, VII (Oct. 1850), 477-78; *Bulwark*, II (Feb. 1853), 218.

[26] *English Presbyterian Messenger*, N.S., I (Jan. 1848), 29; cf. *Wesleyan Methodism, and Religious Education defended from the attacks of John Stores Smith, in his reply to the Revs. H. Stowell and G. Osborne* (Manchester, 1849), p. 12, copy in the National Public Schools Association Papers, MCL, M 136/3/10/4.

[27] *Baptist Magazine*, XXXVI (March 1844), 135, 165-66, XLI (Aug. 1849), 482-85.

[28] The caricature of the accent does not prove prejudice, for the Roman Catholic priests Thomas Sing and Joseph Daniel of Derby published such a story in their periodical (*Catholic Weekly Instructor*, II, 8 Nov. 1845, 539-40).

[29] *Penny Protestant Operative*, III (Jan. 1842), 5; *Protestant Witness*, I (10 Feb. 1849), 88-91; *ibid.* (10 Mar. 1849), 106-8; *Christian's Penny Magazine*, VI (Jan. 1851), 25.

erous, kind-hearted, honest, polite, and attentive to the needs of the less
fortunate.[30] Third, the priests are ever trying to crush these good qualities.
In "Mary Sheridan's First Letter," the Widow Sheridan's eldest son is in
the army in India. Neither she nor her daughter, Mary, can read his letters; Mary wants to learn, and asks to go to "the heretic school." "[O]ld
prejudices were very strong" in the widow's heart, "but love was
stronger," so she lets Mary attend. ("Mrs. Sheridan, in common with all
her countrywomen, had a great respect for learning. . . .") With hard work,
Mary learns to read and write; now she can read the son's letters—and the
Bible—to Mrs. Sheridan. Then the priest finds out what is going on, and
tells Mary to stop attending the school. Mary refuses, and they live happily ever after.[31] "Little Dick, of the Ragged School; or, the Young Protestant," is a similar tale, save that here Dick's parents are simple, kindly, but
"priest-enslaved"; they remove Dick from the school at the wicked Father
Delaney's orders. Dick rebels; Delaney makes him fast; and he dies.[32]

Popular Literature as Cultural Indicator

It is not surprising that organizations dedicated to freeing souls from
popish bondage should romanticize the victims whom they would redeem;
but it is probable that the vast majority of those people who attended
anti-Catholic meetings, signed petitions, and rioted did not read these periodicals. In order to understand what the middle and working classes,
both nationwide and in the areas of local conflict that Joyce and Kirk have
studied, thought about the Roman Catholic Church and the Irish, perhaps
one should turn to what they were reading about those groups in the popular fiction of the day. The audiences for fiction grew in the nineteenth
century, partly because technological developments, especially the steam
press and wood-pulp-based paper, reduced the costs of production, partly
because circulating libraries and large-scale dealers reduced the cost of
distribution, and partly because of changes in attitudes towards fiction itself.

Nonconformists and Evangelical Anglicans, around the start of the
nineteenth century, were suspicious of imaginative fiction, as indeed were
earnest working-class radicals, who thought that "novel-reading, at its
best, [was] only an indifferent substitute for a worse occupation of time."[33]
The strictest Evangelicals thought that fiction was lies and hence sinful;
others thought that it was wicked (as bad as skepticism and the neglect of
private prayer, and just a little better than adultery and the singing of lewd
songs) because it distracted the believer from Bible-reading and focusing
one's mind on God. Liberalization, however, was gradual throughout the
century. The novels of Scott were excepted from the ban, and works such
as George Borrow's *The Bible in Spain* (1843) and Harriet Beecher Stowe's
Uncle Tom's Cabin (1852), as well as anti-Catholic novels, helped to make
fiction acceptable. Charlotte Elizabeth Tonna,[34] one of the most popular

[30] *Penny Protestant Operative*, IV (July 1843), 53-54; *Protestant Watchman*, No. 17 (July 1850), pp. 209-10, *et passim*.
[31] *English Presbyterian Messenger*, n.s., II (April 1850), 302-4; *ibid.* (May 1850), 331-35.
[32] *Protestant Watchman*, No. 21 (Nov. 1850), pp. 253-54; *ibid.*, No. 22 (Dec. 1850), pp. 271-72.
[33] *Northern Star*, 28 Jan. 1843, quoted in James, *English Popular Literature*, p. 38.
[34] Charlotte Elizabeth Browne Phelan Tonna (1790-1846), daughter of a Norwich priest, married an Anglo-Irish army officer who died in 1837; the couple had separated in 1824. She wrote novels

writers of religious fiction, was an exception to this trend. She feared that Satan was using her gift of a vivid imagination "to mislead, by wild unholy fiction, such as should come within the range of its influence." She abandoned fiction in 1841, concluding that the making up of stories that never happened and the recording of prayers never uttered was profanation.[35] Different sorts of Evangelicals reacted in different ways, according to educational level, class, and religion. Working- and middling-class Evangelicals were more hostile to fiction than were the middle and upper classes; Evangelical Nonconformists were more hostile than Evangelical Anglicans. By midcentury, however, fiction was being written for a religiously inclined middle class and reviewed by religious periodicals.[36]

But fiction, like so much else in Victorian society, was class-based. Thirty-one shillings for a triple-decker novel and 2 gns. for a yearly library subscription closed out tradesmen and clerks, and young, well-educated, but poorly paid professionals. Cheaper shilling-a-number serials and reissues in "collective editions" selling between 1s. and 6s. admitted them, but still deterred the working classes. Thus there developed two distinct readerships: what Margaret Stonyk calls "a discerning middlebrow public" for popular writers of the day such as the novelists Dickens, Bulwer Lytton, Kingsley, Elizabeth Gaskell, William Harrison Ainsworth, Margaret Oliphant, Wilkie Collins, Mary Braddon, and R. S. Surtees, and the poets Tennyson, Robert Browning, Thomas Hood, Ebeneezer Elliott, and Martin Tupper; and a "lowbrow" working-class readership of the penny dreadfuls.[37]

We know a great deal about the mental universe of the "middlebrow" readership; for the "lowbrow" readership, we must turn to the cheap, gutter periodicals that "are essential to our understanding of the mid-Victorian world of working-class fantasy and flash, and more relevant to general working-class feeling of the time than any purely radical material."[38] (Sally Mitchell's effective use of these sources to challenge commonly held ideas about what Victorian women thought of their own sexuality demonstrates their value.[39])

Cheap fiction is more a reflection of attitudes than a molder of them; it is said that Edward Lloyd, called "The Father of the Cheap Press," got servants and workers to read his fiction—if they liked it, he ran it.[40] More-

and stories, and edited periodicals including the *Christian Lady's Magazine* (1836-46) and the *Protestant Magazine* (1841-46). She married Lewis Tonna, also an anti-Catholic writer, twenty-two years her junior, in 1841. (*DNB*, XIX, 961-62.) For more on her, see *inf.*, pp. 108-109, 271-73.

[35] L.H.J. Tonna, *Life of Charlotte Elizabeth, as contained in her Personal Recollections, with explanatory notes; and a Memoir, embracing the period from the close of Personal Recollections to her death* (New York, 1851; orig. pub. 1847), pp. 17, 332-33.

[36] Norris Pope, *Dickens and Charity* (New York, 1978), pp. 17-19; Valentine Cunningham, *Everywhere Spoken Against: Dissent in the Victorian Novel* (Oxford, 1975), pp. 48-62.

[37] See Margaret Stonyk, *Nineteenth-Century English Literature* (New York, 1984), pp. 77, 83, 86, 90, 142-43, 161, 185-92, 202, 208; and J. A. Sutherland, *Victorian Novelists and Publishers* (Chicago, 1976), pp. 20-40; for these "middlebrow" writers, modes of production, and prices.

[38] Peter Roger Mountjoy, "The Working-Class Press and Working-Class Conservatism," *Newspaper History from the Seventeenth Century to the Present Day*, ed. George Boyce, James Curran, and Pauline Wingate (London and Beverly Hills, Calif., 1978), p. 267. See Raymond Williams, "Radical and/or Respectable," *The Press We Deserve*, ed. Richard Boston (London, 1970), pp. 14-15, for some interesting comments on the idea of a "gutter" press.

[39] "The Forgotten Woman of the Period: Penny Weekly Family Magazines of the 1840s and 1850s," *A Widening Sphere: Changing Roles of Victorian Women*, ed. Martha Vicinus (Bloomington and London, 1977), pp. 40-51.

[40] Louis James, *Fiction for the Working Man, 1830-1850* (London, 1963), pp. 45-46.

over, one must remember that workers bought periodicals "for a few hours" of pleasure,[41] for "temporary satisfaction."[42] But it is precisely because the gutter press catered, or pandered, to its audience, in order to extract hard-earned pennies, that it may be taken as a good measure of working-class attitudes. If a periodical departed too far from what its intended audience wanted to read, it would not sell. The same is surely true of middlebrow literature, much of which was read on railway trips, on holiday, and in other new Victorian settings.

Circulation figures give a clear idea of which periodicals were popular nationally, and locally in Lancashire, in the middle of the nineteenth century.[43] The most popular periodicals distributed by Abel Heywood's in Manchester[44] and Shepherd's in Liverpool were, of the penny weeklies, Lloyd's romances[45] and the slightly more respectable *Family Herald*,[46] and of the more expensive three-halfpenny weeklies, *Eliza Cook's Journal* and the *Working Man's Friend*. The penny weeklies catered to factory operatives, domestic servants, costermongers, seamstresses, and people "whose education was just sufficient to enable them to read a newspaper, and to grasp the meaning of a not too subtle romance."[47] The three-halfpenny weeklies catered to a more "respectable" audience of self-improving and upwardly mobile artisans and lower middle classes.[48]

An analysis of these publications suggests that the working-, lower-middle-, and middle-class visions of Roman Catholics and Irish are rather more complicated, and ambiguous, than one had thought. The evidence reveals five characteristic attitudes to these outgroups. First, the publications' view of Roman Catholicism was mixed, mostly hostile, sometimes admiring, but always stereotyped. Second, their view of the Irish was even more mixed, publishing significant exceptions to the prevailing unflattering stereotypes. Third, they viewed the Irish in cultural, not racial terms. Fourth, they rarely linked together Roman Catholics and Irish, despite the demographic facts of the day, which showed that the vast majority of Roman Catholics were Irish. And fifth, the middle-class im-

[41] *Ibid.*, pp. 28-29.

[42] Williams, "Radical and/or Respectable," p. 21.

[43] National circulation figures for periodicals are in Richard D. Altick, *The English Common Reader: A Social History of the Mass Reading Public, 1800-1900* (Chicago, 1957), pp. 351-52, 394. Circulation figures for Manchester are in *Protestant Magazine*, XII (May 1850), 76; and for Liverpool, in [Francis Bishop], *Report presented at the fourteenth Annual General Meeting of the Liverpool Domestic Mission Society* (London and Liverpool, 1851), pp. 18-19.

[44] The largest dealer in cheap periodicals, outside London, in England, and possibly in Britain (James, *Fiction for the Working Man*, p. 20; *Biographical Dictionary of English Radicals*, pp. 238-40).

[45] For these, see James, *Fiction for the Working Man*, pp. 36-38; and P.R. Hoggart, "Edward Lloyd, 'The Father of the Cheap Press,'" *Dickensian*, LXXX (1984), 33-38.

[46] For this, see James, *Fiction for the Working Man*, p. 39; Margaret Dalziel, *Popular Fiction 100 Years Ago: An Unexplored Tract of Literary History* (London, 1957), pp. 24-33, 37-40; Bose, III, 634, *s.v.* James Elimalet Smith; and *Biographical Dictionary of English Radicals*, pp. 463-67.

[47] Virginia Stewart Berridge, "Popular Journalism and Working Class Attitudes, 1854-1886: A Study of Reynolds' Newspaper, Lloyd's Weekly Newspaper, and the Weekly Times" (Ph.D. thesis, University of London, 1976), I, 53-54 (quoted). See also Virginia Berridge, "Popular Sunday Papers and Mid-Victorian Society," *Newspaper History*, ed. Boyce, Curran, and Wingate, p. 253; Mitchell, "Forgotten Woman," pp. 29-30, 33-34; and Louis James, "The Trouble with Betsy: Periodicals and the Common Reader in Mid-Nineteenth-Century England," *The Victorian Periodical Press: Samplings and Soundings*, ed. Joanne Shattock and Michael Wolff (Leicester and Toronto, 1982), p. 356.

[48] See Brian Maidment, "Essayists and Artizans—The Making of Nineteenth-Century Self-Taught Poets," *Literature and History*, IX (1983), 77-78; James, *Fiction for the Working Man*, pp. 127-28; and Altick, *English Common Reader*, pp. 302-4.

ages were more nuanced, more moderate, and less stereotypical than were the working- and lower-middle-class images.

Popular Literature on the Roman Catholic Faith

One major strand of Victorian thought was optimism about the future, and the conscious rejection of the past in favor of modernity—especially in the light of the economic achievements of the Industrial Revolution. This attitude lent itself to the rejection of Roman Catholicism, for that religion was identified as outmoded. In *Yeast* (1848), Charles Kingsley has his main character declare that the spinning jenny, railway, and steamship, the sanitary reformer and engineer, have more to contribute to the improvement of society than do the priests and saintly miracles of Roman Catholicism. Other writers such as Thomas Carlyle, Charles Dickens, and J. A. Froude joined in this view.[49]

Not all Victorians cared about Roman Catholicism, of course. R. S. Surtees, who wrote for that tribe whose totems were the fox and hound, ignored the question altogether, save to turn Cardinal Wiseman's name into a slang expression for "being wise."[50] But a spate of novels that took as their main theme the dangers of Roman Catholicism appeared in the 1840s, and continued for the following score of years. These novels, among them William Sewell, *Hawkstone* (1845), Elizabeth Missing Sewell, *Margaret Perceval* (1847), Frances Trollope (who had a remarkable ability to sense changing tastes in the literary marketplace), *Father Eustace* (1847), Elizabeth Harris's *From Oxford to Rome* (1847) and *Rest in the Church* (1848), Jemima Thompson, *The Female Jesuit* (1851), and Catharine Sinclair, *Beatrice* (1852), depicted duplicitous priests, superstitious practices, sinister Jesuits, and the pain of damaged personalities and broken homes. Harriet Martineau had a novel turned down in 1851 on the grounds that it was too sympathetic to Roman Catholicism. A decade later, she published "Sister Anna's Probation" in *Once a Week*; its story line included secret communications between a novice and her lover, a hair-raising flight and pursuit, and a pack of wicked nuns. Others, such as W. M. Thackeray's *Henry Esmond* (1852), gave a positive view of Jesuits.[51] Still others mocked anti-Catholicism, such as Trollope's parody of the convent inspection bills of the 1850s.[52] Some of these tales are more intemperate than others, but none descended to the level of the working-class literature at its lowest.

The lowest of the low were the catchpenny broadsides, written for the most part by working-class authors and sold on the streets. The most popular broadsides dealt with crimes and executions. Religious broadsides avoided controversy in order to sell, and hence were either seasonal sentiments for Christmas and Easter or generalized appeals to religious faith.[53]

---

[49] Houghton, *Victorian Frame of Mind*, pp. 43-46.

[50] R. S. Surtees, *Mr. Sponge's Sporting Tour* (London, 1853), pp. 497, 501, 508, 512.

[51] Raymond Chapman, *Faith and Revolt: Studies in the Literary Influence of the Oxford Movement* (London, 1970), pp. 118-20; Robert Lee Wolff, *Gains and Losses: Novels of Faith and Doubt in Victorian England* (New York and London, 1977), pp. 31-43; Dalziel, *Popular Fiction*, pp. 160-61; Sutherland, *Victorian Novelists and Publishers*, pp. 107-108; Casteras, "Virgin Vows," pp. 149-50.

[52] Anthony Trollope, *The Warden* (New York, 1950; orig. pub. 1855), pp. 68, 149-50.

[53] Victor E. Neuberg, *Popular Literature: A History and Guide from the Beginning of Printing to the Year 1897* (London, 1977), pp. 127-39, 142.

The sheet, "Beware of the Pope!!," is thus interesting because it mocks the anti-Catholic furor of 1850-51.

> Wherever you wander, wherever you steer,
> All old men and women are quaking with fear,
> They are terribly frightened and cry out so queer,
> The Pope is a coming, oh dear! oh dear!

But times are different now, the sheet concludes, so the old folks should cheer up.[54]

The penny press at first glance provides a remarkably even-handed treatment of the Roman Catholic Church. The *Family Herald* (which, like most of the gutter press, was anticlerical, and believed that denominational and theological distinctions were at best meaningless, at worst bad[55]) urged its readers to look at both sides of the religious debate, and not to rely only on anti-Catholic literature.[56] In its view, monasteries preserved learning and made possible "the revival of literature, and the arts, to which modern civilization is so much indebted"; and regretted that Protestantism provided no role for unmarried females in some nonsectarian nunnery.[57] It called John Calvin vindictive and persecuting, and with Lloyd's romances called hierarchies of any kind—Anglican as well as Roman Catholic—corrupt, intolerant, and repressive.[58] The Roman Catholic Church, moreover, was not as powerful as it seemed: Protestantism was based on the principles of political unity, progress, development, and freedom; while Roman Catholic countries opposed each other in policy, and each, at some time, had fought the Pope.[59] All religious sects were right in some respects, but all had fallen short of the truth, and sectarian disputes distracted men from the basic Christian precept—to love one another. What was wanted was love, and a "happy reconciliation of conflicting principles."[60]

But when these popular periodicals were not being consciously tolerant—and many of the pleas for toleration appeared during, and perhaps as a response to, the Papal Aggression crisis—they reproduced the traditional English view of Roman Catholicism as a cruel, superstitious, and hypocritical faith. The "Dark Ages" were "a long reign of foul and ferocious superstition, persecution, and torture by fire and faggot, rack-wheel and thumbscrew."[61] The Protestant Reformation was "the bright day star" of "renewed youth and vigour," "in which human reason escaped from the fetters of an ignorant and besotted spiritual tyranny," of a "blasting thralldom over the minds of men."[62] The early Protestants were noble, brave, and honorable fighters for freedom, while their opponents

---

[54] James, *English Popular Literature*, p. 165.

[55] For anticlericalism and antidenominationalism in these periodicals, see Berridge, "Popular Journalism," I, 353-55; and Dalziel, *Popular Fiction*, pp. 25, 159-66.

[56] *Family Herald*, III (9 Aug. 1845), 216.

[57] *Ibid.*, I (20 May 1843), 30; *ibid.*, VII (27 April 1850), 828-29.

[58] *Ibid.*, XII (9 Sept. 1854), 300; *Lloyd's Penny Weekly Miscellany*, I (1843), 267; *Lloyd's Weekly Miscellany*, I (1849-50), 464; Berridge, "Popular Journalism," I, 353-55.

[59] *Family Herald*, I (1 July 1843), 120-21; *ibid.*, V (19 Feb. 1848), 667; *ibid.*, VIII (23 Nov. 1850), 476-77.

[60] *Ibid.*, VIII (14 Dec. 1850), 524-25; *ibid.* (21 Dec. 1850), 540-41; *ibid.* (4 Jan. 1851), 572-73; *ibid.* (1 Feb. 1851), 636-37; *Lloyd's Entertaining Journal*, V (7 March 1846), 48.

[61] *Lloyd's Entertaining Journal*, VIII (17 Aug. 1850), 252-53; cf. *Lloyd's Weekly Miscellany*, II (1850-52), 1071.

[62] *Family Herald*, II (31 Aug. 1844), 270; *Lloyd's Entertaining Journal*, IV (20 Dec. 1845), 273.

were bigoted, heartless persecuters and torturers.[63] The Roman Catholic faith was a religion of charms, magical relics, fraudulent miracles and exorcisms, winking statues, and swarms of saints.[64] Its cardinals lived amid wealth, comforts, and pomp, and its priests denied the sacraments and other religious rites to those who could not pay for them.[65]

Roman Catholicism, however, was more than a superstitious faith for credulous peasants. Popery was deadly for constitutional reasons; it encouraged despotism and was incompatible with free political institutions, as Italy and Spain demonstrated.[66] And it was bloodthirsty and persecutory. Roman Catholic priests generally, and Jesuits especially, were wicked, scheming, implacable, greedy, cold, evil, sensuous, worldly-minded, expedient men, who constantly plotted to advance their Popish lust for power.[67] During the summer of 1850, the gutter press, London and provincial newspapers, and religious periodicals published the story "Destruction of the Inquisition at Madrid." This was a gory and vivid description of the French army's liberation of the Inquisition in 1809. It recounted the "Jesuitical effrontery" and "cunning villany" of the priests, the dank cells, the torture rooms and their wicked engines, and the maimed and emaciated prisoners. Aroused and enraged, the French troops tortured and slaughtered the priests. The story was a fabrication, but what *frissons* it must have caused![68]

The subtheme of the convent story linked constitutional concerns with sex and death. Convents were gloomy, gravelike places of living death and tomblike silence; the very buildings, corpse-like, moldered away.[69] The heroine of "Juana, a Noviciate in a Portugese Convent," lamented: "long ere the moon sheds her cold silvery beams on yonder grove, I shall bid adieu to home, the world, and all that it contains. No ray of hope to cheer my gloomy cell. . . . The cloister will be my living grave as long as I continue to drag on my miserable existence. To-morrow I take the veil at the convent of Santa Maria."[70] The inmates of these cloisters—young, beautiful girls—were imprisoned against their wills, forced behind the iron bars by unnatural fathers, wicked uncles, or avaricious guardians; so they tried to flee, aided by handsome young men.[71]

"Adeline; or, the Secret of the Abbess," typical of such stories, reminds one of *Henry Esmond* and Harriet Martineau's "Sister Anna." Adeline fled the horrible convent's prison-like cells. The crypt through which she crept

[63] *Lloyd's Penny Weekly Miscellany*, I (1843), 683-84; *Lloyd's Entertaining Journal*, V (18 July 1846), 337 *et passim ad* VI (24 Oct. 1846), 117; *ibid.*, VII (11 Sept. 1847), 384; *Lloyd's Weekly Miscellany*, II (1850-52), 964.
[64] *Family Herald*, II (17 Aug. 1844), 238; *ibid.*, V (9 Oct 1847), 364; *ibid.*, VIII (7 Dec. 1850), 508-9; *Lloyd's Penny Weekly Miscellany*, V (1846), 720; *Lloyd's Weekly Miscellany*, I (1849-50), 824.
[65] *Lloyd's Penny Weekly Miscellany*, II (1844), 505; *ibid.*, V (1846), 733; *Family Herald*, II (19 Oct. 1844), 371.
[66] *Family Herald*, XIV (9 Aug. 1856), 236-37.
[67] *Lloyd's Weekly Miscellany*, II (1850-52), 1049 *et passim ad* 1180; *Lloyd's Entertaining Journal*, III (7 June 1845), 251; *ibid.*, V (20 June 1846), 285; *Family Herald*, I (23 Sept. 1843), 317-18; *ibid.*, XIII (5 May 1855), 13-14.
[68] *Lloyd's Weekly Miscellany*, I (1849-50), 46; Cecil Roth, *The Spanish Inquisition* (New York, 1964), pp. 256-58.
[69] *Family Herald*, o.s., I (24 Dec. 1842); *Lloyd's Penny Weekly Miscellany*, II (1844), 636.
[70] *Lloyd's Penny Weekly Miscellany*, VI (1846), 75.
[71] *Lloyd's Entertaining Journal*, I (4 May 1844), 81-84; *Lloyd's Penny Weekly Miscellany*, V (1846), 595; *ibid.*, VI (1846), 75.

was full of bones; she heard the rats gorging on the corpses of nuns, and she passed niches set in the walls, ready to brick up alive nuns who were caught escaping. Adeline made her way through a garden gate, and fell into the arms of DeLisle, her lover. He and Pierre, his manservant, carried her away, fought off the convent guards, and took passage on a ship that foundered in a furious storm; the lovers survived, only to be recaptured. But it turned out that the abbess was Adeline's mother. She took pity on her daughter; Adeline and DeLisle married, and the cloisters fell into a moldy ruin.[72] Those who were unlucky enough to remain in convents faced the tyranny of bitter abbesses, sexual corruption (for all convents had mysterious tunnels that led to no good end), physical and mental abuse, and death by poisoning.[73]

The story of forbidden love between priest and penitent also was a favorite theme. The priest Bernard de Montalbert and the lady Isadore de Gonzalo fell in love. Isadore went to confession, and Bernard happened to be the confessor. "'Resist the tempter, and he will flee from thee!' said the priest, as he again placed his ear to the grating, where the warm breath from the penitent's ruby mouth, as it touched his cheek, caused every nerve within his frame to vibrate with a ravishing sensation." Bernard and Isadore declared their love for each other, knowing that it could not be consummated, and then died.[74] These tales were set in France, Italy, Spain, Portugal, and Mexico, but one theme unites them all: "At that day which will disclose the secrets of all hearts and homes, neither the haunts of plunder, the palaces of tyranny, nor the dungeons of the oppressor, will plead guilty to one-half the number of crimes which will be charged upon those monasteries, where vice has for ages fixed her deepest lair, and hypocrisy her firmest throne."[75]

Roman Catholicism, then, was an effective vehicle for sex and death, and thus was a convention that the penny dreadful genre had adapted from the gothic tale, historical novel, and theatrical melodrama.[76] The Victorian gutter press, like the *Sun* today with its blend of lurid headlines, leading articles written in simple sentences, and soft-core pornography on page three, or Mills and Boon's Harlequin romances, was in the business of selling—and sex and death sell the best. The working-class press of the second half of the nineteenth century rarely reported colonial news, except for the Indian Mutiny; its Irish reporting matched that for the colonies, save when murderous outrages and Home Rule agitation provided juicy copy. Similarly, Italian news was reported extensively only when Risorgimento blood and gore could be splashed on the front pages.[77]

[72] *Family Herald*, o.s., I (24 Dec. 1842).
[73] *Ibid.*, V (29 April 1848), 825; *Lloyd's Weekly Miscellany*, II (1850-52), 692.
[74] *Lloyd's Weekly Miscellany*, I (1 July 1843), 113-15. Dalziel calls this story "superlatively silly" (*Popular Fiction*, pp. 31-32)—but what *frissons* that line must have caused!
[75] *Lloyd's Entertaining Journal*, IV (13 Dec. 1845), 266.
[76] Dalziel, *Popular Fiction*, pp. 14-20, 107-21; James, *Fiction for the Working Man*, pp. 72-113; Robert Kiely, *The Romantic Novel in England* (Cambridge, Mass., 1972), pp. 30-32, 98-117; Ann B. Tracy, *The Gothic Novel, 1790-1830: Plot Summaries and Index to Motifs* (Lexington, Ky., 1981); and Elliott B. Gose, Jr., *Imagination Indulged: The Irrational in the Nineteenth Century Novel* (Montreal, 1972).
[77] Berridge, "Popular Journalism," I, 291-93, 299-300, 306-308; Berridge, "Popular Sunday Papers," pp. 256-57; Anne Humpherys, "G.W.M. Reynolds: Popular Literature and Popular Politics," *Victorian Periodicals Review*, XVI (1983), 79-89.

The readers of working-class periodicals during the 1840s and 1850s clearly were offered a lurid picture of Roman Catholic doctrine, discipline, and worship; and one ought not to underestimate the impact of such a cumulative exposure. But the picture was not consistent; readers of the gutter press also were exposed to a benign view of Roman Catholicism. Not all priests were wicked; readers encountered a kind abbot, honorable and upright priests who preached against superstition, a wise St. Philip Neri, and a venerable monk whose "mild grey eyes beamed with holiness and humility."[78] And the only real clergyman of any sort whom the gutter press praised was a Roman Catholic priest—Father Mathew, the temperance evangelist. Their Protestant editors were somewhat uncomfortable with him, for he was, after all, "a popish priest," but they judged that he was a "great apostle" with a "God-like mission" and a "holy task," "whose name should be placed in the calendar [of saints] not far below the apostles."[79] Mathew received similar treatment in the middlebrow press.[80]

Two stories, typical tearjerkers, gave as benign a view. The heroine of "Kate Donlavy; or, the Heiress of Castle Connor," remained true to her Roman Catholic faith through abandonments, heartbreaks, betrayals, rejections, and attempted seductions. (The story depicted her faithfulness as her most admirable quality.)[81] Then there was "Maria Rosa, the Pearl of Nemi; or, the Brigand's Daughter." Maria, whose finer feelings, once awakened, revolted from the brutality of her surroundings, went to her only protector, the priest of Gerizano, to confess. The priest advised her to repair to her mother until he could find a convent at Rome for her to enter, if she were willing to become a nun. "Very far from that last condition inspiring Maria Rosa with any fear, the hope of her finding so holy an asylum gave her such joy, that she at first could only express it by tears." She thanked heaven for her deliverance, and returned home happy.[82]

Finally, there is the extraordinary poem, "The Dying Girl's Hymn to the Virgin." It would make a good office hymn for a feast of Our Lady if only it scanned.[83]

> Queen of Heaven! my young star fleets,
> Fainter yet the life pulse beats.
> Hark! I hear bright angels say,
> Mother call thy child away.
>
> Star of the wayworn, Virgin bright,
> Bend from thy glorious home of light;
> List to the dying mourner's plea,
> and bear her soul to light and thee.
>
> In that calm land where thou reignest,

[78] *Family Herald*, I (13 Apr. 1844), 778; *ibid.*, V (4 Dec. 1847), 481-84; *Lloyd's Penny Weekly Miscellany*, I (1843), 296; *ibid.*, IV (1845), 369; *Lloyd's Entertaining Journal*, VII (24 Apr. 1847), 59, *et passim ad* (8 May 1847), 90.

[79] *Family Herald*, I (2 Sept. 1843), 265; *Lloyd's Penny Weekly Miscellany*, I (1843), 244; *ibid.*, II (1844), 136.

[80] *Illustrated London News*, 5 Aug. 1843.

[81] *Family Herald*, XI (19 Nov. 1853), 465, *et passim ad* (7 Jan. 1854), 585.

[82] *Lloyd's Penny Weekly Miscellany*, I (1843), 38; cf. "The Sisters of Charity," a sympathetic account of the French order, in *Lloyd's Weekly Miscellany*, I (1849-50), 295.

[83] *Lloyd's Penny Weekly Miscellany*, V (1846), 599.

Where the bright sun never waneth;
Passing now from pain and strife,
Mary, gain me endless life.
    Pray that all my sins may flee,
    Queen of angels pray for me.

So, although most of the stories with Roman Catholic themes are unfavorable, they are not uniformly unfavorable.

The more respectable three-halfpenny press did not have much to say about Roman Catholicism, and what it did say was ambiguous and contradictory. The Jesuits were wily and conniving, but they were brave and willing "to lead the van of civilization." Samuel Smiles wrote that mediæval monks abused their power, as all institutions do, but fostered learning and piety.[84] All dominant sects, Protestant as well as Roman Catholic, were persecutors; the Church of England was and is persecuting, corrupt, and clerical; Oliver Cromwell was "the warrior-apostle of religious toleration"; the march of civilization had eliminated torture and executions, but it was only twenty years since the worst penalties for religious dissent had been repealed in England.[85] But these views were directed *to* the audience; the authentic view *of* the audience may perhaps be seen in "The Discovery, and Moral, Political, and Religious Effects of Printing," by Andrew Carmichael, Jr., a joiner from Pathhead, Fifeshire. Carmichael tells us that the Bishop of Rome, who is the Antichrist, had put down John Huss; but God introduced printing to bring in truth and enlightenment; it gave us the Reformation, which restored religion to the world.[86]

In contrast to working-class fiction, the middle-class anti-Catholic novel was more "serious," more nuanced, and sometimes less sensationalistic. Elizabeth Harris's *Rest in the Church* (1848) sparked a three-way debate in fictional form among John Henry Newman (*Loss and Gain*, 1848), Charles Kingsley (*Hypatia*, 1853), and Nicholas Wiseman (*Fabiola*, 1854), with Newman replying to both in *Callista* (1855). These historical novels battled over the issues of apostolic authority, patristic infallibility, and the continuity of Classical Christianity with the Roman Catholic Church—a far cry from the motifs in the *Family Herald* and Lloyd's.[87]

More robust anti-Catholicism is found in Kingsley's *Westward Ho!* (1855), a rollicking story of Elizabethan seadogs that vividly transmitted anti-Spanish legends to generations of readers. Its lighthearted violence was especially attractive to boys. Owing much to J. A. Froude's views on the English Reformation, and written in the heat of the Crimean War, *Westward Ho!* connected Protestantism with economic nationalism by stressing the enmity between an expanding England and Roman Catholic Spain. Later, Kingsley returned to the theme in *Hereward the Wake* (1864), which used a variant of the Norman Yoke myth in the service of English anti-Catholic nationalism.[88]

---

[84] *Eliza Cook's Journal*, I (11 Aug. 1849), 229; *ibid.*, IV (18 Jan. 1851), 177-81; *ibid.* (1 March 1851), 288.

[85] *Working Man's Friend*, I (5 Jan. 1850), 4, *et passim ad* III (27 July 1850), 92; *ibid.*, IV (2 Nov. 1850), 124-28; *ibid.*, V (1 Feb. 1851), 126-28.

[86] *Ibid.*, Supplement II (Feb. 1852), 318-19.

[87] Chapman, *Faith and Revolt*, pp. 148-64; Wolff, *Gains and Losses*, pp. 43-71.

[88] Chapman, *Faith and Revolt*, pp. 94-99; Houghton, *Victorian Frame of Mind*, pp. 210-11, 324; Sutherland, *Victorian Novelists and Publishers*, pp. 119-32.

Charlotte Brontë's *Villette* (1853) is a more deeply anti-Catholic novel, perhaps the most anti-Catholic of the fiction called "great" by twentieth-century critics. Based on Brontë's own experiences in Belgium, *Villette* presents an unflattering portrait of how Romanism hides chains with flowers, permitting "large sensual indulgence (so to speak)" in the forms of food and rococo devotion as a counterweight to its spiritual control. In its two best-known scenes, Brontë makes Lucy Snowe confess to Père Silas and, later, discuss religion with M. Paul, her colleague at the Pensionnat Beck. The scenes are ambiguous, for Brontë makes both Silas and Paul to be well-meaning, even decent characters despite their faith. She is at her most sensationalistic only when she has Lucy Snowe faint dramatically when walking home on a dark and stormy night from her confession, and when she mentions in passing a legend of "the bones of a girl whom a monkish conclave of the drear middle ages had here buried alive, for some sin against her vow."[89]

Conventional anti-Catholic images appeared in middlebrow literature from the 1830s through the 1860s. Minor characters in novels were made to utter conventional anti-Catholic sentiments. When the mysterious child in *Salem Chapel* ran off, the governess was sure that she would run into the arms of popery, which for her was a kind of boggart lurking in the bushes.[90] When Lucilla Marjoribanks returned from a Continental trip, a friend called to ask whether she "had not seen something soul-degrading and dishonouring to religion in all the mummeries of Popery."[91] Even a "sensation novel" could not have a character hear a door close with being reminded "of some frail young creature abandoned by her sister n living tomb."[92]

For anti-Catholic poetry, one turns to Martin Tupper, the Royal Family's favorite poet, one of the best-selling Victorian bards, who was a household name on both sides of the Atlantic until tastes changed in the 1860s. Tupper, whose childhood parish priest was Hugh McNeile, prided himself on his Protestantism, and donated anti-Catholic poems to Anglican Evangelical periodicals.[93] Several of his sonnets ("Luther," "Protesting Truth," "Unholy Alliance," "The Papal Aggression," "Toleration") combined Protestantism and nationalism in a Kingsleyesque mix. For Tupper, Britain was the chosen country, "God's Israel to come," "the Sanctuary of Freedom for the World."[94] Hence his dislike of those who would subvert the Protestant Constitution from without, and return to mediæval superstition. "Romish Priestcraft—1851" would not have been out of place at a Hugh Stowell rally, or at Exeter Hall. Five thousand copies of this sonnet were handed out on the streets of Manchester in 1851.

What! after all our charitable pains,
    And long conciliation's liberal hope,
    Can we endure to see this subtle Pope
Scheming to bind our freedom in his chains?

[89] Charlotte Brontë, *Villette*, ed. Herbert Rosengarten and Margaret Smith (Oxford, 1984; orig. pub. 1853), pp. 15, 148, 177, 224-29, 597-609; cf. Robert A. Colby, *Fiction with a Purpose: Major and Minor Nineteenth-Century Novels* (Bloomington, 1967), pp. 178-211.
[90] Oliphant, *Salem Chapel*, p. 410.
[91] Margaret Oliphant, *Miss Marjoribanks* (London, 1969; orig. pub. 1865-66), p. 76.
[92] Mary E. Braddon, *Aurora Floyd* (London, 1984; orig. pub. 1863), p. 89.
[93] Tupper's career is traced in Derek Hudson, *Martin Tupper: His Rise and Fall* (London, 1949).
[94] Martin F. Tupper, *Three Hundred Sonnets* (London, 1860), pp. 9, 13.

Ungrateful, feeble, and perfidious knave!
Never again through Britain's fair domains
  Shall tyrannous old priestcraft make us grope
  In thy dark deep of Intellect's own grave,—
  Never again shalt thou the Mind enslave![95]

In "Tintern Abbey," in my view the best, most thoughtful, and certainly the most interesting of his poems,[96] Tupper rejected Wordsworth's and Turner's romantic visions of the monastic ruins, instead declaring that their derelict state was cause for celebration. For him, the ruins mark a stage in the march of progress towards freedom.

Look on these ruins in a spirit of praise:
  Not only with the painter's well-pleased eye,
  Nor with a poet's glance at times gone by
And all his gilded thoughts of olden days;
But, thankfully regard them as a phase
  Of just Emancipation for the Soul;

Tupper warned that the forces of obscurantism still existed, and that only Britain's Protestant Constitution prevented those forces from resuming power.

For, as the feudal dungeon and its chains
Prison'd the Body of Man, and would again,
  Had English freedom left them strong and whole,—

At the end of the sonnet, Tupper returned to the monastic ruins to look at them in a new way, a way that Turner and Wordsworth had missed.

So held these glorious abbeys grim control
  Over man's Heart and Mind, enslaving both
To crafty monk and superstitious rite:
  Therefore, to find them crush'd be little loth,
But note their ruins with a new delight.

Art kept pace with literature during the same period. There was a big market for engraved versions of paintings on religio-historical topics. Some, such as *John Knox at Calder House*, *Martyrs in Prison* (showing Latimer and Ridley), and *The Acquittal of the Seven Bishops* (imprisoned by James II), focused on great moments in Protestant history, and were extraordinarily popular. Others, such as Alfred Elmore's *Religious Controversy in the Time of Louis XIV*, displayed the conflict between the two systems of belief. In Elmore's work, which created a sensation at the Royal Academy in 1849, a handsome Huguenot, armed only with a Bible, confronts a ranting monk, stacks of lying Roman Catholic literature, and a wily cardinal in the background. The convent theme was as popular as the historical theme. Keepsake annuals and paintings exhibited at the Royal Academy, British Institution, and Society of British Artists used convents and nuns as their subject matter, contrasting the life of the world with the solitude of the cloister and capturing the bittersweet wistfulness of self-immurement.[97]

[95] *Ibid.*, p. 274.
[96] *Ibid.*, p. 5.
[97] Casteras, "Virgin Vows," pp. 140-48; Errington, *Themes in English Art*, pp. 137-38, 162-66.

Popular Literature on Anglo-Catholicism

Anglo-Catholicism, as distinct from Roman Catholicism, hardly appears in the pages of the gutter press. Two short notes listed Anglo-Catholic doctrines, and argued that it and Evangelicalism were opposite extremes (the former led "to Romanism, where formalism exists in the greatest perfection"; the latter led to "fanaticism and individual vagaries"). "A Pusseyite; or, the Old Villa," is a rather pointless story in which the "pusseyite," a spinster of forty years, is a minor villain.[98] The *Family Herald*, in a typically woolly-minded leader on a controversy at Leigh, Lancs,[99] concludes that both sides are right in some respects and wrong in others. The Puseyites only want to restore the Church's discipline over the rich, corrupt, and wicked, who at present can use the Church as they wish, so long as they pay their pew rents; but that discipline originated in "a priestly tyranny." What is wanted is a larger and better idea, of greater moral power.[100]

The theme of conversions to Rome received even less attention—only one tale—even though the departure of the Oxford Converts received close attention in the denominational and the daily press. In "The Convert,"[101] Mr. and Mrs. St. John, true blue English from Northumberland, and their daughter Clara, were in France for Mrs. St. John's health. They attended a Roman Catholic church as tourists, and saw "that gorgeousness of display in which Roman Catholicism loves to deck its ceremonies." Clara, romantic and not very bright, succumbed to "that temptation to religious innovation which a residence in a Roman Catholic country is ever likely to offer." She visited the church again secretly, and saw the handsome young Father Eustache celebrating Mass. Attracted by the beauty of both ceremony and celebrant, she continued to attend, and she decided to convert. One evening, Father Eustache proffered a bowl of holy water. "It was irresistible; Clara stretched out her hand, received the consecrated element, and lowly bowing, signed herself with the cross. The priest's work was accomplished!"

Eustache became her confessor; but then, he was posted elsewhere, replaced by a priest "of dark, sinister appearance . . . whose ambiguous expression was a strange mingling of cold intellect and shifting cunning." Under his guidance, Clara publicly professed her faith (her shattered parents returned to England) and married a middle-aged Frenchman. Disaster followed: Clara suffered a raving, raging fever, but recovered; her husband turned out to hate her; Clara fled for England. On the way, she stopped at a small town, where she read her father's obituary in a newspaper and fell into another fever. The local Protestant Evangelical pastor—who turned out to be Father Eustache, who had seen the light of truth—was summoned; under his guidance, Clara returned to Protestantism and her family, just before she died.

[98] *Lloyd's Penny Weekly Miscellany*, I (1843), 576, V (1846), 589-91; *Family Herald*, III (22 Nov. 1845), 457.

[99] For which, see *inf.*, pp. 145-47.

[100] *Family Herald*, IX, (17 Jan. 1852), 604-5.

[101] *Ibid.*, VII (15 Dec. 1849), 513-18.

She died in her twenty-fourth year; but her sorrowing mother lived to see many a spring green, and many an autumn leaf turn sere in her childless age.

She alone knew the whole of Clara's sad story, and when she heard of conversions to Romanism, the bowed form would have risen erect, and the sorrow-silenced lips have unclosed, to give high and solemn warning against its delusions, but who would listen to the warped views of a prejudiced old woman?

In contrast, the Anglo-Catholic movement gained a good deal of attention in literature aimed at a middle-class audience. Supporters advanced the movement by means of novels; they had to be pro-Puseyite, of course, but they also had to defend themselves from both Evangelicals (who attacked the movement's theology) and Roman Catholics (who denied the movement's Catholicity). Lady Georgiana Fullerton's *Ellen Middleton* (1844), a sympathetic account of confession, was quite a success—readers as diverse as Harriet Martineau, W. E. Gladstone, and Charles Greville liked it—but Fullerton's conversion to Roman Catholicism blunted her effectiveness. More loyally Anglican was Elizabeth Missing Sewell, whose novels, *Margaret Perceval* (1847) and *The Experience of Life; or, Aunt Sarah* (1853), defended Anglo-Catholic practices and warned of the blandishments of Rome. She was joined by William Edward Heygate in *William Blake* (1848), and by Felicia Mary Frances Skene, whose *Use and Abuse* (1849), *St. Albans* (1853), and *Hidden Depths* (1866) were widely read.[102] In the last third of the century, the best (from a literary perspective) of the Anglo-Catholic novelists, Charlotte Mary Yonge, joined their ranks.[103]

What to me is the most interesting treatment of conversions to Rome appears in Margaret Oliphant's *The Perpetual Curate* (1864), because she describes the process through the eyes of the convert's wife. Gerald Wentworth, a clergyman, went through a crisis of faith that he could resolve only by submitting to Rome. Like so many Anglican priest-converts in the real world, however, the fictional Gerald still felt a vocation to the priesthood, but his marriage debarred him from becoming a Roman Catholic priest. Finally, he subdued his will and accepted that conversion would condemn him to lay status.

> I am content to be nothing, as the saints were. The fight has been hard enough, but I am not ashamed of the victory. When the law of the Church and the obedience of the saints ordain me to be nothing, I consent to it.

But what was humility and obedience to Gerald was self-will to his wife, Louisa, who had to suffer the consequences of his choice.

> ". . . now he tells you he is to be nothing!" Mrs. Wentworth stopped to dry her eyes with tremulous haste. "*He* may not mind," said Louisa, "for at least he is having his own way. It is all very well for a man, who can do as he pleases; but it is his poor wife who will have to suffer."[104]

[102] Wolff, *Gains and Losses*, pp. 72-82, 140-54; Joseph Ellis Baker, *The Novel and the Oxford Movement* (New York, 1965), pp. 9-22.

[103] Baker, *The Novel and the Oxford Movement*, pp. 101-13; Chapman, *Faith and Revolt*, pp. 59-79.

[104] Margaret Oliphant, *The Perpetual Curate* (London, 1987; orig. pub. 1864), pp. 141, 145-55, 257-58, 409 (quoted).

Mrs. Oliphant thus injected brutal domestic realism into what was usually treated as a high-minded struggle of principles.

Just as there were anti-Catholic novels, so there were anti-Tractarian novels. Writing from the Evangelical Anglican perspective were Ann Howard (*Mary Spencer*, 1844), Charles Manners Davies (*Philip Paternoster*, 1858), and the prolific Emma Jane Worboise. In *Overdale; or, the Story of a Pervert* (1869), perhaps the most powerful of the anti-Tractarian novels, Mrs. Worboise treated the same theme that the *Family Herald* had treated earlier in "The Convert": the disintegration of a family as the result of the confessional.[105] From a more Broad-Church perspective came William John Coneybeare's *Perversion; or, the Causes and Consequences of Infidelity* (1856), and George Barrow's *Lavengro; The Scholar, The Gypsy, The Priest* (1851) and *The Romany Rye* (1857), which deplored the power of the priesthood over minds, and which condemned Tractarianism for romanticizing the past. A similar work is Charles Kingsley's *Yeast*, which appeared in *Fraser's Magazine* in 1848 and as a book in 1851. Kingsley was concerned to denounce the movement's "unmanly" tendencies towards celibacy.[106] Charles Dickens's most sustained attack on both varieties of Catholicism came in *A Child's History of England* (1852-54), which, like Kingsley's *Westward Ho!*, molded the historical consciousness of several generations of young readers.[107]

The charge of womanly dilettantism forms the basis of what is perhaps the most famous literary attack on Anglo-Catholicism, Charles Dickens's aside in *Bleak House* (1852-53) on

> some ladies and gentlemen of the newest fashion, who have set up a dandyism, in religion. . . Who in mere lackadaisical want of an emotion have agreed upon a little dandy talk about the vulgar wanting faith in things in general, meaning in the things that have been tried and found wanting, as though a low fellow should unaccountably lose faith in a bad shilling after finding it out! Who would make the vulgar very picturesque and faithful by putting back the hands upon the clock of time and cancelling a few hundred years of history.[108]

In contrast, however, Mrs. Oliphant, with her eye for reality, made Frank Wentworth, the perpetual curate of St. Roque's, a sympathetic figure. Both Frank and his brother Gerald were Anglo-Catholics, but while Gerald swam the Tiber, Frank remained loyal to the Church. Many people in Carlingford thought that Frank was "a dilettante Anglican, given over to floral arrangements and ecclesiastical upholstery," but Mrs. Oliphant makes him the only middle-class character who really knew what life was like in the town's Wharfside slum, the only character who was trying to do something concrete to alleviate human needs.[109]

---

[105] Wolff, *Gains and Losses*, pp. 190-91; Baker, *The Novel and the Oxford Movement*, pp. 23-32; Elisabeth Jay, *The Religion of the Heart: Anglican Evangelicalism and the Nineteenth-Century Novel* (Oxford, 1979), pp. 113-14, 129-31.

[106] Chapman, *Faith and Revolt*, pp. 105-7; Baker, *The Novel and the Oxford Movement*, pp. 73-100.

[107] Charles Dickens, *A Child's History of England*, 3 vols. (London, 1852-54).

[108] Charles Dickens, *Bleak House* (New York and Toronto, 1964; orig. pub. 1852-53), p. 174.

[109] Oliphant, *Perpetual Curate*, p. 10.

In his poetry, Martin Tupper denounced "trimmers" and "apostates," and called on the Church to "[w]in back those sheep, half-wandering from thy fold."[110] He would gladly hear the Church, he said:

But where—where is She? who shall strike the truth
Between opposing factions, priest and lay,
The one, to Rome perverting half our youth,
The other leading liberally astray?
Is She indeed embalm'd in magic rite,
And sacramental miracle forsooth,
Resurgent from that mediæval night?[111]

Dickens's reaction to the popular Pre-Raphaelite art of the day also rested on his anti-Catholicism, his dislike of the Middle Ages, and his love of modernity and of what he took to be progress, improvement, and development. He believed that it made no more sense to have a Pre-Raphaelite Brotherhood than it did to have a Pre-Galileo Brotherhood. (Charles Kingsley reacted to the Pre-Raphaelites in much the same way and for much the same reasons.) And yet, not all the Pre-Raphaelites were High-Churchmen. Holman Hunt's *The Hireling Shepherd* (1852), which he began in the summer of 1851, is a devastating attack on Anglican clergymen flirting with the Great Whore of Babylon while their flocks stray. In the painting, the shepherd has his arm around a tarty-looking woman while his flock wanders into another field. As an added touch, the tart is feeding a lamb a green apple, which in real life can kill sheep. Hunt's smaller painting, *Strayed Sheep* (1853), which shows sheep milling about near a cliff, reminds one of the Durham Letter's remarks about clergymen leading their flocks "step by step to the very verge of the precipice." This painting even includes two black sheep, one of which is pushing a white sheep over the cliff's edge. The critic John Ruskin picked up on this theme in his "Notes on the Construction of Sheepfolds," a pamphlet that attacked Anglo-Catholic ideas about authority in matters of doctrine and discipline.[112]

The "discerning middlebrow public" was thus more likely than their "lowbrow" counterparts to encounter Puseyites and perverts, but unlike the latter, they were exposed to positive as well as negative views of Anglo-Catholicism.

Popular Literature on the Irish Character

If the most common stories with a religious focus dealt with Roman Catholicism, the most common stories with an ethnic focus dealt with the Irish. But it is important to note that the gutter press was full of ethnic and cultural stereotypes. The Irish were by no means the only group to be caricatured. Tam and Rab always say "Hoot, mon . . . ye maun ken."[113] Taffy is a crazed Primitive Methodist; Welsh women have "a look of wondering vacancy, that the goats on their own mountains could not have

[110] Tupper, *Sonnets*, p. 275.
[111] *Ibid.*, p. 65.
[112] Errington, *Themes in English Art*, pp. 18-21, 26-28, 54-55, 293-313; Alastair Grieve, "The Pre-Raphaelite Brotherhood and the Anglican High Church," *Burlington Magazine*, CXI (1969), 294-95; John Ruskin, "Notes on the Construction of Sheepfolds," *The Works of John Ruskin*, ed. E. T. Cook and Alexander Wedderburn, 39 vols. (London, 1904), XII, 511-58.
[113] *Lloyd's Penny Weekly Miscellany*, I (1843), 202; *ibid.*, II (1844), 531; *ibid.*, IV (1845), 5.

surpassed."[114] Mordecai, Levy, and Ben Isaac are "avaricious," "grasping," "gripping," "rapacious" pedlars and moneychangers.[115]

Then there were the Americans.[116] Blacks appeared as thick, shuffling, comical, woolly-headed slaves and preachers.[117] Whites were coarse and vulgar; they all whittled; and "Sam Slick," the Yankee dealer, was sharp.[118] (In "A Yankee and his Applesauce," a farmer and a tailor do a trade: a barrel of bad apple cider for an ill-fitting coat.[119]) And as for emigrants: ". . . I squandered our large property; and more, the taint of dishonour fell upon me. We left our home, came to America, the home of the unfortunate. . . ."[120] But the stereotypes were not always consistent: in the same number of one of Lloyd's penny dreadfuls, there were two stories about the American Revolution. In "The Outcasts; or, the Indian Guide," the Rebels were a brutal rabble who tortured and robbed Loyalists; in "The Rescue; a Tale of the American War," the Rebels were noble and genteel South Carolina planters, while the English army officer was a libertine and villain.[121]

Readers of the gutter press also encountered many stories set in France, Italy, Spain, and Portugal, and others of indefinite location, but populated by dagoes. These stories, however, were never written in dago dialect, and often take the form of historical novels. Thus although Irish stories, most written in dialect, were the most common of the ethnic stories during the period, dago stories ran them a close second. And the pages of the penny dreadfuls abounded with other stock ethnic characters.

The image of the Irish character that the gutter press provided was even more inconsistent than its image of Roman Catholicism. There are four themes in this image.

The least common theme was that of the "wild Irishman." Irish beggars were grotesque, filthy, seditious, lazy, and impudent,[122] but only two stories focused on a "wild Irishman."[123] In one, as an emigrant ship was warping in at Boston Harbor, "a tight little bit of an Irishman" dropped from the jib-boom, leapt five feet in the air, whirled his "shillaly" over his head, and screamed: "Hurra for the fra contra, here's Patrick Mullowny, by Jabers; himsel' it is, that's agin the government. . . . It's mysel' I tell ye, Patrick Mullowny, by Jabers, wull iver be agin the government, jist as long as he can twirl a shillaly."[124]

[114] *Ibid.*, I (1843), 709.
[115] *Ibid.*, I (1843), 316, 587, 811-13; *ibid.*, IV (1845), 156; *Lloyd's Entertaining Journal*, VII (17 July 1847), 252-53.
[116] James, *Fiction for the Working Man*, pp. 55-56, 129-36, discusses the interest in America and Americans, both black and white.
[117] *Lloyd's Penny Weekly Miscellany*, I (1843), 216; *ibid.*, II (1844), 412.
[118] *Ibid.*, I (1843), 242; *ibid.*, III (1844), 768; *ibid.*, VI (1846), 48; *Lloyd's Weekly Miscellany*, I (1849-50), 260; *ibid.*, II (1850-52), 116.
[119] *Ibid.*, II (1850-52), 118.
[120] *Lloyd's Penny Weekly Miscellany*, V (1846), 297.
[121] *Ibid.*, III (1844), 369-71, 376-79.
[122] *Family Herald*, II (25 May 1844), 48; *ibid.* (5 April 1845), 766; *Lloyd's Weekly Miscellany*, I (1849-50), 615.
[123] One short story, clipped from *Household Words*, described a "wild Irishman" in a workhouse brawl (*Lloyd's Weekly Miscellany*, II, 1850-52, 109).
[124] *Family Herald*, IX (25 Oct. 1851), 416.

More common was the romantic love story, in which boy met girl,[125] or the supernatural horror tale.[126] The Irish setting, in these tales, lent a certain romantic and exotic atmosphere; but there was nothing uniquely Hibernian about their plots or characters. They were universal stories of love or terror, and could as easily have been set in East Anglia or Transylvania.

Readers were much more likely to encounter the third and most ambiguous theme. In stories such as "Shawn Dhuv," "Kate Dermot, a tale of the Wicklow Mountains," and "Mary O'Rourke, the Cottager's Daughter," some Irishmen and women were honest, frank, manly, respectable, and hardworking, while others were rough, surly, and brutal brigands. There was a love interest, interrupted when disaster struck; the ensuing turmoil was resolved either by a happy ending or by heartbreaking deaths all round.[127]

Two examples illustrate this theme. In "The Irish Daughter," James Burke was "just one's ideal of a warm-hearted, high-spirited, frank, and handsome Irishman"; Mary Conway was fair and blue-eyed. Their engagement was interrupted when Mary's brother—"a noble young man" who did well in America—sent home passage money for the family. But James could not leave his old widowed mother, too weak to survive the passage; so the lovers parted. The emigrants were shipwrecked off the Newfoundland coast, and Mary's parents died in her arms. Mary eventually made her way to her brother in New York state, but, a few years later, he died. Alone and destitute in a foreign land, Mary walked away from her brother's grave. Tears clouded her eyes; she stumbled, and began to sink down in a swoon—when James Burke appeared to clasp her in his manly arms, and they lived happily ever after.[128] The heroine of "Mary Walsh, a Sketch of Irish Life," was a beautiful colleen; her sweetheart, Patrick Haynes, was strong, handsome, and upright. Pat went to Dublin to seek his fortune, but prostitutes tricked him, and he joined the army. Mary, meanwhile, was seduced and jilted by Edward Hall; she committed suicide. Pat heard about it and deserted his regiment to wreak vengence against Hall, who had fled to America. Pat tracked Hall down and killed the latter, but was killed in turn by his own father, who suddenly appeared on the scene. When Pat's father realized what he had done, he went mad; ". . . and thus ended the tale of Mary Walsh."[129]

The most common theme of all, however, was the tale, in a stage-Irish brogue, that showed Paddy, a "machine for turning potatoes into human nature,"[130] to be feckless, comical, blundering, thick, lazy, improvident, devil-may-care, garrulous, naive, and superstitious.[131] Schoolmasters solemnly parade their ignorance, thinking it to be knowledge.[132] People

[125] *Ibid.*, I (17 Feb. 1844), 642; *ibid.*, III (7 Feb. 1846), 625-27; *Eliza Cook's Journal*, IV (14 Dec. 1850), 106, *et passim ad* (28 Dec. 1850), 143.

[126] *Family Herald*, VI (13 May 1848), 23-24.

[127] *Lloyd's Penny Weekly Miscellany*, I (1843), 225-28, 273, *et passim ad* 391, 565-66, 641, *et passim ad* 693, 709-10; *Family Herald*, II (11 May 1844), 5; *ibid.*, III (21 Feb. 1846), 657-59.

[128] *Family Herald*, X (18 Sept. 1852), 323-24.

[129] *Lloyd's Penny Weekly Miscellany*, I (1843), 394-97.

[130] *Ibid.*, p. 88.

[131] *Ibid.*, pp. 107, 136-37; *Family Herald*, I (20 May 1843), 19-20; *ibid.* (30 Sept. 1843), 331; *ibid.*, III (2 Aug. 1845), 193-95; *Lloyd's Entertaining Journal*, VI (16 Jan. 1847), 312-15; *ibid.* (13 Mar. 1847), p. 445; *Lloyd's Weekly Miscellany*, I (1849-50), 127, 327.

[132] *Lloyd's Penny Weekly Miscellany*, III (1844), 91; *Lloyd's Entertaining Journal*, VI (20 Mar. 1847), 464-66.

named Shemus, Paddy, Dinny, and Mick get blind drunk at wakes.[133] In the relic chamber of a convent, Paddy shows a visitor two skulls. One is of St. Patrick; the other, smaller, is of St. Patrick when he was a boy.[134] Teague takes some of his master's books to be bound; the bookbinder tells him that some must be done in Morocco, some in Turkey, and some in Russia. Teague protests; his master had told him to get the work done in Dublin.[135] Some people are walking out, one day, when they hear crying. "I could not for a moment mistake the sob of an Irish voice, it is so deep—so earnest—so altogether abandoned to the grief of the moment." They soon come upon Paddy, weeping, with a dead pig at his feet.[136] These cultural traits are not restricted to the Roman Catholic peasantry; "squireens," and even the Anglo-Irish aristocracy, are just as feckless,[137] and Protestants can be just as wicked.[138]

These periodicals were not too interested in explaining the origin of these cultural traits. The penny *Family Herald* recognized that the Irish Reformation was a religious change imposed by a foreign power on an unwilling and captive people, and suggested that those circumstances helped to explain the extremes of wealth and poverty, virtue and vice, wisdom and folly, industriousness and idleness, that characterized the island and its people.[139] The three-halfpenny press agreed, but in stronger terms; it told its readers that both the "good" (compassionate, patient, generous) and "bad" (impulsive, fickle, improvident) elements in the Irish character, not to mention the Irish reputation for disloyalty, stemmed directly from centuries of English political oppression and religious persecution.[140] But these more thoughtful comments can be counted on the fingers of one hand, and their influence must have been overwhelmed by the "feckless Paddy" tide.[141]

"Peter Mulrooney in America" is a story that shows what the working classes were told about how Paddy looked, sounded, thought, and acted. (And, for lagniappe, we can see what Paddy became when free of British control, and learn what kind of society Brother Jonathan was building.) Peter wore a threadbare suit of black, buttoned up to the chin, a silk hat with the crown stove in, and a pair of patched and repatched dress boots. He encountered an English acquaintance.

> "Sure its a grate gintleman I am since I left sarvice an' set up for myself."
> "A gentleman! What sort of a gentleman, Peter?"

---

[133] *Lloyd's Penny Weekly Miscellany*, V (1846), 234-36.
[134] *Lloyd's Entertaining Journal*, I (11 May 1844), 103.
[135] *Family Herald*, III (25 Oct. 1845), 400.
[136] *Ibid.*, I (16 Dec. 1843), 497.
[137] *Ibid.*, V (19 June 1847), 97-100; *Eliza Cook's Journal*, IV (8 Mar. 1851), 289-95.
[138] *Lloyd's Penny Weekly Miscellany*, II (1844), 235-37, 243-45; *ibid.*, V (1846), 169.
[139] *Family Herald*, III (17 May 1845), 22; *ibid.* (24 May 1845), 35; *ibid.*, IV (27 Feb. 1847), 683-84.
[140] *Working Man's Friend*, V (15 Feb. 1851), 185; *ibid.* (22 Feb. 1851), 208-9; *Eliza Cook's Journal*, I (1 Sept. 1849), 280-81; *ibid.*, VII (9 Oct. 1852), 369.
[141] Not all these tales are trash; they include "Daniel O'Rourke," a delightful story by the Irish antiquary Thomas Crofton Croker (*DNB*, V, 132-34), which has been reprinted for children in the United States (*Through Fairy Halls*, vol. VI of *My Book House*, ed. by Olive Beaupré Miller, 12 vols., Lake Bluff, Ill., 1956, pp. 62-69). I was struck by the ethnic stereotyping when I read the story to my children.

"*Misther* Mulrooney, if ye plase," said he, correcting my familiarity, with one of his droll looks. "Och, but it's a rare counthry this is, anyway. Beyant the wather, it was Pether here an' Pether there, till sorra a bit I know'd of any other name than Pether. But here, the conversation of the ladies an' the gintlemen is illegant in the extreme, and the grate politishuners, in their correspondence wid me, write the beautifullest letters, shuperscribin' them, 'To Misther Mulrooney, Esquire'. . . . I am a profishunal gintleman. . . . It's a politishuner I am wid, a grate janious for fightin'! Och, but it's wonderful busy they kape me 'lecshun days knockin' down the inimy. '

"Which party do you call the inimy?"

"Sorra a bit I know," said Peter, shrugging his shoulders; then, casting towards me one of his queer, sidelong looks, he added, "I'm thinkin', sir, 'tis the *Pat*-riotic party meself does belong to."[142]

That last pun, that shows Pat as politician, Pat as thick, and Pat as rioter, is meant to imply what Irishmen are like, "in their state of nature."[143]

The Irish emigrant offered a good opportunity for weepy sentiment, as in the poem "The Irish Emigrant's Farewell."

Oh, Erin, my country, I love thee, yet leave thee,
For ever I leave thee, dear land of my birth,
No more shall my eyes ever feast on thy beauties,
No more shall my feet ever tread on thy earth.[144]

This ambiguous image of the Irish, a study in contrasts, had its roots in eighteenth-century picaresque fiction, and novels along these lines continued to be written for "middlebrow" readers into the 1850s.[145] Charles Lever made his fortune by writing comic Irish picaresque novels, "rascal autobiographies" of "very free and easy Paddies," and revived his career in the 1840s by turning to stage productions of comic monologues.[146] "Last night we had Lever at the [Manchester] Athenæum making us laugh for two hours, save a ten minute interval, over his Irish Entertainment. The brogue, the action, the look, combined with the fun of his stories was irrisistible [sic]."[147] It is the case, however, that the "discerning middlebrow public" did not have such an extensive exposure to the stereotype of Paddy as did their working-class counterparts.

The visual evidence also suggests that the middlebrow public received a fundamentally sympathetic image of the Irish. It is possible, of course, to assemble an album of "simianized" Irish with prognathous jaws and receding foreheads by carefully sorting through the evidence, avoiding pictures that do not fit one's hypothesis, and ignoring the traditions of political caricature.[148] Such albums are not representative of what was

---

142 *Family Herald*, IX (18 Oct. 1851), 392-93.

143 Read what purports to be a "letter home": "Come to swate Ameriky, and come quickly. Here you can buy paraties two shillings a bushel, whisky and coal same price, because we ain't got no turf here, a dollar a day for digging, and no hanging for staling. Och, now, do come." (*Lloyd's Weekly Miscellany*, II, 1850-52, 1109.)

144 *Lloyd's Penny Weekly Miscellany*, III (1844), 90.

145 Mary Edith Kelley, *The Irishman in the English Novel of the Nineteenth Century* (New York, 1970).

146 Sutherland, *Victorian Novelists and Publishers*, pp. 162-65.

147 Charles Royce to George Royce, 1 Apr. 1846, Royce Family Papers, MCL, M 70/3/8.

148 Gilley, "English Attitudes to the Irish," p. 97; L. P. Curtis, Jr., *Apes and Angels: The Irishman in Victorian Caricature* (Newton Abbot, 1971); John and Selma Appel, *Pat-Riots to Patriots: American Irish in Caricature and Comic Art* (East Lansing, 1990).

drawn. Engravings of Irish life in the *Illustrated London News* show peasants with poor and coarse, but not simianized, features,[149] and show the impish, feckless aspects of Irish life.[150] "The Irish Schoolmaster," by Edmond Fitzgerald, a debate between two hedge schoolmasters, shows them unkempt, unshaven, and even slightly tiddly, but is hardly contemptuous. G.F. Watts painted numerous scenes of Irish life both at home (*The Irish Famine*) and in England (*Found Drowned, The Sempstress*). His paintings show the Irish as fitting objects of pity, not of contempt.[151] Better a thousand words than a picture misread.

The Podsnappian character, who expressed "that hearty contempt and aversion for all *furriners* which is natural to the unsophisticated Briton,"[152] certainly existed in life as well as in art, but middlebrow literature did not pander to him.

Anti-Irish Sentiment and Scientific Racism

The readers of the gutter press, then, and to a lesser extent the middlebrow public, were treated to all sorts of ethnic stereotypes, and the Irish stereotype was the most common. But was this anti-Irish sentiment rooted in racism, as Curtis argues? Did Evangelicals fall "back on their belief in the innate depravity of the Celt" when they found that they could not convert Irish immigrants, as Klaus asserts?[153] What were the English working and middle classes asked to believe about race, during the mid-nineteenth century? And to make things clear, I understand as racism what Jacques Barzun calls "race thinking"—the assertion of any of the following propositions: That humanity "is divided into unchanging natural types, recognizable by physical features"; "That the mental and moral behavior of human beings can be related to physical structure"; That race determines individual and national characteristics, behavior, and capacities.[154]

The gutter press sometimes linked national characteristics with national origins, took physical characteristics to be signs of moral character, and identified stereotypical behavior. The Hungarians are essentially irreligious, while the Irish are naturally devout; both are convinced of their own superiority. Both derive their virtues and vices from their Asiatic origins; but both have lost, somehow, their Oriental seriousness. The Hungarians are more like the Scots in respect of the extent to which the aristocratic element is diffused among the population; i.e., in Ireland the common people are numerous, while in Scotland and Hungary most of the population are lords.[155] The Jewish hawk nose "indicates considerable shrewdness in worldly matters, a deep insight into character, and facility for turning this insight to profitable account"; the Irish snub nose indicates "natural weakness, mean, disagreeable disposition, . . . petty insolence, and

---

[149] *Illustrated London News*, 12 Aug., 7 Oct. 1843, 24 Jan. 1857.
[150] *Ibid.*, 16 Nov. 1844, by Phiz, shows an impish Irishman flirting with two girls.
[151] Errington, *Themes in English Art*, pp. 180-85.
[152] Braddon, *Aurora Floyd*, p. 195.
[153] Klaus, *Pope, Protestants, and Irish*, p. 306.
[154] Jacques Barzun, *Race: A Study in Superstition*, rev. ed. (New York, 1965), pp. 12-13.
[155] *Lloyd's Weekly Miscellany*, I (1849-50), 823; cf. *Eliza Cook's Journal*, V (10 May 1851), 30-31.

divers other characteristics of conscious weakness. . . ."[156] Publications for
a more middle-class audience also did this. The *Kentish Observer* thought
that the Italians (who are Celts) are excitable, reckless, sensual, unprincipled. The Germans (save in the north, where there is an admixture of
Swedish blood) are misled by false prophets, "those apostate Jews who
preach to them of the coming man." The Slavs are simple, believing men
who have not heard the true Gospel ("there is reason to believe that, were
the doctrines and the discipline of the Church of England fairly represented, they would meet an almost universal response").[157] The attempt to
explain the reasons for racial differences, however, plunged these periodicals into theoretical anarchy.

Climate was an obvious cause of racial differences. *Lloyd's* observed
that the Saxon race is energetic, freedom-loving, brave, and self-discip-
lined, in contrast to the "luxurious and effeminate races" who live in the
debilitating ease of "sunny skies, and vine growing lands."[158] In "Why are
there Black Men in the World and What is the Meaning of Africa?," the
Family Herald provided a climatic explanation that is both more sophisticated and more mystical. The earth is a black-and-white planet, because
it rotates on its axis; so it is agreeable with "the harmony of nature" that
the lords of such a planet should be black and white. But at any given
time, more of the planet is in light than in darkness; that fact explains why
whites predominate over blacks. Blacks are natural slaves, "because ignorance is by nature the servant of knowledge, and darkness of light. God
has ordained it." Black and white are associated with south and north:
"Passion and dark complexion burn in the south. Reason and fair complexion calculate in the north." This is why Roman Catholicism in its
purest form is strongest in Italy, Spain, and Portugal, while Protestant
"private judgment and controversial preaching" is strongest among "the
fair nations." By this reckoning, Presbyterian Ulster is superior to the
Roman Catholic south of Ireland, as Scotland is to England: "In Scotland,
preaching and controversial theology prevail. In England, politics and
puseyism."[159]

Not everyone, however, accepted the climatic argument. Climatic differences, the *Working Man's Friend* told its readers, accounted for differences in color and hair, but the fundamental explanation for racial differences lay in skull-shapes: oval-headed Caucasians, pyramid-headed
Mongolians, and prognathous blacks. So there is a hierarchy of races:
Australian aborigines at the bottom, followed by the rest of the prognathous blacks; the North American Indians, Mongolians, and "Indian
branch of the Caucasians"; and at the top the rest of the Caucasians. Yet
the influences of adjacent societies, of changes in the environment, and
even of religious beliefs can change the shape of a people's skulls. African
tribes who convert to Islam also have their skulls converted from prognathous to pyramidal. In Ireland, however, "the people, driven from their
own proper locality into certain widely-different districts of the country,

156 *Lloyd's Weekly Miscellany*, II (1850-52), 1061-62.
157 *Kentish Observer*, 7 Nov. 1850.
158 *Lloyd's Weekly Miscellany*, II (1850-52), 1087.
159 *Family Herald*, o.s., I (7 Jan. 1843).

had not only degenerated in their general bodily conformation, but have actually acquired the prognathous or negro type of cranium."[160]

The same journal, however, also published an article by Benjamin Andrews, a journeyman baker from Wells, that denied that climate affected national character: "Under every view of the subject, we are warranted . . . in assuming that God has ordained every nation, as well as every single individual, with a peculiar character, the expansion of which is favoured or retarded by external circumstances, though it can never become the subject of direct and unerring calculation."[161] And, yet again, the same journal also published the American Elihu Burritt's[162] argument that Saxon superiority is connected with language.

> When a community begins to speak and read the English language, it is half *Saxonized*, even if not a drop of Anglo-Saxon blood runs in its veins. Ireland was never colonized from England, like North America or Australia; but nearly the whole of its seven or eight millions already speak the English language, which is the preparatory state to being entirely absorbed into the Anglo-Saxon race, as one of its most vigorous and useful elements.[163]

We see in these theories no trace of the notion of innate and immutable racial inferiority, and no fear of "mongrelization." Indeed, the *Family Herald* believed that "the black man is destined to improve and perfect the white [and] the one will mingle by degrees with the other till the black and the white become the dark and the fair."[164] "The more advanced and civilised, the less pointed and sharp the outline of the nationality; the more barbarous and savage, the more exclusive and local, national, clannish, and tribish."[165] *Eliza Cook's Journal* gloried in "mongrelization":

> in England, the invidious distinctions of race are rapidly becoming obliterated. We are becoming so mixed up with Germans, Irish, Norman-French, Jews, and people of all countries, that we no longer can pride ourselves on the purity of our "blood." Probably it is all the more vigorous that it is well mixed. . . . Let us hope that the best points of character in all these races will be preserved:—the frank generosity and fine personal qualities of the Celt; the diligence and industry of the Saxon; the valour and love of independence of the Dane; and the gallantry and high sense of honour of the Norman,—and we may well be proud, as indeed we have reason to be already, to bear the name of BRITON.[166]

While the gutter press was groping for some sort of explanation for racial differences, the denominational and anti-Catholic press denied that there were any racial differences to be explained. True, the organ of the English Presbyterian Church once called Scots "real Celts";[167] but then the English Presbyterian Church, because of its own internal needs, wanted to distance itself from its Irish connections and emphasize its links with

---

[160] *Working Man's Friend*, I (5 Jan. 1850), 10-12; *ibid.*, (12 Jan. 1850), 39-41.

[161] *Ibid.*, Supplement I (June 1850), 6-8.

[162] Burritt (1810-1879), a linguist, peace activist, and internationalist, was United States Consul at Birmingham (*Dictionary of American Biography*, III, 328-30).

[163] *Working Man's Friend*, I (30 March 1850), 405; also published in *Eliza Cook's Journal*, IV (29 March 1851), 351.

[164] *Family Herald*, o.s., I (7 Jan. 1843).

[165] *Ibid.*, XII (23 Sept. 1854), 332.

[166] *Eliza Cook's Journal*, VI (3 April 1852), 355.

[167] *English Presbyterian Messenger*, n.s., II (Aug. 1849), 55.

Scotland.[168] Quoting Humboldt, an organ of the Congregational Union maintained "the unity of the human species," and rejected "the depressing assumption of superior and inferior races of man. . . . All are, in like degree, designed for freedom . . . ."[169] Orthodox Christianity had to reject current German scientific thinking on race, which advanced the hypothesis that the different human races were biologically unrelated, for such thinking denied the Biblical account of creation, that all humans were descended from Adam and Eve.

The opinion of the Protestant Association's organ on this subject was made clear in an article, "Italian Superstitions, not 'Celtic Blood', the Cause of Irish Demoralization." A large proportion of the inmates of English jails and workhouses were Irish. They came to England, fleeing destitution and hoping to find a subsistence; but they failed and became a burden on the taxpayer, as either criminals or paupers. This increased the poor-rates and encouraged the English poor to hate their Irish fellow-subjects. Why, one might ask, were the Irish failures at life?

> True, the north of Ireland has been colonized extensively by English and Scottish settlers, whilst the south of Ireland is exclusively inhabited by the Celtic aborigines; but is it to this difference of race—this antagonism of blood, that we are to look for a solution of the great problem of Irish distress. The *Times* may write whole pages upon the necessity of infusing into the Celtic stock the alloy of Saxon enterprise, steadiness, and industry, and some good it might do if the settlers were Protestants: for it is to this fact only, viz., that of the English and Scotch settlers in Ulster being free from the taint of Romanism, that we can assign the cause of the prosperity of Ulster;—for, are not many, a great many, of the inhabitants of the north of Ireland, though descended from the foreign settlers, as good Celts as any to be met with in Munster—or Connaught,—are not numbers descended from the Highland Scottish families who emigrated thither in the latter part of the eighteenth century, and, consequently, as much under the influence of Celtic feelings as their southern neighbours? But they are Protestants,—they are free from the shackles of Popery and unfettered by the iron bondage of superstition.[170]

No, the notion that Celts were an inferior race was absurd: the Cornish, Welsh, Manx, and Scots showed what the Irish could be, if only they were Protestant.

The English working and middle classes, during the mid-nineteenth century, were not being educated in the tenets of scientific racism. On the contrary; they were being asked to absorb an awkward mix of climate, physiology, culture, mysticism, and the will of God. That mix, when boiled down, turned out to be much more about culture than about race. And those groups that were most antipathetic to the Roman Catholic faith were least likely to be told that the adherents of that faith were an inferior race.

Conclusions

The relationship between anti-Irish and anti-Catholic sentiment in the mid-nineteenth century is not so clear-cut as has been thought. The reading public of denominational and anti-Catholic literature was exposed to

---

[168] For this, see *inf.*, pp. 180-82.
[169] *Christian's Penny Magazine*, V (April 1850), 95.
[170] *Protestant Magazine*, XI (Oct. 1849), 154.

a negative view of the Roman Catholic faith, but to a positive view of the Irish. The reading public of working- and middle-class literature was exposed to mixed, although on balance negative, views of both Roman Catholicism and the Irish, but no connection was drawn between the two. For these organs, Roman Catholicism was a bad thing because it was a superstitious, idolatrous, persecuting, and sinister sect, not because most of its adherents in England were Irish. And, although one must not underestimate the impact of the cumulative exposure to these negative views, one must remember that the views were not unrelievedly negative.

Scientific racism had little if anything to do with mid-nineteenth- century views about the Irish. Sheridan Gilley has demonstrated clearly and decisively that L. P. Curtis's racist argument is untenable. It is evident, moreover, that mid-nineteenth-century readers were not being tutored in scientific racism, whatever the governing classes may have been reading; it is also doubtful that the governing classes themselves knew much about scientific racism. When one looks closely at the publication dates of Curtis's sources—and, remember, Curtis claims that his argument holds true for the whole of the nineteenth century—one notices that 43 percent of them appeared in the twenty years from 1880 to 1899, and 30 percent appeared in the twenty years after 1900; the other sixty years of the nineteenth century account for only 27 percent of his sources. The unbalanced distribution of his sources skewed his analysis of the problem, for the debate over how to measure and classify "race" was not settled until the very last years of the century, when linguistic, cultural, and cranial measures were finally rejected.[171]

Out-and-out racism plays little part in the English reception of minorities, at least according to Colin Holmes and Kenneth Lunn. Competition for jobs and for housing played a large part in the reception of Jews, Chinese, and German immigrants in the later nineteenth century, and continues to do so with respect to Asian and Afro-Caribbean immigrants today. And tensions arose (and continue to arise) over non-economic issues—most notably, the threat that immigrant groups pose of transforming the values, customs, religion, and language of the host society. They observe, further, that the receiving society is not monolithic; different sections of the host society react to the immigrants in different ways, and for different reasons.[172] With respect to the reception of the Irish in the period from 1830 to 1870, the attitudes of the various subgroups of the host society to religion was the determining factor.

The decline in the importance of religion—or, at least, the decline of organized religion and its associated theological structures—in the late nineteenth and twentieth centuries may well be the most important element to affect English attitudes toward the Irish. Curtis offers three examples from *Hansard* to illustrate his point, that "the nature of anti-Irish prejudice among the English governing classes underwent no substantial change in its component parts from one end of the nineteenth century to the other." In 1811, John Fuller, M.P. for Sussex, said: "I have no great faith in Catholic emancipation. I think that there is a radical and rooted antipathy

[171] Bolt, *Victorian Attitudes to Race*, pp. 9-26.
[172] Colin Holmes and Kenneth Lunn, "Introduction," *Hosts, Immigrants, and Minorities*, ed. Lunn, pp. 4-6.

between England and Ireland. Well, then, try Catholic emancipation, if you think it will do. I care no more for a Catholic than I do for a Chinese." Twenty-five years later, Lord Lyndhurst opposed Irish municipal reform on the grounds that the Irish were an "alien people" with a different language and religion. In 1893, Sir Ellis Ashmead Bartlett opposed Home Rule because it would put "the best part of [Ireland] under the control of the worst, the loyal under the disloyal, the honest under the dishonest, and the peaceful and the industrious under the idle and thriftless."[173]

Far from showing that what Curtis calls "anti-Irish prejudice" was changeless, "from one end of the nineteenth century to the other," his three examples suggest that there was a slow but profound change. Fuller did not like the Irish because they were Roman Catholic. Lyndhurst did not like the Irish because they were Roman Catholic and because they were un-English in culture. Bartlett did not like the Irish because they were un-English in culture. In other words, the "component parts" of "anti-Irish prejudice" did indeed change; the religious allegiance of the disliked group became increasingly less important a reason to dislike them, and the nature of the group's culture (and politics) became increasingly more important a reason. Perhaps the English, as they became more "secular," stopped disliking the Irish because they were Roman Catholic, and started disliking the Irish because they were Irish.

[173] Curtis, *Anglo-Saxons and Celts*, pp. 26-27.

III

MILITANT ROMAN CATHOLICISM

> Where are now the great boasters? What has
> become of the "No Popery" shouters? They were
> exceedingly noisy and clamorous whilst we were
> asleep,—but when at length we are aroused from
> our apathy and begin to shew signs of life and
> activity, then it would appear they begin to grow
> shy,—to shun the public gaze.—And finding the
> tables turned, and that instead of being any longer
> permitted to insolently attack us,—they are now
> themselves placed upon the defensive, they are
> completely confounded.[1]

> It cheers us to see our walls parading an array of
> Popish controversial lectures. Our liberals can no
> more fling it in our faces that we are always the
> aggressors. Now we are but parrying a blow. It is
> well.[2]

THESE QUOTATIONS, BOTH from Manchester, suggest the disputa-
tious atmosphere of the day in which Roman Catholics met their detrac-
tors head-on, some of the reasons why so much energy was invested in
dispute, and how important local cases are in understanding anti-Catholicism.

Roman Catholicism in the first half of the nineteenth century was decidedly a regional religion as far as its adherents were concerned. If one
draws a line from Lancaster in the northwest to London in the southeast,
most of the Roman Catholic chapels in existence in 1840 fell along it in
three clusters: the cotton district of Lancashire and Cheshire, the West
Midlands with Birmingham at its heart, and London.[3] This regional orientation reflects the unique local conditions that explain the construction
of chapels:

> Chaque cas pose un problème particulier: ici le rôle d'une personnalité,
> prêtre ou laïc, ou d'un groupe de fidèles; ailleurs, des resources financières:
> ou, au contraire, la difficulté éprouvée à acheter ou même à trouver un
> terrain; . . . ces différentes impulsions ou ces freins ont orienté la con-
> struction de ces églises. . . .[4]

It is thus not surprising that local conditions helped dictate the direction
that the Roman Church in England took as it revived in the century, that

---

[1] *Manchester Illuminator and General Catholic Record*, I (2 Feb. 1850), 63.
[2] *Protestant Witness*, I (7 Oct. 1848), 17.
[3] Lesourd, "Catholiques dans la Société Anglaise," I, 605-6.
[4] *Ibid.*, p. 603.

the revival began earlier than the 1840s, and that the Church demonstrated a vigorous local life, surprisingly independent from the central guidance of Eminent Victorian Catholics such as Wiseman and Manning. Moreover, the aggressive, assertive spirit of Victorian Roman Catholicism, usually associated with Wiseman and Manning, can be seen at work at the local level, sparking anti-Catholicism in response.

Roman Catholic Revival and Aggression

As is well known, the English Roman Catholic Church by 1840 had awakened into what John Henry Newman later called "the second spring." It was growth in numbers that stimulated the awakening, caused by Irish immigration. Roman Catholicism grew almost as fast as Methodism before 1840, but, unlike the Methodists, continued its growth throughout the century, as Irish immigration continued. But there was "leakage" or "wastage," at least in the short run, from those Irish who attended Mass occasionally, either because there were no accommodations for them in England or because they had not been habituated to doing so in Ireland, or who were nonpracticing. The 1851 census showed a little over half a million people born in Ireland (most of whom were Roman Catholic), but only a quarter of a million Roman Catholic worshippers (some of whom were English), who may be counted as regular Sunday attenders. Roman Catholicism was a badge of Irish identity in a peasant culture, rather than the object of conscious choice, and the rate of leakage did not drop until the period after 1865.[5]

The ideology that permitted the Roman Catholic Church to capitalize on the numbers was the Romantic ultramontanism and triumphalism of the day, and its most visible expositor after 1840 was Nicholas Wiseman. Wiseman, a former rector of the English College at Rome, became coadjutor to the vicar of the Central District in 1840. A natural master of psychological warfare, he adroitly navigated the shoals of Roman Catholic party politics, cultivated contacts with wavering Anglicans, and encouraged the importation of the most extravagant examples of Italian rococo devotion. His overweening pride matched his physical bulk;[6] his love of the outward display of his rank made him the very stereotype of the proud popish prelate.[7] He wanted to have a territorial hierarchy, primarily for its psychological value in advancing Roman Catholic claims:

> We have gathered together the scattered stones of our profaned sanctuary, and have built them up into a second temple, inferior to the first, but still not without its glories. The fire has been rekindled upon the altar; the priests have sounded again their trumpets, and proselytes have crowded to

[5] *Ibid.*, I, 497, II, 923-46; Gilbert, *Religion and Society*, pp. 45-46, 144; Owen Chadwick, *The Victorian Church*, 2nd ed., Pt. I (London, 1970), p. 272.

[6] "A few days ago Cardinal Wiseman went to call at a house in Hill Street. . . . The door was opened by a maidservant, who, when she heard his name, and realized that he was a Cardinal, prostrated herself on the floor of the stone passage. The Cardinal looked at her for a moment, and then coolly stepped over her, saying, 'This is a faithful creature.'" (Richard Edgcumbe, ed., *The Diary of Frances Lady Shelley, 1818-1873*, 2 vols., New York, 1914, II, 298, 7 Mar. 1851.)

[7] Fundamentally sympathetic assessments of Wiseman's character are in Norman, *English Catholic Church*, pp. 110-57; and in Richard J. Schiefen, *Nicholas Wiseman and the Transformation of English Catholicism* (Shepherdstown, W.Va., 1984). J. Derek Holmes, *More Roman Than Rome: English Catholicism in the Nineteenth Century* (London, 1978), pp. 55-108; and Chadwick, *Victorian Church*, pp. 280-84, are more balanced.

the solemnity. But the rule of the Holy City is not yet restored; the republic of God is under temporary provision of government; its priests and rulers have not yet been fully ordered, classified, or made able, with full efficacy, to display the beauties of their ministry. This is what we now want.[8]

As is also well known, Wiseman and other ultramontane clergy who wanted to revive the English Roman Catholic Church in a Roman image faced opposition from conservative Old Catholic aristocrats who were used to the old days, when clergy, even the bishops, were almost family retainers. Noblemen such as the thirteenth Duke of Norfolk,[9] who opposed societies limited to Roman Catholics, or Lord Beaumont[10] and Lord Camoys,[11] who came to oppose publicly the new hierarchy in 1850, did not like the direction in which their Church was moving, and some eventually conformed to the Church of England.[12] But their future lay in the past.

There also was a conservative "Cisalpine" or "Anglo-Gallican" tradition in English Roman Catholicism that had evolved its own devotional style and that prized its independent, English way of doing things.[13] The Cisalpines had created a lively Roman Catholic community before 1829, one that promoted its own interests by pushing for Roman Catholic Emancipation, and that debated the authority of the vicars over the parochial clergy and the proper relationship between the English Roman Catholics and Rome.[14] But the Cisalpines began to be overshadowed by the ultramontane spirit in the 1830s, and it was not until after the Second Vatican Council a hundred and thirty years later that English Roman Catholics again asked themselves whether they were primarily English or primarily Roman.

A new generation of aristocrats and gentry had arisen, keen to repeal the remaining penal laws, to assert equality with the Established Church, and to demand fair and equitable treatment from the state.[15] By the late 1830s, there was a new generation of Roman Catholic clergy, led by the vicars apostolic, who wished to tighten discipline among the laity by discouraging formerly common latitudinarian practices such as having mar-

[8] Nicholas Wiseman, "A Paper on Ecclesiastical Organization," *Essays on Various Subjects*, 3 vols. (London, 1853), I, 354-55.
[9] Henry Charles Howard, 13th Duke of Norfolk (1791-1856), the first Roman Catholic to sit in the House of Commons; M.P. for Horsham (1829-32) and the Western division of Sussex (1832-41); K.G., 1848; household offices; a staunch Whig and lax Roman Catholic, who had his chaplain reconcile him to Rome on his deathbed (*DNB*, X, 37).
[10] Miles Thomas Stapleton, 8th Lord Beaumont (1805-1854), fought a duel on Wimbledon Common, 1832; summoned to House of Lords by writ as coheir of the barony of Beaumont, 1840; undistinguished (Boase, I, 213).
[11] Thomas Stonor, 3rd Lord Camoys (1797-1881), M.P. for Oxford, 1832-33; summoned to Lords, 1839, when the barony was called out of abeyance, having been dormant since 1746; lord-in-waiting to the Queen during Whig administrations, 1846-74 (Boase, I, 525).
[12] The 13th Duke of Norfolk to Rev. J. H. Parsons, 29 Jan. 1836, Arundel Castle Archives; *Times*, 26 Nov. 1850; 3 *Hansard*, CXIV (1851), 37.
[13] Richard J. Schiefen, "'Anglo-Gallicanism' in Nineteenth-Century England," *Catholic Historical Review*, LXIII (1977), 14-44; James J. Sack, "The Grenvilles' *Eminence Grise*: The Reverend Charles O'Conor and the Latter Days of Anglo-Gallicanism," *Harvard Theological Review*, LXXII (1979), 123-42; Joseph P. Chinnici, *The English Catholic Enlightenment: John Lingard and the Cisalpine Movement, 1780-1850* (Shepherdstown, W.Va., 1980); Josef L. Altholz, *The Liberal Catholic Movement in England: The "Rambler" and its Contributors, 1848-1864* (London, 1962), pp. 1-6.
[14] Brian Carter, "Controversy and Conciliation in the English Catholic Enlightenment, 1790-1840," *Enlightenment and Dissent*, VII (1988), 21.
[15] Paz, "Another Look," p. 49.

riages performed by Anglican clergymen.[16] Henry Granville Fitzalan-Howard, heir of the thirteenth Duke of Norfolk, is a symbol of this change. Unlike his father, he strongly asserted his Church's right to be treated as an equal, and interested himself in questions such as aid to Roman Catholic schools, the provision of chaplains in prisons, the repeal of penal laws, and reform of the law of charitable bequests to accommodate distinctively Roman Catholic practices.[17] Eventually, he broke with his father over the creation of the hierarchy; he was a staunch defender of the hierarchy, while his father conformed to the Church of England.[18]

The English Roman Catholic Church, by the late 1830s, was renewed and vigorous, and indeed anticipated Wiseman's call to greater militance when he took up residence in England in 1840. "It has afforded us great satisfaction to observe," the vicars apostolic declared in 1838,

> that a spirit of well regulated zeal for the vindication of truth and the protection of the oppressed, has of late strikingly manifested amongst us; nor can we doubt that all who see the necessity of defending their religion against the organised assaults of well-educated and powerful traducers, will also see the necessity of training up in our seminaries a strong body of learned men, who, whether they enter the sacred ministry or follow secular pursuits, may, by their superior education, be duly qualified to become the champions of truth.[19]

The awakening of Roman Catholic assertiveness in the 1830s and '40s took several forms.

Worship was the most obvious form. The increase in the number of Roman Catholic places of worship in the 1830s and '40s, and their appearance (larger, more ornate, more "churchly" and less "chapel-like"), were signs of greater self-confidence. Moreover, the worship within those chapels was being assimilated more closely to Continental styles of Italianate piety—rococo devotion to the Blessed Sacrament, to the Sacred Heart of Jesus, and to the Blessed Virgin Mary in some of her more lurid apparitions. The Oxford Converts F. W. Faber and W. G. Ward enjoyed Wiseman's support in promoting this sort of devotion in the middle and late 1840s, but the introduction of this style began earlier.[20]

Organization was another form. There had been several attempts to create national interest groups in the late eighteenth and early nineteenth centuries. The most successful of these was the Associated Catholic Charities, founded in 1811 by the merger of several benevolent societies. More promising as a means of aggressive offense was the Catholic Institute. This had its origins in the Metropolitan Catholic Tract Society, organized in

---

[16] Printed letter, Bishop John Briggs to clergy of the Northern District, 5 Sept. 1837, Archives of the Diocese of Northampton, F1.6; Chadwick, *Victorian Church*, pp. 143-44.

[17] Earl of Arundel and Surrey to Charles Langdale, 24 Apr. 1847 (draft), 13 Feb. 1849, Arundel and Surrey to Sir William Somerville, 11 May 1847, Arundel Castle Archives.

[18] Henry Granville Fitzalan-Howard, 14th Duke (1815-1860), was M.P. for Arundel (1837-51) and Limerick (1851-52); a close friend of the Count de Montalembert, who became his biographer and who called him "the most pious layman of our time"; a staunch supporter of Roman Catholic claims; "administered his vast patrimony with rare liberality" (*DNB*, X, 38-39).

[19] Pastoral letter of the vicars apostolic, 3 Dec. 1838, Archives of the Diocese of Northampton, F1.2(8).

[20] Horton Davies, *Worship and Theology in England*, IV, *From Newman to Martineau, 1850-1900* (Princeton, 1962), 33-35; Ronald Chapman, *Father Faber* (Westminster, Md., 1961); Lynn Hollen Lees, *Exiles of Erin: Irish Migrants to Victorian London* (Manchester and Ithaca, 1979), pp. 166-82; Klaus, *Pope, Protestants, and Irish*, pp. 43-50.

London in the 1820s to circulate cheap tracts among the Irish poor and to counteract Protestant evangelism. Charles Langdale reorganized it in 1838. It was intended to be a national committee to support and guide the fund-raising campaigns of local bodies; it and its local branches also engaged in a certain amount of apologetical and defense work, especially against the Factory Bill, 1843. But it declined after 1843, and was absorbed into the clerically dominated Catholic Poor School Committee in 1847. Certainly the bishops viewed a lay body with suspicion. Also, economic hard times and the growth of Roman Catholic activities in the North reduced subscriptions. And there was competition from the more purely charitable Brotherhood of St. Vincent De Paul, and Frederick Lucas's more overtly political Association of St. Thomas of Canterbury.[21]

Nicholas Wiseman was concerned about the lack of a strong apologetical voice for his Church. The success of his "Lectures on the Connexion between Science and Revealed Religion," which he had given in London in 1835-36, had convinced him that the potential audience for the exposition of Roman doctrine was large. Indeed, he had cofounded the *Dublin Review* in 1836 in large part to present Roman doctrine to educated Englishmen, and to exploit controversies within Anglicanism. There were, moreover, a number of Roman Catholic publishing houses in London and Dublin that supplied Bibles, devotional prayer books, and tracts.[22] But the printed word was passive apologetics; Wiseman wanted trained and aggressive controversialists who could defend against both "the spirit of the times" and Anglican claims. Hence, as is well known, he encouraged the major evangelistic religious orders—Passionists, Redemptorists, Oratorians, and Rosminians—to come to England and give missions in hopes of reaping a harvest of conversions. But although Wiseman, Lucas, and others wanted apologetical societies, the needs of the Irish immigrants required schools, chapels, and refuges. It is ironic, and telling, that the Italian missionary priests who had come to convert Protestants, ended up attempting to stem "leakage" among nominally Roman Catholic Irish.[23] So, the most extensive Roman Catholic voluntary effort took the more common form of philanthropic missions, of which London's has been the most closely studied.[24]

There was no national organization to defend the Church's political interests, no Roman Catholic equivalent of the Protestant Dissenting Deputies or the Wesleyan Methodist Committee of Privileges. Roman Catholics first took a prominent part in political agitation during the campaign against the Factory Bill, 1843, which would have given the control of fac-

---

[21] Bossy, *English Catholic Community*, pp. 349-55; Norman, *English Catholic Church*, pp. 167-68; Sheridan Gilley, "English Catholic Charity and the Irish Poor in London: Part II (1840-1870)," *Recusant History*, XI (1972), pp. 253 ff.; Mary Griset Holland, "The British Catholic Press and the Educational Controversy, 1847-1865" (Ph.D. thesis, Catholic University of America, 1975), pp. 48-51.

[22] Norman, *English Catholic Church*, p. 123; Schiefen, *Wiseman*, pp. 65-70, 145.

[23] Norman, *English Catholic Church*, pp. 223-30; Schiefen, *Wiseman*, pp. 92-93; John Sharp, "Juvenile Holiness: Catholic Revivalism among Children in Victorian Britain," *JEH*, XXXV (1984), 221-25; Robert Kent Donovan, "The Denominational Character of English Catholic Charitable Effort, 1800-1865," *Catholic Historical Review*, LXII (1976), 217-18.

[24] Donovan, "Catholic Charitable Effort,", pp. 201-2, 211-13; Sheridan Gilley, "English Catholic Charity and the Irish Poor in London: Part I: 1700-1840," *Recusant History*, XI (1972), 179-95; Sheridan Gilley, "The Roman Catholic Mission to the Irish in London, 1840-1860," *ibid.*, X (1969), 124 ff.

tory schools to the Church of England. The Catholic Institute attempted to lead the protests, but most took the form of local meetings, and of lobbying by Wiseman. Later in the 1840s, individual Roman Catholic M.P.s such as T. Chisholm Anstey, W. H. Watson, and Charles Langdale were active in Parliament in attempting to remove penal legislation, but there was no attempt to institutionalize this sort of activity.[25] This was largely because the bishops, especially Wiseman, did not want to share their authority and leadership with either the lower clergy or the laity.

It is mistaken to think that "the predominant mood" of English Roman Catholicism before 1850 was "nostalgia," and that during the first half of the century it was "the religion of a cultural and quiescent minority."[26] Far from it. Yet although the national Roman Catholic leadership was eager to proselytize and to combat their enemies, and although in Wiseman they had a formidable paladin, the Church's poverty, exacerbated by the economic depression of the 1840s and the hierarchy's own jealousy of potential rivals for leadership, limited what the hierarchy, even Wiseman, could do.[27]

Defending the Faith on the Local Level

The revival was felt on the local level, as well as on the national, and as early. In many ways, moreover, local manifestations of the "second spring" are at least as important, although less well understood. Five centers of Roman Catholic revival worth examining are Derby, Manchester, Northampton, Leeds, and Birmingham.

As early as 1842, the Roman Catholic priests of Derby, Thomas Sing and Joseph Daniel, began producing cheap tracts for their community; their publishing program drew fire from an anti-Catholic periodical.[28] Sing and Daniel went further in 1844, establishing a newspaper, the *Catholic Weekly Instructor*, designed to supply family reading matter, wean the poor from penny dreadfuls, and lead Protestants to think about Roman Catholicism.[29]

Sing and Daniel published controversial material suitable for a working-class audience. In "Dialogue between a Baptist Minister and one of his Congregation," Mr. Searchwell, about to convert to Roman Catholicism, debates infant baptism with his minister, and along the way vindicates the authority of tradition and the apostolic succession.[30] Other articles included a defense of the Real Presence, extracts from a pastoral letter calling for prayers for the conversion of England, and a letter from Philander Chase, Episcopal Bishop of Illinois, attacking the New York Bible Society for propagating the "leveling effect" of the Bible on human

---

[25] *Leeds Mercury*, 25 Mar. 1843; *Times*, 31 Mar. 1843; *Spectator*, 29 Apr. 1843; *Sheffield Mercury*, 20 May 1843; Schiefen, *Wiseman*, pp. 137-38; Machin, *Politics and the Churches*, pp. 178-79.

[26] H. Davies, *Newman to Martineau*, p. 15; Horton Davies, *Worship and Theology in England*, III, *From Watts and Wesley to Maurice, 1690-1850* (Princeton and London, 1961), 6; cf. Klaus, *Pope, Protestants, and Irish*, pp. 1-2, 11-16.

[27] Holmes, *More Roman Than Rome*, p. 47; Schiefen, *Wiseman*, p. 131; Gerrard Connolly, "The Transubstantiation of Myth: Towards a New Popular History of Nineteenth-Century Catholicism in England," *JEH*, XXXV (1984), 91-92; Lesourd, "Catholiques dans la Société Anglaise,", I, 555-86, II, 763.

[28] *Christian Watchman and Midland Counties' Protestant Magazine*, No. 4 (Sept. 1842), pp. 54-56; *ibid.*, No. 10 (Mar. 1843), pp. 145-53.

[29] *Catholic Weekly Instructor*, I (15 June 1844), 1.

[30] *Ibid.*, III (21 Mar. 1846), 139-40.

society.[31] They also attacked Protestantism directly. The Home Mission
of the Presbyterian Church of Ireland was charged with raising money
through false pretences, by inflating the number of schools that it claimed
to maintain, and by inventing nonexistent teachers.[32] And they printed
advertisements for the sale of livings, with acidic comments from the *English Churchman.*[33] Another way they attacked Protestantism was by contrasting "the good old Catholic Sunday" with grim Evangelical Sabbatarianism.[34]

> Oh, the good old times of England! Ere in her evil day,
> From their Holy Faith and their ancient rites her people fell away;
> When her gentlemen had hands to give, and her yeomen hearts to feel;
> And they raised full many a bead-house, but never a bastile;
>
>   * * *
>
> But times and things are altered now; and Englishmen begin
> To class the beggar with the knave, and poverty with sin.[35]

The *Catholic Weekly Instructor* participated in the national trend of
tightening church discipline. Its readers were encouraged to abandon the
practice of addressing their priests as "Mister" in favor of the Irish and
Continental usage of "Father," and were reminded of the efficacy of the
Blessed Virgin Mary.[36] And the editors thought temperance stories appropriate for their readers.[37]

But, befitting its aims and readership, the *Instructor* printed fiction and
true-adventure stories with a confessional twist. "The Catholic Soldier"
recounts the heroism of a recruit in an Irish regiment who refuses to
change his faith for advancement; and "An Incident at Moodkee" praises
the heroic death of a Roman Catholic chaplain to the 50th Regiment of
Foot in a battle against the Sikhs.[38] "The Demonstration; or, the Day of
the General Turn-Out" is of special interest, for it shows how Sing and
Daniel backed their positive depiction of Roman Catholicism with a conservative social message. The hero, a devout Roman Catholic, refused to
strike against his benevolent Manchester mill-owner, and as a consequence
suffered union violence and lost his job. His baby son died, and he was
saved from the workhouse in the nick of time. Through it all, he stuck to
his principles.[39]

Throughout the life of the *Instructor*, a low circulation hampered Sing
and Daniel's efforts. They lamented the fact that no Roman Catholic serial
publication had ever reached a sale of seven thousand copies per month
(as compared to the *Wesleyan Methodist Magazine*'s and the *Congregational Magazine*'s highest circulations of thirty thousand per month), and
they eventually stopped publication after trying to survive as a monthly.[40]

31 *Ibid.* (21 Feb. 1846), p. 96; *ibid.* (9 May 1846), pp. 220-21; *ibid.,* II (15 Mar. 1845), 131.
32 *Ibid.,* I (12 Nov. 1844), 241-47.
33 *Ibid.,* II (4 Oct. 1845), 479-80.
34 *Ibid.,* I (29 June 1844), 25.
35 *Ibid.* (15 June 1844), p. 5, quoting the Anglican J. M. Neale.
36 *Ibid.,* III (7 Mar. 1846), 116; *ibid.* (27 June 1846), 301-5.
37 *Ibid.,* I (22 June 1844), 19-21.
38 *Ibid.,* III (4 Apr. 1846), 157-59.
39 *Ibid.,* I (9 Nov. 1844), 259-61; *ibid.* (23 Nov. 1844), 281-83.
40 *Ibid.,* IV (Jan. 1847), 2-3; *ibid.* (Dec. 1847), 529.

Sing and Daniel's model for religious controversy was the boy Jesus disputing in the Temple—polite, meek, eschewing hatred and insults.[41] In Manchester,[42] however, both the history of confessional relations and the personalities of the parties involved led to much more dramatic confrontations.

Manchester, Salford, and their out-townships had, in the eighteenth century, a small native Recusant population; beginning in the 1790s, and steadily thereafter, that urban area and other parts of Lancashire as well received an immigration of Irish.[43] Many were from Ulster, and many were Protestant. By the 1850s, Lancashire's Irish community amounted to over two hundred thousand, or 10 percent of the total population. About 85 percent of them were Roman Catholics, and 15 percent were Protestant.[44] Anti-Catholic sentiment and activity began to grow in Manchester after 1800. The Irish brought their communal conflicts with them in the form of the Orange Order, founded in 1808. Voluntary organizations such as the Manchester and Salford Auxiliary of the British and Foreign Bible Society, the Manchester Religious Tract Society, the Protestant Union, and the Society for Promoting Christianity Amongst the Jews increased evangelistic activity and thereby led to encounters and conflicts between Roman Catholics and Protestants. Simultaneously, in political terms, links began to be made among Roman Catholic claims for political rights, political radicalism, and Irish nationalism. And the Catholic Emancipation campaign of the 1820s increased political disputes.

Roman Catholics replied by becoming more aggressive. The Rev. Joseph Curr, assistant at St. Augustine's chapel, Granby Row, during the first half of the 1820s, was a vigorous polemicist by sermon and tract. He opposed both interdenominational cooperation and lay autonomy in the religious sphere, fostering separate Roman Catholic schools, literary societies, and other organizations, and stressing the paramount importance of clerical leadership in the laity's spiritual and institutional lives.[45] Curr was only the most visible participant in a separatist movement that organized Bible societies to print and distribute free or cheap editions of the Douai Version, and that founded the Manchester and Salford Catholic Association in 1824 to protect the community's interests. But these organizations failed. The Bible societies were hampered in part by disputes among Roman Catholic printers over the letting of contracts, but mainly by lack of funds. The Protestant Bible societies had much more money to give out. Divisions that sapped the strength of the Manchester and Salford Catholic Association, moreover, reflected the basic tensions within the community between those, mainly clerical and "respectable" leadership, who wanted

[41] *Ibid.*, I (27 July 1844), 75.

[42] Where I write of "Manchester," I include Salford and the out-townships.

[43] The three following paragraphs are based on Gerard Patrick Connolly, "Catholicism in Manchester and Salford, 1770-1850: The Quest for 'Le Chrétien Quelconque,'" 3 vols. (Ph.D. thesis, University of Manchester, 1980), II, 10-66, 181-229. See also M.A.G. O Tuathaigh, "The Irish in Nineteenth-Century Britain: Problems of Integration," *Transactions of the Royal Historical Society*, 5th ser., XXXI (1981), 149-73.

[44] The total population of Lancashire in 1851 was 2,067,301, of which 191,506 were born in Ireland. But this underestimates the Irish population by not counting those Irish born in England. W. J. Lowe, "The Lancashire Irish and the Catholic Church, 1846-71: The Social Dimension," *Irish Historical Studies*, XX (1976-77), 141.

[45] Connolly, "Transubstantiation of Myth," pp. 95-99.

to focus activity on Roman Catholic claims, and those who also supported Irish and radical claims. These tensions continued into the 1830s.[46]

Organized Roman Catholic activity initially began to dwindle after 1829, but two developments in the next decade gave rise to growing concern on the part of Roman Catholic leadership. A new generation of ostensibly nondenominational but avowedly Protestant charitable organizations such as the Manchester and Salford Town Mission (led mainly by Evangelical Congregationalists), the Manchester and Salford District Provident Society, and the Manchester Domestic Mission Society (mainly Unitarian), appeared. Their concern to attend to the spiritual as well as to the material wants of the poor gave rise to fears of "souperism" and objections to the all-pervasive atmosphere of "institutional Protestantism." And explicitly anti-Catholic organizations such as the Protestant Reformation Society and the Manchester and Salford Protestant Operative Association appeared, having the sole function of opposing and harrassing Roman Catholics. The Tory-Anglican *Manchester Courier* added a powerful voice to the anti-Catholic movement.

Some parts of Lancashire (e.g., Liverpool, Wigan, Preston) had an indigenous Roman Catholic population that was not altogether swamped by the Irish migration, but Manchester did not. Irish, who made up about 85 percent of Manchester's Roman Catholics in the 1830s, grew in numbers during the 1840s and '50s, but declined thereafter.[47] Not all attended Mass, however. Although diocesan officials were more pessimistic about the extent of nonattendance than were the local clergy, it is clear that the practice of religion did not keep pace with the growth of the Roman Catholic population. Nonattendance in Manchester grew, from about 50 percent of baptized Roman Catholics in the 1780s, to somewhat over 80 percent in the 1820s. The Church gradually recovered some of the nonattenders; by the 1860s, nonattenders had declined to around 30 to 40 percent or more (which compares favorably with the 70 percent non-attendance rate that Lees finds for London).[48] Despite their nonpractice, poor Irish were willing to contribute to chapels that they did not attend regularly. Their religion offered them pride, identity, and self-worth, as well as the formal and informal social services of schools, clubs, friendly societies, and alms. And if they did not revere English priests in quite the same way that they had Irish priests (who often were personalities in their own right), they respected them as representatives of the institutional church.[49]

But in the 1830s and '40s, Manchester Roman Catholics became more self-confident, more open about the public practice of their religion, which included the new Italianate devotions. During those two decades, the

[46] Gerard P. Connolly, "The Catholic Church and the First Manchester and Salford Trade Unions in the Age of the Industrial Revolution," *Transactions of the Lancashire and Cheshire Antiquarian Society*, LXXXIII (1985), 125-60.

[47] In 1851, 52,504 of Manchester and Salford's 367,232 inhabitants had been born in Ireland; using a sophisticated method that relates Irish-born to English-born members of Irish families, Lowe estimates that the actual size of the Irish community varied from 79,408 (1851) to 104,329 (1861), to 76,841 (1871). W. J. Lowe, *The Irish in Mid-Victorian Lancashire: The Shaping of a Working-Class Community* (New York, 1989), p. 49.

[48] Connolly, "Transubstantiation of Myth," pp. 88-91; Lowe, "Lancashire Irish," pp. 144-46; Bossy, *English Catholic Community*, pp. 303-8, 424; Lees, *Exiles of Erin*, p. 82. These statistics, based on estimates, must be used with great caution.

[49] Lowe, "Lancashire Irish," pp. 142-43, 147-53; John M. Werly, "The Irish in Manchester, 1832-49," *Irish Historical Studies*, XVIII (1972-73), 350-51.

number of Roman Catholic chapels and schools grew sufficiently to accommodate the number of practicing Roman Catholics, which number
also grew, to about half of all the baptized by mid-century. This self-confidence of growing numbers may be seen in the career of Daniel Hearne,
priest of St. Patrick's chapel, Irish Town, 1842-46. Hearne organized public processions and raised money for a churchbell (both illegal under the
existing penal laws), and punished those of his parishioners who called St.
Patrick's by the servile label, "chapel." In the 1840s, Hearne became active
as a public speaker in the Manchester branch of the Loyal National Repeal Association and the Anti-Corn Law League. (His superiors forced
him to leave Manchester when his language grew increasingly violent, to
the point of provoking faction fights.)[50] By the late 1840s, entertainments
and open houses at Ramsbottom, Bury, and Stalybridge (the last including
a public procession) advertised the progress of Roman Catholicism, promoted communal pride, and "discover[ed] the disposition of others towards
us as a body."[51] The new St. Chad's Roman Catholic chapel, Red Bank,
infuriated Manchester Protestants by its "graven images."[52] St. Wilfred's
chapel, Christ's Church Square, Hulme, gave further offense by a
children's Sunday outing to Blackpool and by the activities of the Confraternity of the Blessed Virgin of Mount Carmel.[53] Placards and handbills
announced the opening of a Roman Catholic school, listed alleged errors
in the Authorized Version, and proclaimed "The Month of May—the
Month of Mary."[54] One could not stroll the pavements without seeing and
hearing evidence of religious militance.

> But a few sundays [sic] ago, in front of the Salford Town Hall, as ev-
> ening was drawing on, two or three Monks, supported by their Irish par-
> tizans, were doing battle subtly and cleaverly [sic] with a Town Missionary
> and two of [sic] three plain working men, on whom they were pressing
> rather hardly, when a gentleman, passing by and attracted by the scene,
> stepped in, took up the gauntlet, and fairly turned the tide of battle.[55]

The main arena of combat, however, was the platform, not the pavements or hoardings; and Manchester was blessed with several experts in
this sort of gladiatorial combat.

When St. John the Evangelist's chapel, Salford, announced a series of
lectures, the Rev. Hugh Stowell, master anti-Catholic orator and leader of
the Manchester and Salford Protestant Operative Association, countered
with his own lectures. The Protestant Operatives regularly sponsored such
lectures, and the Roman Catholics responded in kind: a course of lectures
at St. John's chapel on Marian devotion; a course at St. Patrick's Hall,
Charles Street, on "The Life and Times of Martin Luther," delivered by
William Francis Cleary.[56] Cleary is a shadowy figure. Obviously Irish,

[50] Connolly, "Transubstantiation of Myth," pp. 92-93; G. P. Connolly, "Little Brother Be at
Peace: The Priest as Holy Man in the Nineteenth-Century Ghetto," *Studies in Church History*, XIX
(1982), 192-93, 197-98, 202-5.
[51] *Manchester Illuminator*, I (12 Jan. 1850), 35, (13 April 1850), 142-43, (27 April 1850), 158, (4
May 1850), 166.
[52] *Protestant Witness*, I (19 May 1849), 147.
[53] *Ibid.* (11 Aug. 1849), 198; *Manchester Illuminator*, I (26 Jan. 1850), 51.
[54] *Protestant Witness*, I (4 Nov. 1848), 35, (19 May 1849), 143; *Bulwark*, II (May 1853), 293.
[55] *Protestant Witness*, I (2 Dec. 1848), 49.
[56] *Protestant Witness*, I (18 Nov. 1848), 47, (24 Mar. 1849), 117, (19 May 1849), 143; *Manchester
Illuminator*, I (15 Jan. 1850), 32.

perhaps Irish-born, trained as a schoolmaster, he entered the lists of religious controversy at Liverpool in the mid-1830s.[57] He moved to Manchester at some point in the early or middle 1840s, and soon emerged as the most visible lay defender of Roman Catholic claims, who gave the Protestant Operatives as good as he got. Believing that offense was the best defense, he played David to Stowell's Goliath.

The Rev. J. H. MacGuire of the Protestant Operatives was scheduled to lecture on "Papal Rome Addicted to the Worship of Saints" at the Hope Street School, Salford, on 7 February 1850. On the evening of the lecture, the Roman Catholics got to the school first, and MacGuire had to give up. The Protestant Operatives charged that the Roman Catholics tore down stove-pipes and gas fittings and broke up some forms; one man brought a poker from one of the side rooms into the hall.[58] Cleary denied the story of the poker, pleaded that the pulling down of the stove-pipes "was an unavoidable accident," and observed that if MacGuire had not wanted Roman Catholics to attend, he should have said so on the posters advertising the lectures.

> I remember very well, if Mr. Stowell and his friends do not, that when the friends of secular education called a meeting at the Town-hall, King street, that he and his friends went and upset that meeting. Now what was lawful for Mr. Stowell and his friends in Manchester, was equally lawful for those Catholics who thought proper to go to Hope-street school on the night in question.[59]

Cleary continued his role of gadfly, attending lectures and, when he could, debating speakers such as John Atkinson, Secretary of the Manchester and Salford Protestant Operative Association. He also followed Protestant Operative speakers to Stockport, where the Operatives were mounting a campaign against Mormonism, Roman Catholicism, and Infidelity.[60]

Simultaneously, Cleary was waging a special war against the anti-Catholic lecturer Samuel Condell. Sometimes Cleary spoke in response to an earlier lecture of Condell's, sometimes the two met in open debate.[61] At Openshaw, the landlord backed out of his agreement to rent a room to the debaters, fearing violence perhaps, and the debate was conducted in the open air. "Mr. Cleary addressed the vast assembly from some steps, and afterwards a discussion took place which lasted till eleven o'clock p.m. The public road was completely filled up: the proceedings were highly interesting, and the bigots were completely vanquished."[62]

Cleary sought to meet his opponents head on. He countered a favorite anti-Catholic argument—the degradation of Ireland under popery—by pointing to the degradation of England.

> Yes, the land is covered with Bibles and Parsons—with Churches and Glebe-houses,—and yet the Heathen world does not present such a picture to the human mind as does the moral aspect of this country. Bible societies—and the most atrocious murders; Missionary Societies—and in-

---

[57] William Francis Cleary, *A Letter on the Facility with which a Person, seriously disposed, may ascertain whether he be a member of the True Church or not* (Liverpool, 1836).
[58] *Protestant Witness*, II (9 Feb. 1850), 298-99.
[59] *Manchester Illuminator*, I (16 Feb. 1850), 76.
[60] *Protestant Witness*, II (15 June 1850), 372, (13 July 1850), 390, (21 Sept. 1850), 427-28.
[61] *Manchester Illuminator*, I (16 Mar. 1850), 107, (18 May 1850), 182-83, (15 June 1850), 215.
[62] *Ibid.* (23 Mar. 1850), 115.

fanticides; new Churches—and places of evil resort; the exercise of private judgment—and the withdrawal of youth from parental restraint, stand in juxtaposition, and advance side by side in the same ratio.[63]

No wonder that England—"this land of Bibles and crime"—had been the ruin of many a young Irish Roman Catholic.[64]

Cleary also engaged in controversial journalism. The Protestant Operatives had believed, in 1848, that anti-Catholicism was carrying the day, and that their organ, the *Protestant Witness*, had driven Roman Catholic tracts from the field.[65] So Cleary began the *Manchester Illuminator* to defend the community's interests. "We want a paper," he declared, "to represent our own wants and wishes, and to refute the combined attacks of Stowell and his clique; and we repeat that no journal or periodical could do this but a local one."[66] Besides reporting on meetings and confrontations, the periodical published articles defending points of doctrine such as the authority of the Church and of apostolic tradition, and arguing that submission to authority was compatible with examining the grounds of faith.[67] The periodical also replied directly to the Protestant Operatives, refuting Stowell's "Fourteen Reasons for being a Churchman" and attacking an essay that the Protestant Operative Association had awarded a prize.[68]

No quarter was given in the war between Cleary and the Protestant Operatives. Invective such as "bigots . . . the rottenness of the cause . . . miserable and wretched sophistry . . . the theological quack-doctor M'Neile" characterized the report of speeches by Hugh McNeile, the Liverpool anti-Catholic, and Stowell at the Manchester Free Trade Hall on 7 November 1849.[69] In its turn, the *Protestant Witness* denounced Cleary's "gross abuse and lying representations . . . his natural propensity to calumniate."[70]

These public battles had a certain impact on ordinary Mancunians. Protestant town missionaries in the Irish districts found that although most of their hearers simply listened politely to their message (and a few refused to listen at all), some were prepared to defend their faith.[71]

Cleary faded from the Manchester scene in the mid-1850s,[72] but while he was active, Manchester Roman Catholics had an able, active, and trenchant champion.

Roman Catholicism at Northampton was poor in both money and leadership, and small in numbers. Nevertheless, even there one can detect a rise in energy.

[63] *Ibid.* (22 Oct. 1849), 12.
[64] "Dedicatory Epistle," *ibid.*, iii.
[65] *Protestant Witness*, I (2 Dec. 1848), 49.
[66] "Address of the Editor . . . to the Catholic Body," *Manchester Illuminator*, I (1850), viii.
[67] *Ibid.* (15 Dec. 1849), 5-6, (5 Jan. 1850), 29-30, (26 Jan. 1850), 53-54.
[68] *Ibid.* (16 Feb. 1850), 79-80, (23 Feb. 1850), 84.
[69] *Ibid.* (15 Dec. 1849), 4.
[70] *Protestant Witness*, II (13 July 1850), 390.
[71] Bembridge Journal, 20, 30 Nov., 14 Dec. 1850, MCL, MS. 259.B1.
[72] The *Manchester Illuminator* apparently ceased publishing at some point in the early 1850s, and Cleary's last spoor is a tract on the doctrine of Purgatory, published at Manchester in 1854. The archives of the Roman Catholic Diocese of Salford, admittedly spotty for its early years, have nothing on Cleary, and neither the Rev. David Lannon, its archivist, nor Dr. Gerard Connolly, the leading authority on the Manchester Roman Catholic community, is familiar with his career.

There, as elsewhere, strange and fabulous stories about the behavior of Roman Catholics circulated. It was alleged, early in November of 1850, that two Roman Catholic priests asked the parish clerk of Rothwell for the keys of the church. When the clerk refused to hand them over, the priests, with proper melodramatics, said, "Then, if we cannot get them by fair means we will by foul,—we will get them by blood!"[73] Roman Catholic defenses of the faith focused on repelling stories such as that.

"Escaped nun" stories were popular at midcentury, and one from Nottingham drew fire from William Wareing, the Roman Catholic bishop in Northampton. Despite refutations, Wareing said, the fabrication would be reprinted, "because among a certain class, viz., the Cummings, the M'Neiles, the Hugh Stowells, and their admirers (of whom I am ashamed to say there are a certain few in this town), there is no calumny too gross, no aspersion too false, if only it be vented against Catholics."[74]

Closer to home, John Palmer Kilpin, chairman of the Northampton Board of Guardians and Conservative town councillor, reported the case of a poor servant girl who took a place with a Roman Catholic family, "was enduced" to convert to Roman Catholicism, and joined the "Associates of the Immaculate Conception" (a Marian sodality). But then she took a place in a Protestant household at Weedon, went mad because of her Roman Catholic beliefs, and ended in the Northampton workhouse. This provoked John Dalton, priest of St. Felix's chapel,[75] to repudiate Kilpin's charges. Dalton claimed that the girl had been a Roman Catholic for six years without going mad; rather, she had lost her senses because of persecution by the Protestant family at Weedon. (And, in any case, Kilpin had no business using his official position to interfere with religious matters in the workhouse.) This exchange prompted R. Cupell of Weedon, the girl's former employer, to deny either that Roman Catholicism had driven her mad or that he had persecuted her.[76]

These sorts of calumnies, as well as Hugh Stowell's visit to Northampton, prompted Dalton to become a champion of his faith. He lectured to counter Stowell's message, and he engaged in an extended controversy with the local notables E. S. Greville (Rector of Bonsall), W. D. Ryland (Anglican priest and prominent Tory), Richard Ash Hannaford, and Joseph Pywell (Dissenting minister). Dalton aggressively advanced the soundness of Marian devotion and the religious life, and denounced his opponents' reliance upon the tales of Maria Monk.[77] Dalton managed to retain his sense of humor throughout the no-popery storms. In 1857, he produced a parody, "A Proposed Plan for an Inquisition in England." Dalton proposed to "torture" scripture-readers and no-popery speakers by making them listen to Cardinal Wiseman lecture.[78]

---

[73] *Patriot*, 18 Nov. 1850.

[74] *Northampton Mercury*, 1, 3 Mar. 1851.

[75] Dalton (1814-1874) was Irish, but raised at Coventry; studied at Oscott; served missions at Northampton, Norwich, and Lynn to 1858; published translations of devotional works and biographies from the Spanish, Latin, and German (*DNB*, V, 435).

[76] *Northampton Mercury*, 15, 22 Feb., 1 Mar. 1851.

[77] The controversy can be found in *ibid.* from March through July. Also see the *Northampton Herald*, 22 Feb. 1851. For Ryland, see David Cresap Moore, *The Politics of Deference: A Study of the Mid-Nineteenth Century English Political System* (Hassocks, 1976), pp. 6-7.

[78] *Bulwark*, VI (Jan. 1857), 192-94.

The Irish population of Leeds grew rapidly between 1841 and 1861, almost tripling in size, and amounting to 10 percent of the township's population in 1851.[79] Chapel-building, however, was slow. The original chapel of 1786 was rebuilt as St. Anne's in 1838, and two new chapels, St. Patrick's (1831) and Mount St. Mary's (1857), were added. (The pace of building picked up after 1860, with nine chapels built between then and 1910.)[80] The growth of disputational vigor was faster. Outside lecturers and loyal priests defended Roman Catholicism against the attacks of W. F. Hook (the vicar), Nonconformists, and anti-Catholic lecturers, and correspondents replied to negative articles in the local press. The leading figures here were the Revs. Charles Pratt and George Keasley, the latter an articulate man used to asserting Roman Catholic claims. (Keasley, while pastor of St. Marie's chapel, Sheffield, in the early 1830s, was the first recipient of government aid in England for a Roman Catholic school.)[81]

The vigor also manifested itself in the form of attempting to create community institutions. A great fillip to the community's spirit was the gala opening of St. Anne's Roman Catholic school in January 1841. In addition to the local notables and priests, Daniel O'Connell and J. A. Roebuck (both in town for the Leeds Reform Association meeting) attended and spoke. Nine years later, the community established the Leeds Catholic Literary Institution, secured its own building, and invited Cardinal Wiseman to speak.[82]

Sometimes, defending the faith was rowdy business. The British Reformation Society held a rally on 24 July 1844 at the Music Hall, featuring the Revs. J. H. MacGuire of Manchester and John Cumming of the National Scottish Church, London. MacGuire waved a rosary in the air and denounced prayers to the Virgin Mary and the venality of priests. Cumming defended the wealth of the Church of Ireland, arguing that the Anglican bishops came by their wealth honestly, not by selling Masses or praying souls out of Purgatory. With such a spectacle on the platform, it is not surprising that there was great disorder on the floor. Irish Roman Catholics denounced MacGuire's and Cumming's more outrageous statements, and infidels and Chartists attempted to speak.[83]

Birmingham also shows the pattern of revitalization antedating Wiseman and stimulated by local leaders. Oscott College was near Birmingham, and several Oscott men were missioners in Birmingham and in the Black Country. Missions at Wolverhampton, Walsall, Bloxwich, West Bromwich, and Coventry grew during the period 1800-1840. Birmingham itself was not a major destination of Irish immigrants during the nineteenth century. It had about a thousand English and six thousand Irish Roman Catholics in 1834 (half of the Irish were nonattenders), served by two chapels and two charity schools, all antedating the 1820s. The Roman

---

[79] Where there were 5,027 Irish (5.7%) in a total population of 87,613 in 1841, ten years later there were 10,452 Irish (10.3%) in a total population of 101,051. By 1861 the Irish were 12.6% of Leeds's total 117,566 people, or 14,905. (T. Dillon, "The Irish in Leeds, 1851-1861," *Thoresby Miscellany*, LIV (1979), 3-5, 7-8.)

[80] Nigel Yates, "The Religious Life of Victorian Leeds," *A History of Modern Leeds*, ed. Derek Fraser (Manchester, 1980), p. 256.

[81] *Leeds Times*, 25 Jan., 7 Mar. 1840, 23 Apr. 1842; *Leeds Mercury*, 16 Nov. 1839, 23 Apr. 1842, 14, 21 Jan. 1843, 6, 13 July 1844, 13, 20, 27 June, 11 July 1846; Paz, *Politics of Working-Class Education*, pp. 27-28.

[82] *Leeds Times*, 22 Jan. 1841; *Leeds Mercury*, 27 Nov. 1852, 5 Feb., 4 June 1853.

[83] *Leeds Mercury*, 27 July 1844.

Catholic population had grown to about thirty thousand, half of whom were Irish, by 1851. A bookseller, Michael Maher (1798-1862), served the needs of this community.[84]

This small community ably defended itself against the local British Reformation Society in the period 1828-36. Thomas Michael McDonnell (1792-1869; priest of St. Peter's from 1824) built upon his parish's lay group, the Society of the Sacred Heart, to organize morale-boosting meetings at Birmingham, and travelled throughout the West Midlands (and further afield in Liverpool, Manchester, and York) to debate lecturers from the British Reformation Society. These activities prompted McDonnell to start a periodical, the *Catholic Magazine* (which he published from 1831 to 1836), and to play a role in wider Birmingham life. He was active in the Birmingham Political Union, formed a local branch of the Catholic Association, and spoke for the abolition of church rates. The organizing campaign of the Protestant Association, in 1835-36, drew McDonnell's fire. (The town missionary T. A. Finegan was somewhat more successful in his activities, largely because he made a point of not offending Roman Catholic sensibilities.) By the early 1840s, however, the local anti-Catholic society thought that the Roman Catholics had become less, not more, aggressive.[85]

One can find similar developments elsewhere. The Huddersfield Catholic Guild, a sick and burial friendly society active in the 1840s, combined self-help with apologetics in their annual procession with flags, banners, and music, in direct response to local Tory criticism of Roman Catholic funeral processions.[86] The Roman Catholic community at Shrewsbury showed renewed life in the 1820s, growing in numbers and building a new chapel in 1826. Further growth followed, as Irish navvies came to the area in the 1830s to cut turnpikes and in 1845 to cut the Great Western Railway. Although there were not many public disputations between Roman Catholics and others, the tone of the community was one of increasing self-confidence.[87]

It is clear that the more aggressive Roman Catholicism, which Newman later called the "second spring," manifested itself much earlier than the Oxford Conversions, and even much earlier than the arrival on the scene of Nicholas Wiseman. Moreover, the new assertive spirit sprang up in several localities, independent of central direction. Local leaders maintained their assertiveness in the face of both Protestant hostility and community poverty. Roman Catholic revival in the first half of the century was very

[84] Bossy, *English Catholic Community*, pp. 310, 317-20, 347, 349; Judith F. Champ, "The Demographic Impact of Irish Immigration on Birmingham Catholicism, 1800-1850," *Studies in Church History*, XXV (1989), 237-38; *The Letters and Diaries of John Henry Newman*, ed. Charles Stephen Dessain and Vincent Ferrer Blehl, London, 1963-64, XIII, 515.

[85] Wolffe, "Protestant Societies and Anti-Catholic Agitations," pp. 34-35, 37-39, 55-59, 113-14; Wolffe, *Protestant Crusade*, pp. 46-48, 52-55; Judith F. Champ, "Priesthood and Politics in the Nineteenth Century: The Turbulent Career of Thomas McDonnell," *Recusant History*, XVIII (1987), 289-303; Bossy, *English Catholic Community*, pp. 347, 352 n. 61; Finegan Journal, 10 July 1837, 20 Feb. 1838, Birmingham Reference Library, MS. 312749, pp. 3, 33-34; Birmingham Church of England Lay Association, *4th Annual Report* (1843), pp. 8-9.

[86] *Leeds Times*, 17 Oct. 1840.

[87] Peter Phillips, "A Catholic Community: Shrewsbury. Part I: 1750-1850," *Recusant History*, XX (1990), 251-58.

much a "grass-roots" movement, and active resistance to anti-Catholicism remained strong throughout the 1840s.[88]

Defending the Hierarchy on the Local Level

The storm of abuse stimulated by the creation of the Roman Catholic hierarchy in 1850, and by its unwise method of proclamation, thus fell upon a community by no means unprepared to defend itself.

Cardinal Wiseman himself produced what was accounted an able defense, the thirty-one-page pamphlet *An Appeal to the Good Feeling of the English People, on the Subject of the New Hierarchy*. Wiseman, who had arrived in England on 11 November 1850, finished the pamphlet by the 15th; it was published on the 19th, and appeared in the London papers the next day. It had sold thirty thousand copies by the 25th.[89] Well-argued and clearly written, it has gone down in Roman Catholic historiography as having done much to quell the popular uproar. Wiseman, never hesitant to proclaim his own virtues, thought that he alone had stilled the storm.

> Without any personal feelings on the subject, I believe that if I had not been sent back, there would have been serious difficulties in establishing the hierarchy. I have borne the entire brunt of the excitement; the other bishops have escaped almost unnoticed.[90]

Wiseman's most recent biographer joins with Edward Norman in endorsing this evaluation, as well as in agreeing that the *Appeal* did help to calm the uproar.[91] Derek Holmes, however, judges that the *Appeal* "played only a minor part in moderating the agitation."[92] Although it is true that Wiseman's pamphlet received more national notice than did any other Roman Catholic defense, it was not the only, or even the first, such defense.[93]

Sir George Bowyer, the leading Roman Catholic lawyer, wrote a letter to the *Times* on 16 October, before Wiseman had returned to England. Bowyer's arguments, that the hierarchy exercised no temporal power, that it had been created for reasons purely internal to the English Roman Catholic Church, and that the Roman Catholics had done no more than the Anglicans did with their bishops of Gibraltar and Jerusalem, were the germs of Wiseman's *Appeal*.[94] In order to counter the Protestant memorial drives, Lords Lovat,[95] Dormer,[96] and Vaux[97] presented a loyal address, bearing 255,766 signatures, to the Queen. The memorial declared that the

[88] This is against Wolffe, "Protestant Societies and Anti-Catholic Agitations," p. 298, who believes that resistance to no-popery "had languished somewhat" in the 1840s, until the Papal Aggression crisis revived it.

[89] Wilfrid Ward, *The Life and Times of Cardinal Wiseman*, 3rd ed., 2 vols. (London, 1898), I, 556-57; *Times*, 20 Nov. 1850.

[90] Schiefen, *Wiseman*, p. 197.

[91] *Ibid.*, pp. 190, 196-97; Norman, *English Catholic Church*, pp. 126-27.

[92] Holmes, *More Roman Than Rome*, p. 78.

[93] This is against Lowe, *Irish in Mid-Victorian Lancashire*, pp. 150-51, who claims that there were only a few attempts to defend the new hierarchy.

[94] Letter of "G. B.," *Times*, 19 Oct. 1850.

[95] Thomas Alexander Fraser, 1st Lord Lovat (1802-1875); successor to the 12th Lord Lovat, executed after the '45 (Boase, II, 501).

[96] Joseph Thaddeus Dormer, 11th Lord Dormer (1790-1871); officer in Austrian army; succ. to title in 1826 (Boase, V, 135).

[97] George Charles Mostyn, 6th Lord Vaux De Harrowden (1804-1883); educ. Oscott; Life Guards, 1825-28; abeyance of the title (from 1663) terminated in his favor in 1838 (Boase, VI, 739).

Roman Catholic hierarchy had strictly spiritual powers, and that there had been no intent to infringe upon the Royal Prerogative.[98] But defense on the local level shows the several strategies that Roman Catholics adopted.

At Birmingham, John Henry Newman recommended a firm response. "I hope you will not think me *violent*," he told William Bernard Ullathorne, the new Bishop of Birmingham,

> but my experience tells me that the more you show a bold face to the world, so cowardly is it, the more you gain. It does not appreciate concession. Also, following your Lordship's hint, I think it not a bad move to draw the world's attention on myself, who, not being in a place of authority, cannot suffer from it.[99]

Certainly the "Christ upon the Waters" sermon, which Newman preached at Ullathorne's enthronement on 27 October, was nothing if not firm.[100] A layman wanted to promote the registration of Roman Catholic electors by organizing a "Catholic committee" in every constituency, and to oppose M.P.s who had voted for the Ecclesiastical Titles Bill or the Religious Houses Bill.[101]

Ullathorne, however, pursued a more cautious course. His pastoral letter to the new Diocese of Birmingham (22 October) argued that the papal action was a transaction by Roman Catholics for Roman Catholics, that it applied only to spiritual matters, and that no temporal authority was to be exercised. He argued further that the Scottish Episcopal Church and the Wesleyan Methodist Connexion had their own territorial divisions, and that the Roman Catholics themselves had divided England into vicarates apostolic since 1688. Ullathorne repeated these arguments on the evening of his enthronement, the 27th, in what the press called an "eminently plain and practical" sermon. And the arguments were repeated yet again on 18 November, when the Roman Catholics of Birmingham met to address their fellow-townsmen.[102]

William Wareing, the Roman Catholic Bishop of Northampton, also pursued a mild but firm course. His pastoral letter, issued on 5 November, argued that Roman Catholics had the right to acknowledge the Pope's spiritual supremacy and not that of the Queen, that the authority exercised by Roman Catholic bishops in England depended purely upon the voluntary assent of believers, and that the titles had been selected so as not to violate the law and the government forewarned.[103] But as the furor continued, Wareing addressed an open letter to his fellow townsmen: "Although among my own flock, and according to canon law, I am called Bishop of Northampton, I possess no more power or authority over you now than I did before. . . . [A]s to the title itself, if that offends you, you may give me

[98] *Times*, 14 Feb. 1851; "Number of Addresses," *PP*, 1851, LIX (84), 738; "Copy of An Address presented to Her Majesty from Her Majesty's Roman Catholic Subjects in England," *PP*, 1851, LIX (236), 741.

[99] Newman to Ullathorne, 7 Nov. 1850, Archives of the Roman Catholic Archdiocese of Birmingham, B 2023.

[100] *Sup.*, Introduction.

[101] Draft memorandum in an unknown hand, July 1851, Archives of the Roman Catholic Archdiocese of Birmingham, St. Chad's Cathedral, B 2212.

[102] *Times*, 24, 29 Oct., 19 Nov. 1850; *Birmingham Mercury*, 2 Nov. 1850.

[103] *Northampton Mercury*, 16 Nov. 1850; *Times*, 12 Nov. 1850.

any appellation you please."[104] (Wareing's pastoral was noticed by the Wesleyans and at the great public meeting at Liverpool on 20 November.[105])

Mildness, however, did not necessarily signify passivity, as we have seen with respect to the activities of John Dalton, and of Wareing himself in repelling canards. One of the favorite anti-Catholic charges was that Cardinal Wiseman had taken an oath swearing to burn and persecute heretics. Some Northampton Roman Catholics put out a handbill showing that John Cumming, minister of the Scottish National chapel in London, a leading anti-Catholic who had leveled that charge with great fanfare against Wiseman, had himself signed his adherence to the Westminster Confession, which talked of the duty of suppressing and opposing heretics and schismatics.[106]

Elsewhere, Roman Catholics were also active in defending the hierarchy. The Roman Catholics of Manchester held a meeting on 12 November 1850 to refute the "foul and calumnious statements" of the Protestant Operative Association; about twelve or thirteen hundred people filled the Music Hall, Garratt Road. At the Runcorn public meeting, the Rev. J. Carr, Roman Catholic priest of that place, and E. Daley spoke against the anti-Catholic resolution; at Prescott, the priest Tiernan and the Hon. G. Stapleton spoke. At the Cumberland county meeting, P. H. Howard, M.P., and the priest Brown spoke. And at the Yorkshire county meeting, Charles Langdale made an especially bold and vigorous defense.[107] Sunderland had been visited by two noted anti-popery lecturers, W. W. Sleigh (a medical doctor) and Alessandro Gavazzi, in September and October 1851. The lectures, especially those of Gavazzi, were very well attended and drew much publicity. Philip Kearney, the priest of St. Mary's chapel, Bridge Street, gave his own series of lectures, and a layman, Charles Larkin of Newcastle, lectured at the Athenæum, to contradict Sleigh's and Gavazzi's lectures from the place where they had been given.[108] In London, two well-to-do Irishmen, Patrick Burke Ryan and John Eugene O'Cavanaugh, published the *Catholic Vindicator* in 1851 and 1852. A penny weekly that aimed at London's Irish community, it carried trenchant attacks on Protestant evangelists.[109]

The experience of defending the hierarchy against Protestant attacks in 1850-51 led Roman Catholics to be less willing to tolerate anti-Catholic demonstrations in later years. Despite their treatment at the hands of the Russell Ministry, Roman Catholics turned to the state to demand that the demonstrations be put down. Processions, demonstrations, Guy Fawkes exhibitions, and the putting on of a mock Mass all produced complaints to the Home Office.[110] The complainants pled the danger to public order

[104] *Northampton Mercury*, 30 Nov. 1850.

[105] *Wesleyan Times*, 18 Nov. 1850; *Times*, 21 Nov. 1850.

[106] "The Popery of Protestantism and the Popery of Rome," handbill, Archives of the Roman Catholic Diocese of Northampton, F 1.6.

[107] *Manchester Guardian*, 13 Nov. 1850; *Manchester Courier*, 23 Nov., 7 Dec. 1850; *Times*, 20 Dec. 1850; *Leeds Mercury*, 23 Nov. 1850.

[108] *Sunderland Herald*, 27 Sept., 10, 24 Oct. 1851.

[109] Holland, "British Catholic Press," pp. 101-102.

[110] Thomas Hogan to the Home Office, 6 Nov. 1851, Home Office: Daily Registers: Domestic, PRO, H.O. 46/3, no. 12,228; William Doyle to Spencer Walpole, 30 July 1852, Home Office: Registered Papers, PRO, H.O. 45/4195.

and the encouragement to infidelity that these demonstrations posed, and they demanded their rights as Englishmen.

> Surely, Sir, a continuance of such blasphemous scenes should not be permitted, in a country that prides itself in the pure knowledge of the same Gospel, which St. Peter was commissioned to preach, by Him, who was born of the Blessed Virgin. But, no authority has yet interfered to put a stop to these malicious scandals which during the last twelve months have shocked the feelings of Catholics; &, as her Majesty's Government cannot be ignorant of them, it must be with its consent these things are done.[111]

Both Sir George Grey and Spencer Walpole took these complaints seriously enough to order the police to investigate and to draft replies themselves.[112]

Other Roman Catholics used their official positions to protect their community. The Rev. John Armstrong, travelling lecturer for the Society for English Church Missions to the Roman Catholics, had been scheduled to speak at Walsall on 27 October 1853, but John Whitgreave, a local magistrate (and Roman Catholic), took unsworn testimony from a Roman Catholic priest that a breach of the peace was likely to ensue. Whitgreave and the other J.P.s suggested that the chances of a breach of the peace would be lessened were the lecture to be delivered in the church rather than in the schoolroom, but Armstrong refused to change the place of venue and was forced to give it up. Although Armstrong complained to the Home Office, the decision of the J.P.s was upheld.[113]

Cardinal Wiseman liked to go out of his way to assert Roman Catholic claims, as in 1857 when he quarreled with the *Times* over the Indian Mutiny and Italian unification, claiming that the East India Company discriminated against Roman Catholics. In the same year, when the government proclaimed a general fast for the Indian Mutiny, Wiseman drew criticism for picking a different day for the Roman Catholics to keep the fast.[114] Other bishops also were assertive. Ten years later, the Diocese of Northampton printed up, or obtained from elsewhere and distributed, handbills exposing the misrepresentations of the no-popery lecturer William Murphy, and defending the loyalty and integrity of priests.[115] After Wiseman's death in 1865, Henry Edward Manning, his successor as Archbishop of Westminster, promoted the most triumphalist ultramontanism within his Church. As a public figure, however, he was primarily concerned with temperance and the physical well-being of workers. His major interventions in political life were his condemnation of the Fenians, his support for Home Rule, and his opposition to the seating of the atheist Charles Bradlaugh in the House of Commons. None of these issues was a purely "Protestant versus Catholic" matter, and hence Manning did not spark as much public dislike as had his predecessor.[116]

Of course, not every Roman Catholic defense was telling. John Briggs, the Roman Catholic Bishop of Beverley, produced a turgid pastoral that

[111] Rev. Daniel O'Keefe to Sir George Grey, 8 Dec. 1851, PRO, H.O. 45/3783.

[112] See docketing on *ibid.*, and on Doyle to Walpole, 30 July 1852, PRO, H.O. 45/4195.

[113] PRO, H.O. 45/5128, pp. 580-615.

[114] Timothy J. O'Keefe, "*The Times* and the Roman Catholics: 1857," *Journal of Church and State*, XVIII (1976), 255-71; Janet, "Decline of General Fasts," p. 229.

[115] See five anti-Murphy handbills in the Archives of the Diocese of Northampton, F 1.6.

[116] Holmes, *More Roman Than Rome*, pp. 157-60, 168-69, 176-87.

quelled anti-Catholic attacks only to the extent that it put its hearers to sleep.[117] But Schiefen's belief, which has its origins in Wiseman's *amour-propre*, that most of the bishops "were not well suited for the demanding tasks ahead of them,"[118] certainly does not apply either to Bernard Ullathorne or to William Wareing.

Unfortunately, the spirit of ultramontanism combined with resentment at the often vile nature of anti-Catholic calumnies to harden Roman Catholic attitudes when liberality might have been more effective. Thomas Chisholm Anstey tried to mobilize English Roman Catholic opinion in support of the Madiai's release in 1852-53, but he found that most of his coreligionists were indifferent or hostile to the cause, largely because of the uses to which Evangelical anti-Catholics put it.[119] Later in the decade, English Roman Catholics declined to protest the obvious injustice of the Mortara Affair, again because their anti-Catholic enemies used it for propaganda. Anti-Catholic calumnies drove English Roman Catholics to ignore, and even to defend, injustices committed by Roman Catholics elsewhere during the nineteenth century, just as anti-semitism sometimes affected Jewish responses to the Israeli treatment of Palestinians during the twentieth century.

The Protestant Response

The "second spring," the revival, in ultramontane form, of aggressive Roman Catholic life, angered and even frightened Protestants. "We give them civil and religious liberty *usque ad nauseam*," complained Francis Close, "the Protestant Pope of Cheltenham," "and yet they go on bit by bit, . . . beautiful cathedrals spring up, and the pomps and ceremonies of Popery, with its priests and bishops prevail, until at length comes a scarlet cardinal to take possession of the land. This is Romish gratitude."[120] In short, Protestants complained again and again that Roman Catholics repaid the gift of freedom by exercising it.

It used to be thought, Protestant leaders lamented, that popery had received its death-wound at the Reformation. But alas! the Roman Catholic Church in Great Britain was growing, becoming active, and winning converts. One-third of the population of the United Kingdom, or maybe of England, was Romanist, it was thought; Puseyism was spreading in the universities; and governments of the day were doing nothing to promote Protestantism.[121] Newspapers gave prominence to the opening of new chapels across the land.[122] Romanism in France was growing, too; and if France invaded, as some people feared, in the early 1850s, "it will be like the old Spanish Armada, . . . it will come for the express purpose of extinguishing the Protestant liberties of Britain."[123] And local observers in Lancashire, the West Riding, the Midlands, and elsewhere professed to see

---

[117] *Leeds Mercury*, 23 Nov. 1850.

[118] Schiefen, *Wiseman*, p. 196.

[119] Lohrli, "Madiai," pp. 39-40.

[120] *Cheltenham Free Press*, 16 Nov. 1850; cf. *Protestant Magazine*, XII (Mar. 1850), 40.

[121] Rev. J. M. Cramp, "Special Duties of Protestants in These Times," *Baptist Magazine*, XXXVI (Sept. 1844), 450-52; *British Protestant*, II (1845), 57, 219; *ibid.*, IV (1848), 161-63; *Evangelical Christendom*, I (Aug. 1847), 256; *Preston Pilot*, 7 Dec. 1850; Norman, *Anti-Catholicism*, p. 17.

[122] *Illustrated London News*, 1 July 1843, 31 Aug., 7 Sept. 1844.

[123] *Manchester Courier*, 19 Oct. 1850; *Bulwark*, II (Mar. 1853), 239-40. For this fear, see Emil Daniels, "Die Engländer und die Gefahr einer französischen Landung zur Zeit Louis Philipps und

Popery on the march in their neighborhoods.[124] "The Roman Catholic religion would appear to be making rapid strides in Yorkshire, and proportionately bold appears to be the language held by its dignitaries; and as it is desirable that the public should be aware what expectations are indulged in, we here reprint an account of the proceedings at the opening of a new Roman Catholic church in York. . . ."[125]

Some observers tried to inject a certain reality into the religious question by arguing that the growth of Roman Catholicism had been magnified by both its opponents and advocates. One observer noted that the growth in the number of Roman Catholic chapels between 1826 and 1846—32 percent—simply reflected the same rate of growth in the population between 1821 and 1841.[126] Another pointed to "the progress of evangelical truth" in Ireland, France, and Germany.[127] Yet another welcomed the Roman Revolution of 1848-49 as a sign that Roman Catholicism was changing.[128] "Exertion is required" to defeat popery, "but there is no room for despair."[129]

Militant Roman Catholicism, by midcentury, had shaken English Protestants from their complacency. Quiet recusancy was over, as William Francis Cleary proclaimed.

> We have at length succeeded in arousing our opponents from their apathy and they now begin, but in a very sorry manner, to defend themselves. They have had their own way for a long time, and as we remained quiet, they naturally concluded that things would remain in statu quo to the very end. . . . [T]hey did not suppose that a time could ever arrive in which they themselves would be put on their own defence. But that time has now arrived, and the poor men find themselves placed in an awful "fix."[130]

Napoleons III," *Delbrück-festschrift: Gesammelte Aufsätze, Professor Hans Delbrück zu seinem sechzigsten Geburtstage* (Berlin, 1908), pp. 257-91.
[124] *British Protestant*, II (Dec. 1846), 286-89; *ibid.*, III (May 1847), 73-74; *Protestant Watchman*, No. 12 (Feb. 1850), p. 139.
[125] *Manchester Courier*, 14 Sept. 1850.
[126] *Baptist Magazine*, XXXVIII (Mar. 1846), 142-47.
[127] *British Protestant*, I (Oct. 1845), 221.
[128] *Baptist Magazine*, XLI (Aug. 1849), 482.
[129] *Ibid.*, XXXVIII (Mar. 1846), 144.
[130] *Manchester Illuminator*, I (5 Jan. 1850), 31.

IV

DEFENSIVE ANGLICANISM

> The floodgates on me open wide
> And headlong rushes in the turbulent tide
> Of lusts and heresies; a motly troop they come;
> And old imperial Rome
> Looks up, and lifts again half-dead
> Her seven-domed head,
> And Schism and Superstition, near and far,
> Blend in one pestilent star,
> And shake their horrid locks against the Saints to
> war.[1]

THE CHURCH OF England during the nineteenth century was in revival, recovering from its long Georgian decline, but its self-confidence had suffered an almost mortal wound. In 1740, the Church commanded a practical monopoly on the allegiance of the English people; by 1830, it held the allegiance of perhaps a bare majority. The trend was reversed in the 1830s and '40s: the Church increased its numbers of clergymen, of churches and chapels, and of Easter communicants; it reduced the percentage of its clergy who were nonresident; it initiated a more equitable distribution of ecclesiastical income. The practical work of Sir Robert Peel's Ecclesiastical Commission and the pragmatic statesmanship of Archbishop William Howley and Bishops Charles James Blomfield of London and Samuel Wilberforce of Oxford certainly promoted the needed reform of institutional abuses that was a prerequisite for revival.[2]

Yet, despite its measurable success in coping with its problems, the Church had an embattled mentality, largely because it really was threatened from all sides. Whiggish latitudinarianism threatened to turn the Church into a mere department of state. Working-class indifference and radical infidelity challenged its numerical base of support. Militant Nonconformity and triumphalist Roman Catholicism were potent rivals: The one wished to reduce the Church to being just another denomination; the other wished to replace it as the state church. As a way of responding to these outside threats, Evangelicals within the Church of England transformed themselves into a new, harder type. These new Evangelicals organized themselves for many purposes during the nineteenth century, but the defense against Romanism was one of the main foci for their energies.

---

[1] John Keble, "The Angel of the Church," from *Lyra Apostolica*, quoted by Chadwick, *Victorian Church*, p. 168.

[2] *Ibid.*, pp. 136-37; Gilbert, *Religion and Society*, pp. 27-29, 128-32; Desmond Bowen, *The Idea of the Victorian Church: A Study of the Church of England, 1833-1889* (Montreal, 1968), pp. 18 ff.

Anglican Anti-Catholic Organizations

The two major anti-Catholic organizations that attempted to mobilize mass opposition to the Roman Catholic Church were the British Reformation Society (sometimes called the Protestant Reformation Society), founded in 1827, and the Protestant Association, founded in 1835. (The National Club, founded in 1845, although important for its behind-the-scenes lobbying and for the high social status of its membership, did not attempt to build a base of mass support.) People were always getting the two confused.[3] They differed somewhat in their methods of operation, but shared an anti-Catholic ideology. Their opposition to the Roman Catholic Church was based on theological and constitutional grounds.

The Anglican anti-Catholics were Evangelicals: but they were extreme Evangelicals who reflected the more thoroughgoing Evangelicalism of the 1820s and '30s. Evangelicalism had grown inside the Church of England during the first half of the nineteenth century (Evangelical clergymen grew in number from about one-twentieth of the total in 1800 to a quarter or a third in 1850), but in the process, the movement changed as its understanding of the key doctrines of justification and of the new birth changed. The Clapham Sect, which stood for order, moderation, and loyalty to Anglican formularies, was giving way in leadership to a newer, more aggressive Evangelicalism, the doctrinal interpretations of which ultimately emanated from the postwar Evangelical revivals in Scotland and Geneva. It was the latter group that gave its support to organized anti-Catholicism: Only 17 percent of those clergymen closely connected with the moderate Evangelical Charles Simeon's Trust subscribed to the British Reformation Society, and only 8 percent subscribed to the Protestant Association.[4]

Anglican anti-Catholics believed in justification without the deeds of the law, freely, fully, and once for all, through the blood and atonement of the Redeemer.[5] As a consequence, they found themselves directly in theological conflict with Roman Catholicism, for that Church taught that the individual believer was justified in part by his own works, by the merit of the saints, and by grace supplied through the sacraments. In this connection, they rejected, unequivocally and decisively, the doctrine of baptismal regeneration. That doctrine was to them "the foundation error"; if accepted, it led to belief in a sacramental theology, to the exaltation of the priesthood, and ultimately to the corruption of popery.[6] Although the Claphamite moderates agreed with the hard Evangelicals about justification by grace as opposed to sacramental grace, they were conscious of being surrounded by those who would push the Church towards Dissent, or antinomianism, or towards the Wesleyan doctrines of assurance and perfection that substituted "a presumptuous, over-wrought imagination" for

---

[3] *Christian Observer*, XLII (1842), 144.

[4] Donald M. Lewis, *Lighten Their Darkness: The Evangelical Mission to Working-Class London, 1828-1860* (Westport, Conn., 1986), pp. 5, 11-12, 15; Bebbington, *Evangelicalism*, pp. 2-3, 75-77; Stunt, "Geneva and British Evangelicals," pp. 35-46; Gilbert, *Religion and Society*, p. 53; Wesley Balda, "Simeon's 'Protestant Papists': A Sampling of Moderate Evangelicalism Within the Church of England, 1839-1865," *Fides et Historia*, XVI (1983), 59-60.

[5] *Protestant Witness*, I (21 Oct. 1848), 25.

[6] *British Protestant*, VI (Oct. 1850), 188-90.

"a true and living faith."[7] So they could not quite follow the hard Evangelicals on baptismal regeneration.

The question of baptismal regeneration was perhaps the biggest theological question of the early and middle nineteenth century, and had always been difficult for Anglican Evangelicals to confront. Most moderates had arrived at the notion that the Prayer Book statements about regeneration did not mean what they said, but rather were proleptic (that is, they expressed the pious hope that the child would some day be born again, and represented that future development as if it had already been accomplished). These mental gymnastics were good enough for the moderates, but the hard Evangelicals followed their theology to its logical conclusion.[8]

Their rejection of baptismal regeneration led them to question the authority and truthfulness of the traditional Anglican formularies. The Tractarian Movement, in the 1830s and '40s, was in the process of uncovering the Catholic content of those formularies. Such a process cut the ground out from under the Evangelicals; they replied by denouncing the Tractarians for not believing the "natural sense" of the much more Calvinist Articles of Religion.[9] Yet they themselves were prepared to jettison the formularies, when presented with their "natural sense."

> If we are told that in our Articles baptism means new birth, we reply, in the face of Articles, do our Articles mean all that is in the Bible? That in our Homilies baptism means new birth; do our Homilies mean all that is in the Bible? That baptism in the Prayer-Book and Catechism means regeneration; do they mean all that is in the Bible? We reject every other standard of appeal.[10]

In contrast, the moderates bowed to the formularies, even when they included obnoxious matter such as lessons from the Apocrypha, or even when they included material authorized only by royal decree such as the services for Gunpowder Plot, St. Charles the Martyr, and the Restoration.[11]

Fundamental to the Anglican Evangelical anti-Catholic theology was the need for a conversion experience, for "natural and unconverted man" prefers a religion that allows one to live in the world. Unconverted Protestants attend the forms and ceremonies of the Church, but fail to find "inward peace and satisfaction" there. So, they are "allured" by Tractarians, who stress the importance of apostolic succession, antiquity, tradition, ceremonies, and sacraments. But when they find that the Roman Catholic Church is "pre-eminent in all these excellencies," they apostatize.[12] And this is disastrous to their spiritual health, for popery is soul-blasting error, the Scarlet Lady, the Antichrist. Most moderate Anglican Evangelicals and the more moderate of the Congregationalists did not look for a sudden or specific conversion experience, as the Baptists and Methodists did, but rather expected a gradual change in life. But the more aggressive, Scottish-

---

[7] *Christian Observer*, XLII (1842), 144-47, 290, XLIII (1843), 213-15, XLIV (1844), 12-18 (p. 15 quoted).
[8] Bebbington, *Evangelicalism*, pp. 9-10; Davies, *Watts and Wesley*, pp. 226-27.
[9] *Protestant Magazine*, XII (Sept. 1850), 131.
[10] *Ibid.*, p. 144.
[11] *Christian Observer*, XLIII (1843), 730-31, XLIV (1844), 409, 716-17.
[12] *British Protestant*, II (Oct. 1846), 229-30.

and Geneva-flavored Evangelicals emphasized the role of personal assent in conversion, thereby moving away from the moderate Claphamites.[13]

The Anglican Evangelicals were also anti-Catholic on constitutional grounds. They believed that Protestantism had been the basis of the British Constitution since the reign of King Edward VI, and that the Glorious Revolution had reaffirmed that basis. They also believed that supremacy had to exist somewhere in any human society. ("Take a family, a fleet, an army, an empire, or a Church—there must be somewhere a head, a supreme, an authoritative power, whose decisions others are tacitly or expressly bound respectively to obey.") If If everyone gave orders and claimed to be leaders, then anarchy and chaos would result. In England, the Constitution vested supremacy in all matters of church and state in the Queen under God. But popery did not recognize the supremacy that the English constitution had allocated, "and so it is subversive of order and of English institutions."[14] Roman Catholics, therefore, were an alien body within England. Their loyalty was to the Pope, not the Queen. And the Pope was the puppet of the Austrian emperor, who had the power to veto the choice of the Conclave of Cardinals.[15]

Theological and constitutional concerns came together in Ireland. In the course of chiding British Protestants for their inadequate support of Irish evangelistic missions, the British Reformation Society described "the deadly errors of Romanism"—the confessional, Mariolatry, Purgatory, sacraments—as reasons for heightened exertions. But: "When Christian motives fail, sometimes other arguments are more efficacious." Increased Irish representation in Parliament (most of which would be Papist) was necessary to preserve the Union. But if Ireland remained Roman Catholic, several dire political consequences would follow: The Irish Church establishment would go; the island itself would become ungovernable by a Protestant Parliament; and the English Church establishment would be endangered.[16]

Theological and constitutional concerns also met in England. The Roman Catholic Church, because it had never given up its "Hildebrandine" pretensions to supremacy over the civil power, and because it claimed jurisdiction over all baptized souls, was a threat to freedom. And the threat was the greater because the Roman Catholic Church was concentrating its best efforts and most able men in England, hoping for conversions.[17]

The connection between Church and State, then, was of great concern. Martin Marty believes that the Anglican Evangelicals "were going about their business without much reference to the debate over legal privilege" during the 1850s, and that the "center" for support of the connection was the Broad Church.[18] But that view is erroneous. Precisely because the Tractarians were suspicious of Erastianism, especially in their "radical and

---

[13] *Ibid.* (Sept. 1846), p. 222; Lewis, *Lighten Their Darkness*, pp. 15-17, 29-31; Bebbington, *Evangelicalism*, pp. 6-9; Houghton, *Victorian Frame of Mind*, pp. 63-64; Jay, *Religion of the Heart*, pp. 54-65.

[14] *Protestant Magazine*, XII (Apr. 1850), 56-57.

[15] *Protestant Witness*, I (2 Dec. 1848), 52; *British Protestant*, II (July 1846), 162.

[16] *British Protestant*, II (Aug. 1846), 195-97.

[17] *Ibid.*, I (Feb. 1845), 26; *ibid.*, II (Jan. 1846), 24.

[18] Martin E. Marty, "Living with Establishment and Disestablishment in Nineteenth-Century Anglo-America," *Journal of Church and State*, XVIII (1976), 66.

populist phase" from 1833 to 1836 or 1841,[19] both the hard and the moderate Evangelicals valued the connection as a preservative against popery within the Church. They supported the unregulated private patronage of livings in the name of lay rights and as a weapon against Anglo-Catholicism. They opposed the revival of Convocation because they feared that such a voice independent of the state would be insufficiently Protestant. During the 1850s, they hoped for liturgical revision by a Protestant Parliament to remove from the Prayer Book passages supporting baptismal regeneration, sacramentalism, and sacerdotalism. They formed the strongest opposition to Irish Church disestablishment in the 1860s.[20] The matter was simple for them. The Tractarians wanted to change the Church of England. The state connection prevented such change. So, legal establishment was a Protestant bulwark.[21] This point will be of especial importance when we come to examine the fate of cooperative ecumenical endeavors between Anglican Evangelicals and Nonconformists.

Finally, an element of millenarianism stimulated anti-Catholic activity.[22] The French Revolution had stimulated many Evangelicals to think systematically about the second coming of Jesus, and to ponder the pages of Daniel, Ezekiel, and Revelations. But they came up with all sorts of interpretations. Postmillennialism, the dominant interpretation during the eighteenth century, had the Gospel gradually spreading throughout the world to create a happy Millennium, at the end of which Jesus would descend from Heaven, either in person or figuratively, to wind things up. The French Revolution changed all this. The fall of kingdoms and general commotion described in the apocalyptic literature seemed to be coming to pass in the exploits of Napoleon Bonaparte, and a new interpretation, premillennialism, was invented. Premillennialists had a less pleasant view of what was in store for the world than had the postmillennialists. They denied that the Gospel would save the world, but expected that it would become increasingly wicked, and believed that human history was foretold and knowable. They believed that Jesus would return before, rather than after, the Millennium, although they disagreed as to whether his return would be only spiritual or actually a literal descent from the clouds.

The premillennialists also disagreed as to whether the unpleasant events described in the more hallucinatory parts of Scriptures referred mostly to past and contemporary history (the "Historicists") or mostly to the future, during a time of troubles called the "Tribulation" (the "Futurists"). The Futurists disagreed among themselves as to whether the "Rapture" (when the saved would be whisked away to heaven) would happen before or after the Tribulation. It is not surprising that the strictest Evangelical Nonconformists, too strict to read novels, found in millenarianism "imaginative

[19] Walter H. Conser, Jr., "A Conservative Critique of Church and State: The Case of the Tractarians and Neo-Lutherans," *ibid.*, XXV (1983), 326-31; John R. Griffin, "The Radical Phase of the Oxford Movement," *JEH*, XXVII (1976), 47-56.

[20] M.J.D. Roberts, "Private Patronage and the Church of England, 1800-1900," *JEH*, XXXII (1981), 211; Peter J. Jagger, *Clouded Witness: Initiation in the Church of England in the Mid-Victorian Period, 1850-1875* (Allison Park, Penna., 1982), pp. 7-54, 175-91; P. J. Welsh, "The Revival of an Active Convocation of Canterbury (1852-1855)," *JEH*, X (1959), 189-91; Machin, *Politics and the Churches*, pp. 367-70; *Times*, 18 Aug. 1868.

[21] *British Protestant*, I (Jan. 1845), 4; Lewis, *Lighten Their Darkness*, p. 270.

[22] *Ibid.*, pp. 100-103; Bebbington, *Evangelicalism*, pp. 14, 78-91; Ernest R. Sandeen, *The Roots of Fundamentalism: British and American Millenarianism, 1800-1930* (Chicago, 1970), pp. 3-41, 81-90; D. N. Hempton, "Evangelicalism and Eschatology," *JEH*, XXXI (1980), 179-94.

surrogates for novels." For them, the world was a cosmic arena of struggle between Christ and Antichrist—far more exciting than anything to be got from fiction.[23]

Furthermore, Providentialism provided a link between ideas about the Millennium and ideas about the Constitution. Britain's economic growth and political power after 1815 seemed to show that it was God's chosen country, God's instrument for gathering the nations in the last days. Alternatively, Evangelicals explained disasters such as the Potato Famine and the Crimean War as God's punishment for the toleration of popery and the alliance with popish France. Such views also exalted the importance of the Evangelicals themselves. As Britons, they were doing God's will by extending British power in the secular world. As Evangelicals, they were the ones who could discern the future, they would be saved, and they would rule with Christ over the world to come. Indeed, Mrs. Mary Martha Sherwood, a best-selling popularizer of such ideas, depicted the Millennium as a time when the saved would be the master race over the unregenerate, who would serve them as a subordinate race of slaves.[24]

The role of the Jews was connected with the Millennium. Some Futurists expected the restoration of the Jews to Palestine to mark the Second Coming. A subset of these, most notably the anti-Catholic writer Charlotte Elizabeth Tonna[25] and the Jewish-to-Roman-Catholic-to-Anglican convert Joseph Wolff,[26] believed that Jews should be converted, but should maintain a separate identity within Christendom by retaining circumcision and the dietary laws, and that the restoration of the Jews and the overthrow of the Papacy would together usher in the Millennium.[27]

Changes in ideas about the inspiration of the Christian holy books clearly influenced the changing ideas about the Millennium. The traditional, late eighteenth-century view of inspiration was that there were different levels of inspiration, and that while God had dictated the general sense of the Scriptures, and especially of the more explicitly religious passages, the human writers had supplied the actual forms of expression. This view was challenged by Robert Haldane, an influential Scottish Evangelical, by the Futurists, and by the *Record*, the leading Anglican hard Evangelical newspaper. They favored inerrancy, verbal inspiration, and literal interpretation. Moderate Evangelicals, both Anglican and Nonconformist, were very unhappy about the literal interpretation of apocalyptic passages and about the entire notion of "Christian Jews" (the *Christian Observer*, organ of the Claphamite moderates, sharply criticized Charlotte Elizabeth

---

[23] Cunningham, *Everywhere Spoken Against*, pp. 54-55.

[24] Jay, *Religion of the Heart*, pp. 88-91; Janet, "Decline of General Fasts," pp. 90-91, 228-29.

[25] For Tonna's views on fiction, see *sup.*, pp. 56-57. For the ways in which her career illustrates the gendered nature of anti-Catholicism, see *inf.*, pp. 271-73.

[26] Wolff (1795-1862), the son of a German rabbi, converted to Roman Catholicism in 1812, studied Oriental languages, church history, and theology at Tübingen and Rome, where he met Henry Drummond, and became an Anglican and studied at Cambridge with Charles Simeon. He wandered as a lay missionary, 1821-37, with many adventures, through Anatolia, the Levant, Abyssinia, Arabia, Central Asia, and India. He took orders (American diaconate, Irish priesthood) and held English livings, 1843-62. (*DNB*, XXI, 777-78.)

[27] Jay, *Religion of the Heart*, pp. 94-96. Cf. N. I. Matar, "The Controversy over the Restoration of the Jews: From 1754 until the London Society for Promoting Christianity Among the Jews," *Durham University Journal*, LXXXII (1990), 29-44.

on the latter point), but literal interpretation, at least, began to make headway in the 1830s and '40s.[28]

Anglican Evangelicals, in common with Protestants from the beginnings of that movement, discerned the Pope in the apocalpytical Scriptures; the anti-Catholic Anglicans went further, and believed that the last days were upon them.[29] Without either predicting the immediate Second Coming or entering into the debates about Historicism, Futurism, or the timing of the Rapture, they did believe that the battle between Christ and the Man of Sin was approaching a climax. "[W]hoever may be elected Pope, and however successful may be the efforts of his emissaries in this country, the system itself is doomed. Its destruction is fixed—its sentence is inscribed upon its forehead—it will be consumed by the spirit of the Lord's mouth, and by the brightness of His coming."[30] John Cumming, who although a Presbyterian had close ties with hard Evangelical Anglicans, went further, arguing that the last vial of the Apocalypse would be opened between 1848 and 1867, and seeing in the Crimean War the start of Armageddon.[31]

These millenarian and apocalyptic views were attractive to the general middlebrow public, although the fine theological distinctions no doubt escaped them. Such views burst into the middle-class mind with the exhibiting of John Martin's painting, *Belshazzar's Feast*, in 1820. The work vividly appealed to popular fears of the end of the world; while unknowing revellers continue in their pleasures, Belshazzar and his courtiers, horrified, become aware of God's finger writing their sentence of doom. Martin's work drew large crowds and laudatory reviews when it was exhibited, and in the forms of copies and engravings it continued its popularity for the next half century.[32] By the mid-1850s, Apocalypticism was a not unexpected topic of conversation at vicars' "parish bees": Although the character Katharine Ashton, in the novel of the same name, had forgot the details of the French Revolution, another girl "knew a great deal about it, and talked very learnedly, and gave it as her opinion that the French Revolution was clearly marked out in the Book of Revelations; an observation which [the vicar] allowed to drop without notice."[33] In the same year that Sewell published *Katharine Ashton*, Holman Hunt exhibited *The Light of the World*, which became one of the most popular religious paintings in the English-speaking world. Clothes and eyes glistering, Christ knocks on the door of the human heart. Will he be let in? or will he be turned away, leaving hopeless damnation for those who reject him? Such were the responses that this painting sparked in the minds of its viewers for the next fifty years.[34] Evangelical apocalypticism, albeit in simplified form, thus was a bedrock belief of the Victorian middle classes, one that anti-Catholic societies could appeal to and expect recognition.

If the British Reformation Society and the Protestant Association were as one in their theology, their practice differed. The British Reformation

[28] Sellers, *Nonconformity*, p. 2; *Christian Observer*, XLIII (1843), 801-3, XLIV (1844), 18-20, 34-35.

[29] Paul Misner, "Newman and the Tradition concerning the Papal Antichrist," *CH*, XLII (1973), 377-95.

[30] *British Protestant*, II (July 1846), 162.

[31] Janet, "Decline of General Fasts," pp. 94-95.

[32] Robin Hamlyn, *John Martin, 1789-1854: Belshazzar's Feast, 1820* (London, 1989).

[33] Elizabeth Missing Sewell, *Katharine Ashton*, 2 vols. (New York, 1864; orig. pub. 1854), I, 195.

[34] Jeremy Maas, *Holman Hunt and The Light of the World* (London, 1984).

Society was interested in establishing local "auxiliaries" to conduct inten-
sive work. From time to time, the Irish-born Rev. R. P. Blakeney,[35] led
delegations on speaking tours. In 1845, for instance, he and John Cumming went on a tour of the West Country, "[w]here Tractarianism, Popery,
and Socinianism seem to be in the ascendant." They lectured at Bristol,
Bridgewater, Taunton, Yeovil, Barnstaple, Bideford, Teignmouth, Totnes,
Chudleigh, Torquay, and Exeter. Sometimes they simply lectured; sometimes they debated Unitarians or Roman Catholics.[36] The auxiliaries were
fairly evenly distributed over England (but none in Wales, and only six in
Scotland), which suggests that the interest of incumbents, not the presence
of Roman Catholics, was significant. (Clergymen, in fact, predominated in
the Reformation Society.) It is also clear that most localities could support
only one anti-Catholic organization at a time. Hence, where the Protestant
Association was on the ground, the British Reformation Society could not
grow, and vice versa.[37]

The Reformation Society's auxiliaries were much like the town missions
that flourished in the early Victorian era, in that they were concerned with
individual conversions. The Nottingham Auxiliary was among the most
active, probably because Blakeney lived there. It claimed to own a library
of a thousand volumes and to engage between thirty and forty "Protestant
watchmen," who proselytized and distributed tracts. Other auxiliaries at
Derby and Leicester also made conversions, including that of the Rev. H.
Oxley, priest of the Roman Catholic chapel at Leicester.[38] The society also
attempted to establish "operative auxiliaries" for the working classes.
These were not very active, save in London—Chelsea, Westminster, Lambeth, Bermondsey, and Hammersmith. Their work was similar to that of
the more "respectable" auxiliaries: volunteers went from house to house
"a-tracking,"[39] talking to people, and reading the Bible. They tried to prove
to Roman Catholics the necessity of justification by faith, the evils of
Marian devotion, and the inutility of priests and sacraments as vessels of
divine grace; they talked to Protestants to try to get them to have "born-
again" conversion experiences, to bring them "to a knowledge of Christ
crucified."[40]

The Protestant Association was rather more interested in mobilizing
mass public opinion than in effecting individual conversions; lay leadership
predominated; it was more directly political in its orientation. It disseminated information in the form of theological and historical articles; it
supplied aids for local agitation in the form of sample petitions to be circulated and handbills to be stuck up.[41] And it warned its readership when
emergencies arose. It exposed, for instance, the Roman Catholic plot behind the issuing of the first florin—the Master of the Mint, after all, was

[35] Richard Paul Blakeney (1820-1884), born in Roscommon; curate, St. Paul's, Nottingham,
1843-44; perpetual curate, Hyson Green, Notts, 1844-52; perpetual curate of Christ Church
Claughton, Cheshire, 1852-74 (Boase, I, 305).
[36] *British Protestant*, I (Nov. 1845), 248-67; *ibid.* (Dec. 1845), 272-75.
[37] Wolffe, "Protestant Societies and Anti-Catholic Agitations," pp. 241-42.
[38] *British Protestant*, I (Feb. 1845), 31, (Apr. 1845), 99, II (Sept. 1846), 216-17.
[39] What little boys in poor neighborhoods said when district missionaries handed out tracts (Sewell, *Katharine Ashton*, I, 135).
[40] *British Protestant*, I (May 1845), 114; *ibid.*, II (Aug. 1846), 201-3; *ibid.*, III (May 1847), 73-74.
[41] *Penny Protestant Operative*, III (Feb. 1842), 9-10; *Protestant Magazine*, XII (Dec. 1850), 177.

a Papist. The offending coin omitted the royal titles "gratia Dei" and "Fidei Defensor."[42]

The Protestant Association was also more successful at organizing workers. Its leaders organized "Protestant Operative Associations" in a number of localities and published a monthly magazine, the *Penny Protestant Operative*, during the 1840s. Produced by "the higher classes" for "their less privileged brethren," the periodical attacked "[t]he antichristian doctrines of Popery,—the abominable tenets of Socinianism,—the wicked principles of Chartism, and the filthy notions of Socialism," under the motto, "For God, our Queen, and our Country."[43] Although ostensibly aimed at urban factory and craft workers, it projected a somewhat rosy and romantic view, reminding its readers of the world they had lost. For instance, "The Village Protestant Church," a poem, is illustrated with a woodcut of people carrying their Prayer Books to church in a rural setting.[44]

The magazine was as much for entertainment as for information. The occasional "Paddy story," in a stage-Irish brogue, appears, but the Irish material generally paints a sympathetic portrait of that island's inhabitants.[45]

It is one of the redeeming points of "the finest peasantry in the world," as they are often called, that they are truly and thoroughly hospitable—ready and willing at all times to give a portion of their "bite and sup" to all, and especially strangers, who apply to them. . . . [M]any of the poorer Irish . . . manifest a delicate attention, in this respect, to the hunger of the needy, a lesson which all would do well to learn and copy. . . .[46]

And the periodical pandered to working-class superstition with a page devoted to numerology, showing that various names and titles of popes all add up to the number 666. (Sometimes the letter "E" has the value of 0, sometimes 8, sometimes 5; "I" is sometimes 10, sometimes 1; "D" is sometimes 500, sometimes 4; "N" can be 0 or 50. One need but fiddle to get what one wants.)[47]

But concerns with infidelity and socialism soon gave way to the almost exclusive dwelling upon popery. From 1844 on, the "Intelligence" section at the end of each number printed notices of the growth of popery—the opening of Roman Catholic schools and chapels—in England and elsewhere in the world. From 1845 on, there was an increased concern with politics, a concern that politicians had betrayed Protestantism, and that there was a crisis in affairs. (That, of course, was the year of the Maynooth endowment, which shattered Protestant illusions about the leadership of the Conservative Party.) Thereafter, the magazine reveals more anti-Tractarian articles, more articles about "perverts," more articles about the Church of Ireland, more statements that the power of Rome was increasing—and fewer stories of sixteenth-century martyrdoms, which had been a staple of the earlier years.

[42] *Protestant Magazine*, XI (Nov. 1849), 169-70.
[43] *Penny Protestant Operative* I, (Apr. 1840), 1-2.
[44] *Ibid.*, III (Aug. 1842), 69.
[45] *Ibid.* (Jan. 1842), 5; *ibid.*, IX (Nov. 1848), 125-27; *ibid.* (Dec. 1848), 141.
[46] *Ibid.*, IV (July 1843), 53-54.
[47] *Ibid.*, IV (Jan. 1843), 3. James, *English Popular Literature*, pp. 54-59, discusses the popular almanacs and astrological charts of the day.

Both the British Reformation Society and the Protestant Association had somewhat mixed experiences on the national level. The British Reformation Society's nonpolitical stand made it unattractive to the Ultra-Tories, and its fanaticism made it unattractive to moderate Evangelicals; a few of its officers in the early days were followers of Edward Irving, a Scots Presbyterian minister in London during the late 1820s who started speaking in tongues and practiced faith healing. From these followed its difficulty in establishing a body of supporters, and thus its financial problems. Similarly, the Protestant Association's political activities and its harsh tone displeased the moderate Evangelicals, and its strong support for the Establishment limited its constituency to Ultra-Tories. The incomes of both declined during the 1840s, and neither was able to exercise the leadership that it wished.[48]

Rather, it was on the local level that these anti-Catholic organizations fought important battles, and hoped to score major defeats of the Man of Sin, so one must now turn to these.

Local Anglican Anti-Catholic Organizations

There are a number of places to which one might turn to investigate Anglican anti-Catholicism on the local level. The case of greater London, where both the Protestant Association and the British Reformation Society were active, itself illustrates the extent and variety of anti-Catholic activity and the limitations on its success. Edward Dalton (secretary of the Protestant Association, 1839-44) lived there; there was the local leadership to be found of parish priests such as W. W. Champneys, rector of Whitechapel,[49] J. Horton, rector of St. George's, Southwark, and of lecturers at City parishes such as Tenison Cuffe[50] and M. Hobart Seymour;[51] there lived active laymen, such as the barrister James Lord, involved in organizing branches of the Protestant Operative Association in Southwark, Tower Hamlets, Finsbury, Marylebone, Peckham, and Clerkenwell. Lord succeeded Dalton as secretary of the Protestant Association, and later contested a by-election at Derby in 1848 as a Protestant.[52]

The Reformation Society was active in London from the year of its creation (1827), appointing four Scripture-readers to the St. Giles's rookeries, and distributing tracrs and Bibles. Its activities declined in the 1830s (it reduced the number of Scripture-readers at St. Giles's to one in 1833), but revived during the 1840s. Its London auxiliaries multiplied during that decade—Chelsea, Westminster, Islington, Poplar, St. John's Wood, Southwark, Bermondsey, Woolwich, Greenwich, Lambeth, Somers Town, Deptford, and Hammersmith. These auxiliaries actually tried to make

[48] Wolffe, "Protestant Societies and Anti-Catholic Agitations," pp. 51-54, 65-66, 69-74, 143-47, 243; Wolffe, *Protestant Crusade*, pp. 149-91.

[49] William Weldon Champneys (1807-1875), curate, St. Ebbe's, Oxford, 1831-37; Rector, St. Mary's, Whitechapel, 1837-60; Vicar, St. Pancras, 1860-68; canon of St. Paul's, 1851-68; Dean of Lichfield, 1868-75 (Boase, I, 589-90).

[50] For Cuffe, see *sup.*, pp. 37-38.

[51] Michael Hobart Seymour (1800-1874); Trinity College, Dublin; priest in Ireland, 1824-34; lecturer at St. George the Martyr, Southwark, and St. Anne, Blackfriars; lived at Bath, 1844 to his death; author of numerous polemical works (Boase, III, 507). His two-volume abridgement of *Foxe's Book of Martyrs* (1838) became one of the most popular Victorian editions (Warren W. Wooden, *John Foxe*, Boston, 1983, p. 103).

[52] *Penny Protestant Operative*, I (Apr. 1840)-II (Mar. 1841).

converts—Bermondsey was especially active—by means of systematic house-to-house visitation.[53]

It is difficult to distinguish between the British Reformation Society and the London City Mission (1836), one of the most important Evangelical societies in the Metropolis. Founded by a Scot, David Nasmith, it shared patrons with the British Reformation Society and the Irish missionary societies, but was intended to be nonsectarian. (In fact, Anglicans dominated the London City Mission.) It maintained unpaid missionaries, amounting to 250 by 1850, and encouraged the creation of other missionary and philanthropical societies, especially the Ragged School Union and the Church of England Scripture Readers' Association. Early on, the London City Mission identified Irish Roman Catholics as of special interest, asked the Irish Evangelical and Irish Baptist Societies to open missions, and, when that failed, hired Irish (and sometimes Irish-speaking) Scripture-readers.[54]

Starting in the mid-1840s, several explicitly Anglican anti-Catholic organizations were founded. The Islington Protestant Institute (1846) emerged from the milieu of the Evangelical Daniel Wilson (vicar of St. Mary's, Islington, from 1824). Robert Maguire, an aggressive Irish clergyman,[55] began work for the Institute in 1852. Maguire came into head-on conflict with the Oxford Convert Frederick Oakeley, priest of St. John's Roman Catholic chapel, Islington. The controversy raged until Maguire moved on in 1857.[56]

John Armstrong, perpetual curate of St. Paul's, Bermondsey (and an Irishman), had the greater vision of a purely Anglican organization working throughout London. He and Samuel Garratt, incumbent of the district church of Holy Trinity, St. Giles, got the support of the *Record*, broke away from the British Reformation Society, and formed the Society for English Church Missions to the Roman Catholics in 1853. Armstrong used Erse-speakers and recognized the need to address the material needs of the Irish. His tactics produced a number of converts, including a Roman priest. (The publicity surrounding Daniel Donovan, Roman priest at Southwark, who was convicted of assault for attacking a female convert with an umbrella in 1853, also helped.) But both the British Reformation Society and the London City Mission resented this interloper in what they considered to be their territory, and redoubled their own fundraising. Faced with competition from the better-known societies, the English Church Missions saw its income drop in 1856, and it dissolved in 1858.[57]

Anti-Catholic missions in London competed for attention and financial contributions with a host of other worthy causes, such as missions to exiled Italians and French, antislavery societies, and philanthropic movements. Rivalries among anti-Catholic societies, struggling for access to the same

[53] Wolffe, "Protestant Societies and Anti-Catholic Agitations," pp. 261-71; Sheridan Gilley, "Protestant London, No-Popery and the Irish Poor, 1830-60. I: 1830-1850," *Recusant History*, X (1970), 216-18.

[54] Gilley, "No-Popery and the Irish Poor, 1830-1850," pp. 218-21; Pope, *Dickens and Charity*, pp. 108-22; Lewis, *Lighten Their Darkness*, pp. 49-63, 108-11, 119-49.

[55] Maguire (1826-1890) held a curacy at St. Nicholas's, Cork, 1849-52; after his work at Islington, he combined lectureships at two City parishes, 1856-71, with the perpetual curacy of, St. James's, Clerkenwell, 1857-75; rector, St. Olave's, Southwark, 1875-90; author of numerous polemical works (Boase, II, 692-93).

[56] Sheridan Gilley, "Protestant London, No Popery and the Irish Poor: II (1850-1860)," *Recusant History*, XI (1971), 29-30.

[57] *Ibid.*, pp. 24-28; Lewis, *Lighten Their Darkness*, pp. 197-200.

purse, also hurt. The failure of the missions to convert large numbers of Irish (fewer than two thousand converted between 1850 and 1858) led to a decline in support. And, Sheridan Gilley suggests, only a minority of Evangelicals maintained a serious interest in no-popery after the Protestant excitement of the early 1850s died down.[58]

Town missionaries of all sorts, in London and elsewhere, read passages of Scriptures that taught "the depravity of man, justification by faith alone, the necessity of a change of heart and of holiness of life." They did not accept simple church-going as enough, but asked the churchgoers if they had had a conversion experience. And, of course, Roman Catholics were urged to come out from the Scarlet Woman. Most of the Roman Catholics were polite, but declared their faith, hoping that the missionaries would go away. Only a few were hostile and threatening; only a few converted.[59] For the most part, the missionaries and their essentially middle-class concerns passed through the ken of London's underclass leaving little behind them.[60]

Anti-Catholic activities outside London are equally revealing, as Derby, Manchester, and Birmingham show.

Derbyshire ranked fifteenth among counties in terms of memorialists per thousand of population, and second for petitioners per thousand; and we have noted that Derby town saw a Roman Catholic revival in the 1840s under the leadership of the priests Thomas Sing and Joseph Daniel. It is not surprising, then, to find active there the Derby Protestant Operative Association and the Derby and Derbyshire Protestant Association. The two associations were for all practical purposes indistinguishable. The organizers of Anglican anti-Catholicism at Derby were the Rev. Roseingrave Macklin, incumbent of Christ Church, and George Holden (†1842), pensioner of St. John's College, Cambridge.[61] The men held organizing meetings in October of 1840; once they had established a firm base of operations at Derby, they began holding meetings in the surrounding towns. They were helped in their efforts by visits from Edward Dalton and the Rev. J. H. MacGuire (the latter a coworker of Hugh Stowell's at Manchester), and by the support of local notables such as the Rev. F. G. Greville, Rector of Bonsall (who later debated doctrine with the Roman Catholic priest John Dalton of Northampton).[62]

Under Macklin's direction, the Derby Protestant Operative Association claimed two hundred members, maintained a library, and sponsored monthly lectures on popery that "almost invariably" attracted six or seven hundred listeners. Its members were active in distributing tracts and in carrying anti-Maynooth petitions from house to house.[63] Derbyshire's anti-Catholic activities thus rested on the interplay of active religious controversialists on both sides of the issue.

Lancashire also was a fertile field, with permanent auxiliaries of the Protestant Association established at Liverpool, Manchester, Lancaster,

[58] Gilley, "No Popery and the Irish Poor, 1850-1860," pp. 30-32.

[59] Lewis, *Lighten Their Darkness*, pp. 122 (quote), 124-25, 136-39.

[60] For a more thorough discussion of the impact of domestic missionaries, see *inf.*, pp. 269-71.

[61] J. A. Venn, *Alumni Cantabrigienses*, Pt. II, vol. III, 408.

[62] *Penny Protestant Operative*, I (Nov. 1840), 64; *ibid.*, II (Nov. 1841), 80; *ibid.*, IV (Mar. 1843), 23; *ibid.* (Apr. 1843), 31-32; *ibid.* (Oct. 1843), 80; *ibid.*, VII (May 1846), 45; *Protestant Magazine*, XI (Oct. 1849), 146.

[63] *Penny Protestant Operative*, VII (Jan. 1846), 3-5.

and Warrington.[64] Associations at St. Helen's and Birkenhead had a more fitful life.[65] Manchester anti-Catholicism was dominated by what Joseph Pratt, the anti-Catholic journalist, called the "extraordinary and almost superhuman efforts" of Hugh Stowell. "He has often been styled the 'Lion of Salford', but, hereafter, we believe him justly entitled to the title of the LION OF PROTESTANTISM."[66] Born in the Isle of Man in 1799, Stowell was raised in a decidedly Evangelical household and educated at St. Edmund's Hall, Oxford. Ordained in 1823, he served curacies in the Cotswolds and Huddersfield, and became curate of St. Stephen's, Salford, in 1828. His success was such that Christ Church, Salford, was built for him as a proprietary chapel, and opened in 1831. (The church was owned by trustees elected by the pew-renters, and had no endowment.) He remained there until his death in 1865.[67]

Stowell's success in attracting and keeping a congregation (which rose from 180 to about six hundred communicants between 1831 and 1852) was due in part to his parish's activities. Christ Church was what the late nineteenth century was to call an "institutional church"; it involved its parishioners in pastoral activities. Stowell and his two curates maintained a full worship schedule of three services in the church and two elsewhere on Sundays, a service and lecture on Wednesdays, and frequent schoolroom and cottage lectures. The "Lord's Supper" was celebrated once a month, with a preparatory service the evening before. The parish maintained a panoply of activities for laity: a day school, Sunday schools for both children and adults, a library, and a staff of volunteer district visitors to seek out the poor. And the parish ministered to the poor of Salford with a ragged school, a refuge for prostitutes, a mutual improvement society, and clothing clubs.[68]

But Stowell's success, both as an anti-Catholic leader and as a clergyman whose income depended upon a satisfied congregation, rested upon his oratorical abilities as a preacher. He always spoke extempore;[69] he had a self-confident and commanding pulpit presence. Charles Royce, the young Mancunian intellectual, recorded an incident that illustrates Stowell's daring. At one of the Wednesday services,

> just as Mr. Stowell was giving out his text the gas lights began to grow dim all over the church & very soon went completely out! Then here & there was heard a whistle loud as the railway, frightening all I think but the preacher who went on with his discourse to the end in the dark, merely stopping to explain that the noise (which soon ceased) was occasioned by the air getting into the pipes. . . . I am sure I shall not forget *that* sermon . . . . A man of less nerve than Mr. S. w[oul]d have been put out by the singularity of the scene.[70]

Stowell was an aggressive anti-Catholic, whose attacks brought him national notoriety early on, as a result of a spectacular lawsuit. In 1840,

[64] *Ibid.*, I (Apr. 1840), 8; *ibid.* (June 1840), 24; *ibid.* (Sept. 1840), 49; *ibid.*, II (July 1841), 56; *ibid.*, III (Nov. 1842), 95; *ibid.*, VIII (Apr. 1847), 48; *Manchester Guardian*, 28 Dec. 1850.
[65] *Penny Protestant Operative*, III (Aug. 1842), 71-72; *Chester Courant*, 8 Jan. 1851.
[66] *Protestant Witness*, I (16 Dec. 1848), 62.
[67] John Buxton Marsden, *Memoirs of the Life and Labours of the Rev. Hugh Stowell, M.A.* (London, 1868), pp. 2-3, 14, 32, 34, 40, 273; *DNB*, XIX, 7.
[68] Marsden, *Stowell*, pp. 47, 283.
[69] *Ibid.*, pp. 30-31.
[70] Charles Royce to George Royce, 3 Sept. 1846, Royce Papers, MCL, M 70/3/16.

Stowell charged that the prominent Roman Catholic priest Daniel Hearne[71] had forced John O'Hara, one of his parishioners, to crawl on hands and knees in the roughest part of Smedley Lane, Manchester, for penance. The priest sued for libel in the action *Hearne v. Stowell*, heard in the Nisi Prius Court, Liverpool Assizes, in August 1840. The facts of the matter depended on O'Hara's explanation of his strange behavior to three Manchester policemen, who in their turn ran to tell the tale to Joseph Pratt. But counsel for both Hearne and Stowell acknowledged that O'Hara was a lunatic; "we both well know why he is not called [as a witness] by either of us," said Mr. Cresswell for the defense. So the defense claimed that what a clergyman said in the course of his duties was not libellous, even if untrue, if the clergyman sincerely believed it to be true. Although the jury found Stowell guilty and assigned damages of 40*s.*, Stowell appealed to the Court of Queen's Bench, where the judgement was reversed on the grounds that the judge should have directed the jury to decide for themselves whether the publication was libellous.[72]

Stowell's main anti-Catholic weapon was the Protestant Operative Association. Organized in 1839 as the Salford Operative Protestant Association, it met first, in quarterly meetings, at the Hope Street Infant School, connected with his parish.[73] By 1845, it had expanded its operations across the River Irwell, adding the word "Manchester" to its name. As it grew, it changed its place of venue to the Free Trade Hall, where, on 7 December 1848, its annual general meeting netted over £50 by sale of tickets and the collection.[74] It continued to be active into the 1850s.[75] (The place also had a branch of the Protestant Association,[76] but, as at Derby, it and the Protestant Operatives were indistinguishable.)

The Manchester Protestant Operatives also had a weekly newspaper, the *Protestant Witness*, which began publication on 9 September 1848, under the direction of Joseph Pratt, "a zealous Protestant on principle, and thoroughly Conservative."[77] Commencing in response to the aggressive activities of Manchester Roman Catholics, the *Protestant Witness* became the unofficial organ of the Manchester and Salford Protestant Operative Association. Although Although Pratt pointed occasionally to the constitutional danger that Roman Catholicism posed,[78] he was most concerned with the history of that Church (". . . their intrigues and exterminating Wars . . . St. Bartholomew's Day . . . fires of Smithfield . . . the outboiling blood of the Protestant victims . . . the thraldom of the dark ages . . ."),[79] and with its doctrine. For Pratt, the Bible, the right of private judgement, and the guidance of the Holy Spirit were sufficient to find evangelical truth; yet in the enlightened nineteenth century, Manchester men were threatened with obscurantism.

[71] For Hearne, see *sup.*, p. 90.
[72] Marsden, *Stowell*, pp. 60-61, 102, 119; *Times*, 31 Aug., 11 Sept., 6, 17 Nov. 1840; *Leeds Times*, 5 Sept., 17 Oct. 1840.
[73] *Penny Protestant Operative*, I (Oct. 1840), 55; *ibid.*, II (April 1841), 32; *ibid.*, III (Nov. 1842), 96.
[74] *Ibid.*, VII (Jan. 1846), 9; *Protestant Witness*, I (16 Dec. 1848), 62-63.
[75] Protestant Alliance [Monthly Letter, No. 1], 1 Jan. 1853, Page & Moody Papers, Southampton City Record Office, D/PM 10/5/72.
[76] *Penny Protestant Operative*, IX (Sept. 1848), 101-3.
[77] *Manchester Courier*, 26 Nov. 1859; Boase, II, 1622.
[78] *Protestant Witness*, I (16 Dec. 1848), 62; *ibid.* (13 Jan. 1849), 71.
[79] *Ibid.*, II (16 Nov. 1850), 454—imagine, all that on one page!

Your industry and skill are the pride of England, and the wonder of the world. . . . Let it never be said of Manchester that her sons are slaves—that they have lost every feeling that should pervade the spirit of a free-born Briton—and after giving freedom to the world, are themselves in chains. . . . The very heathen are throwing away their Idols to the moles and bats; and shall we—the enlightened inhabitants of these populous and flourishing towns—set up a whole host of pictures, images, relics, and dead men's bones to be worshipped and adored as Gods? Have our sons and daughters any inclination to be shut up in Monasteries and Convents? or do we need the racks and faggots of the Inquisition to promote our personal comfort and domestic peace?[80]

Stowell was aided in his anti-Catholic work by several secondary figures. The Irish-born Anglican priest J. H. MacGuire[81] was a regular participant in Manchester Protestant Operative activities, and travelled about Lancashire to deliver lectures. In the lecture on "Papal Rome Addicted to the Worship of Saints," which occasioned a dispute with William Francis Cleary, MacGuire denounced "creature worship" and "the cunningly devised fables of the Vatican," and charged that the invocation of saintly merit was "robbing Christ of His glory."[82] Samuel Condell, the Protestant lecturer, was an Irishman, and worked as a packer in a warehouse in the neighborhood of York Street.[83] He enraged the Roman Catholic community by lecturing on "The Pope proved to be Anti-Christ from his own assumptions, the Holy Scriptures, and the voice of the Christian Church for the first six hundred years."[84] John Atkinson, the secretary of the Manchester and Salford Protestant Operative Association, was a mainstay of the anti-Catholic lecture circuit in Manchester. At Stockport, for instance, he attacked transubstantiation "as an awful doctrine, and delusive in tendency. If this doctrine was true, and the body of Christ was literally compressed into a wafer and eaten, it was a greater humiliation of the incarnate Saviour than had hitherto been revealed. . . ."[85]

Finally, Birmingham also had its anti-Catholic organizations. The streets of that town were thronged with preachers, colporteurs, and tract-distributers, and rang with the attendant disorder.[86] "I went into Thomas Street," recorded Thomas Augustin Finegan, evangelist for the Birmingham Town Mission, one Sunday morning in August of 1837,

and there found a man holding forth at one end of the street preaching with Stentorian lungs and agile action of head, arms, and feet. At the other end of the street stood another individual advocating with equal vehemence the cause of *Tee totalism*. It was a scene, on the whole, at variance with my own notion of things, and seeing two of the police about to interfere I had no relish for a share in any of these danties [sic] so I directed my way into John St.—here to my surprise I again saw a *female* spouter,[87]

[80] *Ibid.*, I (9 Sept. 1848), 1.

[81] John Heron MacGuire (†1860), curate of St. Ann's, Manchester, and vicar of St. Luke's, Chorlton-upon-Medlock, 1843-57, (Boase, I, 611).

[82] *Protestant Witness*, II (23 Feb. 1850), 303-4, (23 Mar. 1850), 323-24.

[83] *Manchester Illuminator*, I (16 Mar. 1850), 107.

[84] *Protestant Witness*, II (27 July 1850), 398.

[85] *Ibid.* (19 Oct. 1850), 444.

[86] Geoffrey Robson, "The Failures of Success: Working Class Evangelists in Early Victorian Birmingham," *Studies in Church History*, XV (1978), 382.

[87] Three weeks earlier, Finegan saw "a female ranter screaming," and "prayed secretely [sic], that God would send arrows of conviction to the hearts of the hearers, whether from the bow of a De-

with some 20 or 30[88] female companions concluding a hymn. The street was all in a complete state of disorder in consequence of a fight that just terminated between a party of Irish labourers who came over here to reap the Harvist [sic] and who with their hooks in hand, seemed well disposed to use them upon some thoughtless young men who insulted them and cast reflections on these poor shoeless, and shillingless bogtrotters from Connaught. I was in time to interfere here, and I have reason to be thankful my interference was well timed—for my poor insulted countrymen retired into their lodging houses, and left the field now to me, and the Female preacher who was so untimely and injudiciously squalling out texts of scripture to a barbarian crowd, who neither understood or—or at all cared for what she said. Indeed she would have been treated I fear rather roughly had I not overheard what some persons were saying and one of them said loud enough to be heard by all "*we have women's tongues enough at home, we do not want more of them in the street.*"[89]

Finegan himself was an Irish convert to Anglicanism, although the Birmingham Town Mission was nondenominational, and he was careful to avoid denominational controversy, save when it came to Roman Catholics. He was eager to debate them, and for the most part his relations with them were civil. (Indeed, some of the cleverer Irish relished the debates almost as much as he did.)[90] Rather, it was the Roman Catholic priests who warned their flocks against having anything to do with the missionaries, and who accused converts of being "rice Christians."[91] Sometimes the priests lost self-control, as in 1848, when one burnt an Authorized Version New Testament that had been given to one of his flock. A local Anglican publicized the act, leading the town's Roman Catholic priests to apologize, but to plead provocation.

> Justice, however, requires us to state that the Catholics of Birmingham had suffered constant and great annoyance from the interference of certain Protestant clergymen or others, their agents, who frequently intrude themselves into the houses of poor Catholics, unsought for and uninvited, for the purpose of perverting their faith. It was with the knowledge that such a system was going on, and under the excitement of the moment, that the act, which it is not attempted to justify, took place.[92]

It was not surprising that Roman Catholics should have been annoyed, for Birmingham was home to "some of the most zealous Protestants in the empire," in the judgement of the Scottish Reformation Society;[93] and the first of these was Thomas Ragg.[94]

Ragg's family moved to Birmingham from Nottingham when he was a year old. His father, a hosier and lace manufacturer, was active in radical

borah, or a Barak" (T. A. Finegan Journal, 6 Aug. 1837, Birmingham Reference Library, MS. 312 749, p. 39).

[88] Altered from "seven or eight."

[89] Finegan Journal, 27 Aug. 1837, Birmingham Reference Library, MS. 312 749, pp. 79-80.

[90] *Ibid.*, 27 July, 10 Aug., 6 Sept., 27 Oct. 1837, pp. 22-25, 44-45, 98-99, 154-55; Robson, "Working Class Evangelists," pp. 384-86.

[91] Finegan Journal, 26, 31 July 1837, Birmingham Reference Library, MS. 312 749, pp. 17-18, 33-34; *Protestant Watchman*, No. 2 (Apr. 1849), p. 16; cf. *Manchester Illuminator*, I (26 Jan. 1850), 54.

[92] *Protestant Witness*, I (Dec. 1848), 60.

[93] *Bulwark*, I (Oct. 1851), 77-79.

[94] Ragg (1808-1881) edited the *Birmingham Advertiser*, 1839-45; ordained under special license for nongraduates; perpetual curate of Lawley, Salop, 1865 (*Newman Letters*, XIII, 517); published several books of poetry.

politics. After going bankrupt around 1819, the father set up as a printer
and bookseller, specializing in republican and rationalist publications. (He
was imprisoned twice for uttering seditious and blasphemous publications.) Ragg was apprenticed to his uncle, a Leicester hosier, in 1822. The
uncle, although only an occasional attender himself, made everyone in the
household attend the Rev. S. Wigg's General Baptist chapel; and Ragg
read Brown's Family Bible and *Pilgrim's Progress*, the only books in the
house, out of boredom. He thought about Christianity, but remained a
Deist. In 1826, however, he and his uncle moved to Nottingham, where
he was beset by grave religious doubts. After two years of anxiety, he read
Romans 10:9,[95] believed, and was saved.[96]

> Is *this* religion? What! is this that sad,
> That melancholy thing, which I was wont
> To think so dull and gloomy? Oh, my God!
> 'Tis heaven itself to laud and praise Thy name;
> To lift the soul to Thee, with fervent zeal,
> And sing the blessings of Redeeming Love.
> Lord God Almighty! how shall I express
> The praise Thy grace requires—a wretch like me,
> Who once denied the Cross, and proudly scorned
> My crucified Redeemer? This is bliss
> Beyond my utmost hopes.[97]

Ragg's ambitions obviously extended beyond the knitting frame. As
with other self-taught artisans, words would be the vehicle of his rise in the
world; he began dabbling in the Nottingham literary and journalistic
world. He also turned to the spoken word, becoming an occasional local
preacher in Congregationalist and Baptist chapels. But, even then, he was
friendly with Evangelical Churchmen, did not feel himself "authorised to
administer either of the sacraments," and professed no objections to the
principle of an Establishment.[98]

Ragg became editor of the *Birmingham Advertiser* in 1839, hired by a
group of proprietors who wanted to moderate the newspaper's high Tory
tone and to promote cooperation among Evangelicals, whether Churchmen
or Nonconformists. Ragg at first attended both James Angell James's
Carr's Lane Congregationalist chapel and John George Breay's Christ
Church; but when some of the Carr's Lane people called him a hypocrite
for editing a Church paper while worshipping with Dissenters, he moved
altogether to Church. (He completed his spiritual pilgrimage in 1858, when
the Bishop of Rochester ordained him.)[99]

For Ragg, human history from the fall of Rome to the early nineteenth
century was a grim tale of apostasy, corruption, and infidelity, only occasionally lightened by the lives of a few godly men. (England, however, had

[95] "If on your lips is the confession, 'Jesus is Lord', and in your heart the faith that God raised
him from the dead, then you will find salvation. For the faith that leads to righteousness is in the
heart, and the confession that leads to salvation is upon the lips."
[96] Thomas Ragg, *God's Dealings with an Infidel; or, Grace Triumphant* (London, 1858), pp. ii-viii.
[97] *Ibid.*, pp. vii-ix
[98] *Ibid.*, p.xviii. (Indeed, he wrote poetry praising Constantine and Theodosius for having used
the power of the state to crush pagan gods and to exalt the Christian god.) Thomas Ragg, *The Deity*
(London, 1834), pp. 279-80.
[99] Thomas Ragg, *God's Dealings*, p. xix.

had not a few of the godly.)[100] The Roman Catholic Church, that "blood-cemented Babylon," was Satan's chief weapon against the godly (Islam was his second favorite), but eventually she would fall to the ground "like a dog-worried Jezebel."[101] In his eschatology, Ragg was a Futurist who believed that the end times were upon humanity, and that the Rapture would occur after the Tribulation. The elect would rise into the air to meet their Saviour halfway, but first they would get to watch the fun.

> Wail, O earth!
> Weep forests, hills, and mountains! howl, ye vales!
> The day of vengeance comes! the martyrs' blood,
> That long for retribution cried to heaven,
> Is answered now! The wine-press trodden is,
> Without the city! and the streaming blood
> Reaches the horses' bridles! Gathers fast
> The trumpet of the wrath of God. . .[102]

Ragg thus was a natural leader for Birmingham's Anglican Evangelicals.

Although the organizers of the Protestant Association had visited Birmingham in 1835,[103] the first permanent society there was the Birmingham Church of England Lay Association, founded in May of the same year that Ragg arrived, and lasting until 1847. This organization feared both Nonconformists and Roman Catholics, arguing that they made up "a formidable and heterogenous confederacy, of which the Popish Priests may be considered the main instigators and leaders."[104] Consequently, this organization was as much anti-Nonconformist as anti-Catholic. (Their attitudes reflect the fact that Nonconformity was stronger in Birmingham than in the nation at large.[105]) During the first half of the 1840s, it saw the main threat to the Church as coming from "the restless and ambitious leaders of the Dissenting body."[106] So, it attacked the doctrine and discipline of both Roman Catholicism and Dissent, criticized the amended Factory Bill, 1843, for not giving the Church the educational powers that it deserved, supported by words and money churchwardens who tried to collect church rates against Nonconformist opposition, and circulated petitions against the union of the sees of St. Asaph and Bangor.[107] As an illustration of its approach, one may cite its *4th Annual Report* (1843), which contained eighty-seven pages of attacks on Roman Catholic corruption and idolatry, justifications for Episcopacy, defenses of the Scottish Episcopal Church, rejoicings over the Disruption of what it called the "Presbyterian Church of Scotland," and protests against the nonpayment of church rates.[108] After 1845, however, the threat from Roman Catholicism loomed larger. Anglicans, the organization declared, could no longer

[100] Ragg, *Deity*, pp. 281-91.

[101] Thomas Ragg, *Heber; Records of the Poor; Lays from the Prophets; and Other Poems* (London, 1840), p. 207.

[102] *Deity*, p. 294.

[103] Wolffe, "Protestant Societies and Anti-Catholic Agitations," p. 108.

[104] Birmingham Church of England Lay Association, *8th Annual Report* (1847), p. 7 (quoting from the Preliminary Address of May, 1839).

[105] P. S. Morrish, "The Struggle to Create an Anglican Diocese of Birmingham," *JEH*, XXXI (1980), 61.

[106] Birmingham Church of England Lay Association, *5th Annual Report* (1844), p. 5.

[107] *Idem, 4th Annual Report* (1843), pp. 5-8; *idem, 5th Annual Report* (1844), pp. 5-7.

[108] Pp. 50-137.

trust the Government to guard the Church's "rights, privileges, and property"; it mounted petition drives against the Maynooth grant and against any further relaxation of penal legislation.[109]

The approach of the Birmingham Church of England Lay Association tended to dissipate energies over a wide variety of issues, and to alienate Nonconformists at a time when some thought a united front against the papal threat desirable. To correct this deficiency, the short-lived *Christian Watchman and Midland Counties' Protestant Magazine*, published between June of 1842 and February of 1844, focused its attention exclusively on Romanism. (Although published from London, the periodical's intended audience was in Birmingham and environs.) The periodical is full of hysterical and scurrilous anti-Catholic attacks, taken in large part from the writings of the Rev. Richard Waldo Sibthorp, an Anglican priest who converted and took Roman orders, but who reverted to Anglicanism in 1843. (Sibthorp lived in Birmingham during his two years as a Roman Catholic.) Mean little paragraphs declared that Roman Catholics worship a god of paste and eat Jesus, that Satan was the first Pope, and that popery is wicked, rotten, and idolatrous. And there were stories about Pope Joan and her baby, and about monkish murderers.

In an effort to place anti-Catholicism in Birmingham on a permanent footing, Ragg organized a branch of the Protestant Association in 1847. The clergy, whose support he solicited, were at first reserved, telling him that he must prove himself to be in earnest and show that his association was likely to be more permanent than earlier attempts. Things got off to a slow start, with sixty or seventy members the first year, double that the second, but little change the third.[110] The association's activities brought it publicity, however, and the Papal Aggression crisis brought it a massive infusion of funds. (Its annual receipts jumped from £50 to £540 between 1851 and 1852.) But after that furor died down, and especially after the Crimean War diverted attention and contributions to other causes, the association's income dwindled to below the level of its second year of existence. The excitement of Italian unification, Giuseppe Garibaldi's visits to England, and the question of the Pope's temporal power, however, gave it a new lease of life, and contributions began rising after 1862. (Receipts rose from £20 in 1862 to £140 in 1865.)[111]

The Birmingham Protestant Association attempted to circumvent the problems of the relationship between the Church and Dissent by claiming that all Protestants could work together against the common foe. (It later looked back at the Papal Aggression episode as an example of such cooperation.[112]) "It is not our intention to interfere in the controversy between the Church and the Evangelical Dissenters. Our object is simple and clearly defined, and to that object we intend strictly to keep. Our controversy is with Antichrist, either in its Papal or its Infidel form, and we do not intend mixing in any other warfare."[113] It is a comment on local au-

---

[109] *Idem, 6th Annual Report* (1845), pp. 5-6; *idem, 7th Annual Report* (1846), pp. 9-10.

[110] Ragg, *God's Dealings*, p. xxvi; Birmingham Protestant Association, *1st Annual Report* (1848), pp. 8-9; *Protestant Watchman*, No. 6 (Aug. 1849), p. 72; *ibid.*, No. 18 (Aug. 1850), p. 219.

[111] *Birmingham Protestant Association Record*, No. 1 (Oct. 1866), p. 2.

[112] *Ibid.*, No. 2 (Nov. 1866), p. 5.

[113] *Protestant Watchman*, No. 1 (Mar. 1849), wrapper.

tonomy that this auxiliary of the most strongly Anglican of the mass anti-Catholic societies should claim the pan-Protestant mantle.

The Birmingham Protestant Association's work was helped by Ragg's activities as publisher and editor of the *Protestant Watchman of the Midland District*. Originating as a response to the treatment that organized anti-Catholicism had received from the local Birmingham newspapers, this monthly periodical began with a circulation of five hundred in March 1849; it claimed a circulation of three thousand half a year later.[114] The *Protestant Watchman*, as with most anti-Catholic prints, contained a mix of historical accounts of past papal misdeeds, examples of contemporary corruptions, and controversial articles. A regular feature, "Romish Doings in Birmingham and Neighbourhood," related stories about such matters as petty squabblings over whether a corpse should be buried by Anglican or Roman rites, and charged that the night before the consecration of the Roman Catholic cathedral a group of Roman priests got drunk at the Hen and Chickens and sang "Old King Cole."[115] It retailed gossip: Lord Melbourne had converted to Roman Catholicism; Roman Catholic servants repeat family secrets in the confessional and sprinkle holy water on children when their employers' backs are turned.[116] The Roman Catholic Church claims dominion over all baptized Christians; Papists cannot be loyal to a Protestant Sovereign.[117]

In addition to its journalistic work, the Birmingham Protestant Association stood ready to expose popish conspiracies. Ragg once complained, for instance, that "a blasphemous and popish hymn" had been introduced to a concert, disguised as a solo and chorus from Rossini.[118] But the most notorious example related to William Thomas Jefferys's claims of imprisonment in Mount St. Bernard's Cistercian monastery, founded in 1836 by Ambrose Phillips de Lisle, a well-known convert. (The monastery's growing building program in the 1840s had attracted anti-Catholic attention.)[119]

Jefferys claimed that he had been held against his will at the monastery and had managed to make his escape with only the clothes upon his back; utterly destitute, he was taken in by several anti-Catholics. Ragg was "much edified and instructed" by Jefferys' tale, and published it in the *Watchman*, and as a separate pamphlet (at tuppence) under the title "A Narrative of Six Years' Captivity and Suffering among the Monks of St. Bernard, in the Monastery at Charnwood Forest, Leicestershire."[120] Ragg's pamphlet found its way to Whitwick, within a mile and a half of Mount St. Bernard's Monastery. The Cistercians denied its charges, but it did its work; local colliers and stockingers threatened to burn down the local Roman Catholic school and to blow up the monastery.

Meanwhile, faced with Roman Catholic denials, Ragg began to wonder whether Jefferys's story was true. Further investigation led him to conclude that the "escapee" was an imposter. To Ragg's credit, he then at-

[114] *Ibid.*, No. 6 (Aug. 1849), p. 72.
[115] *Ibid.*, No. 15 (May 1850), pp. 177-80; *ibid.*, No. 21 (Nov. 1850), pp. 251-52.
[116] *Ibid.*, No. 3 (May 1849), p. 38; *ibid.*, No. 8 (Oct. 1849), pp. 95-96.
[117] *Ibid.*, No. 2 (Apr. 1849), pp. 23-24; *ibid.*, No. 5 (July 1849), p. 51.
[118] *Birmingham Mercury*, 10 Jan. 1852.
[119] Norman, *English Catholic Church*, pp. 220-21.
[120] *Protestant Watchman*, No. 3 (May 1849), p. 29; *ibid.*, No. 4 (June 1849), pp. 42-44 and wrapper.

tempted to repair the damage that he had helped to cause. He went to Wednesbury, accompanied by Brother Alexis of the monastery and Michael Maher (Roman Catholic publisher at Birmingham), to try to convince William S. Nayler, who was supplying Jefferys with both moral and financial support. Despite Ragg's endorsement of them, Nayler held the two Roman Catholics in deepest suspicion and told them that they would not be believed upon their oaths. Eventually, Ragg's party, Nayler, and Jefferys went to the monastery itself. "The news of the arrival of the poor runaway monk soon spread in all directions, and the party were in a short time surrounded by an emmense multitude, who followed them to Mount St. Bernard. The Rev. Mr. Cole [the local vicar] had to address the people three times on the road, restraining their anger, and promising a full inquiry." When the party got to the monastery, Jefferys could not even find his way round the building, let alone show the cells and secret passages that he had claimed to have seen; he broke down and cried. Nayler charged him with obtaining goods under false pretenses, and he was committed to Stafford jail for three months as a rogue and vagabond.[121]

Ragg withdrew the "Narrative," and publicly charged Jefferys with being an imposter who lived off anti-Catholics.[122] He became more cautious in accepting anti-Catholic stories, and the feature "Romish Doings in Birmingham and Neighbourhood" was dropped from the *Protestant Watchman* from July 1849 to November 1850. Local Roman Catholics hoped that the affair had discredited Ragg's propaganda,[123] but the damage, once done, could not be undone. By the time of the Papal Aggression crisis, people had forgot about the affair; and even later, on the eve of the Great War, the Hope Trust of Edinburgh (which called itself "Scriptural, Christian and Protestant")[124] reprinted Jefferys's "Narrative," and the Catholic Truth Society was forced to expose the imposture yet again.[125]

As ill-fated, it turned out, was the Birmingham Protestant Association's sponsorship of public speakers. From the ranks of its own members, the Rev. George Stringer Bull (better known as "Parson Bull of Brierly," the factory children's friend) lectured on "The Moral System of Popery," in which he argued that the Roman Catholic Church counselled immorality by permitting dissembling, lying, and the making of false oaths.[126] Other speakers included Giacinto Achilli, the apostate Dominican priest who sued John Henry Newman for libel, and Charles Newdegate, M.P., who made a parliamentary career of denouncing convents.[127] But when the apostate Barnabite and Italian nationalist Alessandro Gavazzi was brought in to address the Birmingham Protestant Association's annual general meeting on 16 October 1851, and to lecture at the Town Hall on the 17th, 20th, and 21st, a public uproar resulted.

---

[121] The story is in *A Full Report of a most Extraordinary Investigation which took place on Tuesday, June 26, 1849, at Mount St. Bernard Monastery, Leicestershire*, 6th ed. (Birmingham, 1849).

[122] *Protestant Watchman*, No. 5 (July 1849), pp. 60-62.

[123] J. H. Newman to George Ryder, 11 July 1849, *Newman Letters*, XIII, 213-14.

[124] Founded by John Hope (b. 1807) to promote teetotalism and to expose the evils of popery (Bruce, *No Pope of Rome*, pp. 36-39).

[125] James Britten, "An 'Escaped Monk': being the story of William Jefferys," *Publications of the Catholic Truth Society*, XCVIII (1914).

[126] *Protestant Watchman*, No. 4 (June 1849), p. 50.

[127] *Ibid.*, No. 16 (June 1850), p. 191; *ibid.*, No. 19 (Sept. 1850), p. 226.

Gavazzi was a dramatic public speaker. His rich, dramatic voice, his equally dramatic habit of black cassock and cape with scarlet cross, his commanding platform presence were such that he could hold audiences enthralled for an hour and a half or more, even though he spoke only Italian. (He had a translator standing by.) In Birmingham, he gave his usual denunciation of Romanism as a religio-political system. But *Aris' Birmingham Gazette*, both political and religious enemy of Ragg's, accused Gavazzi of "red republicanism." In the ensuing controversy, the Revs. G. S. Bull and John Cale Miller resigned from the Birmingham Protestant Association because of Gavazzi's supposed political beliefs, and because they charged that he had no "positive principles" with which to replace popery. (The loss of Miller's support was serious, for he was rector of the principal parish church and active in local affairs.) The controversy raged fiercely for half a month, until the arrival of the Hungarian refugee Louis Kossuth turned public attention to other matters.[128]

All these local anti-Catholic organizations were to play major roles during the winter of 1850-51, in the Papal Aggression agitation.

Opposing the Papal Aggression

Anglican anti-Catholics were quick to challenge the creation of the Roman Catholic hierarchy. The clergy of Westminster led the pack, largely because they had prepared a denunciatory memorial to the Queen in 1848, when rumors of the new hierarchy had first surfaced.[129] Anglican efforts were supported by the *Record*, a semiweekly newspaper that was the voice of the hard Evangelical Anglicans. Besides leading articles attacking Cardinal Wiseman's character and the constitutional implications of the titles,[130] the print called for public protest meetings, explained how to petition Parliament, and printed a sample memorial to the Queen.[131]

The Church of England, however, had no authoritative voice. There was no Convocation; the bishops, owing their appointments to the will of prime ministers, had little sense of corporate identity or hierarchical unity.

> [T]imidity has always been thought to be an episcopal distinction in the Church of England; *Episcopi in Anglia semper pavidissimi*. It certainly was characteristic of the bishops of 1850. In sheer terror of Rome and the Erastianism of Russell, bishop after bishop joined in the general denunciation of Pusey and all who sympathized with him.[132]

The bishops attempted to draft a joint statement, but they were not united in their protests. J. B. Sumner, Archbishop of Canterbury, opposed the idea of requiring candidates for Parliament to bind themselves to repeal Roman Catholic Emancipation and urged laymen to remain in their parishes even if the priest was a ritualizer. Henry Phillpotts, Bishop of Exeter, who hated Whigs as much as Roman Catholics, charged that the Russell Ministry's latitudinarian religious policy had encouraged Pius to proceed

---

[128] *Birmingham Mercury*, 18, 25 Oct., 1 Nov. 1851; David E.H. Mole, "John Cale Miller: A Victorian Rector of Birmingham," *JEH*, XVII (1966), 96-98.

[129] *Record*, 21 Oct. 1850. See draft petitions from the Dean and Chapter of Westminster, 1848, in the Wordsworth Family Papers, Lambeth Palace Library, MS. 2143, f. 315, and MS. 2144, ff. 163-66.

[130] *Record*, 10, 17, 28 Oct. 1850.

[131] *Ibid.*, 24 Oct., 7 Nov. 1850.

[132] Bowen, *Idea of the Victorian Church*, p. 105.

with his scheme. Richard Whateley, the staunch Whig Archbishop of Dublin, on the other hand, refused to sign any address that censured the government.[133] So some bishops acted on their own. Phillpotts and Samuel Wilberforce, Bishop of Oxford, both active in mobilizing their own clergy, also sent protests to every Anglican prelate in the world, for what good it did. (The Bishop of Mississippi, for instance, brought the issue before his diocesan convention and condemned the assumption of titles, but took no official action for fear of seeming to interfere in the domestic affairs of another nation.)[134]

In order to supply a united Anglican voice, Lord Ashley, the philanthropist, and several other Anglican clergy and laymen organized the Protestant Defence Committee, an *ad hoc* committee of correspondence that promoted public meetings and petition drives. Henry Cholmondeley,[135] its secretary, supplied local committees with forms of petition, advised them on strategy, and collected the sheets into a monster memorial, bearing the signatures of 317,692 laymen, which Ashley presented to the Queen.[136] In 1851, when it turned out that the government's Ecclesiastical Titles Bill did not go far enough to suit anti-Catholics, the Protestant Defence Committee produced a model petition to the House of Commons, requesting that the measure be made more stringent, and asked its fifty-five local committees to circulate it.[137] But again there was disunity. The Manchester and Salford local committee promptly adopted the petition, whereas the Southampton committee held off, fearing that "[p]etitions are too much multiplied."[138]

On the local level, however, Protestant Defence Committees blended into Protestant Operative Associations, Reformation Societies, literary societies, and simple meetings of parishioners, in all of which clergymen were prominent. Priests at Blackburn, Manchester, Salford, Liverpool, Chorlton-on-Medlock, Bury, and Rochdale simultaneously preached sermons and laid on lectures about the evils of popery.[139] The meetings at Oldham, Warrington, and Prescott were chaired by the incumbents; the Preston memorial was cooked up at a private meeting of clergy and laity at the Council Chambers.[140] Moreover, clergymen travelled about, attending each others' meetings to encourage the anti-Catholic spirit. Especially active in this respect was the Manchester contingent of Hugh Stowell, James Bardsley, and H. W. McGrath. (Indeed, Stowell was so busy that he had

[133] *Times*, 11, 20 Nov., 14 Dec. 1850; Phillpotts to Francis Close, 19 Nov. 1842, Phillpotts Papers, Exeter Cathedral Library, D&C Exeter/ED/11/14; Phillpotts to H. E. Greaves, 11 Nov. 1850, *ibid.*, ED/11/76; Richard Whateley to J. B. Sumner, 18 Dec. 1850, Edward Copleston Correspondence, Devon Record Office, 1149 M/F 185.

[134] Protest of Samuel Wilberforce, Official Papers of the Diocese (1847-1902), folder 1850, Archives of the Diocese of Mississippi, St. Andrew's Cathedral, Jackson; Declaration of the Exeter Diocesan Synod, 25 June 1851, and William Mercer Green to Wilberforce, 27 Aug. 1851 [draft], Official Papers, folder 1851, *ibid.*

[135] Probably Henry Pitt Cholmondeley (1820-1905), clergyman.

[136] Cholmondeley to Moody, 6, 14 Dec. 1850, Page & Moody Papers, Southampton City Record Office, D/PM 10/1/11; Moody to Ashley, 18 Mar. 1851, *ibid.*, D/PM 10/3/31; *Record*, 10 Apr. 1851; *Christian Witness*, VIII (May 1851), 231.

[137] *Record*, 6 Mar. 1851; *Christian Times*, 8 Mar. 1851.

[138] *Watchman*, 19 Mar. 1851; W. Wilson to Moody, [1851], Page & Moody Papers, Southampton City Record Office, D/PM 10/3/45.

[139] *Manchester Guardian*, 9, 23, 30 Nov., 11 Dec. 1850; *Preston Guardian*, 9 Nov. 1850; *Blackburn Standard*, 13 Nov. 1850.

[140] *Preston Pilot*, 23 Nov. 1850; *Manchester Courier*, 23, 30 Nov. 1850.

to leave the Oldham meeting of 25 November, after his speech, to rush off to another.)[141]

All this activity was intended not simply to repel the Papal Aggression; in the long run, it was hoped that the anti-Catholic energies so unleashed might be institutionalized by creating permanent local branches of the Protestant Association. Several parishes in Manchester established branches during the winter of 1850-51, and branches were organized at Stockport, Ashton-under-Lyne, Oldham, St. Helens, and Preston. Stowell and his Manchester contingent played an important role in this process; the excitement of hearing him speak often led local leaders to organize.[142] Lancashire, certainly, was fertile ground for this sort of endeavor; Evangelicalism had been spreading in Anglican circles there even before the arrival of Prince Lee as first Bishop of Manchester in 1848, and antiritualism thrived there in the 1850s and '60s.[143] And John Foster comments that Anglicanism in the Oldham out-townships merged "in doctrine, as its congregations did in marriage and friendship, with dissent."[144] Lancashire's theological atmosphere was thick with anti-Catholic vapors.

But although local branches formed in the first flush of enthusiasm, their survival over the long haul was problematical. Of the branches named above, only those in St. Thomas' District, Red Bank, Manchester, and Preston lasted. (Manchester had a local branch of the Protestant Alliance in the early 1850s, but its leadership is practically identical with that of the local Protestant Association.[145]) The St. Thomas's District Protestant Association was carried by its incumbent, the Rev. J. A. Boddy, and two dedicated laymen, James Collinge and W. Burnett Coates. The three men presided over regular monthly meetings with speakers and tea, brought in occasional outside speakers such as John Atkinson and James Bardsley of the Manchester and Salford Protestant Operative Association, adopted resolutions, and generally kept its membership active.[146] What went on at these meetings may be gauged by Coates's lecture on "The Rise and Progress of Popery." Coates exposed the evils and tyranny of canon law and expressed the hope that England would thrust aside the craven race who degraded her through cowardice and drive out the Papists.[147] At Preston, the formula of a dedicated clergyman with lay helpers, frequent controversial talks, and outside speakers (in this case, Stowell as well as Bardsley) also worked.[148]

Similar patterns can be discerned elsewhere.

At Birmingham, things were made easy by the presence of Thomas Ragg and the Birmingham Protestant Association. As at Manchester,[149] so

[141] *Manchester Guardian*, 23 Nov. 1850; *Preston Guardian*, 26 Oct. 1850; *Manchester Courier*, 30 Nov. 1850.

[142] *Protestant Witness*, III (19 Apr. 1851), 545; *Manchester Courier*, 9, 30 Nov. 1850, 1 Feb. 1851; *Manchester Guardian*, 27 Nov. 1850; *Lancaster Guardian*, 8 Feb. 1851.

[143] Joyce, *Work, Society, and Politics*, pp. 255-56.

[144] John Foster, *Class Struggle and the Industrial Revolution: Early Industrial Capitalism in Three English towns* (London, 1974), p. 178.

[145] Protestant Alliance Monthly Letter, No. 4, 1 Apr. 1853, Page & Moody Papers, Southampton City Record Office, D/PM 10/2/62.

[146] *Manchester Courier*, 19, 26 Apr., 17 May, 7 June, 18 Oct., 1 Nov. 1851.

[147] *Protestant Witness*, III (17 May 1851), 564.

[148] *Preston Pilot*, 30 Nov. 1850; Protestant Alliance Monthly Letter, No. 4 (1 Apr. 1853), Page & Moody Papers, Southampton City Record Office, D/PM 10/2/62.

[149] *Protestant Witness*, II (2 Nov. 1850).

at Birmingham, the local anti-Catholic periodical became more strident.[150] Clerical activists—I. C. Barrett of St. Mary's, J. C. Miller of St. Martin's, and G. S. Bull of St. Thomas's—sponsored meetings in their own parishes and spoke at each others'. Hugh McNeile was brought in from Liverpool. Other organizations, the Church of England Young-Men's Christian and Missionary-Aid Association, and the local SPCK and SPG auxiliaries, were used as fora. And when the public meeting of the inhabitants of Birmingham, to which all this excitement led, failed to adopt the anti-Catholic resolutions—we shall examine these extraordinary proceedings later—the Birmingham Protestant Association mounted a signature drive to repair the damage.[151]

And as with Birmingham, so with Northampton. Incumbents called parochial meetings, preached controversial sermons, and organized petition drives. The Northampton Religious and Useful Knowledge Society proveded a forum for anti-Catholic rhetoric. Hugh Stowell and Alessandro Gavazzi were brought in to speak. And the British Reformation Society, hoping to capitalize on the excitement, sent R. P. Blakeney to town to try to form a local chapter.[152]

The chief stimuli for protest activities in Lancashire, Birmingham, and Northampton came from local clergy and laymen who had histories of involvement in anti-Catholic societies. The bishops in whose dioceses Lancashire, Birmingham, and Northampton fell were markedly passive and noncommittal in the agitations. The Bishop of Manchester contented himself with stating that he was aware of the dangers that appeared to threaten the Church of England, and that at the proper time he would defend it.[153] The Bishop of Worcester called for greater activity, lest Roman Catholicism take over the colonies; but he offered no leadership.[154] The Bishop of Peterborough was silent throughout the affair. Anglican anti-Catholic agitation in midcentury England clearly was a movement of the lower clergy and the laity, not a creation of the bishops.

The problem of Nonconformity

The biggest obstacle to an effective anti-Catholic response was the relationship between the Church of England and Dissent. The hope of union among true-believing Christians, hearkening back to the mythical unity among the first Christians, has a long history, and some mid-Victorian Englishmen hoped that anti-Catholicism might form the basis for such unity. So, the British Reformation Society claimed to be open to all, and the City of London and Finsbury Protestant Operative Association excluded any discussion of differences among Protestant churches at its meetings.[155]

---

150 *Protestant Watchman*, No. 21 (Nov. 1850), pp. 247-49.

151 *Ibid.*, No. 22 (Dec. 1850), p. 259; *Midland Counties Herald*, 14 Nov. 1850; *Aris' Birmingham Gazette*, 4, 11, 18, 25 Nov., 2, 23 Dec. 1850.

152 *Northampton Mercury*, 2, 9, 16, 23 Nov. 1850, 5 Apr., 5 July 1851; *Northampton Herald*, 22 Feb. 1851.

153 *Preston Guardian*, 26 Oct. 1850.

154 *Aris' Birmingham Gazette*, 4 Nov. 1850.

155 Wolffe, "Protestant Societies and Anti-Catholic Agitations," pp. 66-68; *Penny Protestant Operative*, III (Nov. 1842), 93.

Churchmen attempted to create a united front with Nonconformists during the Papal Aggression crisis of 1850-51. Lord Ashley, the *Record*, and the Stowellites at Manchester all complained because the outcry focused on the interference with the Establishment's hierarchy, and not on popery's Antichrist abominations.[156] At Southampton, the Anglican anti-Catholics succeeded in drafting a memorial acceptable to both Churchmen and Nonconformists; at Preston, however, they were unable to agree among themselves on how to solicit Nonconformist support.[157]

Donald M. Lewis has tried to make out that Anglicans and Nonconformists cooperated much earlier in the century, and much more extensively than is usually thought, but the truth is that Anglican Evangelicals, both hard and moderate, were very suspicious of Nonconformist motives.[158] "It is certainly an historical fact," Thomas Ragg's Birmingham anti-Catholics claimed, "that if Jesuits were not the first fomenters of Dissent, they mixed among the earliest Dissenters, teaching them (as of late) to lose sight of such small things as similarity of faith and principle, in what would now be termed a 'wholesome hatred of the Establishment.'"[159] The London City Mission succeeded in keeping Anglican support because the Anglicans controlled the mission; the Birmingham Town Mission stayed undenominational by pushing out the Anglicans. The Manchester and Salford Town Mission's claim to be nondenominational masked the reality of control by Congregationalists; the Manchester Domestic Missionary Society was Unitarian.[160] At Northampton, and arising directly out of the Papal Aggression, Francis Mulliner attempted to organize a Town Missionary and Scripture Readers Society. Mulliner was an Anglican involved in local Tory politics and in the Anglican-orientated Northampton Religious and Useful Knowledge Society. Yet neither these proofs of his loyalty nor his appeal for unity in the face of infidelity and popery saved his scheme from attack by those who opposed cooperation with Dissent.[161] The case of urban domestic missions appears to show that interdenominational cooperation in evangelizing the masses was little more than a façade.

The Evangelical Alliance was yet another attempt to unite Evangelical Protestants, whether Churchmen or Dissenters, on an anti-Catholic platform. But again, prominent Anglicans such as Stowell of Manchester, Ragg of Birmingham, and Croft Moody of Southampton declined to participate on the grounds that while its supporters called for Christian unity, the chief Nonconformist organs continued to call for spoliation of the Church.[162] "I am more than ever convinced," said Moody, "it is impossible

---

[156] Shaftesbury Diary, 5 Nov. 1850, Broadlands Archives, National Register of Archives, SHA/PD/6; *Record*, 28 Oct. 1850; *Protestant Witness*, II (30 Nov. 1850), 462.

[157] George Grey Cashman to T. H. Croft Moody, [Oct. 1850], Page & Moody Papers, Southampton City Record Office, D/PM 10/2/20; *Preston Pilot*, 23 Nov. 1850; *Preston Guardian*, 23 Nov. 1850.

[158] Lewis, *Lighten Their Darkness*, pp. 2-3.

[159] *Protestant Watchman*, No. 2 (Apr. 1849), wrapper; cf. *Record*, 7 Nov. 1850, and *Christian Observer*, XLIII (1843), 317-19, 347.

[160] H. D. Rack, "Domestic Visitation: A Chapter in Early Nineteenth Century Evangelism," *JEH*, XXIV (1973), 368-69, 370-72.

[161] *Northampton Herald*, 1, 15, 22, 29 Mar. 1851; Wolffe, "Protestant Societies and Anti-Catholic Agitations," p. 268.

[162] Marsden, *Stowell*, pp. 166-68; Birmingham Church of England Lay Association, *8th Annual Report* (1847), pp. 9-10; Croft Moody to John McGregor, 10 Apr. 1851, Page & Moody Papers, Southampton City Record Office, D/PM 10/3/38.

to work with those who oppose Romish endowments & hierarchies not because they are papal but because they are part of a (to them) larger question of ecclesiastical policy."[163]

The self-interest of existing Anglican organizations also discouraged interdenominational cooperation. The British Reformation Society hoped for good things from the Papal Aggression crisis: specifically, more money, more members, and more power. They had all sorts of plans, which never materialized, for expansion.[164] For them, as well as for other Anglican societies, interdenominational cooperation meant reduced support for their own exclusively Anglican work.

In the 1850s, as the hopes for pan-Evangelical anti-Catholic unity dwindled, Anglican anti-Catholics began to turn inward. The three major anti-Catholic societies, faced with declining revenues, engaged in internal debates about interdenominational cooperation. R. P. Blakeney of the British Reformation Society wanted to see closer cooperation along no-popery lines with the Kirk. His idea was that a closer connection with the Church of Scotland would have the dual effect of strengthening Evangelicalism within the Church of England as against the Anglo-Catholics, and of showing that Established churches were better opponents of Rome than were Frees and Voluntarys (who used no-popery to attack Establishments). Blakeney's approach alienated the Scottish Reformation Society, with its Free Church connections, but also alienated some Anglicans, who split off to form the Society for English Church Missions to the Roman Catholics in 1853. A similar debate in the National Club went the other way; proponents of greater openness to Nonconformists were purged from the club's managing committee in 1856, and the club's members elected the narrowly Anglican Marquess of Winchilsea their president instead of the pan-Evangelical Earl of Shaftesbury. Meanwhile, the Protestant Association did little beyond putting out its *Protestant Magazine*; McNeile confined his activities to Liverpool, and Stowell, to Manchester. Accusing it of inaction, the *Record* suggested in 1856 that it merge with the Protestant Alliance, but the Protestant Association refused to give up its distinctively Anglican character. In 1871, however, it merged with the Scottish Reformation Society.[165]

Some anti-Catholics, concerned at the spread of Anglo-Catholicism in the parishes, focused on liturgical reform to excise Catholic doctrine from the Prayer Book. Others joined a new kind of Church association, which focused its energies almost exclusively on matters within the Church of England. The Church Protestant Defence Society, the Church Association, and the Protestant Truth Society had as their goal the purging of Anglo-Catholicism from the Church by means of legal prosecutions and the disruption of church services. And finally, a few West Country Evangelicals, despairing of the Church's ability to Protestantize itself, seceded to form a schismatic group, the Free Church of England.[166] The only Anglican society that gained widespread support across Church party lines was the Church Defence Institution, organized in 1859 to defend church rates

163 Croft Moody to McGregor, 21 Nov. 1851, *ibid.*, D/PM 10/5/1.
164 *British Protestant*, VI (Dec. 1850), 213; *ibid.*, VII (Mar. 1851), 48.
165 Wolffe, *Protestant Crusade*, pp. 254-62, 306; Wolffe, "Protestant Societies and Anti-Catholic Agitations," pp. 284-86, 311-14.
166 See *inf.*, pp. 148-52.

against the Liberation Society.[167] (Anglicans fight over many issues, but almost all can agree that the regular payment of rates, tithes, and offerings is a good thing.) By the end of the 1860s, Anglican anti-Catholics had given up practical hopes of putting down the Pope, as they had their hands full combatting crypto-popery within the Church itself.

[167] M.J.D. Roberts, "Pressure-Group Politics and the Church of England: The Church Defence Institution, 1859-1896," *JEH*, XXXV (1984), 561-62, 564-68.

V

THE TRACTARIAN FACTOR

> Oh what an age for change is this!
> What wonders do appear!—
> The Railroad bears with mighty speed,
> To make the distance near.
>
> Soon as we're in the flying train,
> We find ourselves at home;
> And so *another* railroad runs
> From *Oxford swift to Rome.*[1]

OF COURSE, THE Church of England's internal state had much to do with anti-Catholicism. The Church at midcentury was in the throes of a great conflict over the Catholic revival. The Puseyites, Tractarians, the Oxford Movement—by whatever name, it was the beginnings of Anglo-Catholicism—were dead-set against the Evangelical Movement. And Anglo-Catholicism baffled and frightened Evangelicals; its adherents appeared to be closet Papists, intent on subverting the Protestant character of the Church, working by stealth to take over vital institutions.

Evangelicals feared, as early as 1839 and 1840, that Anglo-Catholics were not simply theological heretics, but conspirators. It was then clear that the National Society, the Church's chief educational institution for the working classes, had been taken over by a group of young people with distinctly un-Protestant views; and the fear of Anglo-Catholicism colored the educational controversies of the 1840s.[2] By 1850, after the dreadful controversies over education, the Gorham Judgement, the Jerusalem Bishopric, and the Hampden appointment, after the devastating apostasies of some Anglo-Catholics, Evangelicals feared that the Church was riddled with traitors.

> [T]he very apostates from the simplicity of their own creed and worship within the pale of the National Church . . . are the prime movers, if not the sole authors, of the present mischief; it is by them that Popery has been enacted, and Papacy emboldened to re-assert its obsolete claims of supremacy; it is by them that the gates have been opened to the enemy of all truth and freedom, and the armies of the destroyer treacherously tempted or invited to enter, and take possession of the betrayed or corrupted citadel.[3]

---

[1] *Penny Protestant Operative*, IV (Apr. 1843), 31.

[2] *The Churchman's Protest Against the National Society* (London, 1840), p. 33; *Christian Observer*, XLIV (1844), 216-19. For the religious dimensions of educational debate, see my *Politics of Working-Class Education*, esp. pp. 62-65.

[3] Daniel Chapman, *The Great Principles Involved in the Present Act of Papal Aggression* (London and Doncaster, 1851), p. 25.

Nonconformists agreed. Anglo-Catholicism, to the Nonconformists, aped Roman Catholic religious paganism, political intolerance, and moral deviousness, but posed a more serious threat, for it also exercised the power of the Establishment. In rural areas, especially, Anglo-Catholic vicars could practice what English Roman Catholic priests only dreamed of: the persecution of Dissenters. And worst of all, the threat to civil and religious liberty, and to spiritual truth, was growing, for "the Church of England is fast drifting towards Rome."[4] Only the Unitarians understood that Anglo-Catholicism represented "a natural development of principles . . . which, though often dormant, have never been dead since the Reformation. . . . The establishment was . . . half-Protestant from the outset."[5]

Anglican anti-Catholic societies also attacked Anglo-Catholicism, for much the same reasons, and organized lectures against the evil, to complement those against Romanism. The *Penny Protestant Operative* began its attacks in 1842, and other Anglican societies soon followed suit. Although anti-Romanism remained the center of these societies' energies during the 1840s, anti-Tractarian attacks came second.[6]

Suspicion of Anglo-Catholicism and of its outward symbols rapidly penetrated the popular consciousness. The cross was especially suspect. To show too great an interest in churchyard crosses was to invite denunciation as a Puseyite. In 1845, a Nonconformist giving testimony at the Leeds Borough Court was handed a Bible with a cross embossed on the binding; he refused to kiss it, declaring that "he was no Papist," and a crossless Bible had to be fetched. Twenty years later, the vicar of St. George's, Leeds, made a thirteen-year-old girl remove the crosses from some Christmas decorations that she had made for the church, because another female member of the congregation had complained that she would not attend church so long as the obnoxious symbol was displayed.[7] Mr. Slope's opinion that "a profane jest-book would not . . . more foully desecrate the church seat of an Christian, than a book of prayer printed with red letters, and ornamented with a cross on the back" was art imitating life.[8] The word "Puseyite" was an insult; and all sorts of stories about Dr. Pusey's unnatural, even diabolical, habits—he taught his children endurance by dripping hot sealing wax on their skin; he sacrificed lambs in his rooms—were current.[9] Politicians had to take care not to get caught up in this sort of thing. Frederick Leveson Gower's election agent at Bodmin said that he had to be seen attending church. But he told Leveson Gower to sit in a pew that faced the altar, so as to offend neither the Low Church party by turning east at the Creed nor the High Church

[4] *Primitive Methodist Magazine*, XXXII (Jan. 1851), 3; *Baptist Magazine*, XXXVI (Jan. 1844), 15-16; *Baptist Reporter*, n.s., VI (Mar. 1849), 105 (quoted); *Wesley Banner*, I (1849), 71; *Wesleyan Review*, II (Jan. 1851), 23-30; *Church*, n.s., I (May 1847), 232-33.

[5] *Inquirer*, 9 Nov. 1850, p. 706.

[6] *Penny Protestant Operative*, III (Aug. 1842), 65-66; *Christian Observer*, XLIII (1843), 779-88, XLIV (1844), 20-22, 35, 64, 84, 87-89; *British Protestant*, I (Jan. 1845), 1-3; *Protestant Magazine*, XII (Sept. 1850), 130-32; *Protestant Witness*, I (24 Feb. 1849), 100-102, (2 June 1849), 156, (16 June 1849), 154-55; Page & Moody Papers, Southampton City Record Office, D/PM 10/2/37 and D/PM 10/6/7.

[7] Joseph Leech, *Rural Rides of the Bristol Churchgoer*, ed. Alan Sutton (Gloucester, 1982), p. 221; *Leeds Mercury*, 29 Nov. 1845; Brian and Dorothy Payne, eds., "Extracts from the Journals of John Deakin Heaton, M.D., of Claremont, Leeds," *Thoresby Miscellany*, LIII (1972), 105.

[8] Anthony Trollope, *Barchester Towers* (New York, 1950; orig. pub. 1857), p. 229.

[9] Surtees, *Mr. Sponge's Sporting Tour*, p. 140; Leech, *Bristol Churchgoer*, pp. 13, 43, 63, 288.

party by refraining from doing so.[10] *Punch's* brilliantly malignant cartoons of Anglo-Catholic priests are visual evidence of this sentiment, at least in middle-class feelings.

Yet opposition to Anglo-Catholicism was only a minor factor in the outcry against Papal Aggression in 1850. A minority of memorialists did indicate its concern with Tractarianism; not quite a third (30.77 percent) of the memorialists went beyond protest against the new hierarchy to deplore Romanizing tendencies within the Church of England. But over two-fifths (43.32 percent) of the anti-Tractarians came from only three great towns: metropolitan London, Bristol, and Birmingham. These, with three more towns (the Plymouth area, Exeter, and Bolton) generated over half (51.37 percent) of the anti-Tractarian signatures. What was the relationship between anti-Catholicism and anti-Tractarianism?

The Spread of Anglo-Catholicism

Thoughtful people began to worry about the spread of Anglo-Catholicism very early on in the 1840s. Although the movement began as a theological enquiry, it soon passed beyond the confines of Oxford common rooms to reach the attention of the educated élite and the middle classes. Robert A. Slaney, Shropshire gentleman, M.P. for Shrewsbury, and promoter of state aid to elementary education, is only one example of many who confided their fears to their diaries.

> The puseyites, cause great alarm at Oxford and elsewhere—wishing to introduce the authority of the Fathers, and other usages of the Roman Catholic Church, and to limit the right of private judgement as to the Scriptures, and requiring generally prostration of the understanding before Authority.[11]

During the 1840s, Anglo-Catholicism's ceremonial and theological implications got mixed up in the debate over the Gothic Revival. For some conservative Evangelicals, the Gothic style was "Popery done in stone." In their opinion, it promoted music, not preaching; its "odd nooks and corners" gave room for shrines, confessionals, and private altars. For them, Protestant worship required that one man be seen and heard by the entire congregation; so they took the lecture-hall as the model for the chapel. Other Evangelicals, especially the more respectable and upwardly mobile, preferred the Gothic style and argued that the odd nooks and corners were good for organ lofts, vestries, and schoolrooms.[12] The taste of the age was favorable to Anglo-Catholic ceremonial.

But it has been common to argue, as Horton Davies does, that "ceremonialism was a later development of Tractarianism, and not expressive of its early genius. . . ," a development of the 1860s or even later.[13] John

---

[10] F. Leveson Gower, *Bygone Years* (New York, 1905), pp. 249-50.

[11] Slaney Journal, Aug. 1843, vol. 9, Morris-Eyton Collection, Shrewsbury Public Library.

[12] *Wesleyan Review*, I (Nov. 1850), 477-85; cf. *Bulwark*, VI (Dec. 1856), 152, on stained glass; Clyde Binfield, *So Down to Prayers: Studies in English Nonconformity, 1780-1920* (London, 1977), pp. 145-49.

[13] Davies, *Watts and Wesley*, p. 244; cf. J.E.B. Munson, "The Oxford Movement by the End of the Nineteenth Century: The Anglo-Catholic Clergy," *Church History*, XLV (1975), 383-84, 394; Bowen, *Idea of the Victorian Church*, pp. 110-11; Nigel Yates, *Leeds and the Oxford Movement: A Study of "High Church" Activity in the Rural Deaneries of Allerton, Armsley, Headingley and Whitkirk in the Diocese of Ripon, 1836-1934*, in *Publications of the Thoresby Society*, LV (1975),

Wolffe maintains that ritualism represented "a substantial discontinuity" between Tractarianism and later Anglo-Catholicism, and that it developed extensively only after 1850.[14] In my view, two reasons explain the connection between Tractarianism and ritualism. The early Tractarians wanted public worship to be conducted in compliance with the Prayer Book rubrics. That meant that they had to pay attention to how worship was to be carried out, in vestments, church furnishings, and ceremonial acts as well as in frequency of services. Tractarians therefore thought about the act of worship and the history worship in ways that were unnecessary for Evangelicals. In addition, Tractarian theological views about the nature of Holy Orders, the Eucharist, and Baptism had liturgical implications, because those concepts found expression in the real world primarily in the form of public worship. Pusey therefore promoted high ceremonial at Christ Church, Albany Street, the Margaret Street Chapel, and St. Saviour's, Leeds, in the late 1830s. Their pupils, who began entering, and affecting, parochial life during the middle and late 1830s, were ready to experiment. Hence, ritualism was neither divorced from, nor later in time than, Tractarianism, and it is possible to catalogue the introduction of church fittings, vestments, and frequent celebrations of the Mass early on.[15] So, the restoration of Catholic ceremonial began to appear early on, in widely distributed parishes; and the people noted it.[16]

It has been common to focus mainly on the Anglo-Catholic parishes in London—St. Barnabas's, Pimlico; St. Alban's, Holborn; and the East End parishes—with occasional reference to St. Saviour's, Leeds, and to Plymouth and Brighton.[17] This London-centered approach does reflect the location of the most advanced Churchmanship, but at the cost of concealing the early spread of Anglo-Catholic Churchmanship elsewhere.

Some scattered examples suggest that there was forward movement early on. The Anglo-Catholic movement in Cambridgeshire, a place that will be examined later in this book, was small and quiet before 1869, but it was there. R. W. Sibthorp vested his choir at St. James's, Ryde, in 1839. When Skipton church, near Doncaster, in the West Riding, was rebuilt in 1839-40, the incumbent replaced the three-decker pulpit with a stone altar, raised the chancel floor, and introduced lights and the eastward position.

4; David Hilliard, "Unenglish and Unmanly: Anglo-Catholicism and Homosexuality," *Victorian Studies*, XXV (1981-82), 189.

[14] Wolffe, *Protestant Crusade*, pp. 284-85, following G. W. Herring's 1984 D.Phil. thesis, "Tractarianism to Ritualism."

[15] W.S.F. Pickering, *Anglo-Catholicism: A Study in Religious Ambiguity* (London and New York, 1989), pp. 19-21; R. W. Franklin, "Pusey and Worship in Industrial Society," *Worship*, LVII (1983), 396-99; L. E. Ellsworth, *Charles Lowder and the Ritualist Movement* (London, 1982), pp. 5-6; Diana McClatchey, *Oxfordshire Clergy, 1777-1869: A Study of the Established Church and of the Role of its Clergy in Local Society* (Oxford, 1960), pp. 80-97, 123-77, 218-20.

[16] Davies, faced with his own evidence (*Watts and Wesley*, pp. 271-73) later modified his contention (*Newman to Martineau*, pp. 118-19).

[17] Nigel Yates, *The Oxford Movement and Parish Life: St. Saviour's, Leeds, 1839-1929*, Borthwick Papers, No. 48 (York, 1975), p. 28; Davies, *Newman to Martineau*, pp. 122-23; Bowen, *Idea of the Victorian Church*, pp. 292-303; Ellsworth, *Lowder*; Geoffrey Rowell, *The Vision Glorious: Themes and Personalities of the Catholic Revival in Anglicanism* (Oxford, 1983), pp. 116-40; Phillip T. Smith, "The London Police and the Holy War: Ritualism and St. George's-in-the-East, London, 1859-1860," *Journal of Church and State*, XXVIII (1986), 107-19; John Shelton Reed, "'Ritualism Rampant in East London': Anglo-Catholicism and the Urban Poor," *Victorian Studies*, XXXI (1987-88), 375-403; J. E. Pinnington, "Bishop Blomfield and St. Barnabas', Pimlico: The Limits of Ecclesiastical Authority," *Church Quarterly Review*, CLXVIII (1967), 289 ff.; Chapman, *Faith and Revolt*, pp. 172-74; Pickering, *Anglo-Catholicism*, pp. 98-105.

Cecil Wray, incumbent of St. Martin's, Liverpool, had to defend himself throughout the 1840s from attacks by Hugh McNeile and by his bishop, who accused him of introducing "unwonted forms and ornaments" and of showing "a tendency to Romish Doctrine." Bernard Smith introduced a processional cross, altar cross, and lights to Leadenham, Lincs, in 1842. The curate of a chapel of ease at Enfield introduced lights and other "Puseyism observances" in 1843. G. A. Denison inherited the custom of preaching in the surplice when he became Vicar of East Brent, Somerset, in 1845, and slowly added more ceremonial. When Charles Royce, the Manchester tutor, visited Lytham (on the Lancashire coast near Preston and Blackpool) in 1847, he heard a "good sermon on the Eye of God being always upon us, but the service altogether is conducted too much in the Puseyitish form to please me." In Northamptonshire, a newly appointed vicar did away with leavened bread, installed candles and a cross on the altar, and then caught one of the churchwardens in the act of removing them. The wardens' complaints were silenced only when the vicar distinguished himself in the congregation's eyes by nursing a family of cottagers who had been taken ill with smallpox. In 1849, the vicar of Lindley, near Huddersfield, preached in the surplice. "Of what was it ominous?" asked a worried parishioner. Charges of "mummeries" and "Puseyite practices" flew at Heyworth, near Gateshead, Durham, and at Houghton-le-Spring, Durham, in 1851.[18] A well-dressed moderate Tractarian at midcentury wore a black cassock, white surplice, academic hood, and tippett.[19] By 1857, Trollope could identify a high ceremonial of lighted candles on the altar, genuflections, surplices, and distinctive clerical garb as "Puseyite practices," and expected his readers to know what he meant.[20]

The rapid spread of Anglo-Catholicism into the parishes during the 1840s and early 1850s was a most significant development, for it seemed to show that Puseyism was a real and present danger, and it affected political and religious behavior in ways that determined the shape of the anti-Catholic movement of the 1840s and '50s. This can be seen by looking at anti-Tractarianism in Leeds and in Lancashire, and then by comparing the patterns thus revealed with those elsewhere in England.

Anti-Tractarianism in Leeds

Walter Farquhar Hook, Vicar of Leeds from 1837 to 1859, came to Leeds claiming to be "to all intents and Purposes an Oxford Tract Man." From the beginning of his tenure at Leeds, he had trouble with the churchwardens, who complained that the introduction of a weekly celebration had increased the size of the wine bill. Local Evangelicals, both Anglican and Nonconformist, attacked his theological position. And, although he

18 *VCH, Cambridge and the Isle of Ely*, ed. L. F. Salzman, II (1967), 194; *Leeds Times*, 22 Feb. 1840; W. F. Hook to Cecil Wray, 4 Apr. 1842, and Bishop of Chester to Wray, 7 Dec. 1850, Claude Jenkins Papers: Cecil Wray Correspondence, Lambeth Palace Library, MS. 1604, ff. 288-89, 228-29; *Illustrated London News*, 1 July 1843; James Bentley, *Ritualism and Politics in Victorian Britain: The Attempt to Legislate for Belief* (Oxford, 1978), pp. 16-17; Charles Royce to George Royce, 26 Sept. 1847, Royce Papers, MCL, M 70/3/21; E. C. Brereton to Rev. Canon Smalley Law, 15 Apr. 1933 (remembering his father), Oundle Papers, Northamptonshire Record Office, Z 49 P/334/381; *Leeds Mercury*, 14 Apr. 1849; *Sunderland Herald*, 10, 17, 24 Jan. 1851.

19 Holman Hunt, *New College Cloisters, 1852* (a portrait of John David Jenkins, Fellow of Jesus College, Oxford), *William Holman Hunt* (Liverpool, 1969), p. 29 and Plate 32.

20 Trollope, *Barchester Towers*, p. 245.

was a Catholic Churchman, he was an independent thinker who quarreled with the Tractarians over their Romanizing wing. His life was complicated, moreover, by the fact that the first two Bishops of Ripon, C. T. Langley (1836-1856) and Robert Bickersteth (1857-1884), were Evangelicals, although the former was somewhat wishy-washy. But all was not opposition. Hook enjoyed support from a considerable segment of his congregation, partly because he was a good preacher, partly because of his intervention in local political and social disputes, partly because he was willing to give up a large part of his large income in order to increase the number of churches, vicarages, and schools in Leeds, and partly because he had a good sense of humor and could laugh at himself.[21]

Hook used his rights of patronage to appoint Catholic High Churchmen to several chapelries and parishes within the Leeds vicarage. He tightened discipline and expanded his control over the committee of the Leeds Parochial Sunday Schools, by testing the Sunday-school teachers' orthodoxy on the doctrine of baptismal regeneration. He and his supporters circulated tracts such as A. P. Perceval's *Reasons Why I am not a member of the Bible Society*, William Dalby's *Reasons why I can no longer hold any fellowship with the Religious Tract Society*, and other Anglo-Catholic productions. His consecration of a grave was castigated as "folly, mummery, and superstitiousness," which meant "that the priests of the Establishment, by means of certain movements of their bodies, render a spot of earth *holier* than it had been left by Him who made it."[22] The Evangelical Nonconformists replied on several fronts. The annual meetings of the Leeds Auxiliaries of the Religious Tract Society and the British and Foreign Bible Society rang with attacks on "Infidelity," "Popery," and "Semi-Popery," denunciations of baptismal regeneration, and praise songs to justification by faith without works. The Rev. John Ely, pastor of the East Parade Congregational chapel, engaged in a pamphlet war with George Ayliffe Poole, one of Hook's curates. And Edward Baines, Jr., editor of the influential *Leeds Mercury* and a member of East Parade chapel, spotlighted these debates and gave extensive adverse publicity to Anglo-Catholicism between 1839 and 1845.[23]

More than religion animated these disputes. Hook sought to influence the Leeds Township Board of Guardians, which supervised the workhouses, in both Conservative and Anglican ways. The Guardians had allowed Dissenting ministers to take turns preaching to paupers on Tuesday evenings and to visit the wards once a week, had permitted Sunday-school teachers to organize classes, and had thrown open the workhouse to the Leeds Town Missionaries. But in 1845, when Hook got himself appointed workhouse chaplain, which gave him control of all public religious services, the Nonconformists were excluded unless individual paupers expressly sent for them. They could no longer go trolling for souls among a captive audience, and they were enraged.[24]

[21] W.R.W. Stephens, *The Life and Letters of Walter Farquhar Hook*, 7th ed. (London, 1885), pp. 220-36, 282-85; Yates, *Leeds and the Oxford Movement*, pp. 11, 13-16.

[22] Yates, *Leeds and the Oxford Movement*, pp. 19-20; *Leeds Mercury*, 16 Nov. 1839, 25 Jan. 1840, 13 July 1844; *Leeds Times*, 11, 18 Sept. 1841 (quoted).

[23] *Leeds Mercury*, 16, 23 Nov., 7, 21 Dec. 1839, 20 Nov. 1841, 9 Nov., 21, 28 Dec. 1844.

[24] *Ibid.*, 28 June, 12 July 1845; Derek Fraser, "Poor Law Politics in Leeds, 1833-1855," *Thoresby Miscellany*, LIII (1971), 23-49.

Attacks on Anglo-Catholicism reached a higher level of vitriol with the opening of St. Saviour's church, which E. B. Pusey had endowed as a memorial to his wife and as a showcase of Tractarian principles.[25] Edward Baines launched a vicious attack on St. Saviour's in the pages of the *Leeds Mercury*, even scoffing at its name (which either reduced the Saviour to a saint, or turned the saints into saviours): ". . . believing, as we do, that Puseyism is *Popery in disguise* and *Treason to Protestantism*, we feel not only solemn regret, but that indignation which disguise and treason naturally provoke."[26]

Controversy within Anglican circles erupted over one of the curates, whose Romanizing practices offended Bishop Longley, Hook, and the town's Evangelical clergy. On the outside, the *Leeds Mercury* kept up steady anti-Tractarian propaganda, and the Leeds Town Mission vowed to combat them. The results were three conversions to Rome and the resignation of the incumbent in January 1847.[27] Turmoil continued, with more Catholic worship, more attacks from Anglican Evangelicals, and with Baines and the Nonconformists doing their best to stir the witches' brew. A second round of secessions occurred in March and April of 1851. Baines printed anything he could find that might cause trouble, even printing an absurd story, which he later had to retract, that the parishioners of St. Saviour's were in the habit of crawling on the floor to gather up "holy dust."[28]

Several denominations attempted to profit from the turmoil at St. Saviour's: the Baptists opened a schoolroom near the church in 1847, and the Wesleyans started a chapel in the neighborhood in 1849, openly declaring their desire to counteract the influences emanating from St. Saviour's. The Roman Catholics, always the poorest, did not open their chapel until 1857, but were active long before.[29] "The Romish priests and the converts are very busy among my poor people just now," wrote John Knott, the incumbent who finally restored peace to the parish, "trying to get up a show of so-called conversions against Easter. The more I see of their tactics the more detestable they seem—and the more their whole religion a mystery."[30]

Although relative quiet had descended on Leeds, at least as far as St. Saviour's was concerned, the hint of Anglo-Catholicism was still enough to provoke trouble elsewhere. In the 1860s, the congregation of St. George's parish, Evangelical by tradition, was rent by quarreling when the church was enlarged by adding a chancel and moving the choir and organ from the loft. The plans came to an impass when it was realized that a choir in street-clothes would not look good, but that to put them into surplices was too popish.[31]

[25] Yates, *Oxford Movement and Parish Life*, pp. 3-5; Bowen, *Idea of the Victorian Church*, pp. 112-18.

[26] *Leeds Mercury*, 25 Oct. 1845.

[27] *Ibid.*, 29 Nov., 20 Dec. 1845, 4 Feb., 4 Apr., 26 Sept., 3 Oct., 12 Dec. 1846, 9 Jan. 1847; Yates, *Oxford Movement and Parish Life*, pp. 6-11.

[28] Yates, *Oxford Movement and Parish Life*, pp. 12-15; *Leeds Mercury*, 1 Jan. 1848, 21 Sept. 1850, 4, 11 Jan., 5 Apr. 1851, 24 Apr., 1 May, 2 Oct. 1852.

[29] Yates, "Religious Life of Victorian Leeds," pp. 256, 263.

[30] John W. Knott to Isaac Williams, 30 Mar. 1852, Isaac Williams Deposit, Lambeth Palace Library, 2/78.

[31] Payne, "Heaton Journals," pp. 105-106.

Anti-Tractarianism in Lancashire

The evidence from Lancashire shows that local circumstances, issues, and personalities affected whether or not memorials mentioned the dangers of Romanizing tendencies within the Church of England.

A small minority of memorialists, 10,590, or 7.66 percent of all the Lancashire signers, protested Tractarianism. But perhaps this seriously underestimates the extent of anti-Tractarian sentiment. When the Orange Order met at Newton-in-the-Willows, just beyond the Liverpool borough limits, all sorts of placards denounced Puseyism, but the gathering adopted no memorial and thus left no countable record of its sentiments.[32] The clergy of the Rural Deanery of Whalley, meeting at Burnley, adopted five memorials, to the Queen, the Bishop of Manchester, Lord John Russell, and to both Houses of Parliament. The memorial to Russell denounced Tractarianism, while that to the Queen did not.[33] Perhaps we should add forty-nine more signatures to the anti-Tractarian total. Three of the four major speakers at the Lancaster public meeting attacked Tractarianism, but the memorial to the Queen did not.[34] Perhaps we should add 1,373 more signatures to the anti-Tractarian total.

More seriously, rhetoric at the Manchester Protestant Operative Society and the Manchester city meetings was anti-Tractarian. "The darkest and deadliest threat to our church and to protestant liberties, had," Hugh Stowell told the Protestant Operatives,

> come from within—he would not say from the church, but from Jesuits and traitors who had nestled in her bosom. . . . [T]he tractarian movement from first to last . . . had been a Rome-ward movement; a pitiful, Jesuitical, dark conspiracy to unprotestantise England, and to ruin us with Rome.[35]

Nine of the fourteen speakers at the big Manchester city meeting attacked Tractarianism.[36]

> But should they not do something to get rid of the enemy within? [asked John Mayson] Was it not monstrous that any clergyman of the Established Church should have been holding out encouragement to the Pope by assimilating the practices and services of the Church of England as nearly as they possibly could to the practices and services of the Church of Rome. Was it not monstrous that they should thus have held out inducements for the recent Popish aggression?—(Hear, hear.) But he confessed he could not see very clearly how this desirable object of getting rid of the enemy within was to be accomplished.—(Several voices raised a shout of "Turn them out," a sentiment which was followed by loud cheers.) But perhaps the Queen and Lord John Russell might know how the object was to be accomplished, and he had every confidence they would.—(Hear, hear.)[37]

Yet neither memorial to the Queen mentioned these enemies within the gates (although that to Lord John Russell did). Perhaps we should add 51,657 more signatures to the anti-Tractarian total.

[32] *Manchester Courier*, 23 Nov. 1850.
[33] *Manchester Guardian*, 20 Nov. 1850.
[34] *Preston Pilot*, 30 Nov. 1850.
[35] *Manchester Guardian*, 6 Nov. 1850; *Manchester Courier*, 9 Nov. 1850.
[36] *Manchester Guardian*, 23 Nov. 1850.
[37] *Manchester Courier*, 23 Nov. 1850.

In that instance, the difference of nuance between memorials to the Queen and to the prime minister may have had to do with the difference between a Sovereign whose Prerogative was infringed and a politician whose Durham Letter had attacked Anglo-Catholicism. But sometimes the omission of anti-Tractarian attacks in memorials stemmed from internal disputes. When the clergy of the Rural Deanery of Bolton met, the Rev. Edward Girdlestone, Vicar of Deane and rabid Evangelical,[38] offered resolutions attacking Tractarianism and praising the Durham Letter. The clergy rejected them by votes of 10-10 and 12-8, desiring, apparently, to secure an address that could be signed unanimously by a body of clergy almost evenly divided between Evangelicals and the more High-Church.[39] In response, the Evangelical clergy of Bolton got up a public meeting, imported Hugh Stowell to warm the audience, and adopted memorials to the Queen (which garnered 4,112 signatures), the prime minister, and the Bishop of Manchester, all of which attacked Puseyism.[40]

Elsewhere, divisions within the clergy were papered over by avoiding the condemnation of Tractarianism. Those divisions led to the abandonment of plans for a public meeting at Bury (which Hugh Stowell had agreed to address). The clergy of Manchester said nothing about it in their meeting, but Prince Lee, their Broad Church bishop, urged them to make sure that their doctrine and ceremonial were true and simple. At Wigan, the divisions, which also had resulted in the abandonment of plans for a public meeting, allowed Dissenters to placard the town with charges of Puseyism.[41]

At Rochdale, a powerful High Church vicar, John Edward Molesworth, prevented attacks on the Anglo-Catholic movement. The memorial, signed by the vicar and 980 inhabitants, did not mention Tractarianism, but instead asked that the Church might have "the unshackled use of her legitimate functions," so as "to make her the consecrating and counselling ally, not the slave, of the state."[42] Molesworth believed that the Church of England's two greatest enemies were Romanism and Puritanism; he maintained that many alleged "Romanizers" were "able and honest Churchmen" who were protecting the interests of the Establishment.[43] The Rochdale memorial's omission of anti-Tractarianism thus reflects the opinions of those who controlled the public meeting there, and especially of the High-Church vicar.

Anti-Tractarianism Elsewhere

Evidence from other places in England confirms the views from Leeds and Lancashire, that local conditions dictated the response to Tractarianism.

Birmingham, one will remember, contributed a considerable number of anti-Tractarian signatures to the national total. The clergy of the Arch-

---

[38] Girdlestone was the author of tracts supporting the Education Committee of the Privy Council's attack on clerical control of Anglican schools and denying the doctrine of the apostolic succession (*DNB*, VII, 1274-75).

[39] *Manchester Guardian*, 20, 30 Nov., 14 Dec. 1850; *Times*, 22 Nov. 1850.

[40] *Manchester Guardian*, 20 Nov. 1850.

[41] *Ibid.*, 7 Dec. 1850; *Manchester Courier*, 16 Nov. 1850; *Preston Guardian*, 14 Dec. 1850.

[42] *Manchester Guardian*, 9 Nov. 1850.

[43] *Manchester Courier*, 18 Jan. 1851.

deaconry of Coventry (in which Birmingham fell) were divided on many issues, especially the doctrine of baptismal regeneration, but most of the speakers at the meeting of over two hundred clergy on 8 November 1850 denounced Tractarianism.[44] The presence in Birmingham of the arch-Tractarian, arch-apostate John Henry Newman must have influenced opinion, although the Oratorian kept a low profile, not attracting much attention outside his new communion until his "Christ Upon the Waters" sermon of October 1850 and his lectures "On the Present Position of the English Catholics" in the Spring of 1851. But there were High Churchmen closer to home. "A Churchman" reminded the Birmingham clergy in 1848 that the required form of service for Guy Fawkes should be used even when the Fifth fell on a Sunday, as it did that year. "Another Churchman" replied (dating his letter "All Saints'-day"), arguing that the service was "annexed" to the Prayer Book, not actually a part of it, that the form carried no authority unless Convocation authorized it, and that it should not be used.[45] A few years later, a feeble and ephemeral Anglo-Catholic Church Union publicly defended the movement.[46]

Thomas Ragg, printer, editor, and founder of the Birmingham Protestant Association, was quite concerned with "Romanizing tendencies," but his concern had to do as much with local developments as with national threats. His concern grew as the number of Anglo-Catholic clergy grew during the score of years after 1850. By the late 1860s, ritualism, especially as practiced at St. Alban's, St. Paul's, and Holy Trinity parishes, had become the main preoccupation of the Birmingham Protestant Association and the local Orange Lodge.[47] The Birmingham anti-Tractarian signatures in 1850, then, were generated by the conjunction of local developments (a momentary Anglo-Catholic presence and the reemergence of Newman into public view) and of a powerful personality (Thomas Ragg) who took an interest in the matter.

The anti-Tractarian signatures from the Plymouth area and Exeter also owe their genesis to local circumstances that created a climate favorable to Anglo-Catholicism and religious controversy. Anglo-Catholic priests appeared early on in the 1840s. Charges of Puseyism flew in Penzance as early as 1843. ("It It is amasing to hear Puseyism talked of so loudly in such a remote corner," Gladstone's brother-in-law remarked.[48]) The activities of the Rev. J. Cocks of Cornwall, who introduced candles, chanting the psalms, and surpliced choirs in procession, gained national attention, as did similar work by G. R. Prynne, vicar of St. Peter's, Plymouth. As is well known, the insistence of Henry Phillpotts, Bishop of Exeter, on strict theological orthodoxy and strict adherence to the rubrics, was misunderstood as Puseyism. (The Devon county meeting in 1850 closed with three groans for the Bishop.) Anglican Evangelicals, who were strong there, circulated memorials to the Queen, complaining of Anglo-Catholic worship,

[44] *Aris' Birmingham Gazette*, 11 Nov. 1850.

[45] *Ibid.*, 30 Oct., 6 Nov. 1848.

[46] Birmingham Church Union, *A Comrade's Harangue* (Birmingham, 1851).

[47] Birmingham Protestant Association, *20th-25th Annual Reports* (1867-1872); *Birmingham Protestant Association Record*, Nos. 1-12 (Oct. 1866-Jan. 1868).

[48] Sir Stephen Glynne to W. E. Gladstone, 17 July [1843], Gladstone-Glynne Papers, Clwyd Record Office.

in 1844 and 1845.[49] Cornwall, because Methodists made up a larger percentage of its population than was the case anywhere else in England, was likely to be upset by anything smacking of Romanism; Plymouth, Devonport, and Saltash, which supplied itinerant preachers to east Cornwall and West Devon, were notable centers of ultra-Evangelicalism.[50]

Elsewhere, organizers of clerical and of county meetings attempted to paper over differences relating to Anglo-Catholicism. The clergy of Northampton town made an unspoken compact (violated when one of the speakers denounced "the fanaticism of Exeter Hall") to say nothing in either speeches or resolutions that might offend party feeling. Similar arrangements for the county meetings of Somerset and Nottingham broke down when Evangelicals carried anti-Tractarian amendments to the main resolutions. Lord Lyttleton refused an invitation to preside over the public meeting at Stourbridge because he did not want Tractarianism to be mentioned. Bishop Samuel Wilberforce of Oxford attempted to control the proposed meeting of the Anglican clergy and laity of Berkshire by laying down stringent limitations as to admission. (He proposed that admission be by ticket obtainable only from J.P.s or clergy, that the number of tickets be limited to a thousand, and that prospective ticket-holders declare that they were members of the Church of England.) When word of the stringent limitations got out, there was so much objection that the plans were dropped in favor of a county meeting.[51]

The Hidden Agenda of Anti-Tractarianism

Local disputes of a nonreligious nature also cropped up in the guise of anti-Tractarianism. The Rev. George Atkinson, vicar of Stow, near Gainsborough, complained that the churchwardens planned to use a parish meeting to protest Romanizing practices within the Church of England as an attack on him. But luckily, the churchwardens could not answer (and could not admit their real motives) when "well-affected working people" pressed them to specify the Romanizing.[52] Hence the charge of "Romanizing" was sometimes little more than a convenient stick with which to beat the vicar in parish-pump warfare. We do not know what was behind the dispute at Stow, but we do know that in certain places opposition to Tractarianism sometimes concealed opposition to Tory-Radical social Christianity. Historians of the Social Gospel in the United States identify three types: conservative social Christianity, which recognized the existence of social problems, but sought to solve them through charity; progressive social Christianity, which challenged existing condi-

---

[49] Tiverton, Devon; St. Stephen's by Saltash, Cornwall; and Exeter; signed by 3,137 people. petitions in Home Office: Registered Papers, PRO, H.O. 45/1010;

[50] David Luker, "Revivalism in Theory and Practice: The Case of Cornish Methodism," *JEH*, XXXVII (1986), 605-8; *British Banner*, 23 Oct. 1850; J. E. Pinnington, "Bishop Phillpotts and the Rubrics," *Church Quarterly Review*, CLXIX (1968), 167-78; John R. Wolffe, "Bishop Henry Phillpotts and the Administration of the Diocese of Exeter, 1830-1869," *Reports and Transactions of the Devonshire Association for the Advancement of Science, Literature, and Art*, CXIV (1982-83), 99-113; John R. H. Moorman, *A History of the Church in England* (New York, 1963), pp. 353, 366-67; Coleman, *Church of England*, p. 24.

[51] *Northampton Herald*, 30 Nov. 1850; *Times*, 23, 30 Nov., 3 Dec. 1850, 4 Jan. 1851.

[52] Atkinson to John Kaye, 9, 17 Dec. 1850, John Kaye Deposit, Lincolnshire Record Office, Cor. B/5/4/91/7.

tions, but was not prepared to advocate sweeping change; and Christian socialism, which did advocate the reordering of economic structures.

I suggest that opposition to Anglo-Catholicism had to do with that movement's criticism of accepted economic orthodoxies, and that the movement early on contained a thread of progressive social Christianity. This argument contradicts the historical truism that the Tractarians "showed little or no interest in the welfare of the common people," or were "utterly blind to the social questions of the day."[53] (Those who accept the truism will admit that a later generation of Anglo-Catholics, Gore and Headlam later in the century, were socially conscious.[54]) That traditional interpretation rests on the assumption that there was a fundamental discontinuity between the Oxford Tractarians and their students in the parishes in social action as well as in liturgics.

Rather, it makes sense to me to follow Desmond Bowen in distinguishing between the more idealist, abstract, and Romanizing wing of the Tractarians, which looked back to the Fathers, the Middle Ages, and the Caroline Divines, and the more pragmatic and English wing, which looked back, too, but which, in looking back, did not neglect its own contemporary world. The former were more conservative in a social sense. Newman believed that rebellion was a sin; Frederick Oakeley said that "the duty of the poor is to submit with cheerfulness . . . and to lend no ear to factious persons who tempt them to break through it." The secession of the Oxford Converts between 1845 and 1850, Bowen argues, left a more socially aware remnant: Pusey himself, and a younger generation including George Rundle Prynne at Plymouth and Arthur Douglas Wagner at Brighton.[55]

The Tractarians knew about one aspect of early industrialization—the depressed cloth trade in the west—from Thomas Keble, whose parish, Bisley, Gloucestershire, had such problems.[56] And they acted upon their knowledge. They were active in the National Society to promote working-class education under the ægis of the Church. Pusey lived an ascetical life, wearing a hair shirt, but also denying himself so that he could use his wealth in charitable endeavors (he gave £5,000 to Bishop Blomfield's Metropolis Churches Fund). He also worked himself, spending the long vacation of 1866 in Bethnal Green, helping to establish a cholera hospital. Isaac Williams was also generous, engaging in a program of disciplined giving to the poor at Bisley.[57]

R. William Franklin argues that Pusey and other early Tractarians went beyond personal benevolence or the alleviation of individual needs. In his view, they pointed to structural problems in the economic system, and wanted to solve those problems by altering the structure of workers' lives. When Pusey called for the building of a new church every day of the year, in September 1833, he had in mind industrial towns as the places

[53] E. Clowes Chorley, *Men and Movements in the American Episcopal Church* (New York, 1950), p. 290; Davies, *Watts and Wesley*, p. 6; cf. Bentley, *Ritualism and Politics*, pp. 89-91; Chapman, *Faith and Revolt*, pp. 1, 75-76; Alan Smith, *The Established Church and Popular Religion, 1750-1850* (London, 1971), p. 75.

[54] Davies, *Watts and Wesley*, p. 262.

[55] Bowen, *Idea of the Victorian Church*, pp. 62-64, 285-90.

[56] Thomas Keble to J. C. Wigram, 21 Oct. 1833, Keble Deposit, Lambeth Palace Library, 5/1/79; Keble to Sir J. Graham, 21 Jan. 1842, *ibid.*, 5/2/8-9; Keble to I. F. Christie, *ibid.*, 4/15.

[57] Isaac Williams to Keble, [9 Feb. 1836], 28 Feb. [1840?], 22 Mar. [1841], Whitmonday [1841?], [n.d.], *ibid.*, 9/5, 26, 36, 47, 48; Bowen, *Idea of the Victorian Church*, pp. 349-51.

where the churches should be built, and he stressed the necessity of attending to the workers' physical wants in the parochial setting. His social thinking rested on the idea that the Anglo-Catholic Movement should counteract the alienating tendencies of industrialization by creating a community centered on the Eucharist. Pusey, and those influenced by him, attempted to make their vision a reality in parishes such as Christ Church, Albany Street, London, and St. Saviour's, Leeds, and they invariably began by abolishing pew rents in favor of free seating—a revolutionary statement in the context of the Victorian era, because it rejected the idea that church seating should reflect class distinctions.[58]

If the older interpretation minimizes the Tractarians' social conscience, a newer interpretation tries to make the Evangelicals out to have been more active in social concerns, as ends in themselves, than has hitherto been thought. Boyd Hilton tries to distinguish between the Claphamites who were laissez-faire and the hard Evangelicals who were more interventionist. Donald Lewis, David Bebbington, and J. Douglas Holladay all point to the Christian Influence Society (founded in 1832 to influence the government and the press on religious matters), list Evangelical benevolent societies, and name Evangelicals such as W. W. Champneys and Charles Girdlestone (who had come to see that the cholera could be dealt with as a public health problem, and not simply prayed away as a divine scourge.) But the Christian Influence Society appears to have had little influence, Christian or otherwise, on anyone. It strains the evidence to see proof of the social gospel in societies to convert the souls of prostitutes and navvies. It flies in the face of the evidence to turn the National Society, controlled by William Ewart Gladstone and his friends since the mid-1830s, and by the High Church Hackney Phalanx before that, into an Evangelical-dominated organization (as Bebbington does). Indeed, Holladay, and Valentine Cunningham for Evangelical Dissent, even advance Evangelical assurances about happiness after death for the saved as evidence for their social concern, because such hope gave some poor people the patience to endure their burdens.[59] To turn the purveying of "pie in the sky when you die" into proof of commitment to social Christianity beats out turning sows' ears into silk purses, as miracles go.

It is no doubt admirable that some Evangelicals in the late twentieth century apparently wanted to find justification for social action in the roots of their tradition, but one must remain true to the evidence, which suggests that Victorian Evangelicals wanted to save souls, not bodies. Although some Evangelicals faced up to social abuses, they saw the abuses as isolated rather than systemic problems, they rarely lived among the poor, and they directed their zeal towards defending the existing social order (which they believed was Providential) and towards looking for conversions.[60] Moderate, Simeonite Evangelicals upheld Sabbatarianism

---

[58] Franklin, "Pusey and Worship," pp. 387-88, 393-96, 402-3.

[59] Boyd Hilton, *The Age of Atonement: The Influence of Evangelicalism on Social and Economic Thought, 1795-1865* (Oxford, 1988), pp. 10-22, 91-100, 211-15; J. Douglas Holladay, "Nineteenth Century Evangelical Activism: From Private Charity to State Intervention," *Historical Magazine of the Protestant Episcopal Church,* LI (1982), 53-79; Lewis, *Lighten Their Darkness,* pp. 74-75, 151-64; Bebbington, *Evangelicalism,* pp. 120-22, 124, 127; Cunningham, *Everywhere Spoken Against,* pp. 88-96.

[60] Bowen, *Idea of the Victorian Church,* pp. 290-91; A. Smith, *Established Church,* p. 75; Jay, *Religion of the Heart,* pp. 50, 169-79.

(among the most blatant pieces of class-based legislation of the nineteenth century[61]), defended rented pews as a good Protestant system, and argued that sobriety among the Irish was "surely purchased too dear" if it came at the hands of Roman Catholic missionaries. Father Mathew's temperance rallies merely showed "the power of one vice to expell another; of superstition to drive out drunkenness." There was little difference between these moderates and the hard Evangelical John Cumming, who believed that it was better to leave poor children untaught than to teach them in Roman Catholic schools.[62] This is not the stuff of which social Christianity is made, and Evangelical philanthropists such as the Earl of Shaftesbury may at most be labeled conservative social Christians.

The career of Charles Lowder, who made his name as vicar of St. Peter's, London Docks, illustrates the continuity of the generations in the Anglo-Catholic movement. He had his first curacy in Street-cum-Walton, Somerset (1843-44). Walton, where Lowder worked, was an agricultural village of 780 inhabitants, so he observed the poverty of farm laborers, an experience that his chaplaincy of the Axbridge Workhouse (1844-45) reinforced. Lowder then became curate of Tetbury, Glos. (1845-51). The population of this town was over 3,000, and its economy was depressed because of the bad weather, and the West Country wool trade was in decline anyway. Finally, as curate of St. Barnabas's, Pimlico (1851-56), Lowder worked in a very poor area; he was responsible for the day and the night schools, industrial and ragged schools, and Sunday school.[63] When he went to the East End, he brought thirteen years' experience in social Christianity with him.

The relationship between Anglo-Catholic theology and social Christianity, and thus the hidden agenda of the anti-Tractarians, appeared most clearly in Wiltshire and Lancashire in 1850.

In Wiltshire, anti-Catholicism and anti-Tractarianism were parts of a party dispute between the High Churchmen (whose strength in the county had been growing since the 1830s) and a combination of Nonconformists and Anglican Evangelicals. Attacks on Puseyism, by identifying a common enemy, helped to forge the alliance among Evangelicals. Simultaneously, hard times in the cloth trade worsened social and political tensions, and Chartism flourished. Active in this turmoil was the Rev. E. J. Phipps, rector of St. Mary's, Devizes (1833-53), a center of the cloth trade, whose "ritualistic observances" led to public protests in 1845 and 1851. His curate preached a sermon on the Real Presence in 1852 that resulted in action in the church courts, and dissidents locked the church doors against him in 1853.[64] So it was that the Wiltshire county meeting in 1850, called to memorialize the Queen, became tumultuous when Phipps rose to ad-

---

[61] Brian Harrison observes that Sabbatarianism received some working-class support, especially from cabmen, postmen, railway workers, and hairdressers, who otherwise would have to work on Sunday. It was thus possible for the Lord's Day Observance Society to trot out working-class speakers at its public meetings. But he also shows "the class bias inherent in mounting Sabbatarian legislation," and observes that Sabbatarianism deprived the working classes of both amusements and opportunities for self-improvement. (*Peaceable Kingdom: Stability and Change in Modern Britain*, Oxford, 1982, pp. 132-34, 138-42, 151, 154.)

[62] *Christian Observer*, XLIII (1843), 21-24, 612-14 (613 quoted), XLIV (1844), 84-87; *British Protestant*, III (May 1847), 65-66.

[63] Ellsworth, *Lowder*, pp. 2-3, 18.

[64] Paul T. Phillips, "Religion and Society in the Cloth Region of Wiltshire, c. 1830-70," *Journal of Religious History*, XI (1980-81), 105-6; R. B. Pugh, "Chartism in Somerset and Wiltshire,"

dress it, and the sheriff had to threaten to suspend proceedings before the priest was given a hearing. "I am a tractarian," he said, "I do hold certain doctrines most decidedly, and make no concealment of the opinions I entertain, but say what I think to be right." And what did Tractarianism mean to him?

He was opposed to Bishops having 5,000*l* a year which he thought a great deal too much. He would carry out the Book of Common Prayer to the fullest extent. He would fearlessly maintain the rubric, and do what that rubric required of him. The Church had not sought enough to administer [sic] to the wants of the poor.[65]

In Devizes, the priest who emphasized high theology, churchly discipline, and social Christianity became the focus of Evangelical animus.

In Lancashire, the hidden agenda was revealed most dramatically at Leigh. This was a town in transition with a mixed economy. Its cheese was noted for its excellence, and it had good pasture land; but silk-weaving was an important source of employment, and coal mining had advanced rapidly since the end of the eighteenth century.[66] Its vicar, James Irvine, was rumored to have "tractarian tendencies."[67]

Irvine sponsored two memorials to the Queen, which did not mention Tractarianism, which protested the assumption of titles on the grounds of the Church's independent canonical rights, not the Royal Supremacy, and which charged that the Russell Ministry's policies hindered the Church's work.[68] He garnered 2,162 signatures. In response, several important parishioners got up a public meeting, which assembled at the town hall on 18 November, to attack the Pope and the vicar. Speakers called the vicar "the little pope of Leigh," "a papist at heart," who "dared not meet a public meeting of the inhabitants of Leigh."[69] This meeting adopted a memorial that protested the assumption of titles, and that went on to ask "that some measures may be taken with respect to those who, subscribing to the articles of the Church of England, lead their congregations with Papistical practices, and give every reason to believe that they themselves are at least infected with the Popish heresy."[70] (Because the churchwardens signed on behalf of the meeting, one does not know how many attended, but a similar memorial from nearby Atherton township got 618 signatures.) The élite of the parish had assembled against their vicar: J. S. Turner Greene (rich barrister of Hall House), William C. Jones (cotton master), Richard Guest (churchwarden of West Leigh, who received his vestry's thanks for "resisting the innovations of the Vicar of Leigh, and protecting the interests of the parishioners"), Richard Marsh (solicitor, clerk to the magistrates,

Chartist Studies, ed. Asa Briggs (London, 1959), pp. 182-84, 210-16; *VCH, Wiltshire*, ed. Elizabeth Crittall, X (1975), 288.

[65] *Salisbury and Winchester Journal*, 7 Dec. 1850 (quoted); *Salisbury and Wiltshire Herald*, 7 Dec. 1850.

[66] *VCH, Lancashire*, 8 vols. (London, 1906-14), III, 414.

[67] Irvine (1791-1874) had fought at Waterloo (probably with the Gordon Highlanders), but then had a change of heart, studied at Aberdeen (M.A., 1819), and became a priest. Although he was not a Scottish Episcopalian, there is some reason to think that that Church's high theology influenced him. (*Ibid.*, p. 420; Donald Clifford Gray, "A Disciple of Discipline: James Irvine, Vicar of Leigh, 1839-1874," M.Phil. thesis, University of Liverpool, 1980, esp. pp. 74-233.)

[68] *Manchester Courier*, 23 Nov. 1850.

[69] *Manchester Guardian*, 16, 30 Nov. 1850.

[70] *Manchester Courier*, 23 Nov. 1850.

Lord of the Manor of Westleigh Old Hall), William Hayes (cotton master), James Pownall (Pennington Hall), James and Joseph Darlington (Bedford Lodge), H. Isherwood (Platt Fold), Charles Widdowes (grocer, cheese factor, pawnbroker), and the Rev. Alfred Hewlett (Calvinist incumbent of nearby Astley, active in agitating against the assumption of titles, who had hoped for the presentation of Leigh in 1839).[71]

Something besides Anglo-Catholic innovations lay behind this attack. J.S. Turner Greene complained:

> The vicar of Leigh was a man who could insult a private individual in private, but he dared not meet them. The vicar of Leigh talked . . . about the freedom of the church, but he prevented their wives and children from being buried in the consecrated church grounds.—(Tremendous cheers.). . . This man, who consigned the soul of the dying man to eternal damnation, because he was not present at the deathbed, dared not meet them. What right had any man to say that a poor being died impenitent, because he was not called in to see the scene on the bed of death. . . . A man who insulted private persons in a private place, and in a manner which prevented them from vindicating their characters,—a man whose brow flushed with anger, and whose lips trembled with the venom that had been spit from them; and who then left the pulpit and went down to administer the holy sacrament—he (Mr. Greene) called that man a nominal churchman.—(Cheers.)

Greene also charged that Irvine "would set man against man, and class against class."

After a war of handbills, Irvine replied in a sermon on 4 December, in which he defended Tractarianism as being solid Church principle. Since coming to the parish, he said, he had sought to improve the temporal and spiritual states of his parishioners. This meant that he built schools, opposed pew-rents, supported the ten-hours movement, and preached on the obligations of employers toward their employees. He regretted that some clergymen

> did not dare to enforce upon their rich congregations the duties which they owed to the poor, and those in their employment; they could be bold enough in a cause which was popular, and say all manner of evil against their brethren, to crowds of ignorant and bigoted people, scarcely one of which was living in close communion with the church to which they professed to belong, and most of them never attended its services; but where were these clergymen, when the cause of the weak against the strong was to be pleaded, of the poor against the rich, of the fatherless and widow against the oppressor, against those who sacrificed them at the shrine of mammon?[72]

The battle continued into the new year. The churchwardens and sidesmen adopted a form of address to the Queen and the Archbishop of Canterbury against Tractarianism. Irvine preached a two-hour-long sermon, defending the Rev. W.J.E. Bennett of St. Barnabas's, Pimlico. The annual meeting of the Leigh Mechanics' Institution (J. S. Turner Greene, president) heard more attacks on the vicar.[73]

[71] Names in *ibid.*; Gray, "Disciple of Discipline," pp. 231-33; *VCH, Lancs*, III, 425; *Lancaster Gazette*, 19 Apr. 1851; *Manchester Guardian*, 2 Apr. 1851.
[72] *Ibid.*, 7 Dec. 1850.
[73] *Ibid.*, 8, 26 Mar. 1851; *Manchester Courier*, 18 Jan. 1851.

What was happening at Leigh was a conflict between a clergyman who emphasized high theology, churchly discipline, and the social implications of Catholic Christianity, and certain of his rich, Protestant-inclined parishioners who were easygoing in their Churchmanship. In worship, Irvine introduced daily Mattins, used a credence table, read the Prayer for the Church Militant, and preached in the surplice. In discipline, he declined to administer private baptisms, required that sponsors at baptism, couples who would be married, and the parish bellringers be regular churchgoers, enforced the rubric in the Visitation of the Sick that required the priest to be notified of those who were ill or dying, and refused to read services in church for Dissenters or the unbaptized. (He read the service in the churchyard.) As for the social dimensions of his Anglo-Catholicism, Irvine extracted free pews in the parish church from Lord Lilford (the patron of the living) and Richard Guest, chaired and addressed short-time meetings and organized petition drives on that issue, campaigned against the relay system, and helped establish a Trustee Savings Bank at Leigh.[74]

The anti-Tractarian signatures from Leigh, then, have as much, or more, to do with the internal concerns, both ecclesiastical and secular, of a specific parish, as with the assumption of titles or any other national development. They certainly reflect the vicar's Anglo-Catholicism, but as certain they reflect the local élite's opposition to the social implications of Anglo-Catholicism, which seemed to them to challenge the social and economic order.

Anglo-Catholic social Christianity in Lancashire gained added support from Joseph Raynor Stephens's weekly magazine, the *Champion*. Stephens was anti-Poor Law, pro-Seven Hours, and attacked Anglican Evangelicals, the Bishop of Manchester, and Nonconformist ministers for their "servile and cringing" service to the cotton masters and to free-market economics. He praised the Rev. W.J.E. Bennett's social service activities at St. Barnabas's, Pimlico; and he welcomed "the recent revival of true religion," which asserted the Church's right and duty "to interpose her mediatorial offices between the rich and the poor." Although Stephens himself never became an Anglican, and certainly was no Anglo-Catholic in theology, his views suggest that James Irvine's was no isolated voice.[75]

Anti-Tractarianism After Midcentury

The charges of Tractarianism and of "popish practices" that flew during midcentury reveal that Anglo-Catholicism was penetrating the parishes much earlier than has been believed, that it could be found elsewhere than in East London, and that its economic implications were being explored early on in the 1840s. Evangelicals felt threatened by this growth, for Anglo-Catholicism challenged both their Protestant theology and their *laissez-faire* economics, so they reacted with savage attacks. It is nonsense to

[74] Gray, "Disciple of Discipline," is a thorough account of Irvine's activities. See also two undated letters from Irvine to William Selby, and Selby's reply, 16 Feb. 1841, about free pews, Lilford Estate Papers, Lancashire Record Office, Preston, DDLi 55; and *Manchester Guardian*, 11 Dec. 1850, about Irvine and the High-Church Additional Curates' Society.

[75] *The Champion of What is True and Right and for the Good of All*, II (6 July 1850), 134-37, (3 Aug. 1850), 194-95, (24 Aug. 1850), 241-46, (19 Oct. 1850), 371; Dale A. Johnson, "Between Evangelicalism and the Social Gospel: The Case of Joseph Rayner Stephens," *Church History*, XLII (1973), 231-38.

claim, as Wesley Balda does, that "evangelical party conflict before 1865 seems to have a great deal to do with the creative imaginations of the more disreputable tractarian apologists."[76] That is to blame the victim. The party conflict was initiated on 2 December 1833, when the *Record* attacked Tractarian language about the apostolic succession. (The *Christian Observer* also joined in.)[77] As the Tractarians developed their theology, and as the Romanizing tendencies of some of the Tractarians became evident, Evangelical fury became more shrill, and public hatred more intense.

Many middle-of-the-road Anglicans during the 1840s and '50s agreed with Joseph Leech, editor of the *Bristol Times*, who thought that Evangelicalism, although it saved the Church from the "dry rot" of the Squarson, would have supplanted "the calm discipline" of Anglicanism "with the excitement of Dissent," had it not been for "another and new movement," the Oxford Movement, which stood for "first principles." But now that new movement in turn was going to excess, offending England's "popular and hereditary Protestant feeling" by introducing ornaments and ceremonial.[78] Yet, although Leech did not like popery, he thought that there was altogether too much harping on the popery of Oxford. Some moderate, Simeonite Evangelicals agreed (as did some in the old high-and-dry party), fearing that the revulsion against Tractarianism might push people to reject altogether the Fathers of the Early Church, Scriptural and orthodox sacramental theology and church order, and even the Establishment itself.[79] These sentiments are little more than the wringing of hands, as compared to the popular sentiment against Anglo-Catholicism.

Lord John Russell, by means of the Durham Letter, did try to focus the public hatred of Popery on the Anglo-Catholic movement, but the attempt did not work; or, rather, it worked only if the local conditions were right. If the vicar were suspected of Anglo-Catholic tendencies, or if those parties that organized the meetings were especially concerned about the growth of Anglo-Catholicism, then the meeting could be expected to produce a memorial that mentioned the danger of Romanizing tendencies within the Church of England. If there were no local sources of Anglo-Catholic irritation, or if those parties that organized the meetings did not wish to object to the growth of Anglo-Catholicism, then the meeting was not likely to produce a memorial that went beyond a protest about the assumption of titles.

Opposition to Anglo-Catholicism was a more central concern among Anglican anti-Catholics after 1850. Although the Protestant Association and the British Reformation Society were busy with their own political and evangelistic concerns, and in any case in financial decline and in disarray over their relations with Evangelical Dissent in the 1850s and '60s, the Church Protestant Defence Society kept anti-Tractarianism alive in the '50s. A reincarnation in 1853 of Lord Ashley's Protestant Defence Com-

---

[76] Balda, "Simeon's Protestant Papists," p. 59.

[77] Chadwick, *Victorian Church*, pp. 73-74.

[78] Leech, *Bristol Churchgoer*, pp. 20-21; see similar comments in the *Illustrated London News*, 7 Dec. 1844; and in the fascinating industrial novel, *The Vicissitudes of Commerce; A Tale of the Cotton Trade*, by Thomas Greenhalgh, 2 vols. (London, 1852), I, 102-5, II, 246-47.

[79] Leech, *Bristol Churchgoer*, p. 100; *Christian Observer*, XLII (1842), 333-37, XLIII (1843), 348-49, XLIV (1844), 26; *Church of England Quarterly Review*, LVII (Jan. 1851), quoted by *Wesleyan Methodist Magazine*, LXXIV (1851), 155.

mittee, which had gone dormant with the creation of the Protestant Alliance, this society focused exclusively on the extirpation of Anglo-Catholicism by means of opposing both Catholic practices and the revival of Convocation. In was active in prosecuting G. A. Denison, vicar of East Brent, for teaching the doctrine of the Real Presence, in a case that lasted from 1853 to 1858.[80] The Scottish Reformation Society joined in, increasing its attacks on Anglican sisterhoods and on ritualism in the parishes.[81]

Anti-Tractarianism also was expressed in the form of the Free Church of England. This schism of ultra-Evangelicals began with the case of James Shore, formerly curate of Berry Pomeroy, Devon. Shore's ultra-Evangelicalism led Bishop Phillpotts to deny him a curate's license in 1844; Shore proclaimed himself a Nonconformist in order to carry on his ministry, and got his chapel listed as a Dissenting place of worship. Phillpotts proceeded against him under the Church Discipline Act, and the case was in the Court of Arches and the Judicial Committee of the Privy Council between 1844 and 1849. Meanwhile, a few other West Country ultra-Evangelicals, who opposed the wearing of surplices, seceded to found free churches: Christ Church, Southernhay, Exeter, was built in 1845-46; other free churches emerged at Totnes (1844), Ilfracombe (1845), Babbacombe (1852), near Torquay (1852), Bovery Tracey (1857), and a few other places. These chapels affiliated and disaffiliated with each other, with the Congregationalists, and with the Countess of Huntingdon's Connexion. Finally, a formal denomination was organized in 1863, and a bishop consecrated by a representative from the Reformed Episcopal Church of the United States[82] in 1876.[83] This schism was numerically and intellectually insignificant.

Other Anglican Evangelicals who were concerned about the spread of Anglo-Catholicism were able to influence the forms of prayer composed for the fast days of the 1850s, and wanted to revise the Prayer Book to expunge passages susceptible of a Catholic interpretation, but their ideas drew no support from men of any consequence, save John Ruskin. The sign of the cross and the language of regeneration in the Order for Baptism, and the use of the word "priest" in the rubrics were favorite targets; the Ordinal and the Occasional Services (especially Visitation of the Sick, which provided for private confession and absolution) needed revision to remove all notions of priesthood—that the clergyman had the power to convey the forgiveness of sins, or that he was in any sense a sacrificing priest. Some partisans hoped for a royal commission to edit the Prayer Book. No prime minister, however, was insane enough to accept such an idea, so others formed the Society for Promoting the Revision of the Li-

[80] Wolffe, "Protestant Societies and Anti-Catholic Agitations," pp. 309-10, 337-39; Machin, *Politics and the Churches*, pp. 255-56.

[81] *Bulwark*, V (1855-56) and VI (1856-57), *passim*.

[82] A schismatic group that left the American Episcopal Church in the early 1870s. The group rejected baptismal regeneration and the apostolic succession, eliminated sacramental and sacrificial language from its version of the Prayer Book, and accepted the validity of non-episcopal ordinations.

[83] Lewis, *Lighten Their Darkness*, p. 99; Allan Brockett, *Nonconformity in Exeter, 1650-1875* (Manchester, 1962), pp. 195, 211-14; *Leeds Mercury*, 15 July 1848, 6 Jan., 31 Mar., 28 Apr., 12 May 1849, 3 July 1852; *Bulwark*, V (Oct. 1855), 112; *Wesleyan Methodist Magazine*, LXXII (1849), 620-28.

turgy in 1854. But liturgical revision was too dangerous to be taken up seriously until the 1920s (and even then proved too dangerous to enact).[84]

The Anglo-Catholics were in a weak position in the face of their enemies, for save the brief period from 1840 to 1844 when Roundell Palmer, then a struggling barrister, wrote pro-Tractarian leaders for the *Times*, they had no powerful sources of support.[85] (The *British Critic*, although important in an intellectual sense, had only a small circulation and was in decline by the 1840s; the *Church Times* did not begin until 1863.) So, some of them organized their own defense groups. The prehistory of the English Church Union (founded in 1860) began with Anglican opposition to the Melbourne Ministry's education scheme of 1839, which posed the threat of government schools along Eerastian and latitudinarian lines. The Bristol Church Union was founded to oppose state control of education, and several other unions, which affiliated themselves to the Bristol Church Union, were organized between 1839 and 1843. After the failure of the Factory Bill, 1843, which would have given the Church a predominating position in working-class education, the unions shifted their activities towards a broader defense of Anglo-Catholicism. By 1859, unions existed in Bristol, Exeter, Chester, Manchester, London, Coventry, Gloucester, Norwich, and York. Late that year, the unions amalgamated to form the English Church Union, which assertively supported Anglo-Catholic advance. The equally assertive *Church Times* began publishing in 1863. Meanwhile, Anglo-Catholic advance occurred in a much quieter way with the Society of the Holy Cross (known as the SSC from its name in Latin), founded in 1855. The SSC was intended to bring together advanced Ritualists by means of a rule of life, prayers, and periodic meetings. Starting with six members, the SSC grew to just under four hundred by the mid-1870s. It probably was the most significant force for the spread of auricular confession. As significant for promoting high eucharistic practices was the Confraternity of the Blessed Sacrament, founded in 1862.[86]

This forward policy led Anglican Evangelicals to form their own aggressive group, the Church Association, in 1864. If the earlier Anglican groups such as the Protestant Association and the British Reformation Society were primarily against Roman Catholics, and only incidentally attacked Anglo-Catholics, the Church Association focused almost exclusively on the Anglo-Catholics. The group published a newspaper, the *Church Intelligencer*, but its energies were devoted mainly to supporting prosecutions in the courts against ritualizers such as James Purchas of St. James's, Brighton, A. H. Mackonochie of St. Alban's, Holborn, and Edward King, Bishop of Lincoln, a tactic enhanced by Disraeli's Public Worship Regulation Act, 1874, and to fomenting riots and disturbances. (Local groups, such as the Orange Order and the Church of England Working Men's Association at Liverpool, could also be used to foment public disturbances at Anglo-Catholic activities.) It also appears to have

---

[84] Ruskin, "Sheepfolds,", pp. 557-58; Janet, "Decline of General Fasts," pp. 71-72, 226-27; Rev. James Turner to Croft Moody, 19 Oct. [1850], Page & Moody Papers, Southampton City Record Office, D/PM/10/1/2; *Leeds Mercury*, 17 June 1854; Bebbington, *Evangelicalism*, pp. 94, 205.

[85] Chadwick, *Victorian Church*, pp. 201-202, 217.

[86] René Kollar, "The Opposition to Ritualism in Victorian England," *Irish Theological Quarterly*, LI (1985), 67-68; Nigel Yates, "'Jesuits in Disguise'? Ritualist Confessors and Their Critics in the 1870s," *JEH*, XXXIX (1988), 202-3; Walsh, *Secret History*, pp. 210-11.

enjoyed a broader support among Anglican Evangelicals—a circumstance attributable to the spread of Anglo-Catholicism. While only a small minority of moderate Evangelicals (as measured by those clergymen associated with Charles Simeon's Trust) had supported the Protestant Association and the British Reformation Society in the 1840s, 44 percent subscribed to the Church Association in the period 1867-72.[87]

In the last decade of the century, the last great Victorian no-popery society, John Kensit's Protestant Truth Society, was formed. Kensit, born in 1853 to an upper working-class family of the sort that the Protestant Operative Society appealed to, sold Evangelical books and tracts for a living, and formed his society in 1889. Kensit specialized in disrupting public church services that he disapproved of. For instance, Kensit attended a Good Friday service at a parish in South Kensington in 1898. The service, one of the most ancient in the history of Christian liturgies, included the "Veneration of the Cross," a devotion in which members of the congregation go up to the altar rail and kiss a cross or crucifix. When it came to be Kensit's turn, he grabbed the cross, waved it around, and ranted against idolatry in the Church of England. Until his death in 1902, Kensit specialized in disrupting Anglican worship, in stealing ornaments from churches, and in vandalizing churchyard crosses.[88] By then, however, the Anglo-Catholic movement was too strong to be extirpated.

In November 1869, the newspapers announced a great, ambitious mission of revival for metropolitan London. Opened with a sermon at St. Paul's Cathedral on 14 November, the mission lasted until Advent Sunday. Participating parishes included All Saints', Margaret Street, St. Alban's, Holborn, St. Barnabas's, Pimlico, St. Peter's, London Docks, and Christ Church, Albany Street; preachers included A. H. Stanton. Among those priests available at stated times to hear confessions was W.J.E. Bennett. The revival mission's final day was marked by street processions with cross, banners, and incense, from St. Augustine's, Hackney Road, and St. Michael's, Shoreditch.[89] This mission marked the coming-of-age of Anglo-Catholicism. "[S]uch a thing has never been attempted since the Reformation," an East Anglian priest rejoiced.[90] It was an outward and very visible sign that Anglo-Catholicism had defeated its enemies and must thereafter be reckoned with as a permanent part of the English religious landscape.

The victory of the Anglo-Catholics, which was a victory in the sense that they were an entrenched Church party by the end of the century, led the Anglican anti-Catholics to become more introverted, to focus more exclusively on what went on within Anglicanism; the two trends combined to push anti-Tractarianism and anti-Catholicism to the margins of Anglican life. There still were anti-Catholics and anti-Tractarians within the Church of England, but in the 1980s and '90s they were marginal: They made nuisances of themselves when the Pope came to visit, or during the national pilgrimage to Walsingham; they wrote crank letters to the *Church*

[87] Kollar, "Opposition to Ritualism," pp. 68-69; Balda, "Simeon's Protestant Papists," p. 60; Bentley, *Ritualism and Politics in Victorian Britain*; F. Neal, *Sectarian Violence*, pp. 187-90; Norman, *Anti-Catholicism*, pp. 105-21.
[88] Machin, "Last Victorian Anti-Ritualist Campaign," pp. 285-90.
[89] *Times*, 5, 15, 25 Nov. 1869.
[90] Armstrong, *Norfolk Diary*, pp. 146-47, 15 Nov. 1869.

Times. There still were Evangelicals within the Church of England, and in the 1980s and '90s they were enjoying something of a revival, but in their outward manifestations they wore Mass vestments, had weekly celebrations, and did not blink at a surpliced choir. Evangelicals had come to accept even the cross as a legitimate Christian symbol.

VI

NONCONFORMITY IN TENSION

> ... the Orangeman raises his howl, and
> Exeter Hall sets up its bray. . . .[1]

THE FIRST HALF of the nineteenth century was of crucial importance
for the history of organized religion in England, for it was then that religion moved into a denominational phase. The rivalry between Anglicanism
and Dissent moved beyond the question of Establishment privilege to include direct competition for members; the rivalry provided one of the
century's staple political questions.[2] Although some late-twentieth-century
scholars find evidence for considerable cooperation in philanthropic endeavors among Nonconformists, and even between Nonconformists and
Anglican Evangelicals,[3] they may have found both more cooperation and
more philanthropy than the evidence warrants. Another scholar thinks
that most Nonconformists at midcentury were more concerned with protecting the civil rights of Roman Catholics and with enjoying the discom-
fiture of their old Anglican rival than with joining in the anti-Catholic
bray.[4]

An examination of what Nonconformists actually said and did about
Roman Catholicism, however, suggests that they did bray, but that the
reality beneath the bray was discordant. That is, Nonconformists did participate in anti-Catholic agitations, and did not place too high a value on
civil rights for Papists. But, different Nonconformist denominations behaved in different ways, partly because of their own internal concerns,
partly because of their relationships with each other. And the question of
the Establishment remained the greatest obstacle to pan-Evangelical cooperation at midcentury, and indeed well beyond.

Nonconformist Behavior

Memorializing in 1850 sprang from different sources and motives than
did petitioning in 1851. (See Table 2 above, p. 45.) Wesleyan Methodist
meetings contributed less than half a percent of the signatures to the memorials, but almost a third of the signatures to the petitions. Anglican

---

[1] T. B. Macaulay, in 3 *Hansard*, LXXIX (1845), 657.

[2] Gilbert, *Religion and Society*, p. 144; cf. Bebbington, *Evangelicalism*, pp. 97-100.

[3] Bebbington, *Evangelicalism*, pp. 120-25; Ian Sellers, *Nineteenth-Century Nonconformity* (London, 1977), pp. 92-98; Lewis, *Lighten Their Darkness*, pp. 2-3.

[4] Norman, *Anti-Catholicism*, pp. 65-67. Norman's mistake was to take as his sole source for evidence of Nonconformist attitudes the *Nonconformist*, an organ of the liberal, anti-state-church Edward Miall.

meetings contributed over a third of the signatures to the memorials, but only three and a half percent of the signatures to the petitions. Old Dissent (Congregationalists, Baptists, Presbyterians) participated hardly at all as distinct corporate entities, although of course as individuals they attended public meetings. A closer look at Nonconformist behavior, correlating memorializing and petitioning with the patterns of religious worship revealed in the Religious Census of 1851, shows more subtle differences among the denominations. The 1851 religious census is a rough-and-ready indicator of the behavior of those who participated in organized religion.[5] (The claim that the census figures for Roman Catholics may have been deliberately distorted or revised downwards, in order to reassure Evangelicals, is nonsense.[6])

The raw attendance figures (Table 4) suggest that about half of the worshippers were Anglican, about a quarter were Methodists of one sort or another, about a fifth were Congregationalists, Baptists, and Presbyterians, and the rest were Roman Catholics, Quakers, Unitarians, and others. The majority of the Methodists were Wesleyans (62 percent), followed by Primitives (21 percent), New Connection, Wesleyan Methodist Association, and Wesleyan Reformers (4 percent each), Bible Christians (3 percent), and Calvinistic Methodists (2 percent). As for Old Dissent, the Congregationalists were the largest body (54 percent), followed by the Baptists (41 per cent.) and the Presbyterians (5 percent).[7] The global figures conceal regional differences. The Church of England was still the National Church in the sense that it was a significant presence everywhere, but it was strongest south of a line drawn from the Bristol Channel to the Wash. The Baptists were strongest in the East Midlands and East Anglia;

TABLE 4

Total Acts of Worship in England, 1851

Faith	N	%
Church of England	4,627,373	50
Old Dissent	1,857,675	20
Wesleyans	1,398,069	15
Other Methodist	875,290	10
Roman Catholic	354,396	4
Other Dissent	128,181	1
Total	9,240,984	100

Source: "Census of Great Britain, 1851: Religious Worship, England and Wales," *PP*, 1852-53, LXXXIX (89)

[5] "Census of Great Britain, 1851: Religious Worship, England and Wales," *PP*, 1852-53, LXXXIX (89). The best discussions of the religious census are K. S. Inglis, "Patterns of Religious Worship in 1851," *JEH*, XI (1960), 74-86; W.S.F. Pickering, "The 1851 Religious Census—A Useless Experiment?," *British Journal of Sociology*, XVIII (1967), 382-407; D. M. Thompson, "The 1851 Religious Census: Problems and Possibilities," *Victorian Studies*, XI (1967-68), 87-97; and Gay, *Geography of Religion*, pp. 45-63. See also my "Popular Anti-Catholicism in England, 1850-1851," *Albion*, XI (1979), 342-43; and Dr. John Vickers's introduction to the returns for Sussex, to be published by that county's Record Society.

[6] Klaus makes this claim (*Pope, Protestants, and Irish*, pp. 7-10), but does not explain how this was done, or by whom.

[7] Gay, *Geography of Religion*, Table 2, p. 223.

half of the Presbyterian attendances were in Northumberland, Durham, and Cumberland, reflecting the pattern of Scottish migration into England; the Congregationalists were strongest in the line of counties from Devonshire to Suffolk and Essex. Methodism was strongest in Yorkshire, Lancashire, the northern Midlands counties, and Cornwall and Devonshire in the West Country.[8]

The biggest problem that the religious census poses is that it does not distinguish among multiple attendances, counting the same people each time they attended church or chapel on census-day. Anglicans commonly attended church once, and that in the morning; while Nonconformists commonly attended more than one service on a Sunday. Multiple church-attendance across denominational lines was not unknown. In urban areas, popular preachers drew crowds to evening services; in rural areas, worship at the parish church in the morning and at a Wesleyan (most commonly) or other chapel in the afternoon or evening was a familiar pattern.[9] Several attempts have been made to turn the raw data of attendances into attenders, but all have their problems.[10] Kenneth Inglis sidesteps the problem of turning attendances into attenders by constructing an "index of attendance" that measures the strengths and weaknesses of each denomination vis-à-vis the general population. He adds together the morning, afternoon, and evening attendances for each denomination, and expresses the sum as a percentage of the total population of an area. His indices thus seek to measure each denomination's strength against the general population.[11]

How different denominations behaved begins to become clear when one correlates memorialists and petitioners per thousand of population with the Inglis indices. The presence of those Methodists who dissented from the Wesleyan Connexion affected petitioning in 1851, and the presence of Roman Catholics affected both memorializing and petitioning. Table 5 shows the results of correlating memorialists and petitioners per thousand with the Inglis indices. It suggests a random distribution of memorialists with Anglicans and Old Dissent,[12] weak negative relations with both categories of Methodists,[13] and weak positive relations with other Dissenting sects[14] and Roman Catholics. Eliminating outliers (especially Northamptonshire) produces correlation coefficients of +.33 for other Dissent,[15] -.17 for other Methodists, -.28 for Wesleyans, and +.38 for Roman Catholics.[16] A similar process with petitioners produces correlation coefficients of +.33 for other Methodists[17] and +.41 for Roman Catholics.[18]

[8] Detailed maps are in *ibid.*, which is essential reading.

[9] Coleman, *Church of England*, p. 6; also see Albion M. Urdank, *Religion and Society in a Cotswold Vale: Nailsworth, Gloucestershire, 1780-1865* (Berkeley, 1990), pp. 99-101.

[10] Inglis, "Patterns of Religious Worship," p. 78; Pickering, "Useless Experiment," pp. 390, 393-94; D. Thompson, "Religious Census," pp. 91-93.

[11] Inglis, "Patterns of Religious Worship," pp. 79-80.

[12] Independents, Baptists, Presbyterians, Unitarians, and Quakers.

[13] Wesleyans, and other Methodists (Lady Huntingdon's Connexion, Primitive Methodists, New Connexion, Association Methodists, Bible Christians, Methodist Protestants, and Wesleyan Reformers).

[14] Besides the independent congregations that Horace Mann aggregated (the identities of which are unknown), I include Mormons, Sandemanians, the Catholic Apostolic Church, and the foreign Protestant congregations in London.

[15] Beds, Hunts, and Northants omitted.

[16] Northants omitted in these last three categories.

[17] Surrey and Cornwall omitted.

[18] Notts omitted.

Nonconformity in Tension

TABLE 5

The Relationship Between Memorialists and Petitioners
and Attendance at Religious Worship

‰ of population	Anglicans	Old Dissent	Wesleyans	Other Methodists	Other Dissent	Roman Catholics
Correlation coefficients with Inglis indices						
Memorialists	+.02	-.03	-.14	-.23	+.01	+.27
Petitioners	-.39	-.35	.0	+.16	-.09	+.36
Correlation coefficients with attendance ratios						
Memorialists	+.16	-.03	-.16	-.23	+.12	+.24
Petitioners	-.20	-.22	.16	+.22	-.02	+.34

Source: "Census of Great Britain, 1851: Religious Worship, England and Wales," *PP*, 1852-53, LXXXIX (89); "Return of the Number of Addresses . . . presented to Her Majesty on the subject of the Recent Measures taken by the Pope for the Establishment of a Roman Catholic Hierarchy in this Country," *PP*, 1851, LIX (84), 649-739; "Census of Great Britain, 1851: Population Tables, I," *PP*, 1852-3, LXXXV [1631], 106; *Report of the Select Committee of the House of Commons on Public Petitions* (Session 1851); K. S. Inglis, "Patterns of Religious Worship in 1851," *JEH*, XI (1960), 74-86.

In an age of growing denominational militance, as the Victorian age was, denominations view the unchurched as a potentially fertile missionary field, but they look upon each other as rivals and enemies. Attendance ratios (ratios of church-attendance by denomination over all attendances) gauge more clearly than do the Inglis indices the relative strength of each denomination vis-à-vis the rest, for they exclude the unchurched from the ratios and assume conflict among denominations. Table 5 shows the result of correlating memorialists and petitioners with attendance ratios for the several denominations. With respect to memorialists, the interesting relations are with Anglicans, Wesleyans, and Roman Catholics.[19] Removing a subgroup of eight counties in which half or more of the attendances were Anglican, but that rank in the lowest quarter of the memorialists,[20] results in a correlation coefficient of +.51. With respect to Roman Catholics, the elimination of Northampton yields a coefficient of +.34. Omitting Northants and four other counties[21] one obtains a coefficient of -.43 for the Wesleyans. As far as petitions are concerned, the elimination of outliers produces coefficients of -.48 for Old Dissent,[22] +.46 for Wesleyans,[23] +.38 for other Methodists,[24] and +.51 for Roman Catholics.[25] These coefficients suggest that Anglicans played an important role in memorializing, while Wesleyans and other Methodist sects were equally important in petitioning. The constant factor in both protests is the presence of Roman Ca-

[19] The negative correlation between memorialists and other Methodists (-.23) is due to Northants having scored highest among memorialists and third from the bottom with respect to other Methodist chapel attendances. With that county eliminated, a coefficient of -.16 shows a much weaker relationship.
[20] Norfolk, Suffolk, Herts, Berks, Oxford, Dorset, Hereford, and Rutland.
[21] Berks, Hereford, Suffolk, East Riding.
[22] Cornwall, Gloucester, and Surrey omitted.
[23] Notts, Surrey, Gloucester, Lancs, Kent, Westmoreland, Staffs, and Derby omitted.
[24] Cornwall, Durham, and Norfolk omitted; if Kent, Glos, and Surrey are also omitted, *r* = +.62.
[25] Derby, Glos, Notts, and Surrey omitted.

TABLE 6

Correlation Coefficients for Memorialists and Petitioners with Rivalry Ratios

	Anglicans to Wesleyans	Roman Catholics to Wesleyans	Roman Catholics to Anglicans	Wesleyans to other Methodists
Memorialists	+.18	+.33	+.17	+.11
(Omitting Northampton)	(+.25)	(+.47)	(+.27)	(+.17)
Petitioners	-.18	+.22	+.34	-.04
(Omitting Nottingham)	(-.13)	(+.28)	(+.38)	(-.01)

Source: See Table 5

tholics: The larger the proportion of Roman Catholic chapel-attendances to all attendances per county, the more likely the county was to memorialize or petition.

The important rivalries are not only between a specific denomination and all denominations, but also between two specific denominations. (That is, suppose that Wesleyans, for example, were more concerned with their numerical standing proportionate to Roman Catholics, say, than to other denominations. If so, then one would expect to find that the greater the ratio was of Roman Catholic to Wesleyan chapel-attendances, the more likely the county was to memorialize.) Table 6 shows the results of comparing the protests with these "rivalry ratios," between Anglicans and Wesleyans, Roman Catholics and Wesleyans, Roman Catholics and Anglicans, and Wesleyans and other Methodists. We see weak positive relationships between memorialists and the ratios of Roman Catholics to Anglicans and Anglicans to Wesleyans, and a moderate relationship with the ratio of Roman Catholics to Wesleyans. The larger the ratio of Roman Catholic to Wesleyan chapel-attendance, the more likely the county was to memorialize.[26] If Northampton, clearly an unusual case, is omitted, the relationships are strengthened. The correlation coefficients for petitioners show similar relationships, except that the ratio of Roman Catholics to Anglicans explains more than the ratio of Roman Catholics to Wesleyans.

But perhaps Roman Catholicness is really a stalking-horse for Irishness. The two are closely related, but the relative influence of each may be separated out and assessed through partial correlation. First-order partial correlation permits the exploration of the relationship between two variables with a third variable controlled. Variable X rarely "explains" all the variation in variable Y; some variation in Y not explained by X may be explained by another variable (Z). Partial correlation correlates X and Y with Z held constant; or, in other words, it estimates the variation "explained" by an extraneous variable, removes it, and then calculates the correlation.

[26] But Wesleyans generated only nine memorials and less than a quarter of a percent of the signatures. The paradox is resolved by noting that Conference leadership asked Wesleyans to attend public town and parochial meetings, rather than to originate distinctively denominational meetings.

If we control for Irish-born per thousand of population, we get coefficients of $+.28$ for memorialists with the Roman Catholic to Wesleyan rivalry ratio, $+.20$ for the Anglican-Wesleyan rivalry ratio, and nil for the Roman Catholic to Anglican rivalry ratio. This means that the two measures of Wesleyan rivalry continue to show moderate to weak relationships with memorializing even after controlling for the Irish presence, while the Roman Catholic to Anglican rivalry ratio explains little indeed of the variation in memorializing. That is, the larger the ratios of Roman Catholic and Anglican attendances to Wesleyan per county, the more likely the county was to memorialize. (And omitting Northampton from the equation strengthens the relationships.) Therefore we may say that Wesleyans tended to be influenced by both the presence of Irish and the presence of Roman Catholics (since the Roman Catholic to Wesleyan ratio continues to explain despite controlling for Irish), while Anglicans were influenced by the presence of Irish alone in 1850. With respect to petitioners, however, the rivalry ratio for Roman Catholic to Anglican church-attendances continues weak but explains more ($r = +.26$) than the rivalry ratio for Roman Catholics to Wesleyans ($r = +.05$).

An examination of Nonconformist behavior in Lancashire may help to put some flesh and blood on the dry statistical bones that we have just gnawed, and may help to carry us along the road down which the statistics directed us. Table 3 (above, p. 46) suggests on its face that Nonconformists, as distinctly separate groups, were not active in the protests of 1850-1851, especially as compared with the national scene. But this is deceptive; Lancashire Nonconformists did object to the Roman Catholic assumption of titles. Dissenting clergy advertised lectures on various aspects of the evils of popery, and the county's Congregational ministers issued a public declaration of protest.[27] The Congregationalist protest, however, was double-edged. They condemned the Roman Catholic Church as unscriptural in its doctrines and intolerant in its civil relations; even though they themselves rejected the Royal Supremacy in things spiritual, they accused Roman Catholics of having "divided loyalties." The Congregationalists went on to claim that the immediate causes of the Papal Aggression were to be found in the Tractarian movement and in the policy of successive governments (granting funds to Maynooth in Ireland and to parochial schools in England, and the recognition of Roman Catholic titles in Ireland and the colonies). The Lancashire Congregationalists offered a solution to the problem: withdraw all government grants from Roman Catholic institutions; turn the universities into "truly national institutions"; and separate church and state, or at least the abolish church courts and tithes.[28] It seems as if the Lancashire Congregationalists condemned the Roman Catholics but reserved punishment for the Anglicans.

The problem, of course, was the Establishment, as two incidents illustrate. There was some objection in the Wigan town council to the proposed resolution condemning the Papal Aggression, for it recognized the Crown's spiritual supremacy, and one councillor proposed to replace the memorial with one requesting the separation of church and state.[29] The Establish-

[27] *Manchester Guardian*, 9, 23 Nov., 7 Dec. 1850; *Preston Pilot*, 30 Nov. 1850.
[28] *Manchester Guardian*, 11 Dec. 1850.
[29] *Manchester Courier*, 21 Dec. 1850.

ment also embarrassed the so-called public meeting at Blackburn: "Several dissenting ministers were expected to take part in the proceedings, but they declined, preferring to oppose popery by preaching, &c., rather than by 'coalescing with those who acknowledge any human supremacy in the church of God.'"[30] To protest against the assumption of titles was to engage in a pro-Anglican activity, for that assumption interfered with the Royal Supremacy. This put Nonconformists between a rock and a hard place. They loathed popery and were happy to grasp the opportunity to attack it, but they did not wish to help prop up the Establishment.

Now public meetings in Lancashire appear to have been tightly organized, with little outlet for disagreement, but elsewhere in England one can see denominational differences at work. At the ten meetings in which the *Times* reported disagreement,[31] twenty Dissenting ministers participated. Four Wesleyan and six Congregationalist ministers supported anti-Catholic memorials. Those who opposed the anti-Catholic memorials were one Wesleyan, two Wesleyan Reformers who had been expelled by Conference, two Congregationalists, three Unitarians, and two Baptists.[32] The Derby town meeting of 17 November 1850 is instructive. James Heygate[33] introduced a resolution, seconded by a Wesleyan preacher, praying the Queen "to take such measures as may prevent such encroachments on the part of the Bishop of Rome." But the Rev. William Griffith, one of the three leading expelled Wesleyan Reformers, proposed an amendment, seconded by the Unitarian Rev. W. Crosskey, that opposed resorts to the civil arm and that labeled any establishment of religion "the essence of popery."[34]

The Lancashire evidence matches this. Of the Nonconformist clergy who participated with Anglican clergy in public anti-Catholic meetings outside Liverpool, nine were Wesleyan Methodists, seven were Congregationalists, one each was English Presbyterian and Unitarian, and the denomination of one was not reported.[35] The "Protestant Nonconformists" of Preston organized their own meeting because the memorial being circulated there recognized the Crown's spiritual supremacy. Of the six speakers at that meeting, two were Congregationalists, two were Wesleyans, one was an Association Methodist, and one was of the Countess of Huntingdon's Connexion.[36] The Rev. James Spence, a Congregationalist, gave the meeting a revealing exposition of Nonconformist views on Roman Catholicism.[37] He argued that Nonconformists did not abandon their traditional views about civil liberty and the Establishment by opposing the assumption of titles. If they were to remain silent, their silence might be construed to mean that they saw no difference between the Pope dividing England into dioceses and the Wesleyan Conference dividing England into districts. To oppose the Roman Catholic hierarchy was actually to pro-

[30] *Manchester Guardian*, 18 Dec. 1850.
[31] St. Leonard's, Shoreditch; Derby borough; Nottingham; Cambridge city; Birmingham; Hexham; Dorset; Stratford-on-Avon; Newcastle-on-Tyne; Berkshire.
[32] *Times*, 29, 30 Nov., 2, 3, 12, 18, 19 Dec. 1850.
[33] Heygate was an M.D. at Derby from 1837 to his death in 1872 (Boase, I, 1456).
[34] *Times*, 18 Nov. 1850.
[35] *Manchester Guardian*, 23, 30 Nov. 1850; *Manchester Courier*, 9, 30 Nov., 7, 14, 28 Dec. 1850, 22 Feb., 8 Mar., 12 Apr. 1851; *Preston Pilot*, 30 Nov. 1850; *Blackburn Standard*, 11 Dec. 1850.
[36] *Preston Guardian*, 7 Dec. 1850.
[37] *Preston Pilot*, 7 Dec. 1850.

mote liberty. Romanism denied access to the Bible, which was "the palladium of their liberty, the foundation of all they enjoyed in civil, intellectual, and religious freedom." Romanism was intolerant, persecutory, and manipulative: "wherever it had attained spiritual supremacy unchecked and uninterrupted, there it had asserted its temporal dominion. Look at Spain, look at Portugal—yea, look to Ireland." Therefore, lovers of liberty must oppose Roman Catholicism. Spence went on to argue that it was important for Nonconformists to hedge about their religious identity by speaking out against Roman Catholicism: "He need not tell them that it was an old combination to talk of Catholics, Dissenters, and Infidels, all in a breath . . . this threefold cord should be broken." For Spence, opposition to Roman Catholicism was a way of clearly defining his own religious identity.

The Preston Dissenters adopted a resolution that professed to support civil liberties, but that opened the door to the narrowest construction of those liberties:

> [W]hile according in the fullest extension of civil and religious liberty to all Roman Catholic fellow-subjects, this meeting considers that the recent Bull . . . is an evidence of the unchanged, arrogant, ambitious, and intolerant character of that system; and is a fresh call on all true Protestants to watch its proceedings, and by intelligence, zeal, and prayer, to resist its encroachments, and seek its overthrow.

Now the responses of the Wesleyans and Congregationalists appear to differ from those of other Nonconformist denominations. Wesleyans were staunchly anti-Catholic, and Congregationalists were only slightly less so. Baptists appeared somewhat divided; and the non-Wesleyan Methodists seemed to doubt the wisdom of the agitation. Let us look more closely at the attitudes of the denominations.

Nonconformist Anti-Catholics

There was something about Nonconformity's frame of mind, Walter Houghton thought, which inclined it to intolerance.

> Puritanism was itself a direct stimulus to belligerence. Though its conception of life as moral warfare led to a struggle *against* the passions in the Victorian conscience, it also inspired a self-righteous intolerance, based on the belief in divine election, that could *release* the passions and justify the most merciless appeal to force. . . . In addition to the inner struggle is the battle against your enemies, political and private as well as national, *who are His enemies, too*, and therefore to be struck down with a good conscience.[38]

This judgement can be tested by examining the anti-Catholic attitudes of the Methodists, the Congregationalists and Baptists, and the Presbyterians.

"[A]nticatholicism," David Hempton argues, "was the most consistent principle in Methodist political involvement from Wesley's lifetime until 1846."[39] John Wesley himself had been labeled a Jacobite, a Papist, in the

---

[38] Houghton, *Victorian Frame of Mind*, p. 213.
[39] David Hempton, "Methodism and Anti-Catholic politics, 1800-1846" (Ph.D. thesis, University of St. Andrews, 1977), p. 7.

pay of Spain, so he defended his movement by embracing no-popery in his *Word to a Protestant* (1742). Disputes with Richard Challoner, vicar apostolic of the London District, that were designed to show that Protestantism was superior to Roman Catholicism, pushed Wesley to deny the apostolic succession. Wesley's twenty-one visits to Ireland reinforced his anti-Catholicism by convincing him that popery was unchanging, persecutory, throve on ignorance, caused backwardness, and was disloyal. Finally, in the period 1778-80, when English Roman Catholics gained some relief from disabilities, and when their numbers grew, Wesley endorsed Lord George Gordon's Protestant Association.[40] "Indeed," Hempton concludes, "Wesley's anti-Catholicism was one of his profound and enduring legacies to the Wesleyan connexion, and the connexion's vigorous anti-Catholicism—in which it genuinely reflected its following—was a most important determinant of Wesleyan political attitudes during the nineteenth century."[41]

Tendencies during the first third of the nineteenth century amplified this legacy. Ireland continued to influence Wesleyan attitudes directly and indirectly. Directly, missions to Ireland, maintained from 1799, allowed Irish (especially Ulster) Protestant voices to be heard in England; by the 1840s, 23 percent of the Wesleyans in the British Isles lived in Ireland. Indirectly, the coincidence of Irish settlement and Methodist growth in the same area—the North of England—led to a heightened consciousness of Roman Catholic militance. Methodism's Evangelical theology, especially as interpreted by "a plentiful supply of half-educated itinerant preachers," further inclined it to anti-Catholicism. Finally, Wesleyans were conservative in politics, and aspired to respectability; so they gravitated to the Tory Party and the Church of England, the two staunchest supporters of the Protestant Constitution.[42]

Wesleyan anti-Catholicism found its most characteristic expression in the education issue. The Connexion's opposition to the 1839 education scheme involved it in its most active politics since Lord Sidmouth's bill of 1811 to put down strolling preachers. The leadership, especially Jabez Bunting,[43] objected to the scheme because it would have permitted state aid for Roman Catholic schools, "in which the errors, the superstitions, and the idolatries of Popery will be inculcated" and "the corrupted Romish translations" of the Scriptures used. The leaders organized opposition in the form of resolutions, a standard form of petition, and publicity in the *Watchman*, the denomination's weekly newspaper.[44]

The Wesleyan Connexion's leaders had cooperated with the Church of England in their opposition to the 1839 education scheme, but the rise of Anglo-Catholicism made such cooperation increasingly difficult. The Tractarians questioned the validity of Wesleyan orders and sacraments, doubted the necessity of a conversion experience (at least, in the form that the Wesleyans experienced it), and dismissed them as mere Dissenters. In

---

[40] David Hempton, *Methodism and Politics in British Society, 1750-1850* (Stanford, 1984), pp. 33-42.

[41] *Ibid.*, pp. 42-43.

[42] *Ibid.*, pp. 15, 117; Hempton, "Methodism and Anti-Catholic Politics," pp. 198, 313-20.

[43] Bunting (1799-1855), a powerful Wesleyan bureaucrat and molder of Victorian Wesleyanism, held many offices and pulled many strings (*DNB*, III, 273-74).

[44] Hempton, "Methodism and Anti-Catholic Politics," pp. 212-16, 230-31; Hempton, *Methodists and Politics*, pp. 160-64; Paz, *Working-Class Education*, p. 85.

their turn, the Wesleyans began to fear that the Church was filled with crypto-papists bent on betraying Protestantism in a Jesuit conspiracy. The *Watchman* attacked the *Tracts for the Times* in 1836, and the Connexion issued its own set of tracts in 1842. The polemics with the Puseyites pushed the Connexion to emphasize justification by faith, to deny the apostolic succession and baptismal regeneration, to try to cooperate with Anglican Evangelicals such as Hugh Stowell, Hugh McNeile, and Francis Close, and to excoriate "the cage of unclean birds" to be found in the bosom of the Church—the secret Romanizers, the "wicked and degraded traitors who have effected a lodgment within her pale, and, like the greedy vampyre, are preying upon her vitals."[45]

The years 1843, 1844, and 1845 were of critical importance for the Wesleyan Connexion. The Factory Bill, 1843, seemed to them to endow Anglo-Catholicism, and the Maynooth grant of 1845 did endow Roman Catholicism. The Dissenters' Chapels Act, 1844, which gave Unitarians firm title to their property, in their view endowed Socinian heresy. The Connexion's leadership wanted to cooperate with the Evangelical anti-Catholic wings of both the Church and Orthodox Dissent, without losing its own independence. Out of this emerged the Evangelical Alliance, which attempted to institutionalize pan-Evangelical cooperation. And the Wesleyans accepted the government's education policy in the Minutes of 1846, which provided state funding for teacher-training in return for a state-dictated syllabus, because Bunting had obtained the best deal for the Connexion as well as the exclusion of Roman Catholic schools from state aid.[46]

Although the Wesleyan Connexion continued to maintain, or to try to maintain, its special relationship as an ex-Anglican, not-quite-Dissenting, not-quite-denomination, a *via media* from Dissent to Anglicanism, it had an increasingly hard time, and it began to abandon its Anglican roots in the Prayer Book.[47] Or, to put it another way, the Wesleyan Connexion found it increasingly difficult to keep its place in what David Hempton calls "this ecclesiastical version of the eternal triangle" of Wesleyanism, Church, and Dissent.[48] This was not a happy position to be in, and Conference leadership, criticized by some because they were not Churchmen and by others because they did not admit to being Nonconformists, compared themselves to "the lamb between the two voracious, carrion-eating vultures, which are both striving to carry off the prize. . . . Herod and Pilate became friends, and then united in the bad work of throwing ignominy on the adorable redeemer."[49]

Wesleyan periodicals were filled with anti-Catholic articles, sermons, and notices during the second half of the 1840s and first half of the 1850s. Anglo-Catholicism came in for attack; the periodicals excoriated what they

[45] Hempton, *Methodism and Politics*, pp. 165-70; Hempton, "Methodism and Anti-Catholic Politics," pp. 184, 240-46, 290-301; *Wesleyan Methodist Magazine*, LXVI (1843), 215-16 (quote), 928-33, LXX (1847), 51-61; *Wesleyan Notices Newspaper*, No. 51 (30 Nov. 1850), p. 214.

[46] Paz, *Working-Class Education*, pp. 120, 134-35; Hempton, *Methodism and Politics*, pp. 172-73, 190; Hempton, "Methodism and Anti-Catholic Politics," pp. 247-66, 276-89, 315; Machin, "Maynooth," pp. 63-64; *Wesleyan Methodist Magazine*, LXVI (1843), 406-8.

[47] Henry D. Rack, "Wesleyan Methodism, 1849-1902," *A History of the Methodist Church in Great Britain*, ed. Rupert Davies, A. Raymond George, and Gordon Rupp, 4 vols. (London, 1965-88), III, 152-53; William Strawson, "Methodist Theology, 1850-1950," *ibid.*, pp. 183-84.

[48] Hempton, "Methodism and Anti-Catholic Politics," p. 9.

[49] *Wesleyan Methodist Magazine*, LXVI (1843), 216.

took to be the excessively pro-Catholic policies of the Peel and Russell ministries; and travel articles described the intellectual and economic evils of popery. But the main focus was on Roman Catholicism's theological paganism and historical persecutory spirit.[50] And the same messages were repeated again and again, in hosts of sermons: Roman Catholicism and Anglo-Catholicism are pagan, persecutory, and un-English; the just are saved by faith alone; sacraments do not invariably convey grace.

It is against this background that the Wesleyan Connexion reacted to the Papal Aggression crisis. The *Watchman* published the offending popish documents, the letters apostolic *Universalis ecclesiæ* and the Flaminian Gate pastoral, and copied leading articles from the *Times*, but at first little was made of the assumption of titles. The legal issues did not seem too important, for the titles did not usurp those of any English prelate, and it did not signify whether Wiseman was Archbishop of Westminster or of Wapping. Englishmen had the right to accept the Pope of Rome or the Grand Lama of Tibet as their spiritual teachers, but it was another matter if the Pope as temporal prince invested Wiseman with secular authority.[51] Very soon, however, the Connexion's leaders convinced themselves that the Pope had done just that: A cardinal is a temporal prince. Wiseman is a cardinal. Therefore, Wiseman will exercise temporal jurisdiction over Englishmen; Wiseman will enjoy the same legal claims and exemptions that a mediæval cardinal legate had. A host of preachers repeated the arguments in local chapels and missionary society meetings.[52]

The Congregationalists and the Baptists had traditions of greater sympathy for the civil rights of Roman Catholics than the Wesleyans had, but they, too, grew increasingly anti-Catholic during the 1830s and '40s. Like the Methodists, the Congregationalists and Baptists reacted to Anglo-Catholicism and the rise of Roman Catholicism by deemphasizing the sacraments as means of grace and the chapel as a corporate fellowship of believers. The agitation over the 1843 Factory Bill was as important for the Congregationalists as for the Wesleyans. It brought the Leeds Congregationalist editor Edward Baines, Jr., to national notice as a leader of the Voluntaryists. It also gave practice in developing the techniques of coordinated press and petition drives that were to be used in later agitations. By the time of the anti-Maynooth agitation of 1846, many Congregationalist and Baptist leaders had abandoned their traditional support of Roman Catholic rights; although they continued to oppose the state endowment of religion, their energies were directed chiefly towards seeing that Roman Catholics were denied a place at the trough.[53]

The main Congregationalist newspapers, the *Patriot*, edited by Josiah Conder,[54] and the *British Banner*, edited by John Campbell,[55] reprinted the

[50] *Wesleyan Methodist Magazine*, LXX (1847), 572-73, 1161-78, LXXII (1849), 147-55, 492-97, LXXIV (1851), 35-44; *Christian Miscellany, and Family Visiter*, I-IX (1846-54), *passim*; Meredith C. Haines, "The Nonconformists and the Nonconformist Periodical Press in Mid-Nineteenth Century England" (Ph.D. thesis, Indiana University, 1966), pp. 76-83.

[51] *Watchman*, 17 July, 16, 23, 30 Oct. 1850.

[52] *Ibid.*, 30 Oct., 6, 13, 20 Nov., 11 Dec. 1850, 15 Jan. 1851; *Wesleyan Methodist Magazine*, LXXIII (1850), 1298-1305; *Preston Pilot*, 7 Dec. 1850.

[53] Sellers, *Nonconformity*, p. 24; Machin, "Maynooth," pp. 64-67; Binfield, *Prayers*, pp. 83-84.

[54] Conder (1789-1855) was an author, bookseller, and editor of the *Patriot* from 1832 (*DNB*, IV, 927-28).

[55] Campbell (1794-1867), minister of the London Tabernacle (second in succession to George Whitefield), was the most visible voice of Congregationalism. He edited the two official organs of the

obnoxious papal documents and denounced the assumption of titles, and numerous Congregationalist preachers used sermons, lectures, and public meetings to combat the aggression.[56]

Congregationalist leaders, like the Wesleyans, managed to convince themselves that the assumption of titles was a temporal, not merely a spiritual, matter, and that therefore their opposition did not really infringe the civil rights of Roman Catholics. The Board of Congregational Ministers of London, meeting on 26 November 1850, declared that although it rejected the Royal Supremacy in things spiritual, it accepted it in things temporal, and therefore opposed "the interference of a foreign potentate"—which the Pope was—"in the affairs of this kingdom." Moreover, although the Board believed in religious freedom, it also believed that popery was "unfavourable to free enquiry" and "averse to constitutional liberty and political freedom"; therefore, to put down the Roman Catholic hierarchy was really to support the free practice of religion.[57]

Other leaders also convinced themselves. Thomas Binney[58] argued that the Roman territorial hierarchy was different from the districts of the Wesleyans or the county associations of the Congregationalists, because the Roman bishops advanced "an implied claim" to spiritual authority over all Englishmen, not just Roman Catholics, and because the Papacy was a temporal power and cardinals were temporal princes. The Rev. Richard Slate[59] argued that Wiseman was a cardinal; Wolsey and Pole were cardinals; therefore, given the chance, Wiseman would behave like Wolsey and Pole. Josiah Conder argued that if the Pope could make an Archbishop of Westminster, he could make a Duke of York.[60] The only prominent dissenting voice in Congregationalist circles was that of the active layman Edward Swaine,[61] who charged that the Anglicans, who cried No Popery the loudest, were themselves popish, and that the biggest encouragement to militant Romanism was the union of church and state.[62] The Congregational leadership thus found the justifications that allowed them to support penal legislation outlawing the hierarchy, and even to brand the Ecclesiastical Titles Bill as "inadequate to vindicate the independence of the Crown and the honour of the country."[63]

Finally, both Presbyterians and Baptists also grew increasingly hostile to both Roman Catholicism and Anglo-Catholicism during the 1830s and '40s. For the Baptists, Roman Catholicism was "one mass of hideous error. It is, in its very nature and design, subversive of the gospel of Christ. It is, and has been all along, Satan's mighty engine for counterworking and

---

Congregational Union (the *Christian Witness* and the *Christian's Penny Magazine*), as well as the *British Banner*, his private newspaper. He was an acerbic and loud personality (the Phillpotts of Independency) and a master religious journalist. (Chadwick, *Victorian Church*, pp. 404-5; *DNB*, III, 839.)

[56] *Patriot*, 24, 30 Oct., 14, 21 Nov., 2 Dec. 1850; *British Banner*, 6 Nov. 1850; *Preston Pilot*, 7 Dec. 1850.

[57] *British Banner*, 4 Dec. 1850.

[58] Binney (1798-1874) was a noted controversialist and pastor of the Weigh House Chapel, London, 1829-69 (*DNB*, II, 519-21).

[59] Slate (1787-1867) was pastor of Grimshaw Street Chapel, Preston, 1826-61, and wrote religious tracts (*DNB*, XVIII, 370).

[60] *British Banner*, 13 Nov. 1850; *Preston Pilot*, 7 Dec. 1850; *Patriot*, 21 Oct. 1850.

[61] Swaine (1795-1862), an insurance agent, was a Congregationalist deacon in Bayswater and amateur author (Boase, VI, 650-51).

[62] Edward Swaine, *'No Popery!' The Cry Examined*, 5th ed. (London, 1850), p. 6;

[63] *British Banner*, 11 Dec. 1850, 19 Feb., 12 Mar., 2 Apr. (quoted), 14 May 1850.

defeating the work of Christ." Its errors were to be found in its priestly mediators, its monasteries as dens of debauchery, its exaltation of tradition above the Bible and of the Blessed Virgin Mary above Christ, and its bloody history of butchery, torture, and murder.[64] The Church of England was hardly better, for

> It tolerates the Puseyites,
> And all their Popish pranks,
>   It dallies with the Pope at Rome
> And bolsters up his ranks.[65]

The English Presbyterians also condemned sacramentalism in both Anglicanism and the Roman Church, and charged that the Prayer Book contained "false doctrine" and gave "poisonous pasture to the lambs of his flock."[66] John Cumming, minister of the Scottish National Church, Crown Court, Covent Garden, and probably the most prominent Scottish Presbyterian in England, took a leading role in the Papal Aggression crisis, lecturing around the country, publishing tracts, and gaining notoriety by claiming that Roman prelates took an oath promising to persecute heretics and schismatics, and calling for the death penalty for the hearing of confessions.[67]

But if Orthodox Nonconformity seemed to speak as with one voice on both Anglo-Catholicism and Roman Catholicism, the strident cries concealed divisions, tensions, rivalries, and fears that go far to explain the nature of Nonconformist anti-Catholicism.

"The pamphlet before us," declared a voice of the Congregationalists, reviewing one of the many anti-Catholic pamphlets that appeared during the Papal Aggression crisis,

> has rendered essential service, and well deserves circulation. One of the lessons which it reads to Protestants is, the necessity of union, and the extraordinary evils of disorganization among the friends of truth. . . . Between true Popery and true Protestantism the war is to the death; the one must fall before the other; reconciliation is impossible.[68]

The call for unity in the face of popery appears again and again during the nineteenth century, from editors of the religious press, from denominational leaders, and from ordinary preachers: let "all true-hearted Protestants . . . merge their differences of opinion" (a Lancashire Congregationalist) and "rally around the one great point of union,—namely, that the man of sin should not take possession of England" (a Chelsea Wesleyan). The call for Protestant unity against popery also could be used to paper over differences and divisions, as when the Leeds Religious Tract Society used it to argue that its nondenominational work merited special support.[69]

These calls for Protestant unity were of course connected with the rise of militant Roman Catholicism and Anglo-Catholicism in the 1830s and

[64] *Church*, n.s., I (Sept. 1847), 325-26.
[65] According to A. M. Stalker, leading Baptist minister of Leeds (*Leeds Mercury*, 28 Dec. 1850).
[66] *English Presbyterian Messenger*, n.s., I (Jan. 1849), 403.
[67] *Patriot*, 11 Nov. 1850.
[68] *Christian Witness*, VIII (Jan. 1851), 19.
[69] *British Protestant*, IV (Feb. 1848), 17; *Manchester Courier*, 14 Dec. 1850; *Watchman*, 6 Nov. 1850; *Leeds Mercury*, 30 Nov. 1850.

'40s; but as important an influence were the changes taking place within Nonconformity itself. The Methodist Arminian revival affected some parts of Protestant Dissent as well as Anglicanism. By the end of the eighteenth century the Congregationalists and many Baptists had joined the Methodists in tasting the revivifying springs of Arminian Evangelicalism; they were joined by Presbyterians, and even by a few Quakers and Unitarians. The growth in numbers and spirit that Evangelicalism stimulated led, in the 1830s and '40s, to a move away from sectarian religious culture and towards denominational forms. Competition for members became stiffer as the Church of England renewed itself, and as economic changes began eliminating skilled artisans and yeoman farmers, Nonconformity's main source of recruits. In response, Nonconformity began developing new priorities—especially the growing theological and sociological distinctions between ministry and laity.[70] The result of all these changes was tension—a tension that might be resolved, deflected, or avoided altogether by beating the no-popery drum.

Internal Rivalry and the No-Popery Cry: The Methodists

Wesleyan Methodism was especially fissiparous; the dramatic expansion in numbers, sustained and rapid from 1740 to 1840, decelerating from 1840 to 1906, concealed numerous schisms. Wesley himself appears to have hoped that remaining within the Church of England would prevent fragmentation, but after his death, the questions that he had papered over reappeared: What was the relationship between Methodism and the Church of England? How was power to be apportioned among preachers, trustees, and ordinary laity? How were the tensions to be resolved between the central Connexional administration and the localities, between conservatives and reformers, rich and poor, the educated and the uneducated, the bureaucratic and the spirit-filled?[71]

The sixty years after John Wesley's death in 1791 saw schism after schism. Alexander Kilham seceded and founded the Methodist New Connexion in 1797 over lay representation in Conference. Poor, religiously conservative enthusiasts came together in the period around Waterloo to form the Primitive Methodist Connexion. In the 1820s, simple, rural folk in the West Country formed the Bible Christians, and simple urban folk in Leeds, who disliked the dominance of Conference over local preachers and of rich trustees over the ordinary laity, seceded to form the Protestant Methodists. Questions relating to the status and education of preachers, the relationship between preachers and laity, and the power exercised by Jabez Bunting and his friends, during the mid-1830s, led to another secession that resulted in the Wesleyan Methodist Association.[72]

Finally, the 1840s saw the so-called Fly-Sheet Controversy, which led to the creation of the Wesleyan Reform Union in 1849-52. The movement had its roots in the power wielded by Jabez Bunting and his friends over Conference, and by Conference over the Wesleyan Connexion. These ten-

[70] Gilbert, *Religion and Society*, pp. 33, 36, 145-48, 150-57.
[71] *Ibid.*, pp. 21, 30; Hempton, *Methodism and Politics*, pp. 58-67, 108, 197-98.
[72] Hempton, *Methodism and Politics*, pp. 67-73; Julia Stewart Werner, *The Primitive Methodist Connexion: Its Background and Early History* (Madison, 1984); W. Ward, *Religion and Society*, pp. 144-47, 159-76; Brockett, *Nonconformity in Exeter*, pp. 198-200.

sions were brought to the surface by the itinerant revivalist James Caughey. Irish-born, but U.S.-raised, Caughey preached in Dublin, Liverpool, the West Riding, Birmingham, and the East Midlands. The tensions were exacerbated by anonymous attacks—the Fly-Sheets—on the motives and leadership of Bunting and his friends. Bunting replied by identifying discontented preachers, and asked them publicly at the 1849 Conference if they had had a hand in the Fly-Sheets. James Everett, William Griffith, and Samuel Dunn were expelled from the Connexion in 1849; James Bromley went in 1850; and a mass exodus of the discontented followed. The Wesleyan Connexion lost about a hundred thousand members, and spent the next score of years reorganizing to cope with the loss of members (and of funds).[73]

Now, what J.C.G. Binfield calls Methodism's "most distinctive facets"—Wesleyanism, the most numerous; the Primitives, the most popular; and the Bible Christians, the most rural—did not compete for membership. Rather, the Wesleyan Connexion's most serious competition for members came from the New Connexion, the Protestant Methodists, the Association Methodists, and the Wesleyan Reformers.[74]

Consequently, neither the Primitives nor the Bible Christians took much notice of affairs within the Methodist tradition, save to remind themselves of how pure, how true to that tradition, they were; and they maintained a complacent neutrality over the disputes within the Wesleyan Methodist Connexion. They were anti-Catholic, of course; but they called for no special anti-papal agitations during the 1840s and '50s.[75] Rather, each of the other Methodist schisms led to tensions within the parent body and among the other schismatic groups. The organizing of the Wesleyan Methodist Association in 1835-37 saw delicate negotiations with the Protestant Methodists that the latter hoped would lead to union. The New Connexion also wooed the Wesleyan Association, hoping to profit from the dispute by attracting adherents. But the New Connexion, although with a half-lay Conference, still stood for the authority of Conference; the Association Methodists wanted a weak Conference, and union did not occur. Other groups also hoped to gain from Methodist disputes. The Church of England was always an option for disaffected Methodists—both Samuel Warren of Manchester and William Byrom of Liverpool ended up as Anglicans. And more exotic fishers of men trolled in those waters: Evangelical Quakers, the Rev. Robert Aitkin's Christian Association, and the Mormons.[76]

At midcentury, the Wesleyan Reformers had to decide what their future was. Should they try to rejoin and reform the Wesleyan Connexion, form a new denomination, or join the New Connexion or the Wesleyan Methodist Association? The Buntingites were not about to let them back in the

[73] W. Ward, *Religion and Society*, pp. 253-72; Richard Carwardine, *Trans-Atlantic Revivalism: Popular Evangelicalism in Britain and America, 1790-1865* (Westport, Conn., 1978), pp. 107 ff.; Chadwick, *Victorian Church*, pp. 380-86; Rack, "Wesleyan Methodism, 1849-1902," pp. 119, 128-31; John T. Wilkinson, "The Non-Wesleyan Traditions from 1849," *Methodist Church in Great Britain*, ed. Davies, George, and Rupp, III, 180.

[74] Binfield, *Prayers*, p. 21.

[75] *Primitive Methodist Magazine*, XXX (1849), iii-iv, XXXI (1850), 1-2, 558-59, 688; *Bible Christian Magazine*, XXX (Jan. 1851), 41-42.

[76] D. A. Gowland, *Methodist Secessions: The Origins of Free Methodism in Three Lancashire Towns: Manchester, Rochdale, Liverpool*, Chetham Society, *Remains*, 3rd Ser., XXVI (Manchester, 1979), 50-51, 57-58, 106-7; W. Ward, *Religion and Society*, pp. 170-71.

Wesleyan Connexion; they were too few in numbers to make a go of it on their own; the New Connexion's omnipotent Conference threatened their desire for local independence. So, they joined the Protestant Methodists and Association Methodists to form the United Methodist Free Church in 1857.[77] But until then, there was turmoil in the Methodist world. The Wesleyan Conference needed to preserve its ecclesiastical authority against both internal and external foes; the Wesleyan Reformers needed to legitimize their revolt against Conference; and lurking in the background were the New Connexion, the Protestant Methodists, and the Wesleyan Association, each hoping that the Wesleyan Reformers would join it—for such an adhesion would increase their own numbers and income, and validate their original revolt against Conference. Anti-Catholicism proved useful for gaining these ends for all concerned.

Conference leadership responded to the crisis by justifying the expulsions as "as righteous an act of ecclesiastical discipline as was ever performed. . . ."[78] They charged that the Reformers drew most of their support from Dissenters, Association Methodists, and other enemies of true Methodism. They contrasted the real freedom to be found in the Wesleyan Connexion with the false freedom of the more democratic connexions. They accused the Reformers of bringing strife into the church, dragging religion into contempt, preventing the salvation of souls, undermining Wesleyan piety, splitting families, and dividing friends.[79] "Many of them are in the Church, what the Red Republicans have shown themselves to be in France;—they are Terrorists, who, by a system of threatening, seek a revolution."[80]

Leadership went on to strengthen the process by which the Wesleyan Connexion was becoming a denomination and repudiating the claims of the Church of England. ("We are a church. We see no good purpose to be answered by blinking this point."[81]) Leadership criticized the Wesleyan Reformers for wanting to turn "the pastoral office," which was of divine institution, into an office open to "Christian tradespeople," into a mere "preaching member" of the congregation rather than "an under-shepherd of Christ."[82] The Wesleyan preacher, "an under-shepherd of Christ," was but a short step from the Roman Catholic priest as *alter Christus,* and bore a standing in the Wesleyan household that the popish confessor did at Rome:

> He is not merely formally, in his public character, admitted into the pulpit, for public duty, but into every family, both as a Minister, and as a friend, a brother, a father. Mingling with them all, and on such terms, he becomes acquainted with their family secrets. He learns their faults as well as their virtues.[83]

This, of course, is almost precisely what a priest does in the confessional, except that in the priest it is a bad thing.

[77] Gowland, *Methodist Secessions,* pp. 18-19.
[78] *Wesleyan Methodist Magazine,* LXXII (1849), 1063.
[79] *Ibid.,* pp. 957-63; *ibid.,* LXXIII (1850), 506-12; *Wesleyan Notices Newspaper,* nos. 33 (4 Jan. 1850), p. 5, 51 (30 Nov. 1850), p. 218, 53 (29 Jan. 1851), pp. 39-44.
[80] *Wesleyan Vindicator,* no. 6 (June 1850), p. 86.
[81] *Wesleyan Methodist Magazine,* LXXII (1849), 617.
[82] *Ibid.,* LXXIII (1850), 717.
[83] *Ibid.,* LXXII (1849), 1064.

Finally, the Wesleyan Methodists did not claim to have an infallible Pope, but they did claim an infallible founder. In devising Connexional discipline, they argued, John Wesley "was wonderfully guided by the great Head of the church, and led to the establishment of a system in all essential points supported by the New Testament, and admirably calculated to promote vital godliness among all who are governed by it."[84]

The popish parallels were too good to pass up. The *Times*, eager to stir up trouble among the Methodists, and to protest a violation of the English sense of fair play, denounced the expulsions as "a step which smacks more of the Inquisition than of British tribunal," and called Conference "as inquisitorial as if Dr. DOMINICK himself were its president."[85] The Wesleyan leadership replied in the same vein by labeling the anonymous publishers of the Fly-Sheets "this Venetian or Spanish conclave of secret conspirators" with their "secret, Venetian, Holy-Office plans."[86] So opened the floodgates. The Wesleyan Reformers charged Conference with "a protestantism which is popish," with being a "priestly conclave," with being "without a parallel save in the history of Papal Rome"; when the Papal Aggression crisis occasioned public meetings, they urged their supporters to use them as a forum to attack "Popery in every form."[87] Conference replied by calling the Reformers popish: They denied the right of private judgement to the vast majority of Wesleyans, who wanted things as they were; they used "Fly-Sheet secrecy" as a weapon of fierce and cruel persecution; they did evil that good might come; they claimed "an individual infallibility, which is worse than a Popish or aggregate one."[88]

Now, we have noticed that Wesleyan Methodists did not participate, as a body, in the memorializing of 1850. This was because the Wesleyan Committee of Privileges, although it itself memorialized the Queen, recommended that its fellow-Wesleyans participate in community memorializing rather than take a separate stand.[89] The Reformers at once charged that the Buntingite leadership was too soft on popery, too solicitous of the Church of England's spiritual claims, and too afraid that Methodists might repudiate their leadership.[90]

> The Clique dare not attempt their old practice of sending out stereotyped petitions for the People to sign. . . . The Committee are evidently afraid of public meetings, as amendments would, in the majority of cases, be moved and carried. The Popery of Methodism is as rank as the Popery of Rome, and must come in for its share of condemnation. . . . We think the Reformers should meet and protest against Popery, not Roman only, but Anglo and Methodistic.[91]

[84] *Ibid.*, LXXIII (1850), 952.
[85] *Times*, 3, 10 Sept. 1849; cf. *Huddersfield Chronicle*, 19 Apr. 1851.
[86] *Wesleyan Methodist Magazine*, LXXII (1849), 1066-68, 1070.
[87] *Wesleyan Times*, 18 Nov., 2 Dec. 1850; *Wesleyan Review*, I (June 1850), 164, (Oct. 1850), 386, (Dec. 1850), 557-64; *Wesley Banner*, III (Jan. 1851), 34; *Local Preachers' Magazine*, I (Aug. 1851), 313.
[88] *Wesleyan Methodist Magazine*, LXXIII (1850), 720; *Wesleyan Vindicator*, nos. 12 (Dec. 1850), p. 216, 13 (Jan. 1851), p. 6, 16 (Apr. 1851), pp. 59-60; *Wesleyan Notices Newspaper*, no. 55 (31 Mar. 1851), p. 71; *Watchman*, 24 Dec. 1850.
[89] *Christian Miscellany*, VI (Feb. 1851), 59-61; *Watchman*, 27 Nov. 1850.
[90] *Wesleyan Times*, 2, 16 Dec. 1850.
[91] *Ibid.*, 25 Nov. 1850.

The Wesleyan Reformers, being Methodists, Evangelicals, Protestants, were anti-Catholic for theological reasons. Like the Wesleyans, they denied that baptism conveyed efficacious rebirth, and maintained that personal faith, not sacramental grace, brought salvation. Their posher journals published theological treatises, while they served up premillennialism, lurid prophecy, and even numerology to their local preachers.[92] Their weekly newspaper vied with that of their Wesleyan enemies for preeminence in publicizing the iniquities of the Papal Aggression. The Reformers were determined to show that *they* were in the forefront of opposition to popery.[93]

Now at this juncture, the New Connexion, which hoped to garner members from the Wesleyan agitation, had internal tensions of its own, as it was tightening up its polity and discipline during the 1840s and '50s. It adopted a constitution that permitted Conference to change polity; it proposed a theological committee to examine probationary preachers; and it decided to found a college, the symbol of a professional ministry, in 1846 (although it did not open until 1864). The results were bickering and loss of members. The New Connexion was conventionally anti-Catholic, of course; but it used the no-popery cry to attack external enemies, subdue internal quarrels, and attract new members.[94] It devoted a quarter of the pages of its connexional magazine to anti-Catholic articles during the first half of 1851, and it sought to put itself in the forefront of opposition to the assumption of titles.[95]

The Wesleyan Reform agitation also brought the New Connexion into conflict with both the Wesleyan Connexion and the Association Methodists. It deplored the controversy and professed to want no part of the spoils, but it reminded all concerned that it had been the first to assert freedom within Methodism, and called upon the Wesleyans to reform themselves. William Cooke, editor of the connexional magazine, published a tract, *Alexander Kilham, the First Methodist Reformer*, which claimed that the New Connexion was much freer than the Wesleyan Conference. The Wesleyans responded by attacking Kilham, founder of the New Connexion; and the Association Methodists charged that the New Connexion was as clerical and dictatorial as the old. Now the Association Methodists just then were tightening their own discipline under the Bunting-like leadership of Robert Eckett. Eckett expelled his chief opponents, James Carveth and David Rowland, and the New Connexion immediately came to their defense.[96]

The same pattern of quarrels, rivalries, and the use of anti-Catholic rhetoric can be discerned at the local level.

Lancashire was very important in Methodist life. In 1830, half of the Wesleyan membership was to be found in the Liverpool, Rochdale, and Manchester circuits. The wealthiest of the Wesleyan laity lived there; but

[92] *Wesleyan Review*, I (1850), 91, 201; *Wesley Banner*, II (Dec. 1850), 467-68; *Local Preachers' Magazine*, I (Oct. 1851), 371-75, and *passim*.

[93] *Wesleyan Times*, 14 Oct., 4, 11, 25 Nov. 1850.

[94] Wilkinson, "Non-Wesleyan Traditions," pp. 167-78; *Methodist New Connexion Magazine*, LIII (Jan. 1850), 26-28, (Apr. 1850), 187-89, (June 1850), 287, LIV (Sept. 1851), 430-31.

[95] *Methodist New Connexion Magazine*, LIII (Dec. 1850), 566-76, LIV (1850), 8-16, 22-29, 63-64, 115-22, 127-29, 161-69, 205-12, 222-26, 233-34, 256-65.

[96] *Ibid.*, LIII (1850), 45-47, 96, 144, 189, 215-20, 375-85, 438-39, LIV (1851), 334, 597; James Carveth, *The Wesleyan Association: Mr. Carveth and the Liverpool Circuit* (London, 1852), pp. 3-5.

these circuits, centers of ecclesiastical and radical politics, saw struggles over the provision of separate communion, over the role of the laity in governance, and over the desirability of revivals.[97] Hence, the Wesleyans focused much of their anti-Catholic activities there during the winter of 1850-51. Numerous Wesleyan preachers, including John Beecham, President of Conference, pounded on the theme that Wesleyanism was in the forefront of the war against popery.[98] But the Wesleyans did not have it all their own way. The New Connexion was attempting to expand its presence; expelled Wesleyan Reformers were active, both at meetings to promote their cause and at public anti-Catholic meetings; and Wesleyan preachers found it necessary to repel charges of popery.[99] The irreligious of Manchester's slums delighted at the spectacle of these fraternal quarrels, as town missionaries found out to their dismay.[100]

At Leeds, Methodism was the *de facto* established religion, at least according to W. F. Hook, the vicar. But it fell on hard times, thanks to Hook (who led the Anglican revival) and to internal schism. Thomas Galland,[101] the most respected Wesleyan clergyman at Leeds, was unsound in Buntingite eyes. Although loyal to Conference, he thought for himself, believed in the free discussion of opposing views, and in politics was a Whig. Moreover, Wesleyan Reformers were strong at Leeds, aggressively used litigation to retain access to Wesleyan chapels, and enjoyed the support of Edward Baines, Jr., editor of the influential *Leeds Mercury*. Thus, the local Buntingite leadership stuck close to Hook during the Papal Aggression agitation, despite his reputation as an Anglo-Catholic. And Wesleyan Reformers disrupted meetings there with denunciations of the Popery of Conference.[102]

Finally, a similar mix was to be found at Birmingham. There the Irish-American revivalist James Caughey was active in the mid-1840s. His revivals were not calculated to gain the approval of the Buntingite respectable, for they exhibited the disorderly and spirit-filled behavior that was reminiscent of Wesleyanism's roots. People knelt before the pulpit, where Caughey was exhorting the meeting with all the power of his lungs. Some of the "inquirers" sighed; others cried, called out Bible verses, wailed, wept, and gnashed their teeth. Each had at least one of Caughey's assistants hovering over her (they were mostly women) in conversation, exhorting her to believe. When an inquirer succumbed to the pressure to believe, an assistant lept to his feet and shouted out, "Glory, glory, she believes! She's saved!" The audience, which all along had been exclaiming in response to Caughey's exhortations, cried out "Glory, Glory! Hallelu-

---

[97] Gowland, *Methodist Secessions*, pp. 20-22.

[98] *Manchester Courier*, 16 Nov. 1850, 1 Feb., 2 Apr. 1851; *Lancaster Guardian*, 22, 29 Mar. 1851.

[99] *Methodist New Connexion Magazine*, LIII (1850), 51-52, 89-91, 342; *Preston Guardian*, 14 Dec. 1850; *Preston Pilot*, 21 Dec. 1850; *Blackburn Standard*, 11 Dec. 1850.

[100] Bembridge Journal, 7 Nov. 1850, MCL, BR MS. 259.B.1

[101] Galland (1791-1843) was intended for the Anglican priesthood, but became a Wesleyan itinerant in 1816 (*Encyclopedia of World Methodism*, I, 893).

[102] Yates, "Religious Life of Victorian Leeds," pp. 251-52, 258; D. Colin Dews, "The Ecclesiastical Returns, 1851: A Study of Methodist Attendances in Leeds," *Proceedings of the Wesley Historical Society*, XXXIX (1974), 113-16; W. Ward, *Religion and Society*, pp. 145, 158; Hempton, *Methodism and Politics*, pp. 163, 183; *Leeds Mercury*, 8, 15 June 1839, 11 Jan., 29 Mar. 1851.

jah! Amen!" The "saved" person then usually fainted, and was hauled away to a room specially prepared for comatose Evangelicals.[103]

The local Birmingham Wesleyans were strongly anti-Catholic—their missionaries would go into Irish courts, call the people idolators and their priests heathen, and then wonder why they got bashed and made few converts[104] —and the addition of Caughey's ecstatic rebirth experiences, which underscored the Protestant dogma of justification by faith alone, and which practically eliminated the need for sacraments, made the anti-Catholic brew more potent. John Barritt Melson,[105] a local preacher whose M.D. degree enhanced his reputation, was both one of the leading enemies of Romanism and Tractarianism, and one of the leading supporters of James Caughey's Birmingham mission.[106] And when the Wesleyan Reform agitation reached Birmingham,[107] Melson joined in, again beating the no-popery drum.

> It is in vain we inveigh against the Tractarian dogma of sacramental effi-
> cacy, if we are prepared to elevate into its place ministerial and ordinantial
> grace: and if the Local Preacher be excluded one day from the presbyteral
> function, he will be in the next from the pulpit.[108]

The New Connexion, which was active at Birmingham,[109] tried to lure the Wesleyan Reformers into its fold. When James Bromley, expelled Wesleyan from Bath, visited the town in June 1850, he was welcomed by William Baggaly, President of the New Connexion and minister of Unett Street chapel. Baggaly told the public meeting that Alexander Kilham, "the first Methodist Reformer," stood for love, freedom, and independence, and opposed the clericalism of Conference. "He thought, and spoke, and wrote freely, as Mr. Bromley has done lately. . . ." Then, Baggaly painted a seductive picture of the New Connexion, to delight Wesleyan Reformers' ears: Ministers and laymen worked together; no one could be expelled without a vote of both; full financial records were published; the Connexion was expanding; there were no internal disputes.[110]

These themes—the resolution of both internal tensions and external rivalries by means of no-popery—appear elsewhere. The Wesleyans at Waltham Street chapel, Hull, unveiled their internal tensions in 1841, when some women presented a gown to their minister, Samuel Waddy.

> We see no reason why this highly esteemed body of Christian ministers
> should not wear the gown as well as their respected brethren the Dissen-
> ters; and are happy to learn from good authority that this opinion is pre-
> vailing very generally amongst the ministers and members of the Wesleyan
> body.[111]

---

[103] *Leeds Mercury*, 18 Apr. 1846. This account reminds one of Mr. Stiggins's preaching services (Charles Dickens, *The Posthumous Papers of the Pickwick Club*, London, n.d., orig. pub. 1836, pp. 364-66), but not all Methodist preachers were ranters (see Borrow, *Lavengro*, pp. 167-69, for a preaching service on a heath).

[104] Finegan Journal, 19 Nov. 1837, Birmingham Central Library Archives, MS. 312 749, p. 179.

[105] Melson (1811-1898), the son of a Wesleyan minister, was a surgeon at Birmingham, 1836-98 (Boase, VI, 194-95).

[106] *Leeds Mercury*, 12 Sept. 1846; *Midland Counties Herald*, 18 Nov. 1847.

[107] *Wesleyan Times*, 23 Dec. 1850; *Birmingham Mercury*, 29 Mar., 26 Apr. 1851.

[108] John Barritt Melson, *The Apostle of the Gentiles, and his Glorying* (London, 1850), p. 39.

[109] *Methodist New Connexion Magazine*, LIII (Jan. 1850), 13.

[110] *Ibid* (Oct. 1850), 455-60.

[111] *Leeds Mercury*, 20 Mar. 1841.

But when Waddy donned the priestly garment on Sunday, many in the congregation, especially the older members, objected.[112]

Wesleyans usually could be relied upon to support anti-Catholic agitations, as at Southampton in 1855, where the local anti-Catholic society kept a list of Wesleyan men for use in anti-Maynooth petitioning.[113] But this discipline slipped during the Wesleyan Reform agitation. A public meeting at the Bethel Wesleyan chapel, Rochester, to hear Father Achilli, was taken over by an alliance of Baptists and Wesleyan Reformers.[114] And the New Connexion lurked in the background, hoping to collect members, as at Cleckheaton, where Joseph Harrison, a Wesleyan Reformer, was invited to join the New Connexion by A. Lynn, the superintendent of its Bradford circuit.[115]

In 1851, Methodists were faced with the question of whether to support the Ecclesiastical Titles Bill—clearly, penal legislation—and they did. Over 30 percent of the signatures to petitions that the bill be made more stringent were affixed to Wesleyan ones. The Wesleyan leadership wanted "not a persecution of the Romanists, but something more than a vindication of the exclusive territorial rank of the Anglican prelates."[116] But both the Committee of Privileges and the *Watchman* believed that there was something so uniquely depraved about Romanism, that the papal system so inextricably linked the temporal and the spiritual, that Wesleyans could in good conscience claim to support religious freedom and still sign petitions asking Parliament to make conferences of Roman Catholic bishops illegal. The Committee of Privileges prepared a standard form of petition in early March 1851 and sent it round the circuits; and the *Watchman* recommended that Wesleyan congregations support the drive, but "without the parade and needless labour of a public meeting."[117]

The Wesleyan Reformers, who also supported a more stringent Ecclesiastical Titles Bill, attacked the Wesleyan Conference for hypocrisy: Conference discouraged public meetings for fear the Wesleyan Reformers would take them over. Conference permitted petitioning to itself only on topics of its own choosing, for only three days in the year, and then only by local preachers and leaders of ten years' standing; in its own way, Conference demanded as much unthinking obedience from the laity as does the Roman Catholic Church.[118] (Having criticized Conference for not memorializing in the autumn of 1850, the Reformers now faulted it for petitioning in the winter of 1851.) Not to be outdone, the New Connexion also prepared to petition Parliament for a more stringent measure.[119]

It is not surprising, then, that the Wesleyan Connexion tried to use anti-Catholicism as a rallying point of unity: Good Protestants, good Methodists, must put aside their petty differences and support Conference in the face of popery. The Committee of Privileges called upon Methodists to put aside their petty jealousies and animosities and stand fast together;

112 *Ibid.*, 3 Apr. 1841.
113 John Philip to T. H. Croft Moody, 30 Apr. 1855, Page & Moody Papers, Southampton City Record Office, D/PM 10/6/29.
114 *Rochester, Chatham, and Stroud Gazette*, 26 Nov. 1850.
115 *Leeds Mercury*, 11 May 1850.
116 *Watchman*, 5 Feb. 1851.
117 *Ibid.*, 27 Nov. 1850, 12, 19 Feb., 5 (quoted), 12, 26 Mar. 1851.
118 *Wesleyan Times*, 10 Feb., 24 Mar. 1851.
119 *Methodist New Connexion Magazine*, LIV (Mar. 1851), 143.

John Beecham, President of Conference, called for special days of fasting and prayer for an end to internal strife in the face of Popery; and numerous preachers called for Protestant unity, that "men may be drawn off from superstitious observances, unscriptural assumptions, and acrimonious controversies."[120]

Thus it was that anti-Catholicism satisfied some basic needs of, and released serious tensions within, Victorian Methodists. The marked exception to this are the Primitive Methodists. That connexion grew more conservative, more respectable, in the 1830s and '40s. Its charismatic founders, Hugh Bourne and William Clowes, were compelled to retire in 1842. Permanent or more substantial chapels began to be constructed in the 1830s, and the pace of building accelerated in the 1840s. Conference began to work at gaining more control over both property and ministers; and ministers began to improve their own status by dressing up in white tie and black coat.[121] Yet they did not suffer serious internal tensions, save in eastern Derbyshire, where conservatives who objected to the growing clericalism organized the Original Methodists, a schism at its height in 1851.[122] The history of the non-Wesleyan connexions, during the nineteenth century, remains unexplored territory. But it may be tentatively advanced that the "Prims" were so far outside the main Methodist currents, and that by choice, that they did not concern themselves with the events that wracked the other connexions at midcentury. Perhaps, too, they had found other ways of resolving their tensions.

Internal Rivalry and the No-Popery Cry: Evangelical Dissent

Orthodox Evangelical Dissent showed a pattern of growth similar to that of the Methodists between the 1780s and 1840. Thereafter, again like the Methodists, their absolute rate of growth slowed and their membership as a percentage of the adult population declined from the middle of the 1880s.[123] And, again like the Methodists, Evangelical Dissent suffered from internal tensions and schisms. The Plymouth Brethren, a fundamentalist and intensely anti-Catholic sect that emerged in the early 1830s, suffered a major schism in 1848, when J. N. Darby's Exclusive Brethren broke away from the Open Brethren. The Exclusives, the larger body, resembled the Strict Baptists; and the Open Brethren were open only by comparison to the Exclusives. But the Brethren of all sorts had only about 150 chapels in 1851.[124] Larger in numbers, more influential in Victorian society, and thus more illustrative of the purposes to which anti-Catholicism were put were the Congregationalists, Baptists, and Presbyterians.

The Independents, or Congregationalists as they were called more frequently as the nineteenth century progressed, had a varied history. Some congregations had their origins in the Commonwealth or in the ejections

120 *Watchman*, 27 Nov. 1850; *Wesleyan Methodist Magazine*, LXXII (1849), 615, 617, LXXIV (1851), 498, 643-49 (quoted).
121 Chadwick, *Victorian Church*, pp. 386-91.
122 Margery Tranter, "Landlords, Labourers, Local Preachers: Rural Nonconformity in Derbyshire, 1772-1851," *Derbyshire Archæological Journal*, CI (1981), 132.
123 Gilbert, *Religion and Society*, pp. 36-39. Valentine Cunningham, sympathetic to Dissent, sees a continued growth during the second half of the century that did not happen (*Everywhere Spoken Against*, p. 106).
124 Sellers, *Nonconformity*, pp. 10-11.

of the 1662 settlement. Others had been Trinitarian Presbyterians. Some were former Wesleyan chapels, or even Anglican proprietary chapels. Some had been founded to belong to no denomination. Loose county associations of Congregationalist chapels had long existed, but in the 1820s and '30s the Congregationalists began developing a central authority to raise funds, to coordinate chapel extension, and to be like everyone else and have a central office in London. While some Congregationalists believed that union beyond the district or county level violated the principle of Congregational autonomy, others were prepared to sacrifice a little autonomy in exchange for efficiency.[125]

The Congregational Union, founded in 1831, got off to a slow start. Its income rarely amounted to much more than £100 p.a., and its debt was large. It was reorganized in 1847, with a new constitution that tied individual congregations more closely to the Union and that improved the collection of contributions from member congregations. Nevertheless, only 218 of the 1,024 Independent chapels licensed for marriages subscribed the modest 10s. fee in 1848; in 1851, only 258 subscribed. The central authority of the Union, feeble as it was, was looked upon in some quarters with a great deal of suspicion indeed.[126]

Yet the circumstances of the 1840s led to the growth of the Congregational Union's ambitions to be the supracongregational leader for the denomination. With the rise of the Anglo-Catholic Movement, the Union's Standing Committee declared that Congregationalists must not "look supinely on" as "the semi-papal doctrines of Apostolic succession and sacramental efficacy" were in process of destroying English souls. The Home Missionary Society, although Independents mostly managed it, was open to anyone, and hence was unconnected with the Congregational Union. After hard work and delicate negotiations, the Home Missionary Society and the Irish Evangelical Society amalgamated with the Union in 1840. So strengthened, the Union attempted to lead the denomination's building campaign by building its own chapels, raising funds, and, in the process, enhancing its own supracongregational leadership role in a denomination that, if its polity meant anything, should not have had any leadership beyond the congregation.[127]

The fear of Catholicism, whether Anglo or Roman, made life difficult for the Congregationalists. The Congregationalists saw very little difference between the Church of England and Roman Catholicism when it came to the doctrines of baptismal regeneration, confirmation, and the Real Presence; and if the Roman Church used the temporal power of the state to enforce its spiritual supremacy when it could, so did the Church of England.[128]

Finally, internal theological debate added to the tensions, as Congregationalists debated among themselves the meaning of the Lord's Supper and Baptism. With respect to the Holy Communion, the "subjectivist" view,

[125] Albert Peel, *These Hundred Years: A History of the Congregational Union of England and Wales, 1831-1931* (London, 1931), pp. 5-69; Chadwick, *Victorian Church*, pp. 400-403.

[126] R. Tudor Jones, *Congregationalism in England, 1662-1962* (London, 1962), pp. 243-44; *The Congregational Yearbook for 1851* (London, 1852), p. 119; Peel, *These Hundred Years*, pp. 20, 118, 163-64, 169, 203.

[127] Peel, *These Hundred Years*, pp. 99-102, 108-15, 148-50.

[128] *Christian's Penny Magazine*, V (Mar. 1850), 67-69, 72-74, (Oct. 1850), 268-69, (Dec. 1850), 309-13, VI (Mar. 1851), 71.

that it was a sign of faith in Jesus and of brotherly love, was gaining
ground over the older, "higher" view that it in some way involved com-
muning with Jesus. With respect to baptism, the question was what it
meant if it did not convey rebirth. Should it be limited to the children of
church members, or should all children be baptized? Should children be
baptized at all?[129] Thinking that English Congregationalism had disputes
enough, the denomination's leading journal refused to review books on the
New Light controversy in the U.S.A., and called for internal unity to meet
the external foe.

> As we have no desire to import the controversy into England, we must
> suffer the matter to drop. These are not times for theological warfare, but
> for the muster of the universal host of God's elect to dissipate darkness,
> and convert men.[130]

Perhaps the denomination's biggest controversy at midcentury was over
Edward White's *Life in Christ* (1846), which questioned the doctrine of
perpetual future punishment. White argued that because immortal life
came only through Christ, the ungodly would be destroyed utterly, or altogether erased from existence, rather than merely tortured for all eternity.
The orthodox criticized White for being too tender towards sinners. In
1850, he rejected pædobaptism, and had himself rebaptized; but although
he resigned his chapel at Hereford, and moved to London where he cooperated with the Baptists, he retained his Congregational affiliation. Five
years later, another Congregational minister, T. T. Lynch, published *The
Rivulet* (1855), a volume of innocuous if bad poetry. A huge controversy
erupted over *The Rivulet*'s supposed pantheism and nature-worship; the
1856 meeting of the Union was postponed; and John Campbell's magazines were officially separated from the Union.[131]

These tensions and concerns were to be found on the local level. The
Lancashire Congregational Union was founded in 1806 over opposition
from those who believed that the Union was designed to promote Evangelical doctrine at the expense of Calvinist predestination and congregationalist polity, and that it betrayed the Independent tradition of loose association. Some also feared an insidious Scottish influence. Once founded,
the Lancashire Union began to grow. With With the growth of population
in the 1830s and '40s, the Union pushed for evangelism in the manufacturing towns and their out-townships, as well as in Liverpool. This, of
course, enhanced the Union's leadership role over the individual chapels.
The history of Congregationalism's transition from sect to denomination
was played out in microcosm in Banbury between 1772 and 1860, in an
Independent chapel that included antinomians, Calvinists, total immersers,
sprinklers, pædobaptists, and believer baptizers. The period saw these
groups sort themselves out into distinct denominations. Each schism, or
hiving off into separate chapels, was accompanied by bad feelings. Sometimes, expansion created problems. The debts contracted during expansion
at Colchester led to disputes over trust-deeds and rivalry for members between Stockwell and Lion Walk chapels, during the 1830s and '40s. Doc-

---

[129] Jones, *Congregationalism*, pp. 226-27.
[130] *Christian Witness*, VII (Oct. 1850), 489.
[131] Jones, *Congregationalism*, pp. 248-49; Frederick Ash Freer, *Edward White, his life and work*
(London, 1902), pp. 11-32; Chadwick, *Victorian Church*, p. 406.

trinal quarrels added to the witches' cauldron, and there followed secessions and the creation of a third chapel, Headgate.[132]

Victorian Baptists were more divided than the Congregationalists. The
Original General Baptists, who thought it wicked to drink blood, had become Unitarian during the eighteenth century; and there were small
groups of Seventh Day Baptists, Scottish Baptists, Welsh Baptists, and
several hundred independent congregations. The most numerous groups,
however, were the New Connexion General Baptists, the Particular Baptists, and the Strict and Particular Baptists.

The New Connexion General Baptists organized their union in 1770,
and formally severed their ties with the Unitarian Original Generals in
1803. They were Arminians, influenced by the Methodist movement, who
believed that Christ had died for all men. They sang hymns, to the dismay
of the Old Generals and the Particulars, and they were evangelists. They
were smaller in number than the Particulars, but more tightly organized.
The Particulars, the most numerous of the Baptist groups, were organized
into several regional associations. The intensity of their Calvinism varied,
but they had come to believe, under Methodist influence, that one could
evangelize and still be Calvinist because only the elect would respond.
Andrew Fuller, who elaborated this view, also supported open communion
(open to Evangelical believers who had not had believer's baptism). Calvinism continued to decline among the Particulars during the nineteenth
century; but as they moved in the direction of Arminianism and open
communion, great debates and splits disturbed their sense of assurance.
The Strict and Particulars rejected Fuller and favored closed communion
(limited to those baptized as adult believers). Developing in reaction to the
liberalization of the Particulars, the Strict and Particulars were loosely organized, linked mainly by the apostate Anglican priest Joseph Charles
Philpot's *Gospel Standard* and the high Calvinist Charles Waters Banks's
Earthen Vessel.[133]

And there were differences that had nothing to do with theology, or
that masqueraded as theology. The two Baptist chapels in Barnoldswick,
for instance, owed their separate existence to business differences between
the preacher and two deacons who were mill-owners. After the split, one
of the chapels was for owners, managers, and overlookers, and the other
was for workers. At any given time, only one of the chapels belonged to the
Yorkshire Association, because where the one belonged, the other avoided.
Similar theological and social issues played themselves out among the
Baptist chapels of Nailsworth, Gloucestershire.[134]

Amid all this disunity, the Baptist Union stood out as "a fragile affair,
without funds, badly supported and with the North grossly underrepre-

[132] Benjamin Nightengale, *The Story of the Lancashire Congregational Union, 1806-1906* (Manchester and London, 1906), pp. 8-16, 63-70; Barrie Trinder, "Schisms and Divisions: The Origins
of Dissenting Congregations in Banbury, 1772-1860," *Cake and Cockhorse*, VIII (1982), 207-21;
Joan Fomin, "Congregationalists in Crisis, 1836-43," *Three Studies in Turbulence*, ed. David
Stephenson, *Colchester Historical Studies*, No. 1 (Colchester, n.d.), pp. 22-32.

[133] Chadwick, *Victorian Church*, p. 413; A. C. Underwood, *A History of the English Baptists*
(London, 1956), pp. 119-39, 153-59, 163-65, 185-88, 202-11, 242-47; Annie Marie Pettyjohn Le-
Barbour, "Victorian Baptists: A Study of Denominational Development" (Ph.D. thesis, University
of Maryland, 1977), pp. 17-18, 167-73.

[134] Keith A. Jones, "The Industrial Revolution: Effects upon the Baptist Community in Barnoldswick and the Resulting 'Split' in the Baptist Church," *Baptist Quarterly*, XXX (1983), 132; Urdank,
Cotswold Vale, pp. 275-304.

sented, a social occasion for London ministers, rather than an administrative dynamo."[135] The Baptist Union existed in name only from its foundation in 1813 to its adoption of a new constitution in 1831. Its objects were to "extend brotherly love and union" among the Baptist chapels that accepted "the sentiments usually denominated evangelical" (thereby fudging the Fullerite question in the interests of unity), to promote "unity of exertion" in the denomination's interests, to collect statistics, and to publish an annual report. But even these modest goals were too much for the Baptists. Attendance at the annual meeting dropped to about forty-five delegates, and its income rarely exceeded £100 p.a. Most of what little support it had came from the Particulars; some New Connexion Generals belonged, but the Strict and Particulars shunned it. It competed with a host of regional associations. (London had five associations in 1851, three for Particulars and two for Generals.)[136]

Despite this ecclesiastical anarchy, events similar to those among the Methodists and the Congregationalists were unfolding at midcentury. Ecclesiastical organizations were becoming more bureaucratic and less personal, developing central mechanisms and structures. The Papal Aggression crisis suggested to the Baptists that England was not necessarily a Protestant country, and underlined the usefulness of a single voice for their denomination—a need that J. P. Mursell, the Leicester Baptist active in the church-rate abolition campaign, as well as other Baptists active in public affairs, had long stressed. The 1851 religious census showed the Baptists that, although Nonconformists were important in national life, many were unchurched and their own denomination was fragmented. Finally, there was doctrinal pressure for unity, from those who feared that extreme congregationalism promoted the spread of heresy.[137] The Baptist Union stood ready to profit from these trends.

Debate over the extent of redemption and the terms of admission to communion raged from the 1830s to the 1860s; and the American evangelist Charles Grandison Finney's mission to Britain in 1849-51, during which he preached mainly in Baptist chapels, raised the volume of debate. Moreover, Baptist preachers were improving their status, becoming more professional, more clerical. During the first half of the century, more associations began insisting that pastors be ordained, that only the ordained preside over the Lord's Supper, and that formal theological training at an academy precede the call to preach. These debates and trends also affected individual congregations. Congregational polity became less exclusive, less rigid, more open to wider, outside influences, and less prepared to control individual lives. Membership and communion became more open; discipline became less strict. The very nature of what it was to be a Baptist thus was in flux; so the stakes were high and the tensions correspondingly high.[138]

Finally, the fear of Catholicism, both Roman and Anglo, led to tensions. The Baptists believed that Romanism was on the march, becoming

[135] Sellers, Nonconformity, p. 4.
[136] Ernest A. Payne, The Baptist Union, a Short History (London, 1958), pp. 61-62; Underwood, English Baptists, pp. 183-84, 211-13; LeBarbour, "Victorian Baptists," pp. 97-99, 142, 145-50.
[137] LeBarbour, "Victorian Baptists," pp. 3-4. 6. 99-100.
[138] Ibid., pp. 38-40, 42-46, 82-84; Payne, Baptist Union, pp. 85-87; Carwardine, Trans-Atlantic Revivalism, pp. 134-39; Binfield, Prayers, p. 25.

more open in its idolatry. In contrast, they lamented the steady decline in the average number of baptisms per chapel since 1841.[139]

> We see Puseyism and Popery, of late, outstripping all the Dissenting churches in their efforts to diffuse their pernicious doctrines. Shall not their church-building zeal, their laborious exertions in domiciliary visiting of the poor, their sacrifices of time and money, and all to supplant the reign of Christ in men's hearts by the reign of the priesthood,—shall not this stir us up to far more self-denial and labours to advance the true knowledge and love of our blessed Lord?[140]

During the 1840s, the Baptist Union attempted to enhance its status by taking the lead in petitioning the House of Commons against state aid to religion. It had already objected to the *Regium Donum* for needy Dissenting ministers in England and Wales, so it was able to oppose the Maynooth grant in 1845 with perfect consistency. The Northern Association also protested against the grant "as unnecessary to the Roman Catholics of Ireland, (whose claim to equal rights with their fellow subjects they would uphold) as well as unjust to the rest of the community." William Groser,[141] editor of the *Baptist Magazine*, argued that Maynooth endowed error, and the training of priests who would oppose scriptural Christianity, but that in any case the endowment of any religion was wrong.[142]

When the Papal Aggression crisis whipped up the rest of the Evangelical world into a frenzy, the Baptists tried to maintain their calm. Groser argued that the participation of Dissenters in the agitation only served to strengthen the Establishment ("from which our fathers and ourselves have severely suffered"), and that the Roman Catholics would emerge from it claiming sympathy as the "victims of calumny and oppression."[143] Edward Bean Underhill, secretary of the Baptist Missionary Society, and John Howard Hinton,[144] secretary of the Baptist Union, argued that the assumption of titles had no consequences for anyone who was not a Roman Catholic, and that the no-popery outcry itself posed the biggest threat to religious freedom.[145]

The Strict and Particulars were somewhat less willing to extend religious freedom to the Roman Catholics, somewhat more willing to see good in the anti-Catholic outcry, than was the Baptist Union leadership. Their magazine argued that Pio Nono's and Cardinal Wiseman's "boastful and lying pretensions" could be dismissed with contempt, were it not for the fact

---

[139] *Baptist Magazine*, XXXVIII (Mar. 1846), 148-50, (June 1846), 333, (July 1846), 418-23, XXXIX (Sept. 1847), 541-45; *Baptist Reporter*, n.s., VII (Dec. 1850), 538; *Church*, n.s., I (Oct. 1846), 68-70.

[140] *Church*, V (Jan. 1851), 3.

[141] Groser (1791-1856), a Baptist minister at Princes Risborough, Maidstone, and London, edited the *Baptist Magazine*, 1839-56 (Boase, V, 519).

[142] *Baptist Magazine*, XXXVI (June 1844), 295, XXXVII (May 1845), 237-43, (June 1845), 303 (quoted), (July 1845), 365.

[143] *Ibid.*, XLII (1850), iii-iv.

[144] A prolific pamphleteer on behalf of Voluntaryism, Hinton (1791-1873) pastored the Devonshire Square chapel, Bishopsgate St., London, 1837-63, and was active in the Liberation Society and in antislavery agitations. (*DNB*, IX, 901-2; Ian Sellers, "John Howard Hinton, Theologian," *Baptist Quarterly*, XXXIII, 1989, 119-32).

[145] *Baptist Magazine*, (Dec. 1850), 765-66, 768, 780, XLIII (Jan. 1851), 11-20, 24-25; John Howard Hinton, *The Romish Hierarchy in England: A Sermon preached at Devonshire Square Chapel, London* (London, 1850), p. iv; Haines, "Nonconformist Periodical Press," pp. 65-68.

that the Roman Catholic Church, not content with its civil and religious freedoms under Catholic Emancipation, wanted dominion. If it ever attained dominion, it would usurp the power of the state and establish despotism. Hence, the popular reaction and Lord John Russell's Durham Letter were good things, for they struck telling blows against Popery. Nevertheless, penal legislation was wrong, and Dissenters should work for the separation of church and state.[146]

Eventually, an official Baptist organ did speak. The Board of Baptist Ministers of London and Westminster adopted a list of resolutions that boiled down to this: Roman Catholicism, bad spiritually, was a persecuting church that claimed dominion over all Christians; hence any assumption of authority was potentially dangerous. But the remedy was to withdraw endowments from the Roman Catholic Church and, ideally, to separate church and state altogether.[147] Baptists at the local level followed this pattern. During midcentury, they often attempted to capture anti-Maynooth and other anti-Catholic meetings to carry amendments calling for the disestablishment of all churches and the separation of church and state.[148]

The third Evangelical denomination to be considered here, the Presbyterians, were markedly different from both the Congregationalists and the Baptists in their history, yet even they show a similar pattern of internal tensions.

The indigenous English Presbyterian tradition dissolved during the eighteenth century as most of the Presbyterian chapels became Unitarian. Of those that remained orthodox on the nature of the Supreme Being, some drifted to the Congregationalists, while others tried to maintain a Presbyterian identity. This last group was revivified, in the last few years of the eighteenth century and the first half-century of the nineteenth, by Scottish immigration (and by Ulster Presbyterians—but very little is known about them). Some of the Scottish immigrants joined the indigenous orthodox Presbyterian chapels; others, Dissenters in Scotland, established their Secession and Relief chapels in England. Most wanted to retain their ties with the Church of Scotland, and established "Scottish National Churches," the chapels in Crown Court and in Regent Square, London, being the most prominent.[149]

The Scottish immigrants wanted formal affiliation with the Kirk, and, acting on the advice of the Kirk's General Assembly, presbyteries in Lancashire and Cumberland formed a synod in 1836. The synod expanded to include London and Newcastle-upon-Tyne in 1839, Berwick in 1840, Northumberland in 1842, and Birmingham in 1848. But the Kirk did not wish to justify Episcopalian Dissent in Scotland by countenancing Presbyterian Dissent in England, and so kept the English synod at arm's length. Then, at the Disruption in 1843, the synod split. Those who supported the Free Church organized the "Presbyterian Church in England" (which included the orthodox indigenous Presbyterian chapels); those who remained loyal to the Kirk formed the "Scottish Synod in England in

[146] *Primitive Church Magzine*, n.s. VII (Dec. 1850), 376-79.
[147] *Baptist Magazine*, XLIII (Feb. 1851), 108-9.
[148] *Rochester, Chatham, and Stroud Gazette*, 26 Nov. 1850; Thomas de Vine to T. H. Croft Moody, 30 Jan. 1852, Page & Moody Papers, Southampton City Record Office, D/PM 10/5/77.
[149] Gilbert, *Religion and Society*, pp. 41-42; Binfield, *Prayers*, p. 7; George G. Cameron, *The Scots Kirk in London* (Oxford, 1979), pp. 90-117.

Connexion with the Church of Scotland" in 1850-51. (The Relief and the Secession chapels, meanwhile, had joined to form the United Presbyterian Church in England in 1840; they joined with the English Presbyterians to form the Presbyterian Church of England in 1876.) The English Presbyterians were the most numerous, with over sixty chapels in 1851.[150]

The English Presbyterians found it hard to maintain their identity as Scots who had no quarrels with an established religion—the Free Church itself, which the English supported, had no objection to a state church—with their reality as Dissenters from an Episcopalian Establishment. Thus, they hated "the enfeebling influence of the Prelatic system . . . the wretched figment of apostolical succession . . . fettered on every side by that Prelatic system . . . the cumbrous, medieval, Prelacy of England"; they declared that Anglican Evangelicals would never do justice to Christ's truth until they abandoned the apostolic succession and separated from the state. Yet they also wanted to show the English Baptists and Congregationalists that they offered scriptural church order.[151] How could they keep to the Establishment principle without becoming Episcopalians? How could they keep to the Presbyterian principle without becoming Nonconformists? Thus the history of the Presbyterian Church in England was marked by tensions inherent in that denomination's "transition, from Scotland to England, and establishment (even if from the Free Church, which considered itself the rightful establishment) to dissent."[152]

A further source of tension came from their fear of popery. They hated Roman Catholic doctrines and opposed anything beyond the most minimal civil rights for Roman Catholics. Some of this animus came from their theological views; some came from their Scottish background. But a significant element in the anti-Catholicism of the English Presbyterians (as with the anti-Catholicism of the English Methodists) was the influence of Ulster Protestantism. Although the English Presbyterians were orientated towards Scotland, some of their ministers, members, and money came from Ulster, and thus brought with them the virulent communal hatreds that expressed themselves in Orange riots and Dolly's Brae shootouts. The English Presbyterians sent deputations to the General Assembly of the Irish Presbyterian Church, and acknowledged their debt to it for ministers; yet they kept the Irish at arm's length.[153]

Finally, quarrels between the English Presbyterians and the Scots Presbyterians in England gave rise to tensions. The latter claimed to be the true Presbyterians because of their connection with the Kirk; the former were quick to point out that the Kirk exercised no jurisdiction south of the Tweed. (The debates over the use of hymnals and organs, which raged within the English Presbyterians during the 1850s, were connected with this rivalry; conservatives, who wanted to stress the Scottish connection, opposed their use as un-Presbyterian innovations.[154]) Money lay behind

[150] Chadwick, *Victorian Church*, pp. 398-99; *English Presbyterian Messenger*, n.s., II (Dec. 1849), 179-83; Cameron, *Scots Kirk*, pp. 241-57.

[151] *English Presbyterian Messenger*, n.s., I (Mar. 1848), 81-83 (quoted), (Feb. 1849), 446.

[152] David Cornick, "'Catch a Scotchman Becoming an Englishman': Nationalism, Theology and Ecumenism in the Presbyterian Church in England, 1845-1876," *Journal of the United Reformed Church Historical Society*, III (May 1985), 203.

[153] *Ibid.*, p. 206; *English Presbyterian Messenger*, n.s., I (Apr. 1848), 126, (June 1848), 184, (Aug. 1848), 238-40, II (Nov. 1849), 141-42, (July 1850), 398, (Aug. 1850), 439.

[154] Cornick, "Catch a Scotchman Becoming an Englishman," pp. 206-208.

this animosity: The two synods were quarreling over money, in the forms of titles to Presbyterian chapels in England and of contributions from philanthropic Presbyterians in Scotland.[155]

But perhaps the greatest source of tension, for the Congregationalists and Baptists as well as for the Presbyterians, were the intense rivalries among them—rivalries that parallel those among the Methodist Connexions. What was at stake was the harvesting of souls, and of the bodies attached to those souls, and of the purses attached to the bodies.

The Baptists and the Congregationalists were great rivals. The two agreed in polity, but not theology; as denominational self-consciousness increased, the divisions between pædobaptists and believer-baptists hardened, and the two unions became rivals in attracting the unaffiliated congregations.[156] "While we ought not to wish to withdraw sheep from the folds of our brethren in a proselyting, self-aggrandizing spirit, yet we ought to wish their churches to become 'even as ours.'"[157] A Particular Baptist open communionist wrote this, but other varieties of Baptists, not to mention Congregationalists and Presbyterians, would have agreed.

The periodicals that spoke for the Baptist Union kept up a steady attack against the Congregationalists, criticizing the "promiscuous" baptism of infants, claiming that the Baptists were really the first congregationalists by polity, and maintaining that Baptists, not Congregationalists, had been the true defenders of religious liberty against Laudian persecution in the early seventeenth century. The attacks ranged from the theological to the personal, and they got especially hot in 1849 and 1850.[158] The Congregationalists fought back, charging that the insistence of the Baptists on the correct amount of water and the correct method of its application amounted to formalism and the exaltation of ceremonial above substance, and hence could lead to "the deadly delusion" of baptismal regeneration.[159]

These rivalries were reflected at the local level. During the Papal Aggression crisis, Edward Baines, Jr., (himself a Congregationalist), tried to organize a joint anti-Catholic meeting of Congregationalists and Baptists at Leeds. No sooner had Baines finished his speech, in which he declared that "we are met to consider the propriety of expressing our sentiments, as Congregationalists," on the question of popish aggression, than the Baptist ministers A. M. Stalker and Robert Brewer rose to say that because the label "Congregationalist" usually referred to pædobaptists who were Dissenters, the phrase "Congregationalists and Baptists" should be used to describe the meeting.[160]

The Congregationalists and the Presbyterians, who agreed in theology but not in polity, were also great rivals. Although the Presbyterians tried to be friends with the Congregationalists, for both shared a common origin in the Puritans, they argued that their polity was better and more scriptural. Congregationalism, they said, turned ministers into either popes or

[155] *English Presbyterian Messenger*, I (Jan. 1848), 31, II (Dec. 1849), 181-82.
[156] Payne, *Baptist Union*, pp. 3, 10-11, 43.
[157] *Church*, n.s., V (Jan. 1851), 3.
[158] *Ibid.*, I (Aug. 1846), 28-30, III (1849), 47-48, 65-67, 110-11, 131-32, 144-45, 233-35, 259, 298-301, IV (Mar. 1850), 75-77, (Apr. 1850), 103-6, V (Jan. 1851), 3; *Baptist Magazine*, XXXVII (Apr. 1845), 194-98, (Aug. 1845), 458-61.
[159] *Confessions of a Convert, from Baptism IN Water, to Baptism WITH Water* (London, 1845), pp. 9, 90, 129.
[160] *Leeds Mercury*, 28 Dec. 1850.

slaves of their chapels, with the results that good men did not enter a ministry that had a "low standard in our days for learning, spirit, and even outward station." Anyway, since Congregationalists in practice have a Presbyterian polity, with their chapel elders (kirk session), local ministers' classis (presbytery), and county union (synod), they might as well become Presbyterians in name. (Some independent chapels tried to put this rivalry to their own use, negotiating with both presbytery and county union to get the best deal.)[161]

Filthy lucre lay behind the dispute. Lady Hewley's Charity, with an income of £4,200 p.a., provided funds for "orthodox English Dissenting" ministers and their widows, according to the trust-deeds of 1704/07. But by the early nineteenth century, many of the trustees were Unitarians. In 1830, some Manchester Congregationalists began a lawsuit, which they won in 1842, arguing that the Unitarians, not being orthodox, should be removed as trustees and denied benefits from the fund.[162] But others of the trustees were English Presbyterians, and the Congregationalists again sued, arguing that the English Presbyterians were really Scots, and hence should also be denied benefits. They won this case in 1848, but the Presbyterians continued to press their claims in courts of law and in the press.[163]

The Congregationalists were also at war with the Wesleyan Methodists. The Congregationalists charged that the Wesleyan Conference amounted to "ministerial despotism, and popular bondage and degradation" by a pack of popes, that if Wesleyans were honest, they would admit that they were Nonconformists, that they should join in the campaign against the Established Church, and that Wesleyan Reformers should become Congregationalists. The Wesleyans denounced "the lugubrious, apathy-stricken, and democratic" Congregationalist periodicals, with their "hybrid, motley, and discordant articles," their "hotch-potch of radicalism and vapid invective," and reminded waverers that Congregationalists, having rejected Arminianism at the Synod of Dort (1618), could hardly provide a home fit for Methodists.[164]

Finally, the Baptists and the Methodists were also at war. Francis Clowes, the Particular Baptist open communionist who claimed not to want to poach on other pastors' flocks, threw his support behind the Wesleyan Reformers, and denounced Wesleyanism as "the very footstool of Episcopal priestcraft," "a blot on evangelical Voluntaryism, similar to that which Slavery is on American Republicanism," "an ecclesiastical system the most *purely and avowedly human* of any since the days of the apostles."[165] The hope, of course, was that disaffected Wesleyans would choose the Baptists rather than the Congregationalists.

---

[161] *English Presbyterian Messenger*, n.s., I (Sept. 1848), 285, (Feb. 1849), 430-32, (June 1849), 566, II (Mar. 1850), 270-71, (July 1850), 414, (Sept. 1850), 468-69, III (Mar. 1851), 74-77, (Apr. 1851), 116.

[162] Earl Morse Wilbur, *A History of Unitarianism*, 2 vols. (Cambridge, Mass., 1945-52), II, 356-62; Chadwick, *Victorian Church*, pp. 392-95.

[163] *English Presbyterian Messenger*, n.s. I (July 1848), 212-13, (Nov. 1848), 347-51.

[164] *Wesleyan Methodist Magazine*, LXVI (1843), 213-14, LXXIII (1850), 742-43, 745, LXXIII (1850), 741; *Christian Miscellany*, II (Apr. 1847), 129-35; *Wesleyan Vindicator*, No. 2 (Feb. 1850), p. 19; *Watchman*, 11 Dec. 1850.

[165] *Church*, n.s., III (Dec. 1849), 334-36, IV (1850), iii, (Feb. 1850), 56.

Anti-Catholicism played an important role in all of these internal and external rivalries, because it provided the justification for the call for unity. "Now," declared the Rev. T. Adkins of Southampton, "if erroneous bodies can combine to propagate their destructive and erroneous principles—if the Church of Rome can unite herself in one federation for the purpose of propagating a species of spiritual harlotry," then surely the Congregationalists, preachers of the true Gospel, ought "to unite to the uttermost."[166] Josiah Conder, another supporter of denominational union under the ægis of the Congregational Union, agreed.[167] The Baptists were somewhat more uncertain. Joseph Foulkes Winks of the *Baptist Reporter*, who eagerly supported the Baptist Union, argued that the General and the Particular Baptists should amalgamate to oppose Roman Catholicism. Francis Clowes doubted that institutional unity would ever be attained on earth; but even he looked for "unity of effort, purpose, aim," unity "in aggressive movements on the dominion of him whose reign is the enslavement of man, and the reproach of the church."[168] Baptist principles were the best antidote to popery, and the Baptist Union was the most efficient engine to broadcast those principles.[169]

Anti-Catholicism thus offered a principle of unity that could be used for a variety of purposes: to quell internal revolts; to legitimize one's own revolt; to legitimize nascent central authorities in traditions of decentralization; to justify poaching on rivals' turf.

The Problem of the Establishment

The desire for unity expressed itself in ecumenical stirrings. If all Evangelicals, or all Protestants, or all Nonconformists could somehow unite, would that not deal the Papal Antichrist such a blow as would send him to the ground? Would that not spread the true Gospel throughout the world? Would that not even hasten the Millennium? Anti-Catholicism thus offered the basis for the origins of the modern-day Ecumenical Movement. Men such as Baptist Noel, John Angell James, Jabez Bunting, and Thomas Chalmers had been searching for a basis of cooperation among Evangelicals, whether Anglican, Scots Presbyterian, or English Nonconformist, since the early 1830s, but the atmosphere of the times was against it.[170] Despite Donald M. Lewis's attempts to argue to the contrary,[171] the 1830s and '40s saw a growing division between Anglican Evangelicals and Nonconformists. Evangelical Anglicans began to value the state connection more, as they became more secure within the Church and as they saw that Erastianism was a weapon against Anglo-Catholicism. For their part, Nonconformists became less kind towards the Anglican Evangelicals as they became more and more convinced that the Church was hopelessly popish. And the pent-up hostility of two centuries of second-class citizenship, directed against the entire Establishment, temporal and spiritual, which expressed itself in the Temperance Movement, an almost exclusively

---

[166] *British Banner*, 14 Mar. 1851.
[167] *Patriot*, 10 Oct. 1850.
[168] *Baptist Reporter*, n.s., II (Feb. 1845), 56; *Church*, n.s., I (July 1846), 5-6.
[169] *Ibid.*, III (1849), iii-iv; *Baptist Reporter*, n.s., VIII (Feb. 1851), 45-46; *Baptist Magazine*, XXXVII (Dec. 1845), 606-607.
[170] Wolffe, "Evangelical Alliance," pp. 334-37; Burritt, *Walks in the Black Country*, p. 35.
[171] Lewis, *Lighten Their Darkness*, pp. 22-25, 89.

Nonconformist movement until the 1860s, also made cooperation difficult.[172]

Evangelical attitudes towards the general fasts of 1847, 1854, and 1855, appointed by royal proclamation to be national days of petitioning for divine favor, illustrate the problem. Many Nonconformists were troubled by the fasts on the grounds that they rested upon the assumption of the Royal Supremacy in things spiritual. The *Record* tried to argue that the fast of 1854 was for general national purposes and therefore that Nonconformists should participate, but the *Eclectic Review*, the *Nonconformist*, and the *Patriot* criticized the whiff of state-churchism in the proclamations.[173]

The Baptists were the most stridently anti-state-church of the Nonconformists. Baptists of all sorts agreed upon the separation of church and state as the best bulwark against Popery, and argued that Dissenters should unite on that issue.[174] The Liberation Society enjoyed considerable support from prominent Baptists such as J. P. Murcell of Leicester; others, such as J. E. Giles of Leeds and J. H. Hinton (secretary of the Baptist Union), were active in the Church Rate Abolition Society and the Religious Freedom Society. Many also participated in movements, such as the Anti-Corn Law League and the Complete Suffrage Union, which, although more purely secular politics, had antiestablishmentarian implications.[175]

The leadership of the Baptist Union was suspicious of the Evangelical Alliance on state-religious grounds. Edward Steane, J. H. Hinton, and William Groser attended the Central Anti-Maynooth Committee in 1845, but eventually withdrew because the committee only objected to the endowment of error, while the Baptists objected to the endowment of anything. When the Evangelical Alliance was formally organized in 1846, the leadership warned that it was unsound on both establishment and slavery. Four years later, although some Baptists tried to argue that Englishmen of all faiths could oppose the Papal Aggression on the grounds of England's independence from foreign control (if the ruler of Rome could exercise power there today, then the ruler of Russia could tomorrow), most agreed that Roman Catholics had as much right to divide up England as did Baptists, Methodists, or Congregationalists.[176]

The Congregationalists also hated the Establishment. John Campbell, the denomination's leading journalist, was a staunch Voluntaryist, a founding member of the Anti-State-Church Association, and opposed to the Evangelical Alliance because he thought it unsound on the state-church question. He filled the pages of his periodicals with examples of Anglican persecution and used the Gorham case to attack the Church. But he weakened sufficiently during the Papal Aggression crisis to argue that the headship of Queen Victoria and the headship of the Pope were vastly

172 Gilbert, *Religion and Society*, p. 169; Bebbington, *Evangelicalism*, pp. 97-99; Sellers, *Nonconformity*, p. 43; Brian Harrison, *Drink and the Victorians: The Temperance Question in England, 1815-1872* (London, 1971), pp. 165, 180-83.
173 Janet, "Decline of General Fasts," pp. 71, 220-23.
174 *Baptist Reporter*, n.s., II (May 1845), 166-67, IV (Apr. 1847), 129-31; *Church*, n.s., I (1846-7), iv, (Aug. 1846), 39-40, II (Oct. 1848), 282-83; *Baptist Magazine*, XXXIX (Sept. 1847), 551-55; *Primitive Church Magazine*, n.s., VIII (Jan. 1851), 11.
175 LeBarbour, "Victorian Baptists," pp. 238-41; Payne, *Baptist Union*, pp. 70, 74, 84.
176 *Baptist Magazine*, XXXVII (July 1845), 367, XXXVIII (Jan. 1846), 23-24, (May 1846), 274-85; *Church*, n.s., I (Dec. 1846), 125, IV (Dec. 1850), 327-28; *British Banner*, 8 Jan. 1851; *Baptist Reporter*, n.s., VIII (Jan. 1851), 2, 4-5.

different.[177] Josiah Conder of the *Patriot* also came to argue that one could support "the supremacy of the Civil Government over all orders and estates in these realms" without thereby owing spiritual allegiance to the Queen.[178]

Other Congregationalist notables were equally ambivalent. Robert Vaughan,[179] the denomination's leading theologian, agreed that "as upholders of the voluntary principle we must certainly maintain the right of Roman Catholics to follow out their system of religion to its full extent; [and to us as Dissenters the establishment of Catholicism among us is no worse an evil than the establishment of Episcopacy itself]." But: "Let bygones be bygones." "The Papal Bull would throw us back again into the night of the middle ages." "Let us aid the Church with a magnanimity which becomes us; yet with the discrimination of Dissenters."[180] Thomas Binney, president of the Congregational Union, thought that the Establishment might be a bulwark of Protestantism. If its Establishment position weakened, Binney warned, the Church might assert exclusive claims about the apostolic succession, priestly powers, and sacramentalism, and, ultimately, might submit to the Pope.[181] Similar ambiguity was to be found among the Protestant Dissenting Deputies and in local Congregationalist chapels.[182]

The Methodists had a hard time cooperating with those who opposed religious establishments. Wesleyans claimed to believe in the "true theory" of state religion: "that it is the duty of a State to acknowledge the existence and supreme dominion of the God and Father of our Lord Jesus Christ, among other ways, by aiding the church of Christ in doing her great work."[183] Since patronage, Erastianism, and certainly Puseyism were not parts of "true" Establishment, the Wesleyans thought it within their rights to interfere in the internal affairs of the Church of England. But they criticized Nonconformists who attacked both Rome and Canterbury on the grounds that Rome was different. The Wesleyan Reformers agreed, chiding Nonconformists for failing to put aside their anti-state-churchism in the face of Papal Aggression.[184]

Anglican Evangelicals also had troubles over the church-state question. Although some, most notably Edward Bickersteth, took prominent roles in the Evangelical Alliance (as did John Cumming, the Scots Presbyterian, who also liked state churches), others did not. The two most famous anti-Catholic Anglicans of the day, Hugh Stowell and Hugh McNeile, refused to join because they did not trust the Alliance to be neutral on the church-state question. Certainly, Sir Culling Eardley Smith (later Eardley), the Alliance's leader, did not inspire confidence: He had founded the Evangelical Voluntary Church Association to coordinate disestablishment in 1840, and he appealed to Voluntaryist sentiment during the anti-May-

[177] Lewis, *Lighten Their Darkness*, pp. 179-80, 183-87; *Christian Witness*, VII (Aug. 1850), 398-400; *British Banner*, 6, 20 Nov. 1850.

[178] *Patriot*, 7, 11, 21 Nov. 1850.

[179] Vaughan (1795-1868), president of the Lancashire Independent College, Manchester, 1843-57, also edited the *British Quarterly Review*, 1845-65 (*DNB*, XX, 175-76).

[180] *Patriot*, 2 Dec. 1850. Vaughan later denied having uttered the words in brackets (*ibid.*, 5 Dec. 1850).

[181] *Christian Times*, 19 Oct. 1850.

[182] *British Banner*, 27 Nov. 1850, 8, 15 Jan. 1851; *Patriot*, 31 Oct. 1850.

[183] *Wesleyan Methodist Magazine*, LXVI (1843), 924.

[184] *Ibid.*, LXXIII (1850), 352, 508, 513, 514; *Wesleyan Review*, I (Dec. 1850), 565.

nooth agitation of 1845. Moreover, the *Record*, which had originally supported the Alliance, fell out with the *Christian Times*, the Alliance's unofficial newspaper; the prints exchanged charges of "Rationalism" and sacramentalism.[185]

The Evangelical Alliance picked its path very carefully through the thicket of church and state. It tried to present itself as a force for unity among Protestants, and even among English-speakers, a body, not exclusive, but for "the living brotherhood" of those who were regenerate in Christ. During the Papal Aggression crisis, the Alliance tried to find grounds on which all anti-Catholics could oppose the assumption of titles. It argued that there was a difference between the spiritual supremacy that the Crown claimed and that claimed by the Papacy; the former rested on Parliamentary will, while the latter rested on tyranny and coercion. Moreover, not to oppose Papal encroachments was to encourage the Anglo-Catholics, who were undermining the Church of England. Yet despite its own arguments, the Alliance's council decided not to memorialize the Queen, lest it alienate those of its supporters who were anti-state-church.[186]

Local evidence, however, shows that the issue of church and state divided Nonconformist ministers. Quarrels broke out in places as far apart as Northampton, South London, Stroud, Suffolk, and Blackburn over whether Nonconformists could in good conscience support the Royal Supremacy.[187] Some Congregationalists decided that they could. William Legg and S. Curwen of Reading said that it was one thing when English Evangelicals like the Wesleyans divided the country into districts; that was all right. It was another thing when the mother of harlots, the mother of abominations did the same thing. Thomas Atkins, at Southampton, agreed.[188] On the other hand, Congregationalist ministers at Kirkham, Burnley, and Lancaster argued that Roman Catholics, as obnoxious as they were, did have religious freedom, and that the Anglican Establishment *in esse* was a more real threat than the Popish Establishment *in posse*.[189] Baptists also supported religious freedom. Preachers preachers at Reading and at Padiham, near Burnley, urged Dissenters not to join in the agitation. At Birmingham, J. R. Mackenzie, English Presbyterian, denounced some Baptists and Congregationalists for dividing Protestantism by linking opposition to popery with opposition to any establishment. Isaac New, of the Bond Street Baptist chapel, replied by taxing Mackenzie for longing for the fleshpots of the Scottish establishment; and the quarrel spread, with Churchmen attacking Dissenters impartially.[190]

The great Nonconformist meeting at Preston on 3 December 1850, which was to have promoted unity along anti-Catholic lines, instead illustrated Nonconformist divisions over the Establishment. W. Walters, a Dissenter (probably a Baptist), had been selected to move the first resol-

[185] *Leeds Mercury*, 24 Jan. 1846; *British Protestant*, II (May 1846), 113-16; *Christian Times*, 1, 8 Feb. 1851; *Manchester Courier*, 9 Nov. 1850; Lewis, *Lighten Their Darkness*, pp. 19, 81; Norman, *Anti-Catholicism*, p. 40.

[186] *Evangelical Christendom*, I (Apr. 1847), 97-99, (Aug. 1847), 249-50, (Dec. 1847), 386; *Christian Times*, 26 Oct., 2, 9, 23 Nov., 14 Dec. 1850.

[187] *Northampton Mercury*, 23 Nov. 1850; *Northampton Herald*, 30 Nov. 1850; *Times*, 25 Nov., 11 Dec. 1850, 17 Jan. 1851; *Preston Guardian*, 21 Dec. 1850; *Blackburn Standard*, 18 Dec. 1850.

[188] *Reading Mercury*, 9 Nov. 1850; *British Banner*, 27 Nov. 1850.

[189] *Preston Guardian*, 23 Nov., 7, 19 Dec. 1850; *Blackburn Standard*, 11 Dec. 1850.

[190] *Reading Mercury*, 9 Nov. 1850; *Preston Guardian*, 14 Dec. 1850; *Birmingham Mercury*, 4, 11, 18 Jan. 1851.

ution, but withdrew upon learning that the mayor, an Anglican, would preside, and that the meeting would be open to Nonconformists "and others." Walters organized his own meeting on 18 December, at which he and J. S. Cuzner proclaimed that the Church of England was as great a persecutor as the Church of Rome, that Dissenters had no business joining the no-popery cry, and that the best way of preventing popish encroachments was to separate church and state. They drew support from the *Preston Guardian*, which reported that two local Quakers had had goods seized for nonpayment of tithes, and which suggested that if an agitation were needed, it should be against the Established Church.[191]

The Evangelical Alliance sought to profit from the Papal Aggression crisis by leading the attack on the watered-down Ecclesiastical Titles Bill, by organizing a meeting of "Evangelical Christians holding the principles of the Protestant Reformation" at Exeter Hall on 27 February 1851, and by trying to focus the debates on theological issues that separated Protestantism from Romanism. But Lord Ashley's Protestant Defence Committee ousted the Evangelical Alliance from the lead by hosting a "combined meeting of Protestants" on 18 March 1851, to consider how to unite the various Protestant bodies against the aggression of the Roman Catholic Church. The Evangelical Alliance at first gave the move only grudging support, fearing a rival society, but became more welcoming when Sir Culling Eardley Eardley, its leader, participated. But the body, known as the Protestant League, evolved in the direction of an anti-Maynooth pressure group; and Eardley's departure for Germany on 31 May ended his involvement in it.[192]

The Evangelical Alliance had failed to become the center of pan-Evangelical, anti-Catholic unity, largely because of the problem of the Establishment.[193] The two new bodies that emerged from the Papal Aggression crisis, the Protestant Alliance (which evolved from the Protestant League) and the Scottish Reformation Society, attempted to get round the problem, in order to achieve Protestant unity, in different ways. First, the two cooperated, with the latter's journal, the *Bulwark*, serving as the unofficial organ of the former. Second, the Protestant Alliance managed to attract the support of Anglicans such as Hugh Stowell, who had avoided the Evangelical Alliance, and focused its efforts on repeal of the Maynooth endowment and the inspection of convents, with an occasional foray into Tuscan intolerance. Third, the Scottish Reformation Society carved out a specialized niche in the anti-Catholic pantheon by purveying more prurient material about the sex life of priests.[194]

For T. H. Croft Moody, the Southampton anti-Catholic activist, as for many others, the Protestant Alliance was the last hope for an ecumenical anti-Catholic association.

> Although not without some misgivings I am desirous of joining the
> Protestant Alliance & to give one more trial to a combined anti-popery

---

[191] *Preston Pilot*, 7 Dec. 1850; *Preston Guardian*, 30 Nov., 7, 14, 21 Dec. 1850.

[192] *Christian Times*, 14 Dec. 1850, 15 Feb., 1, 15, 22, 29 Mar., 5, 12 Apr., 17 May, 7 June 1851.

[193] But also because its sponsorship of Father Achilli brought it into disrepute after the revelations of the *Achilli v. Newman* trial (*Times*, 7 Aug., 4 Sept. 1852).

[194] Protestant Alliance, Monthly Letter Nos. 2 and 3, 1 Feb. and 1 Mar. 1853, Page & Moody Papers, Southampton City Record Office, D/PM 10/2/62; *Bulwark*, I (July 1851), 1, 2, (Sept. 1851), 69, (Dec. 1851), 151; *Times*, 7 June 1852, 10 Jan. 1854.

movement. But in joining it I cannot but express a hope that the alliance will not allow itself to be embarrassed in efforts against Romish endowments or other portions of the Romish organisation by those who are determined to make questions of popery & protestantism subordinate to the question of church & state. I am more than ever convinced it is impossible to work with those who oppose Romish endowments & hierarchies not because they are papal but because they are part of a (to them) larger question of ecclesiastical policy.[195]

But the ecumenical no-popery movement was in disarray again by 1854. A combined conference was held in May of that year, with delegates from the British Reformation Society, the Protestant Association, the Protestant Alliance, Church Protestant Defence Society, Evangelical Alliance, Islington Protestant Institute, Scottish Reformation Society, and the National Club. More meetings followed in 1855, under the chairmanship of the Scottish Tory politician John Campbell Colquhoun, but nothing came of it. In November of 1855, a regional "Protestant Union for the North of England" was attempted at Manchester, under the patronage of the Anglicans Hugh Stowell, Hugh McNeile, Berkeley Addison, and Charles Edward Cawley, the Congregationalists Robert Vaughan and Robert Halley, and Joseph Adshead;[196] but, again, nothing came of it. The Evangelical Alliance, Scottish Reformation Society, and Protestant Alliance were unable to cooperate over the Mortara Affair; each, separately, issued declarations in 1858.[197]

During the later 1850s and 1860s, the Protestant Alliance continued to push the Maynooth and convent questions, tried to block the appointment of Roman Catholic chaplains for workhouses, jails, reformatories, and army regiments, and investigated popish tendencies in schoolbooks on the Education Department's approved list. Perhaps its biggest victory came in 1858, when it got the examiners in law and modern history at Oxford to remove the Roman Catholic historian John Lingard's *History of England* from their approved reading list.[198] During the same period, the Evangelical Alliance focused on sabbatarian proposals to stop Sunday band concerts and to prevent the Sunday opening of the British Museum, National Gallery, and Crystal Palace, and warned against Renan's and Strauss's challenges to orthodoxy.[199]

The issue of state-churchism surfaced again in 1864, when the Baptist Charles Haddon Spurgeon embarrassed the Evangelical Alliance's annual general meeting by denouncing Anglican participation. Spurgeon argued that Anglican Evangelicals supported the doctrine of baptismal regeneration by using the Prayer Book, and therefore were "dishonest" when they subscribed to the Evangelical Alliance. Spurgeon claimed that he was merely stating a fact, and hence not violating the Alliance's rules (which forbade "rash and groundless insinuations, personal imputations, or irri-

---

[195] Moody to John McGregor, 21 Nov. 1851, Page & Moody Papers, Southampton City Record Office, D/PM 10/5/1.
[196] Adshead (1800-1861) was a land agent, mapmaker, and author of numerous improving pamphlets on local social and political issues (Boase, IV, 45).
[197] Docs. in Page & Moody Papers, Southampton City Record Office, D/PM 10/6/4-6; *Bulwark*, V (Dec. 1855), 161; *Times*, 23, 30 Nov., 17, 28 Dec. 1858; cf. Wolffe, "Protestant Societies and Anti-Catholic Agitations," pp. 311, 314, 316.
[198] *Times*, 13 May 1856, 16 May 1857, 25 May 1858, 25 Apr. 1860, 25 May 1870.
[199] *Ibid.*, 26 Aug. 1856, 11 July 1864.

tating allusions" against members). When objections were raised, Spurgeon and his followers resigned.[200]

By 1870, then, both of the ecumenical anti-Catholic alliances were rapidly declining into marginality. The problem of the Establishment remained the insuperable barrier against effective anti-Catholic cooperation. As one disappointed activist at Romsey complained, if he circulated an anti-Maynooth petition, the local Dissenters did the same against Anglican endowments.[201]

Nonconformist Tolerationists

Not all Nonconformists, as we have seen, were willing to participate in the memorializing and petitioning of 1850-51. John Campbell's *British Banner* claimed that the only opposition came from "individuals either of the Romish persuasion, or, without fixed principles upon the subject, or, indeed, a knowledge of it."[202] That, of course, is nonsense. There were two major sources of aggressive opposition (as opposed to simple avoidance) to organized anti-Catholicism at midcentury: what Alan Gilbert calls Old Dissent; and a mixed bag of individuals who were animated by a broad liberalism of thought.

Old Dissent, in Gilbert's terminology made up of the Friends, the Unitarians, and the Original General Baptists, was in a sense what was left over after the Evangelical Revival had done its work. (But there were Evangelicals to be found even among the Quakers and Unitarians.) Basically, it stagnated during the nineteenth century, remaining more or less static in total numbers.[203]

Victorian Quakers were rent by disputes during the nineteenth century, and played little part in "political Dissent," save to oppose the 1843 Factory Bill. They were divided into Evangelicals, who tended to elevate the authority of Scripture over that of the Inner Light, and who looked for a regenerative spiritual experience, be it sudden or gradual, and the old-fashioned quietists, who agreed with the Evangelicals that original sin had ruined human nature, but who continued to obey the Inner Light. The 1830s were years of transition leading to Evangelical domination, which lasted until the mid-1880s. And there was a Unitarian element (the "Hikesites"), condemned from time to time by the Yearly Meeting, but there nonetheless (largely because Quakers and Unitarians came from the same social class). The most extreme of the Quaker Evangelicals followed Isaac Crewdson, a Manchester Friend, into schism in 1835. Crewdson published a tract, *A Beacon to the Society of Friends*, that created an uproar. (Crewdson basically wanted Friends to believe and behave more like Nonconformists.) When the Yearly Meeting recommended that Crewdson be silent in Meeting, he and his supporters quit. Although he organized his own church, many of his supporters ended up in Evangelical Nonconformist denominations.[204] The most prominent Quaker in public life during the middle of the century, John Bright, took a highly visible stand on Ro-

[200] *Ibid.*, 30 Nov. 1864.
[201] C. Avery Moore to Moody, 1 June 1855, Page & Moody Papers, Southampton City Record Office, D/PM 10/6/56;
[202] *British Banner*, 27 Nov. 1850.
[203] Gilbert, *Religion and Society*, pp. 40-41.
[204] Elizabeth Isichei, *Victorian Quakers* (Oxford, 1970), pp. 3-31, 45-49, 196-200.

man Catholic rights—a stand highly obnoxious to anti-Catholics[205] —and Joseph Sturge[206] spoke out at Birmingham against the Papal Aggression outcry, but for the most part Friends did nothing.

In contrast, the Unitarians were much more active. They, too, were split between Evangelicals and rationalists. Evangelical Unitarians were orthodox as to miracles and the plenary inspiration of Scriptures, fervent in their piety, distinguishable from Orthodox Evangelical Dissent only in their belief that the doctrine of the Trinity was unscriptural. The others were the heirs of eighteenth-century Deism and rational religion, who suspected enthusiasm and emotion, and who argued that human reason was the final arbiter of Scriptures. Relations with Orthodox Dissent were tense, partly over doctrinal matters, but largely because of the litigation over Lady Hewley's Charity and other trust deeds, and the bitter disputes over the Dissenters' Chapels Act, 1844.[207] In addition, growing centralization among the Unitarians led to tensions. Unitarians, Old General Baptists, and Old English Presbyterians coexisted uneasily, with a good deal of mutual jealousy and single-minded preservation of one's special heritage. Some Unitarian leaders, however, promoted unity under a central body, the British and Foreign Unitarian Association, founded in 1825. Most congregations, fearing for their independence, were slow to join. In 1826, only thirty-four out of about two hundred congregations belonged; the number never exceeded eighty; and it had declined to thirteen in 1866. Thus the BFUA was not really a union of chapels, like the Baptist or the Congregational Union, but rather a union of individual subscribers.[208]

Despite these tensions, however, Unitarians avoided anti-Catholic activism. The *Inquirer* did not agree with Roman doctrine, of course; but it did not let its disagreement blind it to religious realities. It understood why Anglo-Catholics claimed to be loyal Anglicans. It recognized that the Pope's claim to spiritual supremacy, despite the rhetoric of his assertions in *Universalis ecclesiæ*, applied only to those who chose to be his subjects; and "the terrors of [his] temporal power belong wholly to the imagination." In any case, Roman Catholics were as much brothers in Christ as any other set of Christians. Hence the *Inquirer* condemned the Papal Aggression agitation as sectarian and unchristian.[209]

> The Anti-Papal agitation has taken a turn so coarsely sectarian, and is so obviously becoming a movement for the strengthening of the temporal privileges and advantages of the Established Church, that every man of liberal feeling who has given it the least countenance, ought to find some means of separating himself from those who make Protestantism consist in abuse of the Pope, and propagate hatred in the name of Christianity.[210]

Some Unitarians, such as the Western Unitarian Christian Union, the Lewin's Mead Chapel, Bristol, and the chapels at Bridport and Taunton,

---

[205] *Inf.*, pp. 208-209.

[206] Sturge (1793-1859) contested Nottingham, Leeds, and Birmingham and attempted to cooperate with the Chartists (*DNB*, XIX, 130-31).

[207] Bernard Lord Manning, *The Protestant Dissenting Deputies*, ed. Ormerod Greenwood (Cambridge, 1952), pp. 68-81; Chadwick, *Victorian Church*, pp. 396-97; Binfield, *Prayers*, p. 5; Wilbur, *Unitarianism*, II, 344-45, 368-73.

[208] Wilbur, *Unitarianism*, pp. 351-53; Alan Ruston, "The Omnibus Radical: Rev. Henry Solly (1813-1903)," *Transactions of the Unitarian Historical Society*, XIX (1988), 86-87.

[209] *Inquirer*, 19 Oct., 2, 9 Nov. 1850.

[210] *Ibid.*, 16 Nov. 1850.

focused their attacks on Roman Catholic doctrine.[211] The majority of Unitarians who chose to memorialize the Queen or to participate in public meetings deplored bigotry, opposed penal laws, preached against the agitation, and commended those ministers (such as the minister at Southampton whose effigy got paraded through the streets as "Cardinal Norrington," Henry Solly at the Gloucester county meeting, H. W. Crosskey at Derby) whose stands brought them obloquy.[212] Edward Parry of Battle praised the Roman Catholic Church for "shewing forth the spirit of Christ by [the] self-denial and benevolence" of those who ministered in the cholera-infested slums.[213] Robert W. Taylor of the London District Unitarian Society thought that it was time to petition the Queen for more Roman Catholic rights: "There were still some slight disqualifications under which Catholics laboured, such as Jesuits not being allowed to wear their peculiar dress. This was an injustice; for why should not all alike have the opportunity of dressing so as to make fools of themselves?"[214]

When the British and Foreign Unitarian Association finally pronounced on the assumption of titles, on 11 June 1851, it attempted to satisfy both those who wanted to oppose bigotry and penal laws and those who thought that the Association had no business speaking on the topic at all. It condemned the spirit of "Ecclesiastical assumption and intolerance" that characterized both the Roman and the Anglican Churches, and called for opening the universities to non-Anglicans, releasing the clergy from the requirement of subscribing to the Thirty-Nine Articles, and instituting nonsectarian education.[215]

The second source of aggressive opposition to no-popery at public meetings came from people whose liberal views led them to treat Roman Catholics with fairness. Benjamin Glover, the rather idiosyncratic Radical at Bury, argued that the Pope had done nothing harmful by creating his hierarchy, and that Roman Catholics had as much right to exercise religious liberty as did Protestants.[216] But most working-class Radicals did not care about the Pope and Cardinal Wiseman, and simply used the issue as an excuse to advance their own specific views on other matters.

Similarly, most Wesleyan Reformers hated Roman Catholicism, used no-popery as a weapon in their own warfare with Conference, and did not care about Cardinal Wiseman's religious rights. So, they usually limited their intervention at public meetings to declarations charging that Wesleyan Popes were as wicked as the Pope of Rome. William Griffith, former superintendant of the Ripley Circuit, east Derbyshire, and one of the leading expelled Reformers, was an exception. Himself a member of the Anti-State Church Association, he advanced that group's line at the Derby public meeting on 16 November 1850. He argued that to rely on the secular arm would serve only to produce martyrs and to weaken religion in the eyes of the undecided. Further, he dismissed the uproar as simply a dispute between rival hierarchies. If the Church of England were not established, he averred, no one would object to the Roman Catholic hierarchy.

[211] Ibid., 2, 16 Nov., 14 Dec. 1850.
[212] Cheltenham Free Press, 30 Nov. 1850; Inquirer, 7, 14 Dec. 1850, 18 Jan. 1851.
[213] Inquirer, 26 Oct. 1850.
[214] Ibid., 30 Nov. 1850.
[215] Ibid., 14 June 1851.
[216] The Bury Observer, and Herald of the Good Times Coming, No. 9 (Dec. 1850), pp. 137-39.

Griffith and his followers, aided by support from the Unitarian H. W. Crosskey, managed to carry an amendment opposing any appeal to the civil arm and supporting disestablishment and disendowment.[217]

The Anti-State Church Association, taking the lead from Edward Miall, the Congregationalist minister who was its leading propagandist, tried to defend its Voluntaryism towards religion during the Papal Aggression crisis. Miall used his own newspaper, the *Nonconformist*, to advance the consistent argument that there should be no state interference in or state support for religion. Hence, he opposed the Maynooth grant, but he also defended the Roman Catholic Church's right to have a territorial hierarchy. He went on a speaking tour in Lancashire during November 1850 in which he propagated these views; and other supporters of the Anti-State Church association advanced them during their tours in 1851.[218]

The most spectacular success of the religious tolerationists occurred at Birmingham, when the anti-Catholic meeting in December 1850 failed to adopt a memorial to the Queen, thanks to a combination of anti-state-church men, religious liberals, and Voluntaryists, led by George Dawson.

Dawson,[219] the minister of Mount Zion Baptist chapel, Birmingham, came to believe that an ethical life spent helping others and fighting injustice was more important than correct views on pædobaptism. He also opposed anti-Catholic manifestations and supported full religious toleration for all. In politics, he was a Radical. Eventually, he became too much for the Baptists, and he and his supporters left to start their own chapel, the Church of the Saviour. The chapel had no doctrinal requirements: Its statement of principles said that both sides of every question should be examined, that the Lord's Supper was open to all, and that the individual's informed conscience should be paramount.[220] "True Religion," Dawson believed, was "social, unitive, and brotherly in its spirit: it produces the Church as its social development." For him, Christianity was "a set of fruitful principles," not a code of laws or a theological system.[221]

Such views were anathema to Evangelicals. Thomas Ragg, the Anglican Evangelical leader of the Birmingham Protestant Association, excoriated Dawson's theology as "hero-worship" of "the man deified by God" (i.e., looking to Christ as an example to follow, rather than as a savior to believe in), and exposed the insidious Germanic and Carlylian influences that he was spreading. Furthermore, Dawson's liberal ideas about Sunday observance (he taught that the Sabbath was made for man, and not man for the Sabbath) gave comfort to Sabbath-breakers.[222] The anti-Maynooth agitation of 1845, in which Birmingham was prominent, led Dawson to be-

---

217 *Wesleyan Times*, 25 Nov., 23 Dec. 1850; Tranter, "Landlords, Labourers, Local Preachers," pp. 132-33.

218 Haines, "Nonconformist Periodical Press," pp. 73-76; Binfield, *Prayers*, pp. 101-24; *Preston Guardian*, 26 Oct., 23 Nov. 1850; *Huddersfield Chronicle*, 26 Apr. 1851.

219 Born in London, Dawson (1821-1876) studied at Aberdeen and Glasgow, made his mark in Birmingham in 1844 as "a young, earnest, and eloquent preacher, entirely unconventional in opinions, personal appearance, and style of preaching," and was pastor of the Church of the Saviour from 1845 to his death. One of the most popular travelling lecturers of the day, he was instrumental in popularizing Emerson and Carlyle. (*DNB*, V, 671-73.)

220 Wright Wilson, *The Life of George Dawson* (Birmingham, 1905), pp. 52-61. E. P. Hennock, *Fit and Proper Persons: Ideal and Reality in Nineteenth-Century Urban Government* (Montreal, 1973), pp. 61-79, is the most comprehensive analysis of Dawson's influence.

221 *Church Papers: Printed for the use of the Congregation meeting at the Church of the Saviour, Birmingham*, No. 3 (Aug. 1850), p. 2.

222 *Protestant Watchman*, No. 1 (Mar. 1849), pp. 6-8, wrapper, No. 2 (Apr. 1849), pp. 17-20.

come active in opposing intolerance, thereby giving Ragg and the Evangelicals another reason to hate him. Hugh Stowell found "covert scepticism . . . neological nonsense" in his support for the Ten-Hours movement, and Ragg called him a German mystic and Jesuitical casuist; he called the Birmingham Protestant Association "a set of ignorant fellows."[223]

Five years later, at the Papal Aggression crisis, Dawson displayed the same liberality of spirit.

> Instead of joining in the howl of the Anglican Church, we will welcome, not only the twelve bishops, but as many more as the Pope chooses to send, so long as they are to be found going in and out of the homes of the poor and ignorant, and provided that they show themselves mindful of our civil rights and liberties.[224]

Because Dawson believed that Christianity needed no priests or rituals, no hierarchies, no distinctions between clergy and laity, the controversy over the assumption of titles was meaningless for him.[225]

Thus Dawson took a leading role in organizing opposition to the proposed memorial to the Queen, which denounced the assumption of titles and claimed that the Anglo-Catholic movement had encouraged the Pope in his usurpations. Dawson gained the support of the Quaker philanthropist and Radical politician Joseph Sturge, and of Brewin Grant,[226] who had just left the Highbury Congregational chapel to undertake an independent ministry to the working classes under the patronage of John Angell James and Samuel Morley. Despite the best efforts of J. B. Melson, J. A. James, and Thomas Ragg, the public meeting, which drew between twelve and fourteen thousand inhabitants, negatived both the anti-Catholic resolution and Dawson's protoleration amendment.[227]

This did not end the matter. The anti-Catholics had suffered a serious defeat, for the results of the town meeting were remarked upon throughout England; they attempted to make up for it by increasing their efforts during the early months of 1851. The Wesleyans and the Birmingham Protestant Association gave antipapal lectures, which Brewin Grant and George Dawson replied to with their own lectures; Hugh Stowell, William Sleigh,[228] and Father Gavazzi were brought in, and an Anti-State-Church meeting countered them. By early spring, however, most of the meetings that could have been held, had been held, and other issues began to eclipse no-popery in the public interest—disputes over railways, what to do about the Asylum, was the Birmingham Improvement Bill a good thing, and so on. Birmingham's well-organized anti-Catholics remained active during the 1850s—Father Gavazzi was a fixture of the lecture season—but they

---

[223] *Ibid.*, wrapper; Wilson, *Dawson*, pp. 70, 75; *Report of the Great Meeting of the Protestants of Birmingham, in the Town Hall, to oppose the Endowment of the Popish College at Maynooth, April 17, 1845* (Birmingham, 1845).

[224] George Dawson, *On the Romish Church and her Hierarchy* (Birmingham, 1850), pp. 3-4.

[225] *Church Papers*, No. 5 (Feb. 1851), pp. 1-2.

[226] Grant (1821-1892), a Congregationalist minister at Birmingham, 1848-55, and Sheffield, 1856-68, took Anglican orders and served charges in Bethnal Green, 1870-92 (Boase, V, 470). He came to defend the Irish Establishment as a bulwark against the endowment of the Roman Catholic Church (*Times*, 18 Aug. 1868; Machin, *Politics and the Churches*, pp. 366-67).

[227] *The Catholic Question: Report of the Great Town's Meeting, held in the Town Hall, Birmingham, on Wednesday, December 11, 1850*, 3rd ed. (Birmingham, 1850), pp. 4, 7, 11, 16, 20, 28; Jones, *Congregationalism*, p. 249.

[228] Sleigh (1783-1861) was a Wesleyan minister and author active in anti-Catholic lecturing (Boase, VI, 573).

had failed to accomplish in 1850 what they had done in 1845—to put the town officially on the anti-Catholic side.[229]

So, with but a few exceptions, Evangelical Nonconformity added its distinctive twang to the anti-Catholic bray.[230]

[229] *Birmingham Mercury*, 4, 11, 18, 25 Jan., 1, 8, 15, 22 Feb., 1, 15 Mar. 1851, 13 Nov. 1852; George Dawson, *Two Lectures on the "Papal Aggression" Controversy* (Birmingham, 1851); Brewin Grant, *The Three Shams: The sham Peter, called the Pope; the sham church, called infallible; the sham Bible, Douay & tradition* (London, 1851).

[230] Cunningham's defense of Chadbandian cant (*Everywhere Spoken Against*, pp. 10-12), and Houghton's excoriation of it (*Victorian Frame of Mind*, pp. 407-8), are worth reading.

VII

ANTI-CATHOLICISM AS A POLITICAL ISSUE

> The time is coming when men must hold their opinions with tenacity. . . . The anchorage which will serve for the calm will not serve for the storm. . . . Our day is a day of positivity and decision. . . . Every man is being forced to tell us what he is—what he means—whose side he proposes to take.[1]

CHURCH AND STATE, religion and politics, have always been intertwined in the Christian world—and the nineteenth century was no exception to this. That century especially saw considerable political activity on the parts of laymen and Dissenting ministers. To be sure, some Evangelicals believed that Christian clergymen should be pilgrims on earth, not participants in politics, and that Christian societies departed from their proper function—to spread the Gospel—as they became worldly political associations. But the growing view was that Dissenters had to be political.[2] Being a citizen, *The Church*[3] declared, is "a most solemn and essential part of christian duty." The spread of God's word in the world depends upon how "the affairs of a nation, and especially this nation, are managed. . . ." Whether the people of England will enjoy peace, plenty, and liberty, or war, wretchedness, slavery, and crime; whether, on a larger scale, souls will be saved or lost; whether Christ or Antichrist shall reign: All this "greatly depends, under God, upon the manner in which the affairs of this kingdom are conducted." So it follows that it is mandatory for true Christians and Dissenting ministers to participate in politics.[4]

Given the constitutional and theological opposition to Roman Catholicism, it is not surprising that some anti-Catholics attempted to make their views the object of practical politics. Religious questions were at the center of political life for most of the century, but unfortunately for the anti-Catholics, the most fundamental of the questions was the conflict between the Church, closely connected with Toryism, and Dissent, even more closely connected with Liberalism.[5] Anti-Catholics, then, had the difficult task of bridging the gaps between Liberal and Tory, church and chapel. They hoped that the appeal to shared Protestantism would do that, and thus

---

[1] Hugh Stowell, "The Age We Live In," *Exeter Hall Lectures* (1851), quoted in Houghton, *Victorian Frame of Mind*, pp. 169-70.
[2] Derek Fraser, *Urban Politics in Victorian England: The Structure of Politics in Victorian Cities* (Leicester, 1976), pp. 269-70; Bebbington, *Evangelicalism*, pp. 132-37.
[3] A Baptist magazine edited by Francis Clowes.
[4] *Church*, n.s., I (Sept. 1846), 50-52.
[5] Fraser, *Urban Politics*, pp. 196, 265.

anti-Catholicism offered the possibility of being a force for unity in politics as well as in religion.

Anti-Catholicism was kept alive as a political issue after 1829 by concerns over education and the annual Maynooth grant, and of course it was this annual irritant that ultimately led Peel to make the grant permanent. These issues led to the continued cooperation of Evangelical M.P.s and to the reemergence of Protestantism in the general election of 1835. Appeals appeared in both the *Record* and the *Standard*, calling for "Christian" electors to return Protestant candidates, but most Nonconformist electors remained loyal to the Whigs. (Anti-Catholic sentiment helped defeat Lord John Russell in South Devon, at the by-election required by his assuming office, but the registration of Tories probably counted for more.)[6]

The Protestant Association intervened in the general elections of 1837 and 1841, issuing addresses that urged the return of Protestant candidates, but disavowing support for any specific party. In 1837, the Tories used the anti-Catholic opportunities of the Irish Church bills and Maynooth and the pro-Anglican opportunity of the church-rate bill, but Nonconformists, thankful for civil registration and the church-rate bill, again remained loyal to the Whigs. The big losers were the Radicals. Free trade dominated the 1841 election, but religious issues played a secondary role. Conservative candidates stressed the union of church and state, and attacked Roman Catholicism as a threat to the Constitution; the party's gains came in areas where the Corn Law was the issue. In both elections, the constituencies with the most active Protestant Association auxiliaries, Birmingham, Derby, Manchester, Marylebone, returned Liberal candidates.[7]

The 1847 election was especially complicated because the big questions were the Maynooth endowment, the Education Minutes of 1846, and protection. Voluntaryists, who opposed both Maynooth and the Education Minutes (and most of whom probably also opposed protection), formed a coordinating committee, the Dissenters' Parliamentary Committee, which drew up a list of candidates to stand as Voluntarys, issued an election address, and produced a periodical, the *Nonconformist Elector*. The Anti-State Church Association also organized for electoral politics. Ultra-Protestants, who opposed Maynooth, but most of whom probably liked both protection and, to a lesser extent, the Education Minutes, focused on the activities of the Protestant Association and the National Club. Both issued addresses and pamphlets about the need to return Protestant candidates, but neither raised funds, endorsed candidates, or in any official way engaged in the campaign. The complications are best seen at Liverpool, where the Tory candidates were Sir Digby Mackworth (Protectionist and anti-Catholic) and Lord John Manners (Protectionist, but Tractarian and pro-Maynooth). The split between the two allowed the Liberal Sir Thomas Birch and the Peelite Edward Cardwell to take the seats. The election thus was a contest of a Whig-Peelite center alliance against, on the one hand, Voluntaries and Chartists, and, on the other hand, Protectionists and Ultra-Protestants.[8]

---

[6] Wolffe, *Protestant Crusade*, pp. 65-87.

[7] *Ibid.*, pp. 98-100; Machin, *Politics and the Churches*, pp. 62, 71-72.

[8] Machin, *Politics and the Churches*, pp. 183-92; Hamer, *Politics of Electoral Pressure*, pp. 92-94; Wolffe, "Protestant Societies and Anti-Catholic Agitations," pp. 207-10.

Effective participation in politics required pressure groups to move beyond the educating of public opinion and the lobbying of politicians to the exertion of electoral pressure by means of asking pledges of candidates and of putting up their own candidates. Pressure groups thus had to decide whether to contest general elections, where their resources would be spread thin over the country, their special message drowned out by national issues, and their success more likely to influence the balance of parliamentary power, or whether to contest by-elections, which offered publicity for their message since there were no competing elections for the public eye, but which might be held in constituencies where the pressure group was weak. Moreover, the decision to engage in electoral politics required the pressure group to register voters, challenge names on the list, and convert nonvoters into voters.[9] Yet none of the national Protestant organizations did any of that. Rather, it was almost exclusively local efforts that raised funds, endorsed candidates, and mounted campaigns. Local contexts thus are especially important when one considers anti-Catholicism as a form of political expression.

The Politics of the Platform

Several examples demonstrate the points that local secular political considerations played a role in determining how public meetings were organized, who participated, and what was resolved, and that religion played a role in local secular politics.

When a vacancy occurred in the Bridport town council in 1841, the Liberals put up William Tucker, secretary of the Catholic Institute's local auxiliary. The Tories put up T. Bonner, on the committee of the Protestant Association's local auxiliary. The Protestants raised the no-popery cry, and Bonner, who had been defeated at the last municipal election in November 1840, squeaked in by fifteen votes.[10] At Nottingham, the British Reformation Society fell victim to warfare between Anglicans and the Anti-State Church Society in 1847. The Reformation Society had planned a meeting at the Assembly Rooms, but the town council heeded its members who were anti-state-church men and withdrew permission at the last minute.[11]

It was difficult to navigate the shoals of Whig-Tory politics and High-Low ecclesiology, as the Devon county meeting in 1850 demonstrated. There, Earl Fortescue had prepared a memorial condemning the assumption of titles, but a group of Tories introduced a counteraddress that pointed the finger at the Whig Russell Ministry's policy of accepting the use of Roman titles in Ireland and the colonies. And some Anglican clergy confused matters further by moving an amendment that condemned both Tractarianism and the High Church policies of the Bishop of Exeter.[12]

Evidence from Lancashire confirms the point that nonecclesiastical, political issues often played an important role in public agitations.

Orange politics in Liverpool provide the classic example of this. There, "No-popery" was a vote-getting political slogan for almost a century. Several ingredients made up the devil's cocktail of Liverpudlian politics. So

[9] Hamer, *Politics of Electoral Pressure*, pp. 11, 20-21, 36.
[10] *Penny Protestant Operative*, II (Aug. 1841), 62.
[11] *British Protestant*, IV (Jan. 1848), 1-5.
[12] *Times*, 21 Dec. 1850.

situated as to be the largest British port in the northwest, with daily packet service to Belfast, it attracted Ulstermen of all sorts from middle-class Protestant professionals and clerks to working-class Roman Catholic laborers. (The Irish-born made up 17 percent of Liverpool's population in 1841, and 22 percent in 1851.) Many Irish Evangelical clergymen held livings in Liverpool and Birkenhead. (Hugh McNeile was the dean of the lot.) The indigenous English middle classes were divided by religion and politics. And a large English-speaking working class was attracted from Lancashire, Cheshire, and North Wales.[13]

The Tory-Anglicans discovered in the 1830s that anti-Catholicism was effective in mobilizing the votes to defeat Liberal Nonconformists. The technique was used first in the Schools Controversy. In January 1836, the newly reformed town council, instigated by the Unitarian William Rathbone, proposed to open the corporation schools, then exclusively Anglican, to children of all religious persuasions. The proposal generated considerable public controversy, which reached the national press, and which figured in the parliamentary and the municipal elections of 1837. Hugh McNeile got his start as a public figure in this controversy; the Liberal victory in the corporation elections of November 1837 (which balanced off the Tory victory in the parliamentary election of July and August) led him to found the Liverpool branch of the Protestant Association and to organize Protestant Operative Associations. No-popery dominated the politics of the 1830s and '40s. Once the Tories had learned how to be "matey" with working-class Conservatives, how to pay attention to working-class opinion and leadership, and how to harness the emotive power of Crown, Church, Protestantism, and "true" Englishness, they were able to dominate local politics for most of the century.[14]

The cotton districts of southwest Lancashire also illustrate the mix of anti-Catholic religion, Tory politics, and working-class culture. The Orange Order before 1835, and Protestant Operative Societies afterwards, were constants during the period.[15] The mix reappeared in the public meetings during the Papal Aggression crisis of 1850-51. The Runcorn meeting was brought to a halt when the Rev. J. Barclay, vicar, who had supported earlier clauses of the memorial, objected to the fourth clause because it praised Lord John Russell's "manly" defense of Protestantism. Barclay, who held the prime minister "considerably responsible for what had had happened," moved an amendment that condemned the government. The meeting could not proceed until a compromise was worked out. (Barclay agreed to be satisfied with his oral protest.)[16] The Ashton-under-Lyne meeting became a Tory pep rally when the Rev. S. L. Edgar moved the address to the Queen, and then "read an extract from Blackstone, which treated on the ancient practice of appointing bishops, and he afterwards read a poem entitled 'I'm a Protectionist True.'"[17]

[13] Neal, *Sectarian Violence*, pp. 8-11, 38.
[14] *Ibid.*, pp. 44-53; Paz, *Politics of Working-Class Education*, pp. 87-88; P. J. Waller, *Democracy and Sectarianism: A Political and Social History of Liverpool, 1868-1939* (Liverpool, 1981), pp. 15-19; Fraser, *Urban Politics*, p. 134.
[15] Ward, *Religion and Society*, pp. 209-11.
[16] *Manchester Courier*, 7 Dec. 1850.
[17] *Manchester Guardian*, 7 Dec. 1850.

An interesting transaction took place at the Oldham town council meeting of 9 November 1850. Councillor James Platt moved a resolution of thanks to Lord John Russell for the Durham Letter. The town clerk suggested that it was inappropriate for the council to express opinions on religious or political questions, and Alderman Worthington agreed. It was suggested that a requisition for a public meeting be got up. A majority of the council agreed, and Platt withdrew his resolution.[18] The public Protestant meeting convened at the town hall on 25 November; among the attendees were the Rev. William Lees of the cotton-spinning family, the wealthy cotton-spinners John Duncuft, M.P. for Oldham (and his son), James Rowland, and Aldermen Worthington and Lees, and Henry Tipping, bank manager for many of Oldham's élite families. R. M. Davies, minister of Hope Chapel, was also present, to help bring in the élite families' Congregational sides. The meeting organized a chapter of the Protestant Association. Four days before, the Oldham élite had cemented church-state relations at a testimonial dinner for the mayor; Joseph Jones, Jr., and Alderman Lees attacked the assumption of titles.[19] These events show how anti-Catholicism got caught up in a web of political, religious, business, and family connections. Platt and Worthington were cousins—but the former was a Whig coal and iron master, whose family had only recently abandoned its traditional Presbyterian/Congregationalist heritage; the latter was a Tory coal and cotton master more solidly rooted in Anglicanism.[20] Praise for the Whig prime minister Russell was unacceptable to Tory councillors, who managed to deflect it into another arena. These events represent small thrusts and parries in a bigger political war for control of the borough between Whigs and Tories and between the richer and the smaller masters. Although Oldham's political and economic structures were atypical of other Lancashire cotton towns, the point that the local situation influenced the form that anti-Catholic agitations took remains.

Another source, the editorial opinion of the *Lancaster Gazette*, provides a final example from a more northerly part of the county. Staunchly Protestant, the *Gazette* opposed the assumption of titles from the beginning of the agitation and demanded penal legislation to put down papal pretensions. It admitted that the Ecclesiastical Titles Bill was "a good bill *so far as it* goes," but it wanted stronger legislation. So strong was the print's Protestantism that it abandoned its customary pro-Tory stance during the 1851 Ministerial Crisis. Although it had little confidence in Russell (for Whig pro-Catholic policies had been partly responsible for the Papal Aggression), it feared that Lord Stanley, leader of the Tories, would include Tractarians (i.e., younger Peelites) in any government he might form. So at this juncture the *Gazette* supported Russell's return to office. The print was left high and dry when Russell weakened the provisions of the Ecclesiastical Titles Bill after his return.[21] In this instance, faithfulness to Protestant religious principles rather than to Tory political principles led to disappointment and a sense of betrayal.

---

[18] *Ibid.*, 13 Nov. 1850.
[19] *Manchester Guardian*, 23, 30 Nov. 1850; Foster, *Class Struggle*, pp. 51, 55, 171, 178, 184, 196, 197, 198, 208; Anthony Howe, *The Cotton Masters, 1830-1860* (Oxford, 1984), pp. 109-11.
[20] Foster, *Class Struggle*, pp. 189, 191, 198.
[21] *Lancaster Gazette*, 25 Jan., 15 Feb. (quoted), 8, 15 Mar. 1851.

A year later, in 1852, the Russell Ministry was brought down and a general election followed. Determined to punish those M.P.s who had opposed the Ecclesiastical Titles Bill, the Protestant Association, Protestant Alliance, and Scottish Reformation Society issued election manifestos and rejoiced in the Derby Ministry. Anti-Catholics could taste victory, and Liberal politicians were worried.[22]

William Brown, M.P. for the Southern Division of Lancashire, 1846-1859, a free trader with Anti-Corn Law League backing, had tried to placate both Roman Catholics and anti-Catholics during the Papal Aggression crisis. He attended the mass Protestant meeting at Liverpool, fearing that his absenting himself would make enemies of Hugh McNeile and the Liverpool anti-Catholics; but he tried "to cut [himself] adrift" from the extreme opinions uttered on the platform.[23] In the House of Commons, he voted for the original version of the Ecclesiastical Titles Bill in order to support the Royal Supremacy and to vindicate the principle that British subjects should not accept foreign honors without the consent of the Crown; but he voted against those alterations to the measure that imposed harsh penalties on the holders of papal titles. Brown's strategy succeeded only in alienating both Roman Catholics and anti-Catholics; he worried over rumors that the Liverpool Constitutional Association would put up a Protectionist candidate against him, and that the Liverpool Catholic Registration Committee, determined to oppose any candidate who had voted for the Ecclesiastical Titles Bill, would work against him. Although in the event Brown was returned unopposed, he had some worrisome weeks.[24]

Robert Baynes Armstrong, Liberal M.P. for Lancaster (1848-53), also was in trouble. Having voted against the Ecclesiastical Titles Bill, he earned the enmity of the *Lancaster Gazette*, which declared that he ought to resign and certainly would not stand at the next election. In the event he was returned second in the poll, with only nine votes separating him from his Liberal colleague. But Armstrong's method of overcoming the opposition of anti-Catholics may be deduced from the fact that his election was declared void for bribery and treating (with the hint that he had known what was done).[25]

The July 1852 election at Liverpool saw no-popery at the center of the campaign. The sitting Members, Edward Cardwell the Peelite and Sir Thomas Birch the Liberal,[26] were unacceptable to the Tories because of their support for free trade. Hugh McNeile opted for pragmatism in 1852, deciding to support Lord John Manners (whom he had opposed in 1847 as a Tractarian and unsound on Maynooth). This created a furor, which the Liverpool Constitutional Association ended by selecting a local, Charles Turner (councillor and chairman of the dock trustees) and an

---

[22] *Times*, 13 May 1852; Machin, *Politics and the Churches*, p. 239.

[23] William Brown to George Wilson, 6, 28 Dec. 1850, George Wilson Papers, MCL, M 20/16.

[24] Brown to Wilson, 24 Feb. and 6 Mar. 1852, *ibid.*, M 20/18; Charles R. Dod, *Electoral Facts from 1832 to 1853 Impartially Stated*, ed. H. J. Hanham (Brighton, 1972), p. 173; Hamer, *Politics of Electoral Pressure*, pp. 77, 84.

[25] *Lancaster Gazette*, 29 Mar. 1851; Dod, *Electoral Facts*, p. 174; "Minutes of Evidence taken before the Select Committee on the Lancaster Borough Election Petition," *PP*, 1852-53, XIV (152), 77-123.

[26] Not Sir Joshua Walmsley, as Frank Neal states, for Walmsley, who had failed of election in 1841, did not stand in 1847.

outsider, William Forbes Mackenzie (Conservative M.P. for Peeblesshire, 1837-52). The Liberals were in disarray. Cardwell was reselected, but Birch, who had voted for the Ecclesiastical Titles Bill, was unacceptable to the Roman Catholics. After representations from Richard Sheil of the Catholic Registration Committee, the Liberals dropped Birch in favor of J. C. Ewart. Cardwell and Ewart attempted to focus the campaign on economics, but the Conservatives used the religious question to win the election. Turner, who called himself a "Protestant Free-trader," criticized the Liberals for having bowed to Papist pressure in dropping Birch; Mackenzie promised to vote against Maynooth, and he professed to be sure that Orange processions never resulted in breaches of the peace. This was just what the Protestant electors wanted to hear; 1,120 votes separated Mackenzie from the third-placed Cardwell.[27]

At Preston, no-popery helped decide the outcome. R. Townley Parker, a Conservative who had represented the borough from 1837 to 1841, was defeated in 1841 and again in 1847; two Liberals represented the borough in those years. Parker stood again in 1852. He appealed to no-popery sentiment with a ditty, set to "Hearts of Oak," about vile priests plotting to enslave true-blue freeborn Protestant Englishmen, and was returned at the head of the poll.[28]

The 1852 election probably produced the most success for the anti-Catholics of any election before or since. Besides the results at Liverpool and Preston, negative victories occurred at Ripon where Sir James Graham's patron withdrew his support, and at Plymouth where Roundell Palmer withdrew from the contest. Nevertheless, the election "did not yield the fruits for which ultra-Protestants hoped."[29]

So far, we have concerned ourselves mainly with traditional Whig-Tory rivalries. Other rivalries also manifested themselves as the remnants of the Chartist Movement as well as ultra-Nonconformist radicals tried to take over meetings (as they had done on the free-trade and education questions in 1839 and the 1840s[30]), or in other ways to advance their agenda. Patrick Lloyd Jones[31] tried to address the Ashton-under-Lyne meeting at the Town Hall on 3 December 1850, but was denied the floor because he was not on the program. His supporters tried to start a row when he was expelled from the hall.[32] At Ipswich, William Rushbrook[33] moved an amendment deprecating both the assumption of titles and "similar claims and pretensions made by any other party"; at Ashford, Kent, a person described as "a mechanic" put it more simply: "there were parties in this country as great popes as his Holiness in Rome."[34] Chartists were also active at Huddersfield. Samuel Kydd lectured at the Guildhall in February 1851, advancing a Radical agenda of secular education, the removal of Jewish disabilities, Sunday post delivery, and support for Italian liberals. With

---

[27] Neal, *Sectarian Violence*, pp. 151-54; Dod, *Electoral Facts*, p. 192.
[28] Lesourd, "Catholiques dans la Société Anglaise," II, 824, 877-78; *Electoral Facts*, p. 256.
[29] Machin, *Politics and the Churches*, pp. 240-51.
[30] Donald Read, "Chartism in Manchester," *Chartist Studies*, ed. Asa Briggs (London, 1959), pp. 35-37; McCord, *Anti-Corn Law League*, pp. 51-53, 100-103.
[31] Jones (1811-1886), Owenite, cooperator, journalist, and lecturer (Baylen and Gossman, *Modern British Radicals*, II, 268-73).
[32] *Manchester Courier*, 7 Dec. 1850; *Manchester Guardian*, 7 Dec. 1850.
[33] A tailor, Chartist, and, later, parliamentary reform leader in his town (Dorothy Thompson, *The Chartists: Popular Politics in the Industrial Revolution*, New York, 1984, p. 193).
[34] *Times*, 23, 25 Nov., 12 Dec. 1850.

respect to the Papal Aggression, Kydd argued that the Roman Catholic Church "had as much right to organize their Church government . . . as the Wesleyans or any other body." Henry Vincent lectured on "Civil and Religious Liberty" at the Philosophical Hall in March, using humor to attack the union of church and state and to argue that all churches should be treated equally.[35]

Supporters of the radical Nonconformist agenda could also be found. Two councillors (Messrs. Hilton and Cook) tried to torpedo the Wigan town council's memorial by opposing the inclusion of references to the Queen's spiritual supremacy, arguing for the separation of church and state, and moving that the council take no stand on the matter.[36] At Ulverston, a self-styled "Radical" complained that the no-popery agitation diverted attention from what he considered to be the really important questions of financial reform and separation of church and state.[37]

The instances recounted above suggest that although some public leaders hoped that anti-Catholicism might promote unity, it was not sufficiently strong an issue to bridge political gaps. How and why this was the case can best be seen by looking closely at Manchester, Derby, and Leeds, where anti-Catholics made concerted efforts to capture the representation of all three constituencies.

Anti-Catholic Politics in Manchester

Although divided by the River Irwell, Manchester and Salford were in some ways indistinguishable. Salford never developed the social, cultural, and commercial institutions that might have given it a definite character. It relied upon Manchester for those. In any given year in the mid-nineteenth century, moreover, about a third of the membership of the Salford town council had their business interests in Manchester. Its out-township of Pendleton was a suburb as much of Manchester as of Salford. But unlike Manchester, Salford's population was mainly working-class, and Whigs and Radicals dominated her politics. Joseph Brotherton, a local Radical, was M.P. from 1832 until his death in 1857. Radicals controlled the police commissioners, boroughreeve, and constables before incorporation in 1844, and dominated the town council thereafter.[38]

For all these reasons, Salford was not an especially congenial political arena for Hugh Stowell, even though Christ Church, his proprietary chapel, was located there. Stowell became involved in local politics through the Salford Operative Conservative Association, which he helped form in 1835 to contest control of the select vestry. Whigs and Radicals had gained control of the vestry in 1833, reduced the poor rate, but also reduced the stipend of the workhouse's Anglican chaplain and arranged for the services of unpaid Nonconformist ministers. Stowell cooperated with those politicians who organized the parliamentary campaigns of the Tories William

[35] *Huddersfield Chronicle*, 1 Feb., 5 Apr. 1851.
[36] *Preston Pilot*, 21 Dec. 1850.
[37] *Preston Guardian*, 14 Dec. 1850.
[38] R. L. Greenall, "The Making of the Borough of Salford, 1830-1853," *Victorian Lancashire*, ed. S. P. Bell (Newton Abbot, 1974), pp. 35-37, 43, 50; J. A. Garrard, "Heates, Tumultes and Factions," *Salford: A City and its Past*, ed. Tom Bergin, Dorothy N. Pearce, and Stanley Shaw (Salford, 1974), p. 92.

Garnett in 1832, 1837, and 1841, and John Dugdale in 1835.[39] (Stowell's right-hand man was Stephen Heelis, solicitor, who was both legal advisor to Garnett and amateur anti-Catholic theologian.[40]) But Stowell failed to dislodge the Whig/Radicals from either local office or the town's representation in Parliament. So he turned to Manchester.

There, the Manchester and Salford Protestant Operative Association was the vehicle for his political aspirations. (The Manchester Protestant Operatives turned into the "Operative Conservative Society" for political purposes.) Stowell organized Protestant Operative meetings in Manchester in 1838-39-40, and scored a great coup by obtaining the public backing of Wesleyanism; two of Jabez Bunting's sons appeared on the platform with Stowell. (The Wesleyans were careful to appear at Stowell rallies labelled "British Reformation Society" and "Protestant Operative," rather than "Protestant Association" or "Conservative Operative," in order to adhere to the letter of the connexion's "no politics" rule.) During the 1841 election, the Tories appealed to Wesleyan anti-Catholicism in an unsuccessful attempt to defeat Thomas Milner Gibson.[41] But the Factory Bill, 1843, the Dissenting Chapels' Act, 1844, and the Maynooth endowment of 1845—all policies emanating from the Tory Peel Ministry—disillusioned local Wesleyan leaders, and the Tory-Wesleyan alliance slipped in 1847.[42]

Concurrently, and throughout the 1850s, Stowell was involved in the divisive "Manchester Church Question," which exercised Anglicans between 1837 and the mid-1850s. The Evangelicals wanted to reform the Manchester Collegiate Church, partly because it was inefficient and a poor steward of its wealth, partly because it was controlled by High-and-Dry men who denied Evangelicals a share in their patronage.[43] Thus the Manchester Tory-Anglicans were themselves divided by reason of this internal quarrel, just when they were dividing over the policies of the Peel Ministry.

Stowell intervened in the 1847 Manchester parliamentary elections, testing the candidates on their anti-Catholicism, and finding all wanting. He was a vigorous campaigner against the secular education schemes of the Lancashire Public School Association. And his organ, the *Protestant Witness*, beat the drums against Irish Roman Catholic immigrants.[44]

> Now Ireland contains six millions and a half, and Great Britain two millions of Papists, to which we may add half a million of subjects who are nominal Protestants, that would be ready to join them in any enterprise from which plunder might be expected; and thus we have nine millions altogether, of whose hostility to everything Protestant, and everything loyal, there cannot be the possibility of a doubt; and the result is calculated to produce anything but a comfortable reflection. But to bring the thing

---

[39] Garrard, "Heates, Tumultes and Factions," p. 94; D. Fraser, *Urban Politics*, pp. 62-65. Garnett was a prominent merchant, and Dugdale came from a cotton family with interests including merchanting in Liverpool and calico-printing, spinning, and manufacturing in North Lancashire (Howe, *Cotton Masters*, p. 106).

[40] D. Fraser, *Urban Politics*, p. 169. Heelis (1811-1871) was later Mayor of Salford, 1855-58 (Boase, I, 1416).

[41] Milner Gibson (1806-1884) entered Parliament as a Conservative, but converted to Liberalism; M.P. for Manchester, 1841-57, for Ashton-under-Lyne, 1857-68, after losing his Manchester seat because of his opposition to the Crimean War (*DNB*, VII, 1164).

[42] W. Ward, *Religion and Society*, pp. 212-13; Gowland, *Methodist Secessions*, pp. 133-35.

[43] W. Ward, *Religion and Society*, pp. 220-33.

[44] *Penny Protestant Operative*, VIII (Feb. 1847), 20; *Protestant Witness*, I (23 Sept. 1848), 16, (13 Jan. 1849), 71, (7 Apr. 1849), 119-126.

nearer home, more than one-fourth of the population of this city are Papists, compactly organized, and in close connection with other evil-disposed parties, which render themselves truly formidable.[45]

With such a powerful Church-and-Tory advocate in their midst, Manchester Liberals were understandably nervous on the eve of the Papal Aggression. R. W. Smiles[46] feared the effects of Stowell's enmity, and John Bright, one of the sitting M.P.s, was worried about the state of the electorate. He wanted the Liberals to add two or three thousand names to the electoral register ("numbers will always save the liberal party in Manchester, unless some serious split or mismanagement takes place"), and he carefully avoided anything that might entangle him in personality conflicts (such as the quarrel among Liberals over a portrait of Richard Cobden.)[47]

When the Papal Aggression burst upon England, the *Manchester Courier*, Anglican and Tory, gave it full play by publishing the offending Popish documents and by denouncing it in leaders.

[T]he recent proceedings of the Roman Catholics are not of a nature to be passed over in idle amazement and occasional bursts of indignation. The accumulated instances of the determination of Popery to supplant the principles of the Reformation in this kingdom now amount to a strong and an invincible case, upon which the Government ought to be compelled to act decisively, or be themselves impeached. No half measures will do,—we are past that.[48]

The print trumpeted the Durham Letter and the protest of the Westminster clergy, publicized all of Hugh Stowell's speeches and sermons, and printed a detailed account of Guy Fawkes Day celebrations.[49]

The *Manchester Guardian*, in contrast, took a sensible position on the Papal Aggression.

[W]hat a disproportionate fuss are we making about a matter more worthy of ridicule than of serious apprehension. Because the panic-stricken POPE OF ROME, his head still dizzy with recent political intoxication, has been enduced to give new titles and different coloured hose to the emissaries, whom he has never ceased to send to this country, and because some of them take up the names and the trappings, with all the arrogance which the history and pretentions of their church inspire; there is such a tumult of alarm and indignation as has scarcely been known since the fitting out of the Spanish Armada.[50]

The leading article went on to contend that the assumption of titles made no difference to anyone save Roman Catholics, that the toleration granted to them should include their hierarchy; that the titles violated no law; and that no repressive legislation should be enacted. "In fact," the *Guardian* concluded, "the triumphant insolence of the Romanists is as disproportionate to the occasion as the tumultuous panic of the protestants." It welcomed attacks on Tractarian clergy, and hoped that they would be

[45] *Protestant Witness*, I (13 Jan. 1849), 72.
[46] Robert Wilson Smiles (1816-1890), Secretary of the Manchester Public School Association.
[47] R. W. Smiles to W. J. Fox, 7 Mar. 1850, National Public School Association Papers (hereinafter cited as NPSA), MCL, M 136/2/3/1091; John Bright to George Wilson, 1 July (quotation), 11 Nov. 1850, Wilson Papers, *ibid.*, M 20/16.
[48] *Manchester Courier*, 19 Oct. 1850.
[49] *Ibid.*, 26 Oct., 2, 9 Nov. 1850.
[50] *Manchester Guardian*, 6 Nov. 1850.

forced either to obey or leave the Church. But the *Guardian*'s influence was not powerful enough to dampen the anti-Catholic enthusiasm; so, wisely, it made no further comment on the affair after 9 November.[51]

Stowell entered the fray early on, calling for an outpouring of Protestant sentiment, and pointing to Manchester as a model to follow. He went beyond mere protest; he urged Protestants to prepare for the next parliamentary elections by pledging to vote for only those candidates who were the most uncompromising enemies of Rome.[52] And he proposed to translate this appeal (which appeared in the national Evangelical newspaper, the *Record*) into reality on the local level. The time had come to crush both the pretensions of Rome and those false friends of Protestantism whose unwise concessions had precipitated the crisis—not to mention the chance to crush the Manchester School.

Stowell professed to be nonpolitical—although he mostly managed to support Conservative candidates—but he resented the religious policies of the governments that had held power since 1829. Those policies, he told the Manchester Protestant Operatives, could be summed up as "concession on the one hand, and insatiable demand on the other."[53] Despite Roman Catholic Emancipation, the Maynooth grant, and all the other liberal legislation of the past twenty-five years, he told the Bolton public meeting, "Rome, like the horse-leech, cried 'Give, give, give. . . .'"[54]

It is not surprising, therefore, that he did not fully trust the Russell Ministry. He told the Protestant Operatives that, if Parliament showed "truckling or trimming," the next election should have as its watchword "Protestantism and no Popery"; he asked those present on the platform to promise their votes to anti-Catholic candidates. "It was not a party or political thing—the question at stake was the protection of Protestantism."[55] Stowell was more explicit at the Oldham meeting.

> There was no doubt about the nobleness and manliness of Lord John Russell's [Durham] letter; but let his lordship see that his actions were equally bold, firm, and uncompromising.—(Hear, hear.) He would thank Lord John Russell for his letter, but he would thank him more for firm, resolute, and uncompromising actions.—(Cheers.) And they would not let his lordship forget his promise.—(Loud cheers.)[56]

Stowell and the Lancashire anti-Catholics awaited eagerly 10 December, for that was the day when the London city corporation and the Universities of Oxford and Cambridge were to present their memorials to the Queen; her response would be the first official pronouncement on the Papal Aggression. They were disappointed in the event; the *Manchester Courier* found "a degree of reserve, if not a coldness" in her replies (which it attributed to the Cabinet's "timidity"),[57] and thereafter Stowell became more threatening. Speaking at Warrington at the end of December, Stowell said that Lord John Russell had had ample time to consult his lawyers and

[51] *Ibid.*, 9 Nov. 1850.
[52] *Record*, 31 Oct. 1850.
[53] *Manchester Courier*, 9 Nov. 1850.
[54] *Ibid.*, 23 Nov. 1850.
[55] *Ibid.*, 9 Nov. 1850.
[56] *Ibid.*, 30 Nov. 1850.
[57] *Ibid.*, 14 Dec. 1850. Other Lancashire Protestants also noticed the marked difference in tone between the Durham Letter and the Queen's replies (*Blackburn Standard*, 18 Dec. 1850).

decide what to do, and that "if a man's words and actions did not correspond, he must be reminded of that circumstance." Russell had until Parliament met to prove himself; if the Speech from the Throne were unsatisfactory, or if "a temporising, trimming measure" were introduced, the government would not last six weeks. "He was content to have as prime minister Lord John Russell, until we could find a better, but he was sick of all political partizans, for they had all betrayed us from first to last."[58] On 6 January 1851, at a meeting of the friends of the Protestant mission at the island of Achill, County Mayo, Stowell endorsed Lord Ashley's movement to create Protestant Defence Committees all over England to monitor Parliament;[59] ten days later, he called for such a committee at Manchester.[60]

The government's measure, the Ecclesiastical Titles Bill, disappointed the anti-Catholics; Stephen Heelis, analysing it for the Protestant Defence Committee's Manchester branch, found it to be "altogether deceptive and illusive,"[61] and the *Manchester Courier* faced the awful truth: "It would be worse than idle any longer to attempt to disguise from ourselves or our readers, that the present Ministry have basely betrayed the country on this vital question. Nor can we any longer separate LORD JOHN RUSSELL from his colleagues. He is just as guilty as the rest."[62] The worst blow came, however, when both M.P.s for Manchester, Thomas Milner Gibson and John Bright, voted against the measure. Their action, and that of Richard Cobden, called forth condemnation from the national Evangelical press.[63] Stowell declared war against them at the Church Pastoral Aid Society meeting at the end of February 1851,[64] and called for them to be turfed out at the annual meeting of the Manchester branch, British Reformation Society.

> Protestant electors, don't commit yourselves to their canvassers or their friends. (Hear, hear.) Don't be cajoled or persuaded. Remember if there comes an election on this great question we will find for you two staunch and trustworthy Protestant candidates—(Loud cheers),—men that will echo the views of Manchester upon a gradual and consistent progress in the accommodation of our civil institutions, and to the increasing and development of our national character,—men who will not betray or desert the great Protestant principles that are the foundation, the strength, and the glory of our constitution.—(Applause.) Keep your votes for these men, and I will add, if possible, that they shall be two of your fellow-townsmen. (Applause.) It is a disgrace to this, the mightiest constituency out of London,—it is a disgrace to this intelligent, enlightened, and commercial community, that they should not have a town's-man to represent them, but that they should be obliged to borrow a squire from Cambridgeshire and a nondescript from Rochdale.—(Enthusiastic and prolonged cheering.)[65]

[58] *Manchester Courier*, 28 Dec. 1850.
[59] *Sup.*, p. 125.
[60] *Manchester Guardian*, 8, 22 Jan. 1851.
[61] *Manchester Courier*, 22 Feb. 1851.
[62] *Ibid.*, 15 Mar. 1851.
[63] *Record*, 30 Jan. 1851; *Christian Times*, 1 Feb. 1851.
[64] *Manchester Courier*, 1 Mar. 1851.
[65] *Ibid.*, 8 Mar. 1851.

The anti-Catholic uproar posed a grave threat to the Manchester Liberal Party, and George Wilson[66] wanted Bright and Milner Gibson to speak at a public meeting in order to explain and defuse opposition to their votes on the Ecclesiastical Titles Bill. (Indeed, Wilson wanted a meeting even before Parliament met.) Bright, Milner Gibson, and Richard Cobden, whom they consulted, wanted to wait until the Ecclesiastical Titles Bill had been disposed of;[67] but eventually a compromise was reached, and the two M.P.s for Manchester spoke to a meeting at the Free Trade Hall on 16 April 1851. Milner Gibson met the issue directly:

> . . . although Mr. Hugh Stowell—(A Voice: "Three cheers for him." Loud cheers and counter-cheers, groans, hisses, &c.)—although these gentlemen—(hisses and cheers, cries of "Three cheers for Stowell" and "Stowell for ever," met by hisses, yells and groans)—although these gentlemen may blame the protestantism of my hon. friend and myself, I will undertake to say—(renewed cries and confusion)—that perhaps if it were a question of the protestantism of the respective parties, I should not be surprised if an impartial jury would pronounce the protestantism of my hon. friend Mr. Bright more pure than that of Mr. Hugh Stowell.—(Great cheering, the meeting rising and giving loud hurrahs, drowning some groans and hisses.)[68]

A year later, the Russell Ministry had fallen, and Hugh Stowell threatened to give Milner Gibson and Bright a fight. Cobden was confident of the outcome.

> The result cannot be doubtful. Nor will it require that we should do more than hold ourselves under arms in Manchester. The mere apparatus of the League will be enough.[69]

But this was overconfidence, given that the Manchester Liberals were politically divided, and had been since the late 1830s. The Whiggish *Manchester Guardian* disliked John Bright, considering his principles to be too extreme. The group that the *Guardian* represented were wealthy, moderate Liberals who thought of themselves as the town's natural governing élite, and who wanted to wrest control of the Liberal party machinery from the Anti-Corn Law League. They were much less sympathetic to the plight of the Irish than was Bright. They generally favored state-controlled education, while Bright was a Voluntaryist. Deferential to the landed gentry, they viewed connections with the gentry as a sign of their own acceptability, and hence disliked Bright's anti-aristocratic rhetoric. And they disliked Bright's rather rough personality, and resented the fact that he was an outsider (and from the rival textile town of Rochdale, at that). Hence, when a successor for Mark Philips[70] needed to be found for the 1847 parliamentary election, the *Guardian* approached Richard Cobden and, after he declined, Lord Lincoln.[71] Although Lincoln withdrew and Bright re-

---

[66] Wilson (1808-1870) was secretary of the Anti-Corn Law League until its dissolution and master political organizer for the Manchester Liberals.

[67] Bright to Wilson, 27 Jan., 28 Feb., 11, 28 Mar., 1 Apr. 1851, in Wilson Papers, MCL, M 20/17.

[68] *Manchester Guardian*, 19 Apr. 1851.

[69] Cobden to Baines, 28 Feb. 1852, Baines Family Papers, Leeds City Library.

[70] Philips (1800-1873) was a Mancunian businessman and M.P., 1832-47 (Boase, II, 1495-96).

[71] Henry Pelham-Clinton, 5th Duke of Newcastle (1811-1864); M.P. for South Notts, 1832-46, and the Falkirk Burghs, 1846-51; Peelite and friend of Gladstone's (*DNB*, IV, 554-55).

ceived the nomination, the moderate Liberals accepted him only reluctantly.[72]

The *Guardian* group's opposition to Bright continued after the 1847
election. During the Ministerial Crisis of 1851, the *Guardian* blamed "the
inconsiderate acts of a portion of the liberal party" for bringing down the
Russell Ministry, and argued that the result of "ultra-liberal" opposition
to the Whigs would be a Protectionist government. The newspaper especially blamed Cobden and Bright. It charged that Bright had been "rude
and insolent" to Russell during the debate on Peter Locke King's motion
to extend the franchise, and that he had canvassed Irish M.P.s to vote for
Disraeli's motion for agricultural relief.[73] (The Russell Ministry's poor
showing on these important votes contributed greatly to its fall.) Bright
denied the charges, and a divisive quarrel ensued.[74]

The moderate Liberal élite also disliked Thomas Milner Gibson. They
had welcomed him in 1841, believing that a safe Liberal who was also a
Suffolk squire was just the sort of candidate that Manchester needed; the
more advanced Liberals mistrusted him for those same reasons. But as
things turned out, Milner Gibson became an orthodox follower of the
Manchester School who obeyed the Cobdenite party line emanating from
the *Manchester Examiner* and from George Wilson's offices in Newall's
Buildings.[75] By the end of the 1840s, therefore, Milner Gibson found that
both his supporters and his opponents within the Manchester Liberal
Party had reversed themselves.

But if the Liberals were divided, so were the anti-Catholics. Thomas
Clegg, one of the Manchester Churchwardens, had been on the platform
at the Protestant Operative meeting of 4 November 1850, when Stowell
asked those present to pledge themselves to vote for anti-Catholic candidates, but had remained silent. Then, in the course of his speech at the
Manchester public meeting on 20 November, Clegg declared that it was
not desirable to give such a pledge. Clegg's remarks provoked cries of
"Shame" and "Question"; and one of the people on the platform said
something that led to an uproar and cries of "Turn him out."[76] This episode suggests that some anti-Catholics, although willing to make war on
the Pope and the Cardinal Archbishop, drew the line at the Members for
Manchester.

This point becomes clearer when one looks at the 1852 election. No
poll-books exist for that election; but one can compare the published lists
of supporters of Milner Gibson and Bright, and of their Protestant opponents, with the list of signatories of the requisition for the anti-Catholic
public meeting.[77] Of those who signed the anti-Catholic requisition in 1850
and who also lent their names to candidates in 1852, 85 percent supported
Milner Gibson and Bright, and only 15 percent supported the Protestant

[72] D. Fraser, *Urban Politics*, pp. 191, 203-4, 242-45; John K. Walton, *Lancashire: A Social
History, 1558-1939* (Manchester, 1987), pp. 135-38, 153-58; John Skinner, "The Liberal Nomination Controversy in Manchester, 1847," *Bulletin of the Institute of Historical Research*, LV
(1982), 215-18.

[73] *Manchester Guardian*, 26 Feb. 1851.

[74] *Ibid.*, 1, 5, 12 Mar. 1851; Bright to Wilson, 12 Mar. 1851, Wilson Papers, MCL, M 20/17; Paz,
"Ministerial Crisis of 1851," pp. 34-36.

[75] D. Fraser, *Urban Politics*, pp. 180, 183; Brown, *Victorian News and Newspapers*, pp. 41, 46.

[76] *Manchester Courier*, 23 Nov. 1850.

[77] The lists are in *Manchester Guardian*, 16 Nov. 1850, 5 May, 26 June, and 10 July 1852.

candidates.[78] Those figures do not suggest unity on the anti-Catholic question. Rumors flew, moreover, that some prominent anti-Catholic Mancunians—William Romaine Callender[79] and Samuel Fletcher[80] were named—planned to vote for Bright but against Milner Gibson.[81]

The Protestant opposition, organized as the "Independent Election Committee," had a hard time finding candidates to stand against the entrenched Liberals.They first selected George Loch[82] and Lord Moreton[83] but Moreton withdrew in the middle of May. The Independent Election Committee then sent a deputation to London to find a candidate. They came up with Joseph Denman,[84] a naval officer between commands.[85] Bright at once began digging up these men's pasts, and retailed rumors for use by the *Manchester Examiner*: that Loch had the secret backing of the Earl of Ellesmere and Lord Derby; that Denman was not only a Tory, but also supported W. J. Bennett, ritualist vicar of St. Barnabas's, Pimlico.[86] ("How amusing if Stowell has caught a desperate [sic] *Puseyite* in his search for a candidate!"[87])

The contest began in earnest on 1 May 1852, even before the opposition had found candidates, when Hugh Stowell issued an open letter, *To the Protestant Electors of Manchester*. The manifesto reminded the electors of Bright's and Milner Gibson's behavior during the Papal Aggression crisis, and went on to charge that "their invariable tone of sentiment, and their entire bearing in relation to Protestantism, bespeaks a gross ignorance of the nature, and a sad indifference to the importance, of those great principles on which our Constitution is based, and with which all that is noble and free and glorious in our land is bound up. As Protestants we cannot trust them."[88] The Independent Election Committee attempted to demark a broader field of battle by charging that the sitting M.P.s were too extreme in their legislative programs and ignored the needs and sentiments of their constituency.[89]

Loch's and Denman's own election manifestos make interesting reading, for they support the idea that the two candidates were mismatched. Both men supported free trade, extension of the franchise, and opposition to Roman Catholic aggressions (including the disendowment of Maynooth). Loch went on to favor the reform of institutions while at the same time protecting them from needless experiment; but Denman declared his

[78] Four hundred fifteen signed the requisition; sixty-six of those also supported Milner Gibson and Bright, and twelve supported the Protestant candidates.

[79] Callender (1796-1872), a cotton manufacturer and wholesale draper, was a Liberal city councillor active in the Anti-Corn Law League (H. J. Hanham, *Elections and Party Management: Politics in the Time of Disraeli and Gladstone*, London, 1959, p. 315).

[80] Fletcher (1785-1863), a Manchester merchant and philanthropist, chaired the Manchester branch, London Missionary Society, and was a trustee of Owen's College (Boase, V, 312).

[81] Bright to Wilson, 12, 18 May 1852, and William Brown to Wilson, 19 May 1852, Wilson Papers, MCL, M 20/18.

[82] Loch (1811-1877) contested Falkirk, 1851; later barrister, Q.C., attorney general to the Prince of Wales; M.P., Wick Burghs, 1868-72 (Boase, II, 465).

[83] Henry John Moreton, 3rd Earl of Ducie (1827-1921), M.P. for Stroud, 1852-53 (*Burke's Peerage and Baronetage*, 105th ed., pp. 840-41).

[84] Denman (1810-1875), son of the 1st Lord Denman, went on to have a successful career in the Royal Navy (Boase, I, 859).

[85] *Manchester Guardian*, 1, 15, 19, 22 May 1852.

[86] Bright to Wilson, 20, 31 May 1852, Wilson Papers, MCL, M 20/18.

[87] Bright to Wilson, 24 May 1852, *ibid.*

[88] *Manchester Guardian*, 1 May 1852; Marsden, *Stowell*, pp. 235-36.

[89] *Manchester Guardian*, 5 May 1852.

support for "a liberal, comprehensive and religious system of education."[90] Loch's comments on reform were vague enough to be palatable to electors of Whiggish or Peelite sentiments, but would have alienated Tories and the more radical Liberals, for whom reform had already gone too far, or not yet far enough. Denman's views on education would not have helped his cause, for education was a thorny issue intimately connected with both religious and class rivalries. Denman's views would not satisfy Anglicans, who wished the state to promote education under the auspices of the Established Church, nor Nonconformist Voluntaryists, who opposed the granting of public funds to any denominational schools, nor Manchester Liberals, who believed that secular schools offered the only way to provide education for all English children.

Milner Gibson and Bright, as the sitting candidates, had the advantage of being able to issue innocuous manifestos that simply pointed to their past records and promised that they would continue to act accordingly. This saved them from having to commit themselves to specifics.[91] Instead, both men confronted the religious issue directly. In a mass meeting at the Free Trade Hall on 26 May, Milner Gibson made a sharp attack on the bigotry of Hugh Stowell and Hugh McNeile, and Bright defended his votes against the Ecclesiastical Titles Bill.[92] In contrast, Loch and Denman attempted to focus on religion, but found themselves forced to address other issues. Speaking at a public meeting to promote memorials calling for the government inspection of nunneries, Stowell declared that he had redeemed his promises of 1850 and 1851, to bring forth Protestant candidates.[93] But the Protestant candidates found themselves questioned closely at ward meetings about matters such as the extent to which they would broaden the suffrage, their views on the secret ballot, and the reduction of the military budget; the main theme of their campaign was touched only on the Maynooth endowment.[94]

Organization was at least as important as principles. Here, Milner Gibson and Bright clearly had the advantage. The Newall's Building machine was experienced in registering and canvassing votes, and had district committees in all wards of the constituency.[95] Loch and Denman's Independent Election Committee, in contrast, was thin on the ground, depending mainly on general public meetings rather than on canvassing in the wards.

As the polling day of 9 July approached, Milner Gibson and Bright grew more confident. "Denman wrote to a friend of his a day or two ago," Bright, ever the gossip, observed, "saying he thought he had 'a fair chance' at Manchester. Are Heelis & Bunting[96] cheating their men & getting the £1500 each out of them?"[97] The Tories attempted to renew their political alliance with the Wesleyan leadership. Percy Bunting (Jabez's solicitor son) led a campaign against Bright and Milner Gibson, linking

[90] Loch's manifesto is in *ibid.*, 19 May 1852, and Denman's is in *ibid.*, 22 May 1852.
[91] *Ibid.*, 12, 15 May 1852.
[92] *Ibid.*, 29 May 1852.
[93] *Ibid.*, 22 May 1852.
[94] *Ibid.*, 26 May 1852.
[95] *Ibid.*, 15 May 1852.
[96] Stephen Heelis and T. P. Bunting, Stowellite anti-Catholics and leaders of the Independent Election Committee.
[97] Bright to Wilson, 21 June 1852, Wilson Papers, MCL, M 20/18.

them with the Wesleyan Reformers, and calling the Reformers red republicans—all to scare Wesleyans into voting Tory. The Wesleyan Reformers, themselves, however, had exploited the chasm between Wesleyanism's rich Tory élite and the ordinary Methodists who opposed exclusivity and intolerance.[98] With the Wesleyan Connexion in disarray, this electoral alliance did not much profit the Tories. Milner Gibson and Bright were returned, with the substantial margin of 1,111 votes separating Bright from the third-placed Loch.[99] Stowell's postmortem on the election claimed that most Dissenters had "allowed their sectarianism to outweigh their Protestantism."[100] But in fact that had little to do with Loch's and Denman's defeat.

The split within the ranks of Manchester Liberalism might have become open in the 1852 election. The big warehouseman Sir John Potter, newly knighted and fresh from an unprecedented third year as mayor, had attempted to bring the town's moderate Liberal élite together with the Tories in order to overthrow the Manchester School's political domination. He was the logical candidate to stand in 1852. But he was unsafe on the religious question, since he attended no anti-Catholic meetings nor demonstrated anti-Catholicism in any other way. He was a Unitarian, and thus both theologically heterodox and excessively tolerant, at least in Stowell's eyes.[101] Instead, Hugh Stowell's intervention cast the campaign along lines that compelled Liberal unity, even though he attempted to attract moderate Liberal support by means of his candidates' backgrounds and by appealing to areas of dis-satisfaction with the sitting M.P.s (their "extreme" views, their inadequate attention to the business of the constituency). Militant anti-Catholicism was not enough to outweigh the other political, economic, and social issues that bulked large in Mancunian minds.

Anti-Catholic Politics in Derby

Derby is another borough where anti-Catholic politics intruded. Mid-Victorian Derby was a turbulent town, well known for the popular custom of playing football in the streets on Shrove Tuesday and Ash Wednesday, a custom that usually led to rows and property damage.[102] It was also known for its political radicalism and its corrupt electoral politics, circumstances that worried respectable politicians. As one M.P. put it, "Derby contained many Chartists, and nothing was more likely to turn men to Chartism than seeing drunken electors rolling in the gutter."[103] Less well known is its history of religious disputation in the 1840s.[104] All of these factors converged in the late 1840s and early '50s.

[98] Gowland, *Methodist Secessions*, p. 136; *Wesleyan Review*, I (June 1850), 159-69.

[99] Dod, *Electoral Facts*, p. 207.

[100] Marsden, *Stowell*, p. 241.

[101] D. Fraser, *Urban Politics*, p. 205; Briggs, *Victorian Cities*, p. 127.

[102] Robert Forman to Sir G. Grey, 9 Feb. 1849, Home Office: Registered Papers, PRO, H.O. 45/2923; Forman to Palmerston, 9 Feb. 1853, *ibid.*, H.O. 45/5128, p. 13.

[103] 3 *Hansard*, XCVIII (1847-48), 403.

[104] *Sup.*, Chs. III, §2, and IV, §2.

The Liberal candidates in the 1847 election were Edward Strutt,[105] who had sat for the borough since 1830, and E. F. Leveson Gower,[106] just beginning his political career. Both men were advanced Liberals. Strutt had managed to win a by-election against the Conservative Sir Digby Mackworth the year before, despite his support for Maynooth. Leveson Gower was outspoken in support of extension of the franchise, the secret ballot, free trade, Irish Church disestablishment, and in opposition to church rates.[107] "He was a friend to religious liberty and hated bigotry in whatever shape he found it, whether amongst the Roman Catholic populations of foreign countries, or amongst the No-Popery Protestants of their own land."[108] Although the Liberals defeated their Conservative and Chartist opponents, their supporters had engaged in so much bribery and treating that they were unseated on petition.[109]

The necessary by-election offered local anti-Catholics (who were also Tories) an opening; hoping to fell both Popery and Liberalism at one blow, they put forward two candidates. James William Freshfield (1775-1864), a lawyer with financial interests in the City, had sat as M.P. for Penryn and Falmouth in the 1835-41 Parliament, and contested Wycomb in 1841 and London in 1847. He later sat for Boston (1851-2) and Penryn (1852). In the 1847 election for the City of London, he was the most open anti-Catholic of his colleagues, going beyond criticism of the Maynooth grant to make more general attacks on the religion.[110] James Lord, a barrister who had never stood for Parliament before, had been active in organizing local branches of the Protestant Operative Association in London, went on a provincial lecture tour that included Lancaster and Derby in March 1847, and continued his anti-Catholic activities into the 1850s as secretary of the Protestant Association and editor of the *Protestant Magazine*.[111]

Their opponents were Michael Thomas Bass and Laurence Heyworth, neither of whom had stood for Parliament before. Bass (1799-1884), of the Burton-on-Trent brewing family, was a quiet, moderate Liberal who sat for Derby, 1848-83, who became famous for his substantial public gifts to both Burton and Derby. Heyworth (1786-1872), a woollen manufacturer from Bacup, sat for Derby, 1848-57. He was the author of several works against the Corn Laws and on fiscal legislation, and was a more advanced Liberal than was his colleague.[112]

The Conservatives were cautious. Their election address announced that they supported the Constitution, and declared their friendliness to civil and religious liberty, a revision of the income tax, and the improvement of the working classes. Lord moderated his anti-Catholic rhetoric for the occasion, commenting only that he favored scriptural education and

---

[105] Strutt (1801-1880), friend of Jeremy Bentham and the Mills, later 1st Lord Belper (*DNB*, XIX, 63-64).

[106] Edward Frederick Leveson Gower (1819-1907), barrister, M.P. for Stoke-upon-Trent, 1852-57, and for Bodmin, 1859-85 (*Burke's Peerage and Baronetage*, 105th ed., p. 1160).

[107] Wolffe, "Protestant Societies and Anti-Catholic Agitations," pp. 206-207; *Times*, 24 May 1847.

[108] *Times*, 17 June 1847.

[109] Dod, *Electoral Facts*, p. 81; "Minutes of Evidence taken before the Select Committee on the Derby Election Petition," *PP*, 1847-48, XI (212), 607-732.

[110] Boase, I, 1108; *Penny Protestant Operative*, IX (May 1848), 62-63; Dod, *Electoral Facts*, pp. 30, 81, 193, 246, 355; *Times*, 9, 17, 21, 22 July 1847.

[111] *Penny Protestant Operative*, I, II, *passim*, and VIII (Apr. 1847), 47-8; *Protestant Magazine*, XII (Dec. 1850), 178.

[112] *DNB*, I, 1291-92; Boase, I, 1458-59.

"safe reforms." The Liberals were able to attack Freshfield's record in the House, where he had consistently opposed all reform legislation. Heyworth drew a clear line between the Conservatives and himself, by announcing his support for separation of church and state and for universal manhood suffrage. This appealed to Nonconformists and Chartists, who combined with the borough's Whig and Liberal electors to give Bass and Heyworth the election by a margin of 134 votes.[113]

Freshfield and Lord nursed the constituency for a bit after the election, but had left the scene by the time that Protestants were girding their loins for the 1852 election. Rumor had it that Heyworth would be opposed by the somewhat more moderate Edward Strutt, but in the event the Liberals supported both sitting members. The Conservatives brought in Thomas Berry Horsfall,[114] a merchant who had been Mayor of Liverpool.[115] Horsfall stood for Derby as a free-trade Conservative. He spoke in general terms of the need to reform abuses, opposed the income tax, and tried to depict himself as a reasonable Conservative. "A friend to civil and religious liberty, I am opposed to the grant to Maynooth, because (among other reasons) the grant is made towards the education of the priests of a church which, when it has the power, will not tolerate any other."[116] Bass and Heyworth accused Horsfall of being a secret Protectionist, espousing free trade, but supporting Protectionist candidates at Liverpool against the free traders Edward Cardwell and J. C. Ewart. Horsfall tried to defend himself by explaining that the big question at Liverpool was the preservation of the Protestant Constitution, and that he had opposed Cardwell and Ewart because they were insufficiently Protestant. Although this declaration was not well received, drawing laughs from the audience, Horsfall managed to edge out Heyworth in the poll by seven votes. But it turned out that the votes had been bought by flagrant Tory bribery, and on petition Heyward was returned in Horsfall's place.[117]

Radical politics were of more importance to the Derby electors than Protestantism, but cold cash was the most important of all.

Bainesite Politics in Leeds and the West Riding

Anti-Catholicism affected politics in an unusual way in the West Riding of Yorkshire during the 1840s and '50s; and it entered the arena, ironically, largely through the agency of that paragon of religious freedom and arbiter of Leeds politics, Edward Baines, Jr. Through its newspaper, the *Leeds Mercury*, and through its counsels among West Riding Congregationalists, the Baines family was the leading voice of urban Nonconformist

113 *Times*, 28 Mar., 2 Sept. 1848; Dod, *Electoral Facts*, p. 81; *Penny Protestant Operative*, IX (Oct. 1848), 124.
114 Horsfall (1805-1878) was Mayor of Liverpool, 1847-48, the first president of the Liverpool Chamber of Commerce, and M.P. for Liverpool, 1853-68. Boase, I, 1541.
115 *Penny Protestant Operative* (Dec. 1848), 148; *Bulwark*, I (Apr. 1852), 245-47; *ibid.* (May 1852), 273-78; *Times*, 25 Mar. 1852.
116 *Times*, 21 June 1852.
117 *Ibid.*, 8 July 1852; "Minutes of Evidence taken before the Select Committee on the Derby Election Petition; together with the Proceedings of the Committee," *PP*, 1852-53, XII (219), 9-164; "Report from the Select Committee on Derby Elections (Petition of Inhabitant Householders); together with the Proceedings of the Committee, and Minutes of Evidence," *ibid.* (78), 165-344; 3 *Hansard*, CXXIII (1852), 717-52.

Liberalism during the first three-quarters of the nineteenth century.[118] Edward Baines, Sr.,[119] who had walked from Preston to Leeds as an apprentice printer in 1790, went on to build his influence and retired in 1841 as M.P. for the borough. His son, Edward Baines, Jr.,[120] inherited both the newspaper and his father's political mantle. But Liberal control of Leeds politics was strained during the quarter-century after the mid-1830s, and Baines found it increasingly difficult to maintain his leadership.

The revival of Toryism was the first obstacle to Liberal control. W.F. Hook, the Vicar of Leeds, was the leading, or at least the loudest, figure in the revival, but he was helped by William Beckett[121] of the Tory banking family and J. R. Atkinson, a flax-spinning master. Although the Bainesites dismissed the Leeds Operative Conservative Society as a collection of shop assistants, publicans, and clerks, it enjoyed a certain amount of working-class support. The character of Leeds as a strong Wesleyan town (42 percent of the worshippers in 1851 were Wesleyan) also helped the Tory revival, for there as in Manchester, the Connexion's leadership sought to drum up support for Conservative candidates.[122]

The second and more serious obstacle was splits between Whigs and Radicals and within the middle-class Liberal élite. The Radicalism of Samuel Smiles and the *Leeds Times* was too much for the Bainesites, but not enough for the local Chartist and Short-time movements.[123] Earl Fitzwilliam[124] maintained contacts with prominent Nonconformists in order to influence them in the Whig interest. Yet he also was under pressure from both Anglicans, who had their Church's interests at heart, and extreme Voluntaryists. These tensions periodically split the West Riding Liberals, and much of Fitzwilliam's time was spent trying to paper over the chasm.[125] When Fitzwilliam learned that the Rev. J. E. Giles, prominent Leeds Baptist minister, was urging his congregation to question candidates in the 1841 general election about their views on matters such as church extension and the abolition of church rates and ecclesiastical courts, the Earl called in moderate Nonconformists to restrain Giles.

> The effect of [Giles' tactics] will be to play the game of the Tories, for tho' some of these questions might be answered favorably, others could not. The result of putting questions of this kind at the general election must be most injurious to those who have a *favorable feeling* towards the Dissen-

---

[118] Binfield, *Prayers*, pp. 62, 64, 76-77, 93, is an appreciation of the Baines's religious and civic roles.

[119] The senior Baines (1774-1848) became proprietor of the *Leeds Mercury* in 1801; a civic leader promoting Liberal Nonconformist reforms, he sat as M.P. for Leeds, 1834-41 (*DNB*, I, 910-11).

[120] The son (1800-1890) followed his father in the *Leeds Mercury* trade and in civic leadership; M.P. for Leeds, 1859-74, knighted, 1880 (Boase, IV, 233).

[121] Beckett (1784-1863), principal partner in the banking firm Beckett & Co.; M.P. for Leeds, 1841-52, and for Ripon, 1852-57 (Boase, I, 216-17).

[122] Derek Fraser, "Politics and Society in the Nineteenth Century," *A History of Modern Leeds*, ed. Derek Fraser (Manchester, 1980), pp. 280-90; *Leeds Mercury*, 1 June 1839, 16 Apr. 1842; Binfield, *Prayers*, pp. 59-60.

[123] J.F.C. Harrison, "Chartism in Leeds," *Chartist Studies*, p. 85; Briggs, *Victorian Cities*, p. 141; *Leeds Times*, 3 July 1841.

[124] Charles William Wentworth Fitzwilliam, 3rd Earl Fitzwilliam (1786-1857); advanced Whig politician; M.P. for Yorkshire, Peterborough, and Northamptonshire, 1806 until he succeeded to the peerage in 1833; great power behind the scenes in Yorkshire and East Midlands politics (*DNB*, VII, 224-25).

[125] See Derek Fraser, "Voluntaryism and West Riding Politics in the Mid-Nineteenth Century," *Northern History*, XIII (1977), 199-231; and F.M.L. Thompson, "Whigs and Liberals in the West Riding, 1830-1860," *EHR*, LXXIV (1959), esp. 223-38.

ters, even tho' they do not see every question which interests them in precisely the same light in which they view it themselves. If you can do anything towards quieting this spirit you will do a great service.[126]

The results were controversy and class conflict, exacerbated by the hard times of the 1840s.

Edward Baines, Jr., was a regular supporter of all sorts of Liberal Nonconformist organizations, such as the British and Foreign School Society and the Leeds branches of the London Missionary Society and the Religious Tract Society. But he exited the decade of the 1830s a staunch believer in religious equality. He supported the Whig education scheme of 1839 because it seemed to offer the best chance for nonsectarian schools, and he criticized the fanaticism of no-popery meetings.[127]

> There is no person more firmly opposed to the religious doctrines of the Roman Catholics than ourselves. If those doctrines are gaining ground, whether within the Established Church or out of it, we would encourage every argumentative opposition to them. But to violate the civil rights of the Catholics, and still more to outrage their consciences, is what we abhor. This is persecution; and persecution is as clearly and strongly forbidden in the Bible, . . . as it is in itself hateful, unjust, and practically injurious to the cause of truth.[128]

But political and religious changes in the early 1840s conspired to push Baines into a less tolerant position.

Conservatism was on the upsurge in the early 1840s in both the West Riding and Leeds; in the 1841 general election, the Tories J. Stuart Wortley and Edmund Beckett Denison[129] defeated the Whig Lords Milton (Earl Fitzwilliam's heir) and Morpeth (the Earl of Carlisle's heir). At Leeds, William Beckett headed the poll and Joseph Hume, Baines's candidate, came third. Between 1841 and 1846, Baines grew increasingly concerned about the growth of Tractarianism within the Church of England. The 1843 Factory Bill led him to the conclusion that state-supported education could not be divorced from Anglican control, and that Anglicanism was hopelessly tainted by popery. Baines moved resolutions at the 1845 annual general meeting of the Leeds branch, Religious Tract Society, that deprecated the fact "that fatal errors are now industriously diffused through the press in our own district, and in various other parts of the country." Although Baines did not mention specifics, he declared his support for "evangelical religion" in the warfare "between the forces of truth and the forces of error"; several other speakers alluded to "the spread of semi-popery around us" and to the Ronge movement in Germany.[130] Just at the same time that the West Riding's urban Liberals were exploring ways of cooperating with the Anti-Corn Law League in creating new freeholders,

---

[126] Fitzwilliam to J. C. Gotch, 7 June 1841, Gotch (Kettering) Collection, Northamptonshire Record Office, GK 638.
[127] *Leeds Mercury*, 31 Aug., 7 Sept. 1839.
[128] *Ibid.*, 16 Nov. 1839.
[129] Beckett Denison (1787-1874), M.P. for the West Riding, 1841-47, 1848-59; member of the Leeds banking family; succeeded as 4th baronet, 1872 (Boase, I, 216-17).
[130] *Leeds Mercury*, 22 Nov. 1845.

a program that the Riding's Whig magnates disliked, Baines was splitting the urban Liberals over the cause of Voluntaryism.[131]

The Maynooth grant also was significant in the evolution of Baines's extreme Voluntaryism. Baines vigorously and continuously opposed the grant in 1845. The *Leeds Mercury* began publishing material, such as extracts from travel books and pamphlets from the Religious Tract Society, that promoted a negative picture of Roman Catholic doctrines and practices. Baines also became an ardent supporter of the Evangelical Alliance. Besides using his newspaper to publicize the Alliance's activities throughout the Riding, Baines participated in meetings himself, speaking on the need to promote Christian unity in order to oppose popery.[132]

Baines's views appeared in the political arena first in the Leeds election of 1847, where William Aldam, the sitting Whig-Liberal Member, was ousted because he had supported both the Maynooth grant and state aid to education. As for the Riding, Baines reluctantly supported Richard Cobden against Earl Fitzwilliam's proposal to split the representation between the Whig Morpeth and the Tory Beckett Denison. (Denison declined to ask for a poll, realizing that the Free-trade majority on the registration books could not be overcome.)[133]

But then Morpeth succeeded as Earl of Carlisle in October 1848, and there followed "a struggle for power within the Liberal party, and within the Riding, between aristocratic influence and the middle class of the towns. . . ."[134] Earl Fitzwilliam, who wanted to punish the urban Liberals for having revolted against his authority in 1847, secured Tory neutrality and put forward his son, Charles Fitzwilliam, clearly his father's pawn. But the pawn was withdrawn after most of the urban Liberals refused to accept him. Fitzwilliam and the Whigs then agreed to let the Tories bring in Edmund Beckett Denison unopposed, but at that point, Edward Baines put up his own candidate, Sir Culling Eardley Eardley, a Liberal who had contested Pontefract in 1837 and Edinburgh in 1846.[135] Eardley, of course, was also a leading light in the Evangelical Alliance.

The *Leeds Mercury* tried to depict Eardley as a good reformer, "a friend to Free Trade, to a bold reduction of Expenditure, to an enlarged Franchise, to the protection of the Ballot, to Peace, and to perfect Religious Liberty," and stressed that although he opposed Roman Catholicism for doctrinal reasons, he believed in perfect religious equality and opposed the further endowment of any religious sect.[136] But the intervention of the *Times*, which called Eardley a "religious malignant," changed the direction of the campaign.

---

[131] Derek Fraser, "Edward Baines," *Pressure from Without in Early Victorian England*, ed. Patricia Hollis (New York, 1974), pp. 193-98; D. Fraser, "West Riding Politics," pp. 206-7; Paz, *Politics of Working-Class Education*, pp. 122-25, 133, 136-37; F. Thompson, "Whigs and Liberals in the West Riding," pp. 223-26.

[132] *Leeds Mercury*, 11 July, 29 Aug. 1846, 23 Jan. 1847, 22 Jan. 1848, 20 Jan., 22 Dec. 1849, 2 Feb., 9 Mar. 1850.

[133] F. Thompson, "Whigs and Liberals in the West Riding," pp. 227-29; D. Fraser, "West Riding Politics," pp. 216-20.

[134] F. Thompson, "Whigs and Liberals in the West Riding," p. 233.

[135] *Ibid.*, pp. 231-36; D. Fraser, "West Riding Politics," pp. 220-25.

[136] *Leeds Mercury*, 25 Nov. 1848. In fact, Eardley's opposition to the government's education scheme in 1847 rested on his desire to exclude Roman Catholics from state funds, not so much on a principled opposition to all endowments (*Times*, 19 Apr. 1847).

A populous, wealthy, and intelligent constituency can hardly bear the ignominy of being represented in Parliament by a man whose only pretentions are founded on sectarian bigotry and fanatical acerbity. Sir Culling represents a party which we hope will in a few years become extinct. .
. . The profession of this party is hatred; their faith is negation. They retain
the maxims of Puritanism only to invert and misapply them. Inheriting the
profession of martyrs, they distort it into the practice of persecutors. Living in an age which has recognized the fullest liberty of religious belief,
they go about with sour faces and up-turned eyes, as if they were the victims of a despotism, instead of being its exponents and its executioners.
Clamorous for protection themselves, and combining with every class of
nonconformists so long as the Established Church enjoyed the monopoly
of encouragement, they would now exclude from the privileges which they
enjoy that strong and numerous body of religionists by whose united exertions they were mainly won. . . . In short, they measure all politics by the
standard, as they expound their own in the twang, of the Conventicle. It
is needless to say that a man who represents the ideas of such men can
hardly represent the West Riding of Yorkshire.[137]

The campaign was debated almost exclusively in religious terms, as
Eardley declared again and again that his opposition to Roman Catholicism was limited to the religious sphere, and that he supported fully their
civil liberties.[138] "[I]f, Gentlemen, honestly to believe and zealously to propagate the religious principles which I believe to be right,—if that be religious malignancy, then, indeed, I am a malignant. . . . Gentlemen, away
with the latitudinarianism which tells a man that he is to be enthusiastic
for his fox-hounds, his business, or his farm, but which will not let him be
enthusiastic for his faith."[139] While his No-popery views got him Wesleyan
support, his Voluntaryist views alienated Anglican anti-Catholics; the
Protestant Association accused him of being a democrat. About four
thousand Liberal voters abstained, and about two thousand changed sides
because they could not stomach either Eardley's Voluntaryism or his anti-
Catholicism, but fewer than three thousand votes separated him from the
winner (a small number in this, the largest English constituency).[140] "Un-
happily," the *Leeds Mercury* mourned, "there were not a few to whom he
was strongly distasteful on account of that feature of his character which
is the most honourable and estimable, namely his religious earnestness."[141]
Baines had forgot what he had known a decade before: that to outrage
consciences was persecution.

As a result of the election, the *Leeds Mercury* grew more uncompromising in its opposition to Roman Catholicism. In 1847, before the
election, it had faulted the government for denying aid to Roman Catholic
schools. In 1849, after the election, it gave approving publicity to Eardley's
faulting the government for granting aid to those same schools.[142] Thus,
when the Papal Aggression burst upon England, Baines withdrew somewhat from his extreme Voluntaryism in religion, at least to the extent that
he was willing to see Roman Catholicism treated less equally than other

[137] *Times*, 24 Nov. 1848.
[138] *Leeds Mercury*, 2, 9 Dec. 1848.
[139] *Ibid.*, 2 Dec. 1848.
[140] D. Fraser, "Politics . . . in the nineteenth century," pp. 292-93; D. Fraser, *Urban Politics*, p.
271; *Protestant Magazine*, XI (Jan. 1849), 9; Dod, *Electoral Facts*, p. 360.
[141] *Leeds Mercury*, 16 Dec. 1848.
[142] *Ibid.*, 10 Apr. 1847, 3 Feb. 1849.

faiths. The *Leeds Mercury* gave full publicity to the assumption of titles, the Flaminian Gate pastoral, and the protest meetings, arguing that Roman Catholicism made claims to civil as well as religious supremacy, and praised those anti-Catholic memorials that went on to attack Tractarianism, on the grounds that the assumption of titles would not have taken place had the Establishment preserved its Protestant principles.[143]

When it became necessary to have a county meeting on the Papal Aggression, Earl Fitzwilliam once again had to navigate the West Riding Liberals between the Tories and the Voluntaryists. Fitzwilliam wanted the clergy to stay away from the meeting in order to make clear that the protest originated with the laity; moreover, he wanted the condemnation of Roman titles to promote both Liberal party unity and cooperation with the Riding's Conservatives.[144] But this was not to be. Conservative Anglicans and Wesleyans believed that a mere expression of indignation at the assumption of titles would do little good, for Roman Catholics were indifferent to Protestant opinion. What was wanted was new legislation banning the titles. To oppose such a course would make the entire agitation seem pointless; to favor new legislation would alienate the Bainesite Voluntaryists.[145] Fitzwilliam, and, for the Conservatives, Lord Wharncliffe, revised the resolutions, hoping to satisfy everyone, but succeeded only in alienating them.[146] (So unprofitable was the exercise that the Earl of Carlisle, who as Lord Morpeth had represented the Riding for most of the 1830s, was glad to stay away from the county meeting.[147])

Baines tried to reconcile his disapproval of Popery with his support for religious freedom.

> Yet, as Englishmen and patriots, we are indignant that a paltry Italian Prince should thus virtually set his foot upon the majesty of England. Two wrongs do not make one right. The milder and lesser wrong of the English Establishment is no excuse for the all-consuming and detestable despotism of Rome; and our disapproving of the former would not make us one whit less zealous in opposing the latter. We acknowledge no spiritual allegiance whatever to the Queen; but being affectionately and loyally attached to her as our Sovereign, we cannot with indifference see her treated in a way which the Pope intends, and which she and her people feel, to be an insult.[148]

But the balance was tipped in favor of anti-Catholicism. Baines absented himself from meetings of the Anti-State Church Association, which he had theretofore supported, and chaired a joint meeting of Congregationalists and Baptists that organized denominational opposition to the new hierarchy. Moreover, he argued that neither the Ecclesiastical Titles Bill nor the Religious Houses Bill (which would have required government inspection of convents) really counted as penal legislation.[149] Baines called the Ecclesiastical Titles Bill "prudent in its moderation," "a remedy that meets the

[143] *Ibid.*, 14 Sept., 19, 26 Oct., 2, 16 Nov. 1850.
[144] Fitzwilliam to Earl Wharncliffe, [Nov. 1850], and 15 Nov. 1850, Wharncliffe Muniments, Sheffield City Library, Wh.M. 526(d).
[145] Edward Denison to Wharncliffe, 12 Nov. 1850, *ibid.*
[146] Denison to Wharncliffe, 17, 20 Nov. 1850, and J. W. Copley to Wharncliffe, 20 Nov. 1850, *ibid.*
[147] Carlisle to Edward Baines, Jr., 15 Nov. 1850, Baines Family Papers, Leeds City Archives.
[148] *Leeds Mercury*, 9 Nov. 1850.
[149] *Ibid.*, 16, 23 Nov., 28 Dec. 1850, 17 May 1851.

attempted innovation and wrong," and deplored the truncated compromise version.[150]

Baines continued his anti-Catholic interests into the 1850s. Although he resumed participation in the Liberation Society's Leeds branch, he continued to support the Evangelical Alliance, and gave extensive publicity to both the Protestant Alliance and the Leeds Evangelical Continental Society. (The last, established in 1846, but dormant until 1853, raised funds to support Evangelical Protestantism on the Continent.)[151] He was a staunch supporter of Father Gavazzi,[152] linked support for Italian liberalism with opposition to the Roman Catholic Church,[153] and wrote almost weekly on the Madiai Affair between July 1852 and April 1853.[154]

Baines tried to separate his opposition to state aid for religion from his religious dislike of Roman Catholicism.

> It is a most painful thing to the friends of civil and religious liberty to be forced by false legislation into steps which seem like injustice and hostility either to a nation or to a religious community. We deprecate with all our hearts anything unjust or unfair either towards the Irish as a nation or the Roman Catholics as a religious body.[155]

But the Papal Aggression had tipped the scales for him, so that he lent his voice to the continuing and virulent anti-Maynooth agitations during the 1850s. Richard Cobden criticized Baines's political career for showing "the elasticity of conscience . . . which men of fanatical tempers . . . can exhibit."[156] Baines' changing views towards Roman Catholics is an example of what Cobden had in mind.

Bainesite Liberals, state-education Liberals, and Whig magnates patched up their alliance by the late 1850s, and Baines himself abandoned Voluntaryism by the late 1860s. Nevertheless, the combination of anti-Catholicism and anti-Tractarianism was able to overcome the ideology of Liberal religious freedom in this towering symbol of the middle-class industrial North.

Anti-Catholic Politics after Midcentury

Anti-Catholicism failed to remain at center stage in the general elections of the two decades after 1852, partly because Palmerston's personality was such as to defang the Ultra-Protestants, partly because the most prominent questions, Maynooth and church rates, drove a wedge between Anglicans and Nonconformists.

Palmerston's first ministry had "an air of jaunty Erastianism" about it. His mildly liberal policies satisfied Dissent without conceding anything to their claims. His church patronage, under Shaftesbury's influence, kept both Evangelicals and Broad Churchmen happy. The High Church Peelites in his ministry kept that wing of the Church quiet. So religious issues were muted in the election of 1857. The Protestant Association and the

[150] *Ibid.*, 15 Feb., 15 Mar. 1851.
[151] *Ibid.*, 19, 26 Feb., 3, 24 Sept., 8 Oct., 9 Dec. 1853, 14 Jan., 18 Feb., 1 Apr., 16 Dec. 1854.
[152] *Ibid.*, 3 Apr., 12 June, 21, 28 Aug., 2, 9 Oct. 1852, 5 Feb. 1853.
[153] *Ibid.*, 28 Aug. 1852, 1 Apr., 23 Dec. 1854.
[154] *Ibid.*, 17 July, 25 Sept., 2, 16 Oct., 6, 27 Nov., 11 Dec. 1852, 1, 22, 29 Jan., 5, 12, 19 Feb., 5, 26 Mar., 9 Apr. 1853, 14 Apr. 1855.
[155] *Ibid.*, 16 May 1852.
[156] D. Fraser, "Edward Baines," p. 200.

Scottish Reformation Society raised the Maynooth issue, but to no avail, for all the leading politicians, Derby, Disraeli, Gladstone, and Russell, as well as Palmerston himself, supported the endowment. The *Record* came out for Palmerston, reluctantly, because of his episcopal appointments.[157]

Two years later, religious issues remained muted in the 1859 election. Parliamentary reform and Italian unification attracted attention, and the two perennial issues of Maynooth and church rates were raised. Clearly, however, anti-Catholics and Voluntaryists could not forge a united front on those religious issues. Furthermore, Derby and Disraeli discouraged their own Ultra-Protestant tail in order to foster good relations with Cardinal Wiseman, himself basically conservative in politics, who wanted to support the Tories both in Ireland and at home. Roman Catholic support helped the Tories win South Lancashire, and almost gave them Preston. Anti-Catholicism appeared as an electoral weapon at Hull, where John Harvey Lewis, the eldest son of an Irish landowner, stressed his Protestantism, declaring that a vote cast for him was a vote cast against Puseyism. Lewis accused James Clay, the sitting M.P. since 1847, of leaning towards popery because the latter had voted for the Maynooth grant. But Lewis was defeated, largely because Clay had a record of energetically promoting the borough's economic well-being; many Conservatives split their vote between Clay and J. Hoare, the other Conservative candidate, who also had interests in shipping. Anti-Catholicism could not triumph over economic self-interest, nor was it enough to make an outsider more attractive than an insider.[158]

Parliamentary reform, church rates, and Irish Church disestablishment came to the forefront of political debate during the 1860s. Palmerston was less generous to Evangelicals in his church patronage during this period, showing more favor to moderates. In 1863, his government introduced and secured the passage of legislation that allowed the appointment of paid non-Anglican chaplains to jails, a measure that was of value mainly to Roman Catholics. Ultra-Protestants opposed the measure, but to no avail. The 1865 and 1868 elections were fought over church rates and Irish Church disestablishment, not anti-Catholicism. Tories effected a combination of anti-Catholic, Orange, and Evangelical forces in 1868, which exploited church-chapel and Protestant-Catholic rivalries to win significant victories in Lancashire, including the unseating of Gladstone himself, but the election on the national level was a decisive victory for the combined forces of Liberals, Voluntaryists, Nonconformists, and Roman Catholics. Maynooth, the mainstay of the anti-Catholics, was now disendowed, but as part of a package that also included Irish Church disendowment.[159]

From 1868 on, anti-Catholics found themselves without an attractive issue and without hope of coalescing with Voluntaryists. The inspection of convents, although occupying much parliamentary time during the late 1860s and early 1870s, could not serve as a rally-cry in elections (because

[157] Machin, *Politics and the Churches*, pp. 270-71, 282-85.

[158] *Ibid.*, pp. 295-96; K. Theodore Hoppen, "Tories, Catholics, and the General Election of 1859," *HJ*, XIII (1970), 49, 52, 54, 56-57; W. L. Guttsman, "The General Election of 1859 in the Cities of Yorkshire: A Study of Political Behaviour under the Impact of the Reform Agitation," *International Review of Social History*, II (1957), 238, 242-44.

[159] Machin, *Politics and the Churches*, pp. 300, 305, 330-32, 372-77; J. C. Lowe, "The Tory Triumph of 1868 in Blackburn and in Lancashire," *HJ*, XVI (1973), 740-45; Wallis, "Anti-Maynooth Campaign," p. 190.

it was too much of a crotchet) and could not serve to bring in Nonconformists (because it was state interference in religion). Religious issues, of course, did not disappear from national politics—great battles remained to be fought over temperance and education—but they were issues of church versus chapel, not Protestant versus Catholic. Anti-Catholicism as a political issue was increasingly marginal beyond the confines of Liverpool as the century wore on to its close.

VIII

BONFIRES, REVELS, AND RIOTS

> Bonfire night!
> The Moon shines bright.
> Forty little angels dressed in white.
> Can you eat a biscuit?
> Can you smoke a pipe?
> Can you go a-courting
> At ten O'clock at night?[1]

VICTORIAN ENGLAND, ALTHOUGH more orderly than has been thought,[2] was no peaceable kingdom, eclipsing in terms of people killed and property destroyed the twentieth century's General Strike, Grosvenor Square demos, London School of Economics "Troubles," football hooliganism, Notting Hill, Brixton, and Birmingham race riots, and poll tax riots, but eclipsed by the eighteenth century's Sacheverell, Church and King, and Gordon Riots. Victorian religious violence must thus be viewed against the backdrop of the general level of popular disturbance.

There were two sources of popular disturbances, sustained over extended periods of time, in the 1830s and '40s.[3] These were opposition to the introduction of the New Poor Law, and Chartist (and related industrial) disturbances. The anti-poor-law disturbances took the form of crowds attempting to break up meetings of Boards of Guardians, interfering with the work of Assistant Poor Law Commissioners, and attacking workhouses. Property was destroyed and officials roughed up. The Chartist-related disturbances took several forms. The Chartists themselves threatened violence: "the rhetoric of violence," which threatened a move from "moral force" to "physical force"; the rumors and fears of Chartist arming, drilling, and engaging in threatening processions and meetings; and actual riots, most notably the Birmingham riots of 1839, but also riots in some Welsh towns and the "Newport Rising." Opponents of the Chartists also used violence in the form of riots, especially in the West Country, that aimed at breaking up Chartist meetings. Connected with the Chartist disturbances were the industrial disputes of 1842. There, the motivation was primarily economic, to prevent truck payments and wage cuts, and to that extent harkened back to the stoppages and strikes of the 1810s and '20s and the Swing riots. In contrast to the 1839 Chartist violence, which had

---

[1] *Notes and Queries*, 12th Ser., V (1919), 318.

[2] In large part because patterns of work were more orderly; Mark Harrison, *Crowds and History: Mass Phenomena in English Towns, 1790-1835* (Cambridge, 1988), p. 111.

[3] As opposed to localized, sporadic, and limited violence: e.g., attacks on cholera hospitals and dissection theaters, opposition to the introduction of the new police, fights between Protectionists and Free Traders.

not resulted in fatalities, the 1842 violence did result in deaths: a girl was killed by a brickbat at Stalybridge, mobs killed two constables at Newton and a trooper at Halifax, and soldiers shot five rioters at Preston, one at Burslem, and two at Halifax. In 1848, Chartist disturbances returned to the types of 1839, but with less violence, and without the counterforce of anti-Chartist crowds. After midcentury, the most serious economic and political disturbances happened in Lancashire and Cheshire in February 1854, when Irish strike-breakers were brought in to break the Operative Cotton Spinners strike.[4]

Popular violence related to anti-Catholicism is a phenomenon of the 1850s and '60s, mainly, although there was some violence in the late 1840s. Neville Kirk's examination of the cotton districts of Lancashire and Cheshire finds little working-class ethnic and religious violence before 1848. Kirk argues that the cotton districts saw cooperation between English and Irish Chartists and labor unionists, that the Irish ghettos were not as large or as segregated as some scholars think, that the Irish community was experiencing "a limited process of assimilation," and that "strong and widespread class feeling" transcended ethnic differences. But this picture changed after 1848. Irish immigration increased dramatically in the late 1840s, as did the cholera of 1849 (associated with Irish neighborhoods). These developments coincided with the decline of Lancashire Chartism, the only major force for class unity and against ethnic and religious divisions. Middle-class Conservatives attempted to attach workers to their political and cultural leadership by developing a mass anti-Catholic movement. They were successful. Workers were receptive to the middle-class message because they believed that the Irish immigrants competed for jobs, drove down wages, acted as strike-breakers, and resisted assimilation.[5] The economic realities were that the Irish competed with unskilled migrants from rural England, Wales, and Scotland for the lowest paid jobs, and with the Lancashire cotton operatives for housing, but workers held and acted upon the belief that the Irish were dragging down wages.[6]

In respect of timing, anti-Catholic violence to some extent resembles anti-Mormon violence. Anti-Mormon persecutions in the 1830s and '40s were sporadic, localized in South Wales and the West Midlands, and intended for humiliation, not bodily harm. In the 1850s, however, the campaign against Mormonism became more organized and more widespread. Travelling lecturers such as Dr. John Brindley, Andrew Balfour Hepburn, and William Saunders Parrott inflamed sentiment; Brindley published

---

[4] John Stevenson, *Popular Disturbances in England, 1700-1870* (London, 1979), pp. 245-74, 284.

[5] Neville Kirk, *The Growth of Working Class Reformism in Mid-Victorian England* (Urbana and Chicago, 1985), pp. 45-46, 310, 314-16, 329; Neville Kirk, "Ethnicity, Class and Popular Toryism, 1850-1870," *Hosts, Immigrants, and Minorities: Historical Responses to Newcomers in British Society, 1870-1914*, ed. Kenneth Lunn (Folkestone, 1980), pp. 65-66, 70-73, 76-78, 92-94. Cf. Walton, *Lancashire*, pp. 164-65; and Michael Dury, "The Survival of an Irish Culture in Britain," *Historical Studies*, XX (1982), 22-23. W. Lowe, *Irish in Mid-Victorian Lancashire*, pp. 51-72, and Theodore Koditschek, *Class Formation and Urban Industrial Society: Bradford, 1750-1850* (Cambridge, 1990), pp. 450-51, confirm Kirk's points about ghettos, assimilation, cooperation, and the relatively low level of ethnic violence.

[6] Kirk, *Working Class Reformism*, pp. 333-34; Kirk, "Ethnicity, Class and Popular Toryism," pp. 83-85; W. Lowe, *Irish in Mid-Victorian Lancashire*, pp. 23-24, 96-98.

anti-Mormon propaganda; and violence spread to East Anglia and greater London.[7]

To analyze anti-Catholic violence, one must avoid adopting "social control" theories that view the authorities as manipulative and that define order and disorder as social constructs of the ruling class because, as John Stevenson observes, such approaches "too easily degenerate into a kind of conspiracy theory" that misses "the complexities and subtleties which govern attitudes and responses to events."[8] Crowd behavior sometimes reflected a political agenda, but sometimes not. Sometimes the political agenda was a working-class one, but sometimes it was middle-class, and sometimes landed-class. Sometimes the agenda challenged constituted authority, but sometimes it supported the status quo. Sometimes the authorities put down crowd activities because they did not like the crowd's politics; sometimes they put down the activities because the crowds threatened human life and limb. Sometimes the crowd had a "moral economy" to enforce; sometimes the crowd simply wanted to play.

Stevenson also questions Charles Tilly's quantitative approach because, in his view, it loses the subjective dimension of historical events and confuses big numbers with impact on the contemporary consciousness and statistical significance with historical significance.[9] I would add that Tilly assumes that all collective action is rational, problem-solving behavior,[10] that his sources are inappropriate records for what he wants to measure,[11] that his definition of "contentious gatherings" is so broad as to be meaningless,[12] and that he believes that an elaborate methodology can substitute for a knowledge of the society that he would study.[13]

As to the sorts of crowd activities to be studied, Stevenson and Mark Harrison argue that it is too rigid to exclude "'institutionalised' actions, such as patriotic demonstrations, ritual rebellions, and ceremonial behaviour" from analysis.[14] Finally, Harrison wisely stresses "the importance of local contexts in the reinterpretation of national issues, and the provision of local imperatives and contingencies."[15] I agree with these views.

But the nature of the popular violence related to anti-Catholicism is unclear. As a generalization, one finds two sorts of views. One sort calls this violence "communal": conflicts between two ethnic groups, one Irish immigrants, the other the English working-class host community.[16] An-

---

[7] Malcolm R. Thorp, "Sectarian Violence in Early Victorian Britain: The Mormon Experience, 1837-1860," *Bulletin of the John Rylands University Library of Manchester*, LXX (1988), 138-43.

[8] Stevenson, *Popular Disturbances*, p. 5.

[9] *Ibid.*, pp. 15-16.

[10] Charles Tilly, *As Sociology Meets History* (New York, 1981), p. 151 ff.

[11] It is a mistake to use national sources (the *Times*, the *Morning Chronicle*, the *Gentleman's Magazine*, *Hansard*, and the *Annual Register*) to gather data about meetings and demonstrations outside London.

[12] A contentious gathering is an occasion in which ten or more persons outside the government gather together and make a claim that, if realized, would affect the interests of other people or groups. This is not quite "when two or three are gathered together," but close to it.

[13] He thinks that Middlesex "means, essentially, metropolitan London," when greater London excludes parts of Middlesex and includes parts of Kent and Surrey; his coders recorded an election in "Hustings, Durham." John Boyd, R. A. Schweitzer, and Charles Tilly, "British Contentious Gatherings of 1828," Center for Research on Social Organization, University of Michigan, Working Paper No. 171 (March 1978), pp. 22, 42.

[14] Stevenson, *Popular Disturbances*, p. 8 (quoted); Harrison, *Crowds and History*, p. 142.

[15] Harrison, *Crowds and History*, p. 268.

[16] Joyce, *Work, Society, and Politics*, pp. 251-52; Kirk, "Ethnicity, Class and Popular Toryism," p. 66.

other sees the violence as localized, small-scale rioting, generated by the presence of itinerant anti-Catholic lecturers, directed against Roman Catholics who play the role of victims rather than belligerents, and "not really serious."[17] When one looks at disturbances having a religious component, one sees two types: the antipolice riot, having two subtypes in which either crowds animated ostensibly by anti-Catholic sentiment or Irish Roman Catholic crowds attack the police; and the communal riot, in which English Protestants and Irish Roman Catholics attack each other. The street and pub brawl, often over religion but essentially a private quarrel, is related to the communal riot. I shall first look at Bonfire Night in two specific counties—Northampton and Cambridge—chosen because of how they behaved during the memorializing and petitioning drives of 1850-1851, and then examine the different sorts of revels, rows, and riots.

Bonfire Night in Mid-Victorian Northants

Today an excuse for children to beg and for families to eat sausages and watch Catherine-wheels in the rectory gardens, Guy Fawkes Day was once the most important popular holiday in England, and thus the most common expression of anti-Catholicism.[18] It reaffirmed community solidarity by stressing "English Liberty" (which supposedly transcended class lines),[19] and by linking together the upper classes or notables with the "plebeians"—laborers, artisans, shopkeepers, and tradesmen. Moreover, it was a political activity that both permitted the participation of the unenfranchised and focused, ostensibly, on conflicts between Protestantism and the Roman Catholic Church. Finally, its use of a pyre, the burning of an effigy, and the verbal savaging of the Roman Catholic Church was symbolic violence, and sometimes led to physical violence against people and property.

But in the late eighteenth century, according to Robert Storch, who has studied Bonfire Night in the South of England, élite patronage for these "popular revels" was gradually withdrawn. Local authorities feared fire, but they also wanted to maintain public order and social discipline in the face of Paineite artisanal radicalism. This left the Fifth of November in the hands of the plebeians, who used it as a charivari or skeffington to exercise "popular justice" on local offenders, to act out complaints, and to attack unpopular local political leaders. Guy Fawkes Day thus continued to show political content into the nineteenth century, but that content became "exclusively local." In "old, stable Tory Towns," what Storch calls "arcane upper-class quarrels"—especially opposition to Tractarianism—"could be easily transmitted to crowds and taken up by them," but he denies that the Guy Fawkes crowds were used to promote "narrow political purposes." However, he does admit that links with local party politics may have been "more complex" than he makes out. So, Storch believes, local notables, especially the politically Liberal, socially bourgeois-respectable, and reli-

---

[17] Norman, *English Catholic Church*, pp. 20-21.
[18] Different localities had their special holidays—Lancashire had its wakes and Whitsun walks, Derby its Shrove Tuesday football—but Guy Fawkes Day was the one popular holiday kept universally.
[19] Best, "Popular Protestantism," pp. 120-22.

giously Evangelical, sought to abolish, or, failing that, to emasculate the plebeian ritual.[20]

This brings us to the question of the extent to which popular festivals of all sorts were opposed and repressed by the "improving" middle classes as a means of social control, but defended, sometimes with violence, by the plebeians. There indeed were those who wished to improve popular pastimes out of existence. Their motives, the degree of their success, and the extent to which the disappearance of popular pastimes can be attributed to their activities (as opposed to the consequences of impersonal economic change such as urbanization, industrialization, and the railroad) are matters for spirited debate.[21] As to the extent of working-class resistance, Storch finds "a running battle" between the forces of middle-class repression and the defenders of local custom and popular culture throughout the nineteenth century.[22]

Northamptonshire[23] had its own Bonfire Night traditions, which show connections between popular revels and politics, and which demonstrate class conflict. But the political issues involved, their relationships to party politics, the nature of the class conflict, and the treatment of the popular revels call into question the notion of plebeian resistance to middle-class social control. The results of the Northamptonshire meetings that adopted memorials to the Queen in 1850 and petitions to the House of Commons in 1851 are rather unusual. Northamptonshire ranks first among all English counties in terms of signatures on memorials per thousand of population (generating 120 per thousand), yet the county contained only eight Irish-born per thousand. Why did it behave as it did? Does Victorian anti-Catholicism have little to do with anti-Irish sentiment? Was the county one of those places where "like communism in small-town America, Romanism was the more fearful for being so abstract and remote"?[24]

Northamptonshire was not so remote from Roman Catholicism as mere numbers of adherents might imply. Northampton town, the see of William Wareing, one of the new Roman bishops, had a history of three-way public religious controversy amongst Anglicans, Roman Catholics, and Nonconformists.[25] Moreover, its politics were of such a mix that religious issues

---

[20] Robert D. Storch, "'Please to Remember the Fifth of November': Conflict, Solidarity and Public Order in Southern England, 1815-1900," *Popular Culture and Custom in Nineteenth-Century England*, ed. Robert Robert D. Storch (London, 1982), pp. 71-72, 74, 78, 81, 83, 85, 96.

[21] Brian Harrison, "Religion and Recreation in Nineteenth-Century England," *Past and Present*, No. 38 (Dec. 1967), pp. 98-125; Robert W. Malcolmson, *Popular Recreation in English Society, 1700-1850* (Cambridge, 1973), pp. 89-157; Peter Bailey, *Leisure and Class in Victorian England: Rational Recreation and the Contest for Control, 1830-1885* (London and Toronto, 1978), pp. 170-79; Hugh Cunningham, *Leisure in the Industrial Revolution, c. 1789-c. 1880* (New York, 1980), pp. 116-23; John K. Walton and Robert Poole, "The Lancashire Wakes in the Nineteenth Century," *Popular Culture and Custom*, pp. 116-20.

[22] "The Policeman as Domestic Missionary: Urban Discipline and Popular Culture in Northern England, 1850-1880," *Journal of Social History*, IX (1975-76), 481-509; also his "The Plague of the Blue Locusts: Police Reform and Popular Resistance in Northern England, 1840-57," *International Review of Social History*, XX (1975), 60-90.

[23] Two bits of evidence used here come from outside the county—from Olney, Bucks, and Market Harborough, Leics. These places are only just over the border, within the "catchment area" of the county newspapers, and influenced by Northamptonshire personalities and politics.

[24] Storch, "Fifth of November," p. 82.

[25] *Sup.*, pp. 93, 97-98; "The Popery of Protestantism and the Popery of Rome," handbill, Archives of the Roman Catholic Diocese of Northampton, Bishop's House, Northampton, F 1.6; "A Dialogue in the Streets of Northampton on 'False and True Peace,'" Northampton (Appendix), [A Collection of Cartoons, Squibs, Manifestoes, Newspaper-cuttings, &c., relating to Parliamentary and Municipal Elections at Northampton], British Library pressmark 1851.c.16.

took on great significance. The town was a center for the shoemaking industry, organized in small workshops. The trade was growing; the numbers of workers involved therein more than doubled to over six thousand between 1841 and 1861 as foreign markets expanded in the 1850s, and sales to both North and South in the American Civil War led to more growth. Thus there were many small masters and semi-independent journeymen in town—"the classic breeding ground for independent radicalism," as Edward Royle observes[26] —and shoemakers were the largest single category of voters in the Parliamentary elections of 1831 and 1852. (The town returned Liberal M.P.s throughout the period.) Its population included few immigrants from great distances; 29 percent of the population in 1851 had been born within three miles, and 50 percent between three and twenty miles, of the town. The town also had strong Nonconformist traditions; attendances at evening worship in 1851 were 31 percent church and 57 percent chapel.[27] There was a sizable anti-slavery element, largely Nonconformist, which had links to the Liberal party. Given the town's occupational and religious mix, it is not surprising that its dominant political tradition was an extreme Liberalism of rather greater import than the "surface radicalism" that John Foster sees. And the extreme Liberal-radicals had to combat a Chartist element active in local politics in the 1840s.[28]

In contrast, Conservative landowners dominated county politics. In the Southern Division, Whigs and Nonconformists showed some life from the 1820s onwards, challenging the Tories over issues such as Dissenters' claims, Roman Catholic Emancipation, and church rates. They contested unsuccessfully Tory control of both seats in the 1841, 1847, and 1852 elections. In the Northern Division, Whigs and Tories contested the representation in 1832, split it in 1835, and contested it again, advancing only one candidate, in 1837. Thereafter the Tories returned both Members uncontested until a Liberal stood at a by-election in 1857. Although the interests and sensibilities of the great Whig landowners Earl Fitzwilliam and Earl Spencer were sometimes respected, they could not overcome the influence of the Tory landowners.[29]

The town of Kettering, however, was a Liberal island in the Northern Division. The Whig Lord Sondes was its chief landholder, and it voted Whig or Liberal in the 1831, 1832, 1835, and 1857 parliamentary elections. Old Dissent was strong there, and its notables were self-made men. It was economically depressed, suffering from the collapse of the handloom worsted trade in the 1790s, until the introduction of shoemaking and other manufactories in the 1850s restored economic growth. (Its population grew slowly, from 4,867 in 1841, to 5,198 in 1851, to 5,845 in

[26] Edward Royle, "Charles Bradlaugh, Freethought and Northampton," *Northamptonshire Past and Present*, VI (1980), 142.

[27] Baptists, 25 percent; Wesleyans, 20 percent; Independents, 12 percent.

[28] Foster, *Class Struggle*, pp. 2 (quoted), 76, 85-87, 102-4; Royle, "Bradlaugh," pp. 141-43; Dod, *Electoral Facts*, p. 230; David Waller, "Northampton and the American Civil War," *Northamptonshire Past and Present*, VIII (1990-91), 137-39, 148-49.

[29] Janet Howarth, "Politics and Society in Late Victorian Northamptonshire," *Northamptonshire Past and Present*, IV (1970-71), 269; R. L. Greenall, "Parson as a Man of Affairs: The Rev. Francis Litchfield of Farthinghoe (1792-1876)," *ibid.*, VIII (1990-91), 121-31; Dod, *Electoral Facts*, p. 232; David Cresap Moore, *The Politics of Deference: A Study of the Mid-Nineteenth Century English Political System* (Hassocks, 1976), pp. 105-9, 128-33.

1861.) Hence the political and social climates here were also favorable to radical politics.[30]

Kettering was home to a circle of militant Strict Baptists, centered in the Ebenezer Chapel. John Jenkinson and William Robinson, preachers, and the former's nephew John Jenkinson, Jr., shoe manufacturer, helped organize the Northampton (Chartist) Working Men's Association, belonged to the Anti-State Church (later, the Liberation) Society, participated in local politics, and had their goods seized for nonpayment of church rates.[31] They also published (in 1846-47) the *Citizen*, a monthly magazine that aimed to be to the "cottage" what the *Nonconformist* was to urban Dissent. The influence of the *Citizen* on local views is problematical—it claimed to sell eight or nine hundred copies per month, at a penny—but certainly those who published it represented a significant strand of public opinion, as we shall see.[32]

The *Citizen* treated theological concerns of interest to Baptists, defending believers' baptism and immersion, and attacking doctrines held in common by Roman Catholicism and Anglicanism—sponsors at baptism, confirmation, and the role of tradition—as well as the distinctively Roman doctrine of transubstantiation.[33]

This God is made by incantation—
Words spoken by a priest;
And in the stomach takes his station,
With bacon rank and reest.[34]

Your Pagan makes his God and greets him,
Jove, Juggernaut, or Cupid;
But this, when he has made him, eats him;
Which looks a little stupid.[35]

It was more interested, however, in the social and political consequences of the union of church and state. It attacked the establishment principle, in theory and in the specific cases of the United Kingdom, arguing that as the Church of England grew more "Puseyite" and persecutory, separation of church and state would prevent the rekindling of the fires of Smithfield. Northamptonshire Dissenters, it urged, should prepare for the next elections by forming committees and questioning candidates on their views regarding separation of church and state.[36]

---

[30] R. L. Greenall, "The Rise of Industrial Kettering," *Northamptonshire Past and Present*, V (1975), 253-54, 265; Moore, *Politics of Deference*, maps bet. pp. 112-13; Chadwick, *Victorian Church*, p. 371; *Kettering Vestry Minutes, A.D. 1797-1853*, ed. S. A. Peyton, *Publications of the Northamptonshire Record Society*, VI (Northampton, 1933), iii, xiv-xvi; Chadwick, *Victorian Church*, p. 371.

[31] Articles of Agreement, 27 Feb. 1869, John Jenkinson, Jr., Papers, Northamptonshire Record Office, YZ 5542/5; John Jenkinson, Jr., to F. Ross, [after 1 Mar. 1884], *ibid.*, YZ 5542/14; Greenall, "Kettering," p. 261; R. G. Gammage, *History of the Chartist Movement, 1837-1854*, 2nd ed. (London and Newcastle-on-Tyne, 1894), pp. 36-37; R. L. Greenall, "Baptist as Radical: The Life and Opinions of the Rev. John Jenkinson of Kettering (1799-1876)," *Northamptonshire Past and Present*, VIII (1991-92), 210-26.

[32] *Citizen*, No. 7 (Jan. 1847), p. 49. A run of this magazine from July 1846 to November 1847 is in the Northamptonshire Record Office.

[33] *Ibid.*, No. 12 (June 1847), pp. 92, 96.

[34] Rancid.

[35] *Citizen*, No. 4 (Oct. 1846), p. 29.

[36] *Ibid.*, Nos. 3 (Sept. 1846), p. 21, 4 (Oct. 1846), pp. 25-26, 8 (Feb. 1847), p. 57, and 12 (June 1847), p. 95.

The *Citizen* also sought to promote local discontent by protesting examples of injustice, reporting disputes over church rates, and publicizing internal Anglican quarrels in order to stir up dissension between priest and people. It recounted a dispute at Geddington, three miles from Kettering, which had its origins in rumors that the new incumbent held Puseyite opinions. It reiterated the resentment of some of the parishioners of Kettering about their new rector, in order to make it difficult for clergyman and people to settle their differences. It reported in detail attempts to levy a church rate at Kettering.[37] Finally, it hinted at the social despotism that the establishment principle necessarily encouraged: "in many agricultural villages, Church of Englandism is forced upon the people by influences which we can scarcely designate by softer epithets than those of bribery and intimidation."[38]

The Kettering Nonconformists sought to translate their views into concrete political action during the 1840s. Early in the decade, they used whatever forums they could find to air their grievances. When a public meeting assembled at the National School room on 30 October 1844 to discuss how Kettering should show its loyalty when the Queen passed through the town, William Robinson tried to raise the questions of universal suffrage and the corn laws.[39] Concerned with landlordism, Robinson and the two Jenkinsons supported the Freehold Land Society, the Kettering branch of which was founded in 1851; for all land in the town was copyhold, rather than freehold, a circumstance that limited the business activities of the town's Nonconformist entrepreneurs.[40] The Church of England, of course, was the landed interest at prayer. So Robinson and the Jenkinsons combined their religious and political views by attacking the Church. They encouraged Voluntaryism, and participated in the petition drives against the Education Minutes of 1846, which Edward Baines of Leeds organized. They formed local branches of the Liberation Society in Kettering and its neighborhood. They came very close to defeating a church rate in 1841 and 1845, and actually defeated one in 1848 (before the rector disallowed half of their votes). In 1849 and 1850 they contested the election of the People's Warden. And they sparked uproars at several vestry meetings by challenging rulings of its chairman.[41]

To be sure, Kettering (and Northamptonshire) Nonconformists were not universally behind Robinson and the Jenkinsons. They themselves admitted that what they called "respectable" Dissenters did not attend their meetings; and the Nonconformist notable John Cooper Gotch,[42] who linked his moderate fellows with the Liberal political leadership of Earl Fitzwilliam, opposed them.[43] Their political radicalism was almost as upsetting to Liberal Nonconformists as their religious radicalism was to the Anglicans. Nonetheless, the Kettering group was taken seriously enough, and their

[37] *Ibid.*, Nos. 1 (July 1846), pp. 5-7, 2 (Aug. 1846), pp. 14-15, 3 (Sept. 1846), p. 22, and 13 (July 1847), pp. 99-100.
[38] *Ibid.*, No. 14 (Aug. 1847), p. 108.
[39] *Northampton Herald*, 2 Nov. 1844; *Illustrated London News*, 16 Nov. 1844.
[40] *Citizen*, No. 17 (Nov. 1847), p. 129; Greenall, "Kettering," pp. 255, 264.
[41] *Citizen*, Nos. 7 (Jan. 1847), p. 52, 9 (Mar. 1847), pp. 65-6, and 10 (Apr. 1847), p. 76, 79-80; *Kettering Vestry Minutes*, pp. 142, 155-56, 167-69, 174-76, 188-91, 193-95.
[42] Gotch (1772-1852), footware manufacturer, banker, and member of Fuller Baptist Chapel (from which Jenkinson had seceded).
[43] *Citizen*, No. 10 (Apr. 1847), p. 76; *Northampton Herald*, 2 Nov. 1844; Greenall, "Kettering," pp. 253-54.

influence and allies extended far enough beyond their immediate neighborhood, to provoke an Anglican counterattack. The vehicle for that attack was the Fifth of November.

The Kettering Radicals understood the symbolic power of Bonfire Night, and tried to defuse it by showing how the cruel persecutions of Elizabeth I and James I had goaded some Roman Catholics beyond endurance.[44] Guy Fawkes celebrations in the 1840s, however, were relatively quiet affairs. The county newspapers rarely reported them, even though they were kept. In Northampton town, the local Orange Lodge kept the Fifth with a formal dinner and corporate attendance at St. Katharine's or St. Giles's churches; but they were more interested in remembering King William III's landing day than the Gunpowder Plot.[45] In rural areas, the Fifth was kept in a manner redolent of simple rustic pleasures. At Olney,[46] where the vicar, D. B. Langley, was an active anti-Catholic, the churchbells pealed in the morning, at midday, and at sunset; as soon as work was done and darkness nigh, fireworks were discharged and towballs lit and tossed about. People wandered the streets with their fireworks, but the big show was at the Marketplace. The guy was marched through the streets to the Marketplace, where it was stuck in a barrel of pitch and tossed on the bonfire. People had been working hard and long at the preparations, for the reporter remarked that the guy "shewed much artistic skill."[47]

The Papal Aggression burst upon these simple fêtes, reviving local interest in the holiday,[48] prompting more extensive newspaper coverage, and integrating the celebrations into county politics.

Northampton town saw a much bigger celebration on 5 November 1850 than in previous years. The place of venue shifted from the churches to the streets; boys and men came out to play; and the displays of fireworks and guys outdid any other Fifth in recent memory. The *Northampton Herald*, organ of the town's Anglican Tory classes, saluted the celebration with glee. "If the feeling of Northampton against Popery, and the chance of a return to the darkness of past ages, may be judged of by the displays on Tuesday, the hopes of the 'Holy Father' cannot be of a very sanguine kind."[49] Elsewhere, however, the Fifth was not welcomed. The magistrates of Towcester had sought to suppress the fête for some years, with little success, and prepared for the day in 1850 by summoning extra police. A crowd attempted to lay the fire on the Market Hill, but the police arrested three of the leaders, and the people dispersed. After dark, however, the crowd returned, rocks flew, and the bank's windows were smashed. But someone lit a bonfire in another part of town; the crowd moved there and spent the rest of the evening shouting "No Popery" and singing "Rule Britannia."[50] At Kettering, opposition came from a different source. There, the Rector and "many of the respectable townspeople" organized a fête; but a party or parties mysteriously described as agents of the Liberal

[44] *Citizen*, No. 5 (Nov. 1846), pp. 33-37.
[45] *Northampton Herald*, 6 Nov. 1847, 11 Nov. 1848, 10 Nov. 1849.
[46] In Buckinghamshire, but just over the border.
[47] *Ibid.*, 10 Nov. 1849; Wolffe, "Protestant Societies and Anti-Catholic Agitations," pp. 212-14.
[48] As was the case for the South of England (Storch, "Fifth of November," p. 82).
[49] *Northampton Herald*, 9 Nov. 1850.
[50] *Ibid.; Northampton Mercury*, 9 Nov. 1850.

Northampton Mercury attempted to suppress it.[51] (The hand of the Kettering Radicals may perhaps be seen in this opposition.)

To understand these responses better, we must now turn to the question of how Northamptonshire participated in the anti-Catholic agitation of 1850-51.

The Northampton town corporation failed to adopt a memorial to the Queen, as a direct result of local politics. Liberals and Radicals dominated the corporation, with nineteen members. But there was a tight group of five Conservative councillors, and, in the years just before the Papal Aggression, Chartists (many of whom were small merchants and shopkeepers, Nonconformists, and Liberationists) regularly stood for election.[52] Conservatives grumbled that their council was full of Unitarians, Dissenters, and "Anythingarians."[53]

> Again, we find the Queen persuaded one year to travel with, and another year without, a chaplain, one day to attend an Episcopal, another day a Presbyterian church, whilst Lord John Russell has been so thoroughly be-*Minto'd*,[54] by his last Scotch marriage, that his religious principles have been looked upon as representing the anythingarianism of the day.[55]

For its part, the Conservative leadership included John Slinn, member of the Orange Order, and John Palmer Kilpin, who just then was circulating rumors about a poor servant girl whose conversion to Roman Catholicism had allegedly driven her mad.[56] Kilpin and the Conservative councillors Christopher H. Markham, William Hensman, and Francis Mulliner were active in the Northampton Religious and Useful Knowledge Society, founded in 1839 to combat popery and infidelity by challenging the local Mechanics Institution.[57]

The Liberal councillors determined to move first against the Anglican Conservatives. At council's December meeting, William Dennis (Liberal and Unitarian) moved "that an undue importance has been attached to the papal bull," and that penal legislation ought not to be adopted. Alerted by notice of the motion, many Orangemen attended the meeting. The Conservative councillors, led by William Hensman, knew that they could not defeat Dennis's motion, so they offered obstructionist motions for adjournment, actually left the room at one point, and finally attempted to intimidate the Liberals by calling for the Orangemen to crowd up against the councillors' table. But Dennis's motion passed.[58]

Elsewhere in the county, Nonconformists and Liberals also managed to defeat their Anglican opponents on the Papal Aggression issue. The county nobility and gentry decided not to call for a public meeting of the freeholders (rumor had it out of courtesy to Earl Spencer, Northamptonshire's most

---

[51] *Northampton Herald*, 9 Nov. 1850.

[52] *Ibid.*, 3 Nov. 1849, 2 Nov. 1850; Gammage, *Chartist Movement*, pp. 97, 117, 256-58; Foster, *Class Struggle*, p. 305.

[53] *Northampton Herald*, 30 Nov. 1850.

[54] Referring to Russell's second marriage, to Lady Fanny Elliot, daughter of Gilbert Elliot, 2nd Earl of Minto. Her religious views were Low and Erastian, and she drifted eventually from the Kirk to the Plymouth Brethren.

[55] *Ibid.*, 9 Nov. 1850.

[56] *Sup.*, p. 93.

[57] *Northampton Herald*, 30 Nov. 1850.

[58] *Northampton Mercury*, 7 Dec. 1850.

TABLE 7

Sources of Memorialists and Petitioners, Northants, 1850 and 1851

Source	Memorialists		Petitioners	
	N	%	N	%
Public meetings	24,166	91.29	313	18.88
Anglican meetings	2,306	8.71	81	4.89
Wesleyan Methodists	0	0	1,264	76.24
Total	26,472	100.00	1,658	100.00

Source: See Table 1

prominent nobleman, whose brother, Father Ignatius Spencer, was a notorious convert). Instead, it was determined to circulate a memorial to the Queen privately for signature; 21,065 people signed.[59] A public assembly of the inhabitants of Kettering, meeting at the Independent Chapel, adopted a memorial (with 168 signatures) that repudiated popery, but declared that the Roman Catholics had broken no law and opposed "any departure from the Principles of Civil and Religious Liberty." The public meeting at Market Harborough,[60] after hearing from William Robinson, adopted a memorial (with 152 signatures) similar to Kettering's.[61]

Northamptonshire's Anglican Conservatives, although defeated in these engagements, were determined to fight back. The private memorial circulating in lieu of a county meeting offered one line of attack; the Kettering magistrates secured a copy and left it in their office for signature.[62] Others held countermeetings. The clergy and churchwardens of St. Sepulchre's, St. Katherine's, and All Saints' parishes, Northampton town, adopted memorials to the Queen in 1850, to make up for council's failure to do so. Conservative inhabitants of Market Harborough and Kettering Methodists petitioned the House of Commons in 1851, in order to strike back at Robinson and the Kettering Radicals. Memorials adopted at public meetings in 1850 generated 26,472 signatures. Ninety-one percent of them came from meetings of "Inhabitants"; 9 percent came from meetings of the Anglican priest, churchwardens, and inhabitants. This shows a markedly weaker Anglican participation in the county than was the case nationally (36 percent). In contrast, the Wesleyan Methodist presence in the 1851 petition drives was much stronger in the county (76 percent) than nationally (30 percent). The Northamptonshire Wesleyans were following the lead of their denomination's national leadership, which had organized the collection. of petitions. (See Table 7.)

But the Conservatives' cleverest stroke was to harness popular opinion against ultra-Liberal Dissent by exploiting the symbolic value of the Fifth of November. The new tactic was unveiled at Daventry on New Year's Eve, where about two thousand people watched a ceremonial burning of the Pope and Cardinal Wiseman.[63] The Pope rode backwards on a donkey led by a chimney-sweep's boy; placards with the usual anti-Catholic slo-

[59] *Northampton Herald*, 23, 30 Nov. 1850.
[60] In Leicestershire, but just over the border.
[61] *Northampton Mercury*, 30 Nov., 28 Dec. 1850; "Returns of the Number of Addresses," *PP*, 1851, LIX (84), 737-38.
[62] *Northampton Herald*, 30 Nov. 1850.
[63] *Ibid.*, 4 Jan. 1851.

gans appeared; and a fife and drum played "The Rogue's March" and "The Romish Priest's Delight" (otherwise, "Kiss My Lady"). From time to time the procession halted while the town crier read a satirical proclamation in which "His Unholiness Pope Im-Pious the Last" announced his plans to join the company of the "saints and saintesses Dick Turpin, Jerry Abbershaw, Mother Brownrigg, and Maria Manning." When the procession reached the bonfire, the town crier burnt slips of paper on which were written the titles of objectionable works: the *Morning Chronicle* (a Peelite organ suspected of Tractarian leanings); the *Nonconformist*; two tracts, Edward Miall's "The Pope and the Prelates" and Newman Hall's "Dissent and the Papal Bull" (which argued that Nonconformists should support the religious freedom of Roman Catholics); and, finally, William Robinson's Market Harborough speech. The ceremony ended with three cheers for the Queen, Lord Winchilsea, and Sir Charles Knightly (Conservative M.P. for the county's Southern Division, 1834-52), and a fireworks display.

The elements in the Daventry ceremony—the burning of effigies, a posh version of "rough music," political content of national import, and Conservative Anglican patronage of a popular entertainment—marked the Fifth of November in Northamptonshire during the decade of the 1850s. Bonfire Night was organized not only to attack Liberal and Nonconformist ideas, but also to reply to specific local political situations. The *Northampton Herald* had wanted a county meeting in order to encourage "that patriotism, loyalty and social order which the measures of the Pope have threatened";[64] in Bonfire Night it got all that and more. But, as we shall see, things tended to get out of hand.

Bonfire Night 1851 was kept with spirit in Northampton; at Kettering, the churchbells rang and the authorities, as in past years, offered the Marketplace as the site of Cardinal Wiseman's burning. In contrast, Towcester saw more of the violence that had characterized the Fifth there in earlier years. Some of the "respectable inhabitants" had raised a fund to rent a field away from the town center and to buy fuel for the bonfire. The plan worked, insofar as great fun was had in the field. But after the people returned to town, some of them attempted to enter the Market Hill and a row with the police ensued. Two men were arrested, and the rumor flew that a police truncheon had put out another's eye. This angered many in the crowd, which occupied the Market Hill, drove the police into their headquarters, and smashed the windows of those notables who were thought to be against the customary keeping of the holiday.[65]

In 1852, order started breaking down. At Kettering, where the notables had used Bonfire Night against Robinson and the Jenkinsons, three thousand spectators shouted "Down with Cardinal Wiseman" and "Long Live the Queen" as Guy was burnt, but the evening was marred by accidents. James Foreman, silkweaver, had his shoulder dislocated in the press of the crowd; George Hooper, shoemaker, was seriously burnt when someone pushed him over a burning "jack-in-the-box" and the fireworks in his pockets ignited. And property was endangered when a lighted tow-ball was thrown through the window of a house. An accident also occurred at

---

64 *Ibid.*, 23 Nov. 1850.
65 *Ibid.*, 8 Nov. 1851.

Thrapston, when a firework was thrust into a boy's face. The *Northampton Herald* advised its fellow Tories, "We think it would be much better if a field were chosen for these sports, instead of the market-place and town streets." Things continued badly, at least from the authorities' point of view, in 1853. Although there were no accidents that year at Kettering, the notables reversed themselves and tried to limit the activities. At Towcester, the terse report mentioned only "the usual Protestant demonstrations," as though the authorities hoped that the problem would go away if ignored. And official celebrations sponsored by the Orange Lodge were once again the order of the day at Northampton.[66]

The beginning of the Crimean War gave a new lease of life to the celebrations, and encouraged the Tories to try once again to tame the Fifth for use in their political battles. The Towcester folk were allowed free use of the Market Hill in 1854, with an effigy of Tsar Nicholas substituted for the usual guy, and several notables treated to ale. This strategy reduced violence there to a minimum. At Kettering, the authorities again tried to discourage the popular fête; but some notables hired a brass band, arranged for banners inscribed "Alma," "Down with Sebastopol," and "Old England Forever." (No injuries or damage to property were reported.) The Crimean theme waxed stronger in 1855. The Fifth at Kettering was even more elaborate than the year before. Flags of Turkey, Sardinia, and France, and the Royal Standard were got from London; fifty-six young men, uniformed and bemusketed, put on a mock battle in the Market Square; and the effigy of the Tsar was torn apart by the crowd. Clearly, someone was spending money to turn the Fifth into a loyal demonstration in this Radical-Nonconformist stronghold. (The war also provided the theme at Staverton.)[67]

But once again, things got out of hand. There were more disturbances in 1855 than in 1854. A few "rustics" at Oundle set fire to some tar barrels and managed to roll them down the streets before fleeing the police. At Northampton, William Burgess, nine years old, committed one of those petty crimes associated with Bonfire Night—he stole a shilling from a smaller boy and spent it on fireworks. Things in 1856 were worse still. The Fifth was quiet enough in Wellingborough and Staverton (where the notables treated the village), and almost boring at Kettering ("there was not as much fun as in former years") where there was no guy and no spectacular fireworks. But accidents marred the celebrations. At Kettering, someone set off a piece of a gun barrel stuffed with powder in the Market Hill; it smashed into a chemist's shop, narrowly missing a customer. At Northampton, a squib landed in a carpenter's shop and burnt it to the ground. At Desborough, someone fired a blank pistol into a house, causing a pregnant woman to miscarry.[68] These events, however, were overshadowed by the riot at Irthlingborough.

The respectable people of Irthlingborough had been troubled for some years by what they called "some 'fast' young men" who committed "all

[66] *Ibid.*, 13 Nov. 1852, 12 Nov. 1853.
[67] *Ibid.*, 11 Nov. 1854, 3, 10 Nov. 1855.
[68] *Ibid.*, 10 Nov. 1855, 8, 15 Nov. 1856. Late twentieth-century medical orthodoxy had it that external circumstances did not cause miscarriages. What is important here is that people believed that the sort of behavior common on the Fifth had caused the miscarriage.

sorts of pranks by night."[69] Fearing a row on Bonfire Night, a number of notables, led by Richard Ash Hanniford, the rector, requested of the Chief Constable of Northamptonshire a force sufficient to put down street bonfires and the setting off of fireworks among the thatched cottages. Superintendent Clarke Chambers and a body of constables were despatched, and the result was a riot—a riot started by the police's unprovoked attacks on the villagers, so charged the mysterious J. Saby.[70] Chambers, of course, denied this, and demanded "a full investigation,"[71] which came when several miscreants were hailed before the Wellingborough Petty Sessions.[72]

It is difficult to determine precisely what happened at Irthlingborough, especially since we have only the word of the defendants against that of the police. (All the witnesses for the defense were either related to or friends of those charged.) Nevertheless, a reasonable reconstruction of events and motives can be made.

Some village notables had tried to "reform" Bonfire Night by providing a field and materials for a fire, but it did not work.[73] When Chambers and his men arrived at the village, they found firearms being discharged from pubs, fireworks lit in the streets, and a big bonfire burning in the road. People stood at their doorways, blocking the pavements; a crowd hurled stones at the police, and struck at them with bludgeons, when Chambers led his men towards the bonfire. Having failed to take the bonfire, Chambers tried to clear the streets by marching his men abreast up and down to force people inside their homes. This tactic permitted close contact between police and people; and the exchange of insults reveals that both sides had old scores to settle from past years (and possibly from personal connections, for the police were recruited mainly from local villages[74]). The defendants claimed that the police, hot for action, shouted "Let's go at them," "I recollect you last year, you old humbug," and "We came here last year, and this year we'll do you." The police claimed that William Cox, Sr., one of the defendants, stood in his door and said "You ———, you sha'n't walk here, we pay for this." The defendants claimed that constables tried to push people through their doorways back into their houses, and that they trod on the toes of James West, baker, whose appendages were "just about over the threshold."

Moreover, there was a considerable amount of coming and going, and of drinking. By their own admission, William Cox, Sr., John Saxby, Sr., and John Saxby, Jr., had been in and out of their homes several times during the evening, "to see how things were going on." On at least one of his trips out, Cox fetched a pint of beer apiece for his son, a friend, and himself. Other defendants also had been drinking. John Olney admitted having had two pints in a pub, but claimed to have been sober; James

---

[69] *Ibid.*, 15 Nov. 1856.
[70] Saby's letter is in *ibid.*, 8 Nov. 1856; on the 15th there appears a letter from the notables who had requested the constables, denying that such a person lived in Irthlingborough.
[71] *Ibid.*, 15 Nov. 1856.
[72] The transcript of proceedings, upon which my account is based, appears in the *Northampton Herald*, 29 Nov. 1856. The *Northampton Mercury* of the same date gives only a perfunctory account of the proceedings.
[73] Sup't Chambers, testifying at an application for summonses before the Wellingborough Petty Sessions, 10 Nov. 1856 (*Northampton Herald*, 15 Nov. 1856).
[74] Carolyn Steedman, *Policing the Victorian Community: The Formation of English Provincial Police Forces, 1856-80* (London, 1984), p. 81.

Houghton admitted that "he was not perfectly sober, but said he could walk then as well as he could now."

All this evidence points to the conclusion that both sides were as provocative as they could be. The police probably did want to settle old scores and to provoke illegal acts. But it seems equally likely that the crowd, pot-valiant, sailed as close to the wind as they dared.

Although the defense represented the events at Irthlingborough as a conflict between civil liberties and police repression, the prosecution saw a hidden conflict between more and less respectable elements in the village: "He must take objection to the remark made by the attorney for the defence that the question was one between the police and the public: . . . it was evident it was a question between the superior portion of the inhabitants and another portion. . . ." But the defendants were represented by counsel brought in from Peterborough—most unusual for an offense of this kind in a court of this sort. This suggests that fairly substantial interests stood behind them. The hidden conflict, then, may have had to do with struggles within the village power structure rather than between the power structure and "plebeians."

The violence of 1856 began to do its work, as Tory notables, fearing rows, withdrew their patronage or attempted to "reform" Bonfire Night by providing alternative entertainments. In 1857, the notables of Kettering sponsored a lecture on "Gold, how it is produced, where it is found, how it is got, what becomes of it, and what to do with it"; Market Harborough had a ventriloquist. These attractions probably failed to capture working-class interest, for in 1858, 1859, and 1860, the traditional bonfires and fireworks appeared in Kettering, Market Harborough, Oundle, and Wellingborough. But one can detect a subsidence in the level of popular excitement: bonfires were smaller and guys fewer; and attempts at "reform" seem to have been more successful than in earlier years. After a small row at Market Harborough in 1858, the police managed to transfer the celebrations to a field. At Kettering in 1860, the firing of pistols in volleys and a pyrotechnic display in the grammar school playground also suggest successful reform.[75]

The Guy Fawkes celebrations in Northamptonshire between the early 1840s and 1860 suggest a pattern. By the beginning of the 1840s, the fête, although kept, may well have been moribund. But the Papal Aggression crisis of 1850 revealed its possibilities as a weapon in the warfare between Liberal Nonconformists and Conservative Anglicans, and it was revived under the patronage of the latter group. Quite soon, however, things got out of hand, as the working classes, whose allegiance the fête was intended to secure, found in it the opportunity for "a piss-up and a bovver." The Crimean War allowed the Conservative Anglicans to recapture the fête as a political vehicle; but after a few years, the working classes once again used it for their own purposes. By 1860, the fête's patrons were either withdrawing from participation or "reforming" it. It is interesting to note that the Indian Mutiny, in contrast to the Crimean War, was not adapted to the Fifth. Perhaps the Tory Anglicans feared a repetition of the violence that had frustrated their earlier attempts to use the Fifth. (Certainly the cases of intimidation that characterized the Northampton boot and

[75] *Northampton Herald*, 7 Nov. 1857, 13, 20, 27 Nov. 1858, 12 Nov. 1859, 10 Nov. 1860.

shoemakers' strike in 1857-58 created an atmosphere that might have discouraged notables from providing the opportunity for popular disturbances.[76])

The local "plebeians," as Storch, E. P. Thompson, and others call them, did not use Guy Fawkes Day as a charivari or skeffington to act out grievances or to attack unpopular notables. Only one report of such an instance, at Kettering in 1858, where the effigy of a local notable whom the shoemakers disliked[77] was paraded round the town and burnt, appears in the newspapers.[78] The political content of the Fifth in Northamptonshire, although local in orientation, had to do with national party politics and the struggle for power between middle-class Liberal Nonconformists and the Tory Anglican landed interest, not with "popular" justice, with middle-class attempts to suppress popular culture, or with arcane upper-class quarrels. The attempts to tame or "reform" the Fifth, moreover, which indeed were tried, had to do with the consequences of mixing alcohol and fireworks. The traditional way of keeping the Fifth all too often resulted in missing fingers, scar tissue, and fires.

Finally, we can now see why Northamptonshire generated more signatures to anti-Catholic memorials in 1850 (in proportion to its population) than any other place in England, despite the lack of a statistically significant Irish or Roman Catholic presence. Popular anti-Catholicism in Northamptonshire stemmed not from the abstract fear of a distant and unknown threat, from ethnic conflict between Irish and English, or from class conflict between the workers and the middle class, but rather from the needs of local political battles between ultra-Liberal Nonconformists and Conservative Anglicans.

Bonfire Night in Mid-Victorian Cambridgeshire

The county of Cambridge (and certain nearby places), in contrast to Northants, suggests how local conditions could limit the use of Bonfire Night as a way of whipping up Tory-Anglican sentiment. Cambridge certainly did not lack for political conflicts between Tory Anglicans and Radical Nonconformists, as the politics of city and shire, and the Anti-Corn Law League riot of 1839 illustrate, but the county's agricultural distress during the period 1780-1850 discouraged the mobilization of popular Toryism. Enclosure had turned the peasantry into landless laborers. Wages were low, and high population kept them low. In most parishes, both in the Fenlands and in upland areas, the population density reached its maximum in 1851. The result was rural revolt, at its most spectacular during the "Captain Swing" year (1830), but endemic throughout the 1830s and early 1840s. The introduction of the New Poor Law in 1837 made things worse. Only after 1852, as high farming restored prosperity to the region, did rural protest decline.[79]

---

[76] Stevenson, *Popular Disturbances*, p. 285.

[77] Possibly Charles East (†1875), who introduced the sewing machine into the boot and shoe trade, against great opposition (Greenall, "Kettering," pp. 256-57), or John Plummer, staymaker and writer of anti-trade union verse and pamphlets attacking the limitation of apprenticeships (D. Thompson, *Chartists*, pp. 186-87).

[78] *Northampton Herald*, 13 Nov. 1858.

[79] John E. Archer, *By a Flash and a Scare: Incendiarism, Animal Maiming, and Poaching in East Anglia, 1815-1870* (Oxford, 1990), pp. 7-8; McCord, *Anti-Corn Law League*, pp. 62-63; C. T. Smith,

Although East Anglia was the area most affected by incendiarism, Cambridge participated. Incendiarism, rickburning, and the firing of out-buildings plagued rural areas of the county such as Isleham, Soham, Waterbeach, Cheveley, Kirtling, Chatteris, Fordham, Steeple Morden, Cottenham, and Girton during the 1840s and early 1850s (especially in 1843-44, and in the worst depression years of 1849-52). Nearby villages in Suffolk also saw arson. Some of these incidents represent protests against the reduction of laborers' wages to 7s. per week, but others were arsons to collect insurance, to protest the New Poor Law, or to object to especially brutal or indifferent landowners. On at least one occasion, Bonfire Night provided the cover for arson. Upwood, Hunts,[80] had suffered mysterious burnings in the summer and autumn of 1849. On Bonfire Night, several hayricks were fired shortly after several laborers left a pub, declaring that "the fireworks would soon begin," but no case could be made out against the suspects.[81]

Cambridge city had a rich tradition of rowdy Bonfire Nights. This holiday was the most common time for "town and gown" rows, and the serious disputes between the University and the town corporation over money and legal privileges (disputes not settled until the Cambridge University Act, 1856) exacerbated the rows. But the holiday was quiet in 1849. A few firecrackers were set off at Parker's Piece, near the University Arms, but there were no charges laid in the police court the next day, "a state of affairs unparallelled in Cambridge on the 6th of November."[82] The Papal Aggression changed this momentarily peaceful atmosphere. The *Cambridge Chronicle*, edited by C. W. Naylor, was a Tory-Anglican print. Hence, it denounced the assumption of titles from the first, charging that the papal action had been encouraged by Whig religious policies in Ireland and the colonies, and by "Romanising fooleries that have of late led astray weak-headed enthusiasts." It sneered at what it called the "Uriah Heep" tone of Cardinal Wiseman's *Appeal to the Good Feeling of the English People*. It charged Lord John Russell with hypocrisy in taking advantage of the anti-Catholic feeling, yet putting into the Queen's mouth a tepid response to the memorials of Oxford and Cambridge Universities and the City of London.[83]

As a consequence of the anti-Catholic atmosphere (and also because the on-going disputes between University and town were worsening), Bonfire Night in 1850 was much less placid than it had been the year before. Fearing the prospect of disturbances, both town and University took precautions. Undergraduates were "gated"[84] at nine o'clock that evening, and

---

"The Cambridge region: settlement and population," *The Cambridge Region, 1965*, ed. by J. A. Steers (London, 1965), p. 157; E.J. Hobsbawm and George Rudè, *Captain Swing* (New York, 1968), pp. 284-88; *VCH, Cambridge*, II, 97-99, 116-20; Bruce Galloway, *A History of Cambridgeshire* (Chichester, 1983), pp. 95-103; John Knott, *Popular Opposition to the 1834 Poor Law* (New York, 1986), p. 82.

[80] Near the Bedford Level, Isle of Ely.

[81] *Cambridge Chronicle*, 30 June, 21 July, 4, 18 Aug., 1, 29 Sept., 13, 20 Oct., 12 Nov., 1 Dec. 1849, 23 Mar. 1850, 2, 9, 16, 23 Mar. 1851; David Jones, *Crime, Protest, Community and Police in Nineteenth-Century Britain* (London, 1982), p. 34; Archer, *By a Flash and a Scare*, pp. 102-19, 149.

[82] *Cambridge Chronicle*, 10 Nov. 1849 (quoted); Galloway, *Cambridgeshire*, pp. 118-20; Glynn Thomas and Enid Porter, *Victorian Cambridge* (London, 1969), p. 18; F. A. Reeve, *Cambridge* (New York, 1964), pp. 92-104, 132.

[83] *Cambridge Chronicle*, 19 (quoted), 26 Oct., 2, 23, 30 Nov., 14 Dec. 1850.

[84] Confined to their colleges.

University officials patrolled the streets. But at ten o'clock a group of townsmen left Parker's Piece, paraded the streets, and harassed an undergraduate. The result was a row when other undergraduates, out for a lark, fought back. Another row occurred the next evening when some gownsmen, looking for revenge, met up with some townsmen looking for a fight. And the day after that, a group of townsmen beat up an undergraduate.[85]

The Cambridge Tories, however, found it difficult to turn opposition to the Papal Aggression into anything more lasting than an undergraduate lark. The Roman Catholics themselves fought back when Thomas Quinlivan, priest at Cambridge, read Bishop William Wareing's conciliatory pastoral letter,[86] and preached a sermon on 10 November in which he argued that the new jurisdiction applied to Roman Catholics alone. And many of the local Dissenters, "infected with Mr.-Edward-Miallism," resisted joining the anti-Catholic opposition.[87] Naylor of the *Chronicle* denounced Whigs and Romanists at the Willingham Agricultural Society's annual dinner, and in the new year attacked the Ecclesiastical Titles Bill as "a wretched sham." He was aided by the Rev. Jonathan Holt Titcomb,[88] incumbent of St. Andrew-the-Less, who circulated a memorial to the Queen, used the local auxiliaries of the Church of England Young Men's Society and the Religious Tract Society to vent anti-Catholic rhetoric, and in the new year preached a course of controversial sermons at Christ Church against popery.[89] Their problem was that they did not know how to counter the Papist threat in a positive way.

> The movement of Rome has excited an almost unparallelled feeling of indignation in the public mind. But it runs the risk of being directed into profitless channels, or worse, of degenerating into a senseless crusade. . . . We want to see something practical come out of the declamation that rings around. Something requires to be *done*, and done by the legislature. What is it to be? Can we move consistently except in a backward direction?[90]

The Cambridge Tories eventually got up a meeting of the Protestant inhabitants on 17 December. In the course of moving the first resolution, which protested the Pope's infringement of the Royal Supremacy, Alderman R. M. Fawcett proclaimed that Anglicanism was the bulwark of Protestant truth. He was interrupted by cries of "No State Church," "No Bishops," and "No Church Rates." The Rev. Mr. Bubier, Congregationalist, then came up from the floor to move an amendment opposing interference with religious freedom, arguing that no Nonconformist could support the first resolution, for the very existence of Dissent denied the Queen's spiritual supremacy. Later, Later, the Chartist Henry Hall moved an amendment to the effect that no legislation was required. Although both amendments failed, they indicate the sources of opposition to Tory-Anglican loyalism. (The petition adopted at this meeting was not placed in the Town Hall for signatures until 2 January, by which time one sus-

[85] *Ibid.*, 9 Nov. 1850.
[86] *Sup.*, p. 97.
[87] *Cambridge Chronicle*, 16, 23 Nov. 1850.
[88] Titcomb (1819-1887), moderate Evangelical; curate in Ireland, 1842-44, and perpetual curate of St. Andrew-the-Less, Cambridge, 1845-59, later was the first Bishop of Rangoon, 1877-82, where he fell over a cliff (*DNB*, XIX, 897-98).
[89] *Cambridge Chronicle*, 2, 30 Nov., 7, 14 Dec. 1850, 11 Jan., 15 Feb., 15 Mar. 1851.
[90] *Ibid.*, 23 Nov. 1850.

pects that ardor had cooled.) A county meeting, attended by about three hundred, was held on 1 February 1851. There, it was the Tories who formed the opposition, Alderman Fawcett moving an amendment that attacked concessions to Roman Catholics (especially the Maynooth grant) "by successive governments." The Earl of Hardwicke, who had moved the original resolution, explained that the meeting's organizers, seeking unanimity, had decided to avoid attacks on governments. Fawcett persisted with his amendment, which carried.[91]

Bonfire Night in 1851 returned to relative quiet in Cambridge city. The University authorities restrained the undergraduates, and no political issues arose to inflame sentiment or to inspire rowdies to go out and bash each other.[92]

One other popular holiday, Plough Monday, was available as a forum for loyalist demonstrations. This happened in 1851 at Downham, Isle of Ely, where some notables treated unemployed laborers, arranged for the ceremonial burning of the Pope, and stressed the connections among traditional village fêtes, anti-Catholicism, and opposition to free trade.[93] But it was not safe to do this in Cambridge city, where "Molly dancers," men from outlying villages who by tradition converged on Cambridge with blackened faces and adorned with bells and ribbons, begged money, drank, cracked whips, took over the streets, and then went home tiddly or worse.[94] The chances for insults, insolence, and brawls were numerous.

In Cambridgeshire, in contrast to Northants, the potential for uncontrolled public violence lay too near the surface for Tories to risk exploiting popular revels in their political warfare. Lacking the necessary middle-class and landed political support, fêtes such as Bonfire Night and Plough Monday remained in the limbo of underfunded, spontaneoulsy organized, and thus sporadic, popular customs.

The Anti-Catholic Anti-Police Riot

Elsewhere in England, mass demonstrations using the symbols of Bonfire Night provided an opportunity to affirm loyalty, solidarity, and cultural cohesion. Southern England, where Bonfire Night was common anyway, saw several such demonstrations during the months of November and December 1850.[95] They shared many characteristics: elaborate effigies of Pius IX and Wiseman dressed in "full pontificals" and sometimes horned; men dressed as monks and nuns; a torchlit procession; anti-Catholic, patriotic, and sometimes anti-Tractarian shouts and banners; and a ceremonial burning in a public place, accompanied by patriotic songs.[96]

These demonstrations represent expensive and well-organized efforts, sponsored by the gentry and shopkeepers of the neighborhood. When such a demonstration was planned for Greenwich and Lewisham in December of 1851, F. M. Mallalieu, the alert divisional superintendent of the

---

[91] *Ibid.*, 21 Dec. 1850, 4 Jan., 8 Feb. 1851.
[92] *Ibid.*, 8 Nov. 1851.
[93] *Ibid.*, 18 Jan. 1851.
[94] *Ibid.*, 12 Jan. 1851; Thomas and Porter, *Victorian Cambridge*, p. 10.
[95] Among them were demonstrations at Peckham, Salisbury, Clapham, and Croyden; Tewkesbury (Glos) and Ware (Herts) also had such demonstrations.
[96] *Times*, 14, 15, 21, 25, 30 Nov. 1850; *Illustrated London News*, 30 Nov. 1850; *Manchester Examiner*, 30 Nov. 1850; *Manchester Guardian*, 21 Dec. 1850.

Greenwich Division, Metropolitan Police, investigated and found that tradesmen had collected donations from many of the gentry and organized the march. He warned the tradesmen "of the responsibility they would incur should any disturbance of the peace take place," and got them to reschedule the procession so as not to have it on the same day that the new Roman Catholic chapel at Greenwich was to be opened.[97] Certainly these demonstrations demanded more money than shopkeepers could spare, and therefore required gentry support. But the participation of the working classes—the marchers and torch-bearers—posed the threat of violence; the "herculean fellow" who carried the Pope's effigy on a long pole at Peckham could as easily smash windows or crack skulls. The fear of violence was always there.

Occasionally, the "respectable" clearly controlled the revel, as at Leicester in 1844, where the Collegiate School laid on a bonfire and fireworks, with the Duke of Rutland supplying the band.[98] Local officials always had reason to fear the accidental, thoughtless, or malicious discharge of fireworks, for fireworks caused physical injury, sometimes permanent, to children and adults.[99] Occasionally, local officials were overcautious, as George Martin, superintendent of the Clerkenwell Division, Metropolitan Police, thought, when remembering having been sent, with sixty constables, to put down a bonfire riot at Lewes during the Papal Aggression crisis. Martin thought that the police had been summoned because the year previous the crowd had threatened to chuck an officious interferer into the river; in Martin's opinion, half the number of constables would have been sufficient.[100] Nevertheless, the fear of riot was real, for the most sustained religious disturbances during the nineteenth century were Bonfire Night riots, where crowds were ostensibly Protestant, but directed their violence towards the police, not towards Roman Catholics. This sort of disturbance, as that in Northamptonshire so clearly shows, is connected with problems of local politics, public order, and working-class entertainments.

Bonfire Night appears to have been moribund in much of England during the early nineteenth century. It is true that newspapers did not report consistently Bonfire Night observances, especially when the fête was peaceful or the revellers mainly children. Yet although the holiday may not have been quite so moribund, as phrases such as "as usual," "this annual commemoration," and "countenanced rather more than usual on account of Cardinal Wiseman's late elevation" suggest, it is clear that the Papal Aggression gave it renewed interest.[101] The national working-class press (admittedly with London-centered and vaguely radical perspectives) treated the holiday as a subject fit for nostalgia or ridicule.[102] In one of these penny dreadfuls, Guy Fawkes Day was a hook on which to hang a romantic story, in which Mr. Botherum, Cecily's guardian, would not let

[97] F. M. Mallalieu to Sir R. Mayne, 12 Dec. 1851, Home Office: Registered Papers, PRO, H.O. 45/3783.

[98] *Leicester Journal*, 8 Nov. 1844.

[99] For five examples of physical injury, widely separated in time and place, see *Leicestershire Mercury*, 9 Nov. 1844, *Leeds Mercury*, 8 Nov. 1845, *Cambridge Chronicle*, 10 Nov. 1849, *Preston Pilot*, 9 Nov. 1850, *Birmingham Mercury*, 8 Nov. 1851.

[100] "Second Report from the Select Committee on Police," *PP*, 1852-53, XXXVI (715), 265.

[101] *Leeds Mercury*, 8 Nov. 1845, 9 Nov. 1850; *Cambridge Chronicle*, 10 Nov. 1849.

[102] *Family Herald*, I (4 Nov. 1843), 413-14; *Lloyd's Entertaining Journal*, VI (5 Dec. 1846), 223; *Lloyd's Weekly Miscellany*, II (1850-52), 144.

her marry Charles Chatterley. (Chatterley disguised himself as a guy to get into the garden for a rendezvous with Cecily.) Botherum's Protestantism was presented to the working-class reader as a specimen of humbuggery, pomposity, and silliness. "Bless my heart," Botherum natters,

> yes, it is the fifth of November, and I had quite forgotten it. The fifth of November. The idea now that I should forget the great occasion when the flagrant and abominable attempt was made to blow up the highly protestant parliament of this great and finely-taxed country. The idea of my forgetting the fifth of November.[103]

In some places, however, Bonfire Night was a living tradition that presented serious problems, despite the attempts of the authorities to control it. Riots often followed upon these attempts, as at Wakefield in 1849, when the crowd rolled a flaming tar barrel among the police, besieged them in their station, rescued miscreants from custody, savaged a suspected police spy, and danced and drank about the bonfire in the Bull Ring (a triangular space in front of the Stafford Arms).[104]

In Exeter, a semisecret society ("Young Exeter") put on the Bonfire Night fêtes.[105] Made up of the sons of Tory shopkeepers and merchants, the society promoted an annual night of revelry that had little to do with class conflict and that indeed scandalized Liberals. During the 1840s, however, the *Western Times*, the Liberal newspaper, came to fear Anglo-Catholicism and Roman Catholicism; it joined the Conservative Evangelical *Flying Post* in disliking the policies of Henry Phillpotts, High Church Bishop of Exeter (who was seen, unfairly, as a crypto-Puseyite). Thus both Liberals and Tories came to use Bonfire Night as a weapon in local political disputes. (The cathedral yard, venue of the bonfire, was the perfect place from which to attack the bishop.) These no-popery demonstrations blended into the Surplice Riots of 1844-45 and 1848. Phillpotts had determined to enforce the rubric that required clergymen to preach in the surplice, hoping thereby to deprive the vestment of its significance as an Anglo-Catholic symbol. But the result was protest. Several clergy[106] opposed Phillpotts and cooperated with the bishop's lay political enemies; those clergymen who wore the vestment were mobbed in the streets and howled down in their churches. A clergyman who appealed to the mayor to suppress the demonstrations was told that he had brought it on himself.[107]

The Exeter disturbances were relatively limited in their scope, thanks, no doubt, to the role that they played in local politics. Bonfire Night at Guildford, however, was much more serious.[108] The authorities had with-

103 *Lloyd's Weekly Miscellany*, I (1849-50), 37-38.

104 *Northampton Herald*, 10 Nov. 1849.

105 Storch, "Fifth of November," pp. 76-77, 85, discusses Bonfire Night in Exeter, but must be read with care. See also Robert Newton, *Victorian Exeter, 1837-1914* (Leicester, 1968), pp. 55-58; and Wolffe, "Phillpotts and the Administration of the Diocese of Exeter," pp. 99-113.

106 Including the Rev. J. Bull, Canon of Exeter, who used similar demonstrations in his living at Staverton, Northants, a decade later.

107 John Ingle to Sir George Grey, 15 Nov. 1848, Home Office: Registered Papers, PRO, H.O. 45/2321.

108 See Gavin Morgan, "The Guildford Guy Riots (1842-1865)," *Surrey Archæological Collections*, LXXVI (1985), 61-68; Storch, "Fifth of November," pp. 89, 91-92; and William Taylor (Mayor) to H. Waddington, 12 Nov. 1853, Home Office: Registered Papers, PRO, H.O. 45/5128, pp. 405, 406.

drawn their patronage from the revel during the last quarter of the eighteenth century, and attempted to tame it by forbidding the use of fireworks. Although they gave up the attempt in 1829, public disturbances remained at a tolerably low level during the 1830s and '40s. Members of the secret society (the "Guildford Guys") thought that what they were doing was simply good fun; and some notables supported the revel from feelings of tradition (and, one suspects, of nostalgia for their own lost youth). It became the custom there for men and youths from outlying villages to rendezvous in the town and pull down fences for the bonfire. Groups of men wearing masks and female attire, and carrying clubs, would "beg" from house to house.[109] The Papal Aggression crisis, however, excited the Guildford Guys to a higher level of activity. The bonfires were bigger (which meant that more fences were pulled down), the crowds larger, and a boy was killed playing with fireworks. Several notables complained to the Home Office, and the town authorities determined to suppress the fête. In 1853, the authorities swore in three hundred special constables and got ten Metropolitan Police as leaders; this force kept order. But the Guys replied in 1854 by smashing the windows of prominent townsmen who were thought to be against the revel. Bonfire Night, 1855, was peaceful, but there were riots in 1856 and 1857 when the police and special constables attacked the crowds, leading to charges of police brutality. (One man was killed in 1857.) The authorities withdrew from the battle from 1858 to 1862. Destruction of property continued, but with selectivity, focusing on notables whose unpopularity stemmed from their opposition to the revel.[110]

The Guildford town authorities determined once again to suppress the Guildford Guys in 1863 because the level of violence was beginning to exceed toleration. Bonfire Night in 1862 had resulted in the burning of an unoccupied house; its owner complained to the Home Office, which in turn inquired of the town authorities. Moreover, the Guys appeared to be trying to extend their area of claimed power when they lit a fire in March 1863 for the Prince of Wales's wedding. Finally, the townsmen's custom of throwing chestnuts at one another on the Sunday before the annual St. Catherine's Hill fair in October got out of hand, prompting complaints in the *Times* and the *West Surrey Times*, and to the Home Office. The local magistrates appealed to the Home Office for help from the Metropolitan Police and the army, and armed the town police with cutlasses; invoking these firm measures in 1863, 1864, and 1865 resulted in the suppression of Bonfire Night at Guildford.[111]

Gravesend and Dartford in Kent had similar traditions. At Gravesend, crowds marched by torchlight, carried clubs, wore disguises, lit fireworks, burned effigies, and extorted money by threat of violence. Rival groups of

[109] Morgan, "Guildford Guy Riots," pp. 61-63.

[110] *Ibid.*, pp. 64-65; Rev. W. Walford to S. Walpole, 6 Nov. 1852, Home Office: Registered Papers, PRO, H.O. 45/5128, p. 411; Rev. Henry Shrubb to S. Walpole, 8 Nov. 1852, *ibid.*, p. 408; Guildford Justices to Lord Palmerston, 25 Oct. 1853, *ibid.*, p. 416; Henry Fitzroy to J. H. Smallpiece, 12 Nov. 1853, Home Office: Entry Books: Domestic and General, PRO, H.O. 43/84, p. 4.

[111] Morgan, "Guildford Guy Riots," pp. 65-66; Mark Dowlen to Sir G. Grey, 6 Nov. 1862, Home Office: Registered Papers, PRO, H.O. 45/7324, p. 2; W. Piper (Mayor) to Sir G. Grey, 5 Nov. 1862, *ibid.*, pp. 4-6; Lt. Col. Francis D. Gray to Horse Guards, 4 Nov. 1863, *ibid.*, H.O. 45/7443, pp. 41-42; P. W. Jacob (Mayor) to Sir G. Grey, 22 Nov. 1863, *ibid.*, pp. 96-98; Mark Smallpiece to Sir G. Grey, 15 Dec. 1863, *ibid.*, pp. 2-3.

extorters sometimes fought over begging rights to territory. The Papal Aggression combined with a local circumstance—the purchase of a redundant chapel-of-ease for use as a Roman Catholic chapel—to turn part of the fête in 1852 to window-smashing and the attempted arson of the chapel.[112] At Dartford, the mayor and aldermen attempted to suppress the revel in 1863 against the wishes of the artisans and their employers, and a riot ensued. The officials were more successful in the following year, when they enrolled the employers as special constables, thus compelling them to pressure their own workers.[113]

Although anti-Catholicism was the formal justification for these disturbances, the real concerns of the participants lay elsewhere. Only rarely did Roman Catholics (or Anglo-Catholics) receive the crowd's attentions. Basically, the crowds wanted to have fun by engaging in a time-honored revel that sanctioned exciting explosives and bonfires, public drinking to excess, uninhibited play, and the temporary release of social strictures. From the crowds' point of view, the destruction of property and the occasional injury or death were small prices to pay for the pleasure, especially if it were someone else's property, or if it were someone else's child who was hurt or killed. When the civic authorities or the respectable notables, who placed a higher value on property and life, attempted to reform the revels by forbidding dangerous explosives and fires or by substituting more boring activities, the crowds responded by defending their accustomed play with violence. (And violence against the police offered its own excitement.) Bonfire Night, and the violence associated with it, was void of ideological content, at least insofar as its working-class participants were concerned. When there was ideological content, it was because the fête was part of the ongoing class conflict between the middle and the landed classes.

The Pro-Catholic Anti-Police Riot

The second sort of anti-police riot having a religious dimension is that in which Irish Roman Catholics attacked the police. Here, the catalyst was a public meeting, the purpose of which the Irish Roman Catholics found to be objectionable, and which they attempted to break up.[114] They fought with an ostensibly neutral force—the police—rather than with the organizers and supporters of the meeting. Attempting to take over other people's meetings was a great Victorian pastime,[115] and anti-Catholic organizers were alive to the danger. The organizers of memorial drives at both Preston and St. Helens in 1850 decided to collect signatures privately, rather than call public meetings, because Roman Catholics made up a large proportion of the towns' populations. (The organizers claimed that they feared riots; but they also may have feared that the meetings would be taken over and their resolutions defeated.)[116]

Several major battles between Irish Roman Catholics and the police occurred during the 1850s and early '60s.

112 Gravesend Town Clerk to Ld. Palmerston, 22 Oct. 1853, *ibid.*, H.O. 45/5128, pp. 422-24.

113 Conley, *Unwritten Law*, pp. 35-37.

114 Given the history of violence at public meetings, it is naive to think that they were "a safety-valve channelling emotions to legal and more importantly, peaceful ends" (Klaus, *Pope, Protestants, and Irish*, p. 214).

115 *Sup.*, pp. 24-25.

116 *Preston Pilot*, 23 Nov. 1850; *Manchester Courier*, 14 Dec. 1850.

Hugh McNeile's Liverpool is the obvious place to begin, for it enjoyed the most tense sectarian politics anywhere during the nineteenth century. P. J. Waller calls McNeile, an Ulsterman and incumbent of St. Jude's from 1834, "the real creator" of Liverpool Conservatism.[117] A brilliant and effective anti-Catholic orator, McNeile was a welcome guest on anti-Catholic platforms, and by midcentury was a potent symbol to both Protestants and Roman Catholics. Thus it was that he became the focus of riotous behavior at the Liverpool public meeting of 20 November 1850. The meeting, open to all inhabitants, filled the Amphitheatre; and many present were Irish Roman Catholics. The program included speakers against the anti-Catholic resolutions (including the M.P. Richard Lalor Sheil[118]), and great confusion reigned as partisans among the audience screamed, hissed, and booed. But when Hugh McNeile rose to speak, all hell broke loose. Unable to address the audience, McNeile began dictating his speech to the newspaper reporters. This act of defiance infuriated the Irish Roman Catholics, and they attacked the platform.

[T]he uproar at this moment became deafening. . . . The malcontents . . . jumped from the pit upon the reporters' table and made a *sortis* upon the platform. The confusion at this moment was indescribable. Inkstands were upset, and notebooks and slips of copy were flying about in all directions. The reporters were compelled, of course, to leave their seats and take refuge upon the platform. At this moment a body of the police, armed with their staves, made their appearance, and attempted to drive the invaders back into the pit.[119]

The Liverpool police were not to be trusted as guardians of order when it came to sectarian warfare. Although Edward Rushton, the stipendiary magistrate, Michael Whitley and Matthew Dowling, the chief constables, and several mayors attempted to root out Orangeism in the force, they were unable to bring even-handed law enforcement to Liverpool until July 1852, when Mayor Thomas Littledale and Chief Constable Greig forbade all Orange processions and arrested Orangemen on charges of unlawful assembly. Several members of the Liverpool Watch Committee were brewers, spirit merchants, and publicans, who interfered in the internal administration of the police. The constables themselves were of low literacy, and many of them were Orangemen. This was unfortunate, for the Liverpool police (at 806 officers and men, the largest force outside London in 1851) sometimes came to the aid of the authorities in neighboring towns.[120] Their sectarian biases contributed to the Birkenhead Riot of 27 November 1850.

[117] P. Waller, *Democracy and Sectarianism*, pp. 11-12.

[118] A clever and ambitious Irish Roman Catholic politician, Sheil (1791-1851) wrote plays while a briefless barrister; supported Daniel O'Connell, but also got along well with English Whig politicians; M.P. for Milborne Port, Dorset, 1831, County Louth, 1831-32, County Tipperary, 1832-41, Dungarvan, 1841-50. His ambition for office led him to drift out of touch with his constituents, but his offices (Commissioner of Greenwich Hospital, 1837-38; Vice President, Board of Trade, 1838-41; Master of the Mint, 1846-50; Minister to Tuscany, 1851) did not match his sense of what he deserved. (*DNB*, XVIII, 17-21.)

[119] *Times*, 21 Nov. 1850.

[120] Neal, *Sectarian Violence*, pp. 60-62, 133, 144-46, 156; P. Waller, *Democracy and Sectarianism*, pp. 8, 22; M.M.G. Dowling (Head Constable) to John Bent (Mayor of Liverpool), 7 July 1851, Home Office: Registered Papers, PRO, H.O. 45/3472L-M, pp. 10-12; "A Well Conducted Protestant—a true Whig" to Sir G. Grey, 19 July 1851, *ibid.*, p. 16; evidence of Thomas

The Birkenhead Riot clearly illustrates the interplay of religious prejudices, social stratification, and too ready resort to violence on the part of
both police and Irish—elements that marked other similar riots.[121]

The affair began like any other public meeting, when a group of local
notables, chaired by the Evangelical layman Sir Edward Cust,[122] presented
a requisition for a public meeting of inhabitants to protest the assumption
of titles. The Birkenhead magistrates called a meeting at the Town Hall for
one o'clock in the afternoon of 27 November, but took it upon themselves
to limit the meeting to ratepayers. They also asked for assistance from the
Liverpool police. (Birkenhead had its own force, under the town commissioners, but often asked Liverpool for cooperation.[123]) Meanwhile, a group
of about forty leading Roman Catholics, guided by Edward F. Browne,
the parish priest, and Edward Bretherton, solicitor, prepared counterreso-
lutions, which they intended to introduce at the meeting.

The magistrates assembled at the town hall at nine in the morning of
the 27th, and rushed through their business in about ten or fifteen minutes. They then proceeded to clear and lock the hall; this manoeuvre took
about three-quarters of an hour. The doors were locked at ten o'clock, and
a crowd of about two hundred persons, mainly Irish workers, moved to the
square before the town hall to await admission to the meeting; their numbers swelled to about eight or nine hundred during the following hour. A
detachment of Liverpool police arrived at about eleven, pushed their way
through the crowd into the town hall, and then emerged and attempted to
disperse the crowd. The crowd was both unwilling and (due to the press
of numbers) unable to disperse; so the police used their truncheons and
received a hail of stones in reply. The crowd dispersed; and so ended what
witnesses later called "the first row."

But some of the crowd went to the docks, then under construction, collected spades, iron bars, and sticks, and reassembled at the town hall
around half past noon. Meanwhile, the Roman Catholic committee had
been having a last-minute meeting at Bretherton's law offices. Hearing
that members of the crowd were armed, the parish priest Browne and
Bretherton went to the town hall. Browne addressed the crowd, the majority of which were his parishioners, and asked them to give up their
weapons. Most put their weapons down under the wall upon which
Browne was standing; but many took them up again when the police
moved in to collect them.

At this point, the hour of the meeting having arrived, the Roman Catholic committee, followed by the crowd, attempted to enter the hall.

Heagren Redin, former chief superintendent, North Division, Liverpool Borough Police, "First
Report from the Select Committee on Police," *PP*, 1852-53, XXXVI (603), 94-95.

[121] The riot is reconstructed from statements produced by the leaders of the Birkenhead Roman
Catholic community ("A Statement of the Case respecting the late disturbance in Birkenhead," [ca.
9 Dec. 1850], Home Office: Registered Papers, PRO, H.O. 45/3140, pp. 43-63) and by the Birkenhead town magistrates (Messrs Townsend and Kent to Sir G. Grey, 19 Dec. 1850, *ibid.*, pp. 16-18),
and from the report of the trial of the rioters at the Cheshire Assizes (*Chester Courant*, 9 Apr. 1851).
The report of the riot in the *Times* (29 Nov. 1850) is inaccurate and claims the presence of soldiers
(who were not there).

[122] Cust (1794-1878), an army officer, 1810, half-pay from 1822; M.P., 1818-32; equerry to Prince
Leopold of Saxe-Coburg from 1816; knighted, 1831; master of ceremonies to the Queen, 1847-76;
author of the Evangelical tracts *Noctes Dominicæ, or Sunday night readings* (1848), and *Family
reading, the New Testament narrative* (1850) (Boase, I, 796-97).

[123] "First Report, Select Committee on Police," *PP*, 1852-53, XXXVI (603), 113.

About ten of the Roman Catholics were admitted, but then the police barred the doors to the rest. Pushing and scuffling soon led to the use of truncheons; the police charged the square; and the "second row" began. In about ten minutes of fighting, several policemen were beaten. The Birkenhead magistrates adjourned the meeting "until the Inhabitants can be assembled to express their opinions with the Freedom of Englishmen."[124]

The Roman Catholics complained to the Home Office, and eventually asked for an investigation. For their part, the Birkenhead magistrates blamed the Roman Catholics and determined to prosecute to the fullest. Six men were arrested: John Brown, shoemaker and rate-payer; and Peter Fitzsimmon, Matthew Griffin, William Haggarty, John Feehan, and Edward Smith, all navvies engaged in building the Birkenhead docks. The Roman Catholic community was furious. They believed that Brown, who had been arrested at his home in the middle of the night, had been charged in the hopes that the public would think he was the priest Browne; they resented that the navvies were denied bail. Hauled before Quarter Sessions, the men were charged with conspiracy to riot, and their cases sent to the Assizes.[125]

Although all the witnesses at the trial agreed upon the sequence of events, the evidence against the defendants varied in quality. Fitzsimmon and Griffin brought in witnesses to give them alibis, but the jury did not believe the testimony. Later, Mr. Justice Edward Vaughan Williams,[126] who had tried the case at the Cheshire Assizes, reviewed the proceedings for the Home Office and commented: "although I cannot go so far as to express a decided opinion that the verdict against [Fitzsimmon] was wrong, I certainly feel much doubt whether he was present at the Riot."[127]

More serious, several of the witnesses were clearly prepared to let their anti-Catholicism color their testimony about the roles of Edward Bretherton and the Rev. Edward F. Browne in the "second row." John Grimley of the Liverpool Police, one of those beaten, claimed that Bretherton went into the Town Hall, put his head out the window, and shouted "Now men, now's the time." Thomas Thomlinson, sergeant of the Liverpool Police, described the 'second row' thus:

> After the mob came up from the dock with stones, Priest Brown [sic] addressed the mob. After he had finished, Priest Brown went into the Town Hall. The mob called out, "Are we to come in." Priest Brown said, "Yes all of you come in." A rush was then made at the door, and the second row began.

And Richard Brown, shoemaker of Market Street, Birkenhead, "described the conduct of Priest Brown [sic] and Mr. Bretherton, and from what he saw inferred that they were urging the people to a riot." These witnesses'

[124] Handbill, "Public Notice," 27 Nov. 1850, Home Office: Registered Papers, PRO, H.O. 45/3140, p. 12.

[125] Bretherton to Grey, 9 Dec. 1850, *ibid.*, pp. 37-38; handbill, "Public Notice," 3 Dec. 1850, *ibid.*, p. 76; Townsend and Kent to Grey, 4 Dec. 1850, *ibid.*, pp. 70-71; Bretherton to Grey, 17 Dec. 1850, *ibid.*, p. 21; *Chester Courant*, 1 Jan. 1851.

[126] Vaughan Williams (1797-1875) studied at Lincoln's Inn; barrister, 1823-46; judge, Court of Common Pleas, 1846-65; knighted, 1847; legal scholar and man of letters; "his profound learning combined with an unusual amount of common sense" (*DNB*, XXI, 396-97).

[127] Vaughan Williams to Grey, 16 Apr. 1851, Home Office: Registered Papers, PRO, H.O. 45/3472J-K, p. 22.

use of the construction "Priest Brown" indicates their bias; for such a usage, when referring to a Roman Catholic priest, was common in the anti-Catholic literature of the day, especially that of the Protestant operative societies.

The Birkenhead Roman Catholics attempted a spirited defense of their coreligionists; they briefed John Arthur Roebuck, the noted Q.C. and Radical M.P. Roebuck did his best, charging that the magistrates had been wrong to limit the meeting to ratepayers, and that the police had started the "first row," as they attempted to disperse a legal assembly with excessive force.

> The police came out of the office without any symptom of disturbance in the crowd; and commenced "tapping" the rear ranks of the crowd, to force them backward. They knew what "tapping" by a policeman's stick meant; and the effect of it was such that the crowd, though legally assembled gave way, and were pursued over the ground like dogs hunted from a spot on which they had no right to come, and both men and women were knocked down with inhuman barbarity.

But Roebuck did have to admit that the "second row" was indefensible.

For his part, John Evans, Q.C.,[128] for the prosecution, played the anti-Catholic card.

> Instructed by Roman Catholics his learned friend [Roebuck] seemed to have become embued with their feelings. . . . [B]ecause Rome had attempted to set her sandalled foot on our country, the body of the people had resolved to resist an aggression which as Englishmen they could not brook.

Mr. Justice Williams's summation was about as fair as could be expected. He praised Browne, the Roman Catholic priest, for taking weapons from the crowd and for asking them to be peaceable, but he regretted that Browne had not sent them home. He said that a riot had been proved, and that the question for the jury was whether the defendants had participated. After examining the evidence, the judge called for the jury to be fair in its deliberations, avoiding prejudice against either Roman Catholics or police. The jury acquitted the shoemaker John Brown, but convicted the navvies. Three were sentenced to nine months imprisonment (with credit for three already served), and two received a year.

The Birkenhead Roman Catholics were furious at what they considered to have been an injustice, and renewed their demand that the Home Office investigate the conduct of the Birkenhead magistrates. Now the Home Office had already received a report from Lt. Gen. Earl Cathcart, commanding in Manchester, stating that the riot would not have happened had the magistrates taken the proper precautions of enrolling special constables and summoning the army. And Mr. Justice Williams, although declining to judge the magistrates' conduct, did blame the Liverpool Police for acting injudiciously and unjustifiably in taking "too peremptory & too active measures" against the crowd.[129]

---

[128] Evans (1796-1864); Q.C., 1837; Liberal M.P. for Haverfordwest, 1847-52 (Boase, I, 1004).

[129] Bretherton to Grey, 17 Dec. 1850, *ibid.*, H.O. 45/3140, p. 22; Bretherton to Grey, 10 Apr. 1851, *ibid.*, H.O. 45/3472J-K, p. 16; Cathcart to Grey, 4 Jan. 1851, *ibid.*, H.O. 45/3472A-D, p. 3; Edward Vaughan Williams to Grey, 16 Apr. 1851, *ibid.*, H.O. 45/3472J-K, pp. 19-21.

In the Birkenhead Riot, preexisting religious hatreds and the propensity to use excessive force to settle matters, on the parts of both the Liverpool Police and the Irish navvies, combined with the provocation of a public meeting sure to spew out anti-Catholic rhetoric to make violence almost inevitable. The Birkenhead affair was not an "Attack upon Protestants by a Mob of Irish Papists," as some contemporary newspapers charged.[130] Nor was it "anti-Catholic rioting," as some present-day scholars think.[131] Rather, it was a conflict between two decidedly partisan groups.

Riots along similar lines happened elsewhere and later. At Wolverhampton in June 1858, the anti-Catholic lectures of André Massena (*soi-disant* Baron de Camin) provoked a row. His first lecture was broken up by Irish laborers and colliers. The following night, the crowd stoned the lecture hall and the Riot Act was read, but the crowd withdrew grudgingly, if in relative peace, under pressure from the police. The third lecture went off without violence.[132]

The Garibaldi Riots of 1862 in Hyde Park and Birkenhead were more serious, involving, in the case of London, several weeks of brawls in the park. These instances followed the pattern of the 1850 Birkenhead Riot. An objectionable public meeting roused Irish ire and resulted in a clash between them and the meeting's guardians (the police, or, in the case of the Hyde Park riots, off-duty soldiers). For Italian exiles and English Liberals, Garibaldi and the cause of Italian unification stood for freedom and enlightenment. For Irish, however, those causes stood for anti-Catholicism. In the case of the Birkenhead Garibaldi Riots, Sir Edward Cust, leader of the 1850 anti-Catholic requisitionists, was active in promoting the pro-Garibaldi meeting; the Anglican clergyman in whose parish hall the meeting was held was a known Orangeman. Even the notices of the meeting were printed in orange ink! The meeting, on 8 October, was broken up. Determined not to be intimidated, the organizers rescheduled for the 15th. That night saw a pitched battle between the police and the crowd. Because the parish hall was in an Irish neighborhood, the rioters were able to retreat up side-streets, and the police were pelted by stones and bricks. There was considerable damage to property. Local anti-Catholics accused Roman Catholic leaders of fomenting the disturbances. And Orangemen crossed over from Liverpool, hoping for a fight.[133]

The popular disturbances described here were rather few in number, and occurred either at times of high popular excitement or when an especially nororious or abusive anti-Catholic lecturer provided the spark for violence. Moreover, in a few instances, heavy-handed police behavior was a contributory factor. Finally, at times the Irish community labored under a sense of unfair treatment, as in the case of the 1850 Birkenhead Riot, when the town officials engineered things so as to deny them a hearing.

[130] *Leeds Mercury*, 30 Nov. 1850, copying *Liverpool Times*, 28 Nov. 1850.

[131] Norman, *English Catholic Church*, p. 203 (quoted); Kirk, *Working Class Reformism*, p. 316.

[132] Roger Swift, "Anti-Catholicism and Irish Disturbances: Public Order in Mid-Victorian Wolverhampton," *Midland History*, IX (1984), 90-94.

[133] F. Neal, "The Birkenhead Garibaldi Riots of 1862," *Transactions of the Historic Society of Lancashire and Cheshire*, CXXXI (1981), 87-111; Sheridan Gilley, "The Garibaldi Riots of 1862," *HJ*, XVI (1973), 709-14; P. Smith, *Policing Victorian London*, pp. 150-59; letters to the home secretary (Sir George Grey) from Sir Edward Cust, 16 Oct. 1862, G. K. Dearden, 16 Oct. 1862, T. Johnes Smith (Chief Constable of Cheshire), 25 Oct. 1862, and Charles Bird (Secretary, Birkenhead Auxiliary, Protestant Alliance), 10 Nov. 1862, all in Home Office: Registered Papers, PRO, H.O. 45/7326, pp. 4-14, 19-21, 79, 103.

The Communal Riot

The communal riot, in which English Protestants and Irish Roman Catholics attacked each other's neighborhoods, is the most widely known sort of religious disturbance in the Victorian period. In this sort of rioting, the Roman Catholic community is often seen as the victim. The Stockport Riots of 1852 are often taken to be the model or archetypical form of sectarian violence,[134] and became a specter invoked whenever Roman Catholics feared violence;[135] but actually this type of disturbance was rare.

Liverpool had its own indigenous traditions of communal riots between Orangemen and Irish. After brawls in the 1830s and '40s, there was relative quiet until 12 July 1850, when a riot saw the death of an Irish Roman Catholic. The following year, 14 July 1851, the longest Orange parade in Liverpool's history provoked fights between Orangemen and Irish dockers. Rumors of police collusion incensed the Irish neighborhoods. Two people were killed, and numerous people were seriously injured. Election day (8 July) 1852 saw more riots, as Orange Lodges held parades and as Irish stoned people wearing Conservative colors; a pregnant Irish Roman Catholic died in a police charge. Several shootings and street brawls happened in late July and early August 1852. This provoked the authorities to ban all Orange parades, which now had to be held over the borough boundary (usually in Newton-in-the-Willows); this ended serious riots.[136]

Something like the Stockport Riots happened in Cheltenham in 1850, where the Evangelical Francis Close[137] for many years promoted public anti-Catholic sentiment for both theological and political reasons. For Close, anti-Catholicism was a weapon in his warfare against local Chartists, freethinkers, liberal Nonconformists, and in his attempts to suppress the traditional pastimes of wealthier spa-dwellers (horse racing, the theater, gambling, and drinking).[138] Close organized a Church of England Working Man's Association in 1840, to inculcate what he considered to be "Christian Bible principles" and to oppose Chartism and Owenite free thought. The association held the usual public meetings and imported speakers from Birmingham.[139] "In my humble opinion," Close proclaimed, "the Bible is conservative, the Prayer Book conservative, the Liturgy conservative, the Church conservative, and it is impossible for a minister to open his mouth without being conservative."[140]

As a thorough Evangelical and disciple of Charles Simeon, Close of course opposed both Roman and Anglo-Catholicism on theological

---

[134] Norman, *English Catholic Church*, pp. 203-4.

[135] William Hogarth to Palmerston, 7 July 1853, Home Office: Registered Papers, PRO, H.O. 45/4811.

[136] Neal, *Sectarian Violence*, pp. 129-30, 133-41, 156-57.

[137] "The Protestant Pope of Cheltenham," Close (1797-1882) was a popular preacher and writer of tracts against horse racing, alcohol, tobacco, gothic architecture, and the stage; curate (1824) and incumbent (1826-56) of Cheltenham; Dean of Carlisle, 1856-81. The very stereotype of the narrow, dictatorial, bigoted, puritanical Evangelical clergyman. (*DNB*, IV, 579-80.)

[138] Owen Ashton, "Clerical Control and Radical Responses in Cheltenham Spa, 1838-1848," *Midland History*, VIII (1983), 121, 123, 135-38. For an unconvincing argument from the late twentieth-century Anglican Evangelical perspective, that Close opposed these things only because they were "unscriptural," not because he feared that they threatened the Establishment's political position, see A. F. Munden, "Radicalism versus Evangelicalism in Victorian Cheltenham," *Southern History*, V (1983), 116-19.

[139] Ashton, "Clerical Control," p. 131.

[140] Bebbington, *Evangelicalism*, p. 103.

grounds. As Tractarianism grew in strength and the Oxford Converts made their appearance in the mid-1840s, and as Chartism and Owenism began to wane, Close increasingly turned to anti-Catholicism. He revived the Guy Fawkes Day church service in order to promote anti-Catholic and Conservative "Church and Queen" sentiment (which could be used as easily against those who opposed the levying of church rates as against Anglo-Catholics).[141]

When the Papal Aggression burst upon the English scene, Close endorsed the public agitation and promoted memorializing in Cheltenham. The result, however, was violence. More people had wanted to attend the public meeting than the hall could accommodate, so a second meeting was planned. Meanwhile, a draper in the High Street exhibited an effigy of the Pope "in gaudy pontificals" in one of his windows; and rumor had it that the effigy was to be paraded and burnt after the second meeting. So a crowd gathered to watch the fun. But late in the day, the magistrates forbade no-popery demonstrations and the draper refused to give up the effigy to the crowd. (It turned out that he had thought of the effigy as an attention-getter for his expensive fabrics.) The crowd then turned ugly and smashed his windows. Caught between the magistrates' order and the crowd's wrath, the draper gave the effigy to the police, who stripped it and handed it over to the crowd. The crowd carried it through the streets, burnt it before the Roman Catholic chapel near St. George's Square, smashed the chapel's windows, and looted several shops owned by Roman Catholics.[142]

The Stockport Riots, which happened a year and a half later, were three days of street fighting and serious destruction of property on 28, 29, and 30 June, 1852. The background to the riots is to be found in the fierce political battles between Tories and Liberals for control of Stockport's parliamentary representation and town council. The two parties had split Stockport's M.P.s in 1832, 1835, and 1837. The Liberals carried both seats in 1841, but the Tories regained a seat in 1847. The 1852 contest was especially hot. The Tories had managed to retain control of the town council since 1848, but only with difficulty; and they were on the verge of losing control in the November 1852 local elections. Under the circumstances, Tory leaders and their mouthpiece, the *Stockport Advertiser*, attacked Liberals, Irish, and Roman Catholics in the days immediately before the riot and the parliamentary election. Moreover, there were connections between Tory politicians and the local chapter of the Protestant Association. The Rev. J. Meridyth, incumbent of St. Peter's, Stockport, possibly an Ulsterman and certainly Irish-born, was the Protestant Association's leading light. He attacked John Benjamin Smith, Liberal candidate in the 1852 parliamentary elections, for Smith had opposed the Ecclesiastical Titles Act, 1851, as sitting M.P. for the Stirling District.[143]

[141] Ashton, "Clerical Control," pp. 124-25; *Ibid.*, pp. 124-25; Munden argues that Close believed that "Romanism . . . within the Church of England, and as expressed in the Church of Rome" was a greater threat than radicalism ("Radicalism versus Evangelicalism," p. 118).
[142] *Cheltenham Free Press*, 16, 23 Nov. 1850; *Times*, 25 Nov. 1850; *Illustrated London News*, 30 Nov. 1850; Adams, *Social Atom*, p. 134.
[143] Pauline Millward, "The Stockport Riots of 1852: A Study of Anti-Catholic and Anti-Irish Sentiment," *The Irish in the Victorian City*, ed. Roger Swift and Sheridan Gilley (London, 1985), pp. 209-11.

The town's atmosphere thus was thick with religious animosities when the Derby Ministry issued its famous proclamation on 15 June 1852, which forbade Roman Catholics from displaying their vestments or religious symbols in public.[144] Almost immediately thereafter, copies of the proclamation and Orange placards appeared in Stockport, and anti-Catholic and anti-Irish grafitti were chalked on walls. On Sunday the 27th occurred the annual Roman Catholic Sunday school procession, without religious symbols and with priests in mufti. The procession, escorted by a body of burly Irishmen (an act of defiance, in the opinion of Lt. Gen. Earl Cathcart[145]), went off peacefully. But the next day, rioting began. In the afternoon, the Protestant Association paraded an effigy of a priest. Things remained peaceful until a brawl in the Bishop Blaize pub. William Walker, a local man, started a fight with an Englishman, and was turned out. He went back, started a fight with a group of Irish, and was again beaten up and turned out. He went back again, this time with his mates. The Irish with whom Walker had fought had left the pub, so he and his mates began attacking Irish indiscriminately in Hillgate.

Fighting resumed on the evening of Tuesday, 29 June, in Hillgate and in St. Peter's Square. Irishmen broke the windows of St. Peter's, the anti-Catholic Meridyth's church, but an English crowd chased the Irish back into their neighborhoods, sacked two chapels and twenty-four houses, killed one Irishman, and injured fifty-one. The magistrates read the Riot Act, and a detachment of the 4th Regiment of Foot dispersed the crowds. One hundred eleven Irish and two English were arrested. On Wednesday the 30th, more houses in the Irish Quarter were attacked, but the violence was less.[146]

Pauline Millward, who has studied the Stockport Riots, argues that the rioters had their own concerns, grievances, and goals, and were not simply the "passive instruments" of Tory churchmen and politicians. But the economic explanation, which points to the Irish as competitors for jobs and as cheap labor, does not work, for it was chiefly advanced after the riots. Before the riots, complaints focused on cultural differences—religion, drinking habits, fecklessness, and living conditions. Thus, in her view, the riots "were not simply the product of working-class grievances, but can also be connected with the activities of political and religious groupings outside the working class."[147] In other words, the Stockport English who

[144] The ministry's purpose in issuing this proclamation has never been clearly explained. Walter Arnstein believes that the proclamation was "an immediate response" to the dangers of rioting that the Stockport Riots demonstrated (*Protestant Versus Catholic*, p. 48). The Stockport Riots of course happened after the proclamation appeared, but Arnstein may be thinking of the abstract danger of riot. That is congruent with the "official explanation" of Home Secretary Spencer Walpole, that the holding of processions with vestments, banners, and images was likely to cause a breach of the peace. G.I.T. Machin suggests that the proclamation may have been designed to appease Ultra-Protestant opinion, to make up for the Derby Ministry's scuttling of motions of inquiry into the operations of the Maynooth seminary and the appointment of W.J.E. Bennett to the living of Frome. On the other hand, the proclamation hindered *rapprochement* with Roman Catholics at a time when Tory candidates for Irish constituencies were defending Maynooth. So Machin thinks it possible that the ministry actually believed that the proclamation was needed to prevent disturbances. (*Politics and the Churches*, p. 238.)

[145] Cathcart to Undersecretary, Home Office, 3 July 1852, Home Office: Registered Papers, PRO, H.O. 45/4085H, pp. 132-33.

[146] Millward, "Stockport Riots," pp. 208-209.

[147] *Ibid.*, pp. 213, 215, 217-18.

rioted had noneconomic reasons for disliking the Irish, and to some extent were serving middle-class political interests.

The Stockport Riots may have encouraged violence elsewhere. Election day 1852 (8 July) at Wigan saw street rows between English and Irish, and the magistrates asked for troops, but were able to restore order with their own resources, before the troops arrived. The same month saw brawls in Manchester and Hulme. Hatred simmered during the early 1850s, with minor rows at Oldham, Preston, Blackburn, and Wigan, but the only major riot was at Ashton, in September of 1854, where Irish attacks on English neighborhoods provoked a crowd of about three hundred English operatives to invade the Irish quarter.[148]

The next few years were relatively quiet, but severe violence erupted again in the late 1850s and early '60s. The anti-Catholic lecturer Massena's rhetoric inflamed a crowd at Wigan in 1859 to attack chapels, pubs, and houses. Another of his lecture tours, during the summer and autumn of 1862, led to attacks on Roman Catholic chapels in Wakefield, Bradford, and Leeds. A Roman Catholic chapel at Ashton was stoned in June 1861. Two hundred colliers and Irish brawled at Hurst Brook during wakes week, 1861. An Irish crowd almost lynched a youth who had assaulted the Roman Catholic priest of Stalybridge in May 1862. The biggest riot was that at Oldham in June 1861. Mutual threats and taunts, and rumors that the Irish "should be treated as they were at Stockport," had circulated for some time before the riot. The riot began on a Thursday evening, with the Roman Catholic chapel sacked and the Irish neighborhoods attacked. Anti-Catholic handbills appeared the next day, and a crowd assembled, but the police dispersed it before further damage could be done.[149]

The fiercest and most extensive communal riots, however, did not come until the late 1860s and early '70s, when crowds of English and Irish, enflamed by William Murphy, the no-popery demagogue, battled one another. Murphy is probably the most notorious of the mid-Victorian anti-Catholic lecturers. He was born in Castletown-Conyers, County Limerick, Ireland, in 1834. The family lived a somewhat nomadic life after his father converted to Protestantism. Murphy made a living as a scripture-reader, first for the Irish Society and then for the Irish Society for Church Missions, between 1852 and 1859. After a few unsuccessful years when he tried to find work in secular life, Murphy went to London in 1862, where he was taken up by the Protestant Evangelical Mission and Electoral Union, becoming their star lecturer. His activities between 1862 and 1866 are obscure, but it is known that he lectured in London, Bristol, Bath, Plymouth, and Cardiff. He came to national attention after disturbances in Plymouth (June 1866) and Wolverhampton (February 1867), and from thenceforward was an increasingly troublesome and controversial figure. A group of Irishmen gave him a severe beating at Whitehaven, Cumberland, in April 1871, and he died the following March.[150]

---

[148] Kirk, *Working Class Reformism*, pp. 318-19; Cathcart to Home Office, 4 Aug. 1852, Home Office: Registered Papers, PRO, H.O. 45/4085H, pp. 139-40.
[149] Stevenson, *Popular Disturbances*, p. 280; Kirk, *Working Class Reformism*, p. 320; Foster, *Class Struggle*, pp. 243-46.
[150] Arnstein, *Protestant Versus Catholic*, pp. 88, 90, 105-106.

The Murphy Riots occurred between June 1866 and April 1871. There were about twenty-five actual or anticipated riots, most sparked by Murphy's inflammatory lectures. These often verged on the obscene or pornographic in their allegations about the sexual corruptions of the confessional; and they included the selling of *The Confessional Unmasked*, a pamphlet that compiled passages from the casuist moral theology of St. Alphonsus Liguori and Peter Dens.[151] Murphy usually chose a weekend for his lectures, when Irish were more visible and time available for rioting. Moreover, the riots happened coincidentally with the "Fenian Outrages": the bombing at Clerkenwell Prison that left twelve dead, and the spectacular rescue of two Fenians at Salford. Some of the riots began when English crowds, inflamed by Murphy's rhetoric, attacked Irish neighborhoods; others started when Irish crowds attempted to suppress the lectures. They usually resulted in street battles between the two communities.[152] (Tensions at the time were such that anti-Catholic violence occurred in places where neither Murphy nor his colleagues in the Protestant Electoral Union visited. Crowds broke the windows of the Roman Catholic priest at Ipswich on four occasions between 1864 and 1867, apparently unmotivated by outside events.[153])

Although Murphy's earlier lectures had led to violence, those of 18-22 February 1867 at Wolverhampton gave him national notoriety. His advance men stuck up placards announcing the lectures at the Agricultural Hall. Admission was limited to adult males, and to women who attended confession; tickets cost 1*d.* for unreserved seats and 2*d.* reserved seats. The results were that the hall was packed and that many Irish had been able to afford tickets. Murphy's appearance sparked pandemonium, fights, and a charge at the platform. The lecture was cancelled. The second lecture went off because the audience was limited to Protestants, but several thousand Irish stoned the lecture hall until pushed back by police and the Volunteer Militia. Fearful of violence, the magistrates augmented their forces with detachments from the county police and the 9th Hussars. Thus, the rest of the lectures were delivered, despite the presence of large Irish crowds outside the hall (ten thousand for the last one).[154] Although the Wolverhampton "riots" were rather tame, and share the characteristics of the 1850 Birkenhead Riot, they were the prelude to true communal fighting at Birmingham in June 1867.

Birmingham by 1867 had a thirty-year history of well-organized anti-Catholicism.[155] In the 1860s, moreover, religious tensions had mounted there. The parish of Holy Trinity, Bordesley, was a center of Anglo-Catholicism under the Revs. J. Oldknow (vicar) and C. J. Sneath. The *Record* denounced them throughout the year 1865, and a public meeting on

[151] *Ibid.*, pp. 89-90, 238-39.

[152] For summaries of the riots, see Walter L. Arnstein, "The Murphy Riots: A Victorian Dilemma," *Victorian Studies*, XIX (1975-76), 51-71, which focuses on the riots' constitutional implications; Steedman, *Policing the Victorian Community*, pp. 33-38, which analyzes them as a problem in "policecraft"; Stevenson, *Popular Disturbances*, p. 281; and Kirk, *Working Class Reformism*, pp. 321-22. Donald C. Richter, *Riotous Victorians* (Athens, Ohio, 1981), pp. 35-48, is anecdotal and unanalytical.

[153] Rev. John Charles Kemp to Robert Charles Ransome, 19 Feb. 1867, and S. A. Notcutt to Ransom, 23 Feb. 1867, Robert Charles Ransome Papers, Suffolk Record Office, Ipswich Branch.

[154] Swift, "Anti-Catholicism and Irish Disturbances," pp. 94-98; Arnstein, *Protestant Versus Catholic*, pp. 90-91.

[155] *Sup.*, pp. 117-24.

the subject ended in confusion. A large number of town notables petitioned the rural dean against Tractarianism in Birmingham. The *Birmingham Gazette* deplored the controversy and asked the Anglo-Catholics to submit, but Oldknow refused. Simultaneously, Birmingham Conservatives were exploiting the anti-Catholic issue in the run-up to the 1868 elections, attacking George Dixon, M.P. for the borough, as insufficiently Protestant. (Dixon, also mayor, refused Murphy the use of the Town Hall.) The Anglican clergy and the Birmingham Protestant Association kept their distance from Murphy and the Protestant Electoral Union: They did not openly support him, but they certainly did not discourage him; and they expressed the willingness to be "friendly" towards any local branch of the Electoral Union. (The Protestant Association feared that the Protestant Electoral Union might draw support away from them.) Finally, the fear of Fenianism (probably well founded) within Birmingham's Irish community, and rumors of arming and drilling, contributed to the tensions.[156]

Denied the Town Hall, Murphy constructed a large wooden "tabernacle" (seating three thousand) in Carr's Lane, a street bordering the Roman Catholic St. Mary's neighborhood, as a deliberate provocation. The riots began on Sunday, 16 June, when a crowd of Irish stoned the tabernacle and broke the windows of houses belonging to local Protestant militants. The Irish returned the next day, but were overwhelmed by a Protestant crowd that sacked a pawnshop, a sweets shop, and two pubs near the Bull Ring, and then sacked an Irish neighborhood and a Roman Catholic chapel. The Birmingham police, armed with cutlasses, dealt heavily with the Irish on the Sunday, but were slow to put down the Protestant rioters on the Monday. (The riot began at three o'clock, but the Riot Act was not read until seven that evening; most of those rioters whom the police chose to arrest were Irish.) On Tuesday the 18th, rumors flew of plans to attack St. Chad's Roman Catholic Cathedral, Holy Trinity Anglo-Catholic church, and gunsmiths' shops, but 580 police, six hundred special constables, and four hundred soldiers maintained the peace. The remainder of the lectures were given in relative peace.[157]

Murphy turned to Lancashire for a lecture tour in the spring of 1868, inaugurating another round of communal violence. Street fights and broken windows occurred at Rochdale (March/April), Bacup (April), and Bolton (May), but the most serious outbreaks were at Stalybridge (April), Ashton (mid-May), and Oldham (late May). In each place, anti-Catholic meetings led to the exchange of insults between English and Irish in the streets. The confrontations escalated to the physical, and then crowds of English operatives assembled, attacked Irish districts, ransacked houses, and invaded Roman Catholic chapels to smash altars, pull down confessional booths, and destroy images.[158]

At this point, the authorities, theretofore sensitive to the rights of free speech, began to clamp down on Murphy. He was arrested and prevented from speaking in Manchester in September 1868, and in Birmingham in

---

[156] A. F. Hooper, Typescript on the 1867 Birmingham Riots, pp. 49-53.

[157] *Ibid.*, pp. 53-55; Stevenson, *Popular Disturbances*, p. 281; Arnstein, *Protestant Versus Catholic*, pp. 92-95; Barbara Weinberger, "The Police and the Public in Mid-Nineteenth-Century Warwickshire," *Policing and Punishment in Nineteenth Century Britain*, ed. Victor Bailey (New Brunswick, N.J., 1981), pp. 70-71.

[158] Arnstein, *Protestant Versus Catholic*, pp. 95-99; Kirk, *Working Class Reformism*, pp. 322-23.

June 1869. In the spring of 1869, Murphy toured Tyneside and Northumberland. His lectures provoked a riot in Tynemouth, but local authorities denied him halls in other towns. Although he continued his lecturing in 1870 and 1871, he was excluded from centers of large populations. Thus it was that he met his end in Whitehaven, not Manchester or Birmingham.[159]

Communal riots were as rare as Irish pro-Catholic riots; only in Liverpool can they be said to have typified religious violence. They were spectacular and bloody, the nourishment of demagogues, but they were not the norm.

The Street and Pub Brawl

Ethnic violence in the street, pub, or worksite, although related to the communal riots of the 1850s and '60s, is perhaps more problematical.[160] Violence between Irish and English was infrequent outside Lancashire throughout the nineteenth century, and rare in Lancashire before 1850.[161]

The most common and longest lasting disturbances in rural areas were those involving brawls between Irish and English navvies. Navvies, however, represented a distinct and separate subculture that valued physical strength, drinking to excess, and fighting. Accounts of brawls in Northumberland and the West Riding have several elements in common: They happened on a Saturday or Sunday, heavy drinking was involved, and the brawlers broke property as well as skulls. Moreover, the brawls sometimes were connected with exploitation by labor contractors. (Irish navvies laying track in the Marsden Valley, between Huddersfield and Stanedge Hills, downed tools on 14 April 1849, when the contractors announced that pay day was being postponed. The Irish then attacked the English navvies because the latter went on working.) Sometimes the brawls began among the Irish, and expanded when police or magistrates intervened. Finally, the brawls may have had as much to do with rivalries between railway companies as with ones between ethnic groups. (Thus two groups of Irish navvies employed by rival companies fought a pitched battle at Wolverhampton on 13 July 1850.)[162] Fights between Irish migrant harvesters and English farm laborers were also common. These rows also typically happened in or near public houses, on weekends, after heavy drinking.[163]

The Irish urban working classes did have a reputation for violence, turbulence, and crime, of course; but most of their crime and violence took the form of Saturday-night drinking and brawling rather than more serious offenses. (All three of the Irish rows at Leeds that were big enough to make the newspapers in the week of 17-23 April 1852 began late at night

---

[159] Arnstein, *Protestant Versus Catholic*, pp. 99-101, 105.

[160] John Stevenson calls it "more diffuse" (Stevenson, *Popular Disturbances*, p. 276), and John Foster calls it "labour false consciousness" because it stemmed from nonreligious impulses: specifically, from fears of economic rivalry (Foster, *Class Struggle*, p. 246).

[161] Gilley, "English Attitudes to the Irish," pp. 100-101; Kirk, *Working Class Reformism*, p. 315.

[162] Stevenson, *Popular Disturbances*, pp. 276-78; Roger Swift, "'Another Stafford Street Row': Law, Order and the Irish Presence in Mid-Victorian Wolverhampton," *The Irish in the Victorian City*, ed. Swift and Gilley, pp. 187-88; *Leeds Times*, 15 June 1839; *Leeds Mercury*, 15 June, 27 July, 7 Sept. 1839, 3 July 1841, 21 April, 21, 28 July 1849.

[163] *Leeds Mercury*, 3 Sept. 1842; *Cambridge Chronicle*, 11 Aug. 1849; Rev. John Poore to Sir G. Grey, 4 Aug. 1851, Home Office: Registered Papers, PRO, H.O. 45/3472Q-S, pp. 23-31.

in pubs.[164]) In 1846, the Irish-born, 19 percent of the total population of Manchester, Salford, and their out-townships, contributed 27 percent of all males arrested for common assault, 26 percent of all males arrested for drunk and disorderly behavior, and 16 percent of all males arrested for being drunk and incapable. The percentages were about the same for other Lancashire towns during the period. In Leeds, the Irish, 10 percent of the township's population, were a third of those arrested for common assault, assault on the police, and breach of the peace. Irish criminality in Kent during the period 1859-80 followed the same pattern.[165] Irish immigrants brought to their new homes the customs of drinking to excess, faction fights, and fights with the Royal Irish Constabulary, normal behavior in Ireland.[166]

Changes in police practices also may have helped "cause" Irish violence. There were several major rows between police and Irish in the Caribee Island district of Wolverhampton during the years 1848 and 1849. These were connected with the borough police's growing discipline and militarization (as army officers became chief constables and introduced military-style drill), which resulted in reduced tolerance for disturbances and increased desire to control neighborhoods. There is also some evidence to suggest that fines raised by the apprehending of offenders were used to reduce the cost to the ratepayers of policing. For these reasons, and because Irish neighborhoods were a rich source for minor offenders, the police monitored Irish working-class districts more closely than English ones, and thus had a greater chance of becoming involved in rows.[167]

In his study of crime in Manchester, C. M. DeMotte claims that sectarian rows, in which Irish Roman Catholics attacked Protestants, were common. He asserts that the annual Whitsun walks "usually led to religious conflicts," and that the annual Orange parade on 12 July "always provoked a wave of violence from the Irish quarter." But he offers no evidence of Whitsun violence, and his evidence for Orange violence consists of an attack on the parade in 1834 and two incidents involving rival schoolchildren's gangs in June 1869 and October 1871.[168] In fact, the month of July, at least for the year 1846, was not more violent than other months. Although more males were arrested for drunk and disorderly behavior in that month than in any other single month of the year, (10.87 percent) the number is hardly larger than that for January, the next largest (10.49 percent). Practically the same number of males were arrested for common assault in March (10.85 percent) and in July (10.40 percent), although slightly more were arrested in those two months than in May (9.36 percent), June (9.21 percent), August (9.36 percent), or September (9.81 percent).[169]

[164] *Leeds Mercury*, 24 Apr. 1852.
[165] Watch Committee for the Borough of Manchester, *Criminal and Miscellaneous Statistical Returns of the Manchester Police, for the year 1846* (Manchester, 1847), Table 8; W. Lowe, *Irish in Mid-Victorian Lancashire*, pp. 36-41; Dillon, "Irish in Leeds," pp. 3, 15; Conley, *Unwritten Law*, pp. 158-60.
[166] W. Lowe, *Irish in Mid-Victorian Lancashire*, pp. 126-29.
[167] Swift, "Another Stafford Street Row," pp. 183-87.
[168] Charles M. DeMotte, "The Dark Side of Town: Crime in Manchester and Salford, 1815-1875" (Ph.D. thesis, University of Kansas, 1977), pp. 295-96.
[169] Manchester Watch Committee, *Criminal . . . Statistical Returns, 1846*, Table 1.

English and Irish operatives did not get along together (although they could cooperate in strikes). Some cotton masters segregated them in the mills; others imported Irish strike breakers, thereby creating resentment. Yet Irish-English relations were complex and not reducible to simple dislike.[170] The fiction directed to the working-class audience that told about Irish immigrants in England gave Paddy the same character that he had in Ireland: noble and honest, or feckless.[171] The "informative articles," however, told a different story. The Evangelical Alliance deplored Irish immigration, because the influx augmented the numbers of the Roman Catholic Church.[172] The *Family Herald* feared that Irish labor would compete for work with English operatives, and drive down wages.[173] *Eliza Cook's Jounal* was worried that the large numbers of Irish and Welsh poor ("these Cossacks of civilization") in London, Manchester, Birmingham, Liverpool, and other great towns posed a serious threat to life as they knew it.[174] The remarkable thing, however, is how minor this issue was to the gutter press in terms of the space they devoted to it, even as the Irish population was growing in England.

To what extent did this mutual dislike take the form of violence outside the worksite? It would be a daunting task to read the magistrates' court proceedings for all of England over a twenty- or thirty-year period; but it is possible to suggest that although such brawls did occur, they were not all that common. During the months of April and May 1851 at Manchester, for instance, only one such incident reached the Borough Court. Two brothers, handloom weavers, got to talking, playing dominos, and drinking with an Irish used-clothes dealer in a pub. The conversation turned to the Papal Aggression and grew heated. The result was "a terrific row" in which the brothers used a saw on the Irishman. They were let off with a fine of 10*s*. each. (In contrast, two men, one of whom bit off the tip of a third man's nose in a pub brawl, were fined £5 and 40*s*. respectively; and an Irishman who bruised a woman's hand with a club when she taxed him with tresspassing on her land was fined 20*s*.)[175] This impression is confirmed when one examines the cases of assault brought before the Huddersfield Police Court in 1851. Judging from surnames (a problematical measure, so one must be cautious), it appears to be the case that most of the assaults were between members of the same ethnic group, rather than between English and Irish.[176] "Irish rows" mostly involved fighting among Irish factions, not between the Irish and the English communities; the Irish and the English working classes generally kept to themselves.[177] And

---

[170] Werly, "Irish in Manchester," p. 353; Durey, "Survival of an Irish Culture," pp. 19-21.

[171] *Lloyd's Penny Weekly Miscellany*, I (1843), 709-10; *Family Herald*, I (16 Dec. 1843), 497; *Protestant Watchman*, No. 17 (July 1850), pp. 209-10, No. 21 (Nov. 1850), pp. 253-54, No. 22 (Dec. 1850), pp. 271-72.

[172] *Evangelical Christendom*, II (Mar. 1848), 104.

[173] *Family Herald*, o.s., I (17 Dec. 1842). The *Champion*, Joseph Raynor Stevens's short-lived periodical, published at Ashton-under-Lyne, which also supported the ten-hours movement, was especially concerned about this issue (I, 29 Dec. 1849, 127-28; *ibid.*, 19 Jan. 1850, pp. 168-73; *ibid.*, II, 18 May 1850, 23-24).

[174] *Eliza Cook's Journal*, V (25 Oct. 1851), 403-5; *ibid.*, VI (10 Jan. 1852), 169-71; cf. *Protestant Witness*, III (25 Jan. 1851), 18.

[175] *Manchester Courier*, 12, 19 Apr., 10, 31 May 1851.

[176] *Huddersfield Chronicle*, Feb.-Dec. 1851.

[177] Werly, "Irish in Manchester," pp. 354-56; Kirk, *Working Class Reformism*, p. 315; Gilley, "English Attitudes to the Irish," pp. 100-101; Durey, "Survival of an Irish Culture," pp. 24-25; DeMotte "Dark Side of Town," pp. 294-98; Dillon, "Irish in Leeds," pp. 14-15.

sometimes mixed groups fought. Six drunken young men, four bearing the English surnames Clark, Newby, Kershaw, and Moor (the latter two surnames from the North), and two bearing the Irish names Michael Murphy and Thomas Sirr, entered the Weavers' Arms, Mill Street, Bank, Leeds, at two in the morning of 2 January 1845. When When the landlord refused to serve them, they trashed the pub and assaulted the constables who arrested them.[178]

Conflicts between Irish Protestant and Roman Catholic workers was also a factor, although one difficult to assess. Some of the Irish rows that so scandalized the middle classes may have been battles between these two groups, misinterpreted by those who did not grasp the nuances of Irish communal divisions. (T. A. Finegan, the Birmingham town missionary, remarked that "[m]any persons in this country suppose that an Irishman must necessarily be a Roman Catholic, and all Irishmen, particularly the working classes, are generally considered as such—but the contrary is the fact."[179]) These two groups often lived in the same neighborhoods, and sometimes came into conflict over religious disputes such as the reading of the Bible.

Victorian towns were full of random violence—brawls and rows, exchanges of insults, pushing, assaults, drunk and disorderly conduct—but very little of it had to do with sectarian rivalries. Rather, traditional working-class "machismo" (which defined manliness in terms of the abilities to inflict and withstand physical pain) combined with alcohol abuse and the atmosphere of crowded towns to promote violence.[180] Most criminal behavior in mid-Victorian Portsmouth occurred in pubs, brothels, and alleyways, and was committed by drunk and disorderly soldiers, sailors, and prostitutes. The highest level of anti-police violence in mid-Victorian Birmingham was reached in the hours immediately after closing-time on Saturday nights. During the same period, the small country town of Horncastle, Lincs, had most of its brawls reported after the pubs closed, or in brothels.[181]

Sometimes the violence showed elements of class hostility and ideological conflict as well as the love of violence for its own sake, lads out for a lark, and (at times) incompetence or overreaction on the part of the police. The Hyde Park Sunday Trading riots of 24 June to 15 July 1855 are the best known examples, but there were others. Violence between tenant farmers and urban artisans at the Protectionist meeting at Stafford on 10 January 1850, and at the Dorset Protectionist meeting in February (in which a young man was killed) involved conflict between classes with differing economic interests.[182] Those Birmingham workers who were most

---

[178] *Leeds Mercury*, 4 Jan. 1845.
[179] Finegan Journal, 7 Dec. 1837, Birmingham Reference Library, MS. 312749, p. 195.
[180] DeMotte discusses these issues in an impressionistic way in "The Dark Side of Town," pp. 167-74, 291-98. See also Briggs, *Victorian Cities*, pp. 88-89; Paul Willis, "Shop Floor Culture, Masculinity and the Wage Form," in *Working-Class Culture: Studies in History and Theory*, ed. J. Clarke, C. Critcher, and R. Johnson (New York, 1980), pp. 196-98; and Conley, *Unwritten Law*, pp. 160-61.
[181] John Field, "Police, Power and Community in a Provincial English Town: Portsmouth, 1815-1875," *Policing and Punishment*, ed. Bailey, pp. 45, 51; Weinberger, "Warwickshire," p. 69; B. J. Davey, *Lawless and Immoral: Policing a Country Town, 1838-1857* (Leicester, 1983), passim.
[182] Brian Harrison, "The Sunday Trading Riots of 1855," *HJ*, VIII (1965), 219-45; P. Smith, *Policing Victorian London*, pp. 127-46; Mark Baker, "Aspects of the Life of the Wiltshire Agricul-

likely to assault the police came from the gunmaking and other hardware trades, which were in decline or were characterized by extreme fluctuations in demand, circumstances that suggest economic tensions lay at the root of their behavior; but those trades were also ones in which drinking during working hours was customary.[183] The major rows of the Victorian era were not simply the work of teenagers or of the lumpenproletariat, to be sure;[184] but they were a more complicated mix of motives than some scholars think.

The Leeds Soldiers Riots of 9-11 June 1844 show the mix of motives. The riots began as a pub brawl on the evening of Sunday, 9 June, in which some soldiers of the 70th Foot beat up a civilian and resisted arrest. They were arraigned on Monday the 10th, and another row occurred when about forty of their mates tried to rescue them. Groups of civilians, described as Irish and Chartists, helped the soldiers fight the police. The motives of the civilians appear to have stemmed from the police having prevented them from holding a rally on Sunday night. The soldiers were confined to their barracks on Tuesday the 11th, so the Leeds Irish and Chartists roamed the streets, pelted the police in Kirkgate with stones and bottles, and ultimately were dispersed by police armed with cutlasses.[185] Now, although the disturbances had political, class, and ethnic motives, alcohol, the love of violence, and the mutual hatred between soldiers and police played their parts in this, and in other soldiers' riots.[186]

One can see this in the person of Manasseh Flatow, one of the civilian rioters. Flatow, a Jewish waiter at Ross's Temperance Coffee House, Kirkgate, probably active in the Leeds Total Abstinence Charter Association, and one of the Chartists prevented from meeting on Sunday night, took a leading role in fighting the police. But he was also a violent, or at least an irritable, man. Over a year later, in October 1845, Flatow was fined £1 for attacking a boy with a hammer and his fists at the annual Woodhouse Moor harvest festival. Flatow's temperance booth had been bothered by rowdy boys, who had done £3 damage, and who probably had taunted him with anti-Semitic and anti-temperance gibes, but the boy whom Flatow attacked was not one of them.[187] So, one suspects that Flatow's riotous activity in 1844 cannot be explained on the bases of class conflict or revolutionary ideology alone.[188]

One can find more examples of religious-based or interethnic street and pub violence if one looks at Liverpool, where drink, no-popery orators, and the love of violence combined to have devastating effects on the pub and street, in the view of Chief Constable Matthew Dowling.[189] Frank Neal's recounting of street and pub rows, neighborhood quarrels, fights among fishwives and little boys, and domestic quarrels certainly shows that reli-

tural Labourer, c. 1850," *Wiltshire Archæological Magazine*, LXXIV/LXXV (1979-80), 161; *Leeds Mercury*, 12 Jan. 1850; *Times*, 11 Jan., 25 Feb. 1850.

[183] Weinberger, "Warwickshire," p. 73.

[184] Kirk, "Ethnicity, Class and Popular Toryism," pp. 81-82; Kirk, *Working Class Reformism*, pp. 323-24; Hooper, Birmingham Riots transcript, pp. 55-56.

[185] *Leeds Mercury*, 15, 29 June, 6 July 1844.

[186] As in the affray in Coventry between men of the 7th Hussars and 14th Light Dragoons, who had been drinking in a pub, and the police (*Leeds Times*, 3 Nov. 1838). For soldiers' riots in Kent, see Conley, *Unwritten Law*, pp. 155-57.

[187] *Leeds Mercury*, 4 Oct. 1845; J. Harrison, "Chartism in Leeds," p. 81.

[188] One assumes that alcohol did not play a part in the behavior of this Temperance Chartist.

[189] Neal, *Sectarian Violence*, pp. 113-14.

gious hatreds poisoned the atmosphere of working-class Liverpool, already the most densely populated place in England.[190] Francis Bishop of the Unitarian Liverpool Domestic Mission Society thought that until the Papal Aggression rekindled the no-popery cry, relations between English and Irish had been improving.[191] But Neal argues "that by the end of the 1850s the working class in Liverpool was divided in a way that was unique in England."[192] Liverpool is the exception; without wanting to claim that Protestant lions lay down with Papist lambs, one is struck by how few such incidents there were in the rest of England; one suspects that drunkenness, rather than the ostensible reason, explains brawls.[193]

Not so with attacks on priests. Roman Catholic priests, many of whom wore their distinctive vestments in the streets, were a visible sign of ultramontane aspirations, and one might expect them to be victims of attack during the heightened tensions of the mid-nineteenth century. Indeed, a foreign government alleged just that, which led Foreign Secretary Palmerston to request a report on violence towards Roman Catholic priests within the jurisdiction of the Metropolitan Police during the twelve months from December 1850 to November 1851. Thirteen of the Metropolitan Police's seventeen divisions reported no incidents. Of the five incidents reported, three had to do with disturbances before Roman Catholic property.[194] Only two incidents involved attacks on Roman Catholic priests. Father Ignatius Spencer was insulted in the street; and a priest named Ferrati was assaulted by three men, "supposed Italians," while walking in Baldwin's Gardens between nine and ten in the evening on 25 November 1851. Again, this is small beer; and the attack on Ferrati probably had little to do with the English religious situation. It probably was the prelude to four days of street rows in Baldwin's Gardens in July of 1853, between Irish and exiled Italian nationalists. The Italian nationalists hated the Pope, insulted Roman Catholic priests, and finally pushed one off the pavement. The Irish came to the priests' defense.[195]

Domestic violence related to religious differences was not unknown. Observers at the time were aware of the existence of interfaith marriages, and reported instances of quarrels between husband and wife over these differences.[196] Fights over religion, however, might very well conceal other, more deep-seated, motives for discord, especially within poor families.

Because the crime rate is related to economic change, the prosperity of the 1850s and '60s led to the decline of violent crime against persons and property—at least in Manchester. The 1830s and '40s were the worst times for drunkenness, vagrancy, and assault.[197]

[190] *Ibid.*, pp. 4, 40-43, 55-60, 62, 158-67.

[191] Bishop, *Report, Liverpool Domestic Mission Society*, p. 21.

[192] *Sectarian Violence*, p. 158.

[193] "Give strong drink unto him that is ready to perish, and wine unto those that be of heavy hearts. Let him drink, and forget his poverty, and remember his misery no more." (Proverbs 31:6-7.) Drink, not religion, was the opium of the masses.

[194] A crowd assembled outside Cardinal Wiseman's house in Golden Square and shouted "No Popery"; a man later adjudged insane disturbed a Mass in Clapham; and a disturbance was expected, but failed to happen, when Wiseman said Mass in Islington.

[195] Ld. Stanley of Alderley to H. Waddington, 27 Nov. 1851, and Sir R. Mayne to H. Waddington, 6 Dec. 1851, Home Office: Registered Papers, PRO, H.O. 45/3783; Gilley, "Garibaldi Riots," p. 700.

[196] Finegan Journal, Birmingham Reference Library, MS. 312749, *passim*; Bishop, *Report, Liverpool Domestic Mission Society*, pp. 19-20, 23; *Lloyd's Weekly Miscellany*, II (1850-52), 256.

[197] D. Jones, *Crime, Protest, Community and Police*, pp. 144-71.

I do not assert that radical political motives never lay behind public violence or that ethnic animosities between English and Irish did not exist. I believe, however, that the extent and significance of those elements have been overrated, at least for the period before 1870. And further, I believe that the significance of drink, of competition for the sexual favors of women, and of dislike of the police have been underrated as explanations for early Victorian popular disturbances.

IX

WHO WERE THE ANTI-CATHOLICS?

> woe betide
> The heart that lives on praise! considering nought
> Of Duty's royal edicts, that command
> Thy talents to be lent, thy lamp to shine[1]

> . . . when all other powers have been tried, and
> failed, it will be found that earnestness is the
> fulcrum upon which to rest the moral lever that
> is to raise the world.[2]

> Duty—that's to say complying
> With whate'er's expected here[3]

ORGANIZED ANTI-CATHOLICISM, Lord Ashley thought, was primarily a movement of the middle and working classes. These were the classes that hated "Popery and Puseyism, spiritual fornication, and spiritual adultery." The upper classes inclined towards the High Church, in his view, because that movement had "a more gentlemanlike and conservative air," and because the upper classes believed that Evangelicalism savored of Dissent, and Dissent, of Republicanism.[4] How accurate was Ashley's assessment?

The nature of and motives for working-class participation are problematical, as we have seen. The urban working classes did participate in public disturbances related to religious and sectarian antipathies, but outright communal violence was limited in scope, and the motives for such participation were related to drinking, rivalries for the sexual favors of women, and dislike of the police. The fact of middle-class participation is clearer, but the motives are equally problematical. Organized anti-Catholicism made up only one class of a host of voluntary societies available for Victorians to join. Some joined because they believed in the goals of the societies, but others joined because it was expected, the thing to do. Elisabeth Jay and Frank Prochaska have observed that middle-class men and women learned that they could gain a reputation for piety by appearing on the subscription lists of Evangelical societies. ("Becky Sharp was perhaps the most famous of them all.") So, people who were upwardly mobile, who wanted to associate with prominent men or to retain the trade of the prominent, who wanted to look pious, who wanted to be fashionable, or

---

[1] Tupper, *Sonnets*, p. 97.
[2] Sewell, *Katharine Ashton*, I, 245.
[3] *The Poems of Arthur Hugh Clough*, ed. by F.L. Mulhauser, 2nd ed. (Oxford, 1974), p. 27.
[4] Shaftesbury diary, 27 Jan. 1851, Broadlands Archives, SHA/PD/6.

who wanted to conceal their position in the demimonde subscribed to societies.[5]

Can we be more precise about the social and gender composition of the organized anti-Catholic movement?

The Working Classes

"The lower orders," Edward Royle comments, "had no voice, they were not organized, and were rarely conscious of anything beyond the instincts of the crowd—against the clergy and particularly the Roman Catholics, against dear bread and unemployment, against any attack on their basically conservative outlook."[6] Tory anti-Catholics attempted, as we have seen, to capture these working classes by means of Protestant Operative Associations, pitching their periodicals to what they thought were the tastes and level of comprehension of working-class readers, and scheduling public meetings in the evenings or on Saturday afternoons so that workers could attend.[7] The more pious Evangelical Alliance also attempted to drum up working-class support, offering a prize contest of £20 and £15 for anti-Catholic essays written by working men.[8]

Hugh Stowell was especially concerned to capture the Manchester working classes. He worked hard, organizing the local Protestant Operative and Conservative Operative associations, ragged schools, female refuges, visiting societies, and adult study groups. He organized anti-Catholic and antisecular education rallies for workers, and, according to his biographer, never condescended to his audiences.[9] His opposition to the New Poor Law was well calculated to win working-class support. He argued that the workhouse test was too harsh on those who could not work (the aged, the ill, orphans), and denied the chances for productive labor to those who could work, but who were unemployed from changes in trade or excess population. (He wanted the latter to be put to work clearing waste land or working for wages in workshops, rather than picking oakum or breaking stones in workhouses.)[10]

The anti-Catholics were not especially successful, however, at attracting working-class support. Stowell did use the workers Edward Joynson, John Atkinson, and Samuel Condell as go-betweens for a small working-class following, but the most substantial evidence of such support, a laudatory "Address from the Working Men of Manchester to the Rev. Hugh Stowell" (April 1850), appears to have been got up by Thomas Grieg, a partner in the calico-printers Grieg, Watson, and Grieg, in response to the Lancashire Public Schools Association's program of secular education (although it certainly had working-class support).[11] The sort of worker who

---

[5] Jay, *Religion of the Heart*, pp. 44-46; F. K. Prochaska, *Women and Philanthropy in Nineteenth-Century England* (Oxford, 1980), p. 40.

[6] Royle, *Victorian Infidels*, p. 238.

[7] *Penny Protestant Operative*, I (1840), iii; *ibid.*, II (June 1841), 47; *Protestant Watchman*, No. 3 (May 1849), pp. 31-32; *Blackburn Standard*, 11 Dec. 1850.

[8] Evangelical Alliance, British Organization, *Abstract of Proceedings of the Fifth Annual Conference, held in London, August and September, 1851* (London, 1851), pp. 33-34.

[9] Marsden, *Stowell*, pp. 48, 197, 224-25; *Protestant Witness*, II (21 Dec. 1850), 477; *Manchester Courier*, 21, 28 Dec. 1850.

[10] *Manchester Courier*, 22 Mar. 1851.

[11] *Protestant Witness*, II (1 June 1850), 366; *Manchester Courier*, 7 Dec. 1850; *Manchester Guardian*, 17 Apr., 23 Nov. 1850; Marsden, *Stowell*, pp. 209-11.

was attracted to Protestant Operative activities may likely be gauged by the winner of a £10 Protestant Prize essay in 1849. John Knowles, a cobbler of Hulme, was a convert from "socialism" to Wesleyanism; a local preacher, he was moving upward in life by preparing for the regular Wesleyan ministry.[12] One thinks at once of Thomas Ragg at Birmingham, also an artisan, who also used the written word and the clerical calling to move upwards.

Evidence from elsewhere confirms the impression that Protestant "Operatives" were really clerks, artisans, and shopkeepers. The working men who belonged to the Orange lodges in Northampton were affluent enough to put on elaborate and rich dinners for their William III's Day celebrations.[13] When the Rev. Edward Nangle solicited contributions for the Achill mission from working-class children, he thought it reasonable to ask for 7d. a week.[14] That level of giving represents between 19.4 and 10 percent of a child's weekly wage packet in the Lancashire cotton industry, between 12 and 6 percent of a young person's, and between 6 and 5 percent of a woman's. Societies, especially Baptist and Methodist ones, and the British and Foreign Bible Society, that used children to collect from working-class neighborhoods, asked for a halfpenny or at most a penny a week. When one considers that Lancashire textile families lived close to the bone in the best of times, and that those families most likely to have the young children that Nangle appealed to were also those families most likely to fall below the Rowntree poverty line, it seems highly unlikely that Nangle's intended audience fell below the clerkly and shopkeeping level.[15]

As telling is the cost of the all-day excursion to Richmond that the Metropolitan Protestant Operative Society laid on for its members in 1843: transportation cost half-a-crown (1/6d. for children under ten), with a shilling extra for tea.[16] Those prices were beyond the reach of laboring men, and clearly demark the social stratum of "respectable" skilled workers, clerks, tradesmen, and supervisory workers. (This matches Foster's findings for Oldham, where that stratum was attracted to Methodist chapel-attendance.[17])

If anti-Catholic societies did not directly recruit the working classes to any great extent, did they influence them indirectly by means of the tracts and periodicals that they and town missionaries distributed? Thoughtful observers had doubts about the utility of polemical tracts. When the character Katharine Ashton was about to take over another woman's district visiting, she was made to wonder whether there was any point to handing out tracts. "She had looked into one once, and thought it contained very long, hard words." "'And what is the good of the tracts?' asked Katharine, simply. 'I suppose they may be a good deal of good if the people read them, or if when they read they can understand them,' replied

[12] *Protestant Witness*, I (30 Dec. 1848), 65; *ibid.* (17 Nov. 1849), 252-53.
[13] *Northampton Herald*, 11 Nov. 1843, 9 Nov. 1844, 8 Nov. 1845.
[14] *Penny Protestant Operative*, IX (Nov. 1848), 127.
[15] Michael Anderson, *Family Structure in Nineteenth Century Lancashire* (Cambridge, 1971), pp. 23, 31; Richard K. Fleischman, Jr., *Conditions of Life Among the Cotton Workers of Southeastern Lancashire During the Industrial Revolution (1780-1850)* (New York, 1985), pp. 149-53; Prochaska, *Women and Philanthropy*, pp. 79, 84-85.
[16] *Penny Protestant Operative*, IV (June 1843), 48.
[17] Foster, *Class Struggle*, pp. 214-15.

Jane, 'which sometimes I doubt.'"[18] Dickens, of course, had no doubts, when he had the brickmaker tell Mrs. Pardiggle that he would not read her tracts even if he could read, because tracts were for "babbies," and when he had Jo the crossing-sweep dismiss town missionaries as mysterious beings engaged in debates with one another over issues altogether irrelevant to slum-dwellers.

> Different times there was other genlmen come down Tom-all-Alone's a-prayin, but they all mostly sed as the T'other wuns prayed wrong, and all mostly sounded to be a-talking to theirselves, or a-passing blame on the t'others, and not a-talkin to us. *We* never knowed nothink. *I* never knowd what it wos all about.[19]

A twentieth-century scholar observed that working-class autobiographers who remembered formative influences often mentioned having read chapbooks and broadsides, but never mentioned tracts.[20] Bibles and tracts did fall into the hands of the working classes, but it is significant that there was a small market for the pawning of Bibles and tracts.[21]

Yet despite the low interest in conversion and in attending religious worship—Foster finds 10 percent attending in Oldham; the Manchester and Salford Town Mission found attendances ranging between 10 and 18 percent[22] —town missionaries met a residual interest in religion among urban workers. People claimed a denominational identity, even if they did not attend regularly or at all, and possession of the Bible was common.[23] Thus, it is not surprising to find that anti-Catholic tracts were read, discussed, and even believed by some (because surely no one would print such things if they were false; or because the person who handed out the tracts was a lady or a gentleman, and must know).[24]

The blanket generalization that the anti-Catholic missionaries' activities had a significant influence on urban workers[25] seems doubtful, especially when one remembers the many accounts of reception ranging from polite indifference, through debate and rejection, to bashing. One suspects that the personal style of each missionary determined whether or not he or she would get a hearing. One of the most popular sensation novels of the 1860s featured the character Eliza Floyd, a successful district visitor because she treated the poor with respect. Although "the prim daughters of the second-rate county families fled, tract in hand, discomfited and abashed by the black looks of the half-starved inmates" of the houses of the poor, Eliza was welcomed because "[s]he had the trick of making these people like her before she set to work to reform their evil habits." Her trick was this: "Instead of telling them at once in a candid and Christian-like manner that they were all dirty, degraded, ungrateful, and irreligious, she di-

---

[18] Sewell, *Katharine Ashton*, I, 134-35.

[19] Dickens, *Bleak House*, ch. xlvii.

[20] Neuberg, *Popular Literature*, pp. 259-64.

[21] Prochaska, *Women and Philanthropy*, p. 44.

[22] Foster, *Class Struggle*, pp. 214-15; *14th Annual Report of the Manchester and Salford Town Mission* (1851), p. 17.

[23] Finegan Journal, *passim*, Birmingham Central Library, MS. 312749; Bembridge Journal, *passim*, MCL, BR MS. 259.B1; *3rd Annual Report of the Leicester Town Mission* (1851), p. 6.

[24] *Catholic Weekly Instructor*, I (13 July 1844), 50; [Bishop], *Report, Liverpool Domestic Mission Society*, pp. 19-23; *Protestant Watchman*, No. 16 (June 1850), p. 198, No. 17 (July 1850), p. 208; *Manchester Guardian*, 16 Nov. 1850.

[25] Wolffe, "Protestant Societies and Anti-Catholic Agitations," p. 237.

plomatized and finessed with them as if she had been canvassing the county."[26] In real life, Thomas Augustin Finegan, the Birmingham missionary, knew that a little bit of respect went a long way.

In sum, only a small minority of ideologically motivated workers participated in organized anti-Catholicism. The propagandistic activities of the anti-Catholic societies did penetrate working-class neighborhoods and were listened to by some; but their main effects were to reawaken and reinforce preexisting prejudices and stereotypes. Because the main focus of that propaganda was religious (anti-Catholic) rather than ethnic (anti-Irish), cultural antipathies towards the Irish did not receive positive re-enforcement from that direction.

Women

It is as hard to gauge the level of female participation in organized anti-Catholic activities as it is to gauge that of workers. The most prominent female anti-Catholic activist was Charlotte Elizabeth Tonna, who edited the intensly anti-Catholic *Christian Lady's Magazine*, wrote for the *Churchman's Monthly Review*, belonged to the Christian Influence Society, supported the London City Mission and several Jewish restorationist groups, and edited the *Protestant Magazine*, the organ of the Protestant Association, from 1841 to her death in 1847.[27] She was very much a special case, and it is telling that she was a shadowy, backstage figure as compared to the likes of Thomas Ragg, Lord Ashley, Sir Culling Eardley Eardley, and other males.

Charlotte Elizabeth Browne Phelan Tonna, born in 1790, was the daughter of a minor canon of Norwich and rector of St. Giles's in that city. She was raised in a household in which there was much political discussion of a Tory, anti-Jacobin nature, which discussions she was allowed to hear. The Napoleonic Wars, with their fear of invasion, made a great impression on her, as did the lurid illustrations in the family copy of *Foxe's Book of Martyrs*. She read the newspapers and tracts that her father received, and remembered that her father, who was a large and strong man, once led a group of "gentlemen" to break up a meeting of working-class Jacobins and drive them out of the city. She loved Shakespeare and music; her deafness encouraged her to cultivate a lively imagination and to pretend that she was a Shakespearian heroine. After her father's death, the family removed to London, where she met and married, around 1814, Captain George Phelan of the Rifle Brigade. After spending two years as an army wife in Nova Scotia, she followed Phelan to Ireland, where his property was tied up in a lawsuit. While Phelan was in Dublin, attending to the lawsuit, Tonna lived on the estate.[28]

The chronology of Charlotte Elizabeth Tonna's life is vague, but at this point, in the late 1810s and early 1820s, she had a rebirth experience and her marriage collapsed. In a way typical of Pauline religious terrors, her inner tension grew as she became more and more convinced about the many divine laws that she was violating; the tension was released when she realized that giving herself to Jesus would save her. How this affected her

---

[26] Braddon, *Aurora Floyd*, p. 15.
[27] Lewis, *Lighten Their Darkness*, pp. 88-89.
[28] Tonna, *Life of Charlotte Elizabeth*, pp. 14, 18, 46-52, 73-75.

relationship with Phelan is as unclear as his own character. In later years, Tonna publicly declined to say bad things about him, thereby implying that there were bad things to be said. What we do know is that she refused to accompany her husband when he returned to British North America in 1821; that they separated; that Tonna lived off the profits from writing tracts, articles, and religious novels; and that she turned to anonymous writing in the late 1820s, after her husband asserted his ownership of her copyrights.[29]

Tonna moved to England in 1824, living in Clifton, Bagshot, and Sandhurst until 1831, and in suburban London thereafter. In England, she fell under the influences of Hugh McNeile, the Ulster-born Liverpool anti-Catholic, and William Howells, a popular Evangelical preacher,[30] who convinced her of the truth of premillennialism and of the error of Edward Irving's teachings about miraculous gifts of healing and speaking in tongues. She spent the rest of her life in religious journalism. Her first husband died in 1837, and she married Lewis H. J. Tonna, himself a writer of anti-Catholic literature, in 1841.[31]

Although Tonna "was a more prolific polemicist in the cause of millenarianism than in that of social reform,"[32] what little scholarly attention she has received has focused on her industrial novel, *Helen Fleetwood* (1839-40), one of the earliest of that genre, her essay, *The Perils of the Nation* (1843), which Lord Ashley and the Christian Influence Society commissioned to be the Evangelical answer to social problems, and her miscellaneous writings related to urban slums.[33] Tonna rejected both working-class combination and state intervention (save for the Ten Hours Bill) as solutions to England's social problems. Unionism, she thought, was wicked in and of itself because it administered secret oaths; beyond that, the resort to the strike violated workers' moral and legal obligations to fulfill their contracts. She had doubts about state intervention because she believed that the root problem, a spiritual breakdown in both individuals and society, required a spiritual solution. So, she called upon ladies, whose characters were specially suited for detecting injustice and comforting the unhappy, to influence their fathers, husbands, and sons.[34] Tonna thus falls into the category of conservative social Christian, as a type of the social gospel.

Tonna's concentration on the sufferings of females has led a twentieth-century scholar to see her creating "a force of women working for women."[35] Her emphasis on individual women nurturing right ideas in

---

[29] *Ibid.*, pp. 75-76, 104-13, 123-26, 203-4.

[30] Howells (1778-1832), lessee of the Long Acre Episcopal Chapel, 1817-32; published strongly Evangelical sermons (*DNB*, X, 118).

[31] Tonna, *Life of Charlotte Elizabeth*, pp. 191, 270-75, 281-85, 326.

[32] Ivanka Kovacevic and S. Barbara Kanner, "Blue Book into Novel: The Forgotten Industrial Fiction of Charlotte Elizabeth Tonna," *Nineteenth-Century Fiction*, XXV (1970-71), 155.

[33] *Ibid.*, pp. 160-68, 172-73; Joseph Kestner, *Protest and Reform: The British Social Narrative by Women, 1827-1867* (Madison, 1985), pp. 51, 58, 63-66; Lynn Alexander, "Publishing for Women: Charlotte Elizabeth Tonna and the *Christian Lady's Magazine*," typescript paper read at the Research Society for Victorian Periodicals, November 1990; Lynn Alexander, "Charlotte Elizabeth and the Crusade for Reform," typescript paper read at the Pacific Coast Conference on British Studies, University of Santa Clara, San José, California, March 1991. Dr. Alexander graciously sent me copies of her papers.

[34] Kovacevic and Kanner, "Blue Book into Novel," p. 160; Kestner, *Protest and Reform*, pp. 43-44.

[35] Alexander, "Charlotte Elizabeth."

their male connections in the home context, however, well fits Victorian ideas about domesticity and separate spheres. Indeed, Tonna criticized the preferential hiring of women over men in factories on the grounds that such a practice decreased female domesticity.[36]

The fact was that Evangelical sexual politics limited women to the patriarchal, domestic scene, thereby condemning them to "a somewhat painful sense of uselessness," as "Laica" put it in the *Record*.[37] "Gentlemen can meet, speak, and sign Petitions, but what can *we* do? You will perhaps be disposed to dismiss the question at once by saying 'nothing—there *is* nothing that we *can* do.' Let me intreat you, however, not to rest satisfied with this conclusion." "Laica" then invoked the example of foremothers—the women of Carthage, Jael, and the wise woman who gave up the offender to Joab—to show that there were precedents for female activism. But when it came to offering practical suggestions for combatting popery in the nineteenth century, "Laica" was constrained by the doctrine of separate spheres. "Nothing could give me greater pain than to hear of the women of England doing anything by which they should advance one step out of that modest retirement which is their proper sphere." Rather, women could best combat popery by being nurturers: by keeping alive the issues of the day in their households, by teaching Protestantism to their children, and by encouraging their husbands and brothers to be active in the Protestant cause.

The common view of male religious leaders throughout the nineteenth century was that women had a greater "religious instinct" than men had, a greater "facility for worship."[38] Pierce Connelly neatly separated the spheres when he explained that women were "always the first to feel and to acknowledge their spiritual necessities," but were less fit than men "to choose the remedies they need."[39] Women's role in religious matters was thus acknowledged to be important, distinct, and subordinate, a matter for the heart rather than for the head. Women brought the domestic vocation to their charitable work; they were primarily domestic, fostering creatures, and their work outside the home was domesticity writ large. They were to influence others rather than to exercise power themselves.[40]

In practice, women played a significant role in Victorian organized religion. In England as in the United States, they were more attracted to *membership* than were men. (The membership of Cumbrian Congregationalist chapels ranged from 58 to 68 percent women during the second half of the century.) The proportion of female to male *attendances* was closer, but women still predominated. (York in 1901 showed fifty-one women to forty-nine men at chapel, and sixty-five women to thirty-five men at church; Lambeth in 1902 showed 1.2 women to one man at chapel, and 1.7 women to one man at church.) Women provided workers as well as attenders. The existence of Sunday schools, clubs and guilds, missionary societies, the Mothers' Union, and the Girls' Friendly Society depended

[36] Kestner, *Protest and Reform*, p. 17.

[37] *Record*, 6 Jan. 1851.

[38] Brian Heeney, *The Women's Movement in the Church of England, 1850-1930* (Oxford, 1988), p. 13.

[39] Paz, *Connelly*, p. 89.

[40] Prochaska, *Women and Philanthropy*, pp. 1-17; Heeney, *Women's Movement*, pp. 10-11, 17-18.

upon female volunteers.[41] Women also played an important role as subscribers to voluntary societies. The proportion of female subscribers to
philanthropic societies grew during the nineteenth century. Women made
up between a fifth and a third of the subscribers to the Society for the
Propagation of Christian Knowledge, Prayer-Book and Homily Society,
British and Foreign Bible Society, Religious Tract Society, Society for the
Promotion of Christianity among the Jews, Church Missionary Society,
and Strangers' Friend Society by 1830. Thirty-eight percent of the London
City Mission's subscribers in 1838 were women; this rose during the century, to 42 percent in 1870, and 57 percent in 1904. Because women's financial contributions were in proportion to their numbers, philanthropic
societies grew increasingly dependent upon women as the century wore on.
Finally, women's auxiliaries became commonplace during the century, and
women increasingly were permitted to attend annual general meetings as
recognition that the philanthropic societies increasingly depended upon
women's time and money.[42]

Anti-Catholicism, however, was a more exclusively male activity. Of the
thirty-four lay subscribers to the British Reformation Society from Lancaster, Preston, Leeds, Derby, Birmingham, and Leicester (from March
1849 to March 1853), only nine (27 percent) were women.[43] Of the twenty
laypersons who subscribed directly to the Leicester Auxiliary, British Reformation Society, in 1853, five (25 percent) were women.[44] None of the
members of the Birmingham Auxiliary, Protestant Association, in 1849-50,
were women.[45] The Evangelical Alliance cast its net wider than either the
British Reformation Society or the Protestant Association (which were
mainly Anglican), but it showed even less female participation. Of its 294
lay subscribers in 1850 from Preston, Liverpool, Manchester, Derby,
Birmingham, and Lincoln, 273 (93 percent) were men and only twenty-one
(7 percent) were women.[46]

Those women who did subscribe to anti-Catholic societies were decidedly limited in their active roles. The Birmingham Church of England Lay
Association at first permitted female subscribers to vote at its annual general meeting, but only by proxy; however this right was withdrawn in
1846.[47] Canvassing for petitions was mostly a male activity—the Southampton Protestant Defence Committee instructed its male canvassers not
to accept the signatures of females.[48] On the other hand, the Protestant
Alliance used female canvassers, but only for petitions against
nunneries—thereby preserving women's separate sphere.[49] Women rarely
attended meetings, unless they were held in churches and chapels (their

[41] Bebbington, *Evangelicalism*, p. 12; Heeney, *Women's Movement*, pp. 5-6.
[42] F. K. Prochaska, "Women in English Philanthropy, 1790-1830," *International Review of Social History*, XIX (1974), 428-30; Prochaska, *Women and Philanthropy*, pp. 24-29, 38; Lewis,
Lighten Their Darkness, p. 221.
[43] *British Protestant*, V (June/July 1849), 156-73; *ibid.*, VI (June/July 1850), 111-27; *ibid.*, VII
(June 1851), 94-112; *ibid.*, VIII (July 1852), 80-99; *ibid.*, IX (June 1853), 115-32.
[44] *Ibid.*, IX (June 1853), 136.
[45] *Protestant Watchman*, No. 10 (Dec. 1849), wrapper; *ibid.*, No. 18 (Aug. 1850), p. 220.
[46] Evangelical Alliance, *Abstract of Proceedings of the Fourth Annual Conference, held in Liverpool, October 1850* (1850), pp. 54-68.
[47] Birmingham Church of England Lay Association, *4th Annual Report* (1843), p. 3, *7th Annual
Report* (1846), p. 5.
[48] Undated memorandum, [ca. Jan. 1851], Page & Moody Papers, Southampton County Record
Office, D/PM/10/1/25.
[49] *Bulwark*, II (July 1852).

attendance appears to have been most common at Wesleyan meetings). Their presence at public meetings was rarely commented upon in the press, which likely means that they were rarely present. When they were present, they were likely to be segregated to balconies or windows, like the women who attended the meeting of the Improved Hot Muffin Company.[50] Hugh Stowell rejoiced at the "true Protestant zeal" that he contrived to find among working-class women, and the Protestant Operative Association at first encouraged women's auxiliaries, but he appears to have taken no steps to include them in his band of working-class anti-Catholic activists, and the level of female participation in Protestant Operative activities declined throughout the 1840s.[51]

The first factor that limited female participation in anti-Catholic work was the separate spheres doctrine itself, which limited women to domestic-like work and excluded them from talking about issues. So, as Mrs. Oliphant put it, "when a woman has an active mind, and still does not care for parish work, it is a little hard for her to fill a 'sphere.'"[52] Anti-Catholicism, however, was very much a political issue, and women were unfit to have opinions on political issues. An anti-Catholic at St. Ives became upset when a meeting, advertised as a lecture on popery, adopted a petition to Parliament: "about half the audience was composed of the fair sex and young persons, who, no doubt, attended in the expectation of hearing a *lecture*, devoid of party or sectarian feeling, but were not competent to vote upon *formal resolutions*, at *parish* meetings. . . ."[53] Even so prominent a female anti-Catholic as Charlotte Elizabeth Tonna had to defend herself against criticism for "indulging a taste not considered lady-like."[54] Tonna is an excellent example of Mrs. Oliphant's woman with an active mind who does not care for parish work. She managed to find a place in the anti-Catholic world; but it was against great odds, and stark economic necessity gave her an added source of strength to persevere in her writing.

The second factor that discouraged women from becoming active in anti-Catholic work was the prurient nature of that work. Anti-Catholics had to pay a certain amount of attention to sexual matters, specifically with reference to the sex lives of monks and priests, and to the use of the confessional as a means of seduction. They had to read tracts and listen to lectures that discussed sexual intercourse; they had to consider the sexual implications of everything from casuist moral theology to basement rooms in convents. Anti-Catholic literature used the language of seduction and of perversion to describe conversions to Roman Catholicism. Anti-Catholics assumed as a given that celibacy, being unnatural, was a front for lascivious behavior, and that the relationship between confessor and female penitent was charged with sexuality. There can be no doubt that some male anti-Catholics found in this a godly, uplifting, and acceptable

[50] *Rochester, Chatham, and Stroud Gazette*, 26 Nov. 1850; *Times*, 6, 14 Dec. 1850; *Manchester Guardian*, 13 Nov. 1850; Dickens, *Nicholas Nickleby*, p. 71.
[51] *Times*, 17 June 1841; *Christian Times*, 14 Dec. 1850; *Manchester Guardian*, 26 Feb. 1851.
[52] Oliphant, *Miss Marjoribanks*, p. 395.
[53] *Cambridge Chronicle*, 4 Jan. 1851.
[54] Tonna, *Life of Charlotte Elizabeth*, p. 48.

way of consuming pornography. Women certainly would have to be excluded from that activity.[55]

The third and most important factor that discouraged women from becoming active in anti-Catholic work was the work's implications for gender roles. Anglo-Catholicism and Roman Catholicism ultimately drew opposition because their support for the confessional challenged, and was thought to undermine, the authority of husbands and fathers over their wives and daughters, because their support for the community life for women challenged the middle-class belief that women were unfit to fill leadership roles in religion, and because their support for celibacy and the community life for men challenged the notion that the ideal male was the practicing heterosexual. The Victorian home was sanctified, declared to be a holy place (by such as John Ruskin, Baldwin Brown, Charles Kingsley, Frederic Harrison, John Stuart Mill, and George Eliot). Kingsley maintained, even, that only married men could understand fully the ideas of the Fatherhood of God and of Christ's love for the Church.[56] So, Roman Catholic priests (and celibate Anglo-Catholic priests) were at a disadvantage, for their unmarried state gave them a defective grasp of religion. Because the sexual element in anti-Tractarianism and anti-Catholicism reflects in large part fears about a potential reordering of the sexual politics of the age, it would have been difficult to encourage women to participate fully in those activities.

The confessional, whether Roman Catholic or Anglo-Catholic, drew heavy fire throughout the nineteenth century. Theologically literate Protestants long had objected to the practice because it substituted confession to a priest and priestly absolution for confession to Jesus and his absolution. What especially affronted the Victorian middle classes, however, were the secrecy of the practice and the fact that women went to confession on their own, without the sanction of their fathers, brothers, or husbands.[57] Confession, in the words of William Walsh, "interferes with the confidence which should exist between husband and wife."[58] That is, a woman who confesses has secrets that she does not share with her husband. Furthermore, priests are enjoined not to violate the secrecy of the confessional, not even to admit that they have heard a person's confession. The seal of the confessional is nothing more than lying and perjury.[59] It was thus the duty of Victorian males to restore patriarchal authority in the family, as John Bull is about to do in Fig. 5.

Women's religious orders, which flourished in the nineteenth century as never before, also subverted John Bull's patriarchal authority. Victorian sisterhoods, both Anglo-Catholic and Roman Catholic, were active in the world rather than contemplative in cloisters, and thus offered useful and important things for women to do (useful and important at least as the Victorians defined those terms). Furthermore sisterhoods were republics of women that offered them leadership roles, space, and, at least within the

---

[55] Best, "Popular Protestantism," pp. 117, 124-35; Klaus, *Pope, Protestants, and Irish*, pp. 288-94.

[56] Houghton, *Victorian Frame of Mind*, p. 347.

[57] Yates, "Jesuits in Disguise," pp. 209-14; John Shelton Reed, "'A Female Movement': The Feminization of Nineteenth-Century Anglo-Catholicism," *Anglican and Episcopal History*, LVII (1988), 216-25.

[58] Walsh, *Secret History*, p. 81.

[59] *Ibid.*, pp. 80-92.

PUNCH, OR THE LONDON CHARIVARI, June 26, 1858.

RELIGION À LA MODE.

Mr. Bull. "NO, NO, MR. JACK PRIEST! AFTER ALL I HAVE GONE THROUGH, I'M NOT SUCH A FOOL AS TO STAND ANY OF THIS DISGUSTING NONSENSE!"

Fig. 5

orders, liberation from patriarchal trammells. Deaconesses (who were mainly from the Church of England's Evangelical or Broad Church wings) worked in parishes under the direct supervision of the clergyman, while the authority of the clergyman over nuns was mediated by the authority of the mother foundress or mother superior, and the stories of many religious orders include conflicts between a determined foundress and a male would-be protector.[60]

Anglo-Catholicism attracted women in parish life as well as in sister-hoods. Anglo-Catholic parishes appealed to women more than to men, exaggerating a trend common to Evangelical and middle-of-the-road Anglican parishes. The demographics of spinsterhood were timely for religion, of course, but Anglo-Catholicism was especially attractive for women because of its challenge to the patriarchal authority of husbands and fathers. The elimination of pew rents and the substitution of bench pews for box pews, both of which were marks of the Anglo-Catholic parish, served to break up the authority of the patriarch over the family unit, at least within the precincts of the church.[61] The box pew, enclosed from the outside world by a door, containing domestic comforts like a stove, was a little bit of home space that intruded into the sacred space of the church nave. The patriarch's authority ruled in that space, and consequently the authority of the priest over the sacred space was diminished. Anglo-Catholicism, by turning all the nave's space into sacred space, by making men and women sit side by side facing the altar, and even by separating the sexes (in some parishes), put John Bull on a plane of equality with his wife and daughters, at least with respect to the priest.

John Bull's heterosexuality was also under attack. While Roman Catholic celibacy was viewed as license to fornicate with women, Anglo-Catholic celibacy was viewed as same-sex love. The charge was only hinted at in the nineteenth century, but the hints could be pretty broad. *Punch* turned ritualists into gushing bum-boys, preening in their ecclesiastical finery (Fig. 6). Anglo-Catholicism, and to a lesser extent Roman Catholicism, did challenge prevailing values, did so in a public way, and drew support from groups who rejected those values, including men attracted to other men. Anglo-Catholicism, and to a lesser extent Roman Catholicism, thus were counter-cultures.[62]

The extent and nature of female participation in English voluntary societies remains relatively unexplored territory, especially as compared to their United States counterparts. Voluntary societies played the same function in developing women's self-consciousness in England as they did in the United States; they provided educated middle-class women an opening to exercise leadership and learn administrative skills, and they allowed some women to come to two related conclusions: that voluntaryism

---

[60] Reed, "Female Movement," pp. 226-38; Susan O'Brien, "*Terra Incognita*: The Nun in Nine-teenth-Century England," *Past and Present*, No. 121 (1988), pp. 110-46 (for Roman Catholic orders); and Martha Vicinus, *Independent Women: Work and Community for Single Women, 1850-1920* (Chicago, 1985), pp. 46-84 (for Anglican orders).

[61] Reed, "Female Movement," pp. 201-16.

[62] For discussions of these themes, see Pickering, *Anglo-Catholicism*, pp. 188-91, 194, 201-203; Hilliard, "Unenglish and Unmanly," pp. 184, 192-93; Reed, "Female Movement," p. 200; and John Shelton Reed, "'Giddy Young Men': A Counter-Cultural Aspect of Victorian Anglo-Catholicism," *Comparative Social Research*, XI (1989), 209-26. Prof. Reed was kind enough to show me his book-length typescript, "Revolt Against Common Sense: The Cultural Politics of Victorian Anglo-Catholicism," which explores these and other issues in greater detail.

Fig. 6

HEIGHT OF FASHION
Ardent Ritualist: "Oh, Athanasius, it's charmingly becoming!"

was not sufficient to deal with social problems and that male control limited women. Such a function appears to have come later in England, in the 1870s with Josephine Butler's campaign for repeal of the Contagious Diseases Acts. That campaign opened the doors for women to organize their own associations, to assume the leadership of those groups, to speak in public, and to participate in electoral politics. In contrast to United States temperance and abolitionist societies, which opened those doors to women earlier on in the century, English women's temperance and abolitionist societies were cautious, depended upon male support, and were not as central to the creation of the women's movement.[63]

In Town

Organized anti-Catholicism was primarily an urban activity; the Roman Catholics were there, as were the opportunities for public meetings and petition drives, the infrastructure of town missions and Protestant organizations, the newspapers to report on anti-Catholic activities, not to mention the money to pay for all this. In choosing an urban area to explore, one should move beyond London, about which much has been written, since one of the arguments of this book is that local conditions influence the reception of national issues. The possibilities outside London are rich; we have already touched on the diverse cities and towns of Northampton, Exeter, Derby, Leeds, Liverpool, and Birmingham. I chose Manchester, however, because that town, "the shock city of the age,"[64] was strongly Methodist, but with strong Anglican and Evangelical Nonconformist presences; it had a large Irish population, with a large native population as well. Its leadership had a proudly independent self-consciousness; it had a rich history, but was in the vanguard of the industrial age.

Most of Manchester's anti-Catholics are little more than names on subscription lists, but, rarely, one can discern the people behind the names. Charles Carill Worsley is such a man. The Worsley family was originally Nonconformist, but Thomas Carill Worsley (fl. 1800-48) maintained religious interests in both Anglican and Presbyterian circles. He was Anglican enough to subscribe the substantial sum of 1 gn. p.a. to the British Reformation Society, but he kept an interest in Platt Chapel, Rusholme, which had become Unitarian. Worsley threatened legal action in the 1830s to get control of its trust deeds (presumably on behalf of Trinitarian Presbyterians). A decade later, after the Disruption had split the English Presbyterians between Kirk and Free Church, he sought to block the attempts of Robert Barbour, a Manchester general commission merchant who was a native of Scotland, to capture the chapel for the English Synod of the Church of Scotland.[65] (This action, which dragged on into the 1840s, is of course a local reflection of the national struggle between the two rival

---

[63] Paul McHugh, *Prostitution and Victorian Social Reform* (New York, 1980), pp. 164-67, 265-68; Prochaska, "Women in English Philanthropy," pp. 427, 430-32; Prochaska, *Women and Philanthropy*, pp. 227-30; B. Harrison, *Peaceable Kingdom*, pp. 233-34, 238; Lilian Lewis Shiman, "'Changes Are Dangerous': Women and Temperance in Victorian England," *Religion in the Lives of English Women*, pp. 210-11.

[64] Briggs, *Victorian Cities*, p. 92.

[65] *British Protestant*, I (July 1845), 172; British Reformation Society, *21st Annual Report* (1848), pp. 34-50; bill, Thomas Carill Worsley, to Barrett & Ridgway, 30 Oct. 1834, Carill Worsley Papers, MCL, M 35/9/63/8; bill, Thomas Carill Worsley, to Barrett, Ridgway Ford & Ridgway, 13 May 1844, *ibid.*, M 35/9/63/32.

branches of the Presbyterians.[66]) He was active in the ecumenical movement, serving as co-vice-chairman of the Evangelical Alliance's Northwestern Divisional Committee in 1847.[67]

His son, Charles Carill Worsley (born 1800; still living in 1863), was more solidly Anglican, moving in Hugh Stowell's Evangelical circles. Describing himself as a landed proprietor, he maintained a handsome establishment at Platt Hall, Rusholme, with a butler, groom, cook, two housemaids, and a kitchenmaid to serve the needs of his wife and himself.[68] A good Evangelical, he subscribed 1 gn. p.a. to the Religious Tract Society, and to the Evangelical Alliance, but he reserved his primary benevolence for more explicitly anti-Catholic objects, subscribing £5 p.a. to the British Reformation Society.[69]

It was at the local level, in connection with Hugh Stowell's activities, that Charles Carill Worsley invested the most substantial money and time. He contributed to the salary of James Bembridge, a missionary in St. Philip's District, Manchester, in the 1840s. He subscribed a handsome £10 p.a. to Stowell's Church of England Association for Providing Ministration and Instruction for the Irish Romanists of Manchester and Salford in the 1850s. Another £10 went to help build a Protestant school at Barnes Green and the Blackley side of Mostn Lane (to neutralize an existing Roman Catholic school).[70] Time was money to middle-class Victorians. Hence, the high level of Worsley's commitment led him to invest time as an officer of the Manchester Auxiliary, Church Pastoral-Aid Society, the Manchester and Salford Protestant Operative Association, and the general committee of the Manchester and Salford Protestant Defence Committee. He was chosen to move the first resolution at the Manchester public meeting of 21 November 1850, and he appeared on the platform at many other anti-Catholic rallies during the 1840s and '50s.[71]

Devout Evangelical laymen like Charles Carill Worsley were mainstays of local anti-Catholic organizations, reflecting the "new level of lay engagement in church affairs in urban Lancashire" that Howe finds.[72] Although the clergy provided the leadership, the laity provided the money and the activists. Prominent laymen such as Carill Worsley also drew in other participants who may have found it advantageous to their trade to be seen as active in forwarding worthy causes, and organized anti-Catholicism was such a worthy cause. Thus an analysis of the lay participants in Manchester anti-Catholicism reveals interlocking networks of business relations. Carill Worsley rubbed shoulders at the Church Pastoral-Aid Soci-

[66] *Sup.*, pp. 180-82.
[67] *Evangelical Christendom*, I (Mar. 1847), 96.
[68] Home Office: Census of Population, 1851: Enumerators Books, PRO (Portugal Street), H.O. 107/2219, f. 252.
[69] Subscription receipts, Religious Tract Society, 1857-64, Carill Worsley Papers, MCL, M 35/9/7/227-234; subscription receipts, British Reformation Society, 1859-63, *ibid.*, M 35/9/7/220-224; James Millar to C. C. Worsley, 6 Oct. 1863, *ibid.*, M 35/9/7/226; Evangelical Alliance, British Organization, *Abstract of Proceedings of the Fourth Annual Conference* (1850), pp. 54-68.
[70] Introduction, Bembridge Journals, MCL, BR MS. 259.B1; subscription receipts, 1857-59, Carill Worsley Papers, *ibid.*, M 35/9/7/44-46; Rev. W. R. Keeling to C. C. Worsley, 13 and 19 Feb. 1861, *ibid.*, M 35/9/7/12-13.
[71] *Manchester Courier*, 9, 23 Nov. 1850, 1 Feb., 1 Mar. 1851.
[72] Howe, *Cotton Masters*, p. 65.

ety with Thomas Anderson (his bookseller), and at the Protestant Defence Committee with Anderson and Henry Whaite (his gilder and printseller).[73]

Charles Wolstenholme (born 1810), a land, building, and insurance agent, was another active layman in a web of business deals. Active in the Protestant Operative Association and the Protestant Defence Committee, he had mutual dealings with James and George Holland Ackers (connected with William Ackers, solicitor, on the Protestant Defence Committee), and with William Bowden, builder (also on the Protestant Defence Committee). The Ackers, in their turn, engaged in transactions with Thomas Pittard Bagshaw, solicitor, whom they met at the Protestant Defence Committee.[74] Other dealings involving Protestant Defence Committee members brought together John Taylor, oil merchant, Richard Hargreaves Ingham, druggist, James Stansall Pott, official assignee, and Thomas and John Lomas of John Lomas & Son, calico printers. (The last family was rapidly on its way to Anglican respectability, for John Lomas, grandson of the firm's founder, was described as "late of Strangeways in the County of Lancaster Calico Printer but now of the University of Oxford Gentleman.")[75] Robert Gardner (partner in Gardner & Bazley, cotton spinners) maintained an Evangelical home and was a major contributor to Hugh Stowell. He combined his economic activities with his religion by being a Tory free-trader, and he believed that cotton lords should use their wealth, derived from the working classes, to promote the well-being of those classes.[76] Finally, John Munn (of John Munn & Co., cotton spinners) and William Pearson (general merchant and Munn's managing partner) provided considerable financial support to Hugh Stowell and to the Rev. H.W. McGrath, Stowell's aide in the Church Pastoral-Aid Society and the Protestant Operative Association.[77] For these men, anti-Catholicism neatly combined their duty towards God and their duty towards their neighbor.

But if organized anti-Catholicism brought some of Manchester's textile masters and professional men together in close business harmony, it also included others who ultimately worked at cross purposes against them. We have already noted that many prominent men who lent their names to anti-Catholic activities in 1850 and 1851 abandoned the anti-Catholic party in the parliamentary elections of 1852.[78] Another test of cohesion is the question of secular education. Manchester was home to the Lancashire (later National) Public Schools Association, which wanted to solve the problem of how to provide elementary education for England's industrial society by eliminating all references to religion (the main stumbling block to state provision of education) in schools (which were to be funded out of the local rates and controlled by democratically elected committees). Founded in 1847, the LPSA had connections with the Anti-Corn Law

[73] *Manchester Courier*, 1 Feb., 1 Mar. 1851; bills to Henry Whaite, and Thomas Anderson & Son, Carill Worsley Papers, MCL, M 35/9/51/28 and M/35/9/52/3.
[74] Indenture (draft), 1847, Messrs. Slater, Heelis, Solicitors, MCL, M 159/1/3; indenture, 30 July 1851, *ibid.*, M 159/1/5/1; indenture, 30 July 1851, *ibid.*, M 159/1/5/2.
[75] Indenture, 27 Aug. 1838, *ibid.*, M 159/3/22/3; indenture, 9 Mar. 1844, *ibid.*, M 159/2/11/21; indenture, 13 Feb. 1852, *ibid.*, M 159/2/16/1.
[76] Howe, *Cotton Masters*, pp. 39, 64-66, 212, 302-303.
[77] *Ibid.*, pp. 84-85; Letters of Pearson to McGrath, 5 May 1854, 10 July 1855, 23 Dec. 1856, and Pearson to Stowell, 20 Mar. 1858, Letter Book (1853-58), John Munn & Co. Records, MCL, M 386, Box 2, ff. 56, 109, 169-70, 268.
[78] *Sup.*, pp. 210-11.

League. The aims of the LPSA were anathema to Stowell's Tory Anglican anti-Catholics, who spent as much energy against it as against the Pope.[79]

Some members of the Protestant Defence Committee's general committee, however, were also active in the LPSA. Thomas Ashton, fustian manufacturer and cotton spinner, lent his name to the Protestant Defence Committee, but he also served as a vice president of the LPSA. (So did Elkanah Armitage.)[80] Robert Barbour, "that great benefactor of English Presbyterianism,"[81] who crossed solicitors with Thomas Carill Worsley over the Platt Chapel, but who cooperated with Charles Carill Worsley against the Pope, hesitated to get involved with the LPSA, but was sympathetic. "I am not certain . . . that I could further the Association as my views have always been that it is desirable education should be based on moral and religious principles—at the same time rather than have none I would be willing to promote Secular education alone."[82] William Romaine Callender, who moved into calico-printing via wholesale drapery, was a Nonconformist, active Liberal, town councillor, leader in the Anti-Corn Law League, and enthusiastic subscriber to the LPSA. (He bequeathed his Protestantism, but not his politics, to his son, a key figure in the revived Lancashire Tory party of the 1860s and '70s.)[83] Other anti-Catholics—T. P. Bagshaw and William Joynson, silk manufacturer—subscribed and attended meetings.[84] Still more—William Howarth, drysalter, Frank Jewsbury, insurance agent, and William Medcalf, land agent—were content simply to subscribe.[85] Anti-Catholicism was too broad a movement to focus its energies on much beyond anti-Catholicism itself.

I now turn to a more summary description of Manchester's anti-Catholics. Few memorials or petitions from the agitation of 1850-51 have survived, and none of those is from an urban public meeting.[86] I have thus had to construct a list of 371 anti-Catholics from the names of those who were reported present at the Manchester public meeting, who were on the general committee of the Manchester and Salford Protestant Defence Committee, and who attended Protestant Operative meetings. Sixty-eight men could not be identified in the town directory for 1850. (Not all of these sixty-eight were Mancunians, although their presence meant that they had Manchester connections; they include John and Thomas Clegg, textile mill owners of Bolton, John and William Haslam, textile men from Preston, and James Heald, M.P. for Stockport, 1847-52.) I dropped them

[79] Howe, *Cotton Masters*, pp. 215-29.
[80] *Ibid.*, p. 220; letters of Ashton to R. W. Smiles, 16 Sept. 1851 to 30 Dec. 1853, National Public Schools Association Papers, MCL, M 136/2/3/74-79.
[81] Cornick, "Catch a Scotchman Becoming an Englishman," p. 206.
[82] Robert Barbour to H. K. Forrest, 16 Dec. 1848, National Public Schools Association Papers, MCL, M 136/2/3/147.
[83] W. R. Callender to Frank Espinasse, 6 July 1849, *ibid.*, M 136/2/3/518; Hanham, *Elections and Party Management*, pp. 315-17; Howe, *Cotton Masters*, p. 16.
[84] T. P. Bagshaw to Espinasse, n.d., National Public Schools Association Papers, MCL, M 136/2/3/128; "A Programme of Proceedings in connection with the Sabbath School and Educational Institute, St. Mary Cray, Kent," Sept. 1850, *ibid.*, M 136/3/10/14.
[85] William Howarth to Espinasse, 17 Dec. 1849, *ibid.*, M 136/2/3/1697; Frank Jewsbury to Espinasse, 22 Jan. and 24 Mar. 1849, *ibid.*, M 136/2/3/1817-1818; William Medcalf to Espinasse, 22 Jan. 1849, *ibid.*, M 136/2/3/2348; Medcalf to E. Waugh, 12 Jan. 1849, *ibid.*, M 136/2/3/2345.
[86] H.O. 54/35, Civil Petitions and Addresses (1841-1854), PRO (Kew), contains an anti-Maynooth petition from Bath with the signatures, alas, detached, three memorials signed only by the presiding officer (the mayor and corporation of Woodstock, the Staffordshire county meeting, and the Kirk General Session of Dundee), and eight, all from rural areas, with signatures.

from the survey, leaving 303 men for whom occupational data are available. I located 155 of these men in the 1851 census enumerators' books, and thus have household data for them. (A flood caused serious damage to the enumerators' books when they were kept in the basement of Somerset House; the books for several out-townships and districts of Manchester and Salford are decayed and unfit for production or for filming.)[87]

The area around greater Manchester was dominated by cotton during the period ca. 1830-60. The county was not yet divided between a weaving North and a spinning South, and the combined mill was the norm. Calico-printing, and the related process of bleaching, were centered along the Blackburn-Manchester-Stockport axis. Other manufactures were still important to the region's economy. Among textiles, woollens, worsteds, and flax were on the wane, but silk was growing. Engineering and paper-making were also significant. Finally, the storage and distribution of raw materials and finished products served the cotton trade.[88] The occupations of Manchester's anti-Catholics reflected the town's economic life.

A small number of gentry or would-be gentry lent their names to the Manchester and Salford Protestant Defence Committee. These included the landed proprietors Charles Carill Worsley of Platt Hall, Rusholme, and Col. William Lee Clowes, J.P., of Broughton Old Hall, Cheetham Hill Road. Henry Andrew, of No. 9 Addison Terrace, Victoria Park, Rusholme, called himself a "small landed proprietor & annuitant."[89] The status of others is somewhat more doubtful. *Slater's* Manchester and Salford directory listed William Hall Casson as a slate dealer; he preferred to think of himself as a gentleman who lived off the rents of houses, and so told the enumerator.[90]

TABLE 8

Occupations of Manchester/Salford Anti-Catholics

Occupation	N	%
Cotton	116	38.7
Professional/Service	63	21.0
Retail	52	17.3
Distribution	22	7.3
Other Textiles	19	6.3
Other Manufacturing	19	6.3
Gentlemen	9	3.0
Total	300	99.9

Source: MS. Enumerators' books, 1851 census

[87] The sources for my analysis are *Slater's General and Classified Directory and Street Register of Manchester and Salford, and their Vicinities* (Manchester, 1850); and Home Office: Census of Population, 1851: Enumerators Books, PRO (Portugal Street), H.O. 107/2162, 2218-2235; supplemented by Howe, *Cotton Masters*. The books for Chorlton-cum-Hardy, Withington, Gorton, Didsbury, Burnage, Levenshulme, Rusholme, Openshaw (H.O. 107/2219), Chorlton-on-Medlock (H.O. 107/2220), Salford, Greengate (H.O. 107/2223), Manchester, Deansgate (H.O. 107/2227), Bradford, Newton, Beswick (H.O. 107/2231), and Salford, Pendleton (unnumbered) are decayed or badly faded, unfit for production, and portions are unfilmed. I thank Mr. Norman Evans of the PRO for showing me the original volumes.

[88] Howe, *Cotton Masters*, pp. 1-4; Fleischman, *Conditions of Life*, pp. 15-21.

[89] H.O. 107/2219, f. 276; *Slater*, p. 14.

[90] *Slater*, p. 71; *Manchester Courier*, 1 Feb. 1851; H.O. 107/2222, f. 40.

Of much greater significance are the 116 cotton lords and their smaller counterparts. This group included spinners and weavers such as Thomas Ashton, Herbert Birley, Peter Albert Ermen (of Ermen & Engels[91]), Richard Guest, Matthew Kennedy, John Munn, Thomas Dilworth Crewdson (of the Dacca Twist Co.), and Sir Elkanah Armitage (of Sir E. Armitage & Sons, cotton spinners), who got his knighthood for putting down the Chartists in 1848. Finishers—calico-printers, bleachers, and dyers—included Alderman William Neild, John Lomas, James Slater, and William Farmington Downes (of Smith & Downes, calico printers). Finally, a host of commission agents, dealing mostly in cottons (but many dealt in other textiles, and in other lines of goods)—George Ashworth, Robert Barbour, Hartley Packer Gisborne, Robert Gladstone, Joseph and William Henry Parker, and George Trenbath (of Nicholls & Trenbath, cotton waste dealers) are examples—completed the representation of cotton. Many of these men mixed their occupations, combining spinning, weaving, or finishing with commission work, and it is difficult to sort them into neat categories. Cotton links them all.

The next largest group was made up of sixty-three men who served Manchester's economy in the capacity of professionals and experts. The twenty-one solicitors included Edward Allen, who combined law with insurance sales, Henry Charlwood (Cunliffes, Charlwood & Bury), Charles Cooper and his son John, William Wolley Foster, John Henry Law, William Smalley Rutter (magistrates' clerk and county coroner), Thomas Pittard Bagshaw, Thomas Percival Bunting (a son of Jabez Bunting, Wesleyan Methodism's pope), and Stephen Heelis, prominent follower of Hugh Stowell and Tory stalwart in Salford. The thirteen physicians and surgeons ranged from John Boutflower, John Kenworthy (both F.R.C.S.), and Peter Wood (M.D., Edinburgh), to Daniel Lynch (from a family of chemists). Financial affairs were represented by estate agents (Benjamin Consterdine, Charles Wolstenholme), accountants (John Wolstencroft, James Drew), insurance agents (J. S. Jewsbury), and sharebrokers (Daniel Antrobus, the John Railton family, Bernard Hartley Green), all of whom dabbled in each other's lines of work, and bankers (John Knight Mansell, cashier of the Union Bank). Estate agents overlapped with surveyors and civil engineers (Charles Edward Cawley) and architects (Edwin Hugh Shellard).

The retail trades (fifty-two men) included stationers/booksellers (Thomas Anderson & Son, Hale & Roworth), wine and spirits merchants (William Hadwen, Richard Cope, Jr.), chemists (Richard Hargreaves Ingham, Lynch & Butterworth), grocers (George Critchlow), tailors (Joseph Kidson) and hatters (William Mountcastle), ironmongers (Peter and William Leigh), shoemakers (Henry Holme), cabinet makers (John Wilson), and John Hayward, proprietor of Manchester's leading hotel. The addresses of these men suggest that their custom was in the better parts of town.

The last three groups sum up Manchester's economy. The distribution category includes twenty-two wholesale food merchants (John Chesshyre) and warehousemen (Robert Acheson). Silk, woollens, and linen were represented by nineteen men, including Ebenezer Robert LeMare, John

[91] W. O. Henderson, "The Firm of Ermen & Engels in Manchester," *Internationale Wissenschaftliche Korrespondenz zur Geschichte der deutschen Arbeiterbewegung*, Heft 11-12 (1971), 1-10.

Morley, David Charlesworth, Edward Cheshire and his partner Thomas Parsons (silk mercers), William Joynson (a qualified solicitor active in his family's silk manufacturing firm), and Robert Townend (worsted). Finally, the nineteen men in other large-scale manufacturing included engineering (Sharp Bros. & Co., John Higgins), manufacturing chemists (William Dentith & Co., Hänel & Ellis), paper-makers (James Collinge, Richard Greenhalgh), printers (Henry and W. Blacklock of Bradshaw & Blacklock, who invented the railway timetable; Thomas Sowler, Jr., publisher of the Tory-Anglican *Manchester Courier*), and brewers (James P. Joule, Richard Elliott Mottram).

These men were in the prime of life. Exactly three score years separated the youngest from the oldest, a greybeard of eighty-three, but the largest number (34 percent) fell between the ages of forty-three and fifty-two. That is the age range when men have got established in their occupations and are ready to play a role in civic life, but before they want to retire to private pursuits. Unsurprisingly, the second largest group (28 percent) were aged thirty-five to forty-two, a time when men who are making a go of things are ready to move beyond their daily business. The third largest group, men fifty-three to sixty-two years old, made up 18 percent of the total. The young men from twenty-three to thirty-four (14 percent) and the old men from sixty-three to eighty-three (7 percent) were the least numerous.

Their religious adherence would be difficult to chart without a great deal of research, and even then much evidence is lacking, but it is probably safe to guess that it is comparable to that of the cotton masters. About half of the cotton masters whom Howe studied were Anglican, 23 percent were Methodist, Presbyterian, Congregationalist, and Baptist, and 23 percent were Unitarian and Quaker.[92] A larger percentage of the anti-Catholics probably were Anglican, stimulated by Hugh Stowell's leadership. His leadership may also help to explain why only twelve of these men also subscribed to the Evangelical Alliance (Sir Elkanah Armitage, Robert Barbour, T. P. Bunting, William Romaine Callender, John Fernley, Jabez Johnson, John Johnson, William Neild, Daniel Kay Rea, C. W. Rippon, Peter Wood, and Charles Carill Worsley). Given the tolerant attitudes of Quakers and Unitarians towards Roman Catholics, it is highly unlikely that many of them lent their names to the Manchester and Salford Protestant Defence Committee.

The geographical origins of the anti-Catholics are markedly different from those of the cotton masters, as Table 9 illustrates. Fewer were natives of Lancashire; many more came from the counties adjacent (Cheshire, the West Riding, Derbyshire, Cumberland, Westmoreland), and the larger percentages that came from Scotland and Ireland are especially notable. These men were much more likely to have been migrants than the Lancashire population as a whole. It may be that their uncomfortable status as outsiders led them to become "joiners" as a way of becoming "naturalized" by serving in worthy causes, and as a way of distancing themselves from those other outsiders, Lancashire's Irish Roman Catholic immigrants.

[92] Howe, *Cotton Masters*, p. 62.

TABLE 9

*Geographical Origins of Manchester/Salford Anti-Catholics,
Compared with Cotton Masters*

	Anti-Catholics		Cotton Masters	
Origin	N	%	N	%
Lancashire	77	51.0	265	80.3
Adjacent Counties	35	23.0	26	7.9
Other Northern Counties	3	2.0	5	1.5
Midlands	10	6.6	10	3.0
London, South, and West	11	7.0	6	1.8
Scotland	9	6.0	10	3.0
Ireland	4	2.7	3	0.9
Wales	1	0.7	0	0
Europe	1	0.7	5	1.5
Total	151	99.7	330	99.9

Source: MS. Enumerators' Books, 1851 Census; Howe, *Cotton Masters*, pp. 51-52

The family structures of the anti-Catholics also differed from those of the cotton masters, owing, one suspects, to the inclusion of shopkeepers and professional men in the former group. (See Table 10 below.) The anti-Catholics had three times as many stem families (two or more lineally related, ever-married, living with families or with other kin), but one-third fewer composite families (e.g., unmarried siblings or cousins, living together). And there was a markedly larger incidence of nieces and nephews coresiding with the anti-Catholics than with the cotton masters. (Twenty-three, or 35.4 percent of the sixty-five coresiding kin in anti-Catholic households were nieces or nephews of the head, while only ten, or 19.6 percent of the fifty-one coresiding kin in cotton masters' households were nieces or nephews.) The two groups showed little difference, however, in the incidences of nuclear families and of the head of family living alone.

TABLE 10

*Family Structure, Manchester/Salford Anti-Catholics,
Compared with Cotton Masters*

	Anti-Catholics		Cotton Masters	
Family Type	N	%	N	%
Head alone	6	4	8	7
Nuclear:				
Childless	13	8	10	8
With unmarried children	87	68	76	70
Stem	27	18	7	6
Composite	15	10	21	17
Total	148	99	122	100

Source: MS. Enumerators' Books, 1851 Census; Howe, *Cotton Masters*, pp. 82, 86

TABLE 11

Number of Servants per Household, 1851

Number	Anti-Catholics N	Anti-Catholics %	Cotton Masters N	Cotton Masters %
0	8	5.3	4	3.2
1	31	20.7	16	12.8
2	63	42.0	26	20.8
3	27	18.0	24	19.2
4	8	5.3	24	19.2
5	8	5.3	10	8.0
6 or more	5	3.3	21	16.8
Total	150	99.9	125	100.0

Source: MS. Enumerators' Books, 1851 Census; Howe, *Cotton Masters*, p. 87

The differences between anti-Catholics and cotton masters, however, are most marked with respect to their wealth. The former were less wealthy than the latter, not surprising since the former were more representative of the broader economic structure, while the latter were an élite group. The best measure of wealth for the general population is the number of live-in servants per household. Table 11 shows that a larger percentage of cotton masters' households had more than three live-in servants, as compared to anti-Catholic households, while a larger percentage of anti-Catholic households had fewer than three servants.

One can measure more precisely the wealth of the anti-Catholic households by tallying the sex and age distribution of servants, because male servants were more costly than females, and females were more costly than boys or girls. Table Table 12 compares the age and sex distributions of servants in anti-Catholic households with those in other households in the areas where anti-Catholics lived.[93] To have a little "skivvy" was the basic divide between the working classes and the respectable lower-middle classes; because the number of males in service declined during the century, due to the tax on males (1 gn. p.a. in 1853) and to the broadening opportunities for alternative employment, to keep a male servant meant that one had a substantial income. (Obviously, the wages paid servants and the incomes needed to keep them varied across time and space.)[94] The table aggregates adult and child servants in each category, because no household kept more than two children in addition to the adult servants.

Table 12 shows that the anti-Catholic households (less affluent than the élite cotton masters) were more affluent than the other households in their neighborhoods. A majority of the other households (sixty-nine percent) made do with a skivvy or one female, while a larger percentage of the anti-Catholic households kept two or more female domestics, or kept male

---

[93] I obtained a sample of other households by counting the servants by household on every fifth folio of the census enumerators' books for Broughton, Stretford, Chorlton-on-Medlock, Ardwick, Hulme, Moss Side, Cheetham, Crumpsall, Rusholme, Didsbury, Withington, Chorlton-cum-Hardy, Salford Greengate, Salford, and Bowdon. H.O. 107/2222, 2218, ff. 458-end, 2220, ff. 484-end, 2220, ff. 4-484, 2221, ff. 32-end, 2221, ff. 4-28, 2232, 2219, ff. 204-314, 2219, ff. 81-123, 2219, ff. 27-77, 2219, ff. 4-23, 2223, to f. 181 (very decayed, so I counted all the servant households that I could read), 2224, 2162, ff. 330-362.

[94] See Pamela Horn, *The Rise and Fall of the Victorian Servant* (Dublin, 1975), esp. pp. 7-10, 17-21, 25-27, 124-32.

TABLE 12

Sex Distribution of Manchester/Salford Domestic Servants

Distribution	Anti-Catholic Households		Other Households	
	N	%	N	%
1 or 2 children only	5	3.5	235	16.4
1 female	37	25.7	741	51.7
2 females	56	38.9	249	17.4
3 females	19	13.2	83	5.8
4 females	3	2.1	34	2.4
5 females	4	2.8	2	0.1
6 females	0		2	0.1
1 male	0		4	0.3
1 male + 1-3 females	11	7.6	60	4.2
1 male + 4-7 females	4	2.8	14	1.0
2 males	0		1	0.1
2 or more males + 1 or more females	5	3.5	9	0.6
Total	144	100.1	1,434	100.1

Source: MS. Enumerators' Books, 1851 Census

as well as female domestics. This suggests that Manchester's anti-Catholics were cross-sections of the town's leadership, and of those who served that leadership.

The occupational backgrounds of subscribers to anti-Catholic societies elsewhere confirm that these organizations drew their support from the economic leadership of their locales, supplemented by those who followed the leaders in economics as well as in politics. The lay subscribers to the British Reformation Society from Derby included a landed gentleman, a banker, three solicitors, a brewer, and a wine merchant; Derby's subscribers to the Evangelical Alliance included a solicitor, banker, linen and woollen draper, brickmaker, brewer, two ironmongers, and the clerk to the Board of Guardians.[95] Preston's lay subscribers to the Evangelical Alliance included the flax-spinners T. C. Hincksman (influenced in an Evangelical direction by the Mancunian Robert Gardner) and John Furness, a corn dealer, and a landed proprietor.[96]

Finally, the occupations of the fifty-eight subscribers to the Birmingham auxiliaries of the Evangelical Alliance and the Protestant Association (who can be identified) show the same pattern. Over a quarter (seventeen, or 29 percent) were involved in toymaking, gunsmithing, electroplating, and other branches of the metal trades, so important to Birmingham's economy, but they were mostly smaller masters rather than the larger em-

[95] *British Protestant*, V (June/July 1849), 156-73; *ibid.*, VI (June/July 1850), 111-27; *ibid.*, VII (June 1851), 94-112; *ibid.*, VIII (July 1852), 80-99; *ibid.*, IX (June 1853), 115-32; Evangelical Alliance, *Abstract of Proceedings of the 4th Annual Conference* (1850), pp. 54-68; Samuel Bagshaw, *History, Gazetteer and Directory of Derbyshire* (Sheffield, 1846); *Post Office Directory of Birmingham, with Staffordshire and Worcestershire* (London, 1850); Francis White & Co., *History, Gazetteer and Directory of the County of Derby* (Sheffield, 1857).

[96] *History, Topography, and Directory of the Borough of Preston* (Beverley, 1851); Howe, *Cotton Masters*, pp. 66, 71; Evangelical Alliance, *Abstract of Proceedings of the 4th Annual Conference* (1850), pp. 54-68.

ployers. (Only Henry and John Yates, manufacturers of edged tools, and James James, mayor in 1842, screw manufacturer, employed many workers). Another quarter (seventeen, or 29 percent) were retail shopkeepers, grocers, stationers, butchers, and so on. Nineteen percent (eleven) were professionals or semiprofessionals (bank managers, surgeons and physicians, estate agents, schoolmasters). For the rest, there were five large-scale merchants and factors, five men in miscellaneous trades (paper-making, brewing, house-painting), and three gentlemen.[97]

Anti-Catholic societies, then, were associations that attracted civic-minded men who played or aspired to play leading roles in their towns, and men who stood in a service capacity to that leadership. But local conditions affected this leadership. Birmingham's leadership, many of whom were Unitarian or Quaker, did not appear as prominently as did Manchester's. Other men put down their names because it was the thing to do for men of their profession, or because they wanted to retain the custom of the leaders. At the center were a few activists, committed for reasons of faith or politics.

In the Country

"[T]here never was an address voted by a parish so unanimously as this one," boasted the organizers of the memorial of the rector, churchwardens, and inhabitants of the parish of Kingstone,[98] Kent, near Canterbury.[99] Forgiving the redundant modifier (unanimity is like pregnancy in that it cannot be partial), how true was this? What sort of support did anti-Catholicism get in rural areas? Who was likely to sign memorials, and why?

The eight memorials to the Queen with signatures attached that have survived from the Papal Aggression agitation of 1850 are fairly well distributed across England. Two are from Kent, in the southeast (Kingstone, near Canterbury; West Peckham, near Maidstone), and one from Wiltshire, in the southwest (Horningsham, near Warminster). Three are from the West Midlands (Bucks, Lane End, and Berks, White Waltham, both near High Wycombe; and Warwickshire, Frankton, near Coventry), and one is from the East Midlands (Hunts, Diddington, near Huntingdon). Finally, one is from the West Riding (Kildwick, near Keighley).

Kingstone had a total population of 310 souls in 1851, so the thirty-one signatories to the memorial represent precisely 10 percent of the inhabitants.[100] All the parish gentry signed—Thomas Bartlett, the rector;[101] Ernest A. Stephenson, a fundholder, late of the Paymaster General of the Forces department, occupying the Ileden estate; Mary Montressor, widow of a knight, and her son Captain Montressor, of Denne Hill. Their households

[97] Evangelical Alliance, *Abstract of Proceedings of the 4th Annual Conference* (1850), pp. 54-68; *Protestant Watchman*, No. 10 (Dec. 1849), wrapper; *Post Office Directory of Birmingham*; Francis White & Co., *General and Commercial Directory and Topography of the Borough of Birmingham* (Sheffield, 1855); *Slater's (late Pigot & Co.) Royal National and Commercial Directory and Topography* [of Birmingham] (Manchester and London, 1850).

[98] Now spelled without the "e."

[99] *Kentish Observer*, 12 Dec. 1850.

[100] Rector, Churchwarden, and Inhabitants of the Parish of Kingstone, near Canterbury, to the Queen, PRO, H.O. 54/35; enumerator's book, Registration District 64 (Bridge), Kingstone Parish, PRO, H.O. 107/1623, ff. 246-57.

[101] A staunch Evangelical, Bartlett (1789-1864) held the living of Kingstone, 1816-52, and published numerous Evangelical pamphlets (*DNB*, I, 1255).

also contributed signatures—Stephenson's bailiff, servant, coachman, and gardener; and Lady Montressor's butler, coachman, gardener, and groom. Three of the nine farmers in the parish also signed: Robert Gardner, churchwarden, 290 acres, fourteen laborers; George Smith, Reed Farm, 250 acres, one laborer; William Hooper, Kingswood, forty acres, two laborers. Six of the village's middling sort joined their betters—the publican, miller, smith, carpenter, and two shopkeepers. Only five agricultural laborers signed, however. (Table 13 summarizes the occupations of the signers, and of the rest of the males aged seventeen years and older in the parish.)

All of the signatories were heads of households, save seven (a gardener/groom, who lodged in the village; Stephenson's manservant; Lady Montressor's son, butler, and groom; the occupier of Reed Farm's unmarried son; and the miller's mate). No woman signed, save Lady Montressor herself. Those who could be identified in the enumerator's book amounted to 29 percent (twenty-six) of all the males aged seventeen years or older (ninety).

TABLE 13

Occupations: Kingstone, Kent; West Peckham, Kent; and Lane End, Bucks

Location and	Signers		Nonsigners		Total	
Occupation	N	%	N	%	N	%
Kingstone, Kent						
Gentry	4	14	0	0	4	4
Farmers	3	11	6	9	9	10
Middling sort	6	21	5	8	11	12
Servants	9	32	2	3	11	12
Agricultural workers	6	21	49	77	55	60
No occupation	0	0	2	3	2	2
Total	28	99	64	100	92	100
West Peckham, Kent						
Gentry	3	8	0	0	3	2
Farmers	2	6	0	0	2	2
Middling sort	14	39	8	9	22	17
Servants	3	8	11	12	4	11
Agricultural workers	14	39	73	79	87	67
No occupation	0	0	1	1	1	1
Total	36	100	93	101	129	100
Lane End, Bucks						
Gentry	5	4	2	1	7	2
Farmers	12	9	14	4	26	6
Middling sort	23	17	18	5	41	9
Chair-makers	28	20	17	5	45	10
Agricultural workers	26	19	184	54	210	44
Other workers	41	30	97	29	138	29
No occupation	2	2	6	2	8	2
Total	137	101	338	100	475	102

Source: See Footnotes 100, 102, and 111.

Those who did not sign included two-thirds of the nine farmers, almost half of the middling sort, and 90 percent of the agricultural laborers. The nonsigning farmers included Austin Cooper (Westwood, ten acres), William Featherstone (Pleasant Hill, fourteen acres), George Kelcey (Denne Hill Farm, 640 acres, ten laborers), Charles Whitehead (Lincey Bottom, twenty acres, one laborer), and John Wood (Westwood, 150 acres, nine laborers). The more substantial farmers followed the gentry in signing, but the most substantial farmer of all did not. Three carpenters, a fruiter, and a blacksmith did not sign; nor did a gamekeeper, the postman, and a shepherd.

The memorial from Kingstone, then, was got up by a few gentry and their dependents, 29 percent of the pool of acceptable signatories (males at least seventeen years of age). A significant number of fairly important parishioners chose (for whatever reasons) not to participate.

The memorial from the inhabitants of West Peckham resembles that from Kingstone. (See Table 13.) All of the forty-six signatories were males; all but seven of the thirty-six who can be identified in the enumerators' books were heads of families.[102] They included the local gentry, Maximilian Dalison,[103] Sir William Geary, Bart., and Edward Jones, the vicar (who was generous about forgiving his tithe on hops in bad years[104]), both farmers, and two-thirds of the middling sort. But, unlike at Kingstone, the gentry did not have their servants sign. Few of the farm laborers signed; none of the other workers in the parish (most of whom worked in a paper mill) signed. All told, the signers amounted to 28 percent of the pool of acceptable signatories (males at least twenty years of age), a percentage close to Kingstone's 29 percent.

The parish of Horningsham, Wiltshire, sited in the shadow of Longleat House, had in effect no resident gentry; added to this was a strong Congregationalist presence (the chapel, in continuous use since 1566, was the oldest Nonconformist chapel in England with a resident minister). Thus it was that the perpetual curate, Emmanuel Strickland, had only the help of Thomas Pope, the parish's most substantial farmer (800 acres, fifty men), James Sherring, the bailiff, Thomas Tilbrook, the surveyor, and Thomas Dredge, publican of the Royal Oak, Newbury, and farmer (100 acres, six men), in gathering sixty-seven signatures out of a population of 582 males.[105] Those who did not sign included William Gething, the Congregationalist minister, two of the four publicans, two farmers (200 acres, six men; seventy-five acres, three men), a substantial dairyman, a master chairmaker employing ten hands, and a master pillbox turner employing five hands.

This parish had eight small owners or occupiers (in contrast to the Kentish ones, which had none), and a rather more diversified economy that included a substantial woodworking sector. Yet the majority of small owners/occupiers (six of eight) and workers (ten of thirteen) did not sign.

---

[102] Inhabitants of the Parish of West Peckham, to the Queen, PRO, H.O. 54/35; enumerator's book, Registration District 55 (Malling), West Peckham Parish, PRO, H.O. 107/1612, ff. 222-471.

[103] Burke's Landed Gentry, 17th ed. (1952), p. 596.

[104] Maidstone Journal, 26 Nov. 1850.

[105] VCH, Wilts, III, 99; inhabitants of the Parish of Horningsham to the Queen, PRO, H.O. 54/35; enumerator's book, Registration District 260 (Warminster), Horningsham Parish, PRO, H.O. 107/1843, ff. 363-402.

Of the sixty signers who can be identified in the enumerator's book, forty-seven were heads of households (two more were eldest sons of female heads). Only 25 percent of the male heads of households signed; only 12 percent of those heads who were farm workers signed.

Gentry were thick on the ground in the parishes of Shottesbrook and White Waltham, Berkshire. The Vansittart family of Shottesbrook Park, headed by Arthur Vansittart (1807-1859), a horse-racing enthusiast who founded the Italian Jockey Club in Florence, were lords of both manors and owned the advowson of the united parishes. (Ironically, his third son, Cyril Bexley, 1851-1887, converted to Roman Catholicism and was a chamberlain to Popes Pius IX and Leo XIII.)[106] There were five other landholders in the parish, two gentlemen who lived off the funds, a Royal Navy lieutenant with means beyond his pay, and Charles Vansittart, the vicar. Thirteen tenant farmers and thirty-one of the middling sort (shopkeepers, schoolmasters, skilled craftsmen, publicans, and dealers in agricultural produce) completed the rural economy. Forty-four men affixed their names to the memorial, "unanimously signed by the vicar, churchwardens, and inhabitants."[107]

The driving forces behind the memorial were Charles Vansittart, the vicar, and Charles Sawyer, J.P., of Heywood Lodge. Sawyer was involved in organizing a meeting of the Churchmen of Reading, to be chaired by Samuel Wilberforce, the Bishop of Oxford, but he objected to Wilberforce's demand that the attenders sign a ticket declaring that they were Anglicans and that they would submit to the bishop's authority. So he withdrew and helped organize a county meeting (which he chaired). Charles Vansittart and the Rev. Henry Pole (a cureless priest who was one of the White Waltham landholders) attended the county meeting. Sawyer also chaired the public meeting at Maidenhead, which Charles Vansittart and Berry Doyne (another White Waltham landholder) attended.[108]

Sawyer couched his opposition to Roman Catholicism in political terms ("whether they would suffer a foreign prince to parcel out this country to establish a Roman Catholic hierarchy"), and sought to distinguish between individual Roman Catholics, who were upright men fully deserving of civil equality, and Roman Catholicism as a system. For Sawyer, to defend English Protestantism against popish attack was to defend true freedom, because English freedoms were enshrined in the Protestant Constitution, which in turn rested on "the religion of the bible." Vansittart charged that, although "the old Roman Catholic squire," loyal to Queen and Country, only asked for equality, "they" now aimed at supremacy through priestcraft. But the best way to oppose priestcraft, he thought, was to move with the spirit of the times: to promote sound, liberal education; to reform the universities; to support mechanics' institutions; and to "elevate the condition of the working class." He deplored the spread of Anglo-Catholicism

[106] *VCH, Berks*, III, 166, 170, 172; Boase, VI, 735.

[107] Enumerator's book, Registration District 129 (Cookham), Shottesbrook and White Waltham parishes, PRO, H.O. 107/1694, ff. 30-69; vicar, wardens, and inhabitants of the parishes of White Waltham and Shottesbrook, to the Queen, PRO, H.O. 54/35; *Reading Mercury*, 7 Dec. 1850 (quoted).

[108] *Reading Mercury*, 16, 23, 30 Nov. 1850.

in the Church, and hoped for "the diffusion of a real, sound, vital, spiritual religion amongst all classes of mankind."[109]

When collecting signatures to their memorial, Sawyer and Vansittart did not dip too deep into the parish's social structure. All the gentlemen signed save the naval officer, and all but two of the farmers; about a third (eleven of thirty-one) of the middling sort signed. Two gardeners signed, but four did not. No laborers signed. (Twelve of the forty-nine signatories could not be identified in the enumerator's book.)

Lane End, Buckinghamshire, was made an ecclesiastical district in 1832, out of parts of Great Marlow, Lewknor Uphill, Hambledon, Fingest, and West Wycombe; it was raised to parish status in 1867. (The inhabitants of the northeast side of Wheeler End Common, although not part of the district, participated in Lane End's life.) Its economy was mixed, with wheat and barley grown, but with an iron foundry and extensive chair-making.[110] Its memorial bears 160 signatures. Two signatures are illegible, nineteen are not in the enumerators' books, and two cannot be distinguished from other persons bearing the same name, leaving 137 identifiable memorialists out of a total population of 338 males aged sixteen years or older, or 29 percent of the pool of acceptable signatories.[111] The vast majority of the signatories (103, or 75 percent) were heads of households; twenty-three (17 per cent.) were resident in households with a signing head, and eight (6 per cent.) resided in households with a female head. Only three memorialists (2 percent) lived in households headed by a male nonsigner.

In contrast to the signers of Shottesbrook and White Waltham, those of Lane End reached lower into the social structure. Signatories included the landed gentlemen William Townsend and George Augustus Young, J.P., the iron founder and churchwarden James S. Hobbs, and the master chair-maker William Savage. Along with them signed twenty-eight chair-makers, twenty-six agricultural laborers, and forty-one other laborers. (See Table 13.) A majority of the district's middling sort (publicans, shopkeepers, tailors, and master carpenters, blacksmiths, and shoemakers) signed. Presumably the chair-makers and iron founders signed at their employers' behest; presumably the agricultural laborers Joseph Platt, George Blackwell, Jacob Stops, and George Moors signed because their employer, the farmer Francis Agar, signed.[112]

Deeper in the Midlands lie the two small agricultural parishes of Frankton, Warwickshire (pop. 268), and Diddington, Hunts (pop. 216), each dominated by a single gentry family. The Biddulph family, then headed by the widow Sophia, held both the lordship and advowson of Frankton, while the Thornhill family, headed by George (born in 1783 or 1784; M.P. for Huntingdonshire from 1837 to his death in 1852), were lords of Diddington. Merton College, Oxford, owned the advowson.[113]

---

109 *Ibid.*, 16, 30 Nov., 14 Dec. 1850.

110 *VCH, Bucks*, III, 68, 136.

111 Incumbent, churchwardens, and inhabitants of the district of Lane End, to the Queen, PRO, H.O. 54/35; enumerators' books, Registration District 150 (Wycombe), District of Lane End, PRO, H.O. 107/1719, ff. 353-end, H.O. 107/1720, ff. 4-6, 158-175, H.O. 107/1725, ff. 71-88.

112 *Reading Mercury*, 23 Nov. 1850.

113 *VCH, Warwickshire*, VI, 92, 94; *VCH, Hunts*, II, 270, 272; Dod, *Electoral Facts*, p. 151; Boase, III, 959.

The Frankton memorial is of interest because ten of the thirty-one signatories were women (including one who does not appear in the
enumerator's book), but the women who signed were the lady of the manor
and her daughters, the rector's wife and sister, a farmer's widow who
headed her family, the wives of two signing farmers (the wives of five
signing farmers, and that of the parish clerk, did not sign), and the
schoolmaster's wife. Class thus was at work. Almost two-thirds (nineteen)
of the thirty signatories who can be identified were gentry or farmers; the
rest were of the middling sort (a family of cordwainers, the baker, the tailor, the schoolmaster, a carpenter, a timber-feller, and a gardener). Of the
twenty-six adult male heads of family who did not sign, only one, a carpenter, was respectable; the rest were laborers.[114]

In contrast, the organizers of the Diddington memorial welcomed the
signatures of agricultural laborers. Seventy-four percent (twenty-five) of
the thirty-four signatories who can be identified were agricultural laborers
or other outdoor workers, and four were servants in Diddington Hall; the
rest were the lord of the manor, the vicar, two farmers, and the local
publican. Only eight of the twenty-nine male heads of families in the parish failed to sign the memorial, and the signatories represent 62 percent of
the fifty-five males aged seventeen or older. This tight little village did the
bidding of squire and vicar.[115]

The parish of Kildwick, in the township of Cononley, about five miles
northwest of Keighley in the West Riding, was in a different world. A few
small farms were scattered among the quarries, lead mines, worsted and
cotton mills; families of farmers and hand-loom weavers had children at
the mills.[116] Such an environment was inhospitable to Anglicanism, and the
fifty-two signatories to the memorial of the curate and congregation of St.
Andrew's, Kildwick, amounted to only 4 percent of the total population
(1,272 persons).[117]

That 44 percent (twenty-three of fifty-two) of the signatories were female hints at the marginal nature of memorializing in this cure. Nathaniel
Liberty, the curate (who lodged with the schoolmaster, not having a proper
vicarage) did have the support of a few substantial residents. (Eight of the
signatories were not in the book, and seven could not be identified, leaving
thirty-seven for whom information is to hand.) Among the signers were the
farmers Jonas Spencer (forty acres), George Balme (forty acres), James
Naylor, Jr. (son of the publican, who farmed thirty-four acres), John Par-
kinson (a "landed proprietor" who occupied twenty-two acres), the grocer
Charlotte Smith, and the master tailor John Lee (who kept one boy—his
son). Thomas Peel, the owner of the worsted and cotton mill, employing
eighty hands, probably signed. But Liberty also welcomed the signatures
of two aged paupers, of the pupil teacher, and even of Annie Witham
(sixty-five), the muffin baker, Lucy Watson (fourteen), who ran errands,
and Elizabeth Hudson (twelve), a piecer at the worsted mill. A few hand-

[114] Inhabitants of Frankton, Warwick, to the Queen, PRO, H.O. 54/35; enumerator's book, Registration District 401 (Rugby), Parish of Frankton, PRO, H.O. 107/2070, ff. 341-352.
[115] Inhabitants, Parish of Diddington, Hunts, to the Queen, PRO, H.O. 54/35; enumerator's book,
Registration District 178 (St. Neots), Parish of Diddington, PRO, H.O. 107/1750, ff. 124-139.
[116] *VCH, Yorks*, II, 374.
[117] Curate of Kildwick and congregation assembling at the National School room, Cononley, in
the parish of Kildwick, West Riding, to the Queen, PRO, H.O. 54/35; enumerators' books, Registration District 489 (Skipton), Township of Cononley, PRO, H.O. 107/2278, ff. 324-365.

loom weavers, mill hands, lead miners, and wives completed the signatories.

Reflecting on the memorials from rural areas (Kildwick being the exception), one sees that the concept of "inhabitants" was narrowly understood in practice, when petitioning. One had to be able to sign one's name, perhaps to show that one could read the petition. One had to be male, unless one were a lady, but even gentle status allowed one to sign only if local custom permitted it. One had to be an adult, taking adulthood to begin around the late 'teens. One had to be the head of the household, resident in the household of a signing head, or the eldest male in a household headed by a woman. Last, one had to be "respectable" in the socioeconomic sense. Female, laboring, and child signers were the exception. Not surprisingly, gentry leadership weighed heavy in the securing of signatures. Yet there is little evidence for the dragooning of tenant farmers, tradesmen, or laborers to sign. Petitions, then, in rural areas, appear to express the relatively unfettered opinion of the respectable orders of society.

CONCLUSION

IN SALFORD TODAY, roads feeding traffic to the Albion Way cover the site where Hugh Stowell's church once stood. His parish is dead, and so is his brand of anti-Catholicism. He himself died in 1865, a decade before the controversy over the Vatican decrees in 1874-75 marked what in retrospect can be seen as "the demise of no-popery as an overt issue in English politics."[1] What does anti-Catholicism tell us about Victorian history? What accounts for its demise? Has it any relevance for the late twentieth century?

A comparison with North America may help to highlight the distinctive elements of English anti-Catholicism. During the period ca. 1840-80, Ontario's Methodists, Presbyterians, Baptists, and Anglicans reduced their mutual animosities, developed "a common outlook" on basic issues, and created "an informal Protestant alliance" on those issues. (With the adoption of neo-Gothic architecture, even their buildings looked the same.) The key to the creation of this Protestant culture was the disestablishment of the Anglican and the Presbyterian Churches during the 1840s and '50s, with the secularization of the Clergy Reserves, the growing state control of education, and the elimination of Anglicanism's privileged role in local government.[2] In the United States, of course, there was no state church, Anglicanism having been disestablished and disendowed in the Southern states during the Revolution, and Congregationalism having been disestablished gradually thereafter in New England. Yet the mutual animosities of American Methodists, Presbyterians, and Baptists increased during the antebellum period. All three denominations split along sectional lines over the question of slavery during the 1840s and '50s. Moreover, anti-Catholicism was dragged into the slavery question because many of its leaders, especially in New England and the Midwest, also were abolitionists.[3]

The contrast with England is marked. There, denominational lines grew more rigid during the period ca. 1830-50, and competition among Methodists, Congregationalists, Baptists, Presbyterians, and Anglicans grew more intense. The keys to this difference were the existence of the Establishment and the nonexistence of slavery as divisive issues. Furthermore, Ontario Anglicanism was more uniformly Evangelical in tone than English Anglicanism, and American Anglicanism (save in the South) was rather

---

[1] Altholz, "Vatican Decrees Controversy," p. 593. The year 1875 is in my view a much more appropriate terminus than 1860. I do not see the discontinuities that John Wolffe finds in the latter year (*Protestant Crusade*, p. 8).

[2] William Westfall, *Two Worlds: The Protestant Culture of Nineteenth-Century Ontario* (Kingston and Montreal, 1989), pp. 11 (quoted), 83, 128.

[3] Billington, *Protestant Crusade*, pp. 166-85, 332-33, 390-94, 423-29.

higher than the English Church, one suspects largely as a way of protecting its identity in the new circumstances of purely voluntary religion. Unity along anti-Catholic lines, unity that transcended denominational lines, was thus more easily achievable in Ontario than either in England or in the United States.

Millenarianism was more widely disseminated in Ontario (and in the United States) than in England. Mormons and Millerites crossed over from the United States, and both the Catholic Apostolic Church and the Plymouth Brethren were more visible in Ontario than at home. All these groups preached the Antichrist, which was of course popery. Religion on the Canadian frontier was raw entertainment. A telling measure of the difference between Canadian and English religion is the response to the Rev. James Caughey. Methodist leaders in Ontario considered Caughey to be safe because his revivals were held in chapels rather than in brush arbors, and because they were controlled, lasted for a few hours rather than overnight, and did not threaten resident ministers.[4] In England, however, Caughey disrupted the already shaky control of Wesleyan Methodist leaders because he played into a divisiveness absent in Ontario.

The markedly different fortunes of Orangeism in England and in North America also illustrate the distinctive elements of English anti-Catholicism. In England, Orangeism was reduced to the status of a working-class drinking club after it lost its élite patronage in the 1830s. Only in Lancashire, and especially in Merseyside, did it exert any significant social and political power. In Canada, however, and most notably in Ontario, the Orange Order became a powerful political and social institution. It prospered in Ontario partly because of the province's disproportionately large number of Irish Protestants. (Sixty percent of Ontario's immigrants were Irish, and two-thirds of those were Protestants, during the period 1820-45.) But it rose above and beyond its immigrant base to tap native-born Canadians and non-Irish immigrants for its membership, largely because of its versatile social functions. Lodges in farming and mining areas were community social clubs. In towns they were drinking clubs. Later, the lodges evolved into self-help and insurance clubs. In Toronto and other municipalities, the lodges developed into political patronage machines. The measure of the order's success is that by 1902, Canada had 2,000 lodges, half of which were in Ontario, and Ireland had 1,653 lodges, while Britain had 709.[5]

In contrast, the United States had but 350 Orange lodges in 1902. Lodges were established in New York, Philadelphia, and Boston in the 1820s, but not until 1870 was there a national organization. Because in the United States Irishness was equated with Roman Catholicism, violent behavior, and low social status, Irish Protestants found it easier to assimilate than to preserve their distinctive ethnic identity. (One suspects that Irish Protestant immigrants to England found it easier to assimilate than to preserve their identity for similar reasons.) In addition, the order had to replace its British constitutional and monarchical language with the ideology of being good Protestants in a Protestant republic. But because there

---

[4] Westfall, *Two Worlds*, pp. 73, 166-74.

[5] Cecil J. Houston and William J. Smyth, "Transferred Loyalties: Orangeism in the United States and Ontario", *American Review of Canadian Studies*, XIV (1984), 194, 196-97, 199.

were plenty of genuinely indigenous Protestant republican societies (such as the American and Foreign Christian Union, the American Protestant Association, and the Know-Nothing Party), the Orange Order in the United States failed to become more than an institution for an immigrant minority group.[6]

Ontario was caught between Quebec (Roman Catholic and French) to the east and the United States (Protestant but imperialist) to the south. These entities threatened the hoped-for progress of the British Empire in North America. Thus the defensive mindset of the Orange Order fitted well with the mindset of Ontario itself, in a way that did not work either in England or in the United States. The other side of the coin was that anti-Catholicism threatened the French-Canadian Roman Catholic power structure because it offered through conversion the possibility of assimilation to Anglophone culture.[7]

Anti-Catholicism in the United States was much more violent than in either Canada or England. Large-scale rioting began with the sacking of a convent in Charlestown, Massachusetts, in 1834, and further major riots occurred in Baltimore in 1839, Philadelphia in 1844, in several cities in 1853, and in New York in the early 1870s.[8] In contrast, English anti-Catholic rioting, while probably more frequent (in the form of the Bonfire Night row) than American rioting, was less destructive of lives and property and began later, in the mid-1840s. In part this difference may be because in the United States "gentlemen of property and standing" were much more likely to be found leading crowds for political purposes than was the equivalent class in England. Antebellum riots in the United States, then, harken back to the eighteenth-century riot.

Finally, the pornographic element was more pronounced in the United States than in England. Maria Monk's *Awful Disclosures of the Hotel Dieu Nunnery of Montreal* (1836) is quite literally pornography, since Monk was a prostitute. Although it circulated on both sides of the Atlantic, this extraordinarily popular work was more openly read and cited in North America.

Anti-Catholicism was an integral part of what it meant to be a Victorian. Anti-Catholicism ultimately rested on the Black Legend: the hoary myths of Bloody Mary, the Armada, the Gunpowder Plot, and the Glorious Revolution, but the developments of the first half of the nineteenth century created a distinct climate especially conducive to anti-Catholicism. These developments included the creation of an urban public thirsting for entertainment; the organization of self-improving and voluntary societies; the simultaneous emergence of a new, harder variety of Evangelicalism and a new, romantic Catholicism; the growth of militant denominational identities; the economic, social, and political conflicts and aspirations of the landed gentry, the middling classes, and workers; and the emergence of mass communications and mass culture. But to be a Victorian was still

[6] *Ibid.*, pp. 200-203.
[7] *Ibid.*, pp. 197-98; Paul Laverdure, "Creating an Anti-Catholic Crusader: Charles Chiniquy," *Journal of Religious History*, XV (1988), 94-108; René Hardy, "La Rébellion de 1837-38 et l'Essor du Protestantisme Canadien-Français," *Revue d'Histoire de l'Amérique Français*, XXIX (1975), 163-89.
[8] An extensive literature on nativist and anti-abolitionist rioting in the United States exists, which extends the analysis in Billington, *Protestant Crusade*, esp. pp. 68-76, 195-98, 222-34, 302-11, 420-22.

to be rooted in a region, and thus Victorian anti-Catholicism reflected the ways that these developments appeared in specific locales. Anti-Catholicism mirrors the diversity of nineteenth-century society itself.

The diversity of regionalism helped to determine whether, and to what extent, anti-Catholicism appeared on the local level. The specific circumstances of religious, political, and class conflicts, and even the accident of personality, influenced the very different experiences of places where there were few Roman Catholics and Irish, like Leeds, Northampton, Derby, and Wiltshire, and of places where there were many Roman Catholics and Irish, like Manchester, Liverpool, Birmingham, and London. Historians must take this rich local texture into account when we seek to understand Victorian life.

The last quarter of the century saw a very rapid marginalization of anti-Catholic politics, and indeed of anti-Catholic sentiment, among the middle and working classes. This development had something to do with what Edward Norman calls "the waning of all religious feeling in English society,"[9] although perhaps a better phrase is the waning of orthodox organized Christian feeling. Internal and external religious developments were a factor. The decline in church attendance weakened the political power of the denominations. So did the rise of interest in the promotion of understanding, and even of union, among denominations. Ecumenicism is a symptom of declining self-confidence rather than of strength; and it erases self-identity, blurs distinctiveness, and reduces the rivalries that served as one of the driving forces of anti-Catholicism. At the same time, hard Evangelicalism was being pushed to the margins of the denominations, or even abandoning the denominations as in the case of Spurgeon, and the spread of the Keswick holiness movement fostered the spirit of passive waiting for the Lord to do her will and labeled active struggle as lack of faith. The temper of the times was against denominational politics; working-class politics and the rise of the Labour Party shifted attention to economic matters and secular social reform. The The Education Question drew Tories and Roman Catholics closer together, since both wanted to protect state aid to denominational schools. This rapprochement compelled the Tories to moderate their anti-Catholic line. They also had to moderate their anti-Tractarian line; the operation of Disraeli's Public Worship Regulation Act, 1874, created martyrs and turned public sentiment against the bigotry of the persecuting Church Association.[10]

The rise of alternative sources of entertainment for both the middle and working classes was also a factor in reducing the importance of anti-Catholicism. Anti-Catholicism, whether in the form of the improving lecture or in the form of the riot, was entertainment, and the opportunities for entertainment expanded with the rise of organized paid sports, the music hall, and later the record player and the cinema. John Kensit, founder of the Protestant Truth Society, was able to exploit the entertainment value of anti-Catholic riots by having his mobile bands of "Wycliffites" disrupt

[9] Norman, *Anti-Catholicism*, p. 20.
[10] G.I.T. Machin, *Politics and the Churches in Great Britain, 1869 to 1921* (Oxford, 1987), pp. 8-18, 69-78, 81-86; Bebbington, *Evangelicalism*, pp. 151-80.

Anglican church services during the 1890s,[11] but such tactics rapidly lost their effectiveness after the turn of the century.

Finally, one suspects that the more extreme anti-Catholics helped kill off their movement through the sheer absurdity of their claims. Many of the anti-Catholics' favorite charges—that Jesuits had infiltrated everywhere, that convents were either prisons or brothels, that Irish servants sprinkled holy water on unsuspecting Protestant families—were nonsense.[12] John Cumming claimed to have discovered "an old volume of predictions" that foretold the Crimean War and the end of the world in 1864.

> In twice two hundred years, the Bear
> The Crescent will assail;
> But if the Cock and Bull unite,
> The bear will not prevail.
>
> But mark, in twice ten years again—
> Let Islam know and fear—
> The Cross shall stand, the Crescent wane,
> Dissolve, and disappear.[13]

A few months later, George Eliot's brutally honest dissection of John Cumming's personality appeared in the *Westminster Review*.[14] "[R]eligion apart," Eliot conceded, "he probably appreciates and practises veracity";[15] but when it came to religion, he accepted the false, the superstitious, and the absurd when they matched his preconceptions.

There comes a time when the public can no longer sustain such a mindset, when the vulgarities of anti-Catholicism become too vulgar to tolerate. The response to a Church Association lecture at Dereham, Norfolk, in 1875, illustrates how tastes were changing. The speaker opened his lecture on "Sacerdotalism" by stressing Christ's all-sufficient sacrifice, and then turned to the secrets of the confessional, but when he saw that the subject was repulsing his audience, he quickly switched to the safer topics of the Protestant Constitution and British freedoms.[16] The terrible things that were to happen as the result of the rise of popery, from the collapse of the British Constitution to the Second Coming of Jesus Christ, did not happen. Perhaps the public began to conclude, as Edmund Gosse did, that they were not going to happen.[17]

[11] Pickering, *Anglo-Catholicism*, p. 44.

[12] For these sorts of allegations, see Walsh, *Secret History*, pp. 32-34; *Protestant Witness*, II (13 July 1850), 390, III (25 Jan. 1851), 18; *Primitive Methodist Magazine*, XXXI (Mar. 1850), 173; *Wesleyan Methodist Magazine*, LXXIV (1851), 156; Klaus, *Pope, Protestants, and Irish*, pp. 216-17; *Christian Times*, 29 Mar. 1851; *Watchman*, 2 Apr. 1851; *Record*, 24 Mar. 1851.

[13] *Illustrated London News*, 19 May 1855.

[14] "Evangelical Teaching: Dr. Cumming," George Eliot, *Essays and Leaves from a Note-book* (New York, 1970), vol. 21 of *The Writings of George Eliot*, pp. 125-69 (orig. pub. in the *Westminster Review* for October 1855).

[15] *Ibid.*, p. 136.

[16] Armstrong, *Norfolk Diary*, 20 Jan. 1875, p. 187.

[17] In contrast, John Wolffe finds that "Evangelicals could accommodate extreme charges against Rome within their frame of reference, but when anti-Catholic polemic sank to allegations which were objectively untrue or palpably absurd, their deep sense of moral integrity was outraged" ("Protestant Societies and Anti-Catholic Agitation," p. 144).

Anti-Catholicism was very much marginal in the twentieth-century British Isles, except for Scotland where it was a live issue until after the Second World War, and of course for Ulster and Liverpool.[18] The English religious scene had undergone profound changes in that century; at century's end the Roman Catholic Church was the largest Christian body as measured by regular Sunday attenders, and there were twice as many Muslims as there were Methodists. In contrast, hard Evangelicalism remained much more significant across the Atlantic, and continued to wield social and political power reminiscent of that which Victorian Evangelicalism enjoyed. It is significant that the Ulster clergyman Ian Paisley drew more support from South Carolina than he did from England, and that Victorian anti-Catholic tracts remained in print in the United States. It is equally significant that speaking in tongues and spiritual healing, as well as the hard Evangelical themes of Providentialism, premillennialism, and the United States as God's chosen nation could be encountered daily on national television, and that major politicians including presidents thought it useful to propitiate Evangelical bodies. During the Gulf War of 1991, grocery stores sold books analyzing the question of whether the war was the opening stage of Armageddon.

Yet both Roman Catholics and their Protestant wellwishers in the late twentieth century thought that the most potent anti-Catholic attacks stemmed from agnostics, secularists, and the political Left.[19] What dampened down anti-Catholic outbreaks were the abortion question and Republican party politics, issues that allied ultra-Evangelicals and conservative Roman Catholics. (This alliance reminds one of how free trade linked together otherwise disparate groups in the nineteenth century.) "For the present," a student of American anti-Catholicism observed,

> "born-again" Christianity finds itself allied with Catholicism in affirming the core truths of Christian Revelation, and in opposing the moral emptiness of secularism. It is possible, given an attitude of mutual respect, that these amicable relations may persist into the future. But, historically, this is a religion which has been intensely anti-Catholic, and evidence of that anti-Catholicism has not been lacking.[20]

One hopes that anti-Catholicism remains dampened down. However, the revival of anti-Semitism and clerico-fascism in Eastern Europe after the Velvet Revolutions and the strength of Evangelical Protestantism in North America suggest that toleration can only be attained when the religious state of the United States matches that of England's, for prejudice and superstition are hard to eradicate.

---

[18] See Steve Bruce, *No Pope of Rome*; Tom Gallagher, *Edinburgh Divided: John Cormack and No Popery in the 1930s* (Edinburgh, 1987); and Tom Gallagher, *Glasgow: The Uneasy Peace: Religious Tension in Modern Scotland, 1819-1914* (Manchester, 1987).

[19] John Garvey, "The Ugly Little Secret: Anti-Catholicism with Qualifications," *Commonweal*, CVI (28 Sept. 1979), 520-21; Richard A. Blake, "Christians, Lions, and the Media," *America*, CXLII (12 Jan. 1980), 8-11; Michael Schwartz, *The Persistent Prejudice: Anti-Catholicism in America* (Huntington, Indiana, 1984), esp. pp. 122-39; Martin E. Marty, "The Last Anti-Catholic in America," *Christian Century*, XCVI (31 Oct. 1979), 1071.

[20] Schwartz, *Persistent Prejudice*, p. 135.

BIBLIOGRAPHY

PRIMARY SOURCES

Manuscripts

Arundel Castle Archives. Arundel, Sussex.
Baines Family Papers. Leeds City Archives. Sheepscar Library. Leeds, West Riding.
James Bembridge Journals. Manchester Central Library. BR MS 259.B1.
Archives of the Roman Catholic Archdiocese of Birmingham. St. Chad's Cathedral, Birmingham.
Broadlands Archives. National Register of Archives.
Carill Worsley Papers. Manchester Central Library. M 35.
Edward Copleston Correspondence. Devon Record Office, Exeter.
Journal of Thomas Augustin Finegan, Missionary, Birmingham Town Mission. Birmingham Reference Library. MS 312 749.
Gladstone-Glynne Papers. Clwyd Record Office, Hawarden.
Gotch (Kettering) Collection. Northamptonshire Record Office, Northampton.
Home Office: Census of Population, 1851: Enumerators Books'. Public Record Office (Portugal Street). H.O. 107
Home Office: Civil Petitions and Addresses (1841-1854). Public Record Office (Kew). H.O. 54/35.
Home Office: Daily Registers: Domestic. Public Record Office (Kew). H.O. 46.
Home Office: Entry Books: Domestic and General. Public Record Office (Kew). H.O. 43.
Home Office: Registered Papers. Public Record Office (Kew). H.O. 45.
Claude Jenkins Papers: Cecil Wray Correspondence. Lambeth Palace Library. MS. 1604.
John Jenkinson, Jr., Papers. Northamptonshire Record Office, Northampton. YZ 5542.
John Kaye Deposit. Lincolnshire Record Office, Lincoln.
Keble Deposit. Lambeth Palace Library.
Lilford Estate Papers. Lancashire Record Office, Preston.
Londonderry Papers. Durham County Record Office, Durham.
Archives of the Diocese of Mississippi. St. Andrew's Cathedral, Jackson, Mississippi.
Morris-Eyton Collection. Shrewsbury Public Library.
John Munn & Co. Records. Manchester Central Library. M 386.
National Public School Association Papers. Manchester Central Library. M 136.

Northampton (Appendix). [A Collection of Cartoons, Squibs, Manifestoes, Newspaper-cuttings, &c., relating to Parliamentary and Municipal Elections at Northampton]. British Library. Pressmark 1851.c.16.

Archives of the Roman Catholic Diocese of Northampton. Bishop's House, Northampton.

Archdeaconry of Nottingham Manuscripts. University of Nottingham Library. Misc. 281a.

Oundle Papers. Northamptonshire Record Office, Northampton. Z 49 P.

Messrs. Page & Moody, Solicitors (Protestant Defence Papers). Southampton City Record Office. D/PM/10.

Henry Phillpotts Papers. Exeter Cathedral Library.

Robert Charles Ransome Papers. Suffolk Record Office, Ipswich Branch. County Hall, Ipswich.

Royce Family Papers. Manchester Central Library. M 70.

Messrs. Slater, Heelis, Solicitors. Manchester Central Library. M 159.

Wharncliffe Muniments. Sheffield City Library.

Isaac Williams Deposit. Lambeth Palace Library.

George Wilson Papers. Manchester Central Library. M 20.

Wordsworth Family Papers. Lambeth Palace Library.

Published Documents

"Minutes of Evidence taken before the Select Committee on the Derby Election Petition." *Parliamentary Papers*, 1847-48, XI (212), 607-732.

"Return of the Number of Addresses which have been presented to Her Majesty on the Subject of the Recent Measures taken by the Pope for the Establishment of a Roman Catholic Hierarchy in this Country." *Parliamentary Papers*, 1851, LIX (84), 649-739.

"Copy of an Address presented to Her Majesty from Her Majesty's Roman Catholic Subjects in England." *Parliamentary Papers*, 1851, LIX (236), 741.

"Minutes of Evidence taken before the Select Committee on the Derby Election Petition; together with the Proceedings of the Committee (1853)." *Parliamentary Papers*, 1852-53, XII (219), 9-164.

"Report from the Select Committee on Derby Elections (Petition of Inhabitant Householders); together with the Proceedings of the Committee, and Minutes of Evidence." *Parliamentary Papers*, 1852-53, XII (78), 165-344.

"Minutes of Evidence taken before the Select Committee on the Lancaster Borough Election Petition." *Parliamentary Papers*, 1852-53, XIV (152), 77-123.

"First Report from the Select Committee on Police." *Parliamentary Papers*, 1852-53, XXXVI (603), 1-160.

"Second Report from the Select Committee on Police." *Parliamentary Papers*, 1852-53, XXXVI (715), 161-396.

"Census of Great F..tain, 1851: Population Tables, I." *Parliamentary Papers*, 1852-53, LXXXV [1631].

"Census of Great Britain, 1851: Religious Worship, England and Wales." *Parliamentary Papers*, 1852-53, LXXXIX (89).

"Bonfire Night." *Notes and Queries*, 12th ser., V (1919), 318.

Edgcumbe, Richard, ed. *The Diary of Frances Lady Shelley, 1818-1873*. 2 vols. New York: Charles Scribner's Sons, 1914.

English Historical Documents, 1833-1874. Edited by G. M. Young and W. D. Handcock. Vol. XII, Pt. 1, of *English Historical Documents*. David C. Douglas, General Editor. Oxford University Press, 1956.

Hansard's Parliamentary Debates. 3rd Ser., LXXIX (1845), LXXXII (1845), LXXXIII (1846), XCVIII (1847-48), CXXIII (1852).

James, Louis. *English Popular Literature, 1819-1851*. New York: Columbia University Press, 1976.

Kettering Vestry Minutes, A.D. 1797-1853. Ed. by S. A. Peyton. Publications of the Northamptonshire Record Society, Vol. VI. Northamptonshire Record Society, 1933.

The Letters and Diaries of John Henry Newman. Edited by Charles Stephen Dessain and Vincent Ferrer Blehl. Vols. XIII, XIV, XV. London: Thomas Nelson and Sons Ltd., 1963-64.

Manchester, Watch Committee for the Borough of. *Criminal and Miscellaneous Statistical Returns of the Manchester Police, for the year 1846.* Manchester: Bradshaw and Blacklock, 1847.

A Norfolk Diary: Passages from the Diary of the Rev. Benjamin John Armstrong, Vicar of East Dereham, 1850-88. Edited by Herbert B. J. Armstrong. London: George G. Harrap and Company, Ltd., 1949.

Payne, Brian and Dorothy, eds. "Extracts from the Journals of John Deakin Heaton, M.D., of Claremont, Leeds." *Thoresby Miscellany,* LIII (1972), 93-153.

Reports of the Select Committee of the House of Commons on Public Petitions (Session 1851).

Works of Reference

Bagshaw, Samuel. *History, Gazetteer and Directory of Derbyshire.* Sheffield: Samuel Bagshaw, 1846.

Dod, Charles R. *Electoral Facts from 1832 to 1853 Impartially Stated.* Edited by H. J. Hanham. Brighton: Harvester Press, 1972.

History, Topography, and Directory of the Borough of Preston. Beverley: Manniz & Co., 1851.

Post Office Directory of Birmingham, with Staffordshire and Worcestershire. London: W. Kelly & Co., 1850.

Slater's General and Classified Directory and Street Register of Manchester and Salford, and their Vicinities. Manchester: Isaac Slater, 1850.

Slater's (late Pigot & Co.) Royal National and Commercial Directory and Topography . . . [of Birmingham]. Manchester and London: Isaac Slater, 1850.

White, Francis, & Co. *History, Gazetteer and Directory of the County of Derby.* Sheffield: Francis White & Co., 1857.

_____. *General and Commercial Directory and Topography of the Borough of Birmingham.* Sheffield: Francis White & Co., 1855.

Books and Pamphlets

Adams, W. E. *Memoirs of a Social Atom.* Edited by John Saville. New York: Augustus M. Kelley, Publishers, 1968.

Birmingham Church Union. *A Comrade's Harangue.* Birmingham: William Hodgetts, 1851.

[Bishop, Francis]. *Report presented at the fourteenth Annual General Meeting of the Liverpool Domestic Mission Society.* London and Liverpool, 1851.

Borrow, George. *Lavengro; the Scholar, the Gypsy, the Priest.* London: Macmillan and Co., 1896. (Originally published in 1851.)

Braddon, Mary E. *Aurora Floyd.* London: Virago, 1984. (Originally published in 1863.)

Britten, James. "An 'Escaped Monk': Being the Story of William Jefferys." *Publications of the Catholic Truth Society,* XCVIII (1914).

Brontë, Charlotte. *Villette.* Edited by Herbert Rosengarten and Margaret Smith. Oxford: Clarendon Press, 1984. (Originally published in 1853.)

Burritt, Elihu. *Walks in the Black Country and its Green Borderland.* Foreword by Vivian Bird. Kineton, Warwick: Roundwood Press, 1976. (Originally published in 1868).

Carveth, James. *The Wesleyan Association. Mr. Carveth and the Liverpool Circuit.* . . . London: W. B. King, 1852.

The Catholic Question: Report of the Great Town's Meeting, held in the Town Hall, Birmingham, on Wednesday, December 11, 1850. 3rd ed. Birmingham: Swan Brothers, 1850.

Chapman, Daniel. *The Great Principles Involved in the Present Act of Papal Aggression.* London and Doncaster: Partridge and Oakey, G. & T. Brooke, 1851.

Chiniquy, Charles. *Fifty Years in the Church of Rome.* Chino, Calif.: Chick Publications, Inc., 1985. (Originally published in 1874.)

_____. *The Priest, the Woman, and the Confessional.* Chino, Calif.: Chick Publications, Inc., 1979. (Originally published in 1874.)

The Churchman's Protest Against the National Society. London, 1840.

Cleary, William Francis. *A Letter on the Facility with which a Person, seriously disposed, may ascertain whether he be a member of the True Church or not.* Liverpool: Gardener & Braithwaite, 1836.

Confessions of a Convert, from Baptism IN Water to Baptism WITH Water. London: John Snow, 1845.

The Congregational Yearbook for 1851. London, 1852.

Croker, T. Crofton. "Daniel O'Rourke." *Through Fairy Halls.* Vol. VI of *My Book House.* Edited by Olive Beaupré Miller. 12 vols. Lake Bluff, Ill.: The Book House for Children, 1956. Pp. 62-69.

Dawson, George. *On the Romish Church and her Hierarchy.* Birmingham: J. A. Langford, 1850.

_____. *Two Lectures on the "Papal Aggression" Controversy.* Birmingham: E. C. Osborne, 1851.

Dickens, Charles. *The Annotated Christmas Carol.* Edited by Michael Patrick Hearne. New York: Aveirel Books, 1989. (Originally published in 1843.)

_____. *Bleak House.* New York and Toronto: New American Library, 1964. (Originally published in 1852-53.)

_____. *A Child's History of England.* 3 vols. London: Bradbury & Evans, 1852-54.

_____. *Nicholas Nickleby.* London: Penguin Books, 1978. (Originally published in 1839.)

_____. *The Posthumous Papers of the Pickwick Club.* London: Chapman & Hall, n.d. (Originally published in 1836.)

Eardley, Culling Eardley. *The Imprisonment and Deliverance of Dr. Giacinto Achilli, with some Account of his Previous History and Labours.* London: Partridge and Oakey, 1850.

Eliot, George. "Evangelical Teaching: Dr. Cumming." *Essays and Leaves from a Note-book.* Vol. 21 of *The Writings of George Eliot.* New York: AMS Press, 1970. Pp. 125-69. (Originally published in the *Westminster Review* for October 1855).

A Full Report of a most Extraordinary Investigation which took place on Tuesday, June 26, 1849, at Mount St. Bernard Monastery, Leicestershire. 6th ed. Birmingham: M. Maher, 1849.

Grant, Brewin. *The Three Shams: The sham Peter, called the Pope; the sham church, called infallible; the sham Bible, Douay & tradition.* London: Ward and Co., 1851.

Greenhalgh, Thomas. *The Vicissitudes of Commerce; A Tale of the Cotton Trade.* 2 vols. London: Saunders and Oxley, 1852.

Hinton, John Howard. *The Romish Hierarchy in England: A Sermon preached at Devonshire Square Chapel, London, on the 3rd November, 1850.* London: Houlston and Stoneman, 1850.

Leech, Joseph. *Rural Rides of the Bristol Churchgoer.* Edited by Alan Sutton. Gloucester: Alan Sutton Publishing, Ltd., 1982.

Leveson Gower, F. *Bygone Years.* New York: E. P. Dutton and Company, 1905.

Melson, John Barritt. *The apostle of the Gentiles, and his Glorying: a sermon.* London: Aylott and Jones, 1850.
Merle D'Aubigné, J.-H. *History of the Great Reformation of the Sixteenth Century in Germany, Switzerland, &c.* Philadelphia: James M. Campbell, 1847.
Mulhauser, F. L., ed. *The Poems of Arthur Hugh Clough.* 2nd ed. Oxford: Clarendon Press, 1974.
Newman, John Henry. *Sermons Preached on Various Occasions.* New ed. London: Longmans, Green and Co., 1898.
Oliphant, Margaret. *Miss Marjoribanks.* London: Zodiac Press, 1969. (Originally published in 1865-66.)
_____. *The Perpetual Curate.* London: Virago, 1989. (Originally published in 1864.)
_____. *Salem Chapel.* London: Penguin Books—Virago Press, 1986. (Originally published in 1863.)
Ragg, Thomas. *The Deity.* London: Longman, Rees, Orme, Brown, Green, & Longman, 1834.
_____. *God's Dealings with an Infidel; or, Grace Triumphant.* London: Piper, Stephenson, and Spence, 1858.
_____. *Heber; Records of the Poor; Lays from the Prophets; and Other Poems.* London: Longman, Orme, Brown, Green, & Longman, 1840.
Report of the Great Meeting of the Protestants of Birmingham, in the Town Hall, to oppose the Endowment of the Popish College at Maynooth, April 17, 1845. Birmingham: Thomas Ragg, 1845.
Ruskin, John. "Notes on the Construction of Sheepfolds." *The Works of John Ruskin.* Edited by C. T. Cook and Alexander Wedderburn. 39 vols. London: George Allen, 1904. XII, 511-58.
Sewell, Elizabeth Missing. *Katharine Ashton.* 2 vols. New York: D. Appleton and Company, 1864. (Originally published in 1854.)
Surtees, Robert Smith. *Mr. Sponge's Sporting Tour.* London: Bradbury and Evans, 1853.
Swaine, Edward. *"No Popery!" The Cry Examined.* 5th ed. London: Jackson and Walford, 1850. (Originally published in 1842.)
Tonna, L.H.J. *Life of Charlotte Elizabeth, as Contained in Her Personal Recollections, with Explanatory Notes; and a Memoir, Embracing the Period from the Close of Personal Recollections to her Death.* New York: M. W. Dodd, 1851. (Originally published in 1847.)
Trollope, Anthony. *Barchester Towers.* New York: Modern Library, 1950. (Originally published in 1857.)
_____. *The Warden.* New York: Modern Library, 1950. (Originally published in 1855.)
Tupper, Martin F. *Three Hundred Sonnets.* London: Arthur Hall, Virtue, and Co., 1860.
Walsh, Walter. *The Secret History of the Oxford Movement.* 5th ed. London: Swan Sonnenschein & Co., Ltd., 1899.
Wesleyan Methodism, and Religious Education Defended from the Attacks of John Stores Smith, in his Reply to the Revs. H. Stowell and G. Osborne. Manchester: Joseph Johnson, 1849.
Wiseman, Nicholas. *Essays on Various Subjects.* 3 vols. London: Charles Dolman, 1853.

Periodicals

Annual Register, XCII (1851), XCIII (1852).
Baptist Magazine, XXXVI (1844)-XLIII (1851).
Baptist Reporter, n.s., II (1845)-VIII (1851).
Bible Christian Magazine, XXX (1851).

Birmingham Church of England Lay Association. *Annual Reports.* 4th (1843)-8th (1847).
Birmingham Protestant Association. *Annual Reports.* 1st (1848)-2nd (1849), 20th (1867)-25th (1872).
Birmingham Protestant Association Record. Nos. 1 (Oct. 1866)-12 (Jan. 1868).
The British Protestant; or, Journal of the Religious Principles of the Reformation, I (1845)-IX (1853).
Bulwark, or Reformation Journal, I (1851-52)-VI (1856-57).
Bury Observer, and Herald of the Good Times Coming, No. 9 (1850).
Catholic Weekly Instructor, I (1844)-IV (1847).
The Champion of What is True and Right and for the Good of All, II (1850).
The Christian Miscellany, and Family Visiter, I (1846)-IX (1854).
Christian Observer, XLII (1842)-XLIV (1844).
Christian Watchman and Midland Counties' Protestant Magazine, Nos. 1 (June 1842)-21 (February 1844).
Christian Witness, VII (1850)-VIII (1851).
Christian's Penny Magazine, V (1850)-VI (1851).
The Church, n.s., I (1846-47)-V (1851).
Church Papers: Printed for the Use of the Congregation Meeting at the Church of the Saviour, Birmingham, Nos. 3 (1850)-5 (1851).
Circular of the Protestant Electoral Union. I (1866)-V (1870).
The Citizen, n.s., Nos. 1 (July 1846)-17 (November 1847).
Eliza Cook's Journal, I (1849)-VIII (1853).
English Presbyterian Messenger, n.s., I (1848-49)-III (1850-51).
Evangelical Alliance, British Organization. *Abstract of the Proceedings of the Fourth Annual Conference, held in Liverpool, October, 1850.* London: Partridge and Oakey, 1850.
_____. *Abstract of Proceedings of the Fifth Annual Conference, held in London, August and September 1851.* London: Partridge and Oakey, 1851.
Evangelical Christendom, I (1847)-V (1851).
Family Herald, or Useful Information and Amusement for the Million, o.s., I (1842-43); I (1843-44)-XIV (1856-57).
Inquirer, 1850-1851.
Annual Reports of the Leicester Town Mission, with a list of the Subscribers. (1849-1852).
Lloyd's Entertaining Journal, I (1844)-VII (1847).
Lloyd's Penny Weekly Miscellany of Romance and General Interest, I (1843)-VI (1846).
Lloyd's Weekly Miscellany, I (1849-50)-II (1850-52).
The Local Preachers' Magazine, and Mutual-Aid Association Reporter, I (1851).
Annual Reports of the Manchester and Salford Town Mission. (1837-1853).
Manchester Illuminator and General Catholic Record, I (1849-50).
Methodist New Connexion Magazine, LIII (1850)-LIV (1851).
Penny Protestant Operative, I (1840)-IX (1848).
Primitive Church Magazine, n.s., VII (1850)-VIII (1851).
Primitive Methodist Magazine, XXX (1849)-XXXII (1851).
Protestant Magazine, XI (1849)-XII (1850).
The Protestant Watchman of the Midland District, Nos. 1-22 (1849-50).
Protestant Witness, I (1848-49)-III (1851).
Wesley Banner and Revival Record, I (1849)-III (1851).
Wesleyan Methodist Magazine, LXVI (1843)-LXXIV (1851).
Wesleyan Review and Evangelical Record, I (1850)-II (1851).
Wesleyan Vindicator and Constitutional Methodist, 1850-1851.
Working Man's Friend, and Family Instructor, I (1850)-VI (1852).

Newspapers

Aris' Birmingham Gazette, 1849, 1850.
Birmingham Mercury, 1850-1852.
Blackburn Standard, 1850.
British Banner, 1850-1851.
Cambridge Chronicle, 1849-1852.
Cheltenham Free Press, 1850.
Chester Courant, 1851.
Christian Times, 1850-1851.
Globe and Traveller, 1850.
Huddersfield Chronicle, 1851.
Illustrated London News, 1843-1844, 1850-1851, 1855-1857, 1865-1870.
Kentish Observer, 1850.
Lancaster Gazette, 1851.
Lancaster Guardian, 1851.
Leeds Mercury, 1839-1855.
Leeds Times, 1838-1842.
Leicester Journal, 1844.
Leicestershire Mercury, 1844.
Maidstone Journal, 1850.
Manchester Courier, 1850-1851, 1859.
Manchester Examiner, 1850.
Manchester Guardian, 1850-1852.
Midland Counties Herald, 1847, 1850.
Northampton Herald, 1843-1860.
Northampton Mercury, 1850-1856.
Patriot, 1850.
Preston Guardian, 1850.
Preston Pilot, 1850.
Reading Mercury, 1850.
Record, 1850-1851.
Rochester, Chatham, and Stroud Gazette, 1850.
Salisbury and Wiltshire Herald, 1850.
Salisbury and Winchester Journal, 1850.
Sheffield Mercury, 1843.
Spectator, 1843.
Standard, 1850.
Sunderland Herald, 1851.
Times, 1841-1870.
Watchman and Wesleyan Advertiser, 1850-1851.
Wesleyan Notices Newspaper, 1850-1851.
Wesleyan Times, 1850-1851.
Windsor & Eton Express, 1850.

SECONDARY ACCOUNTS

Works of Reference

Boase, Frederic. *Modern English Biography*. 6 vols. London: Frank Cass & Co., Ltd., 1965.
The Dictionary of National Biography.
Encyclopedia of World Methodism. Edited by Nolan B. Harmon. Nashville, Tenn.: United Methodist Publishing House, 1974.
MacLysaght, Edward. *The Surnames of Ireland*. New York: Barnes & Noble, Inc., 1969.

New Catholic Encyclopedia. 17 vols. New York: McGraw Hill Book Company, 1967.

Reaney, P. H. *A Dictionary of British Surnames.* London: Routledge & Kegan Paul, 1961.

Venn, J. A. *Alumni Cantabrigienses.*

Victoria History of the Counties of England:
    Berkshire, III
    Buckinghamshire, III
    Cambridge and the Isle of Ely, II
    Huntingdonshire, II
    Lancashire, III
    Warwickshire, VI
    Wiltshire, III, X
    Yorkshire: West Riding, II

Monographs

Adelman, Paul. *Victorian Radicalism: The Middle-Class Experience, 1830-1914.* London: Longman, 1984.

Altholz, Josef L. *The Liberal Catholic Movement in England: The "Rambler" and its Contributors, 1848-1864.* London: Burns & Oates, 1962.

_____. *The Religious Press in Britain, 1760-1900* Westport, Conn.: Greenwood Press, 1989.

Altick, Richard D. *The English Common Reader: A Social History of the Mass Reading Public, 1800-1900.* University of Chicago Press, 1957.

Anderson, Michael. *Family Structure in Nineteenth Century Lancashire.* Cambridge University Press, 1971.

Appel, John and Selma. *Pat-Riots to Patriots: American Irish in Caricature and Comic Art.* East Lansing: Michigan State University Museum, 1990.

Archer, John E. *By a Flash and a Scare: Incendiarism, Animal Maiming, and Poaching in East Anglia, 1815-1870.* Oxford: Clarendon Press, 1990.

Arnstein, Walter L. *The Bradlaugh Case: Atheism, Sex, and Politics among the Late Victorians.* Columbia: University of Missouri Press, 1983.

Bailey, Peter. *Leisure and Class in Victorian England: Rational Recreation and the Contest for Control, 1830-1885.* London and Toronto: Routledge & Kegan Paul, University of Toronto Press, 1978.

Baker, Joseph Ellis. *The Novel and the Oxford Movement.* New York: Russell & Russell, Inc., 1965. (Originally published in 1932).

Barnes, Harry Elmer. *A History of Historical Writing.* 2nd ed. New York: Dover Publications, 1963.

Barzun, Jacques. *Race: A Study in Superstition.* Rev. ed. New York: Harper & Row, 1965.

Bebbington, D. W. *Evangelicalism in Modern Britain: A History from the 1730s to the 1980s.* London: Unwin Hyman, 1989.

Bentley, James. *Ritualism and Politics in Victorian Britain: The Attempt to Legislate for Belief.* Oxford University Press, 1978.

Billington, Ray Allen. *The Protestant Crusade, 1800-1860: A Study of the Origins of American Nativism.* New York: Macmillan, 1938.

Binfield, Clyde. *So Down to Prayers: Studies in English Nonconformity, 1780-1920.* London: J. M. Dent & Sons, Ltd., 1977.

Bolt, Christine. *Victorian Attitudes to Race.* London and Toronto: Routledge & Kegan Paul, University of Toronto Press, 1971.

Bossy, John. *The English Catholic Community, 1570-1850.* London: Darton, Longman & Todd, 1975.

Bowen, Desmond. *The Idea of the Victorian Church: A Study of the Church of England, 1833-1889.* Montreal: McGill University Press, 1968.

Briggs, Asa. *Victorian Cities*. American ed. New York: Harper & Row, 1965.
Brock, Michael. *The Great Reform Act*. London: Hutchinson University Library, 1973.
Brockett, Allan. *Nonconformity in Exeter, 1650-1875*. Manchester University Press, 1962.
Brown, Lucy. *Victorian News and Newspapers*. Oxford: Clarendon Press, 1985.
Bruce, Steve. *No Pope of Rome: Anti-Catholicism in Modern Scotland*. Edinburgh: Mainstream Publishing, 1985.
Cameron, George G. *The Scots Kirk in London*. Oxford: Becket Publications, 1979.
Carwardine, Richard. *Trans-Atlantic Revivalism: Popular Evangelicalism in Britain and America, 1790-1865*. Westport, Conn.: Greenwood Press, 1978.
Chadwick, Owen. *The Victorian Church*. 2nd ed., Pt. I. London: Adam & Charles Black, 1970.
Chapman, Raymond. *Faith and Revolt: Studies in the Literary Influence of the Oxford Movement*. London: Weidenfeld and Nicolson, 1970.
Chorley, E. Clowes. *Men and Movements in the American Episcopal Church*. New York: Charles Scribner's Sons, 1950.
Colby, Robert A. *Fiction with a Purpose: Major and Minor Nineteenth-Century Novels*. Bloomington: Indiana University Press, 1967.
Coleman, B. I. *The Church of England in the Mid-Nineteenth Century: A Social Geography*. General Series, No. 98. London: The Historical Association, 1980.
Conley, Carolyn A. *The Unwritten Law: Criminal Justice in Victorian Kent*. New York: Oxford University Press, 1991.
Cunningham, Hugh. *Leisure in the Industrial Revolution, c. 1780-c. 1880*. New York: St. Martin's Press, 1980.
Cunningham, Valentine. *Everywhere Spoken Against: Dissent in the Victorian Novel*. Oxford: Clarendon Press, 1975.
Curtis, Jr., L. P. *Anglo-Saxons and Celts: A Study of Anti-Irish Prejudice in Victorian England*. Bridgeport, Conn.: Conference on British Studies, 1968.
Dalziel, Margaret. *Popular Fiction 100 Years Ago: An Unexplored Tract of Literary History*. London: Cohen & West, 1957.
Davey, B.J. *Lawless and Immoral: Policing a Country Town, 1838-1857*. Leicester University Press, 1983.
Davies, Horton. *Worship and Theology in England*. Vol. III. *From Watts and Wesley to Maurice, 1690-1850*. Princeton University Press, 1961.
_____. *Worship and Theology in England*. Vol. IV. *From Newman to Martineau, 1850-1900*. Princeton University Press, 1962.
Dickens, A. G., and John Tonkin, with Kenneth Powell. *The Reformation in Historical Thought*. Cambridge, Mass.: Harvard University Press, 1985.
Errington, Lindsay. *Social and Religious Themes in English Art, 1840-1860*. New York: Garland Publishing, Inc., 1984.
Fleischman, Jr., Richard K. *Conditions of Life Among the Cotton Workers of Southeastern Lancashire During the Industrial Revolution (1780-1850)*. New York: Garland Publishing, Inc., 1985.
Foster, John. *Class Struggle and the Industrial Revolution: Early Early Industrial Capitalism in Three English Towns*. New York: St. Martin's Press, 1974.
Fraser, Derek. *Urban Politics in Victorian England: The Structure of Politics in Victorian Cities*. Leicester University Press, 1976.
Gallagher, Tom. *Edinburgh Divided: John Cormack and No Popery in the 1930s*. Edinburgh: Polygon, 1987.
_____. *Glasgow: The Uneasy Peace: Religious Tension in Modern Scotland, 1819-1914*. Manchester University Press, 1987.
Galloway, Bruce. *A History of Cambridgeshire*. Chichester: Phillimore, 1983.

Gammage, R.G. *History of the Chartist Movement, 1837-1854.* 2nd ed. London and Newcastle-on-Tyne: Truslove & Hanson, Browne & Browne, 1894.

Gay, John D. *The Geography of Religion in England.* London: Duckworth, 1971.

Gilbert, Alan D. *Religion and Society in Industrial England: Church, Chapel and Social Change, 1740-1914.* London: Longman, 1976.

Golby, J. M., and A. W. Purdue. *The Civilisation of the Crowd: Popular Culture in England, 1750-1900.* New York: Schocken Books, 1985.

Gose, Jr., Elliot B. *Imagination Indulged: The Irrational in the Nineteenth-Century Novel.* Montreal: McGill-Queens University Press, 1972.

Gowland, D. A. *Methodist Secessions: The origins of Free Methodism in three Lancashire towns: Manchester, Rochdale, Liverpool. Remains Historical and Literary connected with the Palatine Counties of Lancashire and Cheshire.* 3rd ser., XXVI. Manchester: Chetham Society, 1979.

Graves, Charles L. *Mr. Punch's History of Modern England.* 4 vols. London: Cassell and Company, Ltd., 1921.

Hamer, D. A. *The Politics of Electoral Pressure: A Study in the History of Victorian Reform Agitations.* Hassocks: Harvester Press, 1977.

Hamlyn, Robin. *John Martin, 1789-1854: Belshazzar's Feast, 1820.* London: The Tate Gallery, 1989.

Hanham, H. J. *Elections and Party Management: Politics in the Time of Gladstone and Disraeli.* London: Longmans, 1959.

Harrison, Brian. *Drink and the Victorians: The Temperance Question in England, 1815-1872.* London: Faber and Faber, 1971.

_____. *Peaceable Kingdom: Stability and Change in Modern Britain.* Oxford: Clarendon Press, 1982.

Harrison, Mark. *Crowds and History: Mass Phenomena in English Towns, 1790-1835.* Cambridge University Press, 1988.

Heeney, Brian. *The Women's Movement in the Church of England, 1850-1930.* Oxford: Clarendon Press, 1988.

Hempton, David. *Methodism and Politics in British Society, 1750-1850.* Stanford University Press, 1984.

Hennock, E. P. *Fit and Proper Persons: Ideal and Reality in Nineteenth-Century Urban Government.* Montreal: McGill-Queen's University Press, 1973.

Hilton, Boyd. *The Age of Atonement: The Influence of Evangelicalism on Social and Economic Thought, 1795-1865.* Oxford: Clarendon Press, 1988.

Hobsbawm, E. J., and George Rudé. *Captain Swing.* New York: Pantheon Books, 1968.

Hole, Robert. *Pulpits, Politics and Public Order in England, 1760-1832.* Cambridge University Press, 1989.

Holmes, J. Derek. *More Roman than Rome: English Catholicism in the Nineteenth Century.* London: Burns & Oates, 1978.

Horn, Pamela. *The Rise and Fall of the Victorian Servant.* Dublin: Gill and Macmillan, 1975.

Houghton, Walter E. *The Victorian Frame of Mind, 1830-1870.* New Haven: Yale University Press, 1957.

Howe, Anthony. *The Cotton Masters, 1830-1860.* Oxford: Clarendon Press, 1984.

Husband, Charles, ed. *"Race" in Britain: Continuity and Change.* London: Hutchinson, 1982.

Isichei, Elizabeth. *Victorian Quakers.* Oxford University Press, 1970.

Jagger, Peter J. *Clouded Witness: Initiation in the Church of England in the Mid-Victorian Period, 1850-1875.* Pittsburgh Theological Monographs, n.s., I. Allison Park, Penna.: Pickwick Publications, 1982.

James, Louis. *Fiction for the Working Man, 1830-1850.* London: Oxford University Press, 1963.

Jay, Elisabeth. *The Religion of the Heart: Anglican Evangelicalism and the Nineteenth-Century Novel.* Oxford: Clarendon Press, 1979.

Jephson, H. D. *The Platform, Its Rise and Progress*. 2 vols. London: Macmillan & Co., 1892.

Jones, David. *Crime, Protest, Community and Police in Nineteenth-Century Britain*. London: Routledge & Kegan Paul, 1982.

Jones, R. Tudor. *Congregationalism in England, 1662-1962*. London: Independent Press Ltd., 1962.

Jordan, Philip D. *The Evangelical Alliance for the United States of America, 1847-1900: Ecumenism, Identity and the Religion of the Republic*. New York and Toronto: Edwin Mellen Press, 1982.

Joyce, Patrick. *Work, Society, and Politics: The Culture of the Factory in Later Victorian England*. New Brunswick, N.J.: Rutgers University Press, 1980.

Kelley, Mary Edith. *The Irishman in the English Novel of the Nineteenth Century*. New York: Haskell House, 1970.

Kestner, Joseph. *Protest and Reform: The British Social Narrative by Women, 1827-1867*. Madison: University of Wisconsin Press, 1985.

Kiely, Robert. *The Romantic Novel in England*. Cambridge, Mass.: Harvard University Press, 1972.

Kirk, Neville. *The Growth of Working-Class Reformism in Mid-Victorian England*. Urbana and Chicago: University of Illinois Press, 1985.

Klaus, Robert James. *The Pope, the Protestants, and the Irish: Papal Aggression and Anti-Catholicism in Mid-Nineteenth Century England*. New York: Garland Publishing, Inc., 1987.

Knott, John. *Popular Opposition to the 1834 Poor Law*. New York: St. Martin's Press, 1986.

Koditschek, Theodore. *Class Formation and Urban-Industrial Society: Bradford, 1750-1850*. Cambridge University Press, 1990.

Lees, Lynn Hollen. *Exiles of Erin: Irish Migrants in Victorian London*. Manchester University Press, 1979.

Lewis, Donald M. *Lighten Their Darkness: The Evangelical Mission to Working-Class London, 1828-1860*. Westport, Conn.: Greenwood Press, 1986.

Lowe, W. J. *The Irish in Mid-Victorian Lancashire: The Shaping of a Working-Class Community*. New York: Peter Lang, 1989.

McClatchey, Diana. *Oxfordshire Clergy, 1777-1869: A Study of the Established Church and of the Role of its Clergy in Local Society*. Oxford: Clarendon Press, 1960.

McCord, Norman. *The Anti-Corn Law League, 1838-1846*. 2nd ed. London: Unwin University Books, 1968.

McHugh, Paul. *Prostitution and Victorian Social Reform*. New York: St. Martin's Press, 1980.

Maas, Jeremy. *Holman Hunt and the Light of the World*. London: Scolar Press, 1984.

Machin, G.I.T. *The Catholic Question in English Politics, 1820 to 1830*. Oxford: Clarendon Press, 1964.

_____. *Politics and the Churches in Great Britain, 1832 to 1868*. Oxford: Clarendon Press, 1977.

_____. *Politics and the Churches in Great Britain, 1869 to 1921*. Oxford: Clarendon Press, 1987.

Malcolmson, Robert W. *Popular Recreation in English Society, 1700-1850*. Cambridge University Press, 1973.

Manning, Bernard Lord. *The Protestant Dissenting Deputies*. Edited by Ormerod Greenwood. Cambridge University Press, 1952.

Moore, David Cresap. *The Politics of Deference: A Study of the Mid-Nineteenth Century English Political System*. Hassocks: Harvester Press, 1976.

Moorman, John R.H. *A History of the Church in England*. New York: Morehouse-Barlow Company, 1963.

Neal, Frank. *Sectarian Violence: The Liverpool Experience, 1819-1914: An Aspect of Anglo-Irish History.* Manchester University Press, 1988.

Neuberg, Victor E. *Popular Literature: A History and Guide from the Beginning to the Year 1897.* London: Woburn Press, 1977.

Newman, Gerald. *The Rise of English Nationalism: A Cultural History, 1740-1830.* New York: St. Martin's Press, 1987.

Newton, Robert. *Victorian Exeter, 1837-1914.* Leicester University Press, 1968.

Nightingale, Benjamin. *The Story of the Lancashire Congregational Union, 1806-1906.* Manchester and London: John Heywood, Ltd., 1906.

Norman, E. R. *Anti-Catholicism in Victorian England.* London: George Allen and Unwin, Ltd., 1968.

_____. *The English Catholic Church in the Nineteenth Century.* Oxford: Clarendon Press, 1984.

Payne, Ernest A. *The Baptist Union, a Short History.* London: Carey Kingsgate Press Limited, 1958.

Paz, D. G. *The Politics of Working-Class Education in Britain, 1830-50.* Manchester University Press, 1980.

Peel, Albert. *These Hundred Years: A History of the Congregational Union of England and Wales, 1831-1931.* London: Congregational Union of England and Wales, 1931.

Pickering, W.S.F. *Anglo-Catholicism: A Study in Religious Ambiguity.* London and New York: Routledge, 1989.

Pope, Norris. *Dickens and Charity.* New York: Columbia University Press, 1978.

Prochaska, F. K. *Women and Philanthropy in Nineteenth-Century England.* Oxford: Clarendon Press, 1980.

Reeve, F. A. *Cambridge.* New York: Hastings House, 1964.

Richter, Donald C. *Riotous Victorians.* Athens: Ohio University Press, 1981.

Roth, Cecil. *The Spanish Inquisition.* New York: W. W. Norton & Company, Inc., 1964.

Rouse, Ruth, and Stephen Charles Neill, eds. *A History of the Ecumenical Movement, 1517-1948.* London: SPCK, 1954.

Rowell, Geoffrey. *The Vision Glorious: Themes and Personalities of the Catholic Revival in Anglicanism.* Oxford University Press, 1983.

Royle, Edward. *Victorian Infidels: The Origins of the British Secularist Movement, 1791-1866.* Manchester University Press, 1974.

Sage, Victor. *Horror Fiction in the Protestant Tradition.* London: Macmillan Press, 1988.

Sandeen, Ernest R. *The Roots of Fundamentalism: British and American Millenarianism, 1800-1930.* University of Chicago Press, 1970.

Schwartz, Michael. *The Persistent Prejudice: Anti-Catholicism in America.* Huntington, Indiana: Our Sunday Visitor, Inc., 1984.

Sellers, Ian. *Nineteenth-Century Nonconformity.* London: Edward Arnold, 1977.

Smith, Alan. *The Established Church and Popular Religion, 1750-1850.* London: Longman, 1971.

Smith, Phillip Thurmond. *Policing Victorian London: Political Policing, Public Order, and the London Metropolitan Police.* Westport, Conn.: Greenwood Press, 1985.

Steedman, Carolyn. *Policing the Victorian Community: The Formation of English Provincial Police Forces, 1856-80.* London: Routledge & Kegan Paul, 1984.

Stevenson, John. *Popular Disturbances in England, 1700-1850.* London: Longmans, 1979.

Stonyk, Margaret. *Nineteenth-Century English Literature.* New York: Schocken Books, 1984.

Sutherland, J. A. *Victorian Novelists and Publishers.* University of Chicago Press, 1976.

Thomas, Glynn, and Enid Porter. *Victorian Cambridge*. London: Dennis Dobson, 1969.
Thompson, Dorothy. *The Chartists: Popular Politics in the Industrial Revolution*. New York: Pantheon Books, 1984.
Tilly, Charles. *As Sociology Meets History*. New York: Academic Press, 1981.
Tracy, Ann B. *The Gothic Novel, 1790-1830: Plot Summaries and Index to Motifs*. Lexington: University Press of Kentucky, 1981.
Underwood, A. C. *A History of the English Baptists*. London: Carey Kingsgate Press, Ltd., 1956.
Urdank, Albion M. *Religion and Society in a Cotswold Vale: Nailsworth, Gloucestershire, 1780-1865*. Berkeley: University of California Press, 1990.
Vicinus, Martha. *Independent Women: Work and Community for Single Women, 1850-1920*. University of Chicago Press, 1985.
Waller, P. J. *Democracy and Sectarianism: A Political and Social History of Liverpool, 1868-1939*. Liverpool University Press, 1981.
Walton, John K. *Lancashire: A Social History, 1558-1939*. Manchester University Press, 1987.
Ward, W. R. *Religion and Society in England, 1790-1850*. London: B. T. Batsford, 1972.
Werner, Julia Stewart. *The Primitive Methodist Connexion: Its Background and Early History*. Madison: University of Wisconsin Press, 1984.
Westfall, William. *Two Worlds: The Protestant Culture of Nineteenth-Century Ontario*. Kingston and Montreal: McGill-Queen's University Press, 1989.
Wilbur, Earl Morse. *A History of Unitarianism*. 2 vols. Cambridge, Mass.: Harvard University Press, 1945-52.
William Holman Hunt. Liverpool: Walker Art Gallery, 1969.
Wolff, Robert Lee. *Gains and Losses: Novels of Faith and Doubt in Victorian England*. New York: Garland Publishing, Inc., 1977.
Wolffe, John R. *The Protestant Crusade in Great Britain, 1828-1860*. Oxford: Clarendon Press, 1991.
Wooden, Warren W. *John Foxe*. Boston: Twayne Publishers, 1983.
Yates, Nigel. *Leeds and the Oxford Movement: A Study of "High Church" Activity in the Rural Deaneries of Allerton, Armley, Headingley and Whitkirk in the Diocese of Ripon, 1836-1934*. Publications of the Thoresby Society, LV (1975).
———. *The Oxford Movement and Parish Life: St. Saviour's, Leeds, 1839-1929*. Borthwick Papers, No. 48. York: Borthwick Institute of Historical Research, 1975.

Biographies

Arnstein, Walter L. *Protestant Versus Catholic in Mid-Victorian England: Mr. Newdegate and the Nuns*. Columbia: University of Missouri Press, 1982.
Chapman, Ronald. *Father Faber*. Westminster, Md.: Newman Press, 1961.
Chinnici, Joseph P. *The English Catholic Enlightenment: John Lingard and the Cisalpine Movement, 1780-1850*. Shepherdstown, W.Va.: Patmos Press, 1980.
Ellsworth, L. E. *Charles Lowder and the Ritualist Movement*. London: Darton, Longman and Todd, 1982.
Freer, Frederick Ash. *Edward White, His Life and Work*. London: Elliot Stock, 1902.
Hudson, Derek. *Martin Tupper: His Rise and Fall*. London: Constable, 1949.
Marsden, John Buxton. *Memoirs of the Life and Labours of the Rev. Hugh Stowell, M.A.* London: Hamilton, Adams, & Co., 1868.
Martina, Giacomo. *Pio IX (1846-1850)*. Rome: Università Gregoriana Editrice, 1974.

Paz, D. G. *The Priesthoods and Apostasies of Pierce Connelly: A Study of Victorian Conversion and Anticatholicism.* Lewiston, N.Y., and Queenston, Ont.: Edwin Mellen Press, 1986.

Prest, John. *Lord John Russell.* London: Macmillan, 1972.

Schiefen, Richard J. *Nicholas Wiseman and the Transformation of English Catholicism.* Shepherdstown, W.Va.: Patmos Press, 1984.

Stephens, W.R.W. *The Life and Letters of Walter Farquhar Hook.* 7th ed. London: Richard Bentley & Son, 1885.

Sylvain, Robert. *Alessandro Gavazzi: Garibaldien, Clerc, Prédicant des Deux Mondes.* 2 vols. Quebec: Le Centre Pédagogique, 1962.

Trevor, Meriol. *Newman: The Pillar of the Cloud.* London: Macmillan & Co., Ltd., 1962.

Ward, Wilfrid. *The Life and Times of Cardinal Wiseman.* 3rd ed. 2 vols. London: Longmans, Green, and Company, 1898.

Wilson, Wright. *The Life of George Dawson.* Birmingham: Percival Jones Limited, 1905.

Articles

Altholz, Josef L. "Truth and Equivocation: Liguori's Moral Theology and Newman's *Apologia.*" *Church History,* XLIV (1975), 73-84.

_____. "The Vatican Decrees Controversy, 1874-1875." *Catholic Historical Review,* LVII (1971-72), 593-605.

_____, and John Powell. "Gladstone, Lord Ripon, and the Vatican Decrees, 1874." *Albion,* XXII (1990), 449-59.

Arnstein, Walter L. "The Murphy Riots: A Victorian Dilemma." *Victorian Studies,* XIX (1975-76), 51-71.

Ashton, Owen. "Clerical Control and Radical Responses in Cheltenham Spa, 1838-1848." *Midland History,* VIII (1983), 121-47.

Baker, Mark. "Aspects of the Life of the Wiltshire Agricultural Labourer, c. 1850." *Wiltshire Archæological Magazine,* LXXIV/LXXV (1979-80), 161-169.

Balda, Wesley. "Simeon's 'Protestant Papists': A Sampling of Moderate Evangelicalism Within the Church of England, 1839-1865." *Fides et Historia,* XVI (1983), 55-67.

Berridge, Virginia. "Popular Sunday Papers and Mid-Victorian Society." *Newspaper History from the Seventeenth Century to the Present Day.* Edited by George Boyce, James Curran, and Pauline Wingate. London and Beverly Hills, Calif.: Constable and Sage Publications, 1978. Pp. 247-64.

Best, G.F.A. "Popular Protestantism in Victorian Britain." *Ideas and Institutions of Victorian Britain: Essays in Honour of George Kitson Clark.* Edited by Robert Robson. London: G. Bell & Sons, Ltd., 1967. Pp. 115-42.

_____. "The Protestant Constitution and its Supporters, 1800-1829." *Transactions of the Royal Historical Society.,* 5th ser., VIII (1958), 105-27.

Blake, Richard A. "Christians, Lions, and the Media." *America,* CXLII (12 Jan. 1980), 8-11.

Bohstedt, John. "Authoritarian Populism: Protestant-Catholic Riots in Edwardian Liverpool." *Riot, Police and Popular Politics in Liverpool, 1800-1914.* Edited by John C. Belchem. Forthcoming 1992.

Cahill, Gilbert A. "Irish Catholicism and English Toryism." *Review of Politics,* XIX (1957), 62-76.

_____. "The Protestant Association and the Anti-Maynooth Agitation of 1845." *Catholic Historical Review,* XLIII (1957), 273-308.

Carter, Brian. "Controversy and Conciliation in the English Catholic Enlightenment, 1790-1840." *Enlightenment and Dissent,* VII (1988), 3-24.

Casteras, Susan P. "Virgin Vows: The Early Victorian Artists' Portrayal of Nuns and Novices." *Religion in the Lives of English Women, 1760-1930.* Edited by Gail Malmgreen. Bloomington: Indiana University Press, 1986. Pp. 129-60.

Champ, Judith F. "The Demographic Impact of Irish Immigration on Birmingham Catholicism, 1800-1850." *Studies in Church History*, XXV (1989), 233-42.

_____. "Priesthood and Politics in the Nineteenth Century: The Turbulent Career of Thomas McDonnell." *Recusant History*, XVIII (1987), 289-303.

Connolly, Gerard P. "The Catholic Church and the First Manchester and Salford Trade Unions in the Age of the Industrial Revolution." *Transactions of the Lancashire and Cheshire Antiquarian Society*, LXXXIII (1985), 125-60.

_____. "Little Brother Be at Peace: The Priest as Holy Man in the Nineteenth-Century Ghetto." *Studies in Church History*, XIX (1982), 191-206.

_____. "The Transubstantiation of Myth: Towards a New Popular History of Nineteenth-Century Catholicism in England." *Journal of Ecclesiastical History*, XXXV (1984), 78-104.

Conser, Jr., Walter H. "A Conservative Critique of Church and State: The Case of the Tractarians and Neo-Lutherans." *Journal of Church and State*, XXV (1983), 323-341.

Cornick, David. "'Catch a Scotchman Becoming an Englishman': Nationalism, Theology and Ecumenism in the Presbyterian Church in England, 1845-1876." *Journal of the United Reformed Church Historical Society*, III (May 1985), 202-15.

Daniels, Emil. "Die Engländer und die Gefahr einer französischen Landung zur Zeit Louis Philipps und Napoleons III." *Delbrück-festschrift: Gesammelte Aufsätze, Professor Hans Delbrück zu seinem sechzigsten Geburtstage.* Berlin, 1908. Pp. 257-91.

Davis, David Brion. "Some Themes of Counter-Subversion: An Analysis of Anti-Masonic, Anti-Catholic, and Anti-Mormon Literature." *Mississippi Valley Historical Review*, XLVII (1960), 205-24.

Detzler, Wayne. "Protest and Schism in Nineteenth-Century German Catholicism: The Ronge-Czerski Movement, 1844-5." *Studies in Church History*, IX (1972), 341-349.

Dews, D. Colin. "The Ecclesiastical Returns, 1851: A Study of Methodist Attendances in Leeds." *Proceedings of the Wesley Historical Society*, XXXIX (1974), 113-16.

Dillon, T. "The Irish in Leeds, 1851-1861." *Thoresby Miscellany*, LIV (1979), 1-28.

Donovan, Robert Kent. "The Denominational Character of English Catholic Charitable Effort, 1800-1865." *Catholic Historical Review*, LXII (1976), 200-223.

Durey, Michael. "The Survival of an Irish Culture in Britain." *Historical Studies*, XX (1982), 14-35.

Ellens, J. P. "Lord John Russell and the Church Rate Conflict: The Struggle for a Broad Church, 1834-1868." *Journal of British Studies*, XXVI (1987), 232-57.

Field, John. "Police, Power and Community in a Provincial English Town: Portsmouth, 1815-1875." *Policing and Punishment in Nineteenth Century Britain.* Edited by Victor Bailey. New Brunswick, N.J.: Rutgers University Press, 1981.

Fomin, Joan. "Congregationalists in Crisis, 1836-43." *Colchester Historical Studies.* No. 1. *Three Studies in Turbulence.* Edited by David Stephenson. Papers of the Colchester Local History Research Group, n.d. Pp. 22-32.

Franklin, R. W. "Pusey and Worship in Industrial Society." *Worship*, LVII (1983), 386-412.

Fraser, Derek. "Edward Baines." *Pressure from Without in Early Victorian England*. Edited by Patricia Hollis. New York: St. Martin's Press, 1974. Pp. 183-209.

_____. "Politics and Society in the Nineteenth Century." *A History of Modern Leeds*. Edited by Derek Fraser. Manchester University Press, 1980. Pp. 270-300.

_____. "Poor Law Politics in Leeds, 1833-1855." *Thoresby Miscellany*, LIII (1971), 23-49.

_____. "Voluntaryism and West Riding Politics in the Mid-Nineteenth Century." *Northern History*, XIII (1977), 199-231.

Fraser, Peter. "Public Petitioning and Parliament Before 1832." 1832. *History*, XLVI (1961), 195-211.

Garrard, J. A. "Heates, Tumultes and Factions." *Salford: A City and Its Past*. Edited by Tom Bergin, Dorothy N. Pearce, and Stanley Shaw. Salford: The City, 1974. Pp. 87-106.

Garvey, John. "The Ugly Little Secret: Anti-Catholicism with Qualifications." *Commonweal*, CVI (28 Sept. 1979), 520-21.

George, Joseph, Jr. "The Lincoln Writings of Charles P. T. Chiniquy." *Journal of the Illinois State Historical Society*, LXIX (1976), 17-25.

Gilley, Sheridan. "English Attitudes to the Irish in England, 1780-1900." *Immigrants and Minorities in British Society*. Edited by Colin Holmes. London: George Allen & Unwin, 1978. Pp. 81-110.

_____. "English Catholic Charity and the Irish Poor in London. Part I: 1700-1840." *Recusant History*, XI (1972), 179-195.

_____. "English Catholic Charity and the Irish Poor in London: Part II (1840-1870)." *Recusant History*, XI (1972), 253-269.

_____. "The Garibaldi Riots of 1862." *Historical Journal*, XVI (1973), 697-732.

_____. "Protestant London, No-Popery and the Irish Poor, 1830-60. I: 1830-1850." *Recusant History*, X (1970), 210-30.

_____. "Protestant London, No-Popery and the Irish Poor: II (1850-1860)." *Recusant History*, XI (1971), 21-46.

_____. "The Roman Catholic Mission to the Irish in London, 1840-1860." *Recusant History*, XI (1969), 123-45.

Greenall, R. L."Baptist as Radical: The Life and Opinions of the Rev. John Jenkinson of Kettering (1799-1876)." *Northamptonshire Past and Present*, VIII (1991-92), 210-26.

_____. "The Making of the Borough of Salford, 1830-1853." *Victorian Lancashire*. Edited by S. P. Bell. Newton Abbot: David & Charles, 1974. Pp. 35-58.

_____. "Parson as Man of Affairs: The Rev. Francis Litchfield of Farthinghoe (1792-1876)." *Northamptonshire Past and Present*, VIII (1990-91), 121-35.

_____. "The Rise of Industrial Kettering." *Northamptonshire Past and Present*, V (1975), 253-66.

Grieve, Alastair. "The Pre-Raphaelite Brotherhood and the Anglican High Church." *Burlington Magazine*, CXI (1969), 194-95.

Griffin, John R. "The Radical Phase of the Oxford Movement." *Journal of Ecclesiastical History*, XXVII (1976), 47-56.

Guttsman, W. L. "The General Election of 1859 in the Cities of Yorkshire: A Study of Political Behaviour under the Impact of the Reform Agitation." *International Review of Social History*, II (1957), 231-58.

Hall, Basil. "Alessandro Gavazzi: A Barnabite Friar and the risorgimento." *Studies in Church History*, XII (1975), 303-56.

Hardy, René. "La Rébellion de 1837-38 et l'Essor du Protestantisme Canadien-Français." *Revue d'Histoire de l'Amérique Français*, XXIX (1975), 163-89.

Harrison, Brian. "Religion and Recreation in Nineteenth-Century England." *Past and Present*, No. 38 (Dec. 1967), pp. 98-125.

_____. "The Sunday Trading Riots of 1855." *Historical Journal*, VIII (1965), 219-45.

Harrison, J.F.C. "Chartism in Leeds." *Chartist Studies*. Edited by Asa Briggs. London: Macmillan, 1959. Pp. 65-98.

Hempton, D. N. "Evangelicalism and Eschatology." *Journal of Ecclesiastical History*, XXXI (1980), 179-94.

Henderson, W. O. "The Firm of Ermen & Engels in Manchester." *Internationale wissenschaftliche Korrespondenz zur Geschichte der deutschen Arbeiterbewegung*, Heft 11-12 (1971), 1-10.

Hilliard, David. "Unenglish and Unmanly: Anglo-Catholicism and Homosexuality." *Victorian Studies*, XXV (1981-2), 181-210.

Hoggart, P. R. "Edward Lloyd, 'The Father of the Cheap Press.'" *Dickensian*, LXXX (Spring 1984), 33-38.

Holladay, J. Douglas. "Nineteenth Century Evangelical Activism: From Private Charity to State Intervention." *Historical Magazine of the Protestant Episcopal Church*, LI (1982), 53-79.

Hoppen, K. Theodore. "Tories, Catholics, and the General Election of 1859." *Historical Journal*, XIII (1970), 48-67.

Houston, Cecil J., and William J. Smyth. "Transferred Loyalties: Orangeism in the United States and Ontario." *American Review of Canadian Studies*, XIV (1984), 193-211.

Howarth, Janet. "Politics and Society in Late Victorian Northamptonshire." *Northamptonshire Past and Present*, IV (1970-71), 269-274.

Humpherys, Anne. "G.W.M. Reynolds: Popular Literature and Popular Politics." *Victorian Periodicals Review*, XVI (Fall-Winter 1983), 79-89.

Inglis, K. S. "Patterns of Religious Worship in 1851." *Journal of Ecclesiastical History*, XI (1960), 74-86.

James, Louis. "The Trouble with Betsy: Periodicals and the Common Reader in Mid-Nineteenth-Century England." *The Victorian Periodical Press: Samplings and Soundings*. Edited by Joanne Shattock and Michael Wolff. Leicester University Press and University of Toronto Press, 1982. Pp. 349-66.

Johnson, Dale A. "Between Evangelicalism and a Social Gospel: The Case of Joseph Rayner Stephens." *Church History*, XLII (1973), 229-42.

Jones, Keith G. "The Industrial Revolution: Effects upon the Baptist Community in Barnoldswick and the Resulting 'Split' in the Baptist Church." *Baptist Quarterly*, XXX (1983), 125-39.

Keith-Lucas, B. "County Meetings." *Law Quarterly Review*, LXX (1954), 109-14.

Kerr, Donal A. "England, Ireland, and Rome, 1847-1848." *Studies in Church History*, XXV (1989), 259-77.

Kirk, Neville. "Ethnicity, Class and Popular Toryism, 1850-1870." *Hosts, Immigrants and Minorities: Historical Responses to Newcomers in British Society, 1870-1914*. Edited by Kenneth Lunn. Folkestone: Dawson, 1980. Pp. 64-106.

Kollar, René. "The Opposition to Ritualism in Victorian England." *Irish Theological Quarterly*, LI (1985), 63-74.

Kovacevic, Ivanka, and S. Barbara Kanner. "Blue Book into Novel: The Forgotten Industrial Fiction of Charlotte Elizabeth Tonna." *Nineteenth-Century Fiction*, XXV (1970-71), 152-73.

Laverdure, Paul. "Creating an Anti-Catholic Crusader: Charles Chiniquy." *Journal of Religious History*, XV (1988), 94-108.

Leys, Colin. "Petitioning in the Nineteenth and Twentieth Centuries." *Political Studies*, III (1955), 45-64.

Lohrli, Anne. "The Madiai: A Forgotten Chapter of Church History." *Victorian Studies*, XXXIII (1989-90), 28-50.

Lowe, J. C. "The Tory Triumph of 1868 in Blackburn and in Lancashire." *Historical Journal*, XVI (1973), 733-48.

Lowe, W. J. "The Lancashire Irish and the Catholic Church, 1846-71: The Social Dimension." *Irish Historical Studies*, XX (1976-7), 129-55.

Luker, David. "Revivalism in Theory and Practice: The Case of Cornish Revivalism." *Journal of Ecclesiastical History*, XXXVII (1986), 603-19.

Machin, G.I.T. "The Last Victorian Anti-Ritualist Campaign, 1895-1906." *Victorian Studies*, XXV (1981-82), 277-302.

_____. "Lord John Russell and the Prelude to the Ecclesiastical Titles Bill, 1846-51." *Journal of Ecclesiastical History*, XXV (1974), 277-95.

_____. "The Maynooth Grant, the Dissenters and Disestablishment, 1845-1847." *English Historical Review*, LXXXII (1967), 61-85.

Maidment, Brian. "Essayists and Artizans—The Making of Nineteenth-Century Self-Taught Poets." *Literature and History*, IX (1983), 74-91.

Marty, Martin E. "The Last Anti-Catholic in America." *Christian Century*, XCVI (31 Oct. 1979), 1071.

_____. "Living with Establishment and Disestablishment in Nineteenth-Century Anglo-America." *Journal of Church and State*, XVIII (1976), 61-77.

Matar, N. J. "The Controversy Over the Restoration of the Jews: From 1754 until the London Society for Promoting Christianity Among the Jews." *Durham University Journal*, LXXXII (1990), 29-44.

Millward, Pauline. "The Stockport Riots of 1852: A Study of Anti-Catholic and Anti-Irish Sentiment." *The Irish in the Victorian City*. Edited by Roger Swift and Sheridan Gilley. London: Croom Helm, 1985. Pp. 207-24.

Misner, Paul. "Newman and the Tradition concerning the Papal Antichrist." *Church History*, XLII (1973), 377-95.

Mitchell, Sally. "The Forgotten Woman of the Period: Penny Weekly Family Magazines of the 1840's and 1850's." *A Widening Sphere: Changing Roles of Victorian Women*. Edited by Martha Vicinus. Bloomington: Indiana University Press, 1977. Pp. 29-51.

Mole, David E.H. "John Cale Miller: a Victorian Rector of Birmingham." *Journal of Ecclesiastical History*, XVII (1966), 95-103.

Morgan, Gavin. "The Guildford Guy Riots (1842-1865)." *Surrey Archæological Collections*, LXXVI (1985), 61-68.

Morrish, P. S. "The Struggle to Create an Anglican Diocese of Birmingham." *Journal of Ecclesiastical History*, XXXI (1980), 59-88.

Mountjoy, Peter Roger. "The working-class press and working-class conservatism." *Newspaper History from the Seventeenth Century to the Present Day*. Edited by George Boyce, James Curran, and Pauline Wingate. London and Beverly Hills, Calif.: Constable and Sage Publications, 1978. Pp. 265-80.

Munden, A. F. "Radicalism versus Evangelicalism in Victorian Cheltenham." *Southern History*, V (1983), 115-21.

Munson, J.E.B. "The Oxford Movement by the End of the Nineteenth Century: The Anglo-Catholic Clergy." *Church History*, XLIV (1975), 382-95.

Neal, F. "The Birkenhead Garibaldi Riots of 1862." *Transactions of the Historic Society of Lancashire and Cheshire*, CXXXI (1981), 87-111.

Nicholls, Robert L. "Surrogate for Democracy: Nineteenth Century British Petitioning." *Maryland Historian*, V (1974), 43-52.

Nikol, John. "The Oxford Movement in Decline: Lord John Russell and the Tractarians, 1846-1852." *Historical Magazine of the Protestant Episcopal Church*, XLIII (1974), 341-58.

Norman, E. R. "The Maynooth Question of 1845." *Irish Historical Studies*, XV (1967), 407-37.

O'Brien, Susan. "*Terra Incognita*: The Nun in Nineteenth-Century England." *Past and Present*, No. 121 (1988), pp. 110-40.

O'Keefe, Timothy J. "The Times and the Roman Catholics: 1857." *Journal of Church and State*, XVIII (1976), 253-72.

Ó Tuathaigh, M.A.G. "The Irish in Nineteenth-Century Britain: Problems of Integration." *Transactions of the Royal Historical Society*, 5th Ser., XXXI (1981), 149-73.

Paz, D. G. "Another Look at Lord John Russell and the Papal Aggression, 1850." *Historian*, XLV (1982-83), 47-64.

_____. "Lord John Russell's Anti-Catholic Dilemma: The Ministerial Crisis of 1851." *Proceedings of the South Carolina Historical Association, 1987*. Pp. 33-43.

_____. "Popular Anti-Catholicism in England, 1850-1851." *Albion*, XI (1979), 331-59.

Phillips, Paul T. "Religion and Society in the Cloth Region of Wiltshire, c. 1830-70." *Journal of Religious History*, XI (1980-81), 95-110.

Phillips, Peter. "A Catholic Community: Shrewsbury. Part I: 1750-1850." *Recusant History*, XX (1990), 239-61.

_____. "A Catholic Community: Shrewsbury. Part II: 1850-1920." *Recusant History*, XX (1991), 380-402.

Pickering, W.S.F. "The 1851 Religious Census—A Useless Experiment?" *British Journal of Sociology*, XVIII (1967), 382-407.

Pinnington, J. E. "Bishop Blomfield and St. Barnabas', Pimlico: The Limits of Ecclesiastical Authority." *Church Quarterly Review*, CLXVIII (1967), 289.

_____. "Bishop Phillpotts and the Rubrics." *Church Quarterly Review*, CLXIX (1968), 167-78.

Prochaska, F. K. "Women in English Philanthropy, 1790-1830." *International Review of Social History*, XIX (1974), 426-45.

Pugh, R. B. "Chartism in Somerset and Wiltshire." *Chartist Studies*. Edited by Asa Briggs. London: Macmillan, 1959. Pp. 174-219.

Rack, H. D. "Domestic Visitation: A Chapter in Early Nineteenth Century Evangelism." *Journal of Ecclesiastical History*, XXIV (1973), 357-76.

_____. "Wesleyan Methodism, 1849-1902." *A History of the Methodist Church in Great Britain*. Edited by Rupert Davies, A. Raymond George, and Gordon Rupp. 4 vols. London: Epworth Press, 1965-88. III, 119-66.

Ralls, Walter. "The Papal Aggression of 1850: A Study in Victorian Anti-Catholicism." *Church History*, XLIII (1974), 242-56.

Read, Donald. "Chartism in Manchester." *Chartist Studies*. Edited by Asa Briggs. London: Macmillan, 1959. Pp. 29-64.

Reed, John Shelton. "'A Female Movement': The Feminization of Nineteenth-Century Anglo-Catholicism." *Anglican and Episcopal History*, LVII (1988), 199-241.

_____. "'Giddy Young Men': A Counter-Cultural Aspect of Victorian Anglo-Catholicism." *Comparative Social Research*, XI (1989), 209-26.

_____. "'Ritualism Rampant in East London': Anglo-Catholicism and the Urban Poor." *Victorian Studies*, XXXI (1987-88), 375-403.

Reynolds, Julian. "Politics vs. Persuasion: The Attempt to Establish Anglo-Roman Diplomatic Relations in 1848." *Catholic Historical Review*, LXXI (1985), 372-93.

Roberts, M.J.D. "Pressure-Group Politics and the Church of England: The Church Defence Institution, 1859-1896." *Journal of Ecclesiastical History*, XXXV (1984), 560-82.

_____. "Private Patronage and the Church of England, 1800-1900." *Journal of Ecclesiastical History*, XXXII (1981), 199-223.

Robson, Geoffrey. "The Failures of Success: Working Class Evangelists in Early Victorian Birmingham." *Studies in Church History*, XV (1978), 381-391.

Royle, Edward. "Charles Bradlaugh, Freethought and Northampton." *Northamptonshire Past and Present*, VI (1980), 141-50.

Russell, David. "The Leeds Rational Recreation Society, 1852-9: 'Music for the People' in a Mid-Victorian City." *Publications of the Thoresby Society*, XVII, Pt. 3 (1981), 137-58.

Ruston, Alan. "The Omnibus Radical: Rev. Henry Solly (1813-1903)." *Transactions of the Unitarian Historical Society*, XIX (1988), 78-91.

Sack, James J. "The Grenvilles' *Eminence Grise*: The Reverend Charles O'Conor and the Latter Days of Anglo-Gallicanism." *Harvard Theological Review*, LXXII (1979), 123-42.

Schiefen, Richard J. "'Anglo-Gallicanism' in Nineteenth-Century England." *Catholic Historical Review*, LXIII (1977), 14-44.

Scott, Donald M. "The Profession that Vanished: Public Lecturing in Mid-Nineteenth-Century America." *Professions and Professional Ideologies in America*. Edited by Gerald L. Geison. Chapel Hill: University of North Carolina Press, 1983. Pp. 12-28.

Sellers, Ian. "John Howard Hinton, Theologian." *Baptist Quarterly*, XXXIII (1989), 119-32.

Sharp, John. "The Influence of St. Alphonsus Liguori in Nineteenth-Century Britain.' *Downside Review*, CI (1983), 60-76.

_____. "Juvenile Holiness: Catholic Revivalism among Children in Victorian Britain." *Journal of Ecclesiastical History*, XXXV (1984), 220-38.

Shiman, Lilian Lewis. "'Changes Are Dangerous': Women and Temperance in Victorian England." *Religion in the Lives of English Women, 1760-1930*. Edited by Gail Malmgreen. Bloomington: Indiana University Press, 1986. Pp. 193-215.

_____. "Temperance and Class in Bradford, 1830-1860." *Yorkshire Archæological Journal*, LVIII (1986), 173-78.

Skinner, John. "The Liberal Nomination Controversy in Manchester, 1847." *Bulletin of the Institute of Historical Research*, LV (1982), 215-18.

Smith, C. T. "The Cambridge Region: Settlement and Population." *The Cambridge Region, 1965*. Edited by J. A. Steers. London: British Association for the Advancement of Science, 1965. Pp.133-62.

Smith, Philip T. "The London Police and the Holy War: Ritualism and St. George's-in-the-East, London, 1859-1860." *Journal of Church and State*, XXVIII (1986), 107-19.

Storch, Robert D. "The Plague of the Blue Locusts: Police Reform and Popular Resistance in Northern England, 1840-57." *International Review of Social History*, XX (1975), 60-90.

_____. "'Please to Remember the Fifth of November': Conflict Solidarity and Public Order in Southern England, 1815-1900." *Popular Culture and Custom in Nineteenth-Century England*. Edited by Robert D. Storch. London: Croom Helm, 1982. Pp. 71-99.

_____. "The Policeman as Domestic Missionary: Urban Discipine and Popular Culture in Northern England, 1850-1880." *Journal of Social History*, IX (1975-76), 481-509.

Strawson, William. "Methodist Theology, 1850-1950." *A History of the Methodist Church in Great Britain*. Edited by Rupert Davies, A. Raymond George, and Gordon Rupp. 4 vols. London: Epworth Press, 1965-88. III, 182-231.

Stunt, Timothy. "Geneva and British Evangelicals in the Early Nineteenth Century." *Journal of Ecclesiastical History*, XXXII (1981), 35-46.

Swift, Roger. "'Another Stafford Street Row': Law, Order, and the Irish Presence in Mid-Victorian Wolverhampton." *The Irish in the Victorian City*. Edited by Roger Swift and Sheridan Gilley London: Croom Helm, 1985. Pp. 179-206.

_____. "Anti-Catholicism and Irish Disturbances: Public Order in Mid-Victorian Wolverhampton." *Midland History*, IX (1984), 87-108.

Thompson, David M. "The 1851 Religious Census: Problems and Possibilities." *Victorian Studies*, XI (1967-68), 87-97.

_____. "The Liberation Society, 1844-1868." *Pressure from Without in Early Victorian England*. Edited by Patricia Hollis. New York: St. Martin's Press, 1974. Pp. 210-38.

Thompson, F.M.L. "Whigs and Liberals in the West Riding, 1830-1860." *English Historical Review*, LXXIV (1959), 214-39.

Thorp, Malcolm R. "Sectarian Violence in Early Victorian Britain: The Mormon Experience, 1837-1860." *Bulletin of the John Rylands University Library of Manchester*, LXX (1988), 135-47.

Tranter, Margery. "Landlords, Labourers, Local Preachers: Rural Nonconformity in Derbyshire, 1772-1851." *Derbyshire Archæological Journal*, CI (1981), 119-38.

Trinder, Barrie. "Schisms and Divisions: The Origins of Dissenting Congregations in Banbury, 1772-1860." *Cake and Cockhorse*, VIII (1982), 207-21.

Wach, Howard M. "Culture and the Middle Classes: Popular Knowledge in Industrial Manchester." *Journal of British Studies*, XXVII (1985), 375-404.

Waller, David. "Northampton and the American Civil War." *Northamptonshire Past and Present*, VIII (1990-91), 137-53.

Wallis, Frank. "The Revival of the Anti-Maynooth Campaign in Britain, 1850-52." *Albion*, XIX (1987), 527-48.

Walton, John K., and Robert Poole. "The Lancashire Wakes in the Nineteenth Century." *Popular Culture and Custom in Nineteenth-Century England*. Edited by Robert D. Storch. London: Croom Helm, 1982. Pp. 100-24.

Weinberger, Barbara. "The Police and the Public in Mid-Nineteenth-Century Warwickshire." *Policing and Punishment in Nineteenth Century Britain*. Edited by Victor Bailey. New Brunswick, N.J.: Rutgers University Press, 1981. Pp. 65-93.

Welch, P. J. "The Revival of an Active Convocation of Canterbury (1852-1855)." *Journal of Ecclesiastical History*, X (1959), 188-97.

Werly, John M. "The Irish in Manchester, 1832-49." *Irish Historical Studies*, XVIII (1972-73), 345-58.

Wilkinson, John T. "The Non-Wesleyan Traditions from 1849." *A History of the Methodist Church in Great Britain*. Edited by Rupert Davies, A. Raymond George, and Gordon Rupp. 4 vols. London: Epworth Press, 1965-88. III, 167-81.

Williams, Raymond. "Radical and/or Respectable." *The Press We Deserve*. Edited by Richard Boston. London: Routledge and Kegan Paul, 1970. Pp. 14-26.

Willis, Paul. "Shop Floor Culture, Masculinity and the Wage Form." *Working-Class Culture: Studies in History and Theory*. Edited by J. Clarke, C. Critcher, and R. Johnson. New York: St. Martin's Press, 1980. Pp. 185-98.

Wolffe, John R. "Bishop Henry Phillpotts and the Administration of the Diocese of Exeter, 1830-1869." *Reports and Transactions of the Devonshire Association for the Advancement of Science, Literature, and Art*, CXIV (1982-3), 99-113.

_____. "The Evangelical Alliance in the 1840s: An Attempt to Institutionalise Christian Unity." *Studies in Church History*, XXIII (1986), 333-46.

Yates, Nigel. "'Jesuits in Disguise'? Ritualist Confessors and their Critics in the 1870s." *Journal of Ecclesiastical History*, XXXIX (1988), 202-16.

_____. "The Religious Life of Victorian Leeds." *A History of Modern Leeds*. Edited by Derek Fraser. Manchester University Press, 1980. Pp. 250-69.

Unpublished Studies

Alexander, Lynn. "Charlotte Elizabeth and the Crusade for Reform." Typescript paper read at the Pacific Coast Conference on British Studies, March 1991.
_____. "Publishing for Women: Charlotte Elizabeth Tonna and the *Christian Lady's Magazine*." Typescript paper read at the Research Society for Victorian Periodicals, November 1990.
Berridge, Virginia Stewart. "Popular Journalism and Working Class Attitudes, 1854-1886: A Study of Reynolds' Newspaper, Lloyd's Weekly Newspaper, and the Weekly Times." Ph.D. thesis, University of London, 1976.
Blass, Homer Harrison. "Popular Anti-Catholicism in England and the Ecclesiastical Titles Bill of 1851." Ph.D. thesis, University of Missouri, 1981.
Boyd, John, R. A. Schweitzer, and Charles Tilly. "British Contentious Gatherings of 1828." Center for Research on Social Organizations, University of Michigan. Working Paper No. 171 (March 1978).
Cahill, Gilbert A. "Irish Catholicism and English Toryism, 1832-1848: A Study in Ideology." Ph.D. thesis, University of Iowa, 1954.
Connolly, Gerard Patrick. "Catholicism in Manchester and Salford, 1770-1850: The Quest for 'Le Chrétien Quelconque.'" 3 vols. Ph.D. thesis, University of Manchester, 1980.
DeMotte, Charles M. "The Dark Side of Town: Crime in Manchester and Salford, 1815-1875." Ph.D. thesis, University of Kansas, 1977.
Ellens, Jacob P. "The Church Rate Conflict in England and Wales, 1832-1868." Ph.D. thesis, University of Toronto, 1983.
Gray, Donald Clifford. "A Disciple of Discipline: James Irvine, Vicar of Leigh, 1839-1874." M.Phil. thesis, University of Liverpool, 1980.
Haines, Meredith C. "The Nonconformists and the Nonconformist Periodical Press in Mid-Nineteenth Century England." Ph.D. thesis, Indiana University, 1966.
Hempton, David Neil. "Methodism and Anti-Catholic Politics, 1800-1846." Ph.D. thesis, University of St. Andrews, 1977.
Holland, Mary Griset. "The British Catholic Press and the Educational Controversy, 1847-1865." Ph.D. thesis, Catholic University of America, 1975.
Hooper, A. F. Typescript on the 1867 Birmingham Riots.
Janet, Richard J. "The Decline of General Fasts in Victorian England, 1832-1857." Ph.D. thesis, University of Notre Dame, 1984.
Joyce, Thomas P. "The Restoration of the Catholic Hierarchy in England and Wales, 1850: A Study of Certain Public Reactions." Ph.D. thesis, Gregorian University, 1966; abstract under that title published, Rome: Officium Libri Catholici, 1966.
LeBarbour, Annie Marie Pettyjohn. "Victorian Baptists: A Study of Denominational Development." Ph.D. thesis, University of Maryland, 1977.
Lesourd, Jean-Alain. "Les Catholiques dans la Société Anglaise, 1765-1865." Ph.D. thesis, University of Lille, 1978.
Nikol, John. "The Oxford Movement in Decline: Lord John Russell, the Tractarians and the Church of England, 1846-1852." Ph.D. thesis, Fordham University, 1972.
Ralls, Walter A. "The Papal Aggression of 1850: Its Background and Meaning." Ph.D. thesis, Columbia University, 1960.
Reed, John Shelton. "Revolt Against Common Sense: The Cultural Politics of Victorian Anglo-Catholicism." Unpublished book-length manuscript.
Wallis, Frank Howard. "The Anti-Maynooth Campaign: A Study in Anti-Catholicism and Politics in the United Kingdom, 1851-69." Ph.D. thesis, University of Illinois, 1987.
Wolffe, John R. "Protestant Societies and Anti-Catholic Agitation in Great Britain, 1829-1860." D.Phil. thesis, University of Oxford, 1985.

INDEX

Library of Congress Cataloging-in-Publication Data

Paz, D. G. (Denis G.)
Popular anti-Catholicism in Mid-Victorian England / D. G. Paz.
    p.   cm.
Includes bibliographical references and index.
ISBN 0-8047-1984-5 (alk. paper):
    1. Anti-Catholicism—England—History—19th century. 2. Catholic
Church—England—History—19th century. 3. England—Church
history—19th century. I. Title.
BR759.P388   1992
305.6'2042'09034—dc20
92–26730
CIP

♾ This book is printed on acid-free paper.

RANDALL LIBRARY-UNCW

3 0490 0433592 %